Clarence A. Berdahl
Illinois. 12/22/30.

HENRY WHITE

THIRTY YEARS OF AMERICAN DIPLOMACY

HENRY WHITE

HENRY WHITE

THIRTY YEARS OF
AMERICAN DIPLOMACY

by

ALLAN NEVINS

AUTHOR OF
"FRÉMONT; *The West's Greatest Adventurer*"

HARPER & BROTHERS PUBLISHERS

NEW YORK AND LONDON

MCMXXX

HENRY WHITE
COPYRIGHT, 1930, BY HARPER & BROTHERS
PRINTED IN THE U. S. A.
SECOND PRINTING
L-E

"The most useful man in the entire diplomatic service, during my Presidency and for many years before, was Henry White; and I say this having in mind the high quality of work done by such admirable ambassadors and ministers as Bacon, Meyer, Straus, O'Brien, Rockhill, and Egan, to name only a few among many."
—THEODORE ROOSEVELT

"I think I am well within bounds when I say that he was the most accomplished diplomatist this country has ever produced."
—COLONEL E. M. HOUSE

"That dearest, best, and most lovable of men."
—LORD CURZON

CONTENTS

Roosevelt on Disarmament, 1906; General Von Falkenhayn on Mobilization; Memorandum on Fiume; A Letter from Henry James.

ILLUSTRATIONS

PREFACE

THIS volume is based in the main upon the extensive collection of Henry White's papers now in the Library of Congress, the papers of Theodore Roosevelt and Henry Cabot Lodge, and the State Department archives. Though it is an authorized biography, the responsibility for every part of it rests exclusively with myself. The materials having been placed at my disposal, I was left to deal with them in absolute independence. The emphasis given certain parts of the narrative, the judgments of public policies, and the views taken of White and all his contemporaries, are entirely my own.

Robert Louis Stevenson in *Prince Otto* tells us that the biographer of an imaginary dignitary of Grünewald drew his hero as "the centerpiece and the cloud-compeller of the whole history." The reader will at once perceive that no attempt has been made to place Henry White in any such false position. But his advantages for observing as well as participating in our diplomacy seemed to justify a rather full account of many sides of our foreign policy after 1890. An effort has been made to give salience to what is new. All the letters quoted are, unless the fact is otherwise indicated, published for the first time. Among other subjects, it is believed that the new material throws light upon the manner in which Secretary Olney handled the Venezuelan affair after he lost faith in Ambassador Bayard; upon the Anglo-American rapprochement at the time of the Spanish War; upon Secretary Hay's handling of the Open Door and Boxer Rebellion; and upon some of the inner history of the Hay-Pauncefote Treaty. Similarly, it perhaps does something to explain Roosevelt's vigorous attitude toward Germany in the difficult Venezuelan imbroglio of 1902-03, and the insistence of the American Government upon gaining all its objectives in the so-called "arbitration" of the Alaskan boundary. There is fresh material upon the Algeciras Conference, and the visit of Roosevelt to Europe in 1910. In Chapter XVIII, the interview with Falkenhayn adds certain details to the record of Germany's entrance into the war, while in the next chapter Ramsay MacDonald's full memorandum upon American entry into the conflict is published for the first time. The story of the Peace Conference as seen by the one Republican member of the American delegation is told in full, and it is hoped that the correspondence with Lodge, Elihu Root, John Jacob Rogers, and others throws some light upon the whole party attitude toward ratification of the Treaty of Versailles. Material is also presented which may help to elucidate the breach between President Wilson and Colonel House.

It is not possible for me, as I should wish, to thank all those who have assisted me in the preparation of this volume. But I must make grateful acknowledgments in particular to Mrs. Henry White, Countess Seherr-Thoss, Mr. John Campbell White, and Mr. W. H. Buckler; to Mrs. Theodore Roosevelt, Mrs. Alice Hay Wadsworth, Mr. Elihu Root, and Mr. John E. Lodge; to Mr. Ray Stannard Baker, Mr. C. S. Hamlin, Mr. J. C. Grew, Mr. Lloyd Griscom, Mr. Frank Polk, Mr. Charles Seymour, Mr. Tyler Dennett, and Mr. Manley O. Hudson; to my colleagues of Columbia University, Mr. Carlton J. H. Hayes, Mr. W. L. Westermann, and Mr. Parker T. Moon; and to Mr. Walter Lippmann of the New York *World*. I am grateful, in addition, for memoranda sent me by Lord Cecil, M. J. J. Jusserand, Count Johann von Bernstorff, President Nicholas Murray Butler, President David Kinley, Mr. Lewis Einstein, Mrs. Richard Aldrich, and Mrs. Corinne Roosevelt Robinson.

NEW YORK CITY,   A. N.
   March 15, 1930

HENRY WHITE

CHAPTER ONE

Maryland and the Civil War

THERE is a strange element of the haphazard, the irrational, and
the unforeseen in all diplomatic history, for the simple reason
that nations have always left their relations largely to chance. Mankind has just begun to make an organized effort to give these
relations greater saneness, foresight, and equity. But throughout the
late nineteenth and early twentieth centuries international transactions were too often the sport of national prejudices, commercial
selfishness, hysterical journalism, the whims of autocrats or parliamentary groups, and the vagaries of mere chance. Enlightened statesmen strove for peace, and the gambler's spirit of a Napoleon III
or Tirpitz, the explosion of a mine in Havana, the crack of a pistol
at Sarajevo, brought war; the Haldanes and Lichnowskys tried to
draw alien peoples into friendship, and saw them insist upon recoil-
ing in hatred; men like McKinley found circumstances and jingoism
too much for them, men like Grey found well-meant agreements
a fatal entrapment. It was in this uncertain and semi-rational world
that the professional diplomatist had to practice his art. The strange
chances, the unpredictable forces, the ever-changing combinations,
were indeed one of the allurements of the profession. On the ad-
venturous, splendid, shabby stage of world diplomacy the United
States long played no real part; it looked rather truculently after
its own specialized interests, and that was all. But late in the century it was forced to undertake a rôle which brought it into touch
with all the Powers, which made it in different crises a world
arbiter, and which gave it in the end a dazzling opportunity for
leadership which it deliberately fumbled. The life of its first professional diplomatist, the man who knew more of this tangled
skein than perhaps any other American, has a decided interest.

Henry White had the fortune to enter diplomacy when the
United States was on the eve of becoming a recognized world
power; he had the ability to become what Roosevelt called "the

most useful man in the entire diplomatic service" just when the United States was beginning to share in a series of important international events. His life from 1890 touches most of these events. The Behring Sea arbitration, the Venezuela boundary, the Spanish War, China and the Open Door, Algeciras, the Pan-American movement—in all these affairs he had a part, sometimes small, sometimes large, but always expert. No one ever took him for a great man, but his astuteness and energy made him what is often far better, a very useful man. He illustrated better than any other American of the time the possibilities of skilled service by a diplomatist of career. Indeed, he was our first eminent "career man" in the field, rising from the humblest posts in the profession to some of the highest. Removed from office in 1909, he returned to public life as a participant in the greatest negotiation of modern times, the Paris Conference which closed the World War. He served the country under five Presidents and both parties, and won the trust of the State Department and the informed public to a greater degree than any of his colleagues.

In still other respects Henry White's career has significance and interest. He possessed something like a genius for friendship, founded upon distinctive and unusual traits of character. For a generation he knew a majority of the leading public men of Europe and America. With many he was on the closest terms. Indeed, he won the intimate confidence of men of the most diverse types. Among those who held him in this special regard were Americans like John Hay, Theodore Roosevelt, Henry Cabot Lodge, and Elihu Root, and Britons like Lord Balfour, Lord Salisbury, Lord Curzon, and Lord Cecil. Men so unlike as Victor Emmanuel III, Lord Bryce, and Richard Olney took to him at once and reposed a complete trust in him. It would be hard to name any American of his time who had more important contacts at home and abroad and whose correspondence was more diverse in its range. He had unusual means of knowing what was going on behind the scenes in the principal nations, and his letters and memoranda furnish some striking glimpses of international affairs.

While he was thus intimate with leaders in government and diplomacy, he saw a great deal more of social life on two continents than is vouchsafed even to much-traveled people. His career was strikingly cosmopolitan. He went to Europe as a lad. Circumstances early threw him into the polite world of England and France, and from the time that he entered the London coterie called "The Souls" till he became an ambassador, he was at home with important social groups in the European capitals in a way that few Americans have ever been. With mere "society" most Americans are rightly a little impatient; with snobbery of any kind White was more impatient than most people. Nevertheless, the relationships he formed supplemented and strengthened his diplomatic work and, as with a number of American representatives from the time of Benjamin Franklin, gave his official activities an invaluable background. The record of his life gains something in color and breadth from his familiarity with people of family, rank, and intellectual distinction in half a dozen lands. He knew many parts of a social world that has almost completely disappeared and that may soon seem as strange as Bourbon France or Stuart England.

Henry White was born precisely at the middle of the century—the year of the Great Compromise, the year of "In Memoriam"; he first saw the light in Baltimore on March 29, 1850, in the home of John Campbell and Eliza Ridgely White, who had been married the previous year.

The family was one of considerable wealth; better, it was also a family of standards and breeding, which had held a recognized place in Maryland for generations. On his father's side Henry White traced his line to a great-grandfather who had emigrated from Ulster. They were of Scotch blood and some members had been Presbyterian clergymen, but this great-grandfather had nevertheless joined the Irish uprising of 1798, and had been imprisoned for a time in Dublin Castle. He was a friend of another Scotch-Irishman, Alexander Brown, who emigrated to the United States at the same time and founded a bank in Baltimore, Brown's three sons becoming known as the Brown Brothers, bankers of Baltimore, Philadelphia, New York, and Liverpool. The American progenitor, John Campbell White, was a shrewd man of business, who established a thriving distillery; by the middle 'thirties, when it was carried on in Center Street under the name of Messrs J. C. White & Sons, it was one of the notable establishments of Baltimore. One of the sons was Henry White, who married Mary LeRoy of the old New York Huguenot family; his son was John Campbell White, father of the Henry White of this biography.

On his mother's side White sprang from the Ridgelys of Hampton, not far from Baltimore, one branch of an extensive family prominent from early Colonial times in Maryland and Delaware. The first of this long line had been a Robert Ridgely, who was a member of the Maryland bar in the late seventeenth century and secretary of the Province in 1676-77. He was one of the considerable number of colonists who received large land patents for bringing in a body of dependent settlers, and at his death left more than five thousand acres. It was a grandson, Colonel Charles Ridgely, who acquired the first lands of the Hampton estate, and a great-grandson, Captain Charles Ridgely, who built the family mansion there. By the Revolution this particular family was one of the best known in the Colony. Its most distinguished member was still another Charles Ridgely, who rose to be a brigadier-general of the state militia and governor of the state in 1815-18, dying at Hampton in 1829. We are told by historians of Maryland that he was a man of wealth, known for his love of the good things of life, for his liberalism in gradually emancipating all his slaves, and for his administrative talents.[1] His granddaughter was the mother of Henry White.

The birthplace of Henry White was an old Colonial house at the junction of Fayette and Holliday Streets in Baltimore, demolished long ago (in 1859) to afford room for the enlargement of Fayette Street and the building of the present City Hall. A few of Henry White's earliest memories cling to this place. He recalled his grandfather and great-uncle, who were carrying on the distillery, as living there. In a Baltimore speech late in life he said that he had a "very vivid recollection of being held up when a little child to the window and seeing, to my inexpressible delight, parades of soldiers and civilians with music, banners, and all the paraphernalia of processions in honor of St. Patrick's Day." But the death of his father in 1853, when Henry White was three years old, resulted in his spending the greater part of his childhood at Hampton, an estate of the border plantation type which was almost ideal for a growing lad.

The house at Hampton, which is one of the largest and finest of

[1] McSherry, James, *History of Maryland*.

its period in Maryland, was at the time of his birth nearly three-quarters of a century old. The Captain Charles Ridgely who built it, a mariner and ironmaster, had begun its erection in 1783, and it had been occupied near the close of 1789. One of the family traditions is of the housewarming held here in 1790. The captain's wife was a devout Methodist, while he was a sailor and politician of convivial tastes; on the day set he invited his cronies to join him around the festive bowl, and was dismayed when he found that Mrs. Ridgely had seized the opportunity to call in numerous fellow-disciples of Bishop Asbury. He solved the problem by staying with his wife and the good Methodists downstairs for religious ceremonies, while his nephew Charles led the wilder spirits to the attic to enjoy their punch and cards undisturbed. Successive owners, and particularly Governor Ridgely, improved the grounds and the furnishings, added to the picture gallery, and made the house a place unusual in comfort and attractiveness.

When the boy Henry White knew it, Hampton was in much the same state as today. With a dignified cupola rising above terraced lawns, it loomed up among the trees of a handsome though roughly gardened park. Carriages drew up before a wide piazza; the ascending visitor was ushered through heavy doors into a central hall of generous dimensions, fully sixty feet long, then as now hung solidly with family portraits and rather old-fashioned landscapes in oils. Among these pictures there stood out a lovely full-length portrait by Sully of Henry White's grandmother, shown as a young girl playing a harp. The hall was high-ceiled and imposing, but somewhat gloomy in cloudy weather. On one side were a roomy library, and a cheerful and still larger sitting-room, both with fine panelling, painted white; in the opposite wing were the dining-room, glittering with old silverware, and two smaller sitting-rooms. At one end of the main structure lay the kitchens, while at the opposite extremity was a room used as the managing office of the estate. At some distance in the grounds stood an older house, built in the early part of the eighteenth century, and an interesting though crude specimen of the architecture of that time. It was called "the lower house" and was surrounded by barns, stables, and negro quarters, for despite the manumissions by General Ridgely, slaves were kept to work the farms. Grain, hay, and live stock made the land, only a dozen miles from the Baltimore markets, profitable, and during Henry White's childhood it was a busy place.

The life of the Ridgelys at Hampton was marked by the dignity and leisure of wealthy landed families of the time in the upper South and border states. Other estates dotted the region about Baltimore and Annapolis and the peninsula between the Chesapeake and the Potomac, and there was much visiting and entertaining. Balls, dinners, receptions, hunting, and political meetings knit the easy-going society together. Henry White's grandmother on the Ridgely side was a woman of hardly more than middle age, still handsome and vigorous, who took an energetic part in social activities, managed the household, and kept up with the intellectual currents of the time. She showed a notable fondness for the boy, who had inherited some distinct traits from her. During the late 'fifties she drove about on frequent visits to country houses or to Baltimore, keeping her four horses at a smart trot, with the colored footman clinging behind if she took the landau, or sitting in a rumble-seat if she used the open calèche. The youngster grew used to accompanying her. Many people thought it strange that he submitted to being dressed in white duck clothing and taken to listen to the talk of adults, when he might have been at play. But, as he wrote late in life, he had simply inherited his grandmother's taste for company and had an inborn "fondness for human nature and for making acquaintances and listening to the conversation of those older than myself, especially if they happened to be people of the world."

It was a rather wide world in which Henry White moved from the outset. Baltimore, which was a handsome city of about 200,000 people, known for its fine monument to Washington and its Battle Monument commemorating the victory of 1814, its Catholic cathedral, equaled only by that in New Orleans, its shipping and banking business, and its aristocratic old families, still regarded itself as a rival of Philadelphia. Its great railway, the Baltimore and Ohio, had united Chesapeake Bay and the Ohio River in 1852. Southern trade was still heavy. No other city in these years had so many national party conventions. It was steadily adding to its attractions—the Peabody Institute was founded in 1857, and Druid Hill Park was opened in 1860. Henry White saw the best side of the city's semi-Southern life, for at least part of the winters was spent there. Early every summer the family went for several weeks to that focus of Southern fashion, the White Sulphur Springs of Virginia. With fifteen hundred visitors often crowding the hotels and cottages, nearly all people of position who had come in their private carriages, the mountain spa offered what Captain Marryat called the best company in America. The boy must have been impressed by the ballrooms, the four-in-hands, the flirtations, and the deference to such social figures as Mrs. Caton of Baltimore, who was the daughter of Charles Carroll of Carrollton, and mother of Lady Wellesley, Lady Stafford, and Lady Caermarthen. A little later each year the family would escape the heat by going to the shore, usually at either Old Point Comfort or Cape May.

One of White's early recollections was of a call which he made with his grandfather in 1856 upon President Franklin Pierce at Old Point Comfort; a call impressed upon him, apparently, by the fact that he had been admonished to take off his hat the moment the President entered the room, and found the strings tied too tightly under his chin. That was the day when boys wore hats with strings! There were also family expeditions far afield in lower Maryland and Virginia; and in 1857 his mother, already troubled by the growing enmity of North and South, took him on the first of his unnumbered trips across the ocean.

The boy's chief happiness, however, was in the long seasons at Hampton, where from April till October or November, with only these excursions as interruptions, he spent the time in outdoor pursuits. It was a superb place for an active lad: a great estate of some five thousand acres over which he, his younger brother Julian, and his cousins roamed at will, swimming in the Gunpowder River, sliding down terraces, riding with his grandfather or uncles, fishing, berrying and nutting. There were old bookshelves where on rainy days he might browse. He could watch the whole cycle of farm operations. He could visit the negroes, whose presence enabled him to study slavery at first hand. Long afterward he set down his tolerant observations upon the "peculiar institution":

There is no doubt that the system was a bad one—increasingly so as this country progressed in civilization and world importance, and more so for the masters and the white people in general than for the negro people. In so far as my recollections go the considerable body of slaves owned by my grandfather were on the whole happy and content. Those about the house and gardens were all personal friends of the children, the older ones being called "uncle" and "aunt," and all of them being kindly treated, with much less to do, on account of their numbers, than a similar number of white people would be expected to accomplish at present. I still remember the younger ones, who at that time were beginning to hear of freedom and the possibilities of education, coming to me at times privately with little primers and asking me to explain the spelling of certain words, or the meaning of certain combinations of letters which they could not understand; begging me at the same time not to let any of my elders know they had done so, one of the principles of slavery being that they should not be taught to read or write. My grandfather used to have services once a week by the Presbyterian minister, named Galbraith (which the family attended in a large square room over the carriage house), for the house and field servants, at which there was a good deal of singing of a melodious character by the slaves. Incidentally, the Reverend Mr. Galbraith, when the war broke out, got himself into trouble with the family, and his ministrations were suspended owing to his having married a mulatto, or at least a person suspected of having negro blood in her veins. He was completely out-lawed, and I never remember to have seen him again.[2]

Though the slaves were considerately treated at Hampton, even there the discipline had its painful features. Henry White added:

There is no doubt, however, that apart from the economic evils of slavery (as its methods were very wasteful and slipshod), it was also bad for the tempers of the owners. I well remember having seen my Grandfather Ridgely lose his temper on one or two occasions, and box the ears of one of the grooms for reasons which seemed to me entirely inadequate, and the incident left a most disagreeable impression on my mind. I remember another punishment, which of course was not really injurious or painful, except to the pride of the victim. This was the cutting off of the hair of a mulatto girl, who was almost white, and

[2] This and other subsequent statements by Henry White relating to his childhood and youth are taken from a manuscript of one hundred typewritten pages entitled *Reminiscences of Henry White*, of which there is a copy deposited in the Library of Congress. It contains a fairly full account of his first twenty years, with some scattered materials on his marriage and entrance into diplomatic life.

THE FAMILY OF HENRY WHITE
(His mother, his father, and a porch
scene at Newport about 1858)

whose hair did not resemble in the least the woolly hair of the negroes. She greatly prided herself on her resemblance in general to the "white folks," and it was a great humiliation that it should be cut off, which of course was the basis for that particular punishment. There were, of course, other much more serious evils connected with slavery even under the most favorable circumstances, which I need not mention. Notwithstanding all this, as I have previously said, my recollection of the system as carried out at Hampton is exceedingly pleasant; many of the objections to which I have referred being, of course, unknown to me at the time.

My grandmother was very particular in having what she was pleased to describe as "marriages" performed by a clergyman between the negro servants; not realizing—certainly I did not at the time—that slaves were unable to perform any civil act, being mere chattels. Consequently, these so-called marriages had no more validity in the eyes of the law than if they had taken place between two animals on the estate. It was perfectly possible, therefore, to part these so-called married couples by selling one or the other to another master, with no hope of their ever meeting again, although no such case ever arose at Hampton. It often did elsewhere, however, even among the best masters, as a result of death and the division of an estate of which the slaves formed part. My grandmother was always very kind in going to see any of the slaves who were ill, and a doctor from the neighboring small settlement then called Towson-town (which has since developed into Towson, the county seat of Baltimore County), was constantly called to attend them.

A boy of seven or eight in Europe—for which Henry White sailed in April, 1857, returning with his mother in August, 1858—is not likely to retain many impressions of importance. He recalled in after years that they went in the comfortable side-wheeler *Argo*, with a fair voyage of a fortnight before they reached Havre; and that on the trip over he suffered a good deal from the estimable lawyer John H. B. Latrobe of Baltimore, who was letting his beard grow (for the dark staterooms and the sea-motion made shaving difficult), and who nevertheless insisted on kissing the boy every morning. He remembered, too, the cow stabled close to the paddle-box for fresh milk, and the coops of live chickens. In Paris they occupied an apartment on the Champs Elysées for a few weeks. Then they visited Geneva, spent the winter in an apartment on the Lung' Arno in Florence—at this time still a half-mediæval city, with the old walls standing—and returned north in the spring to London. Travel in those days was largely by diligence, and it was in this fashion that they made the whole of their trip from Geneva to Florence. In London they took lodgings opposite Paddington Station, where once the boy excitedly watched a train arrive bearing Queen Victoria and Prince Albert. To the end of his days, also, he had a vivid recollection of Junius Spencer Morgan, then the partner of George Peabody, who called several times on Mrs. White. But doubtless Henry White was pleased to get back to the enjoyments of Hampton. For a time, while his Grandfather and Grandmother Ridgely took their turn in Europe, his mother managed the estate, a responsibility for which her energy and strong will amply fitted her.

The year 1860 brought excitement of a new kind. Henry White witnessed, doubtless with a boy's confused interest, the four-sided campaign in which Lincoln, Bell, Breckinridge and Douglas ran for the Presidency; and there is no question that the family's sympathies were not with Lincoln. The Civil War which followed was an unhappy period for all Maryland, and its shadow fell heavily across the Ridgely circle at Hampton. "Even as a child," Henry White wrote later, "I greatly disliked heated discussions between members of the family and their friends, and hardly a day passed that I did not hear one or more such during which the parties thereto frequently lost their tempers, and ended, some of them, by not speaking to one another." The passions of the conflict broke up the old genial social life of Maryland, and its anxieties penetrated within even the quiet walls of Hampton.

Indeed, we are likely to forget to what a tragic extent Maryland was divided by the war and how deep ran the passions of both sides. In literal truth brother was set against brother. When the Confederate ironclad *Merrimac* attacked the Federal fleet at Fortress Monroe, her intrepid commander was a Marylander, Captain Franklin Buchanan; while on the frigate *Congress,* which he sank, the paymaster was his brother, McKean Buchanan. During Stonewall Jackson's immortal Valley campaign, when he so spectacularly worsted Banks, Frémont, Shields, and other Union generals, the battle of Front Royal brought a sharp face-to-face encounter between the First Maryland Regiment, C. S. A., and the First

Maryland, U. S. A. Several thousands of Marylanders, first and last, fought under the Stars and Bars. The people were violently sundered into two hostile camps; family was set against family, friend turned against friend; and over these hatreds stretched a brazen sky of fear and uncertainty. A harsh military tyranny was imposed upon the State, and sympathizers with the Confederacy suffered various forms of proscription. Many were thrust into jail, and even honored judges were imprisoned.

While the boy's paternal grandfather pretended loyalty to the Union, even a youngster could notice that the initial Southern victories gave Grandfather Ridgely marked satisfaction. On the paternal side, Grandfather White, whom he often saw in Baltimore, was reluctant to express any political opinions; but he also seemed to be a Confederate sympathizer. White's mother did not conceal her scorn for the Yankees and her admiration for the embattled South. An uncle actually involved himself in difficulties with the Federal authorities. This was Charles Ridgely of Baltimore, who became captain of a volunteer company of cavalry, raised by him and others to defend the State of Maryland and by implication to fight for the Confederacy. The United States authorities promptly suppressed the company. White always remembered how he was sitting with a book one warm May day in 1861 outside the "little office" at Hampton when a stranger gave him a letter to be delivered instantly to his uncle; this letter proved to be a peremptory warning from a friend to stop the drilling of the company. Grandfather Ridgely was worried, and went to see General John A. Dix, commander of the department, to inquire if there were any official complaint lodged against the captain; to which Dix replied that a warrant had been sworn out for his arrest and that of an associate, Lieutenant John Merryman, but that as yet only the lieutenant would be taken into custody. Merryman was at once arrested, and his detention gave rise to a famous clash between President Lincoln and Chief Justice Taney—a clash in which Taney ineffectually denied the right of military arrest.[3]

[3] Interesting glimpses of Maryland as it was in the spring and summer of 1861 are to be found in W. H. Russell, *My Diary North and South*. From Havre de Grace to Washington he found every station and every bridge guarded by little camps of soldiers. "Sentinels are posted, pickets are thrown

The deep antagonisms created among the people of Maryland by the war, its turmoil and confusion, and an occasional brief glimpse of its blood and bereavements, had one important effect upon Henry White—they helped make him a life-long lover of peace. It was owing largely to the "painful recollections" of the war period, he wrote later, that "I have had a horror of war in general throughout my life. It brings out all that is worst in human nature, and causes friends of a lifetime to become enemies." A number of spirited young men from among the Ridgelys and their cousins the Howards stole away to join the Confederate army, and a much-liked cousin named Ridgely Howard lost his leg in battle. One still September afternoon White, listening on the terrace at Hampton with his awed elders, heard in the distance the rolling beat of the guns at Antietam; and nearly a year later he shared in the excitement which gripped everyone when Lee recrossed the Potomac and swung far north into Pennsylvania, between Maryland and its Northern supports. They waited with eager apprehension for news of the impending battle. Many Marylanders were fighting on each side. When it was learned that the Confederate army had been defeated on the field of Gettysburg, a young cousin who sympathized with the rebel cause, Cornelius Howard, set out in his buggy for the scene of conflict, hoping to find traces of the soldier members of his family. He returned with nothing but a budget of excited impressions, to which the boys of the family listened with rapt attention.[4]

---

out, and in the open fields by the wayside troops are to be seen moving, as though a battle were close at hand. . . . As we approach Baltimore the number of sentinels and camps increases, and earthworks have been thrown up on the high grounds commanding the city." His street car in Baltimore bore the marks of bullets. Strong guards patrolled the thoroughfares; the inhabitants looked sullen and sad; and the police appointed by the Federal authorities were waging a small war against the women, who dressed children and even dolls in the Confederate colors, and wore the Stars and Bars in their ribbons and bows.

[4] During the Civil War, Napoleon III appointed as the French minister to the United States the Baron Mercier de l'Ostende, whom Henry White's family had known in France. Grandmother Ridgely invited the whole Mercier family to spend a summer at Hampton, and they came bag and baggage. "I remember," White wrote to his brother long after, "the Minister used to pay long visits to Washington and return to Hampton in the afternoon,

The conflict laid an embargo on social activities. It scattered the slaves from the estate. Grandmother Ridgely's mind was affected by softening of the brain, and she responded to the anxieties of the war by an asperity which made everybody uncomfortable. Once, for example, she refused to let anyone in the family attend a wedding of old friends because they were adherents of the Union. White's mother also watched the triumph of the North with resentment. "I have on the whole," White wrote long after, "most unhappy memories of the Civil War."

---

saying that he had had interesting interviews with Mr. Lincoln or Mr. Seward. Unfortunately, I was too young then to appreciate the interest which was to be derived from Baron Mercier's accounts; but I do recollect that it became a great nuisance for our Grandfather Ridgely to send him constantly to the station in Baltimore." White to W. H. Buckler, Lenox, August 31, 1925.

CHAPTER TWO

Youthful Days in Europe

I N THE year 1865, with the dawn of a new era in the United
States, a new era dawned also in the life of Henry White. The
old easy, comfortable, Southern style of existence at Hampton, as
at other slaveholding estates of the Chesapeake region, would have
been sharply altered even had there been no family changes, but
decisive changes occurred. Thus far Harry had been partly under
the care of his kindly, social-minded Grandmother Ridgely. Now
her mind and health failed rapidly; it was plain that she and her
husband would not live long—they both died in 1867; and Harry's
mother, a woman of masculine temper, took him firmly under control. Hampton and Maryland were destined quickly to fade into
the background, the estate passing, on his grandfather's death, into
the hands of his uncle Charles; Europe came into the foreground.
Mrs. White took the defeat of the Confederacy keenly to heart.
Her bitterness over the humiliation of the South and the harsh
measures of Reconstruction made the United States an uncongenial
soil. But other factors counted as well in the removal of the family
to Europe.

In the autumn of 1865 Mrs. White was married to Dr. Thomas
Hepburn Buckler, a widower of fifty-three who had long been
one of the best-equipped physicians of Baltimore. He had studied
medicine in the chief clinics of Paris, had acquired a large Maryland
practice, and was so much esteemed that President Buchanan and
Chief Justice Taney were his patients. Later, in 1870, the dying
Robert E. Lee traveled north to consult him.[1] In the 'fifties he had
been one of the first American physicians to treat tuberculosis by
open-air life, rest, and careful nourishment, and his writings on
this and other subjects attracted wide attention. He had also been
something of a civic leader; at one time he had headed a movement

[1] Lee, Captain R. E., *Recollections and Letters of R. E. Lee*, pp. 412,
419, 425.

for filling in the "back basin" of Baltimore, a stagnant tidal area which impeded the city's growth and threatened its health. A man of independent spirit, brilliant mind, and some eccentricities, he had chafed under certain medical jealousies which he felt in Baltimore, and he was a Southern sympathizer.[2] He was hence glad to travel abroad and to renew in Paris the researches of his youth. For Harry's welfare the marriage was of significance because of Dr. Buckler's immediate interest in his education and health. For the first time the lad had a professionally trained man of wide experience to advise his mother and grandfather upon his upbringing.

The dominant fact in the education of Henry White up to this time, his sixteenth year, had been the personality of his mother, a truly remarkable woman. With unflagging zeal she had insisted on teaching each of her children in turn the fundamental branches of knowledge. She had a distrust of such schools as Maryland afforded, and never dreamed of sending her sons north to Phillips Andover or similar academies. Though she sometimes hired a tutor, most of the task she made her own. She was extremely well read; she could write and speak French, Italian, and German fluently; and by taking courses under two classical scholars of the state, she had fitted herself to teach Latin and Greek. Her methods were excellent, for she insisted on strict accuracy, on quality instead of quantity, and on a "thorough grounding." She taught from a quarto *Grandfather's Spelling-Book* dated about 1840, and one of her family always recalled her scorn for a gilt-and-blue substitute called *Reading Without Tears.* She made her pupils face their task without flinching and would listen to their recitations until perfection was attained. Undoubtedly White owed much of the quickness and firmness of his mental grip to this maternal schooling. He used later to say that his mother was one of the few people he had ever met who was able to teach in an interesting way. But there came a time when he needed the associations and discipline of a school.

Dr. Buckler saw the need for a brisker and fuller training, and plans were made to combine education for the children with residence in Europe. Probably no one but Harry's mother, with her

[2] Johnson, Allen, ed., *Dictionary of American Biography,* III, article T. H. Buckler.

intense dislike for the North, guessed how protracted the residence would be. The boy passed his last home Christmas at Hampton (1865) very uncomfortably sick with the measles, and sailed from New York with his Grandfather White in the Cunarder *Java*—called, for her unsteadiness, the *Jumping Java*—to join his mother and stepfather in London. For two or three months the family lived in Cavendish Square. The placid mid-Victorian world of Thackeray lay all about them. An observant youngster, Harry first made the acquaintance of London and began to form the affection for England which was later to be so important. In his fragment of autobiography he writes:

During our stay in London we used to walk about a good deal with my grandfather, who knew the city pretty well, and was able to show us many of the great private houses, public buildings, and other objects of interest. He had come abroad early in his life and had even been on the field of Waterloo about two months after that battle. His account of his experience, and of many of the officers who had taken part therein, and whose descendants were still living, was exceedingly interesting. We frequently walked past Apsley House, which was presented by the British nation to the Duke of Wellington, and at which in after years during my long connection with our legation (and subsequently embassy) I was to be an occasional guest of the third duke and his wife. It is not improbable that the realization that the history of England and our own were the same up to 1776, and that there was far more in common between the two countries than between America and any other, was then implanted in my mind. The London of that day was considerably different from the same city even a few years afterward. The rules of society, that is, of the Victorian epoch, were but little relaxed; no ladies ever drove in hansom cabs, nor did they, so far as I can remember, walk much in the streets. Nearly every lady of importance went out to dinner in what was known as a chariot, a large two-seated carriage swung on C-springs; a coachman sitting on the hammercloth, on the sides of which the family arms or coronet or crest were emblazoned, and one or more footmen standing up behind.

After London came a longer stay in France, first at Versailles and later in a third-floor apartment in Paris, at 6 Rue de Presbourg, facing the Arc de Triomphe. The most important feature of the residence here during 1866-67 was Harry's study at the Institut

Aubert-Savary, a school affiliated with the Lycée Napoléon. Here he perfected his knowledge of French, a tongue he was to find indispensable in his later career; and he was taught also geography, history, mathematics, and French literature. Not least valuable was the strict regimen of the school. The hours were long, the boys were kept in the classroom nearly all day, in the single half-hour allowed for "recreation" no games were permitted, and the highest standard of scholarship was required. White later remembered "passing an examination on a map of France, without any names, which involved a knowledge of the prefectures, eighty-nine in number, the very much larger number of sous-prefectures, all the rivers and railroads, the names of the eighty-nine departments, and much else besides. In looking back upon those days, and over my whole life, I do not think I ever had anything so perfectly pictured upon my brain as the map of France as that country was before the loss of Alsace-Lorraine." Here also he had his first opportunity to become acquainted with the French character, for though there was a small group of American and English boys, all the other pupils were of representative French bourgeois stock.

These were days of what seemed a secure splendor in Paris, but the shadow of vast changes was already rising on the horizon. While the little Prince Imperial was being lifted to hand the Legion of Honor ribbon to visiting statesmen, while Eugénie presided over the gilt-and-plush of the showy court, while tourists admired the avenues created by Baron Haussmann and the operas of Offenbach and Gounod, wars were shaking the surrounding nations. In the spring of Harry's arrival in France, Prussia and Austria plunged into the conflict which ended at Sadowa and which turned French eyes nervously upon Bismarck. As the French Guards were withdrawn from Rome, Garibaldi again took the field. Yet the imperial ceremonies went on with more pomp than ever, and could not but impress a youth of Harry's age. He had a season ticket to the glittering Exhibition of 1867 on the Champ de Mars, and was as curious as everybody else over the locomotives, the sewing-machines, the strange feather-weight metal called aluminum, the new pneumatic tube, the Essen guns, and the Chinese jewelry.[3]

[3] An interesting sketch of Paris as it appeared to Americans in these years may be found in Dix, Morgan, *Memoirs of John A. Dix,* II, 150 ff.

What impressed him still more were the military processions and parades which welcomed one European sovereign after another on visits to the Emperor, who was just emerging from his status of a parvenu among monarchs. Among them were King William of Prussia, shortly to become the first German Emperor, who brought his tall Chancellor, Bismarck, in the *Landwehr* uniform; and the Tsar Alexander II, who sat on horseback in the June sunshine at Longchamps with Napoleon III and the Prussian King to watch Marshal Canrobert's troops march by. At one military review forty thousand troops appeared on parade. The boy saw also the imposing scene in the Palais de l'Industrie when the Emperor distributed the prizes to exhibitors, the guests including the Prince of Wales and the Sultan of Turkey. A state procession about the great hall preceded the imperial speech, but the whole occasion lay under a cloud produced by the sudden news of the execution of Maximilian at Queretaro in Mexico. Some of these ceremonies made a lasting impression upon him. He writes:

In the year 1867, although only a little over seventeen years of age, but being as tall as I have ever been since, I began to go into society. In view of the exceptional opportunities which that year afforded for seeing the world, I attended various important functions connected more or less with the Exhibition. . . . The one of which I have the most distinct recollection as one of the grandest state functions I have ever attended was the great ball given by the prefect of the Seine, Baron Haussmann, and the Municipality of Paris, at the old Hotel de Ville (which was destroyed by the Commune in 1871) to the Emperor Napoleon and the two sovereigns who happened to be visiting him at the time, the Russian Emperor and the King of Prussia. The former was accompanied by Prince Gortschakoff, who was then considered one of the leading statesmen of Europe, and the King by Count Bismarck, Count von Moltke, and other eminent Prussians. The scene was one of great brilliance, and must have cost the municipality an enormous sum. Although having no connection with the American delegation, I remember (as the carriage in which I was seated slowly approached the Hotel de Ville on the way to the ball) seeing that of General Dix, our Minister

---

White and his elders saw a good deal of John A. Dix as our minister to France, and admired him; he made his home in the Rue de Presbourg, near them.

to France, drive by, and convincing the police who were keeping the slow line that I was part of the general's suite; whereupon they let our carriage pull out of line and follow that of the American Minister to the diplomatic entrance of the great building, reaching the ball probably an hour or more earlier than would have been possible had our carriage remained in line. The Avenue Victoria leading up to the Hotel de Ville was brightly illuminated, with lights of every color in festoons and huge stars placed at different points; so was the beautiful façade itself. There were state quadrilles, a state supper for the royalties and distinguished person. in one of the large rooms of the palace, and I was sufficiently entertained to remain till four o'clock in the morning.

The winter of 1867-68 the family spent in Rome, after hesitating between that city and Dresden, with the result that Harry became as proficient in Italian as in French. It meant a good deal to the future diplomatist to see so much of the old Europe, before railways, telegraphs, and tours for the million had quite transformed it. He traveled to Rome by a combination of diligence and train. In other words, he was one of that disappearing race of travelers who heard the crack of the whip as the horses galloped through the French meadows, who saw the sun rise over the central Alps as they toiled up the slopes of the Jura, who knew the lore of post stations and little local inns. Switzerland and Italy were still the countries of Ruskin's *Præterita*, and Rome was unspoiled. The family settled in a large, comfortable apartment in the Via Gregoriana on the Pincian Hill, with a superb view of the city stretching away to St. Peter's dome in the distance. Here they remained six months, Harry exploring the streets on foot with such thoroughness that he soon knew Rome better than he ever knew New York. Injudicious exposure in the raw spring weather brought on the then inevitable sequel, an attack of Roman fever, and after his recovery he was kept closer at home. But his recollections of the Eternal City were happy. Then under the dominion of the popes, it retained the customs of mediæval centuries. The papal guard patrolled the streets in quaint costume. Occasionally the pontiff himself was the dominant figure in some procession that seemed to have stepped straight from the Middle Ages, many participants wearing costumes of the time of Dante or the Borgias; while every

day the cardinals drove by in their scarlet state chariots, with footmen standing behind.

Through an old friend of Harry's family, Miss Emily Harper,
niece of Charles Carroll of Carrollton, they came into contact with
leading figures at the Vatican, among them the astute Cardinal
Antonelli, Papal Secretary of State, who was then laboring with
might and main to avert the absorption of the papal dominions by
the new Kingdom of Italy. These connections enabled Dr. and
Mrs. Buckler and the boys to attend many interesting ceremonies
in the Sistine Chapel and the principal Catholic churches, and
finally to be received by the Pope himself in private audience:

We had an audience with the Pope, Pius IX, whose reign lasted for
many years longer and was, I believe, the longest in the history of the
Papacy. The Pope had a kindly and honest face; but his knowledge of
America was somewhat limited, and I remember his asking after the
health of one or two public men who had been removed to another
sphere several years previously.

The two years which followed were spent in what outwardly
seemed desultory study and travel, Harry being under the supervision now of one member of the family and now another, but
always really under his mother's stern control. The family returned
north in 1868, and he accompanied Dr. Buckler on a tour of
Germany. He always recalled the provincial manners of Berlin,
where at even the most fashionable hotels the guests still dined *en
famille*, with the proprietor sitting at the head of the table. In the
autumn of 1868 his mother and stepfather, with his infant half-
brother William H. Buckler, returned to Baltimore for the winter,
but Harry, Julian, and their grandfather remained, first in England
and later in Paris. In the French capital the boys had as private
tutor Mr. Strother Ancrum Smith, a former fellow of St. Catherine's
College, Cambridge, who coached them well in the classics and
mathematics. He was fond of astronomy, and Harry always carried
with him a memory of his wrinkled old face, with a monocle
screwed into one eye, peering intently out of the window at the
heavens. Among the American families in Paris that winter were
Mr. and Mrs. Benjamin Rush, with their two daughters, who lived
in the same house with the Whites and who took the boys much

into the American circle. A short visit to the United States in the spring of 1869 hardly interrupted Harry's European routine. The family was soon again in Paris, this time taking up more permanent quarters at 11 Rue de Tilsitt, for Grandfather White was ageing rapidly and averse to further movement.

Actually these years were by no means as aimless and undisciplined as they might seem. Harry's mother oversaw almost every detail of his life, and her training was rigid to the point of severity. She was a woman of firm will, fixed prejudices, and not a few peculiarities; one of the "strong-minded" women whom Victorian times produced quite as frequently as it did languishing females. Among her traits were a marked indifference to dress and many other mundane concerns, and an intense interest in religion, benevolence, and personal conduct. She took no pains to preserve her once neat figure, she wore her hair combed back into a small "bun," and she dressed with severe plainness. She went out very little in society. On her sons she imposed a salutary if exacting discipline. She kept them at their books; she insisted that they should master the chief modern tongues, and always spoke and wrote in Italian to Harry. They rose and retired at fixed hours, they had to be usefully occupied, and their behavior was carefully guarded. An atmosphere of piety pervaded the household. All its members were required to be familiar with the Bible—Mrs. Buckler had a way of rapping out sudden questions on small points of Biblical history; grace was said at all meals; and there was family worship both morning and evening. Sunday was observed with great strictness.

It was, moreover, a household interested in works of benevolence. From time to time during the Reconstruction years Mrs. Buckler, still warmly sympathetic with the crushed South, brought over to Paris two or three Southern girls of ruined families and gave them a good education in French schools. These girls, sharing the family home, were also dressed with a total disregard of fashion and kept under a rigorous discipline.

It might have been better for Harry if his regular schooling had lasted longer, but his mother's prejudices made this impossible; she distrusted boarding-schools and vigorously decried universities, saying that her brother at Harvard had learned nothing except to smoke and drink. Yet in later years White's education, though irregularly secured, seemed better than that of most university men, and his mother's iron training must have had its value. Her emphasis on character was most salutary. For mere religious doctrine she cared little, though as a low-church Episcopalian she denounced Puseyism; for truthfulness, simplicity, purity, and temperance she cared everything. In these years Henry White was becoming that rare person, a young man of the world without any of the vices or dissipations of the world. Naturally sunny, light-hearted, and winning, his social traits were kept unspoiled. With plenty of money, plenty of leisure, moving rapidly from one European capital to another, and with no steadying work in college, he might easily have fallen into careless ways. It was Mrs. Buckler, with all her crotchets, who kept him fresh and uncorroded. It was also partly due to her that his simplicity, his warm interest in everyone he met, his ingenuousness and kindliness, were developed steadily. She was, as one of the family later remarked, a lioness who reared her cubs with many growls and rude cuffs, but she reared them in the right way.

Moreover, there was by no means a lack of gayety, for she and Dr. Buckler encouraged Harry to share in such wholesome amusements as riding, driving, dancing, skating, and swimming. He soon knew the little Anglo-American world of Paris, including some distinguished men and women, thoroughly. The winter of 1869-70 was one of constant enjoyment. He attended balls, dinners, receptions, the theater, and the opera, and rode regularly in the Bois de Boulogne.[4] For a time that winter, despite his mother's reluctance, he thought of entering Cambridge University. It happened that in Rome Dr. Buckler had met an English relative, the Rev. Mr. T. B. Rowe, then a house-master at Uppingham School, who had not only strongly advised a course at Cambridge, but had labored

[4] One of the gay and charming American women of the day in Paris was the young Mrs. Charles Moulton, later Mme. Lillie de Hegermann-Lindencrone. Her book, *In the Courts of Memory*, gives the atmosphere of the time and place, with sketches of many people White knew by sight—Auber, Haussmann, Massenet, M. Ollivier, the Duc de Persigny, Gautier, Delsarte, Doré, Jenny Lind; a bright and distinguished world, which was soon to come crashing down in ruin.

Grandfather White   Dr. Buckler

Mrs.
John Steward

John Steward,
of New York

Miss Mary Evans   Henry White

A FAMILY GROUP IN SWITZERLAND

to procure Mrs. Buckler's consent. Negotiations were opened with Trinity College for his entrance and that of his brother Julian. Both had heard enough of English universities to be attracted by their life and were eager for matriculation.

Unfortunately, at this juncture Harry began to show unmistakable symptoms of weak health. His parents were seized with alarm; the incipient phthisis which Dr. Buckler diagnosed seemed a premonition of the pulmonary consumption from which his father had so untimely died. The university plans were in his case hastily given up. At the close of the spring of 1870 a house, the Maison Barbentane, was taken at Trouville on the Normandy coast to give the boy sea air, and Dr. Buckler placed him under careful oversight.[5]

It was from this vantagepoint that he and his elders watched the Franco-Prussian War break over France, and like a terrible storm sweep away the Second Empire. Throughout the summer and fall the news of defeat and disaster came in successive dispatches. Sometimes it was mingled with sudden and unfounded rumors of victory. Harry was at the Deauville races one day, riding his mare Fanny, when he saw the crowd on the grandstand rise in a pandemonium of joy at the news that Marshal MacMahon had captured the Crown Prince and 20,000 German soldiers, thus turning the tide of the war. He at once turned his horse to Trouville, and arriving at the Casino, where all telegrams were received, found the report to have been utterly baseless. A more interesting episode occurred a little later. When the Empress Eugénie was compelled to take flight from Paris, she was secretly driven by the American dentist, Dr. Evans, in his private carriage to Trouville. As White later related the story:

In the harbor at Trouville there was at that time a yacht owned by Sir John Burgoyne, an English baronet, on which I happened to be taking tea on the afternoon of the day on which late in the evening the Empress and Dr. Evans arrived at Trouville, of which circumstance I

[5] Many Americans and Britons came to Havre and Trouville during the war, en route to England. White later recalled his friendship with Mrs. Jerome of New York and her children; particularly the second daughter, who married Lord Randolph Churchill and became the mother of Winston Churchill.

of course had no knowledge. The next morning, which was very stormy, I happened to get up early to look out of my window which faced the sea, and to my surprise, as a heavy gale was blowing at the time, I saw the yacht on which I had been the previous evening sailing out to sea between the wooden piers. I was the more surprised as Sir John Burgoyne had told me that they proposed remaining some time in Trouville, and it struck me as strange that they should change their minds so suddenly, especially in view of the gale which was then blowing. The yacht was a yawl, and not a large one, either, so that my astonishment can be easily understood. However, I thought no more of the matter until three or four days later, when the London *Times* arrived, with a telegram from its correspondent at Ryde, Isle of Wight, saying that the *Gazelle* had arrived there the evening before with the Empress Eugénie on board, after a very stormy passage. It then transpired that I had been a witness of the departure of that august person from France. It seems that Sir John Burgoyne had been induced to take her on board and face the dangers of the Channel, owing to a fear that unless the Empress could be got out of France immediately she would be arrested.

Painfully affected already by the American conflict, White found his sense of the inhumanity of war deepened by his observations of the French *débâcle*. Even at that safe distance from the battle lines, the crowds of refugees, the nervous preparations for an invasion, the gloom which descended upon the country, and the heavy casualty lists constituted a painful experience for anyone who loved the French people. The roads about Trouville were slashed across with deep ditches, covered with a temporary boarding which could be removed if the German armies attempted to advance along them. From the occupied parts of France, and especially from the refugee centers, there came pitiful demands for succor. It was an important part of White's education that twice before he attained his majority he witnessed the crushing defeat of two peoples with whom he had the most sympathetic ties. No small part of his life-long love of peace and his desire to promote it dated from these years.

Amid the excitement of the late autumn of the *année terrible*, the whole household slipped over from France to England, going by way of Havre to Southampton. When they left, Strasbourg had surrendered, the siege of Paris had commenced, and with no real

French armies left in the field, the Government of National Defence had proclaimed a *levée en masse*. France, with the provinces making a desperate effort to maintain the war and with the Commune impending, was no country for American residents. Harry's family and that of his uncle, Charles Ridgely, went for the early winter to Torquay on the Devonshire coast. With this migration to England the Marylander, now a clear-eyed and ruddy-cheeked young fellow, six feet three inches in height, definitely ceased to be a boy and became a man; one period in his life ended and another, more active and interesting, began.

CHAPTER THREE

English Sport and Society: Marriage

IN 1870, when the Buckler-White household removed to England, the Victorian Age was basking in a serene sunlight which sharply contrasted with the storminess of the continental scene. Disraeli was out, Gladstone was in. The Liberal Government was carrying through a long succession of popular reforms. Other European statesmen had to worry over alliances, invasions, wars and preparations for war; but Disraeli in 1870 could give his time to bringing out *Lothair* and Gladstone to publishing his *Juventus Mundi*. The Empire, never greater or more flourishing, everywhere showed signs of healthy development; Canada had just achieved federation, and the Cape Colony was given responsible government in 1871. In the field of letters achievements hardly second to those of the Elizabethan Age were now secure. Dickens had just died; Tennyson and Browning were at the height of their fame; Darwin's theories, diligently expounded by Huxley and Spencer, were reshaping the thought of the world. Livingstone was lost in Central Africa and Stanley was about to locate him. In industry and commerce England yet led the world, while no one even dreamed of a challenge to her financial supremacy. The picture had its shadows in festering slums, in the submerged tenth that Charles Booth was soon to explore, in class antagonisms and Irish troubles; but to foreign observers who saw only the best side, England seemed powerful, wealthy, and preëminently civilized.

Nor was there ever a time when those who had entrance to English society could find more to amuse and interest them. The landed gentry and the rich commercial families had as yet no apprehension of the levies on property and income that were to revolutionize England a generation later. What with politics, literature, and sport, the pursuits of London and of the country houses provided ample diversion for a set of men and women remarkably homogeneous in their tastes. They electioneered and spoke in Parliament, they looked after their estates, they shot and hunted, they attended horse-shows, race-meetings, and polo and cricket matches; during the London season they went to regattas, the opera, balls, picture exhibitions, and political receptions. Except to France and Switzerland, they traveled little abroad. The "season" in London was from May till the August grouse-shooting began. Then sport called the men to the country, and they stayed till the sport had ended, Parliament reopened, and the round in town was under way. It was a society based upon rural life, with country rather than town houses as the centers of its activity. It was also a society where work, paid or unpaid, was not a constant preoccupation, but where every man was expected to do something or to be somebody.

Into this social sphere, though in no sense a closed one, the ordinary American could penetrate only with difficulty, and even when inside he would usually find it as strange as Henry James's hero, Christopher Newman, found the French *grand monde*. It was a society of close-knit local and personal interests, and peculiarly English—not cosmopolitan. But now and then an American with special advantages of personality or of background would be taken into this society at an early age, and in the course of a few years find it completely familiar. Such was the experience of Henry White, and by a strange "ill wind" it was the direct outcome of the tendency to consumption which we have just mentioned. With a view to eradicating this tendency permanently, Dr. Buckler insisted upon Harry's spending the next few winters in the hunting-field. To that medical advice Harry owed his excellent health and his knowledge of town and country life in England.

Both his character and training made him soon feel at home in the social circles to which, through hunting life, he was gradually introduced. The easy, leisurely outdoor existence of his Maryland boyhood, and his love of people and sports, fitted him for the English scene. From boyhood he had been able to ride, swim, shoot, and dance well. Despite his weak lungs, he was an engaging figure, tall, broad-shouldered, and full of vitality. There was something breezily American in his frank affability, his interest in every-one he met, and his warm responsiveness. His acquaintance among county families and hunting-folk grew steadily wider, and he was soon being asked to dinners, dances, and shooting-parties. It was an invaluable introduction to the people with whom he was later to deal. Indeed, late in life he wrote that "the nine winters of fox-hunting were the best preparation which I could have had for the twenty-one years of diplomacy of which I was subsequently (though I little knew it at the time) to have experience in England; not only because of the opportunities for acquiring a thorough knowl-edge of the different classes, but of meeting many of the leading men of the period, and also those who became more or less promi-nent, politically or otherwise, during the years which were to follow."

His first hunting was done with his uncle Charles from Tor-quay, a rather unfavorable country because of the high Devon banks and ditches; soon afterward he hunted from Leamington in Warwickshire. In the autumn of 1871 he took a hunting-box at Market Harborough, in the district made famous by the pen of Whyte-Melville.[1] Here he soon allied himself with his second cousins, Mr. and Mrs. John Steward of New York, and an establish-ment was formed sufficiently large to permit of some entertaining. In the years which followed he and his brother Julian, who joined this household in 1873, kept a considerable stable and hunted all over Leicestershire, Rutlandshire, and Northamptonshire. Harry became acquainted with the "countries" of many famous packs—the Belvoir, the Cottesmore, the Quorn, the Pytchley, and others—and found a growing fascination in following them. He liked the pageantry of the hunt, many of the meets being attended by large fields. It was advisable in those days, in the hunting country proper, or "shires," for any aspirant to Parliament to appear from time to time in the hunting field and be critically appraised by followers of the local hunt. Not infrequently a man's election depended upon the impression he made.

It was not all amusement; it was in part education. Perhaps Henry White, in his enthusiasm for the sport, exaggerated its value as a discipline. "The hunting-field, as I soon realized," he wrote later, "is a wonderful place of training for character, good manners, good temper, and coolness of judgment, and it has played a very impor-tant part in the development of those qualities in the statesmen and

---

[1] Whyte-Melville, G. J., *Market Harborough; or, How Mr. Sawyer Went to the Shires* (1861).

HENRY WHITE AS BOY AND YOUNG MAN

the military—not infrequently also the naval—men of England." He learned some lessons of pluck, self-control, and tact. But the fact of chief importance was that he thus became familiar with the life of the landed families of England. Year after year, until his marriage in 1879, the hunting-box at Market Harborough was kept up, he living there from October to April with his brother and cousins, but traveling at frequent intervals to Paris. His grand-father and mother lived at 2 Rue de Presbourg, at the juncture of the Champs Elysées and Place de l'Etoile, and this Harry regarded as home. Whenever a heavy frost descended upon England and made hunting impossible, he would catch the train for Paris and remain there till a thaw had set in.

Among the mansions within easy reach of Market Harborough and often visited were Althorp, the handsome home of the Spencers; Rockingham Castle, the seat of the Watsons; Cottesbrooke, of the Langham family; Barley Thorpe, near Oakham; and Burley-on-the-hill, the hunting-box of a descendant of Lord Chancellor Hatton. It is a region, indeed, rich in examples of fine mediæval and Elizabethan architecture. Harry formed a special regard for the fifth Earl Spencer, a leading Liberal politician, who was Lord-Lieutenant of Ireland under Gladstone for half a dozen years after 1868. White liked his simple, charming manner, and found him a daring rider in the hunting-field. He was equally fond of the Watsons of Rockingham, who remained his close friends until their premature deaths not many years later. Still another country house was Lamport Hall, eleven miles from Market Harborough, where the owner, old Sir Charles Isham, had developed some harmless peculiarities. Henry White writes:

He had erected a great rockery in the corner of his garden at Lamport, and had scattered there in various caves which he had constructed small figures of gnomes, to which he attributed various powers and which he used to go and talk to, as he fancied, from time to time. Dear old Lady Isham was eminently practical, on the other hand, and particularly desirous of encouraging fox-hunting, which Sir Charles detested, and I have frequently seen him, after she had taken him out to the meet and gotten him on to his horse, galloping home at a furious rate when out of her sight, to escape from following the hounds and not infrequently to confer with the gnomes. They had no son, but two attractive daughters, the younger of whom, known as Emmie, became a great friend of mine, and eventually married the eldest son of McLeod of McLeod, of Dunvegan Castle in the Isle of Skye.

These were happy years in Henry White's life; "years," he wrote later, "or perfect enjoyment without any cares or responsibilities worth mentioning." He saw more and more of the world, rubbed elbows with all kinds of folk, cemented some valuable friendships, and had the pleasure of constantly changing scenes. In addition to his frequent brief trips to Paris he used to spend at least a fortnight there at the Christmas holidays, as well as the spring and part of the autumn; and there were always balls and theater-parties, dinners and visits to friends, which made the time pass in a round of gayety. One summer (1872) he was with his family at Homburg; another (1874) at Biarritz and at Cauterets in the Pyrenees; the next year he was at a villa called "Le Bocage" near Geneva, and in 1876 he divided his time between the Black Forest and Trouville.

Nor did he fail to make friends with stimulating young men of his own age. He knew a few of his brother's college mates at Cambridge, and formed valuable acquaintances at Oxford. A visit to two Baltimore friends who were residents at St. John's College in April, 1871, delighted him. Oxford had then but little changed from its old-time character, and as he wrote in his old age, "the interesting talk in the common rooms of the colleges after dinner, the beautiful services in the college chapels, the boating on the Isis, the semi-monastic character of residence in the old rooms of the colleges, have left in my mind a sense of charm which will remain throughout my life." Among those he met here and who became friends were Maurice de Bunsen, grandson of the great German diplomatist, who was later to be British ambassador to Spain and Austria-Hungary; Lord Seaham, who became Lord Londonderry; and Frederick de Sausmarez, of the island of Guernsey, who in after life was among White's special intimates. He met also two wealthy young Americans of Christ Church—Allen Thorndike Rice and Lloyd Bryce—who were later successive editors of the *North American Review*. These young men formed a more intellectual group than the hunting set, and their contact profited Henry White in a new way.

He was able frequently to return to the United States, and paid short visits to Hampton, Newport, and friends in New York or on the Hudson. He was one of the early members of the Knickerbocker Club, joining that rather exclusive organization in 1876, when it was four years old. He long recalled a visit during the summer of 1873 to the home of Mrs. James H. Jones (*née* Schermerhorn) on the Hudson, and a stay that same season with his cousins, the Chews, in Germantown, in their old house, "Cliveden," marked by the bullets of the battle. These trips to the United States did something to extend his acquaintance with Eastern society, and he soon knew a good many of the younger people. In his brief reminiscences he recalls a coaching party at the Jerome Park races in 1873, on which he accompanied a gay group of young men and women. The men included Thomas Newbold and James H. Jones; the women the Misses Emily Yznaga, Sarah King, and Minnie Stevens, who in after life became, respectively, the Duchess of Manchester, Mrs. Adrian Iselin, and Lady Paget.

Now and then, in this period of almost complete idleness, some sudden display of address and energy would show the capacities which lay beneath Henry White's rather care-free exterior. An incident which illustrated his excutive talents occurred in the middle 'seventies, when he suddenly became interested in a new building for the American Episcopal Church in Paris, of which he was a member. Its old edifice in the Rue Bayard had become too small. For some time the rector, the Reverend Mr. John B. Morgan, had been receiving promises of money for the erection of a new church, but he was hampered by a conservative vestry which refused its consent to any change. White became convinced that it was necessary to turn the vestry out at the next yearly election. These vestrymen had been in the habit of reëlecting themselves in a comfortable Trollopean way every Easter Monday without interference from the indifferent pewholders. But appealing to a number of his friends in the church, including Richard Henry Dana of *Two Years Before the Mast* fame, White rallied a substantial group to his aid. To the astonishment and dismay of the famous dentist, Dr. Evans, and several others of the old vestry, just as they were preparing to go through the annual perfunctory ceremony, some fifteen or twenty pewholders appeared and voted in a new set of men. The

post of senior warden went to Dana; Harrison Ritchie was elected
junior warden; while White himself became a vestryman, and
was soon elected secretary, where he labored diligently for the new
building.

There was no great difficulty in pushing the church to completion, and within a few years it was opened in the Avenue de l'Alma.
White always took pride in his connection with it, and as ambassador to France frequently attended the services. There exists a
letter to him from R. H. Dana, dated September 7th, 1880, when
the author was quitting his Paris residence, in which Dana remarks
that "You have a right to take a large share in the honor of the
achievement, for you have worked hard and faithfully, and nothing
but perseverance and hard work has accomplished it."

By the middle 'seventies Henry White had entirely regained his
health. It is not hard to reconstruct a picture of him, ruddy, active,
overflowing with spirits, and the best of good fellows to everyone;
a young man apparently devoted to amusement, but with a more
serious side somewhere latent. A photograph taken of him with
his family at "Le Bocage" in the summer of 1875 shows a handsome
man of twenty-five, dressed less staidly than anyone else in the
circle—checked trousers, a polka-dot tie, and flaring collar, with a
dark coat and no hat. His tall figure had filled out, so that the
once slender youth had become a person of striking presence; but
a mustache in the continental fashion failed to obscure the engaging
boyishness of his face. To scores of his friends—for he made friends
everywhere—he was simply "Harry." Without being a wit or an
intellectual, he had qualities of strong sense, a vein of merriness,
and a frank sociability which made him good company in all
groups. He had also a solid dependability which everyone recognized and which led people to call him sometimes, even at that
early age, "good old Harry"; a dependability founded on character, and bulwarked by a simple piety which his mother had
instilled into him.

The second decisive turning-point in Henry White's life—for
we may count his mother's prolonged migration to Europe as the
first—was now at hand. In the autumn of 1876, still a trifle lame
from a hunting accident in England the previous winter, which
had cost him a broken leg, he went with his brother Julian to

visit Baltimore and the Centennial Exhibition. On this trip he saw somewhere a photograph of Miss Margaret Stuyvesant Rutherfurd, of a well known New Jersey and New York family, and was greatly struck by it. The next summer he returned to the United States, and not by accident spending some time in Miss Rutherfurd's vicinity at Newport, met her and fell immediately and completely in love. It was not strange that he did so. "Daisy" Rutherfurd was a young woman of really remarkable beauty and poise. She was the sort of girl at whom not only men but other women turned around to look. Forty years after this time, when White was in Paris with President Wilson, an Englishwoman recalled how she had first seen Miss Rutherfurd across a crowded theater and had sat up with a gasp of delight at her loveliness. She was one of those few women whom it gives a man a kind of public distinction to marry.

Margaret Rutherfurd was the eldest daughter of Lewis Morris Rutherfurd, an astronomer of note. Her father, as his name indicated, was descended from Lewis Morris, a signer of the Declaration of Independence; while her mother, who had been Margaret Chanler, was connected with the Stuyvesant family. Educated almost entirely at home, she had been given careful tuition by her father, a scientist of broad tastes. He lived in a large brick house at the corner of Second Avenue and Eleventh Street in New York, where he had mounted a thirteen-inch refracting telescope, one of the best in the East. He was one of the first to practice celestial photography, and was known also for a unique spectroscope which he had devised of flint glass with two crown glass compensating prisms. The family had an estate in New Jersey named Tranquillity, while they spent a good deal of time, especially after the health of the parents began to fail, in foreign travel. The tastes of the household were decidedly intellectual, and Margaret had inherited them. Compared with Henry White she was reserved, while her rigid training had given her a distinctly Puritanical quality. Among her admirers White distinguished himself from the beginning by his impetuosity, and some of his letters to friends overflow with his feelings. When he left the United States in 1877 he was not only a determined but also a declared suitor for her hand.

If it had been necessary to return to America to see Miss Ruther-furd in 1878, White would have done so, but her family saved him the trouble by planning a European tour. He spent the summer at Chaumont, near Neuchatel, going thence to Paris in September to see the Exposition Universelle which registered the recovery of France from the Prussian War. That winter (1878-79) Miss Ruther-furd was at Torquay with her ailing mother—her father often being little better—while White was enjoying his last season of hunting at Market Harborough. Their friendship flourished. He wrote to her frequently, saw her occasionally, and pressed her to visit the Stewards and follow some of the hunts with him; but though her sister went to Market Harborough and enjoyed the outdoor life immensely, Margaret remained with her mother. Later, during the London season, the Rutherfurds went to Malvern. As late as the end of June the letters which the two young people exchanged were semi-formal in style. But before she and her parents sailed at the end of the summer, he had been accepted. The engage-ment was announced at the beginning of October, 1879, and by the middle of that month Henry White's mail was full of letters of congratulation.

On December 3, 1879, the wedding took place at St. Mark's in the Bowery, with the Reverend Dr. (later Bishop) Potter officiat-ing; a church where the bride's mother, grandmother, and great-grandmother had all been married. Henry White, after spending some time with his mother and the rest of the White-Buckler circle in Paris, had been in the United States since the middle of Novem-ber. For a time he had been a busy, hurried, and enormously happy young man, flitting in and out of New York, eating his Thanks-giving dinner at Hampton, and visiting his friend Maurice de Bunsen, now at the British Embassy in Washington. The wedding attracted a large crowd of fashionable people, and we are fortunate in having a description of it from a youthful cousin of the bride:[2]

Into St. Mark's from the Stuyvesant house which overlooked it came the tall bride on the arm of her taller father, his face curiously framed in silver hair worn long. A placid bride; rather eagle-eyed; family laces, French dressmakers, pearls from the bridegroom, did not lessen that

[2] By Mrs. Richard Aldrich of New York.

detachment which seemed to express her favorite hymn, taught not long before to the little cousin who watched her now from a family pew:

"Let all your converse be sincere,
Your conscience as the noonday clear."

There was nothing detached about the expectant bridegroom. Joy shone from the vestry doorway where he waited, joy animated the black-clothed figure soon standing beside the bride. Joy came down the aisles after the solemnization of matrimony had made them man and wife. The handsomest of couples? Not quite; the bride's parents following the four bridesmaids were even handsomer, though not equal in height. . . .

The Stuyvesant house at 175 Second Avenue has been described in one of Fawcett's novels. New York seems always to have contained people who entertained and who did not purchase horsehair for their drawing-rooms; to their tastes, brocades, velvet, and later satin, were likely to display hosts and guests to better advantage. On that day Mrs. Rutherfurd's house was of course unlike itself, for a reception space is more needed than heirlooms. Of the splendid furnishings only the chandeliers seemed to be in place. An afternoon in December is short. While the sun still shone Mrs. Henry White came down the stairs, having exchanged her bridal whiteness for sealskins; and her commanding voice rang out very sweetly as she approached a hall full of emotional relatives—"Mamma last!" Then she somehow reached her mother immediately, we were showering rice through an awning, and the wedding was over.

Just how important this marriage was to prove to his future career neither Henry White nor anyone else could then divine. His wife was perfectly fitted, as the event showed, to give him domestic happiness. But in addition she was a woman of ambition; her father, a man of wealth who might have remained a dilettante, had by hard work achieved rank as an astronomer, and she had the American feeling that everyone should have some useful employment. She at once instilled her views into her husband. He was now twenty-nine; he should embark, she thought, upon some definite career. "Up to the time of my marriage," writes White, "I had lived a life of enjoyment, with no thought of doing any serious work, or of making myself useful in the world other than by the cultivation of friendships, and the promotion thereby of good-fellowship and good feeling among those by whom I was surrounded, both at home and abroad. But shortly after my marriage, my wife, who had an exceptionally interesting mind and a strong sense of public duty, began to talk to me about doing something useful in the world, a matter which we thereupon began to discuss from time to time. Eventually we came to the conclusion that diplomacy would be on the whole the best way in which I could serve my country, especially as she would be of great assistance to me in the pursuit of that profession."

This statement is characteristically generous; actually Henry White's mind, especially since de Bunsen's entrance into diplomacy, had already turned toward that field as a profession. The choice proved so sound that we are likely to forget how bold it was for any young man to make it. Business, the law, almost any other calling, offered firm certitudes; diplomacy was for Americans then all politics, uncertainty, and vagueness.[3] But by this bold choice he converted all his previous training—his travels, his knowledge of different countries, his acquaintance with the English and French character, which otherwise might have been a mere luxury—into an admirable preparation for his future career.

[3] But it is to be noted that President Hayes had displayed an exceptional regard for merit in appointing men to the diplomatic service, and that the advocates of civil-service reform, a movement of growing strength, by no means neglected the diplomatic and consular services of the government. A fight had begun in which White was glad to be enlisted.

MRS. HENRY WHITE
(née Rutherfurd)

CHAPTER FOUR

Mr. Taft and the Viennese Legation

I N HENRY WHITE's life there were few delays which did not in the
end serve a useful purpose. His resolution to embark upon the
diplomatic profession was made at the beginning of 1880, and he
did not actually find his first minor post in a legation till 1883.
Yet the time was not lost. He had unwittingly equipped himself
for his future career by acquiring a wide knowledge of European
countries and languages, and by familiarity with many circles in
England and France. He had greatly increased his potential usefulness in any diplomatic capacity by his marriage. But he was signally
deficient in his knowledge of American politics and politicians, and
this deficiency he was now partly to repair.

During this winter of 1879-80 White, staying in the Second Avenue house of his wife's parents, made a trip to Philadelphia to discuss the possibility of a foreign-service appointment with John
Welsh, a banker who had been minister to England under President Hayes, and of whom White had seen a good deal in his
hunting-days. Welsh naturally advised him to make his wishes
known to all his friends and acquaintances in public life, and to
pull what strings he could in Administration circles. For various
reasons White did not press the matter. The chief of these was
that his grandfather was increasingly feeble; his mind seemed failing, some of his investments were in confusion, and as the next
head of the family, White felt it necessary to devote much time to
the old gentleman and his affairs. The following two years were
therefore spent in European and American society—much more of
American society than ever before—with no fixed occupation. But
it was in these years just after his marriage that he became intimate
with men and agencies later invaluable in promoting his career.

In the spring of 1880, for example, he and his wife made a short
stay in Washington, lodging at Wormley's Hotel, an old-style

Southern caravanserai at the corner of H and Fifteenth Streets which was then a great favorite of Senators and Representatives having no houses of their own.[1] He quickly became intimate with Levi P. Morton, the well-known banker, then just entering upon his long public career by serving a term as Representative from New York. Morton, indeed, he had known in London, where the banker had sometimes come on business, his firm being fiscal agents of the American government. White was repeatedly thrown into contact with John Hay, whom he had known slightly in Paris when Hay was secretary of legation under Minister John Bigelow, and who was now acting for a brief period as Assistant Secretary of State. He also became acquainted with Senators Edmunds of Vermont, Hale of Maine, and Hoar of Massachusetts, and others of lesser importance in both houses of Congress; and he saw something of Sir Edward Thornton and Maxime Outrey, the British and French ministers. Washington was still a small city. Its society was pleasantly informal, and people who were on a friendly footing frequently "dropped in" without invitation at one another's homes in the evenings.

That same winter he was in Ottawa for nearly a week, and several times enjoyed the hospitality of Government House, then presided over by Lord Lorne and his wife, the Princess Louise, fourth daughter of Queen Victoria. The Whites would have gone out still more in Washington and New York but for the sudden death of Mrs. White's sister-in-law, which threw the whole family into mourning. They felt it necessary to spend some time with the bereaved brother, Rutherfurd Stuyvesant, till in late May they sailed for Europe, and accompanied the Buckler household and Grandfather White again to "Les Frémonts" near Trouville for the summer. In the autumn, since the old gentleman's health was more precarious than ever, they took an apartment at 2 Avenue Hoche, which Mrs. White always recalled as charming and which was destined to be their home for the next three years. Here, on October 12, 1880, their first child was born and was christened Muriel.

[1] See the paragraph on the past glories of the Wormley Hotel in Bowers, Claude G., *The Tragic Era*, p. 245. It had housed political leaders like Schuyler Colfax and Caleb Cushing, and fashionable people like the Marquis and Mme. de Noailles.

Here, too, Henry White, with a wife and *ménage* of his own, rapidly extended his circle of French friendships. The first houses in Paris were open to him and he met many picturesque figures of the old and new aristocracies. One of the families he knew best was the extensive Rothschild clan. It included the Baron Alphonse de Rothschild, who owned the house in which Prince Talleyrand had lived and died, opposite the Tuileries; Gastave de Rothschild, with a house surrounded by a large garden opposite the Elysée Palace; and the Baron Nathaniel de Rothschild, whose large *hôtel* stood on the Parc Monceau. "All these Rothschild houses," he writes, "were full of the most beautiful works of art, and they entertained at that time the leading members not only of French society, but of the artistic and literary worlds. Conversation, in which the French in general are so good, was always most interesting at these entertainments, and sometimes of a high order of wit and learning; particularly at the small dinners, which were the more attractive because one was surrounded by everything that was pleasing to the eye."

Among others with whom the Whites became intimate were the famous Countess Mélanie de Pourtalès, one of the beauties of the old Empire and a close friend of the Empress Eugénie; and the Comte de Montsaulnin, husband of Mrs. White's cousin, Anna Morris, a veteran of the Franco-Prussian War and a Deputy in Parliament. They saw a good deal of the German ambassador, Prince Hohenlohe, already one of the important statesmen of Europe. He had been head of the Bavarian Government in the late 'sixties, had done much to bring about the union of North and South Germany, and had been a delegate to the Congress of Berlin in 1878; but the greatest distinction of his long career, the German chancellorship, lay ahead of him. The Whites were frequently invited to the German Embassy in the Rue de Lille, a building interesting as the residence during the Napoleonic period of the Empress Joséphine's son, Prince Eugène de Beauharnais. Walking on the high terrace along the Quai d'Orsay, and admiring the Embassy's beautiful view up and down the Seine, with the Tuileries on the other side, White—as an American citizen—could not but be struck by the contrast it presented to the mean and temporary

quarters of the American minister. Still other friends of this period
were the Spanish ambassador, the Marquis de Molins, and his wife:

They were typical in the best sense of Spaniards of the upper class,
and were at home in their charming Embassy on the Quai d'Orsay near
the Pont de la Concorde, every Monday evening, when there was usually
dancing and a very pleasant assemblage of Paris society. Old Queen
Isabella, who had been deposed from the throne of Spain in 1868 and
had lived in Paris thereafter, was frequently a guest at those parties,
and was a marvel to behold of enormous obesity. Her career as a reigning queen is so well known from the time of the famous "Spanish
marriages" devised by King Louis Philippe and his minister, M. Guizot,
that I need not dwell upon it. It will be remembered that the iniquitous
intention of these two distinguished personages was based on the theory
that, as a result of the Queen's having no children, the crown of Spain
should pass eventually to the King's son, the Duc de Montpensier, and
his wife. Queen Isabella, however, completely foiled their intentions, and
led a life which was not an example of the highest morality. She was
also a victim of endless revolutions, the last of which, under Marshal
Prim, two years before the fall of the French Empire, resulted in her
permanent dismissal from Spain.

This pleasant but rather idle life in Paris would probably soon
have worn upon Henry White. He occupied it by looking after
the family estate, by church duties, by bits of travel, and by getting
his portrait executed by the fashionable Léon Bonnat, and that of
Mrs. White by John S. Sargent, whom Mrs. White selected, though
he was still young and unknown. Sargent, indeed, was not yet
thirty; he had received honorable mention in the Salon of 1878, and
had been given a medal three years later for his "Portrait of a Young
Lady," but it was his fine picture of Miss Burckhardt which determined the Whites to give him the commission. In the summer of
1881 and again in 1882 White went alone for a short visit to the
United States. One unhappy event of these years was Mrs. White's
severe illness with typhoid, followed by a long and tedious con-
valescence at Pau and Cannes. Her husband's letters show that for
a time he was distracted by anxiety, but later he was able to enter
into the life of the Riviera with zest, moving in both the French
and English circles, and spending a good deal of time with old Lord
Clarence Paget, who had a steam yacht at Nice.

Not for a moment did White give up his ambitions, and when Levi P. Morton came to Paris in 1881 as the American minister, while President Garfield retained James Russell Lowell as our minister to Great Britain, his hopes grew stronger. He had met Lowell soon after the latter's arrival in London, while with Morton he was now on a footing of great friendliness. He and Mrs. White were often at the American Legation; the Minister and his wife sometimes came to the apartment on Avenue Hoche. In his talks with Lowell and Morton, White told them that he wanted a secretaryship of legation, preferably in London or Paris. It happened that Lowell's first secretary, E. S. Nadal, later known as a charming if minor essayist, was chafing at his London routine, and eager to obtain a good consulship. Nadal suggested that if wires could be pulled in such a way as to give him the consulship, he would gladly resign his London post in White's favor, and Lowell promised his cordial assent. As for Morton, he was eager to have White connected with the Paris legation, even if nothing but an attachéship could at first be found.

In his visit to the United States in 1881 Henry White spent some days in Washington with Morton, and for the first time met men of the highest political station. He attended one of President Garfield's receptions, and wrote home a brief account of it. "I was surprised," he says, "at the dignity of the President's manner and the almost elegance of his bearing; as also at the greatly improved appearance of the White House, there being a servant, well dressed, inside the glass doors to open them for everyone going in or out. The President was very civil to me." Morton made a formal application to Secretary of State Blaine to have White appointed to his legation, and accompanied by Morton, the young man called upon the Secretary. He writes:

Mr. Blaine was singularly courteous to me; said I was just the man to whom he would like to give a diplomatic appointment, and stated most boldly that he would like to turn out the Berlin man (Everett), who takes on the airs of an Englishman and is practically not an American. He considered the Nadal question in a very favorable light, and thought it could be arranged. His private secretary made notes on the subject, and as we paid a visit afterwards to Hitt, who seems also very anxious on the subject, I imagine something may come of the matter. Hitt took my address most carefully and I am to write to him in the event of our going abroad. I told Blaine plainly that I did not want an attachéship, even if he were disposed to create one, on the ground that I did not consider it a sufficiently serious way of entering the career; of which remark he seemed to think favorably, and expressed a strong desire to make an opening for me.

The wait for action in Washington proved longer than White expected. However, on Christmas Day of 1882 one of his special responsibilities was removed by the sudden death of Grandfather White in Paris. Rising apparently in his usual health, which was remarkable for his eighty-six years, the old gentleman suddenly passed away a half hour later. It was a blow which the grandson felt keenly. "He was gifted with a happy nature and a charming character," writes White, "and was always anxious to make those about him happy. To my brother and me he was the most devoted grandparent, even going to the extent of giving us unlimited credit at the banks." The death brought White certain troublesome duties in the settlement of the estate, which was invested in widely scattered holdings in Europe and America. But for the first time since he had seriously taken up the idea of a career he was foot loose. For the first time, also, he was placed in command of an independent income of from $30,000 to $35,000 a year.

A trip to America to look after the family property was indispensable, and White combined with it a new effort to obtain a diplomatic appointment. In February he was in New York, where he saw Hamilton Fish, Chauncey Depew, Bayard Cutting, and others. He paid a visit to St. Mark's Church, and in a characteristic letter to his wife described the memories with which it had filled him; how they had often taken communion there together, the incidents of their wedding-day, her happy recovery from her illness, and, as he put it, "all my superlative married happiness and the rich blessings which had been showered upon me in the possession of such an ideal treasure of a wife as your own sweet gentle self." In April he was in California, where much of the family funds had been invested. He went out by the Southern Pacific, reading Henry James's *The Siege of London*, finding the "Silver Palace Cars" superior even to Pullmans in their ornate luxury, and seeing evidence along the line of the Indian hostilities then raging in Arizona. In San Francisco he was intensely interested by the new invention of cable-cars, which went up the steep hills like magic. Friends took him out to two show places of the surrounding region —the great 6,000-acre estate of Governor Leland Stanford, where he saw more than five hundred thoroughbred horses in a string of huge stables, and the "marvelous huge house" of Charles Crocker. The scenery of California struck him as magnificent, while he was agreeably surprised to find San Francisco not at all provincial, but a cosmopolitan and luxurious city.

On his return to the East at the beginning of May, White stopped in Washington to see the Secretary of State, Frederick T. Frelinghuysen, who was an old friend and a New Jersey neighbor of the Rutherfurd family. He and his Assistant Secretary, John A. Kasson, promised to do their best to find or make a vacancy in one of the best European legations.[2] They both mentioned the fact of a vacant secretaryship of legation at Vienna, and Kasson pressed White to allow an application to be put in for him. But White feared that the climate would be unfavorable to his wife's health, and made it clear that he would take the place only if nothing better turned up. Before he left, Frelinghuysen made an appointment to introduce him to President Arthur in the White House:

Upon arrival [White wrote to his wife], I was ushered into the East Room, where the Madagascar envoys who had come to Washington the day before were drawn up awaiting the President. I perceived this must be a mistake (the poor envoys being evidently uncertain whether or not I was an official personage of whom they should take notice); I retired, therefore, and told the usher to inquire whether some mistake had not been made, and he then discovered that I was to be sent into the Blue Room. Here, after my waiting some little time, the President and Mr. Frelinghuysen shortly came. The latter presented me as the man whom Mr. Morton had wanted at the Paris legation, and I had quite a friendly

[2] Frelinghuysen, who had been a United States Senator from New Jersey and a member of the Electoral Commission of 1877, had been appointed Minister to England by President Grant, but had declined. Kasson had been First Assistant Postmaster-General under Lincoln; had served repeated terms in Congress from Iowa; had been sent on various special missions abroad, and had been our minister to Austria-Hungary from 1877 to 1881. As Alphonso Taft's predecessor in the post at Vienna, his recommendation of White for a place there would have great weight.

chat with them both. Mr. Frelinghuysen asked very kindly after your father, with whom he went to college. I decided not to say anything about diplomacy, but bide my time and when old Hop's post falls vacant go in for it. I am very glad to have had such a special introduction, and to have had my name specially presented in that way. It will doubtless have its weight at the proper time.

Indeed, the White House visit did bear almost immediate fruit. Secretary Frelinghuysen decided that the young applicant might well take the Vienna secretaryship while waiting for something better. A few weeks later White, having rejoined his wife in Europe, was paying a visit to Ferdinand Rothschild's new house at Waddesdon Manor, in Buckinghamshire, where a great house-warming had been arranged. The guests included the Prince of Wales, later Edward VII, the Duchess of Manchester, and Lady Kildare, later the Duchess of Leinster. White always remembered one instance of the lavish way in which entertainment had been arranged. He and other guests, one afternoon when fireworks had been announced, played tennis on the lawn till nearly eight o'clock; when they retired to dress for dinner there had been no apparent preparation for the coming display; but happening to look out of the window of his room, White suddenly saw a perfect army of workmen creeping out of the bushes in all directions, and beginning to erect frameworks for the various set pieces. They had been kept in hiding in the shrubberies since lunch-time in order to do their work inconspicuously and without delay. At this house-party a telegram was handed him from Alphonso Taft, the American minister to Austria. It inquired whether White had yet been notified of his appointment by President Arthur to be secretary of legation at Vienna, and begged him not to decline until he had heard from Mr. Taft by mail.

In his letter, Minister Taft explained that for some time past the American Government had insisted upon an unfortunate combination of the consul-generalship and secretaryship of legation in Vienna, which the Austrian Government had naturally found inconvenient and against which it had protested. It was a characteristic bit of American cheese-paring. The two posts had now been separated, and Taft hoped that White would accept the secretary-ship. Both Lowell and Morton were consulted, and both urged

White to go. By the middle of July, 1883, he was in Vienna, reporting to Mr. Taft for duty.

To his friends and acquaintances this step seemed merely to
provide a temporary employment, elegant rather than onerous, to
a young man of wealth whose chief interest would always be in
society. Politics in those days, as Henry Adams had learned, did
not offer many opportunities to aspirants of talent but of tender
sensibilities.[3] And politics kept its grimy fist firm upon the diplomatic service. All the offices were part and parcel of the spoils
system, and no position carried a tenure longer than that of the
Administration in power. A quadrennial shake-up ousted one set
of political beneficiaries and replaced them by another. The most
responsible diplomatic position, that of minister to England, might
be filled by a rough poker-playing brigadier like General Schenck,
not above disgracing his country by shady business transactions;
the minor posts might go to any needy hanger-on of some state
boss. As John Hay said later, some Senators combed the list of
Keeley cures for appointees to consulates. But White already had a
vision of an American service which would conform to the efficient standards of the best European diplomacy. The contrast between our diplomatic corps and England's had especially struck
him, and he believed that he might exemplify the usefulness of a
professional-minded staff. As he later wrote:

Being of a hopeful disposition, and having realized the great disadvantage arising to the interests of our country abroad from the appointment to posts in our legations (we had no embassies then) of men backed
by important politicians at home, but without any qualifications whatever
for diplomatic work—not even the knowledge of French or any other
foreign language—I resolved to become the nucleus, if possible, of a
permanent service. Such an idea was considered chimerical by all my
friends, but I had a feeling that it would be possible for the United
States to have, as the other leading Powers of the world then had, a non-
partisan (so far as domestic politics were concerned) service, to which
appointment should be made on the basis of fitness only.

[3] Adams, Henry, *The Education of Henry Adams*, chap. xiv. Henry Adams
disdained diplomacy; as one who had held a position for critical years in the
London legation he "could not beg a post of Secretary at Vienna or Madrid in
order to bore himself doing nothing until the next President should do him
the honor to turn him out."

It was, however, not an easy matter for one whose sole idea was the
service of the nation, and the furtherance of its interests as distinct from
those of one or the other political party at home, to realize this ambition,
and I was given to understand that I might as well make up my mind
to lose the enjoyment of London society for such a period only as the
Republican Administration should remain in power. Notwithstanding
this, I determined to prove the possibility of a genuine professional career
in diplomacy, if possible.

There were other Americans to whom the conception of a foreign
service resting on a professional basis, divorced from politics, had
already occurred. But it was to be many years, till an executive
order of President Roosevelt placed a great part of the diplomatic
and consular service on a merit basis and threw it open to men of
career, before this conception became fact. It is not too much to say
that the resolution to which Henry White committed himself in
1883 was of signal importance in the evolution of our foreign service. With his gifts, his exceptional training in England and France,
and the advantages of his later friendships with Hay and Roosevelt,
he was destined to advance the professional idea in general public
esteem as did no other single man.

Henry White's services as secretary of legation at Vienna filled
only the last six months of 1883, but it was a half year of value in
teaching him the diplomatic routine. Leaving his wife and baby
daughter, first in England and later in Paris, he took rooms at the
Imperial Hotel. He was fortunate in his chief. Alphonso Taft
is now forgotten except as the father of one of our best-loved Presidents, but he deserves to be remembered on his own account. As
White quickly found, he was a blunt, common-sense gentleman of
real cultivation, at seventy-two rounding out a vigorous and varied
career in this rather ornamental office.[4] Though a Vermonter by
birth and a graduate of Yale, he had lived in Cincinnati since the
late 'thirties, and in outlook and manners was thoroughly a Wes-
terner. He had risen to distinction at the Ohio bar and on the bench,
had gained wealth, and had for a short time filled two Cabinet
offices in Grant's second Administration; so that he knew men, and

[4] A considerable number of Taft's letters are in the White papers in the
Library of Congress, and reveal him as a man of fine qualities, extremely
fond of White.

had acquired a practical sagacity of no ordinary kind. White liked him and respected his wisdom and firmness, and liked also the two sons of whom he had glimpses that summer—Henry W. Taft and William Howard Taft, both young lawyers.

With light duties, a congenial chief, and a beautiful capital to study, White found his first berth decidedly pleasant. To be sure, there were drawbacks—the unimportance of the American legation in the Austrian eyes, the snobbishness of the social life of Vienna, and the enforced absence of Mrs. White. The Austrians, whose country Disraeli had not unfairly called "the China of Europe," neither knew nor cared anything about the United States. They regarded it as a far-distant, obscure, and crude republic, curious in about the same way that Persia and Uruguay were curious. The diplomatic business of the legation consisted chiefly of questions of nationality. Austrians or Hungarians by birth who had become naturalized American citizens and had returned to Europe would frequently be arrested for non-performance of army duty, and would at once appeal to Mr. Taft. Despatches to Washington were few and short, and there was seldom any question of sufficient urgency to justify a cablegram.

Some of the taboos of the stiff Viennese society excited White's amusement, and he was alternately charmed and irritated by the life of the capital. At his first interview with Mr. Taft the latter made two requests: first, when he attended the two court theaters, the Opera and the Burg-Theater, he should never sit anywhere except in the two front rows, and, second, that when he took a cab he should use only the two-horse victorias. These were among the many strict points of etiquette connected with the Viennese court. Sure enough, White found that whenever he asked his hotel clerk to engage opera seats, it was taken as a matter of course that he would use only the front rows; and whenever he asked a porter to call a cab, he had to wait till a two-horse fiacre appeared, although the neighboring stands might be full of *Einspänners*. There was a good deal more of hat-touching than White liked, and it was only among the hunting-set and the country gentry, who imitated the English, that he felt really free.[5]

[5] Austria-Hungary had just concluded the Triple Alliance of 1882, and White had an opportunity to begin his study of the balance-of-power system.

One reason for keeping Mrs. White in Folkestone and Paris was that it proved impossible to obtain a furnished house or apartment in Vienna. Another was that the Viennese climate, hot in summer and wet in winter, seemed unfavorable to her precarious health. As the summer passed away, he less and less liked the people. "I don't think they are attractive," he wrote: "narrow-minded to a degree, and most inhospitable to all strangers, unless they be known to have the requisite number of quarterings. The reason, I am told, why they are all so chilly toward the diplomatic corps is that since 1866 they are all more or less in the hands of the Jews, financially, and don't want to show their poverty." Fortunately, he was able to get away on frequent week-end trips to Paris, making the journey on the Orient Express.

Yet many features of Viennese life he did find highly enjoyable. He studied German with a tutor, and made patient progress, going frequently to the theater to perfect his pronunciation. On warm summer evenings he listened to Strauss in the Volksgarten. Soon after his arrival he was elected a member of the Tennis Club, the membership committee of which included Prince Metternich, Prince Arenberg, and Count Czechenyi. The International Exhibition that year afforded some amusement, as well as a place to which he could take Americans who expected to be entertained. When the autumn opened he found opportunity to shoot deer and hares on some of the Austrian estates, and made one of several large parties of pleasure.

As his relations with the Tafts became more intimate, his letters point to a rather amusing anxiety regarding their worldly success. Thus in mid-August a banquet was given at the legation. White wrote to his wife in terms which show that he had been much concerned. "The dinner was well served and well cooked," he states, "but they are not properly mounted as to their own servants, and need a good butler. I told Mrs. Taft so plainly afterward, and myself soundly rated the servant who forgot to light the candles in the dining-room. Mrs. Taft's conduct was admirable and unexceptionable, but Mr. Taft once arose informally from the table to shut a window in a great gust of wind, which somewhat agitated me." The Tafts liked him all the better for his somewhat naïve solicitude. Mr. Taft's decision and energy in managing the legation

ALPHONSO TAFT, HENRY WHITE, AND COMMANDER
T. C. McLEAN, U.S.N.

he often spoke of with praise. He was particularly pleased when the minister summarily shut the door on the agent of Tiffany's in Paris, a pushing man who demanded to be introduced to the Austrian Emperor as he had already been introduced to the King of Italy by our minister in Rome, William Waldorf Astor. He mentioned also Taft's skill in carrying on a correspondence with the Foreign Office for a better interpretation of the Austro-American treaty of commerce.

Had it not been for Mrs. White's absence he might have grown fairly content, but he was frankly homesick for his wife and baby. "I feel that I cannot stay away from you much longer, *coûte que coûte,*" he writes; and again he declares, "What adverse fate caused me to bind myself to stay away from you in this way I cannot imagine; and it worries me very much." While he performed his duties faithfully and went out of his way for such extra tasks as an inventory of the archives of the legation, he felt justified in pressing for a transfer. Late in October he wrote the State Department on the subject, and induced Mr. Taft, who knew that another child was expected in the family, to second his request. The moment was opportune, for Nadal was at last leaving his London post. On November 26, 1883, Taft handed him a telegram which had just come from Secretary Frelinghuysen, offering the second secretaryship with Minister Lowell. White was of course delighted. Both his wife and his mother were equally pleased, and the latter wrote that he would certainly be a minister some day. "I have a sort of feeling," replied White, gayly, "that perhaps I may be, either here or in Rome, with a possible lucky transfer like Mr. Lowell's to London. However, this is somewhat a castle in the air."

He could look back upon the Viennese experience as both diverting and profitable. Taft gave his work warm praise, and sent him a letter expressing his wishes for a successful career. Speaking privately, he said that White ought really to go home and run for Congress, for in politics the opportunities would be far better than in diplomacy. In view of White's later relations with President Taft, interest attaches to his belief that the whole family would prove valuable to his future. William Howard Taft and Henry Taft, he wrote Daisy, were able young men, and would some day hold positions where their friendship might count powerfully in his behalf. The clerk at the legation was extremely depressed by the prospect of White's departure, and when the latter chaffingly remarked that it would be a relief to be rid of so troublesome a secretary, replied: "Mr. White, I would prefer being kicked by you to being flattered by your predecessor." We find in another letter to his wife an amusing passage on this subordinate, which reveals a good deal as to White's own qualities:

The clerk of the legation is terribly low at my approaching departure. He showed me sorrowfully and sentimentally today the telegram announcing the forwarding of my commission, and remarked: "This is a sad souvenir of a short dream of happiness for me." He also said that upon hearing of my appointment he had asked Mr. Taft what sort of person I was. The latter said he did not know; but gave him a letter from Mrs. Schuyler (*née* King, and wife of the minister to Greece) to read. She said that the best description she could give of me was that my presence in a room was like a breath of fresh air, which cheered and freshened up the atmosphere. "Well," said the unfortunate and sorrowful clerk, "this is just what I have found to be the case with you, Mr. White, and I have never come across it in anyone else!"

On December 20th White left Vienna to spend the holidays with his family in Paris, and with the New Year of 1884 he was ready to begin his first important diplomatic training.

Chapter Five

Second Secretary under James Russell Lowell

I F White had been fortunate in having Alphonso Taft for his chief in Vienna, he was still more fortunate in beginning his service in England under so distinguished and considerate a minister as James Russell Lowell. The acquaintanceship between them, already several years old, soon grew into friendship and later affection. Lowell was attracted, not merely by the open-hearted, high-spirited young man, but by his wife; he liked having the "handsome young couple" about him; and it happily fell within White's power to do him personal as well as official service in their year and a half (1884-85) of association.

Lowell had come to London from several years' service in Madrid, and had taken a house at 31 Lowndes Square, not far from Hyde Park. His appointment had peculiarly pleased both Englishmen and Americans by emphasizing the cultural and literary bonds between the two nations. It seemed to revive the traditions of the days when Edward Everett and John Lothrop Motley had served as American ministers in London, and when Hawthorne had been consul at Liverpool. All educated England took Lowell to its heart to such an extent that when Lord Granville, the Foreign Minister, asked him to dine, he said that he felt it was a presumption to give short notice to "the most engaged man in London." When the Whites came over from the Continent, Lowell had already achieved a success as spiritual mediator between the two nations which has seldom been surpassed. His great reputation, his geniality, his brilliance, his felicity in brief after-dinner speeches, and the weightiness of his longer discourses, won the liking of Englishmen and made him in constant demand for both public and private appearance; while he remained ruggedly American at heart, and showed no inclination to retract the criticisms he had sometimes offered of English acts and ways. It was not an unalloyed misfortune that Mrs. Lowell, through the effects of a typhus fever contracted in

Spain, was an invalid, for Lowell, whose purse was modest, could not have gone out so much in society if he had not been freed from the necessity of entertaining in return. The English environment pleased him. "I have only to walk a hundred yards from my door to be in Hyde Park," he wrote, "where, in Kensington Gardens, I can tread on green turf and hear the thrushes sing all winter. As for climate, it suits me better than any I have ever lived in." [1]

There was, of course, no strong intellectual bond between Lowell and Henry White, the latter possessing neither the knowledge nor the literary tastes for such a relationship. Nor had they much in common in their social inclinations. Lowell was a lion; he had long known Englishmen of eminence, notably Leslie Stephen, Thomas Hughes, and Coventry Patmore; and he had been made welcome by the most celebrated authors and artists of the day. [2] Henry White was soon cultivating a distinctly younger and gayer set, led by George Curzon, Arthur Balfour, Henry Cust, Lord and Lady Elcho, and St. John Brodrick. Their paths thus completely diverged. Lowell was at his happiest when he was with some fellow poet, or talking to a kindred scholar, like Dr. Murray, editor of the New Oxford Dictionary. White was happiest on some week-end devoted to riding, tennis, or yachting. Yet they not infrequently met in drawing-rooms as well as the legation office.

For the first time White learned the duties of a large legation, and found that the ill-health of the excellent first secretary, Hoppin, who was now past seventy, threw a large share of them upon him. For the most part his task was writing, writing, writing. He had to manage endless letters on such subjects as the exhuming of John Howard Payne's body, the foot-and-mouth disease in British cattle, pauper emigration from Ireland, the nationality of pretended Americans, trade statistics, methods of theological instruction in England, and details of the international copyright quarrel. When Americans of importance appeared he had to act as

[1] Scudder, Horace E., *James Russell Lowell, A Biography*, vol. ii, p. 259 ff.
[2] "I lunched with Tennyson yesterday," wrote Lowell soon after arriving. "He is getting old and looks seedy. I am going in to take a pipe with him the first free evening. Pipes have more thawing power than anything else."

their esquire in the mazes of social London and hunt suitable entertainment for them. He oversaw the clerks of the legation. He looked
into the cases of distressed Americans, and answered with patient
meticulosity every question which came from the United States,
so that he was always on the search for information. But his leisure
was ample and he was not tied down.

There was, in fact, really no diplomatic business of much importance between England and America at this time.[3] Lord Granville, the Foreign Secretary, and Lowell were on terms of such
cordiality that it almost seemed a pity there was no dispute to
settle; but the only quarrels were those between Lowell and his
Irish-American fellow-citizens. This was the period of the Irish
National League and the agrarian outrages. Numbers of excitable
Irish-Americans, entering the green isle at Dublin or Cork, urged
the people to violence, and when arrested, appealed for American
protection. No one could have been a more zealous defender of
persecuted Americans than Lowell.[4] But he was unwilling to shield
from punishment any American who was really guilty of complic-
ity in treason or sedition, and when an Irish-American who was
arrested on substantial charges could not produce some evidence
of his innocence, Lowell let the law take its course. This policy
was successively indorsed in a very public way by Secretary Blaine
and Secretary Frelinghuysen. But it aroused the antagonism of
the Irish-American leaders and of the politicians who catered to
them; ex-Speaker Samuel J. Randall denounced Lowell for his
"sickening sycophancy to English influence," and a mass-meeting
in Cooper Union loaded him with reproaches. White was an inter-

[3] However, the Venezuela boundary controversy was smoldering. Lowell
took it up, and informed Lord Granville that the United States was "not
without concern as to whatever may affect the interest of a sister Republic of
the American Continent." Cf. Peck, Harry Thurston, *Twenty Years of the
Republic*, p. 415.

[4] Lowell objected vigorously to the so-called Coercion Act. "Its chief object,"
he wrote, "is to enable the authorities to arrest persons whom they suspect
of illegal conduct, without being obliged to produce any proof of their guilt.
Its very substance and main purpose are to deprive suspected persons of the
speedy trial they desire." But since it was the law, it applied to residents of
Ireland whether they were British subjects or American citizens. *Foreign
Relations*, 1881, p. 545.

ested observer of the situation and of the way in which Lowell
handled it in the light of international law and of Lord Lyons's
moderate behavior when Seward was arresting British subjects
during the Civil War. In the end all the Irish-American suspects
save three were set free, and the misunderstandings which might
have arisen were completely avoided.

Lowell's numerous notes to White preserved a record of the ban-
tering and intimate footing on which the two men soon worked.
"Mr. Lowell," wrote Mrs. White to her mother as early as February
19, 1884, "seems devoted to Harry, and calls upon him constantly
for all sorts of things which show his confidence in him; they
gave a large dinner last week, to which Harry went." The minister
rushed up to Edinburgh in April to receive an honorary degree
at the tercentenary celebration of the founding of that university,
and sent back a sprightly epistle, relating how he had been "at
the function at St. Giles's which was like a whole forest of paroquets
with its gorgeous gowns of scarlet, yellow, green, and purple,"
and where he was the only black spot; how he had "forgotten how
picturesque Edinboro' is," and thinks it almost (especially at night)
the most picturesque city of northern Europe; and how "tomorrow
I must make a speech, and have nothing to say. If I could only
say it!" The next day a new note announced that he was just
"going to be capped—don't read it cupped!" He was writing a
little later about his dental troubles. "What dreadful things are
teeth—first in getting them, then in keeping them, and then in
providing something to exercise them on, they take up the whole
of life! This means that I am going down to Windsor tomorrow
with Mrs. Chadwick to a dentist said to be good, and good at least
in this, that he puts gold in the grinders without taking too much
of it from the pocket."

He lamented good-naturedly to White the burden of correspondence from America: "They seem to think us Common Car-
riers or something of the sort. Issachar may be a strong ass (I for
my part admit my share in the noun if not the adjective) but he
won't bear this burden without kicking." He lamented with a less
jocund pen the Irish row. "I shall fall back on my proverbs—'They
say? Let them say!' and 'Peor meneorla,' which I leave in Spanish
as being more savoury in that tongue, and if you don't understand

it you will respect it the more. I am getting tired of the whole business. The worst is that every post brings me a letter of regret at my hard-heartedness, and I have to explain." He refers in one letter to arrangements made for presenting Mrs. White to Queen Victoria. "I have a note from Mme. de Bylandt, joyous at the notion of presenting Mrs. White, and no wonder; if I were the Queen—well, never mind. Word must be sent to that dear old pud-dinghead Sir Francis Seymour, so called because he sees less than any other creature supplied with what are supposed to be eyes." And writing to Mrs. White when in 1885 his retirement had become certain, he indulged in that final evidence of friendship, some atrocious puns. "You must continue to value me in spite of my disposition, for being already an x-professor, I shall rise to the standard of Bass's Stout when I am an xx-cellency, and that, as you know, is the best of its kind—or at least Bass thinks so."

The Whites settled themselves at 22 Hertford Street, and lived quietly during the spring of 1884, for their son, named John Campbell White, was born in March. The house in Paris was given up for good; White renewed his connections with several London clubs—the Marlborough, the St. James's, and the Bach-elors'; and for a time he went about, if at all, without his wife. We find him in August at Cowes, attending a regatta and a ball, and sending back some gossip concerning General Ponsonby, the Queen's private secretary, and the Prince of Wales, with whom he chatted. In December he was in Paris, lunching with the Mortons, and a few days later joined his wife at Biarritz. But for the most part he was at his post in the legation, gaining experience steadily, enjoying his contacts with Lowell, and quarreling a little occasion-ally with the aged and testy Hoppin.

Only at rare intervals was his routine varied by any incident possessing dramatic interest or calling for resourcefulness. Once a poorly dressed woman, unmistakably American and highly re-spectable in bearing, called at the legation in pitiful distress, declar-ing that her life and those of her children were in peril. She had been tricked into marrying an Englishman in Buffalo some years earlier, not learning until they reached England that he had a wife living. White looked at the two marriage certificates which she produced, and telling her that she was quite free, decided to take prompt action. As he wrote Dr. Buckler:

After obtaining Mr. Lowell's permission, I sent off our messenger with her in a cab to remove her and her three little children—the oldest five, the youngest eighteen months—to a fresh hiding-place before the man should return that night; which was safely accomplished, and all went smoothly until the night before last, by which time the fellow had discovered our action, and set after the legation. . . . He is a most brutal, bragging specimen, and thought to intimidate me; but fortunately admitted the only fact of which I wished to be sure, namely, that his real wife was living at the time he contracted a marriage with the American. Each time he spoke of the latter as his wife, I stopped him and said, "She's no more yours than mine," and upon his finally saying, "You don't want to proclaim my children as bastards," I replied, "Nothing I can do will proclaim them more bastards than they are." He finally began to talk about enforcing his will at the pistol's mouth, and I then ordered him out. Mr. Lowell, hearing the noise, came on the scene and did likewise. Upon his refusal, we sent for a policeman and ordered him turned out, which was speedily accomplished. . . .

Fearing complications, however, I decided to take prompt action and to dispatch the poor creature to the United States. Accordingly, I engaged her last night passage in the North German Lloyd steamer sailing today and sent her down to Southampton with our messenger, from whom I have just received the following telegram: "Mrs. Smith (a fictitious name) and children safely on board and sail at four handed her forty-eight dollars all gone off well." I decided to advance the whole amount of passage money, etc., in the interests of justice and mercy. What the poor creature's life must have been words fail me to describe, and I consider it a privilege to have been instrumental in effecting her deliverance.

Mrs. Lowell, who was actually suffering from brain lesion, though no one suspected it at the time, had seemed to grow better during 1884; but a sudden illness in February, 1885, ended in her death. Lowell was almost prostrated by the loss. He wrote White on March 7th that "the stun of so sudden and heavy a blow lasts long, and I have not yet got over it." Acknowledging the kindness of the Whites, the William Darwins, and others, he added: "I have had such good friends as never man had, and I please myself with thinking that nothing so pleased her (generous and self-forgetful as she always was) than that people should be kind to me. But I must not talk about these things. I am as well as I deserve, thank you—only a little shaky about sleep, snatching a bit here, another there, out of different corners of the night as a boy does coppers out of a scramble. 'Tis slow work accumulating capital in this way, but with patience, who knows?" For six weeks at this trying time Hoppin and White bore the chief responsibility of the legation, the former, of course, being nominally in charge, but the latter receiving much more of Lowell's confidence.

Despite this burden of work, the season of 1885 saw the full initiation of the Whites into the social life of London. A letter of Henry White's to his mother-in-law describes his pleasure in getting away from the gold braid of Vienna to the larger English sphere. They had gone with the Prince and Princess of Wales to visit Penshurst, the fourteenth-century residence of the Sidney family, represented at this time by Lord De L'Isle and Dudley, and both had waxed enthusiastic over mediæval paneling, fireplaces, and grillwork. "There is a most interesting portrait there of Queen Elizabeth dancing what appears to be a frantic waltz or even can-can of the present day with Leicester," writes White; "a most curious old picture. He has his arms round the Queen and is squeezing her tight. She appears delighted, and the musicians and bystanders shocked." The Prince of Wales a little later dined with the Whites at the Bachelors' Club, staying till midnight, and seeming to enjoy it hugely. They went to a dinner to meet the Duke of Cambridge; attended balls at the French Embassy and at Lord Fife's, "on both which occasions," reports White, "I danced a valse with the Princess of Wales," enjoyed the state concert at Buckingham Palace, and stayed for a week-end with Lord Salisbury at Hatfield House. A little later we find them writing of an evening at Grosvenor House with the Duke of Westminster, and of a Fourth of July party with Cyrus W. Field. The acquaintanceships thus formed were of great value to White in his professional career.

The election of either Blaine or Cleveland would have meant Lowell's displacement in 1885, for his allegiance to the Mugwump faction of the Republican party insured Blaine's enmity, while Cleveland felt it necessary to give the highest position in the diplomatic service to a Democrat. Lowell's tenure officially ended on June 1st. He was glad to go, for he was heartsore and lonely and wished to be near his old Cambridge intimates.[5] Before he left he had to attend to a few last social duties. "Now don't go and say you are engaged for Friday the fifteenth," he writes in May, "for I want you and Mrs. White to dine here with the Astors. I want two handsome young people and you will answer my purpose perfectly. 'Tis the only evening in the week that is left open, and I shall never forgive you if you don't come." A few days later he canceled the invitation. "Her Majesty has taken it into Her Sacred Head to order me down to Windsor on that day. It is worse than David—my one ewe-lamb, and no Nathan at hand to rebuke her!" He added that Mrs. George Putnam, then in London, had been disappointed at not seeing Mrs. White yesterday. "'Why,' she exclaimed, 'I would have stayed at home all day! She must have looked lovely, perfectly lovely!' I embittered her feelings still more, as our human wont is, by saying, 'She did!'" A black-bordered letter to Mrs. White this same month has another touch of gallantry:

I enclose a note from Lady Brassey (received this morning) by which you will see that I did what I said I would and, what is more to the point, that you can go to the ball whether you get a card or not. I take this precaution because, though Lady Brassey's note to me is dated the 16th, it was not posted till the 20th, and the same accident *may* happen with the card. Moreover, though I must cease to take an official interest in you, that has nothing to do with my personal feeling, and, taking as I do an honest pride in your beauty, I wish as a patriot that the country should have the benefit of being so charmingly represented. Your husband is not ill-looking, but I can't admire him so unreservedly as I should were he a little plainer, or a little shorter. I have always (I may confess it now) looked upon his three inches advantage of me as an indecorum.

I can't end without saying that you have both of you been always good to me and I shall never forget it.

Go then, and dance as long as Cinderella! If some old fellow of sixty-six should ask for a waltz, give him a turn for the sake of one of his contemporaries—I mean coevals—who is affectionately yours, J. R. Lowell.

It had been settled early in 1885 that the new Minister was to be Edward J. Phelps of Vermont, a veteran Democrat, former

[5] Norton, Charles Eliot, *Letters of James Russell Lowell*, vol. ii, p. 296.

president of the American Bar Association, and at this time professor of law in Yale University. Lowell knew something of him, and predicted that he would be an eminently satisfactory chief. It had also been settled that the subordinate force of the legation was to be shaken up. The aged Hoppin was to be offered promotion somewhere on the understanding that he would refuse it and retire, and White was to take his place as first secretary, while Phelps's son was to become second secretary. It was due partly to White's loyal friends, and partly to the new strength of the merit principle, that he received this promotion at the uneasy time of a change of party control in Washington.

The fact is that from the moment of Cleveland's election White had felt a good deal of trepidation regarding his official future, and had hastened to do what he could to protect his position. In this he had the sage advice of Levi P. Morton and the generous help of Lowell. Both interceded with Secretary Frelinghuysen to take steps looking toward Hoppin's promotion, and both approached the incoming Secretary of State, Thomas F. Bayard. White himself made an effort through relatives in Maryland and Delaware to enlist Bayard's influence in his behalf. He also wrote a letter to Bishop Coxe of Buffalo, whom he knew well because of some common labors in Episcopalian matters, asking him to put in a word with Cleveland; he requested the assistance of that stanch Democrat, Governor Robert M. McLane of Maryland, himself to be the next minister to France; and he wrote to Mrs. George H. Pendleton, an old friend, wife of the Ohio Senator whose name is borne by our first effective civil-service law and who had special means of reaching Cleveland. Undoubtedly all this counted. What counted still more was the fact that Cleveland was heartily in favor of restricting the old spoils system, and showed heroism in breasting the flood of Democrats eager to seize every possible office at home and abroad.

By the end of July, 1885, the new chief was settled in the London legation; it was understood that Hoppin was to depart within the next twelvemonth; and with White's advice, Phelps was looking for roomier and more dignified offices. Lowell in departing had charged White with many details of both household and legation business, and his last notes show how much he depended on

the secretary. When Mrs. White sent him an affectionate message
he replied to her in verse from the steamer:

> With many superlative kisses
> A veteran's lips have met,
> But one above all—and this is
> The one that he didn't get!

A little later some rather sad-hearted letters come from him at his
summer home, Deerfoot Farm in Southborough, Massachusetts. In
the first of them he asked White to enter his subscription for a
number of the English weeklies, and added a personal message
with which this chapter may well end:

I am glad to hear such good accounts of you and yours and of the
Legation. Mr. Phelps's success justifies my anticipations. He is in many
and important ways fitter for the post than ever I was—as you perhaps
will remember I said to you. I find myself happier wandering over the
hills here and enjoy the society of my birds and woodchucks immensely;
of my clouds (when we have 'em) particularly, for they never repeat
themselves. The sun has been doing his best of late, to spite the astronom-
ers, I fancy, who have been hinting that he has only thirteen million years'
fuel left. Or is he turning spendthrift in his old age and burning the
candle at both ends? I wear striped flannel shirts in summertime and defy
him and his stokers. The country about me is lovely with pretty views on
every side, and in the northwest a brave undulation of mountains. Were
it not for some friends I had left behind and dearer friends who have
left me behind! . . .

Remember me to everybody who hasn't forgotten me, and keep on
remembering me yourself when you have nothing better to do. Recall
me affectionately to Mrs. White's memory also. Will you kindly explain
to Mrs. Phelps that I did not go to bid her good-by because I *couldn't*?
I have been to my house here but once and stayed but five minutes—
it was so empty and yet so full! I am bracing myself for another visit—
for I need some of my books—but have not mustered the courage yet.
But you knew before that I was a fool in some things.

Chapter Six

Diplomatic Service under Ministers Phelps and Lincoln

THE MAN who served under Cleveland as minister to England in the four years preceding 1889 is little more than a name; the events of Edward J. Phelps's service now seem shadowy and unimportant. There was a hoary dispute between the United States and Canada over the inshore privileges of American fishermen in Newfoundland waters, which somehow seemed to resist all settlement. There was a rather more picturesque quarrel with Canada regarding the seal herds of the Behring Sea, and our claim to exclusive jurisdiction over them in that body of water. Near the end of Mr. Phelps's term there arose the curious Sackville-West incident, creditable to none of the persons concerned. For the rest, the American legation was busied with routine business only, and Minister Phelps with the usual round of speeches and banquets.

Yet Phelps was a man who in a more eventful time might have left a distinct impress upon our diplomatic history. A tall, portly, craggy-faced Vermonter, vigorous though well past sixty, he had a strong intellect cast in an exceedingly conservative mold. He had joined the Democratic party before the Civil War because his native caution warned him of the dangers in the anti-slavery movement; he clung to his party in everything except its soft-money heresies; he was conservative in his legal ideas, in his High Church Episcopalianism, and in his strict code of ethics. He used to say that he cared little for any poetry since Byron, or any novels since Scott. A cultivated man, he had certain literary gifts, manifested in occasional bits of verse and light essays, as well as in his long and studied addresses. One of his qualifications as a negotiator was a vein of stubbornness, and he used to say after his retirement that if President Cleveland and Secretary Bayard had held their ground firmly on the Behring Sea question as he did, Lord Salisbury would have surrendered the Anglo-Canadian contentions. Henry White liked his kindly, old-fashioned, decided ways.[1]

Phelps had ideas of his own as to the dignity befitting the legation, and moved its offices at once to roomier quarters at 103 Victoria Street. Here they had two spacious apartments on the ground floor, each larger than the whole legation in its situation under Lowell, and smaller rooms for the secretaries and *attachés*. He had ideas also as to the management of business, and White was soon writing his friend Welsh that "his strength of character is very marked; poor Mr. Hoppin, between ourselves, has repeatedly been frightened out of his senses." Above all, Phelps chafed over the fact that the American representative in London, though an agent of one of the greatest nations, remained a minister when every other important nation had an ambassador at the English court. In this his views completely coincided with those of White; and early in Phelps's term both men began a systematic campaign to impress leading members of Congress with the importance of raising the London legation to the status of an embassy. At the beginning of 1886 Hoppin resigned his first-secretaryship, and White took his place.

His promotion brought White a decided increase of responsibility, and meant that he was often left for short periods in sole charge of the legation. From the moment that the controversy over the Behring Sea fisheries became important, Phelps and he labored together upon it. The question involved large material interests. For nearly twenty years, since the purchase of Alaska from Russia, the great seal herds of the Pribilov Islands—a part of that territory—had been a valuable American property. An American corporation annually took a limited number of the seals, paying our government a royalty for the privilege. Federal authorities could easily control the slaughter on the islands and in the immediate waters. But the seals made annually a long winter cruise to the southward, and at other times were to be found outside the three-mile limit; so that vessels from Canada, Hawaii, Japan, and other parts of the world

[1] See Phelps, E. J., *Orations and Essays*, with a memoir by J. W. Stewart; and the memoir by M. H. Buckham in *Proceedings of the Vermont Historical Society*, 1901. Phelps's rhymed malediction on Essex Junction should be in every collection of American humorous verse.

could intercept them and threaten their total extermination. In 1881 a United States Treasury order by implication, though not in set terms, declared the eastern half of the Behring Sea part of the territorial waters of the United States and therefore a *mare clausum*. However, pelagic or open-sea sealing by foreign vessels continued. In 1886, therefore, the United States began to seize Canadian and other vessels found sealing in that part of the Pacific, most of them being captured more than sixty miles from land.

The result was a series of British protests, both numerous and vigorous; but the American courts denied the Canadian claimants any redress. In 1887 additional vessels were captured by our revenue cutters, but the warmth of the British representation led in 1888 to a suspension of seizures. Negotiations were meanwhile undertaken by the United States to induce Great Britain, Japan, Russia, and other nations to sign a general convention for the protection of the seal fisheries along the lines laid down by Washington.

It was at this juncture that Phelps's departure for the United States in the spring of 1888 left White to carry on the conversations with the British Government. He held repeated conferences with Lord Salisbury, who was both Prime Minister and Foreign Secretary, and with M. de Staal, the Russian ambassador. At one of these, in April, Salisbury indicated the willingness of the British Government to agree to a convention for the protection of the seals, while de Staal stated that Russia was anxious to have a closed season in not only the Behring Sea, but the Sea of Okhotsk as well. To this Salisbury, as White reported to the State Department, said that he had no objection. He also stated that he had taken steps to prevent the clearance of British vessels to Western Canada for the purpose of hunting seals during the summer of 1888. A few days later White was able to forward to the State Department a draft bill for the protection of the seals, which the Prime Minister thought of introducing into Parliament shortly, and to which it was expected that American legislation would be assimilated. During May, White pressed Salisbury, at a dinner party where they met, to act promptly without waiting to hear from the Canadians. Unfortunately, the Prime Minister had just received a notification from Ottawa that the Dominion Government was preparing a memorandum upon the subject. Under the circumstances, he had nothing to do but wait, and stated frankly that Great Britain would not execute any convention without the concurrence of Canada.

The upshot was that all White's negotiations fell through. The Canadian memorandum, when received, proved to be an emphatic rejection of the American proposals on the ground that they would break up an important industry of British Columbia. The Russians and Americans, argued Ottawa, had their islands on which to kill seals, whereas the Canadians could reach the herds only in the open sea. White in reply pointed out to Salisbury that the admission of any such plea would involve the speedy extermination of the seals from both the open sea and the islands, and with this Salisbury seemed to agree; but the British felt—or professed to feel—that their hands were tied. In the end, though France, Japan, and Russia were quite willing to agree with the United States upon the general terms of a treaty, the Dominion forced the matter to a deadlock. The quarrel dragged on, American cutters seized more Canadian ships in 1889, and the whole issue had finally to be submitted to arbitration in 1892-93—an arbitration in which the United States was signally defeated.[1]

Meanwhile, White was throwing himself enthusiastically into the campaign, already mentioned, for making the London legation our first embassy. This movement dated back to a period previous to his entrance into the service, but as yet it had made no real progress. In 1888 he wrote to Levi P. Morton, a strong supporter of the project, that he had corresponded with dozens of Congressmen on the subject and discussed it "with thousands of fellow-countrymen." He explained to these men that in refusing to make our English representative an ambassador we both crippled his usefulness and compelled England in return to send us second-rate men. When such capable English ministers as Lord Lyons, whom Lincoln valued, and Sir Edward Thornton, had sought promotion to an ambassadorship, they had to return to Europe. They were likely to be replaced by such a weaker envoy as had now come to the

---

[1] The Behring Sea dispute can best be followed through the successive volumes of *Foreign Relations*; J. B. Moore's *International Arbitrations*, vol. i; John W. Foster, *Diplomatic Memoirs*, vol. ii; and S. F. Bemis, editor, *American Secretaries of State and their Diplomacy*, vol. viii. There is a good short account in J. H. Latané, *A History of American Foreign Policy*, pp. 461-472.

United States, Lionel Sackville-West. On all state occasions or in all matters of business, wrote White to Representative William E. Mason of Illinois, a newly arrived minister from the United States had to be ranked below the ministers from Haiti, Venezuela, or Greece, if the latter happened to have been longer in residence. When he was secretary at Vienna, he had actually seen Minister Taft placed at dinner below the minister sent to the Austrian Court by the Prince of Monaco. "Even Spain," added White, indignantly, "is now allowed to send ambassadors, and the great Powers send them to her in return; and I venture to think anyone will admit that there is something radically wrong when the President of the French Republic can dine with the representatives of Russia, Austria, Germany, Italy, Great Britain, and even Spain, but cannot with propriety be entertained by our minister in Paris, owing to the latter's inferior rank, or when the United States minister to Great Britain deems it best for his country's dignity to remain away from state banquets at the Foreign Office and all court functions from which he can absent himself without being absolutely discourteous. No citizen of the United States could fail to be filled with indignation if he could see for himself the second or third rate position in which his country's representative (whatever be the latter's personal merit or distinction) is placed on public occasions, and if it were the fault of the foreign country he would instantly desire such representative's recall."

The Sackville-West affair in the autumn of 1888 did something to illustrate the views of Phelps, Morton, White, and their co-workers, for if England had sent a first-class ambassador he would never have fallen into Sackville-West's error. The main outlines of the episode are familiar. Late in October, 1888, during the campaign between Cleveland and Harrison, the New York *Herald* published a letter which Sackville-West had written to a supposed Charles F. Murchison of California, who represented himself to be a naturalized American of British birth. This "Murchison"—a politician's fiction—had asked how he should vote in the coming election, and Sackville-West had fatuously replied that he regarded Cleveland as more friendly to Great Britain than Harrison. The Republicans hastened to use his letter to enlist the Irish vote on their side, and it produced an international sensation. Sackville-West, called upon for an explanation by Secretary Bayard, declared that his letter to "Murchison" had been strictly private and not intended for publication; but he immediately aggravated his offense by giving an indiscreet interview to a reporter of the New York *Tribune*.

The episode involved the London legation when Mr. Phelps was asked to call upon Lord Salisbury and explain the facts, in order to obtain the recall of Sackville-West. Lord Salisbury, however, declined to take any action until Sackville-West had sent the precise text of his unfortunate letter, with an explanation of his own. The Foreign Office took the ground that the letter in itself appeared to be insufficient to justify Sackville-West's recall, especially since it had become known only through a gross piece of treachery. When the British Government refused to act, President Cleveland felt it necessary to have the unfortunate envoy's passports handed to him. A letter of Secretary Bayard's, preserved among the White papers, presents the American view. The Secretary of State describes his second conversation with the minister:

Lord Sackville, the British Minister, called. His first remark was: "I hope you have no hard feelings and are not angry with me?" I answered, "No; I have no personal feelings on the subject."

He then said: "I have set on foot an investigation, and the *Herald* is also investigating with a view to unearthing this trick in California. I wrote you last night on the subject, and told you that I was taking steps to investigate the conspiracy that induced this letter to me, and obtained from me my reply."

I told him I could only repeat what I had said yesterday morning: that I was amazed he should have been led into so palpable an indiscretion as this; that the letter on its face should have been a warning to him, and I wished now to say to him that I had not before me at the time he came here last the interview which he was alleged to have had with a correspondent of the New York *Tribune*; that that was even worse than the letter; that it impugned the integrity and motives of the President and Senate in respect of international transactions. [Bayard referred to the fur-seal and Canadian fisheries question.]

He asked me again if I was angry with him about it. I said that was not the word; that I did have feelings of amazement and regret that such a thing should have occurred.

The election of Benjamin Harrison to succeed Grover Cleveland brought an immediate change in the London legation. Robert T. Lincoln, the son of the martyred President, who had served as Secretary of War under Garfield and Arthur, was selected as the new minister soon after Harrison's election. For a time there was an interregnum, when White had to fill the gap; Phelps sailed for the United States on January 31, 1889, and Lincoln did not take up the reins until May 15th, so that the first secretary was *chargé d'affaires* for several months. For a time also White feared that the change of party would mean his displacement. A movement to obtain his dismissal was set on foot. Levi P. Morton, the new Vice President, wrote him that a small number of society folk in the East, returning from Europe, had accused both him and Mr. Phelps of neglecting their wishes for entertainment in London. Travel to Europe had greatly increased during the 'eighties, and four or five of the largest London hotels were nearly always filled with Americans during the season. Their demands for letters of introduction and similar favors were troublesome, but the legation had done all that was humanly possible to meet them.[3] Morton immediately after the inauguration called on the new Secretary of State, Blaine, explaining the importance of White's retention; Phelps also from the moment of his return was busy in White's behalf, writing that "if Lincoln is half the man I take him to be he will not permit a valuable secretary he desires to retain to be taken away merely to make a place for some one else." John Hay,

[3] Once an American general came to the legation in great anxiety. He said that he had brought his two daughters to London; they had become unmanageable, refusing pointblank to return to America, and the hotelkeeper supported them in their stand. He begged White's assistance. White advised the general to make it clear to the daughters, the hotelkeeper, and all shopkeepers that no more money would be forthcoming for the expenses of the young women, and the general departed with the air of a man who has seen a great light! Various Americans traveling in Europe wished to use the legation as a mail-forwarding agency, saving the small fee which commercial houses would charge. One nettled gentleman, when White courteously informed him that the legation had no facilities for such work, sent back the crushing note: "Mr. Blank presents his compliments and thanks Mr. White for the information that public servants are not meant to serve the public."

who had recently visited London, wrote indignantly about "so mean an intrigue," and used his influence with Harrison. In the end all came out well. "Do not worry a moment," wrote Hay a little later, "over the exigencies of a lot of idiots who would be unhappy if they didn't take tea every day with the Queen, and would blame you for it. And do not think of trying to satisfy them. You are now as firm as a rock where you are."

White during these years had, as a matter of fact, rendered himself useful to a number of compatriots, and had made new friends while seeing not a little of old ones. Lowell revisited London in the spring of 1886 and again in the autumn of 1888, and he and White, who still corresponded irregularly, had a cordial reunion. Some snatches from Lowell's letters to him are of passing interest:

It is very kind of you to remember me in your New Year wishes [wrote Lowell from Deerfoot Farm, January 19th, 1886]; you and Mrs. White. I have been owing you a letter ever so long to thank you for your kindness in attending to my poor little bits of business over there. But to say sooth, I never understood before what was meant by being a man of letters; I am snowed up with 'em. They gather to me from every corner of the earth as do the ravens to their proper carrions. I can't throw 'em into my waste basket or discharge my mind from them, for some foolish ancestor has bequeathed me a conscience, and in that haunted chamber they rise again and surround me as the ghosts did Richard. I think it must be written somewhere in the Book of Proverbs: "As one nail driveth out another so doth the letter of today drive that of yesterday out of memory." So it was that you were not answered and so it was that your unanswered letter from time to time upbraided me in the regions of the silent thought that is not sweet.

We are covered with snow from Texas to the St. Lawrence, the work of a few hours in a single night. I for the first time fully realized in my consciousness how great a nation we are. Can England do the like of this? Can France? Not they! Ireland only could do it in a jiffy, if I may believe her orators, and has done it a thousand times. We have been having it at twenty, till Mercury begins to think he has been bearded by rascals who have a corner in cold and this is faithful to frost. Our pipes froze (not mine) and the cheeks of one of my grandsons, but I rather like it. It is what Burton would have called courageous weather.

Our politics are something like yours with silver instead of Ireland. At the West and South there are still men who believe that something can be made out of nothing and that not choosing to take eighty cents for a hundred is a villainy of bloated bondholders and bankers like myself. But my faith is not a whit diminished. We shall vanquish this dragon as we did him of the greenback ten years ago. Meanwhile President Cleveland is gaining ground, I think, steadily with all thoughtful persons—who in the long run are the only ones to be reckoned with.

Again Lowell wrote from Cambridge on October 11, 1890:

I have had a wearisome summer of it, climbing slowly up again to where I was before my catastrophe. I had almost begun to despair, but about a fortnight ago I got up one morning with the burden off my shoulders and feeling as if nothing had ever gone wrong with me. So it has been ever since. But I have not yet recovered my sense of security. Whether I shall get across the water again next year, or ever again, I cannot say as yet. London seems very much farther away than it did, and my life there a dream.

I cannot think of Mrs. White as growing stout. She was just right as she was, but I reconcile myself with it on the ground that, the more of her the better.

I do not wonder that you like Mr. Lincoln. I have known him since he was a boy and always thought well of him. He was in one of my classes at Harvard. I don't think he distinguished himself as a scholar—perhaps that may have been my fault as much as his—but he was always an honest fellow with no harm in him and I was sure he would turn out well.

John Hay was in England with his wife in 1887, and again in 1891, and met with much hospitality from White. "Milton found the right description for you in one word," he wrote gratefully during the latter visit. "You are 'an affable archangel.' I never felt so loaded down with kindness." When Henry Adams arrived, White spent much pains in helping him obtain Spanish and British documents for his history. The first meeting between White and Theodore Roosevelt occurred in London in March, 1887. "The other day I happened to hear of your being in London," White wrote him; "as we have a number of mutual friends in New York, I took the liberty of calling upon you with the intention of offering my services." A committee of Parliament had inquired of the legation whether any American citizen then in London would be able to give evidence respecting the provision made in America for the poor, and White asked Roosevelt if he would not serve. He procured for Alvey A. Adee of the State Department, who was an enthusiastic philatelist, a collection of British colonial stamps, and choice seeds for Adee's little Maryland farm. When Senator John C. Spooner arrived in the summer of 1889, White took him to the House of Commons to hear Gladstone speak. Chauncey Depew, Oliver Wendell Holmes during his hundred days in Europe, Don Cameron, the Blaines, who were in England during the summer of 1887, and Hiram Maxim, who brought over his celebrated machine gun to exhibit to European governments, all had White to thank for courtesies.

The period during which Robert Lincoln served as minister was as quiet as the four years of Mr. Phelps. One important and gratifying event was the agreement of the United States and Great Britain in 1891 upon arbitration of the Behring Sea question, a treaty for this purpose being signed on February 29, 1892; though it was not until April, 1893, that the panel of seven judges, representing five nations, met in Paris, and in the meantime friction arose over various contentious points. During Robert Lincoln's absence from London in the summer and autumn of 1892 it fell to White's lot, as *chargé d'affaires*, to lend his hand in straightening out the tangles.

One point of dispute had reference to the procedure to be followed before the court of arbitration, the British proposing a plan which Washington believed would give the United States no fair chance for rebuttal. White called early in October, 1892, upon Lord Rosebery, the new Foreign Minister, conveyed from the Secretary of State a threat of the abandonment of the arbitration proceedings, and obtained a satisfactory adjustment. At an earlier date, while Salisbury was still in power, there arose the question of continuing the *modus vivendi* by which the seals were protected during the pendency of the arbitration. In a letter to his wife (March 30, 1892) White described how he had gone to a party at the Salisburys', arriving late. "Lord Salisbury," wrote White, "said to me that he feared that he should be detained by telegrams to the President, but happily that fear had been removed; to which I replied that in my opinion the Canadians ought certainly to see that he had done his best for them, and subside now under the circumstances, at which he laughed but said nothing." White added: "The long and short of that business is that Lord Salisbury had refused under pressure from Canada to renew the *modus vivendi*, whereby Canadians were prevented from catching seals last year, although an arbitration agreement has been signed; so that while arbitration was going on the seals were to be destroyed. He was therefore informed (in accordance with my urgent counsel to old Foster) that we should simply send ships of war to Behring Sea and protect the seals ourselves, and that this Government would be responsible for any consequences that might ensue. Of course that left but two courses open; either to send British ships there to recapture sealers taken by ours (which meant war) or to back down; and this Lord Salisbury, knowing that this country would not tolerate war for such a purpose, did."

White paid much attention also to two celebrated if minor cases, those of the Irish-American dynamiters and of the famous Mrs. Maybrick. The former involved a set of men who had planned dynamite outrages in Great Britain early in the 'eighties, and had been sentenced to jail for long terms; Dr. Thomas Gallagher, the chief, was in prison for life. Under Irish-American pressure, both President Harrison and President Cleveland caused diplomatic steps to be taken looking toward a possible commutation of sentence. White went to the prison during Phelps's term to attempt to obtain information upon which an appeal for clemency might be founded, but Gallagher refused to see him. Late in 1892, while still *chargé d'affaires* during Mr. Lincoln's absence, he had several confidential conferences with the Home Secretary, H. H. Asquith, on the subject; and as a result, after Asquith had gone into the matter very carefully, it was decided by the Government to release one prisoner at once, and two more shortly afterward. Gallagher was too guilty, however, to be granted any mercy.

Under President Harrison, White was called upon by both Blaine and Foster to intervene—this time unofficially—in the case of Mrs. Maybrick, the American woman who had been convicted, in 1889, as many believed quite unjustly, of poisoning her husband. In America a virtual defense association was established to assist Mrs. Maybrick, in which Gail Hamilton, the cousin of James G. Blaine, was a leading spirit. All representations to the British authorities failed, and Mrs. Maybrick was kept in prison. Later, in

1892, her health, partly because of a self-inflicted wound, became a subject of grave anxiety, and White sent his wife to the prison to talk with her. Of this interview Mrs. White left an interesting record. She found Mrs. Maybrick well cared for in the prison hospital, with a good fire; she was obviously very weak—"her face and hands pale and waxy like those of a person who has lost much blood"; she had a face "denoting absolute calmness, determination, self-control, with manners remarkably quiet and subdued"; and the prison physician told Mrs. White that he considered Mrs. Maybrick "an extremely clever, clear-headed, and very inscrutable woman," who had never betrayed the least sign of emotion and had shown indomitable courage. It was evident that she was suffering no hardship, and she indicated to Mrs. White a certain gratitude that her sentence had been commuted from death to life imprisonment.

It was in such tasks that the four years of White's service under Robert Lincoln passed away. His work was not onerous, and he had ample time for the social enjoyments of which more will be said later. His industry when it was required, sound judgment, and knowledge of English affairs impressed the State Department with his usefulness; while his relations with the successive chiefs in his own legation could not have been more cordial. Phelps wrote that his assistance had been "invaluable," and that "I regard him as better qualified for his post than any other man I ever knew," while Lincoln looked upon him in the same light.

It fell to White, indeed, to do Lincoln much the same service in a time of bereavement that he had done to Lowell. The Lincolns had an only son, John, who they expected would succeed to Robert Lincoln's law practice in Chicago and carry on the great name of the war President. The boy was enjoying a holiday in France in the autumn of 1889 when his parents suddenly received news that he was seized with blood poisoning in the arm. His condition, at first dangerous, grew slowly better, and in the early weeks of 1890 it became possible to move him to London. Then there was a turn for the worse, and at the beginning of March he died at the Lincolns' home, 2 Cromwell Road. During the weeks of illness White, with characteristic kindness, was indefatigable in attendance upon the family. "The end came rather suddenly at last," he wrote his wife. "I was sitting with Mr. Lincoln as usual latterly before going to the legation when poor Mary rushed in and said to her father, 'Go upstairs quickly!' which of course he did, and returned about ten minutes after to say that all was over."

The Lincolns were prostrated by the blow. White had taken charge of the legation, under Mr. Lincoln's direction, and now he not only lifted the official burden from the minister's shoulders, but proved almost another son to the couple in their grief. A letter describing the funeral indicates how heavily they depended upon him. "I sent a wreath in your name," White wrote to his wife. "Mr. Lincoln asked me to go in the carriage with him and the clergyman, which of course I did, returning with him alone. When we got to Kensington Gardens I persuaded him to send away the carriage and walk there, which he did for an hour and enjoyed it. Mrs. Lincoln having earnestly requested me to return to dine and spend the evening, I did so, and evidently cheered them all a good deal. There is no doubt that they have shown a very marked preference for my society over that of others. . . . It certainly is a most horrible break in their lives, and he has been telling me how all his interest in the law business was for Jack's sake only, and to keep the place open for him. He also told me a lot about his trouble with his mother, and seemed generally most confidential."

With the reelection of Cleveland in 1892 there arose once more the question of White's reappointment. The first intimation of possible trouble came from his loyal friend, John Hay. It had been settled early in 1892 that the legation was at last, in accordance with White's hopes, to be raised to the level of an embassy; and immediately after Cleveland's election it was known that the first ambassador was to be Thomas F. Bayard, former Secretary of State. He had let it be known that he hoped to have a continuance of White's services. But from another and unexpected quarter a sudden hostility developed. One of Cleveland's closest associates, Daniel Lamont, who had been his former private secretary and was now to be Secretary of War, believed that during a recent visit to London he had been slighted by White's failure to call upon him. This imagined offense had occurred at a time when White, owing to Lincoln's absence, had been engrossed in the work of the legation.

Shortly after the inauguration, when Bayard had just left for London, John Hay wrote to White in evident worry:[4]

I had it from a sure source several weeks ago that Mr. Bayard knew how valuable your assistance would be to him, and did not wish any change made. I rested in that assurance until a few days ago, when an influential friend told me that some of those subterranean foes who had previously attacked you had again begun their infernal work. Being in the opposition, I knew that anything I could do would be to your disadvantage, if done openly. I said everything that could be said to reach the President and the Secretary, and Mr. Lincoln arriving upon the scene, I consulted him about the matter. He is, as you know, devotedly attached to you, and has already spoken of you to Mr. Bayard in the strongest terms. He is extremely anxious not to interfere with his successor, but at my request had a talk with Gresham (the new Secretary of State) which was satisfactory except in one respect; the Secretary, while thinking highly of you, intimated that he had little to do with making the appointment, the President and Mr. Quincy running that part of the business between them. . . . Everything will be right if they let the matter alone until Mr. Bayard gets to London. He seems at present a little lax and timid about saying what he wants. Before he has been in London a week, he will see that he cannot get on without you, and that, I fancy, will stiffen his spine enough to make him write the President that he must have you.

I feel profoundly humiliated to be obliged to write you in this way. Every man who knows anything about you knows that you are the most valuable man in the service—that you have always given the government tenfold what it has given you. You have long ago earned the highest promotion, and yet any furtive blackguard is able to endanger your standing in Washington. It is not so much my friendship for you as my regard for the service to which I once belonged that fills me with disgust at such a state of things.

Once more White's friends rallied to his defense. Robert Lincoln saw Bayard in New York during May, and Secretary Gresham in Washington later that month; he wrote that Gresham "evidently has the highest opinion of you," but could do nothing. Henry Adams quietly took a hand. The influential editor of the New York *Evening Post*, E. L. Godkin, surprised White by writing that he had entered an emphatic protest with President Cleveland. George W. Smalley

[4] John Hay to White, May 28, 1893.

did what he could through the New York *Tribune*. Unfortunately, most of White's friends were Republicans. When Ambassador Bayard arrived he greeted the first secretary with the utmost cordiality; but as the summer passed, and White went on leave for a brief visit to the United States, he knew that the sword hung by a hair above his head.

CHAPTER SEVEN

London Social Life: The "Souls"

U NTIL his marriage White's acquaintance with English social
life had been confined largely to sporting circles; though
acquainted with some politicians and literary men, he knew best
the people who hunted and shot, who went to the moors in August
and the Riviera in January. From the moment that he brought
Margaret Rutherfurd back to Europe as his wife this began to
change; and it changed very rapidly when he became a secretary of
legation. The Whites, who had settled down after a short time at 9
Grosvenor Crescent, where they took a house adjoining that of
Sir George Trevelyan, soon became familiar with the best drawing-rooms in town. In particular they fell in with one after another of
a remarkable circle of rather young men and women of position,
most of them married, and were shortly adopted as members of
this group.

It was Mrs. White who was responsible for the entrance of her
husband into the "Souls," as the group surrounding Arthur Balfour,
Margot Tennant (later Mrs. Asquith), George Curzon, St. John
Brodrick, and Lord and Lady Elcho were called. She was then at
the height of her beauty and charm. Everyone admired her. It was
not merely that she was lovely to look at; she talked well, with
animation and distinction, and she had grace and poise. "She was
a woman of great beauty and accomplishment," writes Lord Robert
Cecil. "If the word had not been spoilt by unfortunate associations
she would have been rightly called elegant. In the common phrase,
she was asked everywhere." Lady Salisbury was one of those who
thought her incomparable; White reports her in 1892 "fairly beam-
ing about you." Jusserand, according to Mme. Waddington, was
"devoted to Daisy." She seemed the life of her own group. "Get
better quickly, Daisy," implored George Curzon when in the spring
of 1891 she was in Paris for her health; "it is slow without you."
The future Lord Haldane wrote her long letters on literary topics,

76

discussing Zola and Stevenson. When in the summer of 1889 she suffered the loss of valuable jewels by a robbery at Ramslade, the country house of the Whites, the Duke and Duchess of Westminster sent her one of their own jewels in consolation.

But Mrs. White was frequently ailing after the birth of her son, her ill-health keeping her out of society for months at a stretch. Within a short time White was valued quite as much as his wife, and much more universally and unreservedly loved. For loved is not too strong a word. He was not witty, he was not a brilliant talker or writer, he was not a man of deep cultivation, and he had no such resplendent political future before him as Balfour and Curzon. He possessed but comparatively modest wealth. But as always throughout life, his absolute unselfishness and loyalty, his cheeriness and humor, drew everyone to him. "What was it that made him welcome wherever he went?" asks Lord Cecil.[1] "I really think it was his goodness. He never said an ill-natured or bitter thing in his life. He never claimed anything as his due. If there was a dull or disagreeable duty to be done, Harry took it on. Every lame dog naturally turned to him for help. To say that he was unselfish is inadequate. He lived to increase the happiness of others. If he did you a service it was he who seemed the gainer. No wonder he had hosts of friends."

At the beginning of the 'nineties the Gang, as they first called themselves, or the Souls, as they were later named, were at the zenith of their reputation. There has seldom been a more delightful group. They were made interesting by their brilliant social gifts, and by the breadth of their interests. Sport, games, literature, art, philosophy, politics, religion, were all open for discussion at their gatherings. They had wealth, beauty, intellect, and culture at their command. Among them were hostesses who owned some of the most beautiful country houses in England, and at Panshanger, Ashridge, Wilton, and Taplow these congenial spirits would assemble for week-ends. For half a dozen years the charmed circle endured and the coterie sailed on summer seas.[2]

[1] Memorandum by Lord Cecil for the author.
[2] The literature on the "Souls" is voluminous but widely scattered. Special mention should be made of the materials in Lord Haldane, *Autobiography*,

The origin of the Gang, or Souls, may be traced in part to the determination of a few people closely connected with politics not to let the acrimony of the Home Rule controversy spoil their social intercourse. Henry White had just been made first secretary of legation when early in 1886 Gladstone became Prime Minister for the third time. That spring, with the resignation of Joseph Chamberlain and Sir George Trevelyan from Gladstone's Cabinet, it was known that the Ministry was about to bring forward a proposal for full Irish Home Rule. In April, before a crowded House of Commons and in a magnificent speech of three and a half hours, Gladstone introduced his bill. The excitement of the debate which followed, with Chamberlain, Lord Hartington, Lord Randolph Churchill, and Trevelyan leading the opposition, was reflected in nearly every drawing-room of London. A great Liberal peer, the Duke of Westminster, ostentatiously sold his Millais portrait of Gladstone. Men were blackballed at clubs because of their Home Rule views. Hostesses were at their wits' end lest they seat political enemies side by side at dinner parties. The Gladstone Government was quickly defeated in a general election, but the animosities increased during 1887-88 with the outburst of the National League disorders in Ireland. It was under these circumstances that a few of the more independent houses of London resolved not to let public politics obliterate private friendships.

In the half-unconscious grouping of several dozens of kindred spirits into a set of brilliant and gay friends, a few households played a dominant part. One was that of the Earl of Wemyss, with one daughter, Hilda, who married St. John Brodrick, and three sons, Hugo (Lord Elcho), Alan Charteris, and Evan Charteris. One was the Lyttelton family, of whom one son, Alfred, married first Laura Tennant and as his second wife Edith Balfour. A third was the Tennants, comprising no fewer than twelve children, almost all of them talented or at least of striking individuality. Around the younger members of these families was assembled a varied and remarkably constant circle: Harry Cust, George Wyndham, Baron Ferdinand de Rothschild, Mr. and Mrs. John Horner, Lord and Lady Pembroke, Lord and Lady Granby, Godfrey Webb,

in Margot Asquith, *An Autobiography*, vol. ii, and in Lord Ronaldshay, *Life of Lord Curzon,* vol. i.

Mr. and Mrs. Willy Grenfell (later Lord and Lady Desborough), A. G. Liddell, and others.[3]

Since it was the Tennants whom White and his wife first knew well, and who perhaps formed the keystone of this little social arch, a special word may be said of their position. Sir Charles Tennant, a millionaire financier and a Liberal member of Parliament from the Selkirkshire country of Scott and Hogg, had bought a house at 40 Grosvenor Square in 1881. The family estate was the place called The Glen, a great stone mansion in the Scottish baronial style deep among the moors some thirty miles from Edinburgh; its isolation was increased by the chilliness which the Tory gentry of that district showed to a Whig politician. One of the twelve children, Charlotte or Charty, who married Lord Ribblesdale in 1877, was known for her pert tongue. She once asked Lord Rothschild at a dinner, "And do you still believe the Messiah is coming, Lord Natty?" Another sister, Lucy, married Graham Smith of Easton Grey, Malmesbury. Laura, who married Alfred Lyttelton in 1885, died the following year with the advent of her first baby. But the most dashing and famous of all was Margot, who was destined to become the second wife of H. H. Asquith. The beauties of The Glen, the rather peppery brilliance of old Sir Charles, though he cared little for any society but that of financiers and politicians, and above all the attractions of the vivacious daughters, made the castle a resort for all the Souls. When the Whites became familiar with The Glen in 1885 they met there Evan Charteris and his brothers, Arthur Balfour, George Curzon, George Wyndham, Harry Cust—all young men of high and nearly equal promise—and some older figures, such as Mark Napier and Lord Houghton.[4]

By 1886 the Whites were fairly acquainted with the principal future members of the Souls. They knew Arthur Balfour and Lord and Lady Elcho. Curzon had been described as early as 1883, when Mrs. White met him at a country-house party given by Lord and Lady Ripon at Studley Royal. She wrote her mother with some enthusiasm of "Mr. Curzon, the eldest son of Lord Scarsdale. He

[3] Lord Haldane writes that at gatherings of the "Souls" "one or two outside men were welcomed and were frequently guests. Among them were John Morley, Sir Alfred Lyall, Asquith, and myself. We were not 'Souls,' but they liked our company and we liked theirs because of its brilliance."

[4] Cf. Lord Ronaldshay, *Life of Lord Curzon*, vol. i.

is extremely clever and is supposed to be the hope of the Conservative party. He is now Lord Salisbury's private secretary, or one of them, and he is running for the next Parliament. He took all sorts of honors at the university; he writes and speaks extremely well, and is altogether a charming member of society. He uses the quaintest and most original language and is very witty." St. John Brodrick had become a good friend even earlier. After 1886 references multiply in the letters of the Whites to Balfour, familiarly known as Ah Bah—the most distinguished of the Souls, regarded by everyone as a future prime minister; Curzon, always called George; Lord and Lady Elcho, called Hugo and Sweet Mary; and Margot Tennant.

It was in 1886 that the Whites took a house at Ramslade near Bracknell in Berkshire, which for years was a week-end retreat for their friends. By English standards it was modest, though Daisy created some amused perplexity among her American relatives by writing that it contained not only room for themselves, the children, the governess, and twelve servants, but two extra bedrooms; she had to explain that in England twelve servants were not a large retinue. Downstairs there was a large drawing-room, a dining-room, a schoolroom, and a combined billiard-room and green-house. They were only a few miles from Ascot, and in Ascot Week they more than once sublet the house furnished for as much as their whole annual rental unfurnished. Their first visitors were Henry James and George W. Smalley, the London correspondent of the New York *Tribune*. Small groups of the Souls met here, just as larger parties went for week-ends to the great houses where the hostesses were older women, affectionately called the "aunts"— Lady Cowper, Lady Brownlow, and Lady Pembroke.

Because of the cultivation and brilliancy of the Souls the desire for entrance into their ranks was keen; and because many were excluded they became the object of a good deal of envious detraction. Some, including Lord Haldane, who has doubted whether they were on the whole an influence for good, thought they took themselves too seriously. Some thought they took themselves too lightly, and unquestionably, while they had more decorum than most members of the Prince of Wales's set, which was very gay indeed, several were what Margot Tennant called "fast." The

A GROUP OF ENGLISH FRIENDS

Standing, left to right: Sir John Lister-Kaye; Mrs. W. Grenfell; Lord Elcho; George Nathaniel Curzon; Henry White. Sitting, left to right: Duchess of Leinster; W. Grenfell; Margot Tennant.

Whites in their letters indorse what Margot says of Harry Cust, for example: a fine athlete, a rare wit, a man of remarkable learning, who might have gone far but that he "was fatally self-indulgent, and success with my sex damaged his public career." [5] One or two others are mentioned in similar terms. Though nearly all the Souls were above reproach, a significant light is shed upon one side of London society in general by White's remark to Daisy in the fall of 1892, in a letter from Ramslade. "I have just had a delightful hour's talk with ——," he says. "He thinks you very remarkable in having associated with all those people who have lovers without either having your head turned or changing in any way, and yet retaining the respect and admiration of the aforesaid people." But what chiefly distinguished the Souls was their interest in deep and serious discussion. Indeed, their nickname came from Lord Charles Beresford, who remarked at a dinner at Lord Brownlow's in 1888: "You all sit and talk about each others' souls—I shall call you the 'Souls.'"

From the correspondence of the Whites one may select many bits which are mere personal gossip; others which show the tastes of the day in entertaining; and some which bear upon politics. All three ingredients contributed essentially to the diplomatic usefulness of Henry White, and are requisite to an understanding of the background of his work during the 'nineties. He could not have played the effective rôle he did if he had not known important people with genuine intimacy.

Naturally, the gossip is sometimes most entertaining when it is most trivial. Whom should Margot marry? Where would the ambitious George Curzon's passion for travel call him next? Was the quietly astute Asquith really abler than the still quieter Haldane, or would the latter outstrip him? These were three stock topics, and there were others like them. We find White writing Daisy from Lord Elcho's place at Stanway, where he had been hunting, of the charm of "Sweet Mary"—that is, Lady Elcho, whose beauty is preserved in Sargent's picture of the "Three Sisters," the daughters of Percy Wyndham. Again, he writes of Mrs. Horner's comments upon a novel describing one of Harry Cust's love affairs,

[5] Asquith, Margot, *An Autobiography*, vol. ii, p. 55. Henry Cust brilliantly edited the *Pall Mall Gazette* for several years.

penned by the heroine thereof. "She says it is disgusting; also that she does not think Asquith will have a chance of being bagged by ——, as Margot probably will nail him." He refers to the love affair of Margot with Peter Flower, which Mrs. Asquith describes so frankly in her memoirs.[6] "Margot looks ill still, but seemed bright; was very affectionate and sympathetic about you, and went over the Peter story and how much it had cost her, finally agreeing with me that she is much better without him and that she could not have stood him here this season, and that she is much more easy and comfy when he is away." We have frequent comments upon Arthur Balfour's keenness for tennis and golf.

The Souls prided themselves upon the esteem in which they were held, though they did not wish to form too hard-and-fast a clique After a dinner at Joseph Chamberlain's, we find White writing: "George Curzon said last night, 'What a charming dinner party! They're always obliged when they want a really nice dinner to come to our set. Ah Bah never talked brighter nor gayer.'" But the Souls also made mild fun of the way in which some of their circle pursued outside celebrities. During the season of 1891 White writes his wife again:

I had a most delicious evening at Mary's and Pamela's party. Went in and while speaking to Mrs. Wyndham heard shouts from the corner, "There's old Harry," coupled with other murmurs of approval, and was promptly greeted by Ah Bah, George Curzon, George Wyndham, Sweet Mary, and several other friends, who though at a sort of round game actually got up to greet me and ask after you. Lady Grosvenor, Miss Peel, De Vesci, the eldest Hohenlohe, young Wyndham, Mrs. Nevile Lyttelton, Lady Bessborough, Spencer Lyttelton, and Lord Cowper, who seemed in excellent form, with Rennell Rodd and Henry Cadogan, were there. The chief feature of the evening was the extraordinary spirits of Ah Bah, and the eloquent denunciation by George Curzon of what he calls the decadence of our circle by the introduction of the "Cosquiths," a name he has coined out of Oscar Wilde and Asquith to denote the steeplechase after that class whom the fair ones are now pursuing. George confided to me that you and Lady Elcho stand out so tremendously on pedestals for not running after them and I agree with him. Ettie is quite joining in the race, I fear, having announced that she had invited four of them to Taplow, and having been previously dining at

[6] Asquith, Margot, *An Autobiography*, vol. ii, pp. 137-190.

Margot's with some more. George was splendid, and you will hear him when you get back. It was finally proposed by him and Ah Bah as a solution that I should be invited to Taplow on the same occasion, put in a punt with them, and upset it in the hope of drowning them. I must say I am disposed to draw the line at Oscar Wilde, about whom everybody has known for years. I will tell you about it and so will old George when you come. George is looking marvelously well, is living at the Constitutional Club, and retains his rooms at Norwood.

Upon this same subject Curzon commented at length in a letter which he sent to Mrs. White a few days later. He spoke of a debate in the Commons and added:

In the evening we had a great debauch at 44 Belgrave Square. All the friends were there. I am greatly exercised and Harry shares my pain at the novel pursuit of notoriety in any shape (if associated with cleverness) into which some of our friends, notably Lady Charty and Ethel, have plunged. The latest is giving a great Taplow party on Sunday to these new guns, including Mr. and Mrs. Oscar Wilde, Mr. and Mrs. Asquith, and Mr. and Mrs. Beerbohm Tree. Conceive! There is great anxiety to know which of Harry Cust, Oscar Wilde, and Asquith will succeed in outtalking the others. I have christened the three Cosquith, and I solemnly and amid thunders of applause proposed the eternal confusion of Cosquith! Ah, but it means more. It means the dissolution of the fairest and strongest band of friends ever yet allied by ties of affection. Gone forever is the old Gang, and a few magnificent souls like you and Harry, Liddell, Mary Elcho, and myself alone remain. The rest are whirling after new gods and baring their heads in the temple of twopenny Rimmons.

Wilde appears but once or twice in the correspondence and his contacts with the Souls were few. White mentions going in 1893 with Lady Carmarthen to see the first night of "A Woman of No Importance": "The Chamberlains, Lady Randolph Churchill, and Lady Sarah Wilson, the Granbys, George Lewis, and a number of others were there; Arthur Balfour and the George Wyndhams were in a box with Mrs. Oscar. Tree was capital; better, I think, than ever, in get-up and acting, and Mrs. Tree certainly much better than I have ever seen her as the *fin-de-siècle* semi-detached married woman, which one would not have thought her style at all. But she did it very well and was beautifully dressed. There was a rather amusing series of dialogues between the old ladies of society in a country house, and the conversation is full of paradoxes and aphorisms, some of them rather strained and some good. But somehow one does not feel that Oscar's fame has increased or that he has any great depth of dramatic talent. He did not make a speech in spite of the clamors of the audience." Asquith disliked Wilde intensely, and was grateful to the Whites for their efforts to con‑vince Margot of his real character. The Whites' circle included no other men of letters save George Meredith, Jowett, and Henry James, and the first two they saw but seldom.

Asquith was hardly known to the Whites till 1891; thereafter he occasionally dined with them, and was at Ramslade at the end of 1892 to watch the old year out, writing that "I am glad to think that we are more (much more) of friends than we were at its beginning." White occasionally went to the House of Commons to hear him, and was always impressed. Like others of the Souls, he was immensely pleased when in the late summer of 1892 the new Ministry came in and Asquith was made Home Secretary. In‑deed, it was Asquith who, upon the invitation of Gladstone, moved the amendment which caused the Salisbury Ministry to fall; and his inclusion in Gladstone's fourth and last Cabinet was a matter of course. He was on the eve of his fortieth birthday, and was henceforth to be one of the important Liberal leaders. Since As‑quith and Balfour were on opposite sides of the political fence, members of the Souls took a warm interest in their occasional clashes. Thus in the spring of 1892 White wrote that he had just heard a debate on the Irish Local Government bill. "Asquith made a brilliant and most successful speech. He was eloquent and more fortunate in his gestures than the last time he spoke. He made some capital points, especially when he parodied Arthur Balfour's speech at Belfast."

Of matchmaking there could be little among the Souls, for most of the members were already married; and for this reason the circle watched with increased interest the progress of the romance between Asquith and Margot Tennant. As late as April, 1892, White felt his doubts about the match. Margot at that time, George Curzon told him, "had her hooks into" more suitors than ever. Witty, incalculable, unconventional, no one could predict what she would do. "As regards Margot," White wrote his wife, "I think it quite likely she may not marry Asquith, although I have not seen them enough together to judge. I don't think she seems in love with him, but fancies his strong character." When the engagement was announced in 1893, White heard of it in New York. The news met with much disapproval among friends on both sides; but White was delighted, and his comment was much the same as that which Margot's friend Dr. Jowett made. "I certainly do not believe she will ever again be so deeply cared for by anyone else," he confided to Mrs. White. "I hope she will marry him, as it will be an excellent discipline for her and give her plenty of congenial and legitimate occupation to further his interests."

It is difficult to convey in brief space the flavor of a period, and especially a period and place so crowded with personalities, events, and movements as London at the turn of the 'nineties. These were the years of the Queen's Jubilee, of Irish Relief and Irish Land bills and agitations, of Salisbury's exchange of Heligoland for Zanzibar, of General Booth's *Darkest England*, of the Parnellites, of the Baring failure, of *Robert Elsmere* and *Plain Tales from the Hills*, of dock strikes and "Ta-ra-ra-boom-de-ay." Of it all White was an intent observer, and his sympathies were much less limited to one class than were his contacts. The best way to indicate the persons and occasions which made up his life outside of office hours is to quote some typical passages from his letters. In April, 1892, for example, he writes of a meal with his distinguished next-door neighbor:

This morning I breakfasted with Trevelyan, a club breakfast, there being present Sir Mountstuart Grant Duff, whom Jusserand used to know very well, old Mr. Leveson Jones, Courtney the deputy Speaker, and I; very pleasant. Trevelyan talked of a visit he has recently been paying to the quarters at Hampstead occupied by Keats and the Brawnes, which he described very well. Then they talked of the numerous records of Byron to be found at the Pisa post office, which are still preserved. It appears that the authorities there were very suspicious of him, opened his letters, etc., all of which is still recorded there, and the record is on view. . . . It seems also that the Grand Old Man, when recently in Paris, met Taine, and does not appear to be much elated with the interview. Probably Taine did not make up to him.

A little later there was an amusing dinner with Lord and Lady Airlie:

Lady Airlie told many stories and was in capital form. She certainly is very agreeable. It appears that Jowett (with whom she has recently been staying) has been writing for some years past farewell letters to his friends and keeping them. When he thought himself dying not long ago he had them posted. This reminded Charty of the one he had written Margot, which contained something offensive to her about her worldliness, on the authority of the Duchess of Bedford, whom Jowett quoted. Margot being determined to get the opinion modified and feeling no time was to be lost, telegraphed old Jowett that she would not have the offensive observation as his last words (so cheerful this last for a dying man), and imploring him to write something else, which he appears to have done. His fondness for gossip and ignorance of the ways of the world were commented upon.

Another letter, dated in April, 1893, describes one of White's days of release from the cares of the embassy:

I had a pleasant breakfast this morning with old Brodrick, St. John Brodrick, Alfred Milner, Sir Mountstuart Grant Duff, president of the Geographical Society, a man called Gibbs and another called Mallet. Old Brodrick is certainly most extraordinary to look at, but interesting to talk to; he told me his experiences when upon a commission to investigate the treatment of Irish prisoners in England long ago, and other kindred topics. I have played golf this afternoon and dined at the Beefsteak Club; very pleasant men there. Afterwards I went to hear Asquith make a speech which never came off for want of time; but I heard Courtney make an excellent one, which, although nearly one and a half hours long, interested me from beginning to end. No exaggeration about it; but merely putting the objections calmly. The Grand Old Man fairly winced at times, but John Morley remained in excellent humor, as did the Irish even. Still it was most telling.

Frequently White met Sir William Vernon Harcourt, in whose burly, lovable, elemental nature he took great pleasure; a man then regarded as heir apparent to Gladstone in the leadership of the Liberal party, but whose defects of temper gave the succession to Lord Rosebery.[7] One of these occasions was in 1890, when the

[7] Bearing on White's friendship with Harcourt, see Gardiner, A. G., *Life of Sir William Harcourt*, vol. ii, p. 402.

débâcle of Parnell through the exposure of his relations with Mrs. O'Shea had done so much to shatter the hopes of the Liberal party and the Home Rule cause. Some of the ensuing bitterness in the Liberal ranks is apparent in White's record:

Ferdy's [Ferdinand Rothschild's] dinner was most pleasant and would have been remarkable and most amusing had Richard Power, an Irish M. P. and supporter of Parnell, who was expected but had to back out at the last moment, been present. Sir William Vernon Harcourt and Henry James were the *pièces de resistance*, the other guests being old Sir H. Hoare and Lady Hamilton. We sat till past eleven. Both the *pièces* were in excellent form, and it really was comical to hear old Sir William talking of the Irish *in private*. It appears that Labby [Labouchère, editor of *Truth* and Liberal leader] says he will have no more leaders unless they are emasculated, and suddenly told old Mundella, who it appears is particularly straitlaced, that he should not even trust him unless he should submit to the operation! What do you think also of Parliament getting through its work, owing to the Irish row, already, and being able to adjourn possibly next Friday; certainly on Tuesday?—There were some amusing stories told about Mrs. O'Shea, who, it appears, began her career before she was married, and had one or two "results," of which O'Shea must have been cognizant; so that they must have been a rare couple altogether.

Gladstone, the Grand Old Man himself, is seen usually at second hand in the correspondence of the Whites; but three or four times they sat at dinner with him. One meeting is of special interest. The Right Honorable Arthur Peel, who was Speaker of the House of Commons for eleven years following 1884, used to give Mrs. White admission to the gallery of the House at practically all times, and she often attended. Her report of the debates interested her young son, and he asked many questions. As White years later wrote: [8]

One day Miss Julia Peel very kindly asked him whether he would like to come down to her gallery (her mother had died shortly before) and hear a debate. Of course he accepted the invitation with alacrity, and it was arranged that on a certain day I should take him to Miss Peel's gallery and leave him there; and that I should call for him at the Speaker's house in the Palace of Westminster about half past five o'clock,

[8] Undated memorandum by Henry White.

after he had taken tea with her. This arrangement was carried out, and when I went to take the boy home I was surprised and interested, upon entering the Speaker's library, to find Mr. Gladstone addressing himself to Jack with considerable earnestness on the subject of dogs; the Speaker, who was a very tall and imposing man, standing before a fire in the great fireplace in his robes and wig—a very striking and picturesque scene.

It seems that when Jack had been brought down from the gallery for tea, the Speaker, who had heard of a favorite fox terrier of his called Spot, had asked him about his pet, which started a conversation on dogs, and something was said by the boy which aroused Mr. Gladstone's interest. Mr. Gladstone had the singular faculty of turning his mind abruptly and with great earnestness to any question, however insignificant or unimportant, which might suddenly occur in conversation, and on which he differed from an opinion expressed by some one else. On these occasions, of which I was several times a witness at dinner parties and elsewhere, he would often discourse at considerable length and with great eloquence. It was in the midst of just such an occasion that I entered the Speaker's library. The interesting part of it to me was not only that Mr. Gladstone should be talking to my youthful son in such an earnest and eloquent manner, but more particularly that a casual remark made by a little fellow of his tender years should have aroused the great British statesman as it did, and I shall never forget the scene. I have no recollection of the question at issue, but I remember Jack's asking one or two questions, which only seemed to increase Mr. Gladstone's interest and eloquence.

In another letter White describes how the G. O. M. was once his table companion:

Last night Mr. Gladstone sat next to me and made himself most agreeable. He told me among other things that he always told Mrs. Gladstone all his state secrets and that she had never even hinted at the knowledge. He also said that one of his rules through life had always been never to talk over and if possible never to think of exciting or disagreeable things late at night or in bed, but always to wait for the morning, and it had now become second habit. Then he talked about his correspondence. In the course of his career to the Queen alone he had written 2,000 letters, and his yearly average of letters received, not counting those of special departments during office, is about 20,000. Besides all the writing done by his secretaries, he writes by hand (only letters) about four hours a day; and yet he reads everything and leads all his political life besides.

Now and then White, in his visits to the House of Commons, would witness an incident of dramatic value. One is recorded in a letter of April 22, 1893, to a friend:

The Grand Old Man, who rose at ten minutes to twelve and spoke for more than an hour, was in his best form; he seemed as fresh and combative and full of gesture as I have ever seen him. One specially interesting incident took place. A few days ago Austen Chamberlain made what everybody seems to think a brilliant maiden speech, some of the arguments of which Mr. Gladstone dealt with; but in referring to the speech he praised it and said, turning round with emphasis to the elder Chamberlain, "I can only say that the speech must have been *very* dear to a father's heart." The effect of this was like an electric shock to Joseph Chamberlain, who started and buried his eyes in his hands, and shortly afterwards I saw him brushing away the tears of emotion which could not be kept back. I can give no idea of the manner and gesture of Mr. Gladstone in saying these words; but they of course produced more effect, coupled with Joe's emotion, than the words themselves.

Encounters with royalty in these years were rare and unimportant. Twice or thrice the Prince of Wales, later Edward VII, dined with the Whites, but they formed no novel impression of him. Of Queen Victoria they had mere occasional glimpses. The most extended record of her preserved in the Whites' papers is a bit of reminiscence by Mrs. White, referring to a visit which they paid in October, 1897, at Balmoral. They drove over from Braemar, being invited for dinner at 8:45 in the evening. Mrs. White writes: [9]

I wore my black brocade Worth dress, with tulle sleeves and a big yoke on one side, a diamond and pearl chain, and diamond collar with a row of pearls; an aigrette in my hair. Lady Lytton said I looked nice! She took me into the household drawing-room where they all assemble, and from the door of which on the passage one makes one's obeisance to the Queen as she passes into the dining-room leaning on the arm of her Indians and followed tonight by Princess Beatrice, Prince Christian, and the Hohenlohes. I curtsied to the Queen and kissed her hand and she said she hoped I was not tired after the long drive. She looks wonderfully well; not so red as she used and a little thinner, and such a happy, peaceful expression; but very stiff and lame, walking with real difficulty and apparently shorter than ever. She is tiny! But her dignity is wonder-

[9] Undated memorandum by Mrs. White.

ful. It almost amounts to being abstract, so little is it helped by her personal appearance. I sat at dinner between Fritz Ponsonby, so nice and clever, and Joseph Chamberlain. Princess Hohenlohe looked so fresh and pretty in pink satin trimmed with fur and diamonds. The Queen sat between Prince Christian and Hohenlohe. For the most part they talked German together, and neither continuously nor much. Harry was placed between Princess Beatrice and Lady Lytton; he made Princess Beatrice talk quite glibly. After dinner we went to the drawing-room. I forgot to say that the Queen's two Indians looked very splendid in gold and scarlet at dinner, and waited on her chiefly, but also on everyone. A chair was put near the center table for the Queen, and next it a magnifying glass and one or two little objects that I did not make out.

First Lady Lytton went to talk to her, and during that time Princess Beatrice, Princess Hohenlohe, and I, standing near the fireplace, all talked together. By and by Lady Lytton came over for me and I went around and stood by the Queen and had the longest talk I have ever had with her and the easiest except for the physical effort of leaning down to her, I being standing and tall and she being seated and so short. I think I must have stood there quite twenty-five minutes. The Queen first asked me exactly where Carrie Fergie is. She said she didn't know the house. I told her it was the last house on the left on the Spittal Road, near the Black Gate leading into her forest. "Oh no, that is not my gate; it is Farquhar's." Then she said, "I understand that you have been a sufferer for some time and you came here for your health five years ago; I hope this place is doing you good." I told her a little about my poor health and how it had to my everlasting disappointment prevented me from attending her Jubilee at St. Paul's, and how bitterly sorry I was to have missed that great occasion.

I then told her that there had been much rejoicing in America over her Jubilee, in spite of some Jingo propensities, and she laughed and said: "Yes, they have always had a kind personal feeling for me, and I don't know why." Then I told her that the President had wanted to send Harry to Spain as minister, but that I had rather prevented this because I wished to stay in England, and I asked her if she thought I had done wrong. She said: "Oh no. Where one is happy one is best." I told her I had just been reading her letters and Tennyson's in the Memoir by his son, and asked her about Tennyson. "I have the book," she said, "but have not read it. Tennyson was a very gruff man in manner and was often misunderstood through this, but he was always very kind to me. He was like a person who had never been contradicted or disciplined, but he had noble thoughts."

Browning she said she had seen only once and thought his poetry very difficult to understand. She preferred Mrs. Browning's writings, and thought the "Sonnets from the Portuguese" very beautiful. Then she asked me if there was any new or coming poet in America, to take the place of Longfellow, Lowell, and the others. I told her I feared so far there was no one. We talked of golf. She said she had never really seen a game; that she had always been particularly stupid at mastering games, but she had seen people walking about with sticks in the distance, and it looked very dull. . . . And by and by the Queen gave her little bow and smile which means dismissal, and I retired to talk to Princess Beatrice and the others.

Then she talked to Harry. She told Lady Lytton she thought I had such a pleasant voice and speech (I suppose this she does not expect from Americans) and that she thinks me very pretty! Before she left the room I again kissed her hand.

A definite part was played in the social life of the Whites by numerous Americans visiting London, who fell into two groups; those political personages whom they entertained chiefly from a sense of duty, and the friends whom they took to Ramslade or had to dinner in London because of genuine personal esteem. We have already mentioned several of the latter, notably John Hay and his wife, and Henry Adams, who came over with Don Cameron and the fascinating Mrs. Cameron. When Hay visited London at the same time one year as Chauncey Depew, White asked them to a bachelor dinner to meet Gladstone and Trevelyan; and Trevelyan always remembered one of Chauncey Depew's inimitably told stories, which he said was like nothing he had ever heard in life save perhaps an after-lunch piece by Coquelin *jeune*. Another visitor, with whom White's relations were shortly to be much closer, was Joseph Choate, who pleased the Secretary by saying they ought to make him minister. Senator Hoar, spending some days in London in 1893, brought a little partisan gossip regarding the President. "He says that Cleveland is a man who can be intimidated into making appointments, and instanced the case of Mr. Phelps, respecting whose confirmation by the Senate, if appointed, he himself had been approached by Cleveland, who fully intended appointing him until threatened by the Irish, two or three of whom went to Washington to stop it and were successful."

There can be no question that Henry James's friendship, unlike

Lowell's, was chiefly for Mrs. White, whose beauty, charm, and lively intelligence awakened his gallant regard when in the middle 'eighties they first met. He wrote to both, but his letters to her were longer—sometimes in his rambling fashion very long indeed— and warmer than to her husband. He liked to come down to Rams- lade at least once a summer, and to drop in at her town house for tea. When he replied to their letters of condolence upon the death of his sister in the spring of 1892, it was to her that he unburdened his heart:

My sister's death makes a great difference in my daily existence, because she was a great element of interest, of society, of talk, and a singularly remunerative and delightful one, whenever she was in Lon- don. I went to see her every day, and that in itself is a difference, though the smallest. Her extinction, however, is also the end of so many years of acute suffering that the consciousness that all this is over is almost, for one's self, like a cessation of personal pain. I should deplore more the necessary duration of your absence if I were not myself preparing to leave town for the whole period of the session. I don't even yet, indeed, know where I shall go; whether abroad, or somewhere in the British Islands. Probably the former, and in this case to Italy, my well-beloved. I have followed you in imagination to Bordighera, though I confess that faculty has not been particularly kindled in me by the general sense of the little court taking place there. It mainly makes me utter—oh, such a philosophical sigh! London has emptied itself with its sheeplike unanimity for Easter, and left me as usual behind, like a straying black mutton of the social flock. What I do deplore, dear Mrs. White, is the fact that you have to dedicate yourself to a cure. What has such a happy creation and delightful work of nature to be cured of? Leave that to the failures, the female botches—and at any rate part with as few as possible of the valued signs by which you are known, dear Mrs. White, to your very faithful old friend, Henry James.

This letter is characteristic of a dozen others, and in a later con- nection we shall quote some self-revelatory passages, fuller and more intimate. To Mrs. White he gave the study that a novelist gives a distinct and perfected type, and it is possible that some of her intellectual qualities may be reproduced in Maria Gostrey of *The Ambassadors,* or some other traits in Maggie Verver of *The Golden Bowl.* The Whites would have seen more of him but for his industry. Writing doggedly at his fiction, he used to lament that "I am a vile, impracticable brute, who has so fatally arranged his life that he is tied to the leg of his table"; that "It is a thousand years since I have seen you—but I have ceased to live, anyhow."

When White's diplomatic career suffered its check in 1894, James was deeply interested in their return to the United States. He had then been absent from London for some months.

I was swept off into Italian out-of-the-wayness [he explained] and all my ingenuity, for several months, was squeezed into keeping still. There seemed nothing more sonorous than writing to you, and a certain sympathetic taciturnity forbade it. But my behaviour was not heroic. I returned to England the other day, but came almost straight out of town again—where I shall continue to be up to October 1. I was, however, in London long enough to hear the strange legend of your intention of spending next winter in the United States. That will be a drama indeed —and how I should like a front seat to see it. I myself, personally, never thought to return to my native land (I may whisper), but I think I would go, to be present at your dealings with it. We must talk it over. How many things I want to talk over with you!

But it was to be more than a decade before he brought himself, with a distinctly literary intention, to revisit the American scene.[10]

It was, in a sense, a wonderful "opportunity" which Henry White enjoyed in these years—an opportunity of knowing so many men and women intellectually distinguished; of meeting on a footing of comradeship future rulers of empire like Balfour, Asquith, and

[10] Mrs. White preserved among her papers some brief reminiscences of Matthew Arnold, dated September 19, 1888. She met him first at a luncheon, where they had little conversation. "My first impression of his personal appearance was that he was ugly, but this soon disappeared. He was tall, broad in figure without being stout, dark, and manly-looking; with very thick dark hair, gray eyes, and a smile that was delightful, illuminating his whole face. His voice was particularly rich and mellow and his manner, although stately and dignified, was extremely genial." He told Lady Ribblesdale that Mrs. White was the nicest American he knew. "The best and longest memory I have of him," Mrs. White's memorandum continues, "is of spending an afternoon and evening with him and his family at Cobham, his little house; quite a cottage on a green lawn, neat, homelike, and English. He was charming and I wish I could remember more details about it all. His wife was a small, gentle, motherly, quick woman, not a woman of the world as he was a man of the world."

Curzon; of easy social contact with Cabinet Ministers, members of Parliament, and others. He did not regard it self-consciously. He took his social life and its advantages as he had taken the benefits of his earlier career. He and his wife neither journalized upon their contacts with eminent people nor noted them down mentally for future reminiscences, and the record would have been almost entirely lost but for Mrs. White's frequent absences in search of health and White's devoted letter-writing. But the value to White of all his experience lay beyond the pleasure and profit of the moment. As he had previously known the brighter, gayer side of European life, so now he saw the most distinguished side in the European nation where men worked hardest and their interests were broadest.[11] His knowledge of English life and affairs was of far-reaching advantage to him in all his diplomatic contacts. It was not, unfortunately, an unmixed advantage, for by the completeness of his identification with English circles he seemed to some of his countrymen to lose that rigid Americanism which they thought essential to an ambassador in London, and thus raised up an impediment to his own promotion.

All social groups in fast-moving centers are evanescent, and the wonder is not that the Souls gradually dissolved, but that their circle remained fairly intact for so long a period. The marriage of Margot and Asquith in 1894, the absence of George Curzon on his trip of 1892-93 around the world, the departure of St. John Brodrick for an Australian tour, and White's loss of his official position, were all centrifugal influences which rent the intimate fellowship apart. The beginning of the end may be dated from the departure of Curzon and White from England in the summer of 1892, the former on the first part of his circuit of the globe, the latter

[11] The diary of White's daughter for the early 'nineties offers much evidence of the informality of social contacts. Once there was a bicycling party at a country house. "Mrs. Grenfell and Mr. Balfour teased each other playfully all the way. The greatest people are often the simplest. Mr. Balfour seems like a schoolboy during his holidays. Most of the day he spent on his back under a tree, reading a book." Jusserand used to come to Ramslade to play tennis, and leaped about the court with indescribable agility and quickness; White's two children called him "the little gentleman that dances." It was indeed White who taught him tennis, an accomplishment of which he made good use in Roosevelt's "tennis cabinet."

to attend to business in America. The Whites had always regarded Curzon with unqualified affection. His brilliant parts, his self-confidence, his enormous powers of work, his imagination regarding his own career, impressed them, and they never felt conscious of his *amour propre*, as some did. On this Atlantic voyage White and Curzon enjoyed themselves hugely. They shared the state apartment on the upper deck of the Hamburg-American liner *Fürst Bismarck*, which happened to be vacant and was given them at no extra charge. They jested about the misspelling of Curzon's name on the seating-list at table; about the bride of a Presbyterian clergyman, whom Curzon dubbed "the little Wesleyan," and with whom he pretended that White was carrying on a flirtation; and about an emotional woman who boarded the vessel in New York Bay and, taking White from the rear for her husband, embraced him with the joyous cry, "Is that you?" Both wrote high-spirited letters to Mrs. White detailing incidents of the passage. Curzon continued sending high-spirited notes from various points on his long journey. For example, he wrote from Seoul in the following October:

I don't suppose you ever heard of this place, so I shall add to your geographical knowledge at the time that I call to your mind the remote traveller. It is a great city, with 20,000 people, a King, and a court. I am going to see the King this afternoon. When I went to call upon the Minister for Foreign Affairs, he said to me: "I presume you are nearly related to the royal family?"—that being his idea of official eminence in England. Here no one gets office but the Queen's relations. I replied that I was not yet married, and that there was still a chance of establishing the requisite connection!

That winter Mrs. White and the children stayed at Ramslade until February, and in April both White and his wife went on a trip to Spain. In the autumn of 1893 they returned to the United States together, visiting friends in New York and Baltimore, and attending the Columbian Exposition in Chicago. Cleveland was now President, Bayard was ambassador in London, and in October, 1893, as we shall see, White was dismissed from the service.

CHAPTER EIGHT

American Years: The Venezuela Affair

FOLLOWING Ambassador Bayard's arrival in London in April, 1893, White had spared no pains to make him feel at home and to assist him in mastering the technical details of the embassy's work. Himself always candid, friendly, and whole-heartedly helpful, White harbored no suspicion of his new chief and wished only to make himself useful. Bayard came with high credentials. Now sixty-five, he was a man of much greater political reputation than his predecessors, Lowell, Phelps, and Lincoln. For fifteen years he had been one of the Democratic leaders in the Senate, where his legal expertness, conservative views on financial questions, and aggressive opposition to all class legislation had given him increasing influence. Twice he had received a considerable vote in Democratic conventions for the Presidential nomination—though Presidents are never elected from Delaware. He had served with real credit as Cleveland's first Secretary of State. He was a man of the world, a cultured gentleman, and a representative of one of the great American families. His tall, dignified figure, polished speech, and austere courtesy seemed to mark him as a natural diplomatist. It would have required a more critical person than White to perceive at once that his dignity masked a good deal of egotism, and his grave deliberation a slowness of mind. It took White some time to conclude, as the Cleveland Administration eventually did, that Bayard's appointment was a mistake.[1]

But despite White's friendliness to his chief, he quickly saw that Bayard was not thoroughly friendly to him. He soon felt a reserve in Bayard's manner; and he had no difficulty in learning

[1] White never doubted Bayard's good intentions or devotion to the Republic. He would have agreed with John W. Foster's tribute to Bayard's high ideals and exalted patriotism; *Diplomatic Memoirs*, vol. ii, p. 265. For an appreciation of Bayard see G. F. Parker in the *Contemporary Review*, vol. xxiv, p. 675 ff.

the reason from Lloyd Griscom, Bayard's private secretary. The ambassador had come to England convinced that Robert Lincoln had governed the embassy with such a slack hand that little work was done by any of the staff; suspicious that White wished to make use of his position for social advancement, and apprehensive that with his superior experience White would try to "manage" him. Characteristically, White felt most indignant regarding the first of these preconceptions. "That such an accusation should be leveled against dear, bustling, hard-working, most accurate Linky is indeed too bad!" he wrote his wife.

By working long hours at the embassy, by showing his grasp of laborious details, and by doing a good deal to enlarge Bayard's social contacts, White partially dispelled the ambassador's prejudices. Bayard was often peppery, would seldom take advice from anyone, and had some irritating mannerisms, such as a way of snatching papers from his assistants' hands. But the first secretary never lost his poise. Mrs. White also labored to be agreeable. Lloyd Griscom was soon reporting that she was the only person whom he had ever known to excite Mrs. Bayard's enthusiasm, and that Mrs. Bayard "can never say enough of you and admires you beyond words."

If Bayard had insisted on White's retention, he might have been kept in London; but Bayard was not a man to insist. Cleveland's Administration had political debts to pay, and the Assistant Secretary of State who served briefly at the beginning, Josiah Quincy of Massachusetts, was active in paying them. Several of the diplomatic appointments, notably that of an erratic Texan named Colonel A. W. Terrell to be minister to Turkey, where he at once offered to tell the Sultan Abdul Hamid that he ought to institute a constitutional government on the American system, caused much amusement. Secretary Lamont's prejudice against White marked him for slaughter. Moreover, there was an alert aspirant for his post in James A. Roosevelt of New York, a Democrat who had made large party contributions. The consequence was that when in September, 1893, White prepared to depart for America on leave, Bayard told him that the President wished his resignation. Drafting it at once, White took it with him to present. Just as premature rumors of his dismissal had caused such men as Pierpont Morgan,

E. L. Godkin, Phelps, and John Hay to protest, so now a number of indignant letters poured in upon White. It is sufficient to quote one from Henry James:[2]

I can't withhold the expression of the distress and disgust, the deep resentment and sorrow, with which I have just heard the horrible news of your recall from the embassy. There is no point of view from which it isn't for your friends and compatriots a lamentation and a humiliation; but I feel it, frankly, most as a dark day in my own life. I rejoiced, without modification, in your being there, and I am as ashamed of your departure as I am grieved by it. It seems the end of the golden age—I mean of the long honorable, tranquil time during which one was at blissful peace about your office or about the Legation. Whatever befell, your being there was always so much to the good. I beg you, therefore, my dear White, to believe in my very friendliest and heartiest and most permanent regrets. Please ask your wife to do the same, and tell her how many recollections crowd upon me at this hour, of kindness and hospitality, at her hands and yours, each more charming than the last, filling all the backward-reaching years, and making me conscious again of a loss and gloom whenever I failed fully to avail myself of them. That loss and that gloom cover all the prospect now. But I refuse to believe we are really losing you. We shall keep you on some other footing and still console ourselves with you. London holds you by too many hands. However, all that is for the future. For the moment I only want to assure you both of the sympathy, the indignation, and the very faithful attachment of yours most truly, Henry James.

So much pressure was exerted in his behalf that White still had faint hopes of being retained; he thought it barely possible that on reaching Washington he might find his dismissal had been revoked. Arriving at the capital late in October, and learning that his resignation had not been formally demanded, he went at once to the State Department. He found Secretary Gresham cordial. He found also that President Cleveland, who was convinced that White had spoken disrespectfully of him, was adamant. Gresham asked for the resignation, and telling White that he would use such arguments as he could for its refusal, took it to Cleveland. The sequel, as White described it to his wife, throws a curious light on one of our really great Presidents:

[2] Henry James to White, London, September 2, 1893.

Mr. Gresham again took me into his private room [wrote the first secretary],[3] and in the kindest way reported to me the following interview with the President. He handed him my letter of resignation, and Mr. Bayard's letter, after which Mr. Cleveland remarked, "This resignation is accepted." Mr. Gresham then read him a very strong letter which he appears to have received from Pierpont Morgan, earnestly requesting for various good reasons that I be retained, and Gresham then said that if I could not retain the London post that I should like and my friends would like me to be given some other equally good appointment, or such promotion as I could accept after vacating such a post as London; to which Cleveland still vouchsafed no reply whatever. Mr. Gresham then told him what I had heard as the reasons for the removal, and that it was absolutely untrue that I had ever spoken disrespectfully of him and that I should be glad to have the opportunity of saying so to him, quite irrespective of any desire for employment under his Administration, to which the President still made no reply. Thereupon Gresham said he thought it best to drop the subject, which he did by saying: "I suppose, Mr. President, that I am to infer from your silence that Mr. White need not count upon further employment under this Administration"; to which there was still no reply, and nothing more appears to have been said on the subject.

For the moment White's diplomatic service was ended. His resignation of October 27, 1893, terminated his labors—so far as he could see—for at least four years.

It has been remarked that some of White's best strokes of luck came to him in the guise of misfortune; and this was one. Though he had not realized it, he had been in danger of becoming, if not Anglicized, at least identified with an Anglicized element; he needed an enforced sojourn in the United States, and more friends there. He knew that the Republicans were likely to return to power in 1897. He knew that he had stanch well-wishers—Morton, Lincoln, Hay, Roosevelt, Depew—among the Republican leaders. It was his Washington residence in the next three years, in which he cemented his friendship with the party's future leaders, and especially with Roosevelt and Hay, which made his later promotion and usefulness possible.

Returning to England in the late fall of 1893, White had for a few months a life of entire leisure. His diary, a jotting of brief

[3] White to Mrs. White, Washington, October 30, 1893.

disjointed notes, shows that he saw much of Alfred Lyttelton and Arthur Balfour, walked with Margot Asquith, played golf with John Horner, talked bimetallism with Sir William Vernon Harcourt, and twice was at Hatfield for week-end parties given by the Salisburys. Asquith repeatedly stayed with the Whites at Loseley. Among entries for February and March, 1894, we find: "Asquith returned for the night. Talked about the Grand Old Man's alleged resignation." (This was on February 2, when Gladstone's impending retirement, finally announced on the 28th, was being discussed.) "Long visit from Hodson—old Bayard's peculiarities." "Dined alone with George Curzon." "Lady Airlie arrived. Rosebery's speech. Daisy went with Haldane to see George Meredith." It was a pleasant interlude of freedom from work or care. But in March White received word that his mother was very ill in Baltimore, and before the end of the month she died. One of the mournful compensations for such deaths is that they occasion a family reunion, and once more he had an opportunity to see his brother, half-brother, stepfather, aunt, and other relatives all gathered together. Since it was determined to bury his mother at Hampton, he left his wife and children at Loseley, and after executing some urgent business sailed for the United States.

The gloom of this voyage was in some degree lightened by his shipmates. They included Lawrence Godkin, son of the editor, who told him that White's dismissal was the only regret his father felt in connection with the new Administration; and Mark Twain, gayly coming back from France to face the financial difficulties of his publishing house, Charles L. Webster & Company. Mark Twain and White found each other congenial, and the latter wrote to his wife:

Mark Twain seems to have taken quite a fancy to me, having changed his seat from the captain's table to sit next to me, with young Godkin on the other side. He is a quaint, rough, and rather uncouth sort of person in manner, very frank and open in expressing his opinions. Today he hooked his arm into mine and took a long walk. He has taken a great aversion to a common Englishman whom Winty and I call "the hog," who sat between him and Bartlett Tripp, the minister to Austria, and who had the effect of shutting him up, much as unsympathetic people used to make Lowell quite silent when in the room with them. After he got to our table, which is opposite the Captain's, he went into fits of delight at seeing the hog begin to talk most genially with the steward, and remarked to me, "That d——d fellow has at last found his level. I could not get a word nor even a smile out of him, but the moment he gets some one of his own calibre to talk to there's a perfect diarrhœa of conversation."

Today we got on the Copyright Act, for which he worked hard, and he said that his chief interest in it was the hope that it would prevent cheap editions of foreign literature, English included, from being read in the United States. He declares that the reading of English novels, Walter Scott included, has imbued the whole American people with a worship for royalty and aristocracy which he considers most unfortunate, and that he would keep out all foreign literature for fifty years if he could! He took occasion not long afterward to mention that he had dined with Princey and with the Emperor of Germany; so I don't quite know how much he meant of what he said; but he has a quaint emphatic way—sometimes quite profane—of giving utterance to his views, which is amusing. He said, by the bye, when he first met me, that he had often heard of me, and thought my removal a great outrage. Tripp, minister to Austria, said the same thing, and appears to be emphatically of the opinion that secretaries should be promoted to be ministers and ambassadors. . . . He said my removal was the greatest surprise to him and to the service generally, as Cleveland had told him that he wanted to have secretaries in the service who could be retained and eventually be promoted.

Nearly all White's time during this visit to America, though he stayed several days with Phelps in New Haven, was spent in arranging his business affairs. On April 17th Mrs. Buckler was buried at Hampton beside her first husband, the body being carried from the vault by her three sons. White's diary records simply that he "spent day at Hampton," but we may imagine the emotions he felt in revisiting the family mansion where he had spent so happy a childhood with his mother, now laid to rest beneath its elms and maples. Thereafter he passed a fortnight in or near Baltimore, arranging for the disposal of furniture and personal effects, signing legal papers, and coming to an agreement with Dr. Buckler regarding an annuity to be paid the latter. Since White's career would not have been possible except for his financial independence, it may be noted that he was now a man of means. The estate was

conservatively valued at $1,559,000; his share was more than $500,-
000; and though part of the property was realty which paid no income, his resources were at once augmented by more than $15,000
a year, while he had a net addition of $25,000 or $30,000 annually
in prospect.[4] Previously his expenses had closely approached his
income, but after this year he never had a moment of financial
anxiety.

A visit to Washington enabled White not only to make plans
for a home there the following winter, but to see a good many
people. His acquaintanceship in the capital was already fairly large,
and a succession of dinners and receptions gave him an antepast
of Washington life. He dined the first day with the Leiters, Senator
Higgins being of the party; the second day, April 30th, he attended
Miss Harriet Blaine's wedding, meeting Senators Hoar and Hale,
Representative Hitt, and other political figures. Among those men-
tioned frequently in his diary are Senator Don Cameron and his
wife—the latter always delighted White—the Lodges, Morton
Frewen, Mrs. Sartoris, Senator Henderson, and Senator Jones of
Nevada. Theodore Roosevelt, now a member of the Civil Service
Commission, he met twice or thrice; Roosevelt wrote him later that
"I need hardly say how I enjoyed seeing you here in Washington,
and how we look forward to having you here next winter, though
I trust it will not be too long before we again see you in our
diplomatic service." Hay was in England, after a winter spent
in Italy with the Charles Eliot Nortons, and White had a number of
his letters posted in London. He described how he had been at
Fairford, Gloucestershire, to see the huge studio where Edwin A.
Abbey and John Sargent were at work on their murals for the
Boston Public Library; how he caught a distant view of Mrs. White
at the Asquith wedding; and how he wished White were there—
"I feel myself missing you every day, when I want to ask a question which neither books nor journals, nor anything but tact and
experience can answer."[5]

In Washington, where Senator Morgan of Alabama had introduced a bill on the subject, White found there was a good deal of
talk about consular reform; and disagreeing with some of Senator

[4] White to Mrs. White, Baltimore, April 17, 1894.
[5] Hay to White, London, May 16, 1894.

Morgan's proposals for placing the service on a professional basis, he wrote an article which appeared in the December (1894) issue of the *North American Review*. He dealt so thoroughly with the history of the American consular service, the organization of European services, and the means of making our consular work a career for able men, that the essay was reprinted a few years later in Harper's Cyclopædia of United States History. Pending its appearance, he wrote a long letter on the subject to Senator Morgan, sending a copy to Roosevelt. These efforts seemed for a time likely to bear fruit. Roosevelt went over Morgan's bill in connection with the letter and suggested changes. Lodge, he wrote White, would probably introduce the amended bill.[6] But it was still too early for really constructive legislation on consular affairs.

The second week in January, 1895, saw White's family settled in a commodious house at 1812 I Street in Washington. He and Mrs. White had taken their temporary farewell of England at a luncheon party in London on New Year's Day, which Henry James attended. How little time they lost in entering the decidedly informal life of the capital, a much smaller and more intimate place than today, may be gathered from White's diary entry of his first day, January 13: "Spent morning rearranging furniture. Lunched with the Camerons to meet the Lodges, Roosevelt, Reeds, Mrs. Adair, and Mrs. Hatch."

Washington during the recent years had greatly improved in appearance and gained in wealth; so greatly that, as Henry Adams remarked later in his autobiography, it was now becoming habitable according to the standards of fashion. "Slowly, a certain society had built itself up about the government; houses had been opened, and there was much dining, much calling, much leaving of cards, but a solitary man counted for less than in 1868. Society seemed hardly more at home than he. Both Executive and Congress held it aloof." Adams tells us that no one in society, whether the Democrats or Republicans were in power, seemed to have the ear of the government; nobody in the government felt inclined, as was the way in London and Paris, to consult the world of society. But there were some exceedingly pleasant circles in Washington. Diplomatic entertainments, since a number of legations had been

[6] Roosevelt to White, Washington, December 12, 1894.

raised to embassies, had a new splendor. Among those who entertained most brilliantly and frequently were the Hays, the Don
Camerons, Senator Calvin Brice and his wife, the Nelson Aldriches,
the Allisons, and the Lodges. Still active, but what some called
"venerable figures" and others "elder statesmen," were Senator John
Sherman of Ohio, with his elevation—and humiliation—as Secretary of State still before him, and William M. Evarts of New York.
George F. Hoar appeared frequently at dinners, though he loved
better to sit at home over Thucydides or Gibbon. His friend, John
T. Morgan of Alabama, had somewhat less of mellowness and culture but rather more force. Roosevelt was frequently to be seen at
various houses. Foreigners of distinction came and went. It was in
these years that Rudyard Kipling used to go to the Cosmos Club
and listen to Roosevelt's torrent of animated talk on affairs "till
the world seemed spinning round and round, and Roosevelt was
the spinner."

It was a fortunate circumstance that all three members of that
closely-linked trio, John Hay, Clarence King, and Henry Adams,
were in Washington during the spring of 1895, for they gave society
an intellectual focus otherwise lacking. King and Adams had been
rambling lazily together in picturesque, troubled Cuba the previous
year, while Hay and Adams had spent the summer of 1894 in the
Yellowstone, camping and riding. Of both Hay and Adams, but
especially the former, White saw a good deal. Their two houses,
with the private connecting door, were the centre of a special
group of Washington people. Mrs. Don Cameron, influential by
virtue of being a niece of Senator and General Sherman as well as
wife of the reigning sovereign of Pennsylvania, divided the pre-
eminence among hostesses with Mrs. Lodge. The English ambassador, Sir Julian Pauncefote, and his popular young secretary of
embassy, Cecil Spring-Rice, were frequently seen at dinners. Finally,
an important place in Washington society was held by Senator
Edward Wolcott of Colorado, a silverite of brilliant talents.

Altogether, Washington seemed full of interesting people to
White that winter and spring. Since Mrs. White was with him, we
lack the description of parties and individual contacts with which
he would have filled his letters had she been away; and in his
diary he did little more than jot down lists of names. There is a

certain monotony about these names. One night at dinner he would meet the Lodges, Montsaulnins, Roosevelt, Miss Leiter, Spring-Rice, and George W. Smalley; the next night the party would include the Leiters, Pauncefote, Sir Rivers Wilson, Smalley, Hay, Tom Reed, and the Roger Wolcotts; on a third night he would meet Roosevelt, Senator Cushman Davis, Lodge, Hoar, Bellamy Storer, and the Bonapartes. When the ordinary entertainments palled, White had the diversion of travel. On April 17th he made a trip to New York to meet George Curzon, who arrived on the *Majestic* and whom he proudly brought to the I Street house in Washington, where that night the Roosevelts, Lodges, and former-minister Phelps dined with them. Five days later he attended Curzon's marriage in St. John's Church to Mary Leiter, "a beautiful wedding." This was the wedding where Mr. Leiter, having gotten on the wrong side of his daughter, electrified the spectators by jumping across her long train. Washington was soon after deserted in anticipation of the heat, and White's family had planned to go back to England for the summer. The night before he sailed early in June he went out with Roosevelt, who had become Police Commissioner of New York, to Oyster Bay, a visit of which his diary records nothing save that Miss Carow was there.

The friendship with Roosevelt had now become sufficiently close, it may be observed, for a constant interchange of letters. Roosevelt trusted and liked White from the beginning, and the fact is evident in his plain-spoken, cordial epistles. During the summer of 1895 he wrote a good deal about his work with the Police Board and the city and state campaigns of that year. He and his strict enforcement of the liquor laws were political storm centers. For years the saloons of New York had evaded the Sunday-closing law by locking their front doors and opening the side doors. Roosevelt, with characteristic courage, had locked both doors. He was now fighting hard for the election of Seth Low to head another reform administration. It was only on Sundays and occasional nights, he said, that he got out to Sagamore Hill. "A couple of evenings a week, or oftener, I have had to speak, usually to East Side audiences; in hot, crowded rooms, but usually to friendly audiences, though they generally contain enough of the enemy to make it lively by questions and altercations. We have certainly made a success of this policy so far as the actual administration is concerned. We have materially improved the condition of the force, while crime has diminished, and we have enforced the law in ways no man had deemed possible." Politically, he added, no one could foretell the result of this vigorous law enforcement, but he believed that Tammany would sweep New York city in the fall election, and that the Republicans would carry the state. Both predictions proved to be correct.

Just before election, "nearly driven to death," he wrote White again. "My own story is a perfectly monotonous one of working day and night in this department and on the stump. Odds are against us, thanks partly to the misconduct of the Republican machine managers; partly to the idiocy of some of the Good Government men; and partly to the misbehavior of the Germans, who, not content with wishing the [Sunday closing] law repealed, insist on demanding that it be dishonestly enforced." Though Roosevelt put the police force to work with great effectiveness to stop fraudulent registration, Tammany carried the city for Robert Van Wyck by 40,000 votes, and the reform administration of Mayor Strong was left with a tenure of only two months.[7]

Later, though Roosevelt was still "almost driven to death, especially as I am striving to finish the fourth volume of *The Winning of the West*," there came other letters. "Tammany's victory has immensely increased my labor; but I have come to the conclusion, on the whole, that the New York papers, headed by the *World*, with the *Herald* a good second, are worse than Tammany. They are doing everything in their power to make me swerve from my course; but they will fail signally; I shall not flinch one hand's-breadth." He thought that "Bayard seems to me to be rapidly becoming a prize fool." Early in December he wrote that he was frenziedly laboring to complete *The Winning of the West* by January 1st, that he was too busy to see any friends, having had the merest glimpse of Lodge since the latter's return from Europe, and that, though there could not be a much more difficult job than the presidency of the Police Board under the existing conditions, he really enjoyed it. He had met Horace Plunkett, a Dublin

[7] Cf. Wheeler, E. P., *Sixty Years of American Life*, p. 343 ff. The notorious Van Wyck administration was about to begin.

Unionist and "a very good fellow," and had talked with George W. Smalley, "a charming man, though I think he is weak on what he regards as our jingo sentiment." After this year, as we shall see, Roosevelt and White exchanged letters with fair regularity till the end of Roosevelt's life.

When White had awakened in 1893 to the fact that, like Othello, his occupation was gone, he had not expected to resume it before 1897. He was a man of but one calling; when poiitics deprived him of office, he could not turn, as most officeholders did, to law, journalism, or business. Fortunately, the resumption of his diplomatic work was nearer than he supposed. While he was spending a quiet summer and fall in England, playing golf at The Glen with Sir Charles Tennant and Lord Ribblesdale, shooting grouse with Godfrey Webb, deer-stalking in Scotland, and bringing Arthur Balfour and Senator Lodge together to discuss international bimetallism, clouds of Anglo-American difficulty were mounting in the sky. As yet few suspected their existence. Most Englishmen and Americans did not perceive them until in the closing days of 1895 the sudden peal of thunder—Cleveland's Venezuela message—showed that a storm was imminent. It was, of course, common knowledge that Venezuela and British Guiana possessed a long-disputed boundary. Most people knew that Venezuela had several years earlier suspended diplomatic relations with Great Britain; that the British Government had repeatedly refused arbitration; and that the United States had several times tendered its good offices, only to meet a rebuff. But few supposed that the dispute was dangerous.

White had paid more attention to the controversy than most Englishmen or Americans, for Senator Lodge had expressed to him some belligerent views on the subject. They had discussed the question that spring in Washington while Lodge was writing an article on it for the *North American Review*, and early in the summer Lodge had amplified his opinions in a personal note:[8]

Your very kind letter came to me here [Nahant], by way of Washington, last evening—too late to catch you with a line on this side. I was extremely pleased that you liked my Venezuelan article, and you were very good to write and take the trouble to tell me so. The historical detail . . . made it difficult to deal with the question in such a limited

[8] Lodge to White, Nahant, June 5, 1895.

space. There is hardly room to turn around. So I am especially glad
that you thought the case clearly and intelligently put. It is not a pretty
story. A worse case of land-grabbing from an inoffensive and weak state
it would be hard to find. I wanted first to call attention to the facts but
little known here, and second, to pave the way for a stiff declaration of
the Monroe Doctrine by the next Congress. You know that has never
been done. The next Congress will do it, and we shall serve notice on the
world that we shall regard an infringement of the Doctrine as an act of
hostility. This will have, I think, a wholesome effect, and if you will
pardon the vernacular, will make some of the brethren sit up and take
notice. We are here at home for two or three weeks, with no notepaper
among other things, as you may infer from these sheets. It looks as if
Olney were to be Secretary of State without much doubt. As long as
Cleveland is obliged to take a man in sympathy with his foreign policy,
he could not do better—Olney is a gentleman, a man of training and
education, and a very able lawyer.

Richard Olney, who had been Attorney-General under Cleveland, succeeded Walter Q. Gresham as Secretary of State on the
latter's death, taking office in June, 1895. Another of White's
friends, W. W. Rockhill, hinted to him that the foreign policy
of the United States would now be given increased vigor. "We are
all much amused," he wrote, "at the suggestions contained in the
English papers of an alliance between Great Britain and the United
States, and of the absolute impossibility of our ever coming to
blows. The article in the *Spectator* of October 26th is a fair example of this stuff. England certainly wants an alliance of some sort,
and my old friend Sir Henry Howorth has been suggesting one
with Russia on the ground of the community of interest between
the two countries!"[9] Olney possessed courage,[10] as he had shown
in handling labor cases for the Administration; he had already
given the Venezuelan tangle careful study, and his character in-

[9] Rockhill to White, November 7, 1895.

[10] One of Olney's displays of courage which especially interested White
was in ordering non-competitive examinations for entrance to the consular
service. Roosevelt thought little of this. Like President Harrison's rules regulating promotions, he wrote, such orders "amount to absolutely nothing in
point of permanence or in point of ruling out political pressure, while they
work real harm in persuading good people that something has actually been
done and that therefore there is no further cause for agitation."—Roosevelt
to White, New York, September 25, 1895.

cluded a good deal of inborn pugnacity. But the determination to push the issue was really that of the blunt and vigorous President Cleveland. He became convinced that the Monroe Doctrine was involved, and he suspected the "imperialistic" tendencies of Great Britain and other European Powers, to which he meant to give a sharp check.

White's letters from England did not mention the dispute. A long communication which he sent to Speaker Reed from London early in November was concerned entirely with bimetallism, for he had spent some time with Balfour at Whittinghame, and Balfour thought the United States should call a conference of Great Britain, France, Germany, and India to establish a bimetallic league.[11] But the Venezuela squall which suddenly burst in December was no surprise to him. On December 17, 1895, Cleveland sent his famous message to Congress, asserting that the Monroe Doctrine applied to this dispute, recommending that Congress appropriate money for an investigating commission—to determine the true boundary, and declaring that when the commission made its report, it would be the duty of the United States to resist by every means in its power any attempt by Great Britain to appropriate territory which the commission assigned to Venezuela. In brief, the United States was to fix and defend Venezuela's boundary line.

The two nations seemed suddenly on the verge of war. White at the moment was in London. He felt the excitement which ran through both countries. But certain that peace would be preserved, he went on calmly with his preparations for a trip to Egypt. He thought, as he often said later in life, that the purpose of Cleveland's message was sound and statesmanlike, and that it was necessary to give England a distinct shock, but that some of the President's sentences were too rough and untactful. His considered view was expressed in a letter to his half-brother, William H. Buckler, from his boat on the Nile:[12]

[11] White to Thomas B. Reed, London, November 8, 1895.
[12] White to W. H. Buckler, February 21, 1896. White had written earlier (December 22, 1895): "Cleveland's methods are remarkable and show absolute lack of diplomatic knowledge or training. But I have spent my time in Paris in defending his recent action, all of our compatriots there being dead against

As regards the famous Cleveland message, it is only another proof of his ignorance of diplomacy. I don't think he had realized the extent of the international tempest which the message would occasion. I think he was right to insist on arbitration, or on some means of determining how far British Guiana extended. But the form in which the last part of the message was couched was in bad taste, and calculated to render a modification of the English position more difficult. On the other hand, the British Government miscalculated the force of American sentiment on the subject of the Monroe Doctrine in general, and the question of Venezuela in particular—as to which last the British public has not the slightest notion. If Cleveland had understood the British mentality sufficiently to send a message to Congress saying that he was going to make another effort to obtain a modification of the English position (without threat, or creating his commission, which is absurd from an international point of view), he would have brought the matter before the attention of the British public. The latter, having a profound horror (as you and I knew in advance, and as they have now sufficiently shown since Cleveland's message) of a war with the United States, would have put such pressure on the Foreign Office that Lord Salisbury's dispatches would never have been written in a sense opposed to the concession.

As to the Monroe Doctrine, I do not find the modern interpretation extravagant, considering the great power of the United States. It is evidently not a piece of international law, but what matter so long as the United States has the power to maintain it as a policy? It is quite untrue that Lodge, whom I know very well, wants war with England. I read his speech in the Senate of October 30th last, and I did not find a word which could justly be considered hostile or offensive to England. I think it is in the interest of both branches of the Anglo-Saxon race that we should be supreme on both American continents, otherwise there will always be questions between the two countries. Our government does not contend that Venezuela is right, and merely asks that the truth should be established. I must say that while I was at the Legation in London I had a pretty pronounced conviction that the Guiana frontier had recently been considerably extended. But the English side of the question has never been stated. We shall soon have it. In any case I think the result of the clash will be a better understanding of one another by the two nations. Great Britain will realize how serious our determination is to maintain the Monroe Doctrine, and I cannot help hoping that our

---

it, and the diplomatists to a man; you know that I approve of sustaining the Monroe Doctrine and bringing the Venezuela business to a head. It has dragged on long enough."

people will realize the profound horror with which England would regard a war with us. But that will be rather in spite of, than because of, the Cleveland diplomacy.

Though as yet White was a mere spectator, the time was at hand when his services were to be commandeered by the very Administration which had shelved him. Late in March, 1896, he was back in London, after the usual experiences of a tourist in the Egypt of that day. He had visited Luxor and Karnak, lunched with Lord Cromer, received the then Colonel Kitchener aboard his private steamer at Assuan, spent some agreeable days with the novelist E. F. Benson (the author of *Dodo*) and Rennell Rodd, and shown the sights to his children. From England he sailed for America, leaving his wife in London.

In Washington he had the fortune to fall in at once with Secretary Olney, with the result that the two men formed a lasting friendship. Once more, as soon as he was in the capital, he was engaged nearly every night; the Hays and the Lodges gave dinners for him, the former asking among others Sir Julian Pauncefote, Senator Wolcott and his wife, Clarence King, and Speaker Reed and his wife, while Lodge included Secretary Olney among his guests.

There being three men over [White wrote his wife],[13] I was put next to Olney, with whom I had an agreeable talk and who talked mostly to me, Clarence King being on the other side. . . . I very soon discovered that he realizes how utterly useless old Bayard is, and he told me that he gives him nothing whatever to do. I also discovered that Joseph Chamberlain put himself forward in the Venezuela business unknown to Lord Salisbury, with a view to getting the credit of patching it up, and that he was sat upon by Lord Salisbury. Olney very soon saw that I am well up in what has been going on in this bailiwick, and was quite communicative and even confidential. I told him how disgraceful I considered Cleveland's treatment of the consular service had been, and he admitted it; he said that the moment he came in he instituted the present examination system, which had resulted (he said confidentially) in turning down most of those recommended to Cleveland for appointment to consular offices. He seems a very intelligent man, keen, rather rugged, and, unlike his predecessor, of ability and force.

[13] White to Mrs. White, Washington, May 8, 1896.

White added that Olney had touched but lightly at the dinner
upon the Venezuelan question, "but he has asked me to come and
see him at the Department of State, which I shall do tomorrow."
He was to enter without being announced. "I took good care to
let Olney know," concluded White, "that none of the London people see much of the leading men of England in private life, and I
think he was impressed by the knowledge I showed in matters of
which they are deficient in experience." It was true that Bayard's
position lacked the needed sympathy with the American point of
view. On the eve of the crisis, in May, 1895, he had written that
"There is no question now open between the United States and
Great Britain that needs any but frank, amicable, and just treatment." After Cleveland's message he had exploded to White about
"that man Cleveland." He added that Olney was thwarting all his
efforts to maintain good relations "with this g-r-e-a-t country." Nor,
though he enjoyed supposed popularity among the English people, did he see much of men like Salisbury, Chamberlain, or Harcourt, or receive confidences from the oustanding British leaders.
Compared with its position when White was first secretary, the
American embassy was poorly informed.

The result of Olney's discovery of White was that when the
latter sailed for England at the end of May, it was understood that
he was to see the important members of the government, interpret
the American position to them, and report back his impressions. He
had a semi-official status. Olney suggested that if his relations with
the embassy were sufficiently cordial, he should use its cipher in
transmitting his messages—which he did. At the moment the negotiations for arbitration were at a standstill, and though all danger
of war had blown over, the difficulties seemed great.

Venezuela had intrusted all the negotiations in her behalf to the
United States. President Cleveland, whose chief wish was for peace,
desired the whole question to be submitted to arbitral decision; but
the British Government declared that it would consent to arbitration only on those parts of the disputed territory which were not
already settled by British subjects. To this Olney had objected
(January 22, 1896) that it was hardly feasible to define what were
real settlements in advance of the arbitration. Meanwhile, an effort
was being made by Olney and Sir Julian Pauncefote to draft a

general treaty of arbitration, which was not to affect the Venezuelan settlement; but this also was meeting with obstacles. On February 27, 1896, Lord Salisbury consented to transfer into Pauncefote's hands in Washington all the Venezuela negotiations. Side by side, he and Olney were thus trying to push forward both an *ad hoc* arrangement in the Venezuela matter, and a broad permanent treaty of general arbitration. It was because he needed a trustworthy agent in London that Olney turned to White.

Within ten days after he landed in England on June 3rd, White had seen every English leader important for his purposes, without making any special appointments, at dinners or receptions. He had lunched with Arthur Balfour, and had taken him down to his country place for the week-end; he had spent a second week-end at a country place where H. H. Asquith was present; he had talked with Lord Rothschild, a leader of great financial interests, and Sir William Harcourt, the head of the Opposition; and Lord Salisbury, the Prime Minister, had asked him down to Hatfield for a day. White was thus able to furnish our Government expert reports on the situation. In replying to the first two reports, Olney wrote with asperity, under the heading "strictly personal," that his letters showed "most significantly how this Government has been handicapped by having in England a diplomatic agent who has not sympathized with its policy, and who through sentiment, self-conceit, physical infirmity, and otherwise, has been practically disabled from rendering the services rightfully expected of him." [14]

When White left America, Lord Salisbury was still refusing to let Pauncefote modify his original reservation of the "settled" territory. He had proposed a commission of four to determine the facts, to be succeeded by an arbitral tribunal of three to determine the conclusion from these facts, but with the proviso that no territory occupied by British subjects on January 1, 1887, should be affected. To this Olney demurred, insisting that the settled districts be included; while he also pointed out that the commission of four might divide two and two, and thus prove not only useless, but dangerous. As for the general arbitration treaty, an entirely separate matter, Lord Salisbury had proved unwilling to go as far as Cleveland and Olney. He had suggested that in an arbitration affect-

[14] Olney to White, Washington, June 30, 1896; "strictly personal."

ing territorial claims, the country which lost might protest the decision even if the arbitrators were unanimous; and had proposed for an appeal in such cases to a new court consisting of six judges, three from the highest court of each nation—a vote of five to one being required to sustain the award. This seemed to Olney altogether too timid an application of the principle of arbitration.

White, addressing himself exclusively to the Venezuelan dispute, found by the time he reached England that some slight progress had been made. The British Ministry had tentatively decided, on the cabled suggestion of Pauncefote, to submit the question of sovereignty over even the settled districts to a special form of arbitration proposed by Pauncefote. That is, an arbitral tribunal was to be set up; if either the United States or Great Britain felt that the decision was not in accord with the evidence, it was to appeal to its own Supreme Court on the issue; and if the court sustained the objection, then negotiations between the two nations were to be reopened. This plan, however, was, of course, unacceptable to Olney.

Since White's object was to act as a clarifying influence, he explained the American position at length to Salisbury, Balfour, and Lord Rothschild. He showed that the inflammable material which caused the warlike explosion of American feeling still existed, and that the flames would burst out again the moment the public learned there was any serious hitch in the negotiations; particularly if the American boundary commission now hard at work reported against the British claims, and Cleveland had to execute the threat in his message. He explained that no successor of Cleveland's, in view of the state of public sentiment, could modify his position in any material respect; that old resentments and the Irish question kept a strong anti-British feeling latent in America; and that it would be well to lift the subject out of the impending presidential campaign.

Salisbury, talking with White as they walked across a turnip-field, was impressed. He said he would be glad to settle the question, but that he considered compulsory arbitration a dangerous precedent for the British Empire; for claims to territory might constantly be made against it by countries having nothing to lose and everything to gain. Moreover, he disliked leaving such far-reaching questions to the ultimate decision of one fallible man, and that man a foreigner. From the remarks of Salisbury and Balfour, White felt that he could lay his finger on certain other causes of delay. He wrote to Olney:[15]

In the first place, I have good reason to believe that the government has been advised through American channels, which I have as yet been unable to trace, that being an eminent lawyer and not a diplomatist, you are likely to take, in any international difficulty, the extreme view of an advocate anxious to win his case in court, and are more desirous to make out a good legal case in the Venezuelan matter than to settle it; that you are animated, moreover, by feelings of hostility to this country, and if, as seemed probable from some of Smalley's telegrams to the *Times*, you had recently appeared anxious to arrive at a settlement, it was merely in order to obtain for the Democratic party (and for yourself in particular) during the approaching presidential campaign, the credit of having compelled this country to give in. I was therefore careful, during my conversation with Lord Salisbury, without making any allusion to this rumor, to say that I had met you several times while in Washington, and had never heard a word hostile to Great Britain or to himself fall from your lips; that you had spoken of the Venezuela question in a broad and statesmanlike manner, and that, while I had no authority to speak for you, my impression was that you thought it desirable in the interest of both countries, that it should be kept out of the presidential campaign by being settled.

Another reason for delay is, I think, the alarm said to have been caused in Canada by the remark in your dispatch to Mr. Bayard as to the inexpediency of "any permanent political union between a European and an American state." Strong representations were made, I understand, to Mr. Chamberlain from that quarter, to the effect that if arbitration were assented to in the matter of Venezuela, and territory should thereby be lost to British Guiana, there would be a loss of prestige throughout the Empire and particularly in Canada.

I have no means of ascertaining to what extent these and other causes have operated in favor of delay, but our ambassador has done nothing to counteract them, if indeed he has ever heard of them.

By the middle of July White felt that the chief obstacle to a settlement lay in Joseph Chamberlain, the Colonial Secretary. The two had a long talk at one of the Queen's garden parties, and

[15] White to Olney, Harrogate, June 17, 1896.

Chamberlain said that in view of the innumerable claims that
would crop up against many parts of the Empire, England ought
never to arbitrate upon the settled districts. "He added," White
wrote Olney,[16] "that if your Administration would not in any
respect modify its demands in the matter, they must wait and
see whether the next one would be more reasonable. I at once
assured him that I did not believe for a moment the next Administration could afford to or would modify the position taken by
you, and he then said: 'Well, I am afraid that, sickening as is the
prospect, we shall have to look forward to war. That is a terrible
alternative, but better than laying ourselves open to being arbi-
trated out of our possessions in different parts of the world without
appeal.'" Though this was a clumsy attempt at bluff, it should
be remembered that later on Joseph Chamberlain's bellicose tendencies really had much to do with dragging England into the
Boer War. While Chamberlain said that the whole Venezuela
affair was none of America's business, Salisbury, whose attitude was
at no time so stiff as his subordinate's, assured White that the
United States had perfect justification for intervening.[17] When
White took Chamberlain's remark about war to the Duke of
Devonshire, the latter naturally made light of it.

The brief of the Venezuelan Government on the boundary question, made by James J. Storrow of Boston, reached London at this
juncture, and with some difficulty White arranged for its simultaneous publication in all the leading newspapers. The *Times*
brought it out in full, five columns, and with it a column leader.
On the day it appeared White went to Sir William Harcourt,
leader of the Liberal Opposition, told him that the negotiations still
seemed to be at a deadlock, and suggested that he should arrange
with the leader of the House for a discussion of the subject; and
Harcourt made the arrangement that same afternoon. Then White
dropped in for lunch and a talk with Lord and Lady Salisbury.[18]
Nor was this all:

From there I went to Devonshire House and had a talk with the
Duke, who has great influence with the Ministry and whose views have

[16] White to Olney, London, July 17, 1896.
[17] White to Olney, London, July 18, 1896.
[18] White to Olney, July 29, 1896.

great weight in the country. I repeated to him my apprehensions in respect to the present condition of things and how important I thought a settlement would be for England, and told him that I was absolutely sure our government would not consent to any arbitral agreement on the Venezuela question the award of which should not be final. I repeated to him Chamberlain's talk with me (which I wrote to you, and which by the bye Sir William Harcourt, to whom I also related it, says was bluffing on his part). I found the Duke of Devonshire very reasonable. He said much more than I should be justified in ever loading this letter with, but I shall hope to tell you of it when we meet, which I hope may be before long. He realizes that war is out of the question, expressed the same anxiety that his colleagues feel lest a yielding to our position would affect the Government's prestige throughout the Empire—particularly Canada—and suggested what seemed to him the least detrimental way (from a British point of view) of escaping from what he quite admitted to be almost a deadlock, and one from which, as matters now stand, neither side can recede without loss of prestige.

With this work done, White sailed for the United States at the end of July, gratified that an Administration which had dismissed him should thus have turned again to him for assistance. Olney was quite frank about the reliance he placed upon him. "It ought not to be so, but you will understand why, for any assistance in England, I am obliged to rely upon non-official persons," he wrote. "My own implicit trust could not be more strongly demonstrated than by the unreserved manner in which I write you."[19] The two men met shortly in Newport, where the Whites in September had a house-party including Lord Russell of Killowen, Lady Russell, Secretary Olney, Speaker Reed, Bourke Cockran, and Senator Lodge. Meanwhile, the seeds White had sowed in England showed evidences of germination. In August there came a note from Sir William Harcourt:

I have made the strongest representations to the Government urging the acceptance of Olney's proviso as to the dealing with settled districts by the arbitrators, and only abstained from making a speech in that sense on the Appropriation Bill on being satisfied that the negotiation would proceed on that footing and would be brought to a speedy and satisfactory conclusion. Pauncefote is here, and the government allowed him to communicate with me. His views are entirely in accordance with mine. I

[19] Olney to White, Washington, July 10, 1896.

received from Pauncefote the distinct assurance that the instructions he is taking back with him will remove all the difficulties which have hitherto delayed the business. The Government here are now fully impressed with the necessity of an immediate settlement of the arbitration with the present Administration of the United States, and before the United States Commission reports. I am myself satisfied with the assurance that I have received and with the answer given by Balfour to my question yesterday, which means even more than it says.

Chamberlain leaves England for the United States on the 26th and told me yesterday that he means to see Olney, and added that he should be very peaceable. I hope that may be so, but I confess I should have been better pleased if the matter had been left in Pauncefote's hands.

As a matter of fact Sir William Harcourt, when Pauncefote came to him, had dictated a formula according to which he thought Great Britain ought to announce the reference of the whole Venezuelan question to arbitration. This formula Pauncefote took to Lord Salisbury. There followed a succession of conferences between Pauncefote and Harcourt, the conversation turning chiefly on the troublesome question of the "settled districts," where Lord Salisbury still showed reluctance to yield. Harcourt wrote to White, mentioning his talks with Pauncefote and saying that "the latter is extremely reasonable and anxious for a settlement on the basis you and I desire. And I finally received assurances which to me were quite satisfactory, and Pauncefote informed me that he had no doubt would lead at once to a final and conclusive arrangement." He suggested that White use his influence to induce Olney also to recede, "now that the substance of the matter is conceded."

The result was a completely satisfactory settlement, the United States agreeing to except from the arbitration settlements of fifty years' duration. The tribunal created was to consist of two members nominated by the Supreme Court of the United States, and two by the British Supreme Court of Judicature, with a president to be chosen by these four, or, if they failed to agree, by the King of Norway and Sweden. This arrangement, which represented a triumph for the views of Cleveland and Olney, was concluded before the end of 1896, though the treaty embodying it was not signed until February 2, 1897. With this the controversy came to an end. When President Cleveland's Commission appointed to find "the true di-

vision line" made its report on March 1, 1897, it refrained from
fixing a boundary line, and contented itself with laying before
Congress and the court of arbitration some fourteen volumes of
material, with an atlas containing about seventy-five maps—a valuable contribution to the arbitrators' work. The final award was
mainly in favor of Great Britain, though there were some substantial concessions to Venezuela's claims.[20]

Both Lodge and Roosevelt followed the Venezuela negotiations
with interest, and sent White some frank comments on the course
of events. Roosevelt praised Lodge's position, saying that it "has
really been entirely proper throughout this Venezuelan controversy;
but the Anglomaniac press, and of course Smalley, have utterly
misrepresented him. I wish I had sent you a little article I wrote for
Winty Chanler's magazine, the *Bachelor of Arts*. I am very glad our
House has at last passed a decent appropriation bill for battleships
and for fortifications. . . . I feel very strongly that while our foreign policy should be free from bluster, yet it should emphatically
be vigorous." All England's troubles in the Transvaal, he thought,
were traceable to her having at first disregarded the rights of the
Boers, and then under Gladstone's leadership made a cowardly retreat before them. "I am very sorry for this, for though I greatly
admire the Boers, I feel it is to the interest of civilization that the
English-speaking race should be dominant in South Africa, exactly
as it is for the interest of civilization that the United States themselves, the greatest branch of the English-speaking race, should be
dominant in the Western Hemisphere."

As for Lodge, he was characteristically vigorous. "The fact is,"
he proclaimed early in the crisis,[21] "that outside of the moneyed
interests in New York and Boston, the American people, like Congress and the press, are solidly behind the President in defense of
the Monroe Doctrine. We shall carry our point, and there will be
no war either." Later he wrote, jubilantly: "I think we have carried
our point pretty well and that we have impressed upon the world
the Monroe Doctrine so thoroughly that we shall not be troubled
in that direction again. Of course if we had had a minister like Mr.
Adams, for example, in London, Lord Salisbury's letter, which

[20] McElroy, R. M., *Grover Cleveland, The Man and the Statesman*, vol.
ii, pp. 201, 202.   [21] Lodge to White, Washington, January 10, 1896.

made all the trouble, would never have been written. If the American feeling had been properly represented to Lord Salisbury by the American ambassador, all this trouble would have been avoided."

White watched the presidential campaign of 1896 from his Newport residence, and was excited by the struggle over silver. It seemed to him, as he wrote Olney, the most critical election since 1860. For the first time he sent the Republican party a campaign contribution. His letters to England reflected his anxiety, and the day after McKinley's election he received a telegram from Sir William Harcourt reading, "Thanking God with you, dear friend." He felt fairly confident that the Republican victory would bring him and his friends—notably Hay and Roosevelt—back into office. In the early stages of the campaign Hay told White that if McKinley were elected, he would come in with fewer promises than any of his recent predecessors, but the more cynical Lodge, who was chagrined by the collapse of the boom for Speaker Reed's nomination, declared that the McKinley people had promised all the offices a dozen times over. Immediately after the election White went West, paying a visit to McKinley and Hanna in Ohio.

When McKinley took office there were various Republican aspirants for the position of ambassador to Great Britain, notably Don Cameron and Whitelaw Reid. But it soon became known that Hay would be sent to London. There was more doubt concerning Roosevelt's fate. White knew that he wished the post of Assistant Secretary of the Navy, and used what influence he possessed in Roosevelt's behalf.[22] From T. R. he had a series of notes on the situation:

[22] Roosevelt had followed with great interest White's activities in England. He wrote to his sister of "Harry White's special and really extraordinary fitness for and service as a diplomat in London—fitness and service which would entitle him to a far higher position if they were all that were to be considered. Phelps and Lincoln are never tired of singing his praises; but the conclusive testimony has been given within the last year. . . . I have as my authority the letters I have seen from Salisbury, Harcourt, and Balfour and what Olney and Rockhill have themselves told me. White knows the very men whom it is all-important that he should know; and he knows them in just the right way for the purposes of the position. During the exceedingly delicate negotiations of the last ten months he has rendered invaluable services, and has been trusted as no man not in official life has before been trusted."—Roosevelt to Anna Roosevelt Cowles, January 8, 1897.

ROOSEVELT TO WHITE

[March 8, 1897.]—In view of John Hay's selection, I hope I may regard your matter as settled; at least it seems perfectly incredible to me that there should be any other possible solution than your reappointment. As for myself, I have been so absorbed in the fight here that I have had little time to think of my chances as Assistant Secretary of the Navy; and during the last month or so, I have become convinced that they are very small, because neither the Platt nor the anti-Platt people of New York feel that I am a useful ally; and in this feeling they are quite right. I know they have industriously sought to persuade the President and Secretary Long that I would be headstrong, impractical, and insubordinate. As a matter of fact, were I appointed, the very qualities that have made me insist on the obedience of my subordinates would also render me prompt in carrying out the policy of my superior officer. . . .

Lodge is not only my dearest friend, but is also the most faithful and loyal man I have ever known. I am deeply touched by what he is doing.

[March 11th.]—Lodge has just written me telling me how disinterestedly you have concerned yourself on my behalf, in the middle of all your affairs; it touched me very much. Now, old man, don't you bother about me. I can say quite sincerely that I am much more anxious to have you go back to London as First Secretary than I am to be Assistant Secretary of the Navy, for I think that it is a much more important thing that you should go back, and as for me, I am pretty well accustomed to the buffeting of American political life, and take things with much philosophy. I try to give as good as I get.

[April 16th.]—As soon as I received the news of my appointment I thought of you, and knew you would be pleased. Of course, it was Lodge who engineered it, at the end as at the beginning; working with his usual untiring loyalty and energy. Platt did his best to defeat me; and Gorman, with the help of the Populists, came near causing serious trouble in the Senate. However, I went through; and without making a promise, or even request of any kind, save to ask Olcott and Doty to vouch for my efficiency, etc., as you know. I am very glad to get out of this place [the Police Commissionership]; for I have done all that could be done, and now the situation has become literally intolerable. I do not object to any amount of work and worry, where I have a fair chance to win or lose on my merits; but here, at the last, I was playing against stacked cards. Now that I am going, all the good people are utterly cast down, and cannot say enough of my virtues!

President McKinley gave White his choice between the minister-ship to Spain, then a post of the greatest responsibility, and the first secretaryship in London. He urged White to take the former. He thought that by placing him in Madrid and a good man in Havana in place of Consul-General Lee, war might be avoided. On the evening of March 10th, Hay and White were together at the White House. After a few minutes' conversation the President remarked: "What am I going to do about the Spanish mission? I must have a trained diplomatist there. I wish very much, Mr. White, that I could persuade Colonel Hay to let me send you there. It is a great opportunity for a diplomatist to keep us out of trouble, and if successful it might lead to any position in the public service."[23] The temptation to go was strong. It is to be wished that White had accepted—he might have induced the Spanish Gov-ernment to yield earlier to our main demands, and so have averted the conflict. But he knew the Spanish climate would wreck his wife's health. He feared that it would be difficult to educate his children in Spain. His heart was in England, and though some of his friends, like Senator Wolcott, expostulated vigorously, he chose London instead of Madrid.

[23] White to Mrs. White, Washington, March 11, 1897.

CHAPTER NINE

John Hay as Ambassador: The Spanish War

SINCE John Hay did not arrive in England until April 21, 1897, White, who took over the embassy from Mr. Bayard at the end of March, was in sole charge for some three weeks. He at once set to work with his usual competence and energy. In the next fortnight he renewed his relations with the Foreign Office and sent to Washington a dozen despatches, the chief dealing with the Behring Sea question and bimetallism. When his new chief arrived on the *St. Paul*, accompanied by Henry Adams, White took Henry James down to Southampton to greet them. He helped Hay establish himself comfortably at No. 5 Carlton House Terrace, master the routine of the embassy, and enlarge his acquaintance among English statesmen. He had done all this for new ministers before, but never with such pleasure, for never before had he had so congenial an associate. The year and a half during which he and Hay were to serve together was to be a period of the pleasantest companionship. Perhaps he had made a mistake in declining the post of minister to Spain; but he never regretted it.

Though Anglo-American relations were not in the halcyon state in which they had sometimes been, the questions between the two countries were neither of major importance nor of pressing urgency. Those which were most troublesome concerned the Canadians and their interests—the Alaskan boundary, the continued slaughter of the seals in the Behring Sea, and the Newfoundland fisheries. They could drag on a while longer, and as a matter of fact they did drag on. A good deal of the débris of the Venezuelan dispute had to be cleared up and the arbitration ended, though nobody felt much concerned with the issue. The McKinley Administration was bound by its campaign platform to go through the empty motions of trying to negotiate an "international agreement with the leading commercial nations" for the free coinage of silver, and was making perfunctory gestures to that end. Meanwhile, the

123

higher American tariff of the Dingley bill, which Congress was debating in April and McKinley signed in July, had irritated commercial interests abroad. Our difficulties with Spain were creating tension in the relations with the chief continental Powers, and rendered it expedient to court the good will of Great Britain. In all this White knew just where to take steps and avoid missteps.

The general arbitration treaty between America and Great Britain, a structure carefully designed by Olney and Pauncefote, and hopefully dedicated as a temple of peace by President Cleveland and Lord Salisbury, was received with international plaudits when disclosed to view in January, 1897. But immediately thereafter the Senate fell upon it with ax and hammer and quickly demolished it. By this course they almost broke Pauncefote's heart and bitterly grieved both Olney and Hay.[1] A number of references by White during the months early in 1897 when most people still hoped that the treaty, cordially indorsed by President McKinley, would succeed, show how enthusiastically all his associates regarded it. He wrote to Olney on January 13th, offering his congratulations. Lady Salisbury told him that her husband had "worked like a nigger" over it; and when White lunched soon after with Gladstone at Hawarden, the latter expressed the warmest approval, though he added that he had never been a believer in any great result from international arbitration. The discouraging debate in the Senate warned both nations of what was about to happen. On May 5, 1897, the treaty failed of a two-thirds majority, the vote being 43 to 26, and White wrote to Olney in condolence.[2] He was sorry for the failure, he said, but it had been discounted and had created little comment. "It is better from the point of view of good feeling between the two countries that the treaty should have failed to pass the Senate, than that it should be rejected upon its return here in a more or less mutilated condition, which latter might have aroused protest and ill-feeling on our side of the water."

Olney in high indignation sent White a memorandum on the

[1] The text of this general arbitration treaty is in James, Henry, *Richard Olney and His Public Service*, p. 280 ff. For Olney's attitude see the same volume, p. 143 ff. For Pauncefote's see Mowat, R. B., *Life of Lord Pauncefote*, p. 160 ff.

[2] White to Olney, London, May 22, 1897.

treaty, to be shown to the secretary's English friends; and when White took it to Balfour, the latter found it so interesting that it was circulated to the whole Cabinet.[3] Declaring that the rejection of the treaty was a calamity "of world-wide proportions," Olney was anxious to have it understood that the great majority of Americans both loved peace and liked Great Britain.[4] He bade the English leaders disregard the "mouthings" of cheap politicians and the "lurid utterances of the political exiles and convicts who infest our large cities." The truth was, he said, "that the American people are proud of their lineage; set the highest value upon the laws, the institutions, the literature, and the language they have inherited; glory in all the achievements of the Anglo-Saxon race, in war, in politics, in science, in literature, and in art; and feel themselves to be not merely in name but in fact, part of one great English-speaking family whose proud destiny it is to lead and control the world." He explained the defeat of the treaty by a variety of reasons, among which were individual jingoism, partisan dislike of anything emanating from the Cleveland Administration, and pressure from shipbuilding interests anxious to see the navy increased. But beyond this there were two paramount reasons for its rejection.

One reason was that the Senate was steadily asserting itself as the dominant power in the Government; it was aggressively encroaching on the other branches, and when it dealt with a treaty, it insisted that "it must be either altogether defeated or so altered as to bear the unmistakable Senate stamp—and thus be the means both of humiliating the executive and of showing to the world the greatness of the Senate." Second among reasons for the defeat Olney placed the irritation of the silverite Senators against Great Britain as the most conspicuous and efficient supporter of the gold standard; and he quoted Mr. Lodge's violent speech on the subject as showing how this spirit had infected even the Eastern members. As a third explanation he mentioned the unfortunate behavior of Mr. Bayard, who was apparently "unable to understand that to conciliate one country by a process which simultaneously alienates

[3] White to Olney, London, July 12, 1897.
[4] Olney to White, Boston, May 8, 1897. This memorandum of Olney's has not before been published or summarized.

another is not the best way to make the two countries friends."
He believed that Bayard's continuous stream of gush over England
and the English, with its implied comparisons to the disadvantage
of America, had caused a resentment which had not a little to do
with the downfall of the treaty. But on the whole, Olney too
optimistically felt that the cause of general arbitration between the
two countries had received but a temporary setback, and would
yet triumph.

Not only was there no misunderstanding of the situation and
no resentment in England, but the English feeling toward the
United States was now one of almost unprecedented friendliness.
During the Queen's "Diamond Jubilee" in 1897 general use was
made of the American flag in decorating the houses of both rich
and poor in London, and in the great parade vociferous cheers
rolled down the streets with the carriage in which Whitelaw Reid
was driving as special representative of the United States. White
was gratified by all this and in his letters makes numerous comments on the cordiality. Even the costermongers' carts were decorated with American and British flags together, and wherever the
special representatives appeared Whitelaw Reid was received with
much more cordiality than the envoys of France or Italy. The
luckless German envoy at one point on the great day was hissed,
and there was some trouble in persuading newspaper correspondents
to suppress the fact. The Jubilee impressed White rather more than
it did Hay, who called it a Welsh-rabbit dream. Incidentally, both
White and Hay, in spite of what the latter's biographer, William
Roscoe Thayer, says on the subject, thoroughly approved of Whitelaw Reid's presence.[5] It was a season of much speech-making, in
which Hay cultivated a reticence all the more brilliant after Mr.
Bayard's continuous oratory. "He has refused thirty-two invitations to make speeches," White wrote approvingly on July 12th.

While these events were passing and Hay was familiarizing himself with embassy business, White was resuming the social life
which had suffered so many interruptions in the past four years. To
Mrs. White, again in the country for her health, he wrote constantly,

[5] White to Olney, London, July 12, 1897. Cf. Cortissoz, Royal, *Life of
Whitelaw Reid*, vol. ii, p. 215 ff.

JOHN HAY AS AMBASSADOR TO GREAT BRITAIN

and though most of his news is of work, he found frequent snatches
of relaxation:

WHITE TO MRS. WHITE

[From Mells Park, Frome, May 23, 1897.]—Here I am and in a
delicious spot, too. I came down here with the Asquiths and found here
on arrival Lady Edward Cecil, Haldane, and the Aggy Jekylls. . . . Margot got pretty worn out coming down in the train. I ascertain from her
that she will be a snake-charmer in an Oriental dress with a serpent on
her forehead and wings spreading out on each side thereof. Asquith will
be a Roundhead (Oliver Cromwell), which is, I think, an excellent
selection for him. Haldane is very non-committal as to whether he will
go or not; but it seems his costume is having Lady Decies' anxious consideration, so Asquith says! Haldane is evidently amused at old Mrs.
Horner's suggestion that he had better make up as Napoleon. Mary
Curzon writes a kind note suggesting that I pay them a visit at the
Priory during the Whitsuntide holidays, which I shall probably do. . . .

A little later: I have had a delightful walk and luncheon is over, which
was gay and cheerful, all talking merrily—Asquith, Haldane, and Mrs.
Horner very amusing, Herbert Paul and Rhoda Broughton the chief
topics. An amusing story about Rhoda Broughton's engagement. It appears that she was once engaged to a man much younger than herself,
and after some time his parents persuaded him to break it off. When
he did so, Rhoda Broughton was furious, and by way of showing it sent
him a mug inscribed, "For a good boy."

[London, May 25th.]—I had John W. Foster on my hands this morning; took him to Stead's, and on Saturday he leaves, not to return until
after the Jubilee. The papers announce Whitelaw Reid's appointment as
special ambassador, which will, I think, be creditable and satisfactory.

[London, May 27th.]—I have been dining at the Spanish Embassy—
a dull dinner, save for the Staals and Hays, including Helen, whom I
took down to dinner and with whom I had a nice talk, the only one
almost since she has been here. She still wishes "beautiful" were here
(being you), and evidently longs to impart to you her impressions and
to obtain guidance. . . . I have looked in at Lady Ancaster's ball, where
were the Hays again. I took Helen one turn and introduced her to
Prince Christian and Princess Victoria, who were both there. She made a
very nice little curtsy and so did Mrs. Hay afterwards to Prince Christian, who looked her up after John Hay had spoken to him. The Hays
conduct themselves admirably; perfectly simple, but go up and speak
to the royalty and such people as they should talk to.

[London, June 15th.]—The House of Lords was interesting and looked rather like old times, with a considerable number of peers present. . . . Londonderry has got to be quite a fluent and rather good speaker. He put his own view well, I thought. Asquith was present and listened to the frequent mention of his own name. I went to Arthur Balfour's to breakfast. I had a short walk with Arthur in the garden alone and told him the history of the dispatch, which he does not seem to think will do much harm. He thinks, apparently, that the success of our bimetallists depends upon whether France is really in earnest or not, as to which he appears to feel a little skeptical. He was as charming as ever; asked particularly about you.

Throughout 1897 White was much engaged with the fast-dying cause of international bimetallism. President McKinley in April appointed three men, Senator Edward O. Wolcott of Colorado, Adlai E. Stevenson, and General Paine, to visit Europe and try to arrange a bimetallic conference, and their arrival attracted much attention. There was considerable sentiment for bimetallism in England, embracing Lancashire, part of Yorkshire, many farmers, most of those engaged in commerce with the silver-using nations, and most Anglo-Indian officials. It tended to rise, as the London *Times* remarked, whenever foreign trade declined, and to fall when trade was good. Arthur Balfour and Sir Michael Hicks-Beach had persuaded the Government to take a favorable attitude toward a worldwide agreement for a bimetallic currency. But all efforts to come to such an agreement broke down. The Indian Government was adamant, declaring that if it was found impossible to maintain the parity of the two metals, the United States and Europe could withdraw without severe loss, but India could not.[6] Balfour told White that the attitude of India was silly and stupid, and Henry Chaplin added that it was beneath contempt, but nothing could be done about it. France also was disposed to insist on the ratio of 15½ to 1, which other nations rejected. Finally Balfour gave up in the autumn, telling White that it was useless for Wolcott and his colleagues to push the matter further. Apparently Wolcott had already lost confidence.[7] He had sent a letter through White to the painter, G. F. Watts, inquiring if the forlorn canvas called "Hope" did not represent the free-silver cause. As he said, the pathetic blind female

[6] White to Hay, North Berwick, October 5, 1897.
[7] White to Hay, Braemar, October 8, 1897.

figure, bending to catch a faint chord from a harp of which all the strings but one were broken, looked to him much like Bimetallism listening for the dying echo of "Sixteen to One."

As 1898 opened the danger of war with Spain had clearly become great; as February and March passed the conflict seemed imminent, though a strong stand by President McKinley at the critical moment might have averted it. The State Department, controlled by Assistant-Secretary Day rather than by the aged and nerveless hand of Secretary Sherman, directed Hay and White to prepare a critical appraisal of the British attitude, political, diplomatic, and financial. Most of the burden of this fell upon White, for Hay left him in charge of the embassy while, with Henry Adams and other friends, he paid a winter visit to Egypt, leaving London January 18th and not returning until March 21st. White and Hay were able to make a series of optimistic reports.[8] A new and brighter era was dawning in Anglo-American relations; an era brought about by numerous factors and not to be described by the simple terms used by Henry Adams when he says that it was caused by the "sudden appearance of Germany as the grizzly terror which in twenty years effected what Adamses had tried for two hundred in vain." It was true that suspicion of Germany and hostility for her had been steadily growing in England; White had noticed the fact when he came back to England, and had written repeatedly of it. He had said a year earlier that "There seems to be but one opinion of the conduct of the German Emperor and his hostility to this country, which seems to impel him to all manner of disagreeable actions."[9] But even had Germany been all smiles and complaisance, the feeling for the United States would have grown.

[8] State Department Files, Great Britain, vol. clxxxi, dispatches 345, 348, 372, etc.

[9] The "disagreeable action" which White had in mind at the moment was some interference by the Kaiser in delaying the Turko-Greek armistice; White to his wife, London, May 18, 1897. Soon afterward White wrote to his wife of efforts which were on foot to draft a new Anglo-American arbitration treaty, and of the wish in both Washington and London to keep them secret from the German Government. The Kaiser was very shortly to become the victim of a fixed delusion that some kind of alliance existed between England and the United States.—White to Mrs. White, Taplow Court, May 29, 1897.

White sent to the State Department a copy of the somewhat unin-
spired verses of the Poet Laureate, Alfred Austin:

> Yes, this is the Voice on the bluff March gale,
>   "We severed have been too long:
> But now we have done with a worn-out tale,
>   The tale of an ancient wrong,
> And our friendship shall last long as Love doth last,
>   And be stronger than death is strong."

Of this feeling there was ample evidence in these rather anxious
days. When White called on Lord Salisbury on another matter early
in February, Salisbury volunteered the information that the Spanish ambassador had just been in and had attacked the United
States savagely because the battleship *Maine* had been sent to
Havana. (Incidentally, in a letter of curiously prophetic phraseology, Senator Lodge had just written White that "there may be an
explosion any day in Cuba which would settle a great many
things. We have got a battleship in the harbor of Havana, and our
fleet, which overmatches anything the Spaniards have, is masked at
the Dry Tortugas.") [10] A few days later came the destruction of the
Maine and the embassy was deluged with letters and telegrams
of condolence. White and the Spanish ambassador shortly met at a
levee, and the latter was profuse in his expressions of sympathy,
adding that his Government wanted peace, but of course the Ministers would be powerless if the people decided to go to war as in the
Napoleonic days. To this White replied that the calm and dignified
course of the President showed that he was only too anxious to
let Spain restore order in Cuba, but that if the people of the
United States determined to go to war no President could stop
them! [11] Various British leaders kindly saw that White was furnished the fullest information on international affairs. When he
went one day to breakfast with Arthur Balfour (March 31st),
the Permanent Under-Secretary for Foreign Affairs, Sir Thomas
Sanderson, arrived with dispatches, and was disconcerted to see
White present. "Come in, Sanderson," said Balfour; "we have no

[10] Lodge to White, Washington, January 31, 1898.
[11] White to Hay, London, February 21, 1898.

secrets from Harry White." Sanderson thereupon sat down and declared his whole business in White's presence.[12] Not a little came to White at second hand, but freshly and accurately, from the British Minister to Spain, a close observer friendly to the Americans.

One of White's duties was to negotiate the purchase of two Brazilian cruisers, the *Amazonas* and the *Almirante Abreu*, the first at Gravesend ready to sail and the second within eight months of completion at Armstrong's. He learned on February 27th, through Hiram S. Maxim, that they might be bought, telegraphed to Washington, and received authority to treat for an option.[13] By March 15th, thanks to his prompt action, both vessels were in the possession of the United States. For a time the United States hoped also to buy some British warships; but though Joseph Chamberlain would gladly have sold them, other members of the Government objected to this as a breach of neutrality. To Roosevelt, then Assistant Secretary of the Navy, White wrote on his purchases and on the nuisance of naval unpreparedness, and had in return some interesting letters:

NAVY DEPARTMENT, WASHINGTON, March 9, 1898.
MY DEAR WHITE:

I am very glad to hear from you. Our feeling of grief at the loss of the *Maine* in this Department has been sunk in a very eager desire to find out the cause of the disaster and to avenge it if it is due to outside work. What the cause was no one can yet say; but in confidence I may mention that the officers on the spot outside of the Board, and the chief of our representatives of the State Department there, are confident that it is due to an outside explosion. Of course, I have nothing to say as to the policy of the Government, but I earnestly hope that this incident will not be treated by itself, but as part of the whole Cuban business. There is absolutely but one possible solution of a permanent nature to that affair, and that is Cuban independence. The sooner we make up our minds to this the better. If we can attain our object peacefully, of course we should try to do so; but we should attain it one way or the other, anyhow.

[12] White to Mrs. White, London, April 1, 1898.
[13] State Department Files, *Great Britain*, vols. cxc, cxci, telegram February 26th, dispatch March 2nd. White signed the contracts for the American Government, involving a payment of £347,194.

Yes, I know about those Brazilian cruisers. I suppose we shall purchase them. I am not myself very much in favor of purchasing anything
but first-class armored cruisers or battleships, and large sea-going torpedo
craft of the destroyer type. It would be a mistake to lumber our navy
up with valueless craft. A year ago we could have ended a war with
Spain with very little difficulty. The delay has steadily been to our
disadvantage, but we can still end it without much difficulty if we act
with promptness and decision. Of course, the real time to strike was a
year and a half ago, when we had most excuse and could have struck
to most advantage.

I am sure that the English have genuinely sympathized with us. I am
glad there seems to be so friendly a feeling between the two countries,
though I don't believe that we ought to have an alliance. . . .

Faithfully Yours,
THEODORE ROOSEVELT.

NAVY DEPARTMENT, WASHINGTON, March 30, 1898.

MY DEAR WHITE:

Your letter was most interesting, and I congratulate you upon having
been left alone during such an important crisis, and upon the way you
have acquitted yourself while thus left alone.

Indeed I more than agree with what you say. If we ever want an
illustration of the futility of not preparing for war in advance, it will
be furnished by the frantic efforts that have been made to purchase ships
at this time, with the net result that after two months' work we get one
good unarmored cruiser, and two second-rate torpedo-boats, together with
a dozen tugs, yachts, and merchant steamers.

I am, of course, a strong advocate of immediate action against Spain.
I do not think half-measures will avail anything; nothing short of recognition of independence, accompanied by armed intervention on our part.
It is of course the greatest misfortune that we did not interfere last
December. We had ample cause thrice over for this interference. The
Spaniards then had no torpedo-boats, and but five sea-going armorclads
against our seven. The weather would have been admirable, and we
would have saved all the hideous misery which the Cubans have suffered
this winter. However, I am not conducting our foreign affairs, and I
say this for your ear alone. . . .

I see a great deal of the Lodges—also of all the Senate Committee on
Foreign Affairs, with whom I am in entire sympathy.

Very Faithfully Yours,
THEODORE ROOSEVELT.

White sailed for the United States early in April, 1898, and was in Washington on April 16th, attending a dinner given by the Lodges at which Fitzhugh Lee, recently consul-general in Cuba, furnished a heartrending account of the sufferings of the Cuban *reconcentrados*. White was interested in the mounting war fever, but still more in the altered feeling toward Great Britain. "I am surprised," he wrote his wife, "to find a complete change of sentiment here with regard to England; particularly in Congress, where they seem really to appreciate England's action in refusing to mediate or to join other Powers in mediating. As to Lodge, he is not only highly favorable to a good understanding, but wants to be known as a promoter of it. Yesterday, on my representing to him (and a letter arriving from John Hay on the same subject) that the Canadian award ought to be paid, he at once introduced a bill to do so, made a speech himself commendatory of it, and got Senator Morgan, who is supposed to be particularly hostile to England, to do so likewise. They all seem surprised to find (except perhaps Lodge) that the feeling which we have always known exists in England, really does so, and having ascertained this to be the case they are tremendously appreciative of it." White naturally did his utmost to give impetus to this new current of friendliness—the friendliness of a country shivering a little to find herself out in the great arena of world affairs, feeling the chill hostility of all the continental nations, and glad for once to meet John Bull halfway.[14]

Twice, on the invitation of President McKinley, White visited the White House to talk with him. The President asked him to assure everyone in England that he abhorred war, and that the conflict then about to open with Spain would be waged, so far as he was concerned, in the cause of humanity and to put an end to the cruel maltreatment of thousands of Cubans. McKinley added that there would be no privateering, and that he was deeply interested

[14] White wrote to Hay on April 22nd that "Senators Frye and Morgan have completely changed their opinion of Great Britain. They both told me that although they had given England many hard knocks in the press, they now recognize the practical and cordial sympathy she has recently shown us and are pro-English (Senator Morgan's words), believing joint action and a good understanding to be perfectly possible. . . . These Senatorial opinions were expressed to me voluntarily, not in reply to questions from me."

in maintaining and cultivating friendly relations with England.[15] Immediately afterward there came the Spanish declaration of war, the news of Manila Bay, and the rush of preparations for fighting in Cuba; amid which excitement White prepared to travel back to his post. But he took time for a final call on various Senators. "To my amazement," he wrote his wife, "I found those hitherto most unfriendly to England, *viz.*, Frye of Maine and Morgan of Alabama, as well as Davis of Minnesota, all eminently friendly and assuring me that while they have given that country many hard knocks in the past, they now recognize that she has availed herself of the opportunity to show us sympathy, which is all that we want, and that they are therefore in favor of being friendly with Great Britain. Foraker of Ohio, Hanna's enemy and colleague, told me that his only regret is that we did not join England in stopping Russia in China."

In coming to America on the *Etruria*, White had met the Canadian Minister of Trade and Commerce, and talked with him regarding American-Canadian relations, while in Washington he also chatted with Pauncefote. As a result he was able to make some suggestions to McKinley and Assistant-Secretary Day. Friendly conferences had been carried on with Canada regarding the sealing and other questions through a special commissioner, John W. Foster; he was not liked, and White had Kasson substituted for him at the Canadians' request. Dining in New York late in April with Levi P. Morton, Bourke Cockran, and G. W. Smalley, White heard them discuss the tonnage dues in the new war-revenue bill, which would have increased eightfold the tax paid by all foreign vessels entering our ports. The Cunard and White Star lines would have been especially hard hit. Feeling that Representative Dingley had inserted this provision without thinking of the ill-feeling it might arouse, White returned to Washington, spoke to members of Congress, and secured its omission. These

[15] McKinley at the first meeting talked confidentially with White, showing great reluctance about the war. He expressed decided regret that Congress was not inclined to give him more discretion about opening hostilities, and showed great satisfaction in Hay's work. Then, wrote White, his brother Abner came in "and sat down as though the place belonged to him, and promptly shut the President up."

matters of Anglo-American relations struck him as hardly less important than the Spanish War. Indeed, he wrote that if the war "be followed by a good understanding with England it will indeed be a blessing in disguise." For many years he had made Anglo-American friendship the chief object of his life, and now he saw his best hopes being suddenly realized.

Naturally, White's visit was seized upon by part of the press as a secret diplomatic mission, having for its aim the sounding of the United States upon a new treaty of arbitration—and perhaps something still broader. The New York *Herald* carried two-column headlines over a front-page Washington dispatch which declared that he was bringing assurances of the friendliness of Great Britain in the crisis and of its willingness to go "to any extent" to prove it; and that his inquiries touched no less a subject than a possible treaty of alliance. He was close to Balfour, to Salisbury, to Lansdowne; he was "in high favor" with the Prince of Wales; and he had been sent to strike while the iron was hot. Out of the blaze of Anglo-American cordiality created by the little Spanish War was to emerge a mighty alliance of the two English-speaking nations. White quickly deflated these reports in an interview in Baltimore, saying that he was charged with no negotiations and that a treaty of alliance would be undesirable for either nation. "A thorough understanding can only, in my opinion, be based upon a conviction on the part of each country that it has the sympathy, and is likely, in certain contingencies, to have at least the moral support of the other."

In early summer White was back in London and had resumed his usual official and social round. He played golf at Hall Barn with Balfour; shot partridges with Lord Rosebery at Mentmore; dined with the Asquiths, Sir Alfred Lyall, and others; visited the army maneuvers on Salisbury Plain; and had various meetings with Edmund Gosse, with whom he stayed for a time at John Hay's country place. Meanwhile, the American forces were winning their rapid victories in Cuba and the Philippines, and in London the popular enthusiasm for the United States was mounting. White carried on an animated correspondence with Senator Lodge, whom he kept informed of the efforts of the German and Austrian ambassadors in London to arouse ill-feeling between

Great Britain and America. He wrote to other Senators and Secretary Day on the state of English feeling.

Senator Lodge was of course elated by the war and the emergence of the United States as an imperial power, and his jubilant letters have no little interest. He wrote to White on May 4th, four days after Dewey's victory at Manila, that "we must on no account let the islands go," that "they must be ours under the treaty of peace," and that "the American flag is up and it must stay." He added that "We hold the other side of the Pacific, and the value to this country is almost beyond imagination." From the beginning he was nervous lest the United States should give up the Philippines, or at least part of them, and anxious to influence everyone he could reach for their retention.[16] By his letters to White he hoped to place his views before Hay, for he expected Hay to be one of the peace commissioners. All this came out clearly in subsequent correspondence:

LODGE TO WHITE, WASHINGTON, AUGUST 12, 1898

As to what we shall do in the East the Administration is hesitating. The problem is undoubtedly difficult, but two things are clear in my mind. One is that the country would strongly object, after winning the islands, to hand them back to Spain, and the other that the country would never forgive giving up Manila. Public opinion is so pronounced that I do not see why there should be hesitation, and yet it looks as if it might be the intention to withdraw as much as possible, which would be to my thinking a great mistake, not only with a view to the interests of the country but on account of the immediate political effects. As the Ambassador will probably be one of the peace commissioners, I wish you would say this to him for me. There is no question about the popular feeling, and we want to be very careful how we draw out in the East. We ought certainly to keep Manila, and I think Luzon. The other islands are not so important. Of course all this that I have just said is in strict confidence and only for yourself and the Ambassador.

Already, Lodge rejoiced, certain great fruits of the war were secure:

[16] Secretary Day told Lodge in June that Cuba must be ceded to the United States in trust and Porto Rico outright, and that the only question was to the Philippines. "You see how the Administration has advanced since you left," wrote Lodge.—Lodge to White, Washington, June 21, 1898.

One of the most important is the friendly relations which have been established with England. Another is the expulsion of Spain from this hemisphere. Another is our entrance into the Pacific by the annexation of Hawaii and our securing a foothold at last in the East—for that much I think we shall obtain. Lastly, we have risen to be one of the great world powers, and I think we have made an impression on Europe which will be lasting. We are certainly going to have a very powerful navy.

Later came another urgent plea for the use of White's influence: [17]

Thanks for your most interesting letter of September 10. There is no doubt about the President's attitude in regard to Cuba. He is going to take firm military possession, then look about him. In regard to Porto Rico the case is equally clear. The islands are ours now and the Spaniards pretty well out of it. The doubt has been all along in regard to the Philippines. I think that it is pretty well settled that no one thinks of giving up Manila. That means that the island of Luzon goes with it and that this is the minimum demand of our commissioners, from which they will not recede. This may force our possession of the rest of the group, but we can let that take care of itself. I hope whenever you have an opportunity you will put in a strong word with any of the Commissioners for the retention of Manila and Luzon.

With the close of fighting in Cuba during July, for the war was practically ended by the destruction of Cervera's fleet and the capture of Santiago, the question of the terms of peace became a subject of general discussion. Ambassador Hay was repeatedly asked to advise the State Department during June and July, and wrote to Secretary Day approving the tentative terms formulated in Washington—the retention of Porto Rico, the liberation of Cuba, and the annexation of at least part of the Philippines. As he reported, the British Government wished the United States to keep the Philippines, or failing that, to insist on an option in the event of their future sale. The continental powers were by no means of this view. Late in June or early in July, White had a talk with Jusserand on the subject, the substance of which he preserved in an undated memorandum:

Said he wished peace could be made. I replied it could be on easy terms for Spain if the latter would sue for it. Said Pauncefote had been

[17] Lodge to White, Washington, September 23, 1898.

talking with French, German, and Austrian representatives at Washington and giving it as his opinion that such was the case; practically on same terms as we know. But he thought a coaling station in Philippines would be required, and if so that this would prolong the war indefinitely as none of the Continental Powers would advise Spain to accede to that for fear of European complications—in which France he hoped would have no direct interest but might become involved. That Germany, it is known, is stirring in the matter and is very anxious. That whatever we do about the Philippines there is no chance of Spain being allowed to remain there and that there would probably be a fight over them between Germany and England, which the United States would do well to keep out of. On the other hand he thinks that if that point were abandoned peace might be made at once—Spain undoubtedly anxious for it. The reported alliance between France, Spain and Japan all bosh. Not true France very hostile to America, but merely sorry for Spain, although misgovernment in Cuba thoroughly appreciated and condemned. Admitted, however, that the report was doing great harm to French trade, a merchant of his acquaintance having requested from the United States not to mark goods as of French origin.

Said he thought we should be very unwise to become implicated with Philippine affairs by having a coaling station out there. Said Pauncefote was not acting squarely—but talked one way to us and another to Day at Washington.

He thinks Spanish government would not consent to make peace if Philippine point omitted, as pressure would be brought by European powers. Said anything may happen in Italy; whole state of Europe rotten.

Before the American peace commissioners arrived in Europe, White was again in sole charge at the embassy. The recall of Hay to become Secretary of State was by no means unexpected. When White was in Washington the matter had been discussed in connection with Secretary Sherman's resignation and he had thrown as much cold water on the proposal as he dared, for he did not believe Hay's health equal to the strain. But on August 14th Hay suddenly received a telegram from McKinley offering him the Secretaryship. Day was to go to Paris as one of the peace commissioners, and it was desirable to have Hay in Washington immediately. In great anxiety the ambassador, who was resting in the country, talked the matter over with White. He was "utterly depressed." He told White that he was "quite sure the State Department would kill him in six months"—he was then suffering from pain in the kidneys. All the work he had done to make the ambassadorship useful to him seemed wasted, and he dreaded the routine drudgery of the new office; he would miss the social gayety of London; but, he concluded, there was no getting out of it, for his relations with McKinley were such that he would have to go. White had seldom seen him in a state of such perturbation and discouragement.[18]

It seemed wise to White that Hay be allowed a breathing-space for consideration before accepting the promotion. He made up his mind to intervene and on August 15th sent to Secretary Day the following message:

I think it my duty to let the President and you know that it is very doubtful whether the Ambassador's present condition of health is equal to onerous duties of your office; in fact, certain it is not. But such are his devotion and desire to be with the President that he will not tell him so. He has been in the country for the past few days and still is resting there. Could not immediate vacancy be avoided by your going to Paris as Secretary of State, for which there are several precedents, notably Castlereagh at Vienna and Beaconsfield and Lord Salisbury at Berlin? Time would thus be allowed for careful consultation with his doctor, who is absent from London, and you could satisfy yourself as to his condition when you are here, which might then have greatly improved. He does not know I am sending you this. I will write you fully by next mail.

White on the same day confessed to Hay what he had done. "I know it was a great responsibility," he wrote him, "but such is my deep attachment for you that I decided to risk it, and to say what I am convinced is the truth. Your life is besides too valuable from an international point of view. . . . 'The office' is greatly delighted that I sent it, but the responsibility is entirely my own." [19] Though Hay had resolved to give a conditional acceptance, which was cabled on August 16th, he perfectly approved of the message, and it did suffice to win him a brief delay. But for it he would have been ordered home forthwith; now McKinley asked him merely to sail at his earliest convenience, which was not till a month later.

[18] White to Mrs. White, London, August 14, 15, 1898.
[19] White to Hay, London, August 15, 1898.

On September 14th White sadly saw him off from Liverpool. Once more—this time for a considerable period, with his responsibilities more serious and numerous than ever before—he was *chargé* and, in all but name, ambassador.

When the American peace delegation passed through London on its way to Paris, White saw and chatted with the members—Judge Day, Senator Cushman K. Davis, Senator William P. Frye, George Gray, and Whitelaw Reid. The negotiations in Paris were long drawn out, for it took more than two months to induce the Spanish commissioners to accept the American terms; and the serious hitch came upon the Philippines. The British were keenly interested in the subject, and eager that the United States should take the whole archipelago. In October White spent four days with Arthur Balfour at Whittinghame, playing golf and discussing the impressions which Balfour had formed during a trip he had just made to Germany. His host reported that while there was no doubt about Germany's "perfect craze" for colonial expansion, she had an equally great if not greater desire to remain on good terms with the United States. She considered that she had no *locus standi* in peace negotiations, and could claim no rights in the Philippines so long as the Americans remained there. But, said Balfour, if the United States relinquished any part of the islands, Germany would at once try to establish a footing; if Great Britain or any other Power were ceded part of them, she would instantly intervene. As a matter of fact, the American ambassador to Germany, Andrew D. White, had foolishly encouraged the hopes of Berlin that Germany might gain part or all of the islands. Henry White asked Balfour if he could suggest a way in which the United States could retain effective control over any unannexed part of the Philippines without assuming a protectorate. He replied that the only way would be to guarantee the unannexed portion to Spain against all other nations; this, he added, would require free trade between the American and Spanish islands, and the United States would have to reserve control over the external tariff of the whole archipelago. Of course White told him that the United States would never guarantee any of Spain's possessions.

The recall of Hay left the ambassadorship a prize for the aspirations of half a dozen ambitious Americans. One candidate "mentioned" for the place—especially by himself—was Chauncey Depew; another was Whitelaw Reid, who at first had the support of Ex-Secretary Day; a third was Horace Porter; and in a sense White was himself a candidate. Hay had said, on leaving London, quite sincerely, that he would go much more happily if he knew that White would succeed him, and he did what he could in Washington to further the movement in White's favor. The American press correspondents in London, led by G. W. Smalley, also did everything in their power for the first secretary. But he lacked the organized political support in the United States which was essential to an appointment from McKinley. Late in October, Hay wrote him that the President was more and more inclining to the choice of Joseph H. Choate. McKinley had gone over the names of the principal aspirants—Porter, Reid, Senator Wolcott, Robert Lincoln, and others—and decided against them all, while all proposals for promoting men already in the service he had summarily dismissed. "He sees in Choate all the qualities he wants: a great lawyer, a great orator, a great citizen, who as president of the Constitutional Convention of New York made a national reputation as a jurist and publicist. . . . Of course I could not but agree with everything he said of Choate, whatever may have been my private preferences." Nor, though Choate was politically so conservative that he might be called a reactionary, could anyone else question his fitness. To White it was an appointment more welcome than would have been that of any other of the leading men suggested.

In the six months which elapsed before Choate's arrival, White undertook a series of important negotiations with the British Government, which we shall describe later. It may be mentioned here that the fall and winter, the last before Mrs. White fell gravely ill, were socially busy. There was a dinner with the Asquiths, a dinner with the Queen and the Empress Frederick of Germany at Windsor Castle, a week-end at Cliveden with William Waldorf Astor, a visit to Lord-Lieutenant and Lady Cadogan in Dublin, and so on. The troubles with the Boers, the Fashoda incident, and the Dreyfus affair were the topics of the day. "I had quite a talk last night with Lord Salisbury after dinner," White wrote his wife, "from which it would seem that Delcassé has been the chief obstacle to the settlement of the Fashoda question, and that the

Cabinet's efforts have been chiefly devoted to bringing him into line, which was at last accomplished yesterday. There was much ironical laughter (in which Lord Salisbury indulged also privately to me after dinner) at the announcement of the way the French Government has suddenly discovered that the occupation of Fashoda is of no use to them." The dinner in question was one to Kitchener, and was attended by Lord Rosebery.

Other letters describe a farewell party (December 3, 1898) at Wilton House for George Curzon, who was about to go out to India as Viceroy, the guests including Rosebery, Balfour, Kitchener, and the Duke of Devonshire. In December the Whites attended the wedding of Margot Asquith's father, Sir Charles Tennant, and among the minor gossip of the letters is a history of the event for John Hay's edification. "All the children were there, the old boy looking somewhat agitated but happy," wrote White. "They went to The Glen for the honeymoon, whence one of the grandchildren wrote (innocently enough) a really comic letter to Margot. On the first day all was bliss, on the second things were rather piano, but on the third he was very irritable and proceeded to find fault with everything—the bride in particular, whom he blew up for eating a pear with a fork! In short, said the Asquith girl, aged eleven, 'Whereas all was heaven on the first day, all was hell on the third!' " [20]

At the beginning of March, 1899, the Choates, at last arrived, were dining with the Whites. But on March 6th Mrs. White was suddenly seized with an attack of polyneuritis, one of the most severe she had yet experienced.

[20] White to Hay, London, December 29, 1898.

CHAPTER TEN

The Isthmian Canal and the Hay-Pauncefote Treaty

THE Spanish War was over within a few weeks after it began, and Americans looked about them to see how marvelously their horizons had expanded. Their nation was now a World Power. That term, hardly known ten years earlier, suddenly became a commonplace of discussion. There leaped up in the United States an acrimonious debate between imperialists and anti-imperialists, Roosevelt and Lodge vigorously demanding that we make the most of our new opportunities, while Bryan, Hoar, and Schurz denounced the lust for dominion. Men disputed whether the Constitution followed the flag, and rejoiced in the fact that trade certainly did so. Before Americans had ceased feeling proud of themselves as the liberators of Cuba and the Philippines, they were fighting a vicious guerrilla war with the Filipinos and facing a sudden hostility in Havana. Our relations with every quarter of the globe were altered by our victories, our acquisition of new territory, and our subsequent rapid emergence as the leading industrial and exporting nation of the world. For the first time we were definitely plunged into Far Eastern affairs, with a stake on the confused Asiatic chessboard. All Latin America, as we went to work in Cuba and Porto Rico, viewed us with a new uneasiness. Our relations with Europe possessed a more practical character and were tinged with new emotions. The mere suggestion of a hostile league of continental Powers had stirred the anger of many Americans, and a resentment against Germany in particular persisted. But English neutrality having been of the friendliest kind, Americans suddenly felt a kindlier sentiment toward Great Britain than at any moment since 1776.

In the crowded years after the Spanish War one diplomatic event pressed upon another. With Hay and Root in the State Department, with Roosevelt shortly in the presidential chair, and with the American people ready to take pride in energetic action, the old policy of passivity and semi-isolation was left far behind. Before the Isthmian Canal question was fairly taken up the Open Door and the Boxer Rebellion demanded attention. The adjustment of pressing difficulties with Canada was not out of the way before there was a new Venezuelan dispute, involving both Great Britain and Germany. With the Anglo-French quarrel over Morocco and the Algeciras Conference of 1906, even Americans perceived the danger of a general European war. The work of American diplomatists was lifted to a new significance. White, who had reached his late forties with few chances to deal with important affairs, now found himself able to render services of increasing value. We shall take up in succession, beginning with the Isthmian Canal Treaty, the chief transactions in which he figured.

Before the Spanish War many Americans had vaguely wished for an inter-oceanic canal under their own control, and had not regretted the breakdown of the French undertaking. One episode of the war, the voyage of the *Oregon,* vividly illuminated the necessity for the new waterway. When the conflict ended, Americans realized that they had insular possessions in both the Atlantic and Pacific to defend, that in any future naval war a division of the fleet might be fatal, and that for our new commerce with the Orient the canal was urgent. It was clear that no corporation could undertake such a vast work without Government aid, and that the tolls would for some years be inadequate to meet the maintenance costs and capital charges; in other words, it was a task for the Government itself. A Federal commission had been appointed in 1895 and another in 1897 to study the routes, and Congress would soon be ready to act. The moment had come for revising the old Clayton-Bulwer treaty of 1850, which gave Great Britain far-reaching restrictive rights over any Nicaraguan or Panama canal built by the United States.

White, as *chargé,* received instructions early in December, 1898, to sound the British Ministry on the subject.[1] He had been invited that week-end to stay at Hatfield with the Prime Minister, and talked with Lord Salisbury immediately after breakfast. "He was much pleased with the manner in which we have brought the

[1] Hay to White, December 7, 1898; Instruction No. 976.

matter up," wrote White to Hay,[2] "and described your instruction after I had read it to him as admirable. . . . Nothing could have been more favorable than the preliminary or cursory view taken later privately by Lord Salisbury, in a brief confidential conversation which we had after it was settled that, as I was not in a position to state our Government's views, Pauncefote should ascertain them and endeavor to come to an arrangement. The Prime Minister quite realizes (1) that the canal can only be built by a Government, and that no company can be expected to undertake it alone, and that it is desirable that it be built; (2) that it is better for it to be under our protection than that of any other Power—and better, in the abstract, under the protection of one than of two or more Powers; (3) he is of opinion—and said so privately to me—that the canal is of comparatively little importance to England now that they have the Suez Canal; which, as I pointed out to him, though nominally neutralized, is practically under British control, as the Spanish admiral had discovered when he tried to coal there." Lord Salisbury evidently did not think the retention of the existing treaty rights a matter of serious importance to Great Britain.

At Chatsworth White also talked with the Duke of Devonshire, while he saw Arthur Balfour, whom he reported to be "quite sound." Before the new year he had thus not only brought matters to a point where the drafting of a treaty could be undertaken, but had done something to create a favorable English atmosphere. The principal negotiations were then transferred to Washington, where Hay and Pauncefote set diligently to work.

Unfortunately, a hitch shortly developed. White in his first letter had warned Hay that "one never knows what influence may be brought to bear. The Canadians would like to get a share in the control, which I imagine you will not consider for a moment." A member of the Canadian Cabinet, Mr. R. R. Dobell, came to White with a suggestion that the United States, Great Britain, and Canada should all unite in building and controlling the canal; he said that Prime Minister Laurier had been favorably struck by the idea. This proposal was of course absurd. But a very real difficulty did lie in the dispute between Canada and the United States over the Alaskan boundary, which had been referred during 1898

[2] White to Hay, London, December 23, 1898.

to a Joint High Commission without result. The British showed a disposition to insist that if they made concessions in the matter of the Isthmian Canal, Washington should make concessions regarding the Alaskan line. They argued that the two questions should be settled together, and maintained that England could hardly agree to a canal which would double the strength of the American fleet at a time when trouble might develop over a boundary on the Pacific Slope. Hence the early weeks of 1889 found the Joint Commission in a deadlock, with both sides indulging in somewhat bitter recriminations.

For a time, while both the Prime Minister and the Colonial Secretary, Joseph Chamberlain, took a distinctly reserved attitude, the outlook for a new canal treaty was dark. Chamberlain, eager to obtain a settlement of the Alaskan boundary, asked White if he could not bring pressure on the American members of the Joint High Commission while he, Chamberlain, did the same with the British representatives. "Personally," he wrote,[3] "I care very little for the points in dispute, but I care immensely for the consequential advantages of a thorough understanding between the two countries and the removal of these trumpery causes of irritation." Though White passed this suggestion on to Hay, nothing came of it. When the Joint Commission held its last sitting on February 20, 1899, the deadlock was still unbroken. Meanwhile, the draft of the canal treaty drawn up by Hay and Pauncefote had gone to the Foreign Office, where it reposed in neglect. When White asked Lord Salisbury point blank what might be expected of it, Salisbury replied sarcastically that he could not help contrasting the slow and precarious negotiations of the Americans upon the Alaskan question with the swift decision expected upon the canal. At this Hay was disgusted, writing to White that "I think it is deplorable that the British Government insists on making the Clayton-Bulwer matter depend on the successful issue of the Canadian negotiations." But after all, Lord Salisbury did not quite mean what his statement to White implied; his growl was always worse than his bite. In a final interview just before Choate arrived White ascertained that even if

[3] White to Chamberlain, London, December 26, 1898; Chamberlain to White, December 27.

no agreement were reached on the Canadian issues, Salisbury would not refuse his assent to the abrogation of the Clayton-Bulwer treaty.

The British leaders felt that there was no immediate hurry, since American opinion was still divided between the rival Panama and Nicaraguan routes, while Chairman Cannon of the House Appropriations Committee had said that the heavy treasury deficit forbade any early expenditure for a canal. They told White, moreover, that they had to protect their position before a critical Parliament. Joseph Chamberlain was particularly frank upon this.[4] As White wrote to Hay:

Chamberlain said that it would be really a great advantage to the Government if we could in return for their assent to "waive their rights" under the Clayton-Bulwer treaty come to a settlement on other matters; that there is a certain feeling here that of late we have usually got the best of any arrangement between the United States and this country, and that he feared that this feeling might be aggravated if so large a concession without any *quid pro quo* were to be announced; that while we undoubtedly have our Senate to look out for, they also have their croakers in Parliament who might under the circumstances aforesaid make it awkward for the Government in the House of Commons.

Despite Choate's arrival on March 2nd, White had a busy and responsible summer. There were a number of conferences in the spring with Sir Julian Pauncefote (who had come over especially from Washington) and others, at which Choate insisted on White's presence. The visit of ex-President Harrison to London necessitated some rather elaborate entertaining. Near the close of the year Hay, at the suggestion of an official Danish agent named Christian, commissioned White to go to Copenhagen to sound the Danish Government upon the possibility of a purchase of the Virgin Islands. White reported to the State Department in a telegram which, Hay wrote him,[5] "was exactly what I wanted, clear, comprehensive, and satisfactory throughout. The President was delighted with it, and old Adee said once more, 'White is the most valuable man in the service.' To which I replied, '*A qui le dites vous?*' You were the only man I would have asked to undertake such an errand, and it was done precisely as I wished."

[4] White, Memorandum for Hay, February 4, 1899.
[5] Hay to White, Washington, December 27, 1899.

The friendship with Hay, which had come to mean so much to White during 1898, was kept green and flourishing by a constant interchange of letters. Indeed, Hay seems to have found in White a man to whom he could confide all his anxieties and resentments in the office which he called his "place of punishment." He enjoyed the knowledge that his labor as Secretary of State was important, but he did not enjoy the labor itself. "No human being ever approaches me but to 'work' me for some purpose or other," he burst out.[6] In August, a year after "the fatal summons," he wrote an anniversary epistle of humorously bitter tone. He was still alive, he reported, and not much the worse for wear, but all his other forebodings had been realized.[7] "It is impossible to exaggerate the petty worries and cares which, added to the really important matters, make the office of Secretary of State almost intolerable. The unrestricted freedom of access which members of Congress, and especially Senators, insist upon; the venomous greed with which they demand, and quarrel over, every scrap of patronage that falls in; the clamor of private claimants and their attorneys, for pressure to be applied to poverty-stricken dago-states who may, or may not, owe them money; all these things, which are outside my legitimate work, would take every hour of my day, if allowed." He enumerated the numerous questions of actual weight pressing upon the department—questions with Canada, Italy, Germany, and China. There was so little social life to mitigate his hard lot that "there has hardly been an hour of real enjoyment in the whole year." Washington, with Mrs. Cameron living in the South, Henry Adams hardly ever there, Clarence King vanished into the underworld of Western mines, Whitelaw Reid always busy in New York, and Billy Philips dead, seemed to him a dull city. "Really, your letters give to me and my wife more glimpses of personal interest than anything we get elsewhere."

In this and other letters Hay expatiated upon his fear, contempt, and dislike of that august body the United States Senate. It was the specter of the frowning Senate which gave him most uneasiness in the Canadian boundary controversy. He and Lord Salisbury could draw up in twenty-four hours a settlement perfectly satisfac-

[6] Hay to White, Washington, January 10, 1899.
[7] Hay to White, Newbury, N. H., August 11, 1899.

tory to both, but the chances were two to one that Canada would reject it and the Senate tear it to shreds.[8] "You may work for months on a treaty," he complained, "and at last get everything perfectly arranged, and send it into the Senate, where it is met by every man who wants to get a political advantage, or to satisfy a personal grudge, everyone who has asked for an office and not got it, everyone whose wife may think mine has not been attentive enough— and if they can muster one-third of the Senate plus one, your treaty is lost without any reference to its merits." President McKinley and the Cabinet had told him to go ahead and take his chances. "But I must feel of my ground somewhat before risking a defeat in the Senate, which ought to involve my continuance in the Government. I would gladly go out, on such an issue, if it were not to damage the President next year." When White had apparently smoothed the road for the purchase of the Danish West Indies, Hay wrote that he had slyly thought that he might elude the two-thirds vote in the Senate by having the transaction accomplished by joint resolution.[9] He felt sure of a majority in both houses. But he had to talk with Chairman Cushman K. Davis of the Foreign Relations Committee first. "So I went to him and put the case before him and asked him squarely which procedure offered the better chance of success. I could see he feels as I did—that the joint resolution was preferable. But being a Senator he could not at once bring his mind to pass over the Senate—so he asked for a few days to make up his mind. I am afraid he will decide for the Senate."

These were the complaints, like Olney's, of a man as yet unused to politics; and events lay just ahead which, while showing that Hay's apprehension of the Senate was justified, showed also that the veto power of the Senate is sometimes used to advantage. As the year 1899 closed the Clayton-Bulwer Treaty was still unabrogated. But as White wrote repeatedly, both Salisbury and Chamberlain had given him private assurances that they were ready to consent.[10] These assurances they made good. On February 5, 1900,

[8] Hay to White, Newbury, August 11, 1899.

[9] Hay to White, Washington, December 27, 1899.

[10] White to Hay, London, August 29, 1899. They gave similar assurances to Choate.

Pauncefote and Hay signed in Washington a convention for the abrogation of the Clayton-Bulwer compact, which it was known that Parliament was ready to ratify. The British asked for no *quid pro quo*, and their generosity was praised by the American press. But as the convention was more carefully studied, objections to it appeared in many American minds. It neutralized the canal, laid down rules for the complete freedom of international traffic, even during a war in which the United States was engaged, provided for the adherence of other Powers to the convention, and stipulated that "no fortifications shall be erected commanding the canal or the waters adjacent." Leading Senators at once attacked a number of these provisions. By April, 1900, a campaign against the convention was in full swing.

Of the nature of this campaign it is unnecessary to speak. Theodore Roosevelt, then Governor of New York, wrote to Secretary Hay a letter, which has been often printed,[11] stating that he had two chief objections to the convention: first, by forbidding us to fortify the canal or close it in time of war it rendered us more vulnerable than before, and second, the requirement for the adherence of other Powers trenched upon the Monroe Doctrine. Others felt as he did, and Senator Cushman K. Davis led the attack with an amendment providing that the restrictions upon the use of the canal should not apply to measures which the United States might adopt for its own defense or for the maintenance of public order along the route. Several lesser amendments followed. Much of the criticism was abusive and unjustified. Hay, hot with resentment, expressed his feelings in a series of letters to White:[12]

DEPARTMENT OF STATE, WASHINGTON,
February 27th, 1900.

MY DEAR WHITE:

. . . I can say nothing as yet about the fate of my negotiations. I have never seen such an exhibition of craven cowardice, ignorance, and prejudice. I am old enough to have foreseen it, but I confess it never entered into my mind that anyone out of a madhouse could have

[11] It is given in Dennis, A. L. P., *Adventures in American Diplomacy*, pp. 160, 161.

[12] These letters supplement the material given in Thayer, W. R., *Life and Letters of John Hay*, vol. ii, chap. xxv.

objected to the Canal Convention. It gained all we have longed for and worked for for twenty years, and without an atom of compensation. Yet the cranks are all yelping as if they had been skinned alive. —— comes out today in the *Tribune* saying it will be the death of the Republican Party, if the treaty goes through—the frantic little lunatic. I can only let the storm blow itself out. You will be sorry to learn that Lodge, after accepting and applauding the treaty, has suddenly lost his nerve, and wants it rejected. . . .

Yours Faithfully,

J. H.

———

DEPARTMENT OF STATE, WASHINGTON,

March 18th, 1900.

MY DEAR WHITE:

I judge from the tone of the English newspapers and that of some of the American correspondence that our transmittal of the Boer message was not very well received at the Foreign Office. It was, of course, received and answered precisely as I had anticipated—any other answer would have been out of the question. On the other hand, it was impossible for us to have done otherwise. The public mind on this side is for the moment in a state far from satisfactory. The Irish and the Germans, for the first time in my knowledge, seem to have joined their several lunacies in one common attack against England and incidentally against the Administration for being too friendly to England. I do not imagine that this coalition can survive many months, but for the moment it lifts all our light-weight politicians off their feet. You would hardly believe, if I told you, how it has affected, not only men habitually timid, like Lodge and ——, but men like Davis and Cullom, who are anxious about their home vote, and men like —— who are mad for popularity, and shout always with what seems the voice of the crowd. There is not a man in either House (excepting perhaps Wolcott) who would, I think, be willing to express the feeling of most men of sense, that the fight of England in South Africa is the fight of civilization and progress, and that all our interests are bound up in her success. This being the case, we can only wait for the present dust-storm to blow over. To oppose it actively, at this moment, would defeat our own purpose. For this reason, I saw there was nothing to be done with the Boer message but to send it on to you with an expression of the President's platonic desire for peace. If I had done otherwise there would have been a joint resolution rushed through Congress advising us to do it, couched in language which could not have failed to be offensive and injurious. For the present we seem to have spiked their guns.

You can form some idea from what I have said, of the disgusting position we are in, in regard to the pending Canal Treaty. Nearly every member of the Foreign Relations Committee approved the treaty and promised his support—but the *Sun* and the *Journal* began their furious attack which met with so much response from the papers in Chicago, who are cross with the President for personal reasons, that it frightened the weak sisters out of their wits. Lodge was the first to flop—then Cullom, who is a candidate for reëlection, and in great danger of failing. They have worked on Davis, who is too indolent to make a strong fight. Wolcott, who is all right, is most of the time in New York, and was of no use. So they hit on the idiotic expedient of working into the treaty the utterly inapplicable and futile tenth article of the Suez Act. They thought they would save the treaty by placating the howling fools in the Senate, and that England, seeing how silly and ineffective the amendment is, might contemptously accept it. I do not know what will happen next. I resigned my place as Secretary of State in profound disgust; the President, in a most touching and beautiful letter refused to accept it, and would not even communicate it to the Cabinet. So I must stay for the present. If they ratify the treaty with the amendment I shall have to present it to the British Government with whatever nausea I may feel. I only hope they may surmise what I cannot properly express— that the amendment is a weak resort of ignorance and cowardice, that it does not mean anything in particular, that long before it shall become a practical question, calling for interpretation and action, we shall all be dead, and the face of the world much changed. I think the amendment deforms the treaty, makes it ridiculous from our point of view, but that it does not materially change its spirit and intention, nor make it impossible for England to accept it, if they see fit.

You know what I have for years thought of the Senate. I am profoundly grieved that I saw so clearly.

We are in the worst of our *giboulées de Mars*, physically and morally. We have a snowstorm nearly every day; and a ridiculous little tempest quite as often in Congress and the newspapers. But we shall live through it. We shall get what legislation we need. McKinley and Bryan will be nominated in the summer and we shall have the fight of four years ago all over again with the same result.

In spite of what you see in the newspapers and in the speeches of the cranks there is deep and sincere satisfaction at the recent English successes. When the job is finished, as I hope it will be soon, the public opinion here will settle down to the conviction that this was the only issue compatible with the honor of Great Britain or with our own future interests. . . .

Yours faithfully,
JOHN HAY

White, talking with Arthur Balfour early in April—for during Lord Salisbury's absence abroad Balfour was in charge of the Foreign Office—found him favorable to acceptance of the treaty with the proposed Senate amendments. This, he gathered, was also Salisbury's view; but there was a general feeling that the matter would have to stand over till after the presidential election. In fact, there was really nothing else to do; the Senate adjourned in March of 1900 without a final vote, and did not sit again till December.[13] In May White made one of his brief trips to the United States again, and found opinion on the treaty much divided. Roosevelt was emphatically against it; Senator Nelson Aldrich was for it, and believed that it would certainly be ratified without amendment after the election. Whitelaw Reid told him that there was a strong pro-Boer feeling in the West, based chiefly on the old-time anti-British feeling, but that the country was slowly appreciating the real merits of the South African conflict.

In December, when the Senate reconvened, the final blow fell— the treaty was ratified with amendments sufficiently far-reaching to permit the United States to police the canal and close it in war against any enemy, and to safeguard the Monroe Doctrine. Hay

---

[13] For a short time there was hope that the Senate would change its position. White wrote to Hay from London on May 16, 1900: "I dined last night with Whitelaw Reid, who spoke in a manner as strongly commendatory as your best friend could have wished, of your course in general, and of the magnitude of the feat accomplished by the Open Door arrangement. He entirely agreed with us about the Hay-Pauncefote Treaty, and intimated that the real cause of Davis's action was an aggrieved feeling at not having been consulted beforehand; I mean before the Treaty was sent in if not actually before it was negotiated. I saw Senator Aldrich in New York, who assured me that it will certainly be ratified without the amendment after the election. He also thinks the pro-Boer wave has spent its greatest force. Reid says there is a strong pro-Boer feeling in the West chiefly based on the old anti-British feeling, but he thinks the country is getting on to the merits of the case slowly."

was bitterly grieved, and for a time there was a decided coolness between him and Senator Lodge. He wrote White that the treaty would have been ratified intact "if our people had any pluck, or if Lodge had acted squarely." Lodge, he added, had come out with a carefully prepared interview, saying that a treaty when sent to the Senate is not properly a treaty at all, but a project. "That is to say that if France and the United States make a treaty, after careful study and negotiation, it is nothing more, when sent to the Senate, than a petition from the two nations to that body to make a real treaty for them. The attitude of the Senate toward public affairs makes all serious negotiation impossible." In sad perplexity about his future course, Hay had again tried to resign, and McKinley had again refused to permit him. "Apparently, no one desires my resignation except the *Sun* and the 'yellows' and myself," he concluded bitterly in his letter to White. "I am sick to the heart of the whole business, and shall gladly get out at the first opportunity. And when I go, it will be final. I shall never again accept office at home or abroad." Fortunately—for Hay at the time was almost indispensable and some of his greatest services lay ahead—this feeling of chagrin soon passed away.

While the Secretary was thus writing to White, Henry Cabot Lodge was unburdening himself in equally frank letters:

LODGE TO WHITE, DECEMBER 18, 1900

No one appreciates more fully than myself Mr. Hay's conception and motives in making that treaty in the form in which he did make it. I understand what he aimed at, and I know that there is no more patriotic man, as there is no more accomplished diplomatist, than he. The attacks upon him in the newspapers on account of this treaty have been as cruel as they have been unjustifiable, but when I came to examine the Hay-Pauncefote treaty with Davis last spring I came to the conclusion, very reluctantly, that we made a promise there which we ought not to make. We engage to keep the canal open in time of war as in time of peace, and thereby to allow an enemy's fleet, if we were at war, to pass unmolested through the canal if they could get within the three-mile limit. We either meant to keep that promise, or we meant, under stress of war, to break it. In either event I was against it. . . .

. . . The plain facts of the case are these: The American people will never consent to building a canal at their own expense, which they shall guard and protect for the benefit of the world's commerce, unless they have virtually complete control. There is no use arguing about the wisdom of this attitude. This is what the American people and the American press, without a dissenting voice, demand, and it is that sentiment which the Senate is representing. If England should reject the Senate amendments it is just as certain as the coming of the day that we shall abrogate the treaty by resolution of Congress and go on with the building of the canal. The American people mean to have the canal and they mean to control it. Now England does not care enough about it to go to war to prevent our building it, and it would be ruinous if she did make war on us. As she is not prepared to go to war, why is it not better that the canal should be built under the Hay-Pauncefote Treaty with her assent to the amendments than to have her refuse the amendments and force the United States to abrogate the treaty and then build the canal? A prompt assent to the Senate amendments would have an admirable effect on the relations of the two countries.

Unquestionably the Senate had correctly interpreted the majority opinion in the United States when it amended the treaty, and its amendments constituted a distinct improvement. Undoubtedly also Secretary Hay's treaty, even in its original form, represented an important gain by American diplomacy; and if its defeat had meant no treaty at all, as Hay and others feared, it would have been better to accept it with its defects. For a time the outlook for a new agreement with England was gloomy. In another letter to White,[14] Senator Lodge wrote that if Great Britain refused to accept the amendments her action would do more than anything else to drive forward the construction of the canal, for the American public would leap to the conclusion that the British had some sinister motive in using the Clayton-Bulwer treaty to hamper the United States. White forwarded extracts from Lodge's letters to Arthur Balfour, urging that the American amendments would work no practical disadvantage to Great Britain and that the Senate had not acted in an offensive spirit.[15] But the British press attacked the amendments, the public disliked them, and Salisbury finally turned his back on them. For a time the deadlock seemed complete.

[14] Lodge to White, Washington, December 24, 1900. Lodge denied that the Senate's action was in any way influenced by the transcontinental railroads.

[15] White to Balfour, London, December, 1900; day not stated.

Fortunately this was for only a short time. Feeling that the country was determined upon the canal and fearing that the irritable Senate would abrogate the existing treaty as roughly as Lodge had threatened, Hay set to work to draft a second and better agreement. Alvey A. Adee, at his instance, in April, 1901, sketched the terms of a new treaty. Both Ambassador Choate and White worked during the summer and early autumn with Lord Lansdowne (now the Foreign Secretary) and Pauncefote to hammer the various clauses into shape. During the latter part of the summer Lord Lansdowne sent Hay a confidential memorandum of his own views. With more political shrewdness than he had previously displayed, Hay consulted some of the leading Senators and thus won their confidence in advance. White, again visiting the United States in the spring of 1901, lent what hand he could in influencing public men; and among others he saw the new Vice President, Theodore Roosevelt, whom he was glad to find standing heartily behind the effort for a new treaty. White wrote to Hay from New York on April 24th:

I spent last night with Teddy, who was in capital form and in a very friendly mood to the treaty and favorable to the Panama route. He thinks a treaty providing for the passage of vessels of commerce of all nations through the canal, on the same terms as to tolls, etc., in peace or war (including merchant ships of a country at war with us) and saying nothing about ships of war, would pass the Senate (the Clayton-Bulwer Treaty being at the same time abrogated).

At the same time he sent to Mrs. White a fuller report of what Roosevelt had said:

He was most reasonable on international affairs and seems to favor the Panama rather than the Nicaragua route, as also to be very strongly in favor of coming to an agreement with England this summer. He thinks that a treaty providing for abolition of the Clayton-Bulwer Treaty (about which, as I understand the situation, England does not care particularly provided neutrality be guaranteed) and guaranteeing the free passage of merchant ships of all nations in peace or war at all times and at the same rates of toll, etc., and saying nothing about ships of war, will certainly pass the Senate (which agrees with what Senators have told me); and he says he would work tooth and nail for such a treaty. He says it is impossible if this country spends all the money and gives all the protection and incurs the risk of loss, etc., to expect us to allow warships of a Power at war with us to go through the canal and to get quickly from one of our coasts to the other, but certainly the merchant ships of such a Power might be allowed to go through. He says as regards warships, England need not mind, as if by any terrible mishap she should be at war with us, there is no possible doubt that her navy would be strong enough to capture both ends of the canal and thereby take complete possession of it; a view which I have always taken. But there is not the faintest chance of the Senate's agreeing to a clause providing for the invitation of other Powers to participate in a guarantee, and I don't think England attaches importance to that either. I am beginning to be quite hopeful of reaching an agreement.

A few months after this conversation, Roosevelt was President. For a week following McKinley's death there was some uncertainty whether the new Executive would retain Hay as Secretary of State. Hay felt it himself, and writing to White on October 1, 1901, of "this last horrible fortnight," was frank in speaking about it. As Roosevelt journeyed from Buffalo to Washington, he stated, the less responsible newspapers had been full of reports that the Secretary was to be dropped because his ideas on foreign policy were incompatible with the President's, that Lodge was to be appointed in his stead, and that if Lodge declined, Root would be chosen. Partly crediting these rumors, two of Lodge's friends, Eugene Hale and William H. Moody, with his son-in-law Augustus P. Gardner, wrote the Senator in Europe to hasten home, which Lodge sensibly declined to do. We have been told by H. H. Kohlsaat in his memoirs that Roosevelt actually did hesitate; but not for long. "When the President arrived," wrote Hay, "he said to me in the station, without a moment's delay, that he wished me to stay with him 'not temporarily but as long as I shall be here.' I said I would stay as long as I could." Lunching together on the two following days, Roosevelt and Hay went carefully over the principal questions in our foreign relations, and as Hay wrote to White, they found themselves in hearty agreement upon every point. He would have a free hand, he thought, in matters of principle, but in appointments not a voice. The sordid necessities of the situation, as he put it, would be controlling, and he smote White's hopes of early advancement to an embassy by saying that Myron T. Herrick was to be sent to Rome when the recently-appointed incumbent there, George von Lengerke Meyer, resigned, and that Roosevelt's plan was to appoint Bellamy Storer to Paris as soon as General Horace Porter left. There were vague reports that Andrew D. White was about to give up Berlin. "I can only say '*Credat Judæus,*' " wrote Hay. "To see him out and to see you in his place, I would give a lot."

During the fall of 1901 Ambassador Choate, whose hard work had brought the new canal treaty into final shape, sailed for the United States, leaving White in charge.[16] Choate wrote back expressing his pleasure that John Hay looked in excellent health though sad, saying that President Roosevelt "is wonderfully well and cool, calm, and collected," and predicting a successful Administration. Pauncefote also returned to Washington that fall, and most of the final touches were put on the treaty in our capital, though some were settled in October between White and Lansdowne.[17] Lord Lansdowne naïvely suggested to White that the treaty might be submitted to the Senate before it was signed, whereupon White explained the constitutional and political objections to such a step. As it was, Hay had consulted more than enough Senators. In October the main terms of the new agreement leaked out through some of them; it became known that the United States would be practically though not explicitly placed at liberty to fortify the canal; and some American newspapers raised vulgar shouts over "our triumph." Hay wrote White that he hoped the British would pay no attention to these vain boastings. "If we keep negotiations secret from leading Senators, we incur their ill-will and oppo-

[16] Hay wrote to White that the British ought to know—White had told them often enough—that if the two governments could not agree on a treaty before December, nothing could prevent a violent legislative abrogation of the old Clayton-Bulwer agreement.—Hay to White, Washington, June 18, 1901. With this letter in his pocket, White went to Hatfield for a week-end in July, and talked with Salisbury of the treaty. Salisbury mentioned compensations on the Alaska boundary. White emphatically protested. "Lord Salisbury said, 'You really feel that way, do you?' to which I replied, 'Most decidedly,' and he then said: 'Well, there would be this advantage in dealing with the canal question alone, that we should have only one antagonist, whereas in respect to Alaska there would be two—yourselves and Canada.' "—White to Hay, London, July 24, 1901.

[17] Choate to White, New York, October 26, 1901; White to Hay, London, October 26, 1901, on his negotiations with Lansdowne on certain treaty clauses.

sition. If we tell them confidentially what we are doing and thus secure their coöperation—their vanity leads them to blab everything to some newspaper, to show that they are 'in it.'"

At the beginning of November White was able to cable the State Department Lord Lansdowne's official acceptance of the treaty; and the instrument, signed on November 18th, went to the Senate under the most favorable auspices. White had done a good deal in London during the summer to confirm Lodge's support, a fact for which Hay was grateful:

I am glad [he wrote, October 14th, 1901] that you have got Cabot so thoroughly committed that there can now be no drawing back. It is amusing to see how enthusiastic the President is in favor of the treaty. He gave Billy Mason a drastic calling-down the other day. It is not known what effect it will have. . . . The Senators are already worrying Theodore like gadflies over their petty little consulates. He has a lot of good ideas, which I hope he may be able to work out. But I wish we could see this treaty through before he begins to take the Senate by the collar. Did you see the long article on "The Senate as a Treaty-making Power" which Mr. Choate cut from the [London] *Times* and sent me? It was written by Maurice Low, the correspondent of the *Chronicle*.

In the Senate the treaty was swiftly and easily carried. As Lodge wrote to White, the opposition had been quite shattered by the palpable fact that England had made all the concessions which the American critics had demanded.[18] The day after Christmas, Hay was able to send White a letter rejoicing in the completion of the whole business. Lodge, he said, who had felt himself particularly responsible for the wreck of the old treaty, had put his back into promoting the new one. The President had likewise been extremely zealous in rounding up the doubtful Senators, and all having fallen in line except the "irreclaimable cranks," the final vote was 72 to 6.[19] This was a gleam of sunshine after a most unhappy year for Hay. He had lost his son Adelbert, a staggering blow; he had lost his chief, McKinley; he had lost Clarence King and his old collaborator, John Nicolay, both after illnesses which involved terrible suffering. But he could rejoice that the way was now clear, so

[18] Lodge to White, Washington, November 21, 1909.
[19] Hay to White, Washington, December 26, 1901.

far as Great Britain was concerned, for the construction of the inter-oceanic canal, and White rejoiced with him. The canal was to be built by the United States or under its auspices; the "general principle of neutralization" was to be maintained; but it was to be policed by the United States, and by implication it might be fortified. In short, from the American point of view the treaty was thoroughly satisfactory.

The whole episode of the Isthmian treaty, as White could look back on it, had several instructive aspects. Once more the Senate had shown its insistence upon holding the whip hand over treaties, and had used its power well. Once more the United States had demanded the full measure of its rights, without counter-concessions. Once more, also, Great Britain had manifested its eagerness to maintain cordial relations with the United States by assenting to all these demands. Venezuela, the Spanish War, the Hay-Pauncefote Treaty, were so many milestones on the road to full Anglo-American agreement, destined to be so important in the future. Meanwhile, still another chapter was being written in the record of friendly relations between the two countries, and to it we shall now turn.

CHAPTER ELEVEN

Sidelights on the Open Door and Boxer Rebellion

As the Spanish War led naturally to the building of the Panama Canal, so it led also to a more vigorous policy in the Far East. Until the acquisition of the Philippines, the American people had been for the most part indifferent to Oriental affairs. China was very distant and very alien—in another world entirely. We carried on a certain amount of trade with the Far East, which concerned a small number of importers, but very few exporters. For the rest, the Orient was a region with which we were content to have little to do. We had indeed been at great pains in the 'eighties to shut Chinese immigration out of the country. The outbreak of the Chino-Japanese War in 1894 aroused a certain interest in Far Eastern politics, American sympathy being generally on the side of Japan. Now this interest was greatly stimulated by the hoisting of the American flag over the Philippines, and by a marked increase in American trade with that part of the world. We had an Asiatic foothold of importance; our exports to China rose from less than three million dollars in 1890 to fifteen and a quarter millions in 1900, and bade fair to rise much higher.

The whole world, in fact, after 1895 focused a new attention upon the Far East. The complete defeat of the Chinese in the Chino-Japanese conflict was a signal for a general rush of the Powers to obtain commercial concessions in the huge, helpless, and rich Chinese Empire. Both the United States and Great Britain wished to preserve the principle of the Open Door, with equal commercial privileges to all; indeed, American devotion to that principle dated from 1843, when Secretary of State Webster gave his instructions to Caleb Cushing, American commissioner to China.[1] But for a time there seemed no likelihood of a check to the seizures. Germany in 1897 occupied Tsingtau, and as a recompense for the murder of two missionaries forced China in 1898 to lease her that

[1] Fuess, C. M., *The Life of Caleb Cushing*, vol. i, p. 397 ff.

port for ninety-nine years, and to give her a dominant economic position in the province of Shantung. Immediately afterward Russia acquired a lease of Port Arthur; France a lease of Kwang-chuan; and Great Britain a lease of Wei-hai-wei and of Kowloon on the mainland opposite Hong-kong. All the great birds of prey seemed swooping down to rend the carcass of China. Great Britain, which acted last and more or less reluctantly in this competition, made it clear through Sir Michael Hicks-Beach and Arthur Balfour that she regretted the orgy of spoliation, and wished the integrity of China maintained.[2] But the alarmed and indignant dispatches of the American minister in Peking, Mr. Denby, met little response in the United States, preoccupied as it was with Cuba. Only when the Spanish War was over were we ready to take a determined stand.

It was while Hay was travelling in Egypt in March, 1898, that Great Britain first confidentially suggested that it and the United States coöperate in opposing any action by foreign Powers antagonistic to free Chinese trade, whether this action involved merely the lease of parts of the Chinese coast or the acquisition of Chinese ports outright. In effect, it was a proposal that the two should act together in maintaining the Open Door. White wrote to Hay that the British were convinced of the necessity of checking the continental Powers. He had been talking to the two principal members of the Ministry next to Lord Salisbury himself:

WHITE TO HAY, LONDON, MARCH 6, 1898

I don't know whether I wrote you that Joseph Chamberlain in addition to Arthur Balfour had spoken to me of the importance of our taking some sort of action in support of England's policy in China, which I

[2] As *chargé*, White on March 2, 1897, reported the Commons debate of the preceding day on the motion "That it is of vital importance for British commerce and influence that the independence of Chinese territory should be maintained." This resolution was agreed to without a division. The *Times* and other newspapers carried vigorous leaders expressing uneasiness lest Germany and Russia block up the Open Door; Sir William Harcourt, leader of the Opposition, and Curzon, Under Secretary for Foreign Affairs, both made strong speeches; and the latter declared that regard for the integrity of China was the cardinal basis of British policy.—State Department Files, Great Britain, vol. cxci, despatch No. 287.

duly wrote to Porter. Chamberlain says that he does not believe the promises of Germany and Russia with regard to their ports would hold good any longer than it suited the convenience of those Powers, and in view of Germany's recent action of objecting to—practically vetoing —the proposed railroad from Tien-Tsin to Chia-Kiang on the Yang-tse (which is or was to be constructed with American and British capital) unless it be of German material and built by German engineers, on the ground that Germany considers the whole province of Shantung for commercial purposes a German province, it would seem that what-ever her intention may be about the freedom of the port of Kiau-chau, she certainly does not mean the province of Shantung to be open to the rest of the world on equal terms. Kiau-chau and the territory ceded with it to Germany occupy a small spot on the coast of that province, through a limited portion of the western part of which the projected railway was to pass. I imagine it to be one of the many contemplated railways and other Chinese investments in which Calvin Brice and his friends are interested.

Two days after this letter was mailed, on March 8, 1898, the British Government presented through Sir Julian Pauncefote its formal but secret proposal to Washington regarding the Open Door. White was at once told all about it. "You will be interested to hear," he wrote Hay, "that Sir Julian Pauncefote's visit to the President, of which so much was made in the papers, was to propose joint action in China for the maintenance of free trade to all the world, to which the President appears to have replied, with his usual pru-dence and reserve, most politely, but committing himself to noth-ing. Arthur Balfour, who told me of it this morning, promised to send me Pauncefote's telegram stating what had occurred, but he has not yet done so." To the disappointment of the British, Secre-tary Sherman's response was chilly. Our government had no evi-dence of interference with commercial equality in China, he declared; the German ambassador had given unofficial assurance that the bay of Kiau-chau would be open to everyone; and the United States saw no reason for departing from its traditional policy of avoiding European complications. English opinion had not ex-pected such a reply. White had written Secretary Sherman six weeks earlier that it was the general British view that our people and probably our Government also would be with them in standing for the Open Door. But with the outbreak at this juncture of the Spanish conflict, the whole matter was dropped.

It was taken up again immediately after Hay's appointment as Secretary of State. Hay was of course thoroughly familiar with the British point of view. He grasped clearly the new situation presented by our acquisition of Oriental possessions, and he was a man of imagination. He was the first American Secretary, as his friend George W. Smalley has written, to take the lead in a world-embracing policy, and to unite the Powers of western Europe behind it. He did more; he extorted a pledge even from Russia, and brought half-reluctant Japan to join the other nations in guaranteeing China her territorial integrity and her commercial freedom. Many factors entered into the formulation of what is called Hay's Open Door policy. They included the ideas expressed by Balfour and Joseph Chamberlain in English speeches, and those contained in the British memorandum presented by Sir Julian Pauncefote; the ideas of a robust, high-spirited, loquacious Englishman of considerable Oriental travel, Admiral Charles Beresford; and those of W. W. Rockhill, who after much Far Eastern experience was now in Washington.[3] Secretary Hay was busy in 1898 with the peace negotiations with Spain and the Hay-Pauncefote Treaty, and probably thought little of China. But the subject cropped up repeatedly in White's letters to him. He wrote Hay, for example, on November 2nd, of a visit to the Russian Ambassador to Great Britain:

This morning I dropped in on my bicycle to see old Staal, who was exceedingly festive and most amusing. . . . He gave me an account of a visit he had received from the Russian military *attaché* with our forces at Santiago, who had come back full of admiration of our regular army and of the navy—saying that he is sure there are no better or more courageous troops in the world, but that the mismanagement of everything connected with moving the troops and with the volunteers was fearful. The military *attachés* were treated no worse than anyone else, but were herded in with negroes and subjected to all manner of discomfort and privations, owing, he says, to faulty arrangements and the incapacity of those in charge. General Shafter he reported as "*très*

[3] Cf. Dennis, A. L. P., *Adventures in American Diplomacy*; Thayer, W. R., *Life and Letters of John Hay*, vol. ii, p. 231 ff.

grossier et pas du tout à la hauteur de la situation." Of course he told me all this in the strictest confidence, which pray consider it.

Staal then went on to say that "*On dit que ce cher Hay est retourné très anglophile. J'espère qu'avec cette question de vos Philippines, etc., etc., nous n'allons pas être autrement qu'anciens amis comme toujours, en Chine surtout.*" To which I answered, "*On n'a pas besoin d'être russophobe parcequ'on est anglophile,*" and that I hoped he would keep his Russians well in the North in order to avoid any possibility of friction, and I assured him that your sentiments toward Russia are of the friendliest. He added that he has great difficulty in keeping things smooth with this country owing to British excitability with Russia. He then let off a few jokes in his best style and I was obliged to leave him to his imperial service. You will have seen that the German Emperor is returning, which looks squally. Lord Salisbury said, by the by, that if we had taken Luzon and left the rest of the Philippines, we should "undoubtedly have had another Kiau-chau" very soon on our hands.

Later that month White again wrote to Hay of the British interest in the maintenance of the Open Door for commerce everywhere, including the Philippines. He had been shooting at Panshanger, Lord Cowper's place near Hertford:

There was a particularly pleasant party there, including Arthur Balfour and St. John Brodrick, both of them particularly interested in maintaining the most intimate relations possible with us. Brodrick told me that he had received so many letters from the chambers of commerce and the commercial community throughout the country about the probability of our establishing differential duties and extending our navigation laws in Cuba and the Philippines that he was very much afraid lest the feeling of this country, in the event of those projects being carried out, instead of remaining as now particularly friendly to American expansion, might assume a lukewarm if not actually hostile attitude to it. He showed me a copy of a despatch perfectly unobjectionable in tone which Lord Salisbury is sending to Pauncefote today directing him to make representations to you as to the great hardship which would result to the British shipping interest if vessels from this country should be unable to take a cargo to a port in the United States and be unable to take another thence to the Philippines. I replied that I knew nothing of what is to happen in that respect but supposed that if the Philippines should actually be annexed to the United States as Porto Rico is and Cuba is not, the President would have no alternative but to apply our tariff and navigation laws to them until Congress should otherwise order it.

Apparently British trade is very considerable with the Philippines—much less with Cuba; but of course I can quite see the hardship should the navigation laws be applied to the Philippines and I hope this may not be necessary if, as the newspapers announce, we are going to make a protectorate and not absolutely annex them. Arthur Balfour said that he would never question the right of any country to make just such arrangements in these matters as might seem most expedient and least of all would he ever do so in our case; but that of course if it should ever turn out that the result of American expansion, upon which the people of this country now look with such particular favor, is the crippling of British trade, undoubtedly there will be a considerable change in public opinion here on that point, which would be regrettable to those desirous of seeing the closest possible intimacy between the two countries.

I showed him your telegram explaining what the open door means, and he said that of course there could be no more complete open door than the admission of all nations to trade in the Philippines on equal terms. So that their minds are quite at rest on that point.

White also kept Senator Lodge informed of the British opposition to any partition of China, and Lodge expressed his sympathy for this position. Indeed, at the beginning of 1898 he had written to White in vigorous terms. "If I had my way," he stated, "I should be glad to have the United States to say to England that we would stand by her in, her declaration that the ports of China must be opened to all nations equally or to none, and if England takes that attitude firmly I am in hopes this may come about, although our foreign policy is always more haphazard than I like to see it. Senator Teller advocated this action on our part in a public interview, and I cordially agree with him. Some of the large mercantile bodies are also beginning to move in the same direction."

It was true that American commercial bodies were interested, for more than half the import trade of northern China was in American hands. During the summer of 1899 Hay was aroused to take action. Admiral Charles Beresford had expounded, in his trip across the United States, a number of ideas on the Open Door; and since Rockhill was critical of some of his proposals, Hay had Rockhill draw up a memorandum on the subject. It was this memorandum, completed on August 28, 1899, which Hay made the basis for his doctrine of the Open Door as laid down in the identic notes that on September 6th he sent to Great Britain, Germany, and Russia. In these notes he called upon each Power claiming a sphere of influence in China (for copies were shortly sent to France, Italy, and Japan) to adhere to the principle that all treaty ports should be kept open on equal terms, that no special tariffs or harbor dues should be levied, and that railway charges should be equal for all nationalities. By adroit maneuvering in the closing months of 1899 Secretary Hay secured the consent of the six nations named, though in some instances conditional and vague, to this principle of the Open Door. It was a timely stroke, and one of the greatest of Hay's achievements.

The achievement was universally acclaimed in England, now engrossed in the Boer War but still eager to see her views as regards China given effective application. White was able to report general applause. The Prime Minister expressed himself freely. "With regard to the Open Door correspondence," White wrote to Hay, "Lord Salisbury said that he thought you had accomplished a work of great importance and utility to the world and especially to our respective countries. I asked him whether after reading the different replies to your proposals he had any criticism to make upon any of them on the score of inadequacy or evasiveness, and he replied 'none whatever'; that they seemed to cover the ground exactly." Sir William Harcourt sent White a charming letter of congratulation, saying that the Open Door agreement was a great service to the world, and adding: "I know how largely you have yourself contributed for many years in maintaining the good will between England and the United States, and I feel how much you must rejoice in the happy consummation of a policy which is the common object of both nations." [4] British observers particularly appreciated the address with which Hay had outmaneuvered the Russians. He had taken their unsatisfactory note on the Open Door, treated it as satisfactory, and proclaimed to the world that Russia as well as the five other Powers had come to a "final and definitive" agreement on the subject.

Hay himself was gayly pleased with what he had done, and wrote White a characteristically playful letter on the way he had managed the unwilling Russian Government:

[4] Harcourt to White, London, March 28, 1900.

DEPARTMENT OF STATE, WASHINGTON,
April 2, 1900.

MY DEAR WHITE:

I have received your letter of the 23rd of March. Your report of what
Bertie said coincides with some very curious things that have come to
me here. I do not quite know what line Russia is going to take in the
matter. She was opposed to the whole business from the beginning;
did what she could to block our game. Cassini consistently opposed it
here, assured me over and over that it would never get through, especially that it would be suicidal on the part of England to yield on our
proposals, said the same thing about Germany and France, and continually asserted to me: "You don't know what you are asking; you
are attempting something impossible; you have no idea of the extent
of your propositions." In spite of this, I thought I had some idea of
what I was doing, and when, at last, I gave up trying to convince
Cassini, I transferred the negotiations to St. Petersburg. Tower carried
them on with excellent judgment and tact, and gained the desired result.
Cassini then gave way, wrote me a gushing, affectionate letter of congratulation, and all seemed well. The other day, however, after the
publication of the correspondence, he came to me with a face as long
as the moral law, and with ghostly solemnity said: "I have not a word
to say in regard to the matter. I only hope that my government will
accept it." He gave no explanation of these mysterious words, and I said
to him: "We made certain propositions to you; you made a reply; we
thanked you for the reply and have published it; I do not see there is
anything pending."

What they mean by it is hard to say. There are three or four hy-
potheses, but the one I most favor is that Cassini, being bitterly opposed
to the whole business and having been turned down by his government,
is suffering from a severe attack of *amour-propre froissé*. I do not see
what they can possibly do at St. Petersburg except to withdraw or
modify their letter, or to explain it away by limiting its application.
If they do that I shall be compelled to publish what Mouravieff said
to Tower while the negotiations were going on, that Russia would agree
to anything that France would agree to. When, afterwards, Tower referred to this engagement of Russia, Mouravieff flew into a passion, and
insisted upon it that Russia would never bind herself that way, that
whatever she did she would do alone and without the concurrence of
France. Still, he did say it, he did promise, and he did enter into just
that engagement. It is possible that he did so thinking that France would
not come in, and that other powers would not. If now they choose to

take a stand in opposition to the entire civilized world, we shall then make up our minds what to do about it. At present I am not bothering much.

. . . I am glad to hear continually better news about Mrs. White. All the family send love, and I am always,

Sincerely yours,
JOHN HAY.

Hay had secured guaranties of the integrity of China none too soon. Even as the last Power, Italy, announced her adherence to the Open Door policy on January 6, 1900, ominous clouds were rolling up on the Chinese horizon. The storm of the Boxer Rebellion was rapidly brewing. This was essentially a popular outburst against the foreigners who were exploiting Chinese territory at a dozen points, and it was all the more violent and explosive because of the impotence of the central government of China in Peking. In no sense a surprise, it came as a natural response to the voracity of Europe, and warning was given of its approach by a succession of local outbreaks against foreigners. The patriotic Chinese society which conducted the uprising was called by its members the "Fists of Righteous Union"—whence the name Boxers. It is impossible now to refuse some sympathy to the cause of the Boxers, but at the time their patriotic aims were obscured by the cruelty and disorder which they used, and the outbreak shook the civilized world. The United States had been given timely notice by our minister in Peking, Edwin H. Conger. He had sent frequent dispatches upon the early growth of the Boxer society, in March, 1900, he had urged our Government to make a naval demonstration in North Chinese waters unless the Peking authorities agreed to check the incipient disorders, and he reported in May that the Government either secretly sympathized with the Boxers or was afraid of them. At the beginning of June the legations in Peking were suddenly cut off and besieged by the Boxer forces. During July the siege continued. Meanwhile the Powers hastily accumulated a joint army of about 20,000 men. With the whole world in suspense, it began its march in July, and by a nip-and-tuck effort reached Peking in the middle of August and relieved the legations.

The blame for this spasmodic Chinese revolt rested upon all the European Powers which had engaged in grabbing concessions and

spheres of influence, and even now it is not easy to apportion it.
But in view of the chicanery and trickery used in Far Eastern
affairs, it was natural for each nation to suspect some neighbor of
playing a double game. White at first wrote to Hay that Russian
agents had probably egged on the Boxers. The Russian Government, he argued, wished to seize Manchuria, it saw that England
and the United States were acting in concert to prevent the partition of China, and it knew that the end of the Boer War and of
the presidential campaign of 1900 would make it possible for both
nations to take strong measures. But a week later White was writing that the British Foreign Office took a different view. It believed that Germany was at the bottom of the crisis—on the theory
that Germany was dissatisfied with Kiau-chau and wished to fish
in troubled waters for something better.[5] St. John Brodrick told
White that the Chinese upheaval had really come too soon for
Russia, which would have preferred to wait for the completion
of the Trans-Siberian Railroad before showing her hand or coming
into collision with the other Powers. These theories of double-
dealing are not convincing, but they are illuminating as to the
current conceptions of international morality. Some American leaders, as a letter from Henry Cabot Lodge showed, partook of White's
suspicions of Russia. Lodge wrote:[6]

The Chinese question is upon us with a vengeance. I have expected
it, but as always happens, it has come more suddenly than I expected
and in a totally different way. If Russia stirred up the Boxers she over-
did it, for it is evidently a great popular movement, and has resulted in
bringing all the Powers upon the scene, which is just what Russia could
not have wanted. The Administration has acted, I think, with great
wisdom, caution, and vigor. One regiment, as you know, has already
gone from Manila, two more are to go from this country, and Chaffee,
who is one of our best men, is to command. Our fleet is large, and we
can exercise a large influence in the final settlement when it comes,
which is, to my mind, of the last importance. We shall inevitably act
with England and Japan, and from indications thus far I should say
that France would be with us. If we act properly together we can prevent the absorption of China by Russia, and keep the Empire open for

[5] White to Hay, London, June 9, June 16, 1900.
[6] Lodge to White, Nahant, June 29, 1900.

our trade and commerce, which is all we want. Under these circumstances to have the country handed over to Bryan and his gang would
be a hideous misfortune, for they have no foreign policy and understand
no foreign questions.

White thought it unfortunate that the Chinese crisis occurred
in a presidential year; but Lodge assured him that this made no
difference—that nine-tenths of the country was with the Administration in its vigorous policy.

The drama of the beleaguered legations interested the American
people, as Henry Adams has said, as much as if it were a novel by
Alexandre Dumas. By the middle of July nearly every one took it
for granted that the legation staffs had been massacred. White gave
up hope along with the others. In England a memorial service for
the slain was planned in St. Paul's Cathedral. Most observers assumed that Secretary Hay's Open Door plan had been massacred
along with the legations, and that out of the turmoil in China would
emerge new schemes of partition. But Hay never lost hope for
either the foreigners in Peking or his Open Door principle. From
his asylum in New Hampshire, where a lapse in health and the heat
of Washington drove him that summer, he wrote to White in confident terms. Part of this confidence was promptly justified when
the allied relief expedition reached Peking, fought its brief battle at
the walls, and entered the city, from which the Empress Dowager
had taken her flight. "I congratulate you," wrote White,[7] "on being
the only man of any position who was right as to the foreign
ministers being alive in Peking some little time ago. I confess that
I could not bring myself to believe in that first message of Mr.
Conger's, but I rejoice that you have come out right on the subject.
It has still further enhanced the great reputation which you already
have for sagacity—I mean in Europe." There remained the question
whether the Open Door could be saved along with the diplomatists,
and for an anxious year this seemed dubious.

As our State Department had taken the initiative in obtaining
general adherence to the Open Door, so now it assumed a position
of leadership in protecting China from spoliation and destruction,
and in fixing due limits to her punishment. Secretary Hay on July

[7] White to Hay, London, August 11, 1900.

1st wrote to all the American representatives abroad that the
United States intended to remain in peace and friendship with
China, and that in helping cut short the Boxer disorders, it desired
"to ensure the permanent safety and peace of China, and to preserve
her territory and administrative entity." He was willing to exact
reparations and punishment, but he was determined to oppose to
the last any dismemberment of China. Most people thought dismemberment certain, seeing no way to prevent it; Henry Adams
"saw none and laughed at Hay for his helplessness." [8] But Hay,
undaunted, sent Rockhill to China as Special Commissioner, and
insisted that the Powers should recognize Li Hung-Chang as a
bona-fide plenipotentiary of China for the purposes of negotiation.
He had to face the prospect of all sorts of intrigues by the continental Powers. Germany objected to treating with Li Hung-Chang; the
German Government was sending out Marshal von Waldersee to
command the allied forces, and with him was going a glittering
new contingent of troops. Russia meanwhile was drawing off her
legation staff and troops from Peking, and begging the United
States and other nations to do likewise; her intention being to
undertake secret negotiations with China and ask for territorial
concessions in Manchuria on the ground that she had persuaded
the allied nations to evacuate their forces. Hay refused this Russian
invitation, for he had no desire to play the Muscovite game. A
letter which he sent to White showed how well he was aware of
the maneuvering by the other Governments:

NEWBURY, NEW HAMPSHIRE.
September 7, 1900.

MY DEAR WHITE:

I am slowly crawling back to my usual form and looking forward
with more or less dread to plunging once more into the autumnal heat
and worry of Washington.

I am sorry some of the press in England think we have changed our
point of view in China, and have taken up one more friendly to Russia
than to England. Nothing could be more erroneous. We have steadily
withstood every overture—and there have been many—on the part of
Russia and Germany for a more intimate understanding to the disadvantage of Great Britain. Germany at the time of the Shanghai matter

[8] Adams, Henry, *The Education of Henry Adams*, chap. 26.

was very pressing. But we have not given way an inch. When Russia took possession of New Chwang, I addressed a very serious inquiry to Blessbury asking what their purposes were as to permanency of occupation and as to the Open Door. I got a most positive and satisfactory reply—so far as words go. Of course we know that Russia will not be bound for an hour by promises which it is more convenient to break. But we must take care that it shall be inconvenient. As to the proposition of withdrawal from Peking: If Russia withdraws, the concert is broken by that act, and we should be very unwilling to force an alliance with Germany for the conquest of China—which is evidently what the Emperor wants. To me the most ominous feature of the situation is the understanding between Japan and Russia, of which I see many symptoms. The Emperor of Germany is trying, in his vociferous style, to give the impression that he controls the policy of Russia, but I do not believe a word of it. I was rather afraid of the contrary, but I am less so of late.

Some English papers attack me for my "guileless confidence in Li Hung-Chang." This is nonsense. We must deal with some one and he has been chosen by the government to negotiate. He is of course a great scoundrel—but I know of no Chinese saint available. I get great profit by treating him as if I believed in him, and there is no other way of dealing with Li. Our policy is still the policy of our note of the 3rd of July. We have no unavowed aims or purposes. We want to limit the war as closely as possible, and to withdraw our troops as soon as consistent with the objects for which we went there. We want no territory and should regret to see China despoiled. Above all we want the Open Door.

As to vengeance—what would glut some people? We have killed ten for one at least; we have looted and destroyed many millions of property. The story is enough to sicken a Zulu.

I am heartily glad the war in South Africa is virtually ended. I have told Del he may come home when he likes.

Yours faithfully,

J. H.

Hay and the McKinley Administration wished the American troops withdrawn at the earliest favorable moment; but they did not wish to seem forced out, or frightened out, or to lose their proper influence in the final negotiations. If they left the Germans and English in Peking, and retired with the Russians, who had already made their secret bargain with China, they would gain the resentment of the two former Powers and no help from the third.

And as Hay wrote Choate,[9] quoting from a letter Root had sent him, "the approach of the much-prepared Waldersee seemed a peril. There was danger that after all the Emperor's windy eloquence he might feel the necessity of kicking up a row to justify the appointment of Waldersee."

Ambassador Choate being absent from London during the late summer of 1900, White kept close at the embassy to deal with Chinese affairs. On September 18th he showed the Prime Minister one of Hay's letters: and although Lord Salisbury's mind was full of the approaching general elections, he chatted confidentially about China.[10] The Prime Minister thought that the first necessity was to "exhaust Waldersee"; that since the Kaiser with much bombastic speechmaking had sent over the marshal, the pair must first find that they could really do nothing in China and make themselves a bit absurd, and then a discussion of terms with the Chinese might begin. Salisbury quite agreed with Secretary Hay on the questions of dismemberment and vengeance; he would resist both to the utmost. He thought that China might be asked to furnish, as a guaranty to the future safety of the legations, a site at Taku for a little group of forts garrisoned by the Powers, to support the foreigners in Peking and to furnish a police guard in any emergency. One of Salisbury's pet aversions was the Kaiser. Now he was highly amusing, wrote White, on the subject of the vociferous German Emperor, "whom he thinks very like Li Hung-Chang, only with Li's chief characteristics more fully developed." In the retention of the troops in Peking for the time being and their withdrawal as soon as a settlement was reached, he was willing to act with the United States.

Both White and Salisbury spoke frankly of their distrust of Russia and their dislike of Germany's rather bullying Far Eastern tactics, and White closed his letter with the remark: "I have long since arrived at the conclusion that the chief aim and object of the diplomacy of these countries since the Spanish War is to break up the good understanding between this country and ours, and I

[9] Hay to Choate, Newbury, N. H., September 8, 1900. It must be remembered, in judging Germany's policy, that the German minister in Peking had been murdered by the Chinese.

[10] White to Hay, Wilton Park, September 18, 1900.

quite understand it from their point of view; for so long as Anglo-Saxondom is acting harmoniously, they are quite powerless to do very much harm."

The day of this interview was the very day on which the Kaiser issued a note that fell, as A. A. Adee said, "like a bomb in the allied camp." He proposed that as a *sine qua non* to the opening of negotiations, China should be required to hand over to the Powers the chief perpetrators of the crimes against international law committed in Peking, to be punished by the Western Governments. Of course this personal vengeance was odious to the United States. Hay at once replied to Berlin with a stern refusal. At the same time, as White ascertained in two calls upon Lord Salisbury, the British Government indicated a tacit but no less vigorous dissent; whereupon the German Emperor made a second proposal which contained no stipulation as to punishment and was acceptable. The letters of White to Hay on his conversations with Lord Salisbury are of more than usual interest in showing how the Kaiser was then regarded in London, and two extracts of some length may be given:

WHITE TO HAY, LONDON, OCTOBER 3, 1900

I have had two interviews with Lord Salisbury since I last wrote—and neither of them was of a nature to be reported in a despatch, save in the brief form in which I worded my confidential despatch of the 26th. . . .

Lord Salisbury was as usual, in the interview briefly reported by that telegram, humorous about the German Emperor and the Chinese. He commented on the extraordinary procedure of the Kaiser in throwing such a bombshell of a suggestion among the Powers without consulting anyone but said that he nevertheless wanted to save his susceptibilities as much as possible, toward which he admitted that our reply to his circular had been of considerable assistance. He emphatically stated and reiterated also that nothing would induce him to assent to a proposal to enter into no negotiations until the leaders of the Boxer outrages should be caught and handed over to the Powers, whereby he said British commerce might be seriously hampered for years—or at all events for a very considerable period, as the whole thing would end in not catching anyone probably. When I saw him he intended sending his reply "in a day or two," but he saw Hatzfeldt after me and the latter persuaded him, after learning the nature of his proposed reply, to postpone it until the opinion of McDonald [British minister to China] could be obtained as to the feasibility of the Emperor's proposal. McDonald's answer was received only yesterday afternoon, just before I again saw Lord Salisbury. Its substance, the latter told me, is that it is very easy to designate the leaders and probably all the foreign representatives at Peking would agree upon the same men; but that it will be very difficult if not impossible to catch them. He was as emphatic yesterday as on the previous Tuesday in saying that nothing would induce him to assent to the German Emperor's proposal making surrender for punishing a preliminary to negotiations.

WHITE TO HAY, LONDON, OCTOBER 5, 1900

I went to see Sanderson. . . . Sanderson took occasion to tell me that this government had availed themselves of the German Emperor's modified proposal just issued to telegraph and accept it, being glad to get anything feasible from him, and that they had telegraphed McDonald to act upon its lines. I also gathered from him that no answer will now be necessary to the Emperor's proposal of September 17th making punishment a preliminary to negotiations. There is no doubt that your reply to that proposal followed by the information derived from Lord Salisbury by Hatzfeldt as to the answer England would send made the Emperor climb down, as he undoubtedly has done, and doubtless Hatzfeldt and the German Foreign Office are proud of having eased off the British answer until it should no longer be necessary to send it. I have no doubt that they would rather have done almost anything than have the world know that we and England had refused the Emperor's proposal in identical terms which was, as I have written and telegraphed you, Lord Salisbury's intention. Thus you have again been leading the concert of the Powers.

Hay naturally replied to these communications in good spirits. With Salisbury supporting him, he had checked the Kaiser and the prospects for preserving the Open Door seemed brighter and brighter. Again he sent White an almost gay letter:

DEPARTMENT OF STATE, WASHINGTON,
October 16th, 1900.

MY DEAR WHITE:
I have a thousand things to talk to you about, but impossible to do it today. I write especially to ask you to buy for me a bag like the historic

one which you gave me before I left London, neither of us knowing how weighty its contents were to be in the future. I want one for Adee about Christmas time. Have the name A. A. Adee stamped on it.

What you say about your conversations with the great Cecil is most interesting to me. The success we had in stopping the first preposterous German movement when the whole world seemed likely to join it, when the entire press of the Continent and a great many on this side were in favor of it, will always be a source of gratification to me. The German Government, which is generally brutal but seldom silly, recovered its senses, climbed down off its perch, and presented another proposition which was exactly in line with our own position.

I own I am amazed at Smalley. I find in the despatches in the London *Times* of the 4th of October that he says our rejection of the first proposition was due to timidity, and our acceptance of the second to a desire to ingratiate ourselves with the Powers. I cannot imagine where he gets these idiotic impressions unless by reading the yellow journals at the clubs. Everything seemed to be going well until this promenade of Waldersee's to Tao Ping, which I fear will have very unfavorable results upon the rest of China. The great viceroys, to secure whose assistance was our first effort and our first success, have been standing by us splendidly for the last four months. How much longer they can hold their turbulent populations quiet in the face of these constant incitements to disturbance which Germany and Russia are giving is hard to conjecture.

Yours faithfully,
JOHN HAY.

Meanwhile, Senator Lodge was sending letter after letter on the situation to White, expressing his approval of Hay's course and his dissatisfaction that Great Britain should be so slow to support the American Government in the protection of China. At this White expostulated. While he admitted that Great Britain was not precipitate, he argued that she would act in her own good time in harmony with the United States. It is impossible, in reading Lodge's correspondence, to avoid the impression that throughout this period of his life he had an ineradicable prejudice against the British. "What is the matter with England?" he querulously demanded on September 3rd. "It seems as if the Ministry had completely lost its wits and utterly failed to understand the situation in China. Our policy . . . is to prevent a partition of the Empire, set up a decent

government under proper guarantees, and keep an open market
for all China, and this obviously is the policy which England
wants, yet instead of standing by us and insisting on this policy she
seems to be perfectly helpless and not to know what to do." This,
as the British action early in October showed, was rather unfair.
White and the march of events persuaded Lodge of the fact, but
he was still irritable. "What I criticized," he grumbled to White a
month later,[11] "was the vacillation and uncertainty which seemed
to characterize all British action. They ought to have been with
us at the start instead of coming in after we had forced the hand
of the Powers. I do not think that anyone here has any confidence
in the friendship of Russia, and I have no doubt that they are
going to hold on to Manchuria. At the same time our policy is to
prevent the partition of China and retain the open market. In order
to attain this object it was essential to bring the war to an end,
prevent the breakdown of the Chinese Government, and get them
into such shape that we could treat with them and secure a general
agreement. What I wanted was that England should have been
with us at the beginning instead of at the end." Lodge's influence
in the party and Senate and his position on the Foreign Relations
Committee made his attitude important, and White felt it part of
his duty in promoting Anglo-American amity to dispel the miscon-
ceptions which Lodge too easily formed.

One by one the various crises in the Chinese situation were met
and passed. The Russian proposal that the United States withdraw
its troops from Peking was thrust aside by Hay, despite the fact that
President McKinley for a time wished to get out with the least
possible delay. Germany's proposal for punishment of the criminal
leaders was supported by France, Austria, and Italy, while Japan
straddled; but it was vetoed by the United States, Great Britain,
and Russia. Then came a new development, the Anglo-German
agreement of October 16, 1900, which fortunately turned out to
be unimportant. This provided for the Open Door in China, and

[11] Lodge to White, Nahant, October 6, 1900. Lodge added some political
comments. "I think McKinley will be elected by a larger electoral majority
than before, but there is so much at stake that I am profoundly anxious. The
campaign generally is looking well except in Indiana, whence come disquieting reports."

pledged the two countries to take no advantage of her troubles to secure territorial gains for themselves. The third article declared that if another Power should press China for territorial advantages under any form whatever, Germany and Great Britain might consult with each other and take what steps were necessary to protect their own interests. Hay was pleased by the general agreement, but he was concerned lest the third article might conceal some secret understanding. White, after talking with Foreign Office officials, sent him a reassuring word: [12]

As regards the third clause about which you are inquiring, Eric Barrington says that it means just what it says—that is, precious little; in fact, he spoke of the whole agreement as not half so important as it sounds and as the Continent seems disposed to make it out. Old Tommy Sanderson says its meaning is this: that if any Power (Russia being probably referred to) should seize territory, England, Germany, and the other Powers assenting to the agreement should not do likewise nor take any steps until they had conferred together; in fact, that such seizure by one Power should not cause a rush on the part of all the others for a slice of land also.

Meanwhile, in far-off Peking, still garrisoned by the troops of six Powers, the diplomatic corps was endeavoring throughout November and December to agree upon demands to be laid before the Chinese Government, as represented by Li Hung-Chang and Prince Ching. This difficult task was not made any easier by the delays and bother of cabling to six different capitals. The German Government, with that brutality which Hay ascribed to it, proposed that an "irrevocable condition" should be laid down, requiring the Chinese authorities to put certain specified persons, including several princes of the blood, to death, and this proposal was supported by France. The Americans, British, Japanese, and Russians successfully opposed it. Then the Germans proposed another "irrevocable condition"—the severe punishment of these leaders named. Hay objected to the word "irrevocable" as savoring too much of an ultimatum, which he and McKinley disliked. Unfortunately for him, this objection was nullified by an exceptionally irritating accident

[12] White to Hay, October 27, 1900.

of diplomacy. He sent White an account of the accident, marked "very confidential," which if only as a diverting tragi-comic incident is worth preserving. Wrote Hay: [13]

Just three weeks ago Conger [the American minister to Peking] wired us that the joint note was ready to sign, on the terms at last agreed on, after infinite labor. He sent us a copy of it in which the word "irrevocable" did not appear. He said the majority of his colleagues wished to retain it, but would yield, if we insisted. I instantly wired him, "Sign joint note as transmitted." I had an instinctive fear of the cipher and so avoided all mention of the objectionable word. Now what does fate do but change one digit of the group meaning "transmitted" so that Conger read it "majority." It made no sense, was incoherent and ungrammatical, but the unhappy Conger, instead of asking us to repeat the telegram, jumped at the conclusion that it was an authorization for him to make a graceful concession to the "majority" of his colleagues, and ran cackling around to them with the agreeable news. So for ten days we heard nothing—thought everything was satisfactorily arranged—while all the ministers were getting authority from their governments to sign the note with "irrevocable" restored to the text. England held out, but was reported by the press to be insisting on the *retention* of the word. At last, as the result of frantic inquiries at London and Peking, I found out the facts. I instantly wired a sharp instruction to Conger to undo his mistake, and I asked England to persist in the course she was pursuing. But it was too late. Conger told me it was impossible to make his colleagues change again. England had at last given way and ordered Satow to sign. Peking and London both said that delay would endanger everything, and that as we had gained our other points, "irrevocable" was no longer harmful. Still I held out, and once more ordered Conger to insist. I held up the signature three days— at the end of which Conger wired he had done his utmost, and that the whole negotiation would fall if we refused to sign. All the others had already signed. Finally Rockhill, in whose judgment I have great confidence, cabled me that no other course was possible than to sign— that the conditions were ominous and delay highly dangerous. So I had to give Conger the final order.

It is maddening, but when your tools break in your hands and electricity goes back on you, *que voulez-vous?* I now find we are not

[13] Hay to White, Washington, December 23; Hay sent the same letter to a newspaper friend.

FOUR ENGLISH FRIENDS

Arthur J. Balfour
Lord Salisbury

St. John Brodrick
Sir Julian Pauncefote

alone in our troubles. Both Pichon and Satow misunderstood their instructions, and only after Pichon had signed did Delcassé learn the facts.

The press, or part of it, criticized Hay severely. And Hay accepted the censure meekly, for as he said, bad luck is, and must be, punished more harshly than intentional sin.

Thus the note of the Powers to China, defining the preliminaries of negotiation, was finally ready as 1900 closed—and in the nick of time, for as Rockhill had cabled Hay, the situation was growing dangerous. The bellicose Germans were ready to indulge in punitive military expeditions, which offered an opportunity for loot and adventure, and they were supported by other Powers.[14] On the side of peace, the Americans, British, and Japanese were drawing into one camp. On the side of continued war, the Germans, Russians, and French, with their satellites, were forming another group. There was also danger that some Power would undertake separate negotiations with China. It was still necessary for the United States to stand up boldly for Chinese integrity, and she did so with such success that even Russia's assumption of a position of recognized supremacy in Manchuria was for the time being prevented. The troublesome Waldersee was recalled in May, 1901. Finally, on September 7, 1901, the terms agreed on by the Powers and China were formally signed at Peking; terms which provided for apologies to various of the Powers, indemnities, the punishment of the Boxer leaders, the razing of the Taku forts, and so on, but which left the Open Door doctrine still alive and effective. It had survived two years of turmoil, but its future was dubious.

White was intensely interested in all this and pleased at the almost perfect harmony between England and America upon Chinese policy. He had called once on Lord Salisbury when part of the British press was criticizing Hay's policy, and found "not a shadow of foundation for the suggestion that this government shares the feeling expressed in certain newspapers as to our line in China. He pronounced it absolute 'bosh' and considers that the two governments are in perfect accord." This substantial agreement of England and America was the strongest support which the Open Door had.

[14] Dennis, A. L. P., *Adventures in American Diplomacy*, p. 240 ff.

Of subsequent events in the Far East White was an inactive rather than active observer. An inexorable chain of circumstances led to the eclipse and humiliation of Russia and the rise of Japan as the dominant Oriental power. The failure of the selfish and designing Russian Government to carry out its promises to evacuate Manchuria; the growing friction between the Russians there and the Japanese in Korea; the signing (January 30, 1902) of the Anglo-Japanese alliance; the rising impatience of Japan as Russia refused to settle the Manchurian question; and finally, in February, 1904, the outbreak of the Russo-Japanese War—all these events concerned the United States but slightly. Hay's policy was to hold aloof from the Russo-Japanese quarrel. Our course was to bide our time, do what we could for the Open Door, and see whether Japan could really defeat the Russian colossus.

However, White's correspondence with Hay on the crowded events of these years contains much that is interesting. He saw at once, as few other American diplomatists did, the profound importance of the Anglo-Japanese alliance in its bearing upon the future balance of the world. He kept his eye in 1903-04 upon the boiling Oriental pot, and made sure that Hay was informed even of rumors. When in 1903 he congratulated Hay upon the progress he had made in having the Manchurian ports of Mukden and Antung opened to commerce, he added that the outlook for peace seemed ominous. "There is considerable anxiety here all the time about Manchuria," he wrote, "and especially at a report which seems to be credited that Russia is pouring more troops into the province and that Japan is making constant preparations for war. It is difficult to discriminate between the different rumors, and there is always the feeling that Russia has no compunction about going back upon solemn promises and assurances when it suits her." It was a pity, in White's opinion, that the United States was still in the grip of the Civil War legend about Russia's special friendship for her. The Government in St. Petersburg and its ambassador in Washington, Cassini, he thoroughly distrusted.

This distrust was shared by Secretary Hay. His letters to White are full of it. When Russia in 1903 tried to force seven demands upon China as conditions to the evacuation of Manchuria, and the

United States lodged a protest, the Russians attempted to wriggle out of the affair. Hay wrote to White in caustic terms:

I have not seen Cassini for several days. He is in a great state of nervous agitation and depression on account of, first, the Manchuria matter, and now, the Kishineff massacre. He has been talking very indiscretely for publication, and, in consequence, the American press are after him in full cry, the most savage attacks emanating from the unhappy and persecuted Jews. I get, of course, my share of abuse for not launching a *brutum fulmen* against Russia; but when I have a chance to talk with one of the Jews in private, he is unable to tell me what possible advantage it will be to the Jews or to this country to make remarks to Russia about the massacre, and be told to mind our own business and control our own mobs.

The Manchurian matter is far more delicate and more troublesome. Russia, as you know, has given us the most positive assurance that the famous "convention of seven points" never existed. We have a verbatim copy of it as it was presented, with preamble and appendix, by M. Plançon to the Chinese Government. If they choose to disavow Plançon, and to discontinue their attempts to violate their agreements, we shall be all right; but, if the lie they have told was intended to serve only a week or two, the situation will become a serious one.

Till the last moment our minister in Peking, Mr. Conger, labored to obtain promises from China regarding commercial freedom which the Russians blocked, while our representatives in St. Petersburg put up an equally futile fight to protect American interests in Manchuria. When finally Japan struck and the war was on, the American Government had no sympathy for Russia. Roosevelt wrote appreciatively that the Japs had shown themselves past masters of David Harum's famous gloss on the "Do unto others" injunction— "They did it fust!" There was equally little sympathy in Great Britain. White saw Lord Lansdowne in February, 1904, just as hostilities were beginning. "He seemed much gratified," wrote White to Hay, "to know that public opinion in our country is in such entire accord with British feeling on the Far Eastern question, and he does not think that England is likely to be drawn into the war." Lansdowne added confidentially that from what he had heard, an attempt would soon be made to induce the United States to mediate or offer its friendly services. France would first be approached as the nearest friend of Russia, and she would probably ask England to bring pressure to bear on the Japanese; but as England could not place herself in the position of advising her ally to withdraw her rightful claims in the Orient, the next step would be to persuade Washington to act. Within the next few weeks Hay made inquiries and discussed the subject of mediation with Takahira, Cassini, Speck von Sternburg, and Jusserand. He notified White late in May that he had learned that both sides would resent any interference.[15]

In letter after letter Hay expressed his irritation with Russian policy and with the tactics pursued by Cassini.[16] Even as Russia was being beaten in successive engagements, he feared, as he wrote White, that she was planning some sculduggery. For example:

DEPARTMENT OF STATE, WASHINGTON,
May 5th, 1904.

MY DEAR HARRY:

I answered this morning by wire your telegram of yesterday. On the 29th of April Cassini came to me in great distress of mind, fearing, or pretending to fear, that China was going to join with the Japanese against Russia. A long experience in Russian diplomacy has not yet sufficiently educated me to make me sure when they are in a panic or when they are simulating a terror for diplomatic reasons. It is altogether possible that they fear a fire in the rear from General Ma, and it is also possible that, with the singular dual construction of their minds, they may be at the same time scared to death and absolutely sure of a complete final victory. In the latter case, after they have annexed Manchuria and Korea and dictated a peaceful disarmament in Tokio, they may think it may be handy to have in the house a pretext of grievance against China. In any case, I felt it would do no harm to comply with their urgent request, and I instructed Mr. Conger to impress once more upon Prince Ching the vital necessity of observing strict neutrality, and

[15] Hay to White, Washington, May 24, 1904.

[16] For example, Hay in March was irritated because, following the sending of American consuls to Mukden and Antung in accordance with the American treaty with China, some Russian newspapers protested against their errand. "It is utterly impossible for us to please the Russians, especially in the present circumstances. Every time they get a kick from Japan, instead of kicking back, they begin to whimper and whine that it is our fault."

giving to neither party any just ground of offence. I received yesterday, as I wired you this morning, a report from Mr. Conger that the Chinese Government was determined to observe strict neutrality.

The words and deeds of the Russians in this crisis afford a subject of interesting study, both from the point of view of psychology and politics. Cassini, especially, showed up very well under these trying circumstances. The air of flippancy with which he welcomed the prospect of war has entirely gone, but he preserves a dignified and philosophic attitude in the midst of the misfortunes of the Russian arms. Every time they meet with a reverse, he simply says that it will make the war longer, and at the end there will be a more thorough rearrangement of the attitude of the two powers. He never admits for an instant the possibility of anything but a complete Russian triumph. . . .

Yours faithfully,
John Hay.

A little later he was writing that "The most important thing on hand with Cassini just now is that a Japanese *attaché* went to a dinner party and said *banzai*. I do not think the Count regards it as a *casus belli*, but something perilously near."

The constant interchange of letters between White and Hay on Far Eastern topics had for its main object the harmonization, so far as they could effect it, of British and American policy in that part of the world. White could at least see that the Secretary of State understood the English view, and that the British leaders understood Hay. Roosevelt was frequently impatient with British policy, regarding it as hesitant and confused, but thanks to White's rôle as informant and mediator, any sharp disagreement was avoided.

Chapter Twelve

Canada and the Alaskan Boundary Quarrel

FROM Great Britain, as we have seen, the United States gained all the concessions it required for building the Panama Canal. In the Far East it worked in harmonious coöperation with Great Britain. These were years, thanks to Hay and Salisbury, of a decided Anglo-American rapprochement. The massy foundations were being laid which made possible a union of effort in the World War, and the victory of the Allies in the greatest struggle of modern times. But there were points at which the two nations came into serious conflict and which caused long weeks of worry, fuming, and search for expedients, long months and even years of negotiation, before a settlement was reached. Two issues, one affecting half-frozen Alaska and the other tropical Venezuela, and both closely observed by White, require examination in some detail.

There are several reasons why the Alaskan boundary dispute is one of the most interesting episodes of these years. It is interesting in its origin, for its immediate cause lay in the Klondike gold discoveries of 1896-97. There was a wild rush to this remote corner of northwest Canada, adjoining Alaska. A population of 30,000 sprang up within a few years, and gold-hunters found that the easiest route to the fields lay through the southern strip of Alaska by way of Dyea and Skagway. Questions of jurisdiction at once arose, for no boundary line had been surveyed between the coastal strip and British Columbia. The dispute is interesting, again, as revealing the growing national consciousness of Canada. Canadians were ready to insist on partial control of their own foreign affairs, and the British Government felt constrained to grant them a decided voice in the question. Finally, it is interesting because of the brusqueness with which the American Government insisted upon having its own way. Washington would yield nothing, and in the end the United States, to the chagrin of Canada, won every contention.

As we have seen, at first the Alaskan boundary question was

wrapped with a number of others, such as the sealing dispute and the Newfoundland fisheries dispute, for blanket settlement by an Anglo-American Joint High Commission, which contained American, British, and Canadian members.[1] Indeed, to this body were hopefully referred no fewer than twelve controversies. It was not a happy method of treating important questions. Neither side showed a conciliatory temper, and John W. Foster of the American panel and Lord Herschell of the British group were decidedly contentious. A good many Americans believed, like President Polk when the Oregon question was pending in the 'forties, that John Bull had to be faced belligerently. "I do not agree with you about the Foster dispatch," wrote Senator Lodge to White when in 1897 John W. Foster had published a brusque note to the British commissioners on the sealing question.[2] "It was able and I admit rough, but we can never get anything from England, not even attention, unless we are rough. She has only herself to thank for our tone."

Under these circumstances, on the main issues a deadlock rapidly developed. On the sealing question, the British and Canadians would have consented to prohibit deep-sea sealing if the United States had agreed to pay the Canadians a large money compensation, but the United States refused. On the Newfoundland fisheries question, Canada would have agreed to recognize the old American privileges in return for the free entry of Canadian fish into the American market, but here again the United States stood fast.[3] As for the Alaskan boundary, in essence the Canadians and British wanted a compromise, while the Americans declared they would yield nothing.

In the closing days of 1898 White received letters from Senator Lodge and Secretary Hay, both denouncing Lord Herschell as "cantankerous" and "the principal obstacle to a favorable arrangement." Lord Salisbury, Arthur Balfour, and Joseph Chamberlain, complained Hay, had all given private assurances that Herschell would be used to bring the Canadian commissioners to reasonable terms; instead, wrote Lodge, he is "technical, sharp, often violent." Both men wished White to give the British Government a strong

[1] Dennis, A. L. P., *Adventures in American Diplomacy*, p. 134.
[2] Lodge to White, November 19, 1897.
[3] Lord Herschell's Memorandum to Senator Fairbanks, December 21, 1898.

hint on the subject. White at once used the most open kind of diplomacy. He wrote frankly to the Colonial Secretary, Joseph Chamberlain, saying that he had heard from high authority in Washington that Lord Herschell was impracticable; and in return he got an equally frank letter defending Herschell and attacking some of the American members, notably Foster. When Hay heard of this interchange he was somewhat ruffled. His letter is indorsed by White as "the nearest approach to a rebuke I ever received from him." "I must confess," he wrote,[4] "it gave me a little shiver to see all those things in black and white. *Litera scripta manet*—and I imagine that sooner or later Herschell will see your letter. My idea was rather to place you in possession of the facts so that, by confidential conversation, you might perhaps induce people in London to suggest that Lord Herschell should moderate somewhat the keenness of his lawyer-like zeal." From this time forward the breakdown of the negotiations was seen to be almost inevitable.

The Alaskan question, by far the most serious of those involved, was an outgrowth of the vague terms of an Anglo-Russian treaty of 1825 which stated that the boundary of southern Alaska—the long coastal extension—should follow the crests of the mountains in such a fashion as to leave Russia a territorial strip thirty miles wide along the coast. But the coast was highly irregular and pierced by deep inlets. The question was whether this boundary should traverse the mouths of the inlets, or run inland behind them. Some of the inlets possessed valuable harbors and led to passes reaching the interior. The Canadians, of course, maintained that the boundary should run across the inlets, leaving their heads and ports in Canadian possession, and the United States of course denied this.

The most important of the inlets which penetrate more than thirty miles was the Lynn Canal, which runs nearly a hundred miles into the mainland. Towards its northerly end it splits into two narrow forks, the waters of which, deep between high white stone cliffs, crowned with firs, lead to the principal landings on this part of the coast. The Lynn Canal thus forms two harbors. On one lie the two towns of Dyea and Skagway, closely adjacent to each other and marking the entrances to the parallel passes known as the Chilkoot and Skagway. The other and less frequented

[4] Hay to White, Washington, January 10, 1899.

harbor, called Pyramid Harbor, gives access by a third pass to the Dalton Trail, which leads to Fort Selkirk, some 250 miles distant. Over the Skagway Trail, by which it was only forty miles to the first navigable waters of the interior, a railway was built in 1898-1900 to the head of navigation on the Yukon. The Canadian contention was that all the landing-places, lying well beyond what they regarded as the thirty-mile limit, were in Canadian territory. But badly as Canada wanted the deeper inlets, Hay was emphatic that she had no shadow of a right to them. He wrote to White:[5]

In the case of Alaska, it is hard to treat with patience the claim set up by Lord Herschell that virtually the whole coast belongs to England, leaving us only a few jutting promontories without communication with each other. Without going into the historical or legal argument, as a mere matter of common sense it is impossible that any nation should ever have conceded, or any nation have accepted, the cession of such a ridiculous and preposterous boundary line. We are absolutely driven to the conclusion that Lord Herschell put forward a claim that he had no belief or confidence in, for the mere purpose of trading it off for something substantial. And yet, the slightest suggestion that his claim is unfounded throws him into a fury.

Lord Herschell and his Canadian colleagues made one demand in particular. They suggested that even if Dyea and Skagway were denied to Canada on one branch of the Lynn Canal, on the other she should be allowed the port of Pyramid Harbor, with a connecting corridor of land behind. This, they argued, would save the Dominion from being cut off here entirely from the sea, while it would cost the United States almost nothing; for the port and strip were of use only for the purpose of passage into Canadian territory. But such a concession the American commissioners flatly refused to grant. "We are ready to compromise the boundary," Lodge wrote to White,[6] with a rather elastic use of the word compromise, "by giving them access to the sea and a free port with places for their buildings, etc., but no territorial sovereignty. We will not assent to breaking our coast line with another Halifax or Esquimault, and as what they want is access to the sea and a free port, this is more than a fair promise, for under the Russian treaty they

[5] Hay to White, Washington, January 3, 1899; "personal and confidential."
[6] Lodge to White, Washington, January 7, 1899.

have not, as regards the Alaskan boundary question, a leg to stand on. Their whole case is manufactured." Lodge was vexed that the negotiations should be blocked in this way, for, as he said, Anglo-American amity and coöperation were becoming an object of the greatest moment in China. "It is most important, with a view to our general relations in the East, which are of infinitely greater importance than all these Canadian difficulties put together, that the two countries should arrive at some agreement, even if it is only a partial one, with a view to its effect upon other Powers. Russia is watching these negotiations here with the utmost close-ness, and with a hardly concealed anxiety that they should fail. At the same time Russia is going out of her way just now to make herself conciliatory and pleasant to us."

In an effort to dispose of all the issues together, the British Gov-ernment suggested early in February, 1899, that the other disputes might be adjusted if the United States would only agree to arbitrate the Alaskan boundary, providing an umpire "to insure certainty and finality." The Clayton-Bulwer treaty would be revised, all the petty irritations about fisheries and sealing would be brushed aside, and the two nations could then act with the utmost cordiality in both Oriental and Occidental affairs. It was a tempting suggestion, but Hay refused his consent. He was confident that the Americans had a perfect case upon the Alaskan boundary, he believed they should maintain their stand unshaken, and he feared that the foreign umpire on an arbitral tribunal would bring in a compromise de-cision, sacrificing the fair legal rights of the United States. As a counter offer, the American commissioners proposed that the boundary question should be submitted to the six jurists, three on each side, without any umpire. When the British refused, the nego-tiations temporarily ended, (February 22, 1899). Hay wrote to White in some chagrin:[7]

I am sure you will see on a diligent reading of the last few pages [of the final Protocol] that our commissioners went to the very verge of concessions to induce the Canadians to make a treaty. They refused to consider any form of arbitration, except that which they themselves proposed. Even the scheme that Lord Salisbury and Sir Julian thought so well of—that is, three arbitrators on a side—they entirely refused to

[7] Hay to White, Washington, February 21, 1899.

consider, and finally they refused to consider the proposition to isolate the Alaskan question and to agree upon all the rest, leaving that open for future negotiations, although much progress had been made in the discussion of the other matters that an agreement was, in almost every one of them, almost in sight. . . . My only explanation of their obstinate refusal to agree to close up matters is that they prefer to stand alone before the Canadian Parliament in the attitude of stout defenders of Canadian rights and interests rather than as signers of a treaty which would not meet the views of their advanced supporters.

In another letter he put this view still more sharply:

The Canadian matter is in a nutshell this: Laurier preferred to pose before his Parliament as a stout defender of Canadian rights and interests against Yankee selfishness, rather than have the trouble to defend himself against the attacks of the Opposition for having made a just and reasonable treaty—which was within his reach. Our people went as far, in the way of concession, as even I could have wished—but there was no real desire among the Canadians to have matters closed.

A *modus vivendi* line being arranged that fall, the whole Alaskan dispute was allowed to drift for several years. This temporary line met the principal American contentions and was satisfactory to Hay. "I shall be savagely attacked on the Pacific Coast, as a matter of course," he wrote White,[8] "but on the other hand we have pushed the Canadians back fifteen miles from tidewater, and drawing the line north of Klukwan we have got them even away from canoe navigation." The whole Lynn Canal, under this arrangement, was held under American sovereignty, the boundary on the Dyea and Skagway trails being fixed along the summits of the Chilkoot and White passes. The rights and privileges of the citizens of each country received a mutual guaranty. It was a good working arrangement, for it was fairly obvious that time was on the side of the United States. The American Government remained as determined as ever to hold its own interpretation of the Anglo-Russian treaty; the Canadian Government, on the other hand, became less and less inclined to insist on its extreme stand. The outlook immensely pleased Henry Cabot Lodge, always an intense nationalist, who wrote to White that he was glad to see Canada given her

[8] Hay to White, Newbury, N. H., September 9, 1899.

deserts.[9] "England may as well make up her mind that she will get no more, for the feeling is that all the rights are ours, and that she is trying, very unwisely as I think, to crowd us. She let the accepted time go by last winter, and she will never, I believe, get as good terms as our commissioners were then ready to concede."

During 1900 and 1901 the question of the Alaskan boundary was allowed to rest. When Roosevelt succeeded McKinley, he felt that there was no urgency about the issue, and said to Ambassador Choate in January, 1902, "Let sleeping dogs lie." But it was nevertheless desirable that the controversy be given a final settlement, and White was the instrument by which it was reopened in the early summer of 1902. The opportunity appeared suddenly and almost by accident. It happened in June that both Sir Wilfred Laurier, the Prime Minister of Canada, and Lord Minto, the Governor-General, were in London. White went to see the former, and reported the result to Secretary Hay.

WHITE TO HAY, LONDON, JUNE 28, 1902

My chief object in today's letter is to report an interview I had a few days ago with Sir Wilfred Laurier, whom I went to see as an act of courtesy, having known him before. I had of course no idea of alluding to the Alaskan boundary question, but I had not been with him many minutes before he introduced the subject by saying: "I wish you would help me to settle the Alaska boundary question, which is full of danger, if left open, owing to the possibility of gold being found there at any moment." This enabled me to say in reply, that as he had mentioned the subject, I might say that I had recently been informed from a non-official source (thinking of what I wrote you that Cabot had written me) that his government is most anxious to settle the question by adopting our view but that they had been prevented doing so by the government here—all of which Sir Wilfred said is of course nonsense, which I knew it must be. He went on, however, to say that he is a practical man and knows that it will be impossible to turn us out of Skagway, however much the Canadians may believe—as he does believe—that it is in their territory, and that what he would like is an arbitration in order to "save his face," so to speak, vis-à-vis his people; his idea being that if the arbitrators were to decide that our view of the boundary is correct, there would be an end to the whole business (which I gathered

[9] Lodge to White, November 19, 1899.

he would not regret) and he could say that he had done his best for them. If on the other hand the arbitrators should decide that our view was not the correct interpretation of the treaty, Canada would be entitled to compensation elsewhere, either in land or in *money*, for the Skagway district, which he fully admits can never be restored to Canada. I said to him that of course I had no authority to discuss the matter with him, but should take due note of what he had said, and meanwhile I might say that our view as to the boundary question is embodied in a note from Mr. Choate of two years ago or thereabouts, to which no answer had yet been received. He said he remembered reading it, and had at once sent a reply to this Government which he had imagined they had duly sent to us, in respect of which I of course told him he was mistaken.

Just about this time Michael Herbert, the new ambassador, was announced, and I left him and Sir Wilfred together. I take it that the latter is really anxious to settle the matter and will go as far as he can in the way of concessions which he can make his people swallow toward the end. The suggestion of financial compensation is to me a new one. At all events I transmit what he said. He added that he is well aware of your difficulties in respect to the Senate, with any negotiation of that kind. I have not yet seen Minto, who is also here and may speak on the subject when we meet. If he does I shall send you a summary of what he says. Meanwhile, Herbert is seeing Minto, Laurier, and Lansdowne, on the subject, and when he arrives, which he hopes to do in September (latter part), he will be in a position to discuss the matter with you.

This letter, indicating that both Laurier and Lansdowne wished to have the boundary settled and showing that Laurier had lost hope of obtaining the Lynn Canal, caused a stir in the State Department. Secretary Hay sent it to President Roosevelt with a note pointing out its significance. Before Lord Minto sailed back, White had a full talk with him, which he summarized for Hay's benefit. The Governor-General expressed the hope that some compromise might be arranged with regard to the southern portion of the boundary; but when White told him that he believed no American concessions would be possible, he did not seem surprised.[10] Thus the matter stood when Sir Michael Herbert became ambassador.

[10] White to Hay, London, August 12, 1902.

As White had said in his letters to Hay, Herbert expected to
make every effort to close the dispute. His success was destined to
be the chief monument to his tragically brief ambassadorship. He
held long discussions with Hay, a treaty took shape, and on January 23, 1903, it was signed. Sir Michael, as Hay put it, wished
to signalize his promotion, Laurier was willing to consent, and
though when the treaty went to the Senate, Cullom and some
others "kicked awhile," the arrangement was ratified in February.
It was substantially the same solution which Great Britain had
rejected three years earlier. A joint commission of "six impartial
jurists of repute" was to be appointed, three on each side—with no
umpire. The British-Canadian members, when the time came, were
selected according to the terms of the agreement—Lord Alverstone,
the Lord Chief Justice of England; Sir Louis Jette, formerly of
the Quebec Supreme Court; and A. B. Aylesworth, a respected
barrister of Ontario. President Roosevelt could have chosen similar
men in America. But he had no intention of running any risks.
The result was that, after the gesture of inviting Supreme Court
justices to act, he named as our panel Secretary of War Root,
Senator Lodge, and Senator Turner of Washington. These were
our "impartial jurists"! The announcement of their names caused
a burst of American laughter mingled with criticism. The Brooklyn
Eagle remarked that the chance of Canadian success before this
tribunal was about equal to the chance of a "thaw in Hades." The
Springfield *Republican* said that three less impartial men could
not have been found. In Canada there was an outburst of anger.[11]
England showed a milder resentment, which White described in a
letter to Hay:[12]

I am sorry to tell you that although nothing has been said officially to
Mr. Choate about our appointments to the Alaska Arbitration Tribunal,
they have caused a good deal of embarrassment and some dismay as well
as great surprise. Chamberlain spoke to me quite seriously on the subject yesterday, and said that he feared very much, now, that the whole
scheme will prove abortive. Canada of course has been making great

[11] "It was largely political," wrote Lodge to White, and it also arose from
the fact, he believed, that the Canadians knew they really had no case.—Lodge
to White, Washington, March 15, 1903.
[12] White to Hay, London, April 1, 1903.

protests on the subject, and it is very difficult—not to say impossible—for the British Government to maintain that Cabot is an "impartial jurist of repute" or that Root or Turner are impartial in the sense required by the treaty, the former being a member of the Government which maintains the fallacy of the Canadian claim, and the latter a well-known opponent thereof, like all the other inhabitants of his section of the country. Chamberlain was quite ready to admit that many people in this country consider we are quite right, and that our claim is so strong (as of course it is) as to be irrefutable, but for that very reason he said it would have been so much easier (and would have commanded so much more confidence) if we had appointed judges or lawyers who were not connected with the Government or who had not committed themselves publicly against the Canadian claim. He added that had our appointments been of this nature the British Government would have insisted upon two of their three members being from this country; whereas, under existing circumstances, had he been left alone he said he would have allowed the Canadians to appoint all three. Of course I consider the difficulty of getting anything through the Senate, and I only mention these facts because I think you ought to know what is being said and felt here in the matter.

From the outset it was realized on both sides that while all six men were called arbitrators, the real arbitrator would be Lord Alverstone.[13] The three Americans would stand tenaciously on al-

[13] Hay replied to White that he could well understand the British objections to the American appointees, "but the President thought it was impossible to get the treaty through the Senate without the earnest and devoted assistance of Lodge and Turner and of the groups which they represented." Root he believed to be unexceptionable; next to Choate he was the first lawyer in America, and a statesman as well. "Of course, the presence of Lodge on the Tribunal is from many points of view regrettable, and as if the devil were inspiring him, he took occasion last week to make a speech in Boston, one-half of it filled with abuse of the Canadians and the other half of it filled with attacks on the State Department. He is a clever man and a man of a great deal of force in the Senate, but the infirmity of his mind and character is that he never sees but one subject at a time, and just at present it is the acceptability of his son-in-law to the voters of Gloucester. Of course, you know his very intimate relations with the President, which make it almost impossible that the President should deny him anything he has to give him, and he insisted upon this appointment on the tribunal." Hay deeply regretted that the justices of the Supreme Court had refused to serve on the tribunal.—Hay to White, Washington, April 10, 1903.

most every point, the two Canadians would be equally firm for the Dominion's claim, and the Lord Chief Justice would have to decide.

The American Government pinned its faith on Lord Alverstone's fairness—and on his response to some plain hints as to America's determination to have her way. "Everything," wrote Hay, "now depends on whether Lord Alverstone goes on the bench with an imperative mandate or not. If he goes there with an open mind, we consider our case won." White did not at all like the American appointments; he had particularly wished to have Choate named as a member of the tribunal, for he felt that it was necessary to bring a tactful form of pressure against Lord Alverstone. "I do not disguise my anxiety as to the outcome of the sitting of the tribunal," [14] he wrote, "and I very much fear that even Mr. Choate himself could not have made Lord Alverstone take upon himself the responsibility of being alone in differing from the views of the other British Commissioners and siding with us against them. I am hoping for an opportunity of letting him know privately our view of the situation, which is that we have consented to the arbitration in order to afford this country a loophole to escape from an untenable position (which Laurier as good as admitted it to be to me in private conversation last year), but no such opportunity has yet presented itself, and of course it would be a very delicate operation at best to do so, with a man like Lord Alverstone." He made up his mind to have a good confidential talk with his old friend Arthur Balfour, who had become Prime Minister in 1902, and he did so. From this time forward, indeed, he kept in close touch with members of the British Government, and lost no opportunity of impressing upon them the American attitude.

The sittings were to be held in London; and various Canadian and British efforts to delay the meeting of the tribunal were dealt with summarily by President Roosevelt, who wrote some sharp letters on the subject. He told Hay in July that if England would not come to an adjudication at once, "nothing will be left the United States but to act in a way which will necessarily wound British pride"; while he wrote to Lodge that if the British resorted

[14] White to Hay, London, May 13, 1903.

to unfair delays he would imitate Cleveland in the Venezuela affair
—"the thing to do is to declare the negotiations off, recite our case
in the message to Congress, and ask for an appropriation to run
the boundary as we deem it should be run." [15] These views White
privately communicated to the British in August, and as a result
the tribunal duly met in September.

From the outset White was confident that the decision would be
favorable to the United States. "Alverstone is getting daily into
closer personal touch with Cabot and Root and has already spoken
quite freely to them," he wrote Hay on September 19th.[16] "There
seems to be unanimity in thinking the Canadians have a good case
upon the Portland Canal or channel, and Alverstone has intimated
that he is with us on the main question. Root says that Turner
will give way about the Portland Channel and Prince of Wales
Island; all of which is of course confidential." A week later he
confirmed this hopeful view. Alverstone, he reported, would surrender to the chief American contention, that the boundary ran
around the heads of the inlets instead of crossing them; the Americans would give way on the Portland Channel; and the only
point where the British would "attempt to squeeze us is in respect
to the amount of territory between the boundary line and the Lynn
Canal and coast." Even Lodge, he said, was now an optimist. He
might well be. The concession which the Americans made regarding the Portland Canal was slight. This was the inlet at the very
southern tip of the Alaskan coastal strip, and there was some question as to the exact course of the boundary through it. The Americans waived their claim, and gave the Canadians also some small
islands at the mouth of the inlet. But on the all-important question
of a solid Alaskan *lisière*, keeping the Canadians away from the
coast at all points north of 55°, they stood adamant.

It was well that the tribunal was coming to a decision so favorable to the United States. We know from Roosevelt's letters to
Lodge that he was ready to fight rather than give up the Alaskan
panhandle. Already he had sent troops to Alaska. He and Hay both
replied to White's letters in terms showing an immovable stand.
Hay wrote:

[15] Dennis, A. L. P., *Adventures in American Diplomacy*, p. 145.
[16] White to Hay, London, September 19, 1903.

Newbury, New Hampshire,
September 20th, 1903.

Dear Harry:

I have read with the greatest interest your letter of the third. In spite of the pessimistic prophecies we have heard in such plenty, the Tribunal is in session at the time appointed, with a fair prospect of getting through its work with reasonable despatch. As to the result, we can only hope—the time is too short for convenient prophecy. For my part I cannot see how a man of Lord Alverstone's ability and clearness of vision can avoid giving a verdict in our favor. I see the Canadians are clamoring that he shall decide not according to the facts, but "in view of the imperial interests involved." Even in that view he should decide in our favor. For this is the last time we shall admit this question to any form of judicature. The land in question is ours. It was held by Russia in accordance with the treaty from 1825 to 1867, and has been held by us ever since. We shall never think of giving it up. No administration could abandon it and live a minute. If this Tribunal breaks up without deciding the question, we shall stand on our presentation of the case, and resist any attempt to take the territory from us.

We have never had the slightest doubt of our right. The President, at my earnest persuasion, consented to this tribunal, because I felt sure we could convince any great English lawyer that our contention was just. He was not so sanguine, but agreed to try the experiment to enable the British Government to get out of an absolutely untenable position with dignity and honor. If the Tribunal should disagree he will feel that he has done his utmost, and will make no further effort to settle the controversy. He will hold the territory, as we have held it since 1867, and will emphasize the assertion of our sovereignty in a way which cannot but be disagreeable to the Canadians. And all the labor of the last two years, to bring about a closer friendship between the two governments, will have gone for nothing. And this, after I have heard from Laurier and Pauncefote directly *that they know that they have no case.* I will not believe it till the verdict is in.

Yours faithfully,

John Hay.

Roosevelt had written confidentially to Messrs. Root, Lodge, and Turner just after their appointment that the Canadian claim to Skagway, Dyea, and Pyramid Harbor on the Lynn Canal could not in his opinion be considered open to discussion. He also told them that the treaty of 1825 was undoubtedly intended to cut off the

British access to the sea, and that "in the principle involved there will of course be no compromise." This was in effect an instruction to our arbitrators, tying their hands. Now in a letter to White he showed just what he intended to do if a deadlock occurred.

OYSTER BAY, NEW YORK,
September 26, 1903.

Personal.

MY DEAR WHITE:

Many thanks for your interesting letter. I was particularly delighted with what you say about the Canadian business. I most earnestly hope that your forecast is true. The Canadians have had some very ugly articles published, which I was afraid might influence English opinion. This would be unfortunate. It would be a bad thing for us if there was a deadlock in the present Commission; but it would be a very much worse thing for the Canadians and English, because it would leave me with no alternative but to declare as courteously, but as strongly as possible, that the effort to reach an agreement having failed, I should be obliged to treat the territory as ours, as being for the most part in our possession, and the remainder to be reduced to possession as soon as in our judgment it was advisable—and to declare furthermore that no additional negotiations of any kind would be entered into.

I look forward to seeing Hamilton, Ribblesdale, and Poynter, and especially to seeing you Christmas. I hope Jack enjoys Harvard. Give my warm regards to Mrs. White. I was greatly interested in Balfour's masterly pamphlet; it is a noteworthy article.

Faithfully yours,
THEODORE ROOSEVELT.

It is evident that White was expected to convey the gist of these letters to members of the British Government, and as years later he wrote to Mr. Worthington C. Ford, he did so. He also intervened, before the final decision was reached, in a more direct fashion, using the diplomatic methods which were peculiarly his own and were so often useful to the United States. Lord Alverstone during September began to complain confidentially to the Americans of the intense Canadian pressure on the question of the inlets; he said that he was in a most trying and disagreeable position, and hardly knew what to do. The Canadians vehemently assured him that Messrs. Lodge, Root, and Turner would insist that the British surrender upon the main issue of the inlets, and that once they had obtained this would refuse to yield any compensatory ground on the minor questions. On October 2nd Lodge wrote two rather frantic letters in hot succession to White—letters which Root read and approved—suggesting that White should see the Prime Minister at once. He declared that the Tribunal was "in danger of breaking" and must be rescued without delay; White was on intimate terms with Mr. Balfour and could talk to him freely. The overbearing attempts of Canada to influence the situation, declared Lodge, made it highly desirable that the facts should be brought to Balfour's attention, and that he should be urged to let Lord Alverstone know that the Ministry would support him in a firm stand.

At once acting on this suggestion, White traveled north to Whittinghame and remained with Balfour over the week-end. "I took occasion on Sunday afternoon, the 4th," he wrote to Secretary Hay,[17] "to have a long talk with him during which I left no doubt upon his mind as to the importance of a settlement nor as to the result of a failure to agree. He said that he attached far more importance to the agreement of the Tribunal than to any of the Cabinet questions and complications with which he was then bothered, and that he thought it would be little short of a disaster if the Tribunal broke up without a decision. I then explained to him the rock on which I thought they might come to grief, and he said he would consider what he would do. I explained to him very fully the position of Alverstone, and intimated that I thought it would be very desirable that he should be told that the Government, without in any way wishing to influence him, was very anxious for a decision. I never heard directly whether he did anything nor if so what; but two days afterwards his confidential secretary, Saunders, who is a friend of mine, let me know very confidentially that he had had two interviews with Lord Alverstone. Subsequently on Friday the 9th A. J. B. himself was in London on Cabinet business, and Cabot having intimated a desire to see him, he came to tea with me to meet Cabot, who expatiated at length and with perfect lucidity and good temper on the same theme, only manifesting more anxiety than I should as to the probability of failure. Whenever things seemed to be approaching a deadlock—

[17] White to Hay, London, November 20, 1903.

as they did once or twice during the past week—I only attributed it to Lord Alverstone's very natural and proper desire to do the best and make all the fight possible for the Canadians on the question of the width of the *lisière*, and I never for a moment doubted that the undercurrent of diplomacy, the force and quiet working of which you and I appreciate more than those who have not been trained as we have to that profession, would bring about a decision in the end."

On October 20, 1903, the day White wrote this letter, every essential point had been decided. Lord Alverstone gave his vote in favor of the American view regarding the inlets, and the boundary was determined to the entire satisfaction of the United States. Public opinion in Canada was resentful and disappointed. The two Canadian arbitrators refused to sign the award. A storm of criticism burst upon Lord Alverstone's head; to which he made the stout reply that if in any arbitration the Canadians did not want a decision based on the law and the evidence, they must not put a British judge on the tribunal. White wrote to Hay a confidential review of the work of the American commissioners: [18]

All of our Commissoners have produced a most favorable impression, and it may surprise you to hear that of the three Cabot is the one who seemed to be the most appreciated by Alverstone. They became positively intimate, and whenever anything of a delicate nature was to be said to Alverstone it was always Cabot who was deputed to do it. He has shown great tact and considerable diplomacy throughout, and Turner had gradually gained the esteem of everyone and proved himself to be a very able and strong man. He has also shown plenty of breadth of mind, and was prepared to go quite as far, notwithstanding his position as a resident of that section of the country where feeling in the matter is so strong, in the way of concessions as any of the others. Of course you know Mr. Root so well, and his ability and broad-minded way of looking at things, that I need not tell you about him. The three made a very strong team. General Foster has been very conciliatory and has, I think, modified the antagonistic view of him taken at the Foreign Office.

Few can review the Alaskan dispute at this later day without feeling that President Roosevelt's threatening tactics were both improper and unnecessary. The pains he took to warn the British

[18] White to Hay, *ut supra*.

Government of his militant purposes through Lodge, Choate, Justice Oliver Wendell Holmes, and White reflected, beyond doubt, his conviction that the United States was entirely right. But he might have trusted to the righteousness of the American case— particularly after he placed on the tribunal three representatives committed in advance to the American contentions. The final decision, impartial students have told us, was substantially fair. Canada's case was weak, and she received almost if not quite all that she was entitled to get. But it was unfortunate that Roosevelt's method of handling the problem planted in the breasts of Canadians a conviction that a powerful nation had used its strength to take advantage of a weaker neighbor. The fortunate aspect of the whole matter was that Anglo-American relations were left on a friendlier basis than ever. England, faced by a hostile Europe and aware of Germany's fast growing strength, retained what she so earnestly desired, the friendship of the United States. A few rocky, uninhabited islands on the lower Alaskan coast, a reduction of a few miles here and there in the *lisière*, were all that Canada might fairly have gained; her claim to the inlets was untenable. These possible acquisitions in territory paled into insignificance when compared with the amicable settlement of a question which offered perennial opportunities for arousing discord between two great kindred nations.[19] So White felt, and so history must declare.

[19] White, in a letter to Worthington C. Ford on November 17, 1926, declared that it was not quite fair to say that Roosevelt determined there would be no real arbitration. "On the contrary, he wrote to me that, while he did not believe in partisan tribunals with three advocates on either side, he would nevertheless abide by any decision, whatever it might be, at which the Alaskan Boundary Tribunal might arrive. What he really dreaded was that the Tribunal would arrive at no decision, and it was to obviate the latter contingency that I took certain steps of a private and confidential nature which turned out to be successful." White's own opinion was that in the main the Canadian claims were "preposterous," and although neither Lord Alverstone nor any member of the British Government ever told him so, he believed they held the same view.

CHAPTER THIRTEEN

Germany, the Danish Islands, and Venezuela

IN THESE years at the turn of the century the lusty young German Empire was regarded with suspicion in both the United States and Great Britain. Both countries began to see in Germany an aggressive Power with ambitions which might conflict with their own. This attitude was unfortunate but inevitable. The United States, after a long century of friendship, had quarreled slightly with the Germans over Samoa in 1888; but that dispute had been easily settled by a treaty which guaranteed the independence of the islands under a protectorate of both nations and Great Britain. Ten years later, the position taken by Germany during the Spanish War had been a much more unpleasant shock to America. Not only was German sentiment overwhelmingly on the side of Spain; Germany sent an unnecessarily powerful squadron under Admiral Diedrichs to Manila, and its behavior there was worrisome and offensive.[1] Later still, the American public strongly disapproved of Germany's seizure of Kiau-chau, and of the harsh German policy during the Boxer Rebellion. Powerful undercurrents seemed to be slowly alienating the two nations. The fact grieved sensible people in both lands, and the Kaiser dispatched Prince Henry to America with an olive branch; but the feeling of rivalry and suspicion continued.

White had plenty of opportunity to learn of the popular American distrust of Germany, which Hay shared; and he had equal opportunity to feel the pervading atmosphere of suspicion in Eng-

[1] There is no evidence that the German Government or Diedrichs had improper intentions; most of the attacks upon their attitude at Manila, when historically analyzed, boil down to zero. Dewey had no armor and had shot away nearly all his ammunition; the presence of the untactful Germans with their armored battleship *Kaiser* gave him an attack of nerves. The whole incident was exaggerated.

land. There had been a considerable British feeling against Germany from the time of the Kruger telegram and the Boer War. It was aggravated by the increase in the German navy, the pressure of German commercial rivalry, the press jingoism on both sides, and the unfortunate Bülow-Chamberlain controversy. Of course White knew that many of the British were only too glad to impress Americans with the dangerous character of German aims, and he discounted much of the talk that he heard.[2] His own feeling toward Germany was entirely friendly. It would be possible to quote numerous passages from his letters expressing admiration for the great industrial and scientific achievements of Germany. But he was a curious and alert observer of relations between Washington and Berlin. In two episodes of the time, the attempted American purchase of the Danish West Indies and the Venezuelan imbroglio of 1902, he had some experience, indirect rather than direct, with German tactics.[3]

The first of these may be rapidly passed over. We have seen that late in 1899 White made a flying visit to Copenhagen to negotiate for the purchase of the Virgin Islands. They were wanted for use as coaling stations, and incidentally to prevent their acquisition by any other Power. By interviews with the Danish authorities, White learned that the islands were really for sale, that the Danes would like to get $4,500,000 for them, and that an offer of $3,500,000 would probably be accepted. When he reported this to Hay, the latter had a treaty drafted for purchase at the lower of the two

[2] White's papers offer much evidence of this; they also offer much evidence that he had to discount German insinuations against England. The Kaiser, as we have said, believed there was a virtual Anglo-American alliance. White wrote to Hay (January 27, 1899) of Hatzfeldt's efforts to stir up ill will for America in England. Hatzfeldt was repeating everywhere quotations from an anti-British speech by Justice Harlan and the remark of a California Congressman that "we shall whip England if necessary as we whipped Spain."

[3] With Samoa he had little to do. The tripartite protectorate of Samoa by Germany, Great Britain, and the United States had worked very badly. Cleveland wished to get out of Samoa altogether. Hay thought this a great mistake, and wanted to keep a foothold in Samoa "in the interest of our Pacific work." Germany wished to wind up the affair in a manner hurtful to England, and England hurtful to Germany; Hay was desirous of playing fair with both.—Hay to White, September 24, 1899.

figures. For a long year the negotiations dragged on, being unnecessarily tangled by the quarreling of the American minister and American consul in Copenhagen. In the summer of 1901 White went back to straighten affairs out, and met with some success. Hay finally increased the American offer to $5,000,000, a treaty was signed in Washington, and on February 17, 1902, it was ratified by the Senate. It then came before the Danish upper chamber. After long uncertainty this body, on October 22, 1902, by a close margin refused to ratify. The plan for the purchase thus failed. The question was, why did the treaty fall short of the votes needed and expected in the Landsthing?

Undoubtedly most of the Danish opponents of the sale were actuated by patriotic reasons, or a feeling that the price was too low; by waiting fifteen years, Denmark actually got $25,000,000. Some Danes also believed that the islands should be kept to be traded to Germany for part of Schleswig, and that a sale for mere money was foolish. But White concluded that the few deciding votes had been won by other considerations. For some time he had felt that the Germans were playing the rôle of trouble-makers for the United States. During the summer of 1902 he had informed Hay of the reports he heard from Berlin. "Lloyd Griscom went yachting with the Emperor," he wrote, "and had a good deal of talk with him; there is no doubt that he is very anxious to make up to us, and is trying to understand us, but with very imperfect success so far, and meanwhile he does all that he can to create irritation in this country against us, with equal lack of success. I am told that much of the opposition to the Atlantic combine emanated from him, or rather was inspired by his orders. What we want there now is an American ambassador who speaks German fluently, and without being prejudiced against the Germans, will nevertheless not be unduly influenced by the blandishments of the Emperor." When the Danish negotiations ended in defeat, White felt sure the Germans had a finger in the pie. He wrote to Hay:[4]

[4] White to Hay, London, November 4, 1902. Many years later, it may be noted here, some Danes proposed that their government should cede the Virgin Islands to the United States; that the United States should cede part of the Philippines to Denmark; and that Denmark should then give its Philippine territory to Germany in exchange for Schleswig—a neat all-round trade!

Of course, I am much disappointed at the upshot of all our efforts in respect to the Danish islands, and especially as it was owing to the devices resorted to in bringing two dotards with nurses into the Landsthing and getting them to vote. I have little doubt that the result is largely due to German intrigue, and F. Bertie agrees with me. He says they are at it everywhere, all the time, against England as well as us, and that they are chiefly responsible for preventing Russia from getting on better terms with England, which I quite believe. I have not yet been able to see Bille [the Danish minister to Great Britain], who is away at The Hague presenting his credentials to the Queen of Holland, to whom he is accredited also, but I understand that the member of the Landsthing for the district adjoining Schleswig was induced to change his vote at the last moment, which of course decided the question. You may also have observed that the very morning after the rejection a company was started for promoting trade between the islands and German Baltic ports, and shortly afterward the crown prince paid his state visit to Germany, where he now is. Of course we can afford to wait and for us it is a mere question of time, and Denmark will be the loser in the end. The islands eventually must come to us, and for less money probably—for with our tariff against them they cannot be made to pay, nor will the line of steamers pay, either.

A little later he heard on good authority that the German Government had secretly offered strong inducements to Princess Waldemar of Denmark to use her influence, which was decisive with several members of the Landsthing, to defeat the Danish treaty. It seemed to him rather a suspicious fact that the German Emperor shortly visited Copenhagen, and was especially cordial to the princess, who had been the chief agitator against the treaty. "In view of what Mr. Choate wrote you recently as to the German Emperor's designs upon two harbors in southern California," White again informed Hay,[5] "and of the mention made by several members of the Danish royal family of his probable intentions with regard to the Danish islands, I don't think it requires a great stretch of the imagination to realize that he had a hand in the defeat of our purchase scheme and that he is fairly lying awake nights wondering how he can possibly get hold of them." Prince Charles of Denmark, talking with White in the spring of 1902, had said he favored selling the islands, which were a drain on the Danish

[5] White to Hay, London, April 7, 1903.

treasury and which Denmark could never protect against any power "such as Germany"; and he asked White pointedly what the United States would do if the Germans should try to take or buy the islands. White was emphatic in his reply. Queen Alexandra also mentioned Germany to White in connection with the Danish islands. As White told the story in a letter to Hay dated April 7, 1903:

When I chanced to meet the King and Queen of England at luncheon some time ago at the Carringtons', in Buckinghamshire, the latter (next to whom I sat) and I had some chaff about the islands. She said that she could not help being delighted that they had been preserved to her country, that we do not really want them, etc., etc. and in reply to my suggestion that we had only come into the matter at all in order to relieve Denmark of a burden upon her treasury, the Queen said: "It was all bad management; with the new management you will see how the islands will flourish and be made to pay"; to which I replied that I feared she was mistaken but hoped she might not be, as we have not the least desire to dispossess Denmark of them. She then added, "But I hope you will never let Germany have the islands; that's what we (the Danes) would dread above all things," to which I replied that her majesty might make herself quite easy on that point, as it would be the grossest infringement of the Monroe Doctrine, which our country would spare no expense to put a stop to. Curiously enough her brother, the Crown Prince, as I think I wrote you at the time, had asked me the very same question last year when he was here for the coronation. The King, hearing the conversation between the Queen and me across the table (we were only about eight or nine) broke in, saying: "I hope you know, my dear White, that I have always been in favor of your having the islands, and you'll have them yet. It was a great mistake in Denmark to reject the treaty, and she will soon see it."

Hay sent this note to President Roosevelt. A little later, in 1905, Senator Lodge and others were much disturbed by a report that the Hamburg-American Company was about to establish a great coaling station in the Danish West Indies. Indeed, there was and is evidence of various kinds that the German militarists and big-navy men were eager to possess themselves of a foothold, if only a small naval station, somewhere in the Western Hemisphere. Meanwhile, the ill feeling between England and Germany resulted in a steady increase of propaganda on both sides. British newspapers

and agents were busy assuring the United States that Codlin was
the friend, not Short; and German agents and German-American
newspapers were vehemently reversing the assurance. Lord Lansdowne, who was now British Foreign Minister, labored earnestly
for friendly relations with Germany, but in 1902 the Bagdad Railway negotiations furnished a new source of trouble. Roosevelt
regarded German policy with some uneasiness, and in 1902 specially
requested White to ask Balfour what the British would do if Germany annexed or absorbed Holland. White, inviting the Prime
Minister to dine with him, was told that annexation would never
be permitted. Apparently Roosevelt feared that if Queen Wilhelmina
died, Germany might try to seize Dutch Guiana; in which event, as
White told the Prime Minister, he would have intervened under the
Monroe Doctrine.

It was against this background that there occurred the so-called
Venezuelan affair of 1902-03. In this dramatic controversy, which
involved Venezuela, Germany, Italy, Great Britain, and the United
States, White was a modest participant; for when the crisis became
acute in November of 1902, he was *chargé d'affaires* in the absence
of Mr. Choate. The story of the affair has often been told, and there
is no need to rehearse its details; but upon some of its most striking
features White's correspondence throws light.

The controversy arose from the fact that Germany, Great Britain,
and Italy all had financial claims against Venezuela which the
government of that republic, under the irresponsible dictatorship
of President Castro, refused to satisfy. The German claims were
large, including arrears of interest on Venezuelan bonds owned by
German citizens, dividends guaranteed by the Venezuelan Government upon a $20,000,000 railway, and the compensation of
German subjects for forced loans. While under international law
these claims were a dubious ground for German intervention,
they were obligations which Venezuela had no moral right to deny.
When the financial interests involved demanded action, the three
European countries were justified in exerting pressure, and the
world had no sympathy for the scoundrelly Castro. In the spring
of 1901 Germany and Great Britain proposed arbitration to Castro,
which he rejected. Thereupon, on December 11, 1901, the German
Ambassador brought the claims to the attention of the United

States, and suggested that some measure of coercion might be necessary; adding that under no circumstances would Germany consider
the permanent occupation of Venezuelan territory. To this Hay
replied by quoting a recent message of Roosevelt's to Congress—a
message in which the President had said that the Monroe Doctrine
did not protect any American nation from punishment if it misbe-
haved itself, but that the punishment must not take the form of
the acquisition of territory by any non-American Power.

In the steps for the actual employment of force Great Britain,
according to our recent information from European archives, led
the way. Germany at once—July 23, 1902—intimated her wish to
be associated with England. Pressure from investment interests in
both countries was heavy. Lansdowne suggested a naval demonstration and the seizure of the Venezuelan gunboats, but the Germans
wished in addition to establish a blockade. In November Hay
was informed by the British of their plan of action. Both governments sent ultimatums to Venezuela, dispatched warships to her
waters, and joined in seizing some armed craft of Venezuela's.
Castro then hastily backed down, and on December 9th proposed
to accept arbitration. While he was thus belatedly trying to escape
from the consequences of his greed and folly, the Germans and
British announced a blockade of the Venezuelan ports, which became effective on Christmas Day. Thus far the American Government had tacitly acquiesced. But when the German naval commander, ignoring his agreement to take no separate action, sank
several gunboats and fired some shots at a Venezuelan fortress,
the American attitude changed. Public opinion in the United States
reacted strongly against the steps taken by Germany and Great
Britain—particularly the former—a feeling spread that the Monroe
Doctrine was in danger, and signs of popular excitement appeared.

As the cables informed the British public of this American uneasiness, it was promptly matched by a similar state of apprehension
and disturbance in Great Britain. It would never do, in the eyes
of the average Briton, to risk a breach with the United States over
some paltry South American debts; it would certainly never do
to pull Germany's chestnuts out of the fire. Ever since the Kruger
telegram and the Boer War Germany had been growing more
unpopular, and joint action with her was almost universally dis-

approved and condemned. While Sir Michael Herbert sent strong
warnings to Lansdowne from Washington, a debate in Parliament
on December 15th revealed a general spirit of criticism.

As the crisis developed, White, who had special means of judging public opinion in Great Britain, felt sure that popular pressure
would cause the Government to recede. He took pains to see the
Prime Minister, Arthur Balfour, and Lord Lansdowne. He was emphatic in urging upon them and other officials that Castro's offer
of arbitration, which had been transmitted by the United States,
should be accepted; while he gave warning that if hostilities began,
Great Britain would almost certainly be drawn into acts which
would antagonize American feeling. "You will probably have inferred," he wrote Hay on December 13th, "that much of the private
information I have cabled you is based upon conversations with the
Prime Minister, to whom I unburdened very frankly on Monday
at his private room at the House of Commons my feelings of
anxiety at the whole situation and my earnest hope that he would
not allow his government to be led by Germany into doing anything to exacerbate our public opinion. I have also seen him since.
I think it partly due to my talk that he persuaded the Cabinet to
publish the statement made yesterday by Lansdowne which I
cabled you as to not landing troops on Venezuelan soil. On Monday they meant to keep it secret in order not to let Venezuela know
it, lest the fear of armed invasion being removed, she should become obdurate."

Not only did Lansdowne assure White that the British would
put no troops or marines ashore, but the Cabinet publicly committed itself to this statement. Balfour told White, with the request that his words be repeated to Hay, that he "would consider it
a positive calamity to be obliged to land an armed force." On December 15th White was able to add: "I am inclined to think whole
Venezuelan matter, especially British acting with Germans, unpopular in this country. Sinking of ships certainly is. Consequently
I am not without hope something may come of our transmission
of arbitration proposal." He was still urging the danger of a
collision.

Under these circumstances, the British Government made up its
mind to recede. It decided to arbitrate, and when Count Metternich,

the German ambassador, saw Lansdowne on December 16th, he was tactfully informed of this intention. The German Government vigorously opposed any such concession, and the Kaiser annotated Metternich's dispatch on the subject with the scornful remark, *"Serenissimus verliert Nerven! Das hätte Grossmamma nie gesagt!"* [6] But within a few days, word having come from Washington that Roosevelt was prepared to use the Big Stick in a summary way, the Germans also gave way. Berlin and London simultaneously announced their acceptance of arbitration. This decision was received by the American and English publics with a sigh of relief. The Venezuelan question, after occupying for days the chief place in the London press, suddenly gave way to Curzon's triumphal entry into Delhi. White wrote of all this to Hay on December 31st, saying:

. . . But there is no doubt that for a week or more the whole country was in a state of great uneasiness lest the alliance or agreement with Germany should in some way bring them into conflict with American public opinion and possibly diminish the good feeling which they hope exists on our side towards this country; besides a strong feeling of hostility to being in any way connected with Germany in any foreign enterprises; there being a very marked hostility to that country in the British public mind since the attacks continually emanating from the German press during the late war. I have reason to believe that the Ministry have been entirely taken aback by the great unpopularity of their agreement with Germany, but all this has been of advantage to us, and has furthered the acceptance of our advice as to the best way of getting out, with the least discredit, of a very disagreeable predicament. It was bad enough to have to face an outburst of American sentiment, but when it came to having to encounter a stronger and even more hostile one here, the situation was impossible.

I need scarcely say that throughout the whole business Lord Lansdowne's courtesy has been perfect, and his desire to conform as far as possible to our views and wishes very great. I saw him every day the week before Christmas, and nearly every day last week, and he lets me invade him at Lansdowne House whenever I like in the morning. I think it not unlikely—indeed I have pretty good reason to believe—that

[6] "His royal majesty has lost his nerve! Grandmother would never have said that!" As Lord Newton says in his *Lord Lansdowne: A Biography*, the Kaiser had the mistaken impression that Edward VII was in personal control of British foreign policy.

those reassuring statements in Parliament by him and Arthur Balfour were the result of my urgent representations. . . .

It was not merely the British public which objected to acting with Germany, but the sovereign as well. A month later White was writing his wife of a luncheon with King Edward.[7] "The latter took me aside almost the moment he arrived," he wrote, "and talked about the Venezuelan business, and was generally rather hostile to the 'Ally,' but most friendly to us and full of praises to Burgess, which I shall be able to write him. His Majesty was really very outspoken."

During January, 1903, White did his utmost to persuade the Balfour Ministry to cut short the Venezuelan blockade, but the Government, fearing Castro's duplicity, was unwilling to recall its warships. There was danger that some headstrong naval commander would spill the fat into the fire, and the English leaders frankly recognized it. On January 17th, White advised Hay to use pressure on the two countries to withdraw their squadrons. "I cannot imagine," he wrote, "and have not yet succeeded in ascertaining, what ever possessed this government to go in with Germany, and if the whole matter is not settled before Parliament meets, you may be certain that they will have a pretty time of it when that body assembles." As he tried repeatedly to impress upon Balfour and Lansdowne the risks of protracted coöperation with Germany, and made no secret of what he was doing, his activities attracted the attention of Berlin, which concluded that he, perhaps with the encouragement of Secretary Hay, was trying to drive a wedge between Germany and Great Britain. Through Charlemagne Tower, the American Ambassador in Berlin, the German Foreign Office let out a squeal of protest. "You stirred them all up considerably," wrote Hay.[8] Berlin complained that according to its representative in London, White had been attacking the whole German position, and particularly the insistence of Germany that certain preferential claims should be settled outside of the proposed arbitration. This particular charge was untrue, and White denied it.

[7] White to Mrs. White, London, January 29, 1903.

[8] Hay to White, March 15, 1903. Hay praised White's work. "I do not need to tell you, at this late date," he wrote, "that I always take it for granted that you have done exactly what is right and judicious."

Washington paid no attention to the German grumbling, and Berlin was in no position to press its complaint. At this juncture occurred the mysterious and ruthless removal of Holleben, who received a cablegram from the Kaiser ordering him to feign illness and come home, which he obeyed within twenty-four hours; and as his career thus ended in disgrace, his place was taken by Speck von Sternburg, a personal representative of the Emperor. White was delighted when in the middle of February, on British initiative, the blockade was lifted.[9] "There is no doubt," was his final word to Hay, "that the German connection has been a tremendous lesson to them here for the future." This was indeed the last instance of active Anglo-German coöperation before the World War.

Though the Venezuelan affair added nothing to the prestige of either Great Britain or Germany, the final adjustment did settle the claims of both. During the summer of 1903 ten mixed commissions sat at Caracas to adjudicate the bills offered by as many nations against Venezuela, and in the end the British received awards of nearly ten million bolivars, the Germans of a little more than two millions. If any Germans had hoped to use the affair to becloud Anglo-American relations or to gain a foothold on the South American coast, they were disappointed. Three years later the Chilean minister in Paris, Edwardes, told White that the Germans had been zealously and systematically trying to sow discord between the South American republics and the United States, chiefly by raising the bogey of American aggression. But for the moment all seemed well. Two of Hay's final letters to White on Venezuela may be quoted, the second referring to the troubles of the well-liked Sternburg:

[February 16, 1903.]—I think that the thing that rankles most in the German official mind is what Bowen [10] said to Sternburg: "Very well, I

[9] White to Hay, London, March 4, 1903. On Holleben's dismissal, cf. *The Education of Henry Adams,* p. 437. White wrote later of Sternburg that he was the only German representative in his time "who understood us and had the courage to tell his own government plain truths, however unpalatable, in the hope of making its members and their sovereign understand us better, in which he achieved a good deal of success." White to Roosevelt, September 1, 1908.

[10] Herbert W. Bowen, American Minister to Venezuela, was representing Venezuelan interests.

will pay this money which you demand, because I am not in position to refuse, but I give you warning that for every thousand dollars which you exact in this way, you will lose a million in South American trade." Michael Herbert's action throughout has been in the highest degree judicious and correct.

[March 5, 1903.]—We are well and happily out of the whole affair— with considerable net gain to us, and more or less damage to Germany. My advices from South America show a grateful feeling to the United States and a certain resentment toward the Kaiser which may lead to practical results hereafter.

Sternburg has had a terrible time—first in inducing his Foreign Office to allow him to make peace, and secondly in fighting a boycott in his own embassy. I never heard of anything so extraordinary. His counsellor, Quadt, and his second secretary, Ritter, refused to recognize him or his wife, socially or officially, on the ground of his inferior social standing. He has had them both recalled. I don't know how long he can make head against such a cabal, as I hear Von Bülow is himself unfriendly. But the President is his Dutzbruder, and the Emperor seems inclined to keep him, as a *persona gratissima*.

It remains to record the most interesting episode of the whole Venezuelan imbroglio. We have mentioned that at a critical moment in December President Roosevelt seized the Big Stick, and that his gesture was decisive in persuading Germany to yield to arbitration. The alleged facts of his dramatic intervention did not come to light until years later. The President, in studying the situation through White's dispatches and other information, had arrived at the conclusion that England was a half-hearted associate of Germany, dragged rather unwillingly at her side in the later phases of the affair, and eager not to offend the United States; he knew that she would remain neutral if a clash occurred between Germany and America. He became convinced also that the ruling group in Germany had no real desire for a peaceable settlement with Castro; that they were secretly eager to seize some Venezuelan harbor, fortify it, and hold it on the model of Kiau-chau, to enable Germany to exercise an influence over the surrounding area and the projected Isthmian Canal. The German refusal early in December to arbitrate impressed him as a confirmation of this theory. As he has told the story, he was unwilling to let the situation drift and resolved to take sharp measures to bring the Imperial Government to its senses. Hence, assembling the American battle-fleet, including every battleship and torpedo-boat under our flag, in Porto Rican waters as if for a maneuver, he sent orders to Admiral Dewey to be ready for action at an hour's notice. Then, feeling prepared for any emergency, he called the German Ambassador to the White House and told him that unless Germany consented to arbitrate, the American fleet would be given orders, by noon ten days later, to proceed to the Venezuelan coast and protect Venezuela from any aggression.

According to Roosevelt's statement made years afterward, and placed on record in two letters, one to White and one to William Roscoe Thayer, a second interview occurred about a week later. The dates are not given, and unfortunately no contemporary record was made of the meetings. At the second Roosevelt delivered a virtual ultimatum—Germany would either accept arbitration, receiving his congratulations for her generous action, or he would have Dewey's fleet sail at once. The Kaiser, according to his story, at once yielded. Roosevelt wrote to White in his letter of 1906:

At the time of the Venezuelan business I saw the German Ambassador privately myself; told him to tell the Kaiser that I had put Dewey in charge of our fleet to manœuver in West Indian waters; that the world at large should know of this merely as a manœuver, and that we should strive in every way to appear simply as coöperating with the Germans; but that I regretted to say that the popular feeling was such that I should be obliged to interfere, by force if necessary, if the Germans took any action which looked like the acquisition of territory there or elsewhere along the Caribbean; that this was not in any way intended as a threat; but as the position on the part of the government which the American people would demand, and that I wanted him to understand it before the two nations drifted into such a position that trouble might come. I do not know whether it was a case of *post hoc* or *propter hoc*, but immediately afterward the Kaiser made to me the proposition that I should arbitrate myself, which I finally got him to modify so that it was sent to The Hague.

Such a telling demonstration of the Big Stick would have been thoroughly characteristic of Roosevelt. Unfortunately, the story as Roosevelt tells it lacks corroboration. There is nothing whatever in the German archives to sustain it. It seems altogether unlikely that the incident was quite so dramatic as the President pictured it in 1906. His imagination had heightened its colors. It also seems likely, however, that he gave Holleben a clear warning of some kind, and that the ambassador transmitted it to the Kaiser. He would hardly have dared to do even this but for White's explicit assurances that the British Ministry held to very moderate aims, and would under no circumstances join Germany in defying the United States. Acting alone, the German navy could do nothing; acting together, the British and German navies could do as they pleased. White's dispatches had made it plain that there was no danger of such joint action.

Perhaps the best review of the whole episode is that which White embodied in a letter to Hay, in which he sagaciously remarked:[11] "I do not regret the Venezuelan incident, which has served to further still more the acceptance of the Monroe Doctrine, and indeed to establish it on a very firm footing; and it has also been an object lesson as to the danger of tampering with the American continent, besides enhancing still further the prestige—already great, as you know—of the President, and increasing your reputation."

[11] White to Hay, London, December 31, 1902.

CHAPTER FOURTEEN

Adviser, Observer, and Friend

OFFICIALLY, Henry White's position in these years was not high. We have seen that his intimate acquaintance with the leaders in British politics, his knowledge of British opinion, and his long experience of diplomatic precedent, gave his work a value out of all proportion to his rank in the service. Our successive ambassadors found him literally indispensable, and when they were absent, he could take up their work as *chargé* without the slightest break. He filled a unique rôle in the diplomatic service. But his unofficial activities were also of importance. He held a position of peculiar usefulness in Anglo-American affairs merely as a friend of conspicuous men on both sides of the water, a go-between in all sorts of exchanges, a source of information and an interpreter for both countries. To the general public he was little known. To many men of affairs—capitalists, politicians, journalists, writers, people of fashion—who traveled much between England and America, hardly anybody was better known.

For Secretary Hay in particular White after 1898 was eyes and ears in London, and his stream of confidential letters, answered by letters which were often equally intimate, must have been invaluable in giving Hay the atmosphere of British affairs. At times he wrote almost weekly. He constantly saw people of importance, he constantly heard facts unknown to the public, and he let Hay have the benefit of his observations. An entertaining small volume could be made of these letters; but to quote salient passages from merely a few will indicate their general character. We may begin with the autumn of 1898, when the Spanish War was just ending:

WHITE TO HAY

[September 28, 1898.]—The Peace Commission have come and gone. They wisely decided that it would be better for them not to see Lord Salisbury, who however sent them a message through me, expressing the hope that they would stop in London on the way home and allow him an opportunity of showing them hospitality. I shall see that he does not forget this.

You will be amused to hear that the Spaniards are firmly convinced that Chamberlain was sent to our country for the purpose of negotiating an agreement with us whereby we shall retain the whole of the Philippines and give England half of them. I understand that old Rascon has actually protested against this perfidy on the part of His Majesty's Government. Under these circumstances it seemed just as well—in fact, much better—to me that the Commissioners and Lord Salisbury should not meet, and I think the latter was of that mind also. The Commissioners would neither dine in London with me nor pay me a country visit. But I saw them constantly and took some of them to the Abbey on Sunday and to the National Gallery. I also dined with them and thereby hangs a brief tale which may amuse you. By dinner time Mrs. Senator Davis had waxed quite enthusiastic about the sights of London, which she had seen with me, and her enthusiasm assumed the form not only of thinking, but unfortunately of announcing in a sonorous tone of voice (with Mr. Whitelaw Reid on the other side of her!) that I was the proper person for Ambassador, and she intended "speaking to the Senator" about it that night. The only thing for me to say was that it was very good of her, but I wanted Mr. Reid to have it, and she must not thwart my projects; whereupon Mr. Reid, who had been listening, chimed in with: "And the worst of it is that the appointing power seems to pay no attention to either of us!"

He was writing to Hay a few weeks later of a visit to the Duke of Buccleugh, where he had talked with the Secretary of State for India:

[October 14, 1898.]—George Hamilton was very chatty, and I had several good talks with him. He confided to me just before I left that the Government have had recent telegrams from MacDonald at Pekin saying that the present reactionary movement in China is not brought about by Russia nor any other Power nor in the interest of any, but is for the most part purely Chinese and caused by a feeling that the Emperor is going much too fast in the direction of modern ideas; but that so drastic are the Empress-Dowager's methods that a counterrevolution may shortly be expected. Meanwhile, however, I fear from all accounts that the poor Emperor will have been removed to another sphere. . . .

St. John Brodrick's appointment as Parliamentary Under-Secretary for Foreign Affairs is gazetted today. He is a very old friend of mine, as you know, and I much prefer to have him there than George Curzon, as he is much more interested than the latter in our country and its affairs, and, without George Curzon's brilliancy, is an able and hard-working fellow who will do well in that place and is liked by the House of Commons.

I have treated you to a dissertation in a despatch on the relations between this country and France relative to Fashoda. There is no doubt that the relations are very strained, but I scarcely think that war is to be apprehended. So far, however, the French don't seem disposed to yield, and it is certain that they won't budge nor hear of any compromise here—and rightly so, I think. The chief element of danger in the situation of course lies in the weakness of the French Government just now, coupled with the internal dissensions in that country. Considering that the British Government has to be depended upon for enabling the French to communicate with Marchand and for supplying the latter and his men with food and that they can squeeze him out at any moment, it is difficult to see what can be done to maintain by force the position France seems disposed to assume in regard to him.

Early in 1899 there was a meeting between two striking figures of the day. White wrote:

[March 28, 1899.] You will be interested to hear that the meeting between the German Emperor and Cecil Rhodes was exceedingly cordial. They are both so much alike that each appreciates the other. The Emperor said to Rhodes, "If only you were my Prime Minister, I should be the greatest sovereign in the world." They discussed everything without reserve, including the Emperor's famous telegram to Kruger, in respect to which Rhodes said: "The mistake you made was in trying to thrash me. I was a naughty boy and the English people meant to do so, but they would not allow anyone else to assume that rôle, and the moment you attempted it, they resented it and became my friends."

Later that year, with the Boer War raging, he naturally made many references to South African affairs. His sympathies, like Hay's and Roosevelt's, were all with England:

[November 3, 1899.] This whole country is of course entirely engrossed by the war and can think of nothing else. There is a general yearning for American sympathy and approval, in respect to which of course no

expression of opinion is ever extracted from us. But the feeling is growing in the newspapers that American sympathy is with the British arms.
There can be no doubt, I fancy, that the Boers have long been preparing
for the conflict, and that they never meant to make any concessions to
the Uitlanders which might at any future time endanger Dutch supremacy. This has been much more patent since the war began than
before, I think. I fear the slaughter will be fearful before they have done,
and most of the leading families are sending out sons; Lansdowne's two
(and only) sons have both gone.

Secretary Hay was somewhat disturbed in the spring of 1900 by
the visit of a delegation of Boers to the United States, whom he
and President McKinley received politely but without any promises. White wrote in praise of his tact:

[May 26, 1900.] I arrived safely on the 23rd, and just in time to
attend the Duchess of Devonshire's party, where a perfect chorus was
sung and long continued over your handling of the Boer matter. The
Duke stopped me on my way upstairs to say how admirable they
thought your reception of them had been and to ask particulars as to
American feeling, etc., on the subject of the war, which I told him
very frankly, and was fortunately able to report that the pro-Boer wave
is receding. If any further proof of the latter fact were needed it would
be found in the lack of protests in the United States against your reply
to the envoys, of which I am glad to see that even the Chicago *Tribune*
approves. People here are all very much amused at the President's having
conducted the envoys to the back of the White House to see the
Potomac and Washington Monument. How exactly the whole thing
went off as you foreshadowed it would! It was the first news that I
read at Queenstown, and by no means the least clever part of the whole
affair was the written statement in which I recognized your master hand
—as did A. J. Balfour—wherein the facts were conveyed to the public.
A. J. Balfour says he adheres more than ever to the opinion he expressed
to me before I sailed of you, and which he repeated with emphasis.
He also said some nice things of the President.
I paid him a visit at the House of Commons at his request to tell
him all that I could about affairs in our country and particularly the
President's prospects of reëlection, which I was fortunately able to report
in a favorable light. They are deeply interested in it here and quite
understand that they must not let this feeling be known. If any
proof were needed of the extraordinary eagerness manifested here with

respect to American opinion, I might mention that the old Duchess of Devonshire, who until recently thought and cared as much of what was going on in the United States as in Persia or the moon, called me aside in the middle of her party the other evening and made me sit down in the corner beside her to "tell me all about what they think in America." By the by, Arthur Balfour said, "Why could not Hay come over on a visit next year after the election? Other ministers of foreign affairs visit foreign countries occasionally, and he would have a wonderful reception if he were to come."

From the letters of 1901 we may select excerpts upon a variety of topics—the funeral of Queen Victoria, American prosperity, a conversation with Lord Salisbury:

[January 30, 1901.] I hope you are well again and not worrying too much about the Senate and the "yellows." Apropos of the latter you may be amused to know that the *Journal's* correspondent wrote a peremptory demand to be admitted, as the leading New York newspaper, to St. George's Chapel in the Ambassador's suite! Your telegram of yesterday about Mr. Choate's representative functions was exactly right, but it was some time before I could quite get it into his head that it made him special envoy and thereby entitled him to ride in the procession, which caused him quite a flutter when he finally became convinced of it after I had been to the Foreign Office where, upon receiving the information, they at once said, "The King offers him a horse to ride with the princes and other foreign representatives." As he rides well, he naturally would have liked very much to do this and I should also have liked it for him. But of course he cannot ride in a dress suit or in a frock coat and tall hat. . . . We have ordered a beautiful wreath for the President which cost fifty guineas—the cheapest which we could get in any way worthy of a chief of state. Mr. Choate and I gave it much consideration and I think it will be worthy of him. Even Portugal spent a hundred guineas on her King's tribute, and Russia, we are told, one hundred and fifty guineas. . . . Did I write you that a worthy man from Kalamazoo called recently on Mr. Choate and solicited formally his good offices with a view to obtaining permission for him to embalm the Queen's body? This was too much for the Ambassador, who fairly turned upon and rent him. . . .

[October 23, 1901.] John Morley confided to my wife the other day that Moberly Bell has just returned from his visit to our country in a state of profound depression at the condition of his own in comparison therewith from almost every point of view except the journalistic. You will also be glad to hear that Admiral Seymour, who has just returned from China, tells his friends confidentially, some of whom have passed it on to me, that our fellows, both naval and military—meaning the men as well as the officers—were by far the best out there, not even excepting the British, which from his point of view is a very strong admission.

[November 25, 1901.] I spent three very pleasant days last week with Lord Salisbury at Hatfield. He seemed in particularly good form, and has made a bicycle gravel-and-asphalt path, beautifully engineered like a miniature railway, with cuttings—one of them quite deep—bridges, levellings-up, etc., in the Park, three miles long, of which he makes a round on his machine every morning. There is no doubt that this exercise has done him a lot of good, as he looks less stout and much clearer as to the skin. When in London he makes a tour of Buckingham Palace Gardens. I got him into some very pleasant talk, during which, as usual, he spoke with great freedom on many topics. I found that he is delighted at the recognition made by the German Ambassador, on his return recently from his holiday, of the Monroe Doctrine; and indeed he is always delighted when the German Emperor, who is not sympathetic to him, gets a snub or has to climb down. He also admitted to me that the Senate was quite within its right in its amendment of the first Hay-Pauncefote Treaty, and that there was nothing necessarily offensive to this country in its manner of so doing.

White's zeal in behalf of Anglo-American friendship involved many small and half-amusing, half-irritating cares. During 1900 Senator Lodge took a violent dislike to Gerald Lowther, first secretary of the British embassy, who had been in the diplomatic service since 1879 and later became ambassador to Turkey. According to the Senator, Lowther was tactless, had made various offensive remarks, and ought to be recalled. In reply, White defended Lowther, and though the secretary received an admonition from London, he succeeded in smoothing matters over. Early in the century an American polo team visited the British Isles and won a series of victories, whereupon Lord Shrewsbury charged that the Americans had been guilty of unsportsmanlike conduct; a small storm blew up, but White, who saw Edward VII in person, quickly dissipated it by obtaining from the critic a disclaimer and apology. He was the medium through whom American public men frequently had corrections made in the British press. In 1899, for example,

Senator Mark Hanna was indignant over a London *Times* story about a "deal" which Hanna was alleged to have made with McKinley for the appointment of Alger as Secretary of War. "I never asked the President to appoint Alger or any other member of the Cabinet," Hanna wrote White [1]—and White had the story corrected. No detail was too small for White's attention. Take, for instance, his protest to Hay against some presumptuous American requests of Great Britain:

I wonder if you had time to read over the circular instruction of last February issued in your name in which we are instructed to ask the British Government to do an enormous amount of statistical work for the New York Public Library. I should think it would take one man more than a month to look up and compile all that is therein suggested. And the worst of it is that in the final paragraph it is stated that "the replies to this instruction will be printed in a special number of the Consular Reports," the result of which will be to bring down every library in the country upon the Department or upon this Embassy (for I don't suppose they care much for other government publications in foreign languages). Already we have another from Seth Low on the same subject for the library of Columbia, forwarded by you. I am working at the matter through the Treasury and other semi-official sources and hope to get something up to send him. But the same request for the gift of government publications to a public library has already been refused in Mr. Bayard's time, which does not make it any easier now.

Or take, again, a little warning he sent to Roosevelt in 1903:

I see that Jusserand has arrived, and I hope you will find him to equal my description of him. I am sure you will greatly enjoy talking with him on all sorts of literary and other questions—there are very few which he cannot discuss in an interesting way. He is fully alive, moreover, to the great responsibilities of his new post and means to do his best to be worthy of them. He is, as I told you, extremely prejudiced against this country and attributes deep designs and base perfidy to its policy, which are usually without the least foundation. As you know, they blunder into things here—witness this German alliance against Venezuela—and do not carry out many great policies after long reflection. It is the more curious as he knows England so well and most of his writings are about England in the olden time.

[1] Mark Hanna to White, July 25, 1899. "Another cussed letter from Smalley," is the way Hanna spoke of the *Times* dispatch.

Much more important was the attention which White gave to the representation of Great Britain in Washington, a subject upon which he was several times able to advise the British Government. In the fall of 1900 he and Secretary Hay were disturbed by reports that under the rule of rotation Lord Pauncefote, the very ideal of an ambassador, might not be retained another year. White saw Lord Lansdowne, impressed on him the importance of keeping Pauncefote in the United States, and had the pleasure of seeing his appointment extended. "I have had several conversations with Lord Salisbury on the subject," he wrote Hay, "and vetoed several members of the service whom he suggested as possibilities. Some day I shall tell you about it." Pauncefote's term in Washington came to an end only with his death. Hay wrote White that he never again expected to find an ambassador or a dean of the Diplomatic Corps with whom it would be so pleasant to work, and President Roosevelt broke precedent by having the flag half-staffed on the White House and sending the body home on an American battleship; not, he said, "because he was British ambassador, but because he was a damn good fellow!" [2] For some time the British Ministry hesitated in choosing a successor. White urged, as forcibly as he could, that the place be given to his friend Sir Michael Herbert. This Lansdowne was reluctant to do, for he had in mind the appointment of an old subordinate in India, Sir Mortimer Durand, who possessed a special admiration for America and her institutions. [3] But ultimately Herbert was appointed. He was deeply touched, writing White that he did not know how to thank him enough. "One thing is certain, that I should never have got it without you, and that it is chiefly due to your unremitting and tactful efforts on my behalf. I am not modest enough to compare myself to the mouse in the fable, but I earnestly hope that some day I may imitate the

[2] Mowat, R. B., *The Life of Lord Pauncefote*, p. 297. Roosevelt had two reasons for making his tribute forcible—personal affection, and his resentment of the charges made by the German ambassador, Dr. von Holleben, against Pauncefote. The latter early in 1902 accused Pauncefote of having engaged at the beginning of the Spanish conflict in an intrigue against the United States, and the anguish caused by the charges hastened the aged Pauncefote's death. All of von Holleben's accusations fell flat, American opinion rejecting them utterly.

[3] Durand was British Ambassador at Madrid.

example of that thankful little rodent whenever I get the chance of being useful to you." Herbert was an instant success, and as Henry Adams said, he counted for double an ordinary diplomatist.

Once more, when Sir Mortimer Durand succeeded Herbert, White was able to lend a helping hand. For some reason President Roosevelt did not get on well with Durand. The two men did not understand each other, and while Jusserand and Sternburg became intimate with the President and were often at the White House, Durand was never in favor. Late in 1904, when Roosevelt was trying to mold a successful Far Eastern policy and had hopes of making peace between Japan and Russia, he sent an appeal to White.[4] "Now I wonder if you could arrange to have the Foreign Office send Spring-Rice over here to see me for a week?" he wrote. "I understand he is in London for a little while. There is no one in the British Embassy to whom I can talk freely, and I would like to have the people at the Foreign Office understand just my position in the Far East, and I would like to know what theirs is. I do not have much faith in the tenacity or willingness to stand punishment of either the English Government or the English people, and as it is impossible to foretell what conditions will arise, and therefore what position our people will be willing to take, I think that all that can be done at present is to try to get a clear idea of the respective mental attitudes of the two governments. But I think it would be an advantage to have this clear idea. I do not know whether it is my fault or Sir Mortimer's, but our minds do not meet; and in any event I should be unwilling to speak with such freedom as I desire to anyone in whom I have not such absolute trust as I have in Spring-Rice, both as regards his intelligence, his discretion, and his loyalty." White was able to arrange for Spring-Rice's visit. The Foreign Office also gave Durand some plain hints, and he made an effort, partly successful, to come to better terms with Roosevelt.[5]

[4] Roosevelt to White, Washington, December 27, 1904.

[5] It may also be noted here that White had not a little to do with securing Bernstorff's appointment as German ambassador. During the later years of his secretaryship in London, Bernstorff was Councilor of the German embassy there (1902-06). White learned to have a high regard for him. In 1908 his name and that of some one else were suggested to Roosevelt as possible appointees to the embassy; Roosevelt consulted White, who warmly recom-

The routine of the embassy was seldom laborious. White frequently worked there eight, ten, or twelve hours a day; but he could usually command his week-ends, and he could leave his desk in mid-afternoon if occasion required it. He excelled in entertaining, and his superiors handed over to him numerous eminent American visitors to England. His infallible instinct for the right way of dealing with any question of social form or precedence was indispensable. At the time of the coronation of Edward VII the Roosevelt family gave consideration to a suggestion that Alice Roosevelt should attend; White advised against it, and his information that she would inevitably be treated as a royal princess reinforced the President's determination not to let her go. Whenever personal influence in London was desired, application was almost certain to be made to White. In 1902 Senator Lodge wrote him that everyone, including the President, was eager to have Roosevelt's portrait for the White House painted by Sargent, but that the sum available, only $800 being appropriated by Congress, was so small that they feared to apply to the artist. White ascertained that Sargent would gladly paint Roosevelt for any fee or none, and received delighted letters from both Roosevelt and Lodge. After all, it was found that $2,500 was really obtainable from Congress, so that Sargent's fee was not so mean as had been feared.[6]

For Secretary Hay White bought rare books, valuable pictures and manuscripts, including the manuscript of Stevenson's *Markheim*, for which he paid £85 at Sotheran's. It fell to White, who had looked after Mrs. Maybrick just after her trial, to make the arrangements for her departure from prison in 1904, when she was allowed to take refuge in France. When the Pilgrims' Club of London elected Roosevelt a member in 1902, it was White who advised him, for special reasons, to decline the membership. The American squadron happening to pay a visit to Kiel in 1903, Edward VII was anxious that it should touch at some port on its return, and Francis Villiers of the Foreign Office called thrice in

mended Bernstorff, and the latter was chosen. White admired Bernstorff's work during the World War, and always believed that if the Berlin Government had taken proper advantage of his advice, he would have effected a peace by American mediation.

[6] Lodge to White, Washington, March 27, May 5, 1902.

one week to learn if this could be arranged; it was White who arranged it. It was he who obtained for Roosevelt the original of Bernard Partridge's famous Rough Rider cartoon in *Punch*. When he was on a trip to Scotland in 1901 he hurried back to see Senator Lodge off from Southampton. "I want to see," he wrote Hay, "that he starts home in a right frame of mind about the Canal and other matters, and shall spend the day with him probably."

White keenly enjoyed his life and all the little humors attendant upon it.[7] He enjoyed seeing the young German Kaiser review the troops at Aldershot, wearing a British uniform and affectedly kissing the hand of the Duke of Connaught. He enjoyed showing men so different as President Harrison, Bishop Potter, and Senator Jones of Nevada about London. He enjoyed talking with Andrew Carnegie even at a time when the great capitalist was positive that Roosevelt and Hay were wrong about everything, including the Panama Canal, which was not needed and would never be built. White commented to Hay, "Carnegie's vanity is stupendous, is it not?" He enjoyed such duties as conveying to his old neighbor, Sir George Trevelyan, Roosevelt's congratulations on his history of the American Revolution, together with an invitation to visit the White House—an invitation to which Trevelyan replied in warm terms:

Your letter gave me great pleasure, and made me exceedingly proud. It is impossible to imagine a more interesting project than a visit to the President, and such a President, at the White House; and I have clung to the hope that I could accept his very kind invitation—but only in imagination. In reality I am fully persuaded that I am not up to a journey to, and especially a stay in, the United States. I should be sorry to name the amount of money I would pay down to find myself for a week in Washington, a week in and about Boston, and for a couple of days at Trenton, and a couple more at Gettysburg, but I am not strong enough for a tour in the States and all that it would involve. I please myself

[7] White described the coronation of Edward VII for Hay's benefit. "The old Duchess of Devonshire," he wrote, "came a cropper on the way out of the Abbey, not seeing a step and falling over it headlong, her coronet, which was on at the time, rolling off to some distance. There was a very comic side to this incident, as you may imagine. The venerable lady has made no allusion to it since to anyone whom she has seen, and no one has ventured to mention it to her!"—White to Hay, August 12, 1902.

with the idea that, when my book is finished (and after its reception there I must try and finish it now), I may see the great country at last, when it will not matter whether I am the worse for it in health. But that is only an idea, however fascinating a one, and I must make it serve for the reality as best I may. I have received a letter from the President about my book, which I value very highly.

Some days which White spent in 1903 in guiding William Jennings Bryan's explorations of London and assisting him to meet prominent Englishmen were pleasanter than he had expected. He felt that Bryan, whom some six million American voters had twice supported for the Presidency, deserved every honor and consideration, but he feared that he would be a bore. Instead, he found to his surprise that the Democratic leader was an extremely good fellow, with an active and inquiring mind. When he lunched or dined with the rather curious British statesmen, he talked ably and interestingly—better than he listened. Of history, art, and letters, it is true, his knowledge was rather scanty. Thus in viewing Whitehall, Bryan asked when it had been built, and upon being told that several of the Stuarts and King William had lived there, he demanded, "William the Conqueror?" When he was shown through Hampton Court Palace he was immensely pleased by the fine wood-carvings of Grinling Gibbons; but the reason why they pleased him was merely that he knew a craftsman in Lincoln, Nebraska, who did work of somewhat similar type. Again, in dining with the Whites he expressed intense interest in Tolstoy, saying that one of his principal objects in his travels on the Continent would be to pay that great teacher a visit at Yasnaya Polyana. Mrs. White, naturally enough, asked him which of Tolstoy's books had most impressed him, to which Bryan replied: "Oh, I have not read Tolstoy's works; but I have read a great many articles in the magazines and the Sunday newspapers about him." But White liked him and felt the magnetism of the man.[8]

[8] Memorandum by White, 1926. While Ambassador to Italy, White in 1906 entertained Bryan in Venice. "He asked me whether I was a Democrat, to which I replied that I was a diplomatist, and consequently a servant of the nation, and not of any particular party. Mr. Bryan thereupon expressed great regret regarding what I had said, because he said he felt that there would not improbably be a change of Administration before long in the United States, and he would much have liked to have me remain in the public

As the years passed, White's circle was of course changing. Many of his old English friends had now risen to high station, while some, like Sir William Harcourt, had died. He frequently saw Balfour, whose ministry lasted till late in 1905. He heard regularly from Curzon in India, and at one time thought of going with Mrs. White to visit the Viceroy. Curzon complained of overwork and intellectual loneliness, and was severe in criticism of some aspects of Anglo-Indian social life. "I have had a letter from George Curzon," White wrote to Hay, "who is disposed to animadvert upon the tendency to flirtation of the British subaltern in India, and says that his own moral code has suffered since he has been there to an extent which his friends would not recognize." Of St. John Brodrick he saw a good deal, and much of Mrs. Asquith, though Asquith himself is seldom mentioned in his letters. Among Americans White corresponded irregularly with E. J. Phelps, Robert Lincoln, and Levi P. Morton. But his principal correspondence was with Hay, Henry Cabot Lodge, and Roosevelt—particularly the first two, for after 1901 Roosevelt was one of the busiest men on the planet.

The closest of all his American friends just after the turn of the century was unquestionably Hay, and their intimacy is attested by many letters. The two men had grown extremely fond of each other during their year and a half together in London; Hay, quick-witted, mercurial, highly gifted artistically, and always needing affection, found comfort in White's sympathetic and less emotional nature. In 1901, when as we have noted Hay lost his son Adelbert as well as John Nicolay, Clarence King, and President McKinley, he wrote to White as probably to no one except Henry Adams. Adelbert Hay, after his work for British prisoners in Boer territory and as consul at Pretoria had returned to London, where he stayed with White, and had then in March, 1901, gone to New York. "I am most grateful to you, and to all of you, for your kindness to him while he was in London," wrote Hay. "I have no idea what he will do next, and shall not press him to make any decision until later

---

service, intimating, however, that such a course would be impossible for those in charge of a Democratic Administration, as all places similar to that which I then occupied would have to be given to loyal supporters of the Democratic party."

in the year." Some weeks later arrived news that he was to have an important White House appointment. Immediately thereafter came word of his death. Hay wrote to White:

NEWBURY, NEW HAMPSHIRE,
June 30th, 1901.

MY DEAR WHITE:

I thank you for your kind telegram. We are overwhelmed with kindness from every quarter. If sympathy could help, our sorrow would be brief.

But every word of praise and affection which we hear of our dead boy, but gives a keener edge to our grief. Why should he go, I stupidly ask, with his splendid health and strength, his courage, his hopes, his cheery smile which made everybody like him at sight, and I be left, with my short remnant of life, of little use to my friends and none to myself? Yet I know this is a wild and stupid way to rail at fate. I must face the facts. My boy is gone, and the whole face of the world is changed in a moment.

Have you heard how it happened? The night was frightfully hot and close. He sat on the window-sill, to get cool before turning in, and fell asleep. He was the soundest sleeper I ever knew. He probably did not wake.

The President had just appointed him—without my advice—to be one of his secretaries—the medium of communication with Congress and the departments. Del had great hesitation about accepting it. I would not help him even with a word. He finally took it, and was full of preparations for it. He was not going to the White House till autumn, and meantime intended to make a cruise in Col. Payne's yacht and was thinking of surprising you with a visit.

All this is dust and ashes.

Mrs. Hay and Helen are bearing up wonderfully. I feared for both of them—they idolized him. But they show more strength than I do.

I go to Washington Tuesday to put things in order for a longish vacation. Adee has gone back, and the work of the department is in very good shape. I am very glad we have this hermitage where we can hide our misery for a while.

Give our love to Mrs. White.

J. H.

During the summer and autumn Hay wrote several times in great depression. He had been asked to accept an honorary degree at Yale University late in October; even then he said it was agony to go, but he felt that it would seem surly to decline so great an honor on so notable an occasion, the bi-centenary of Yale; and he would be there but he would not speak. Then in 1902 and 1903 letters began to come penned with some of his old defiant gayety.

Hay, it is evident, felt free to comment more frankly to White than to anyone else in the diplomatic service upon men and events. "Congress begins work on the first [of December]," he wrote in the autumn of 1902, "and I anticipate a series of defeats for the State Department. Mr. Cullom is staunch and resolute—says he will force the treaties to a vote. But the result seems reasonably certain—nothing will pass that anyone is opposed to." Senator Lodge had told him that it broke his heart to oppose the Newfoundland fisheries treaty which Hay was sponsoring, but that the wishes of the Gloucester fishermen, who had volunteered nobly in the war with Spain, were sacred. Progress was being made upon a treaty with Cuba, but the negotiations with Colombia for the Panama strip were slow. "Colombia is as slippery as an eel," wrote Hay. "I cannot believe they want the negotiations to fail, but they act as no reasonable creatures would act, save on that supposition. I have stopped talking with Concha [the Colombian minister] for the moment, to see what a period of silence and *recueillement* may operate in his so-called mind. The press have taken up the matter and are rabid against Colombia, and getting quite friendly again to Nicaragua. I hope Concha reads them. Happily, I don't care a hoot what the Senate does. I am not personally engaged in any of the treaties now pending, though they are all good things for us and ought to pass." Of such candor there was a great deal in the letters. Frequently he mentioned three of White's friends— Senator Wolcott, Lodge, and Roosevelt—and their relations with one another. Thus he wrote in the summer of 1903:

Helen had a dinner party last night—all friends of yours. Everybody spoke pleasantly of you and Mrs. White. Wolcott was here in good condition, but sore at heart with the President's unfriendliness to him in Colorado—which is absolutely inexplicable to me—the President having given his entire confidence, and the control of patronage, to a bitter enemy of Wolcott named Phil Stewart.

Our relations with Russia are getting badly smashed in spite of all my efforts. I thought I had everything arranged when I left Washington, but the war of *communiqués* has broken out since, worse than ever.

I am glad Lodge is going to England soon. He worries the President with querulous complaints of the Department being too easy with England in the Alaska business, when the Lord knows we have been rigorous to the point of discourtesy. Lodge always behaves himself better in England than here.

With equal candor Hay described his feelings as to his own future and discussed the vexations of his office. A succession of letters in 1904 treats of the presidential campaign, his probable career after the election, and his troubles with Russia and other nations. It is sufficient to take a few extracts:

[July 9th.]—I have been to Michigan and got back alive, after a journey which was unusually and unexpectedly pleasant. We had a great meeting, some ten thousand people, in a beautiful grove, who listened with exemplary patience from noon till night to the eloquence of yours truly, and Fairbanks and Cannon, and a lot of others. I spoke an hour and a half with perfect ease to myself, however the audience may have suffered.

The St. Louis convention has nominated Parker and evidently squared Bryan by rejecting both his and Hill's money plank. They have absolutely dodged or straddled all the important issues, and the net result is the nomination of which everyone was certain beforehand, and two lamentable campaign speeches by Williams and Champ Clark which offered a melancholy contrast to the two great speeches in which Root and Taft set forth the Republican programme.

[July 31st.]—I do not know what Wolcott's sources of information may be, in regard to my plans. I am getting old and tired, it is true, but I have never told anybody I intended to retire in March. I shall be propelled out on the 5th of March, if the Parker-Hill-Gorman combination comes in. But Roosevelt—at present at least—will not listen to my suggestions of retiring, and I do not discuss the matter with anyone else—except my wife, and she is reasonable about it, and will agree to whatsoever seems best. She makes only one condition: If I stay on next year, I am to take a vacation of a few months abroad. I shall cease to be Vice-President next spring, and shall feel a little freer in my movements, if I have health and strength left to go anywhere. . . .

The President's speech of acceptance was a great success and has been splendidly received. The Boston *Herald* has a furious article against it, saying that the President, being a lawless, violent, unscrupulous man, has no right to make a speech so sober, sound, and judicious!—and intimates that Root and I made him do it! The pitiful fools—they are unconscious of the exhibition they are making of themselves.

———

[August 11th.]—Everything seems favorable to us. The President's speech of acceptance made a splendid impression on the country, and Parker's speech made yesterday is weak and puerile to the last degree. On the subject of the currency he says nothing but to repeat his telegram, and in regard to the tariff he says he is in favor of some reasonable reduction of the tariff which will not interfere with business, and, at the same time, he winks at the tariff men in the party and says that you must not forget that the Republicans have got the Senate and nothing that we say in the matter will have the slightest practical effect. As to the Philippines, he says he is in favor of giving them self-government as soon as they are ready for it. Neither Root nor Taft nor Roosevelt say anything different from that. The rest of the speech is a mass of inane platitudes.

Roosevelt's letter of acceptance, on the contrary—which I went over with him yesterday—is an admirable document, clear, straightforward, and comprehensible to anyone who can read. I think he will lose very few Republican votes, and, on the other hand, he is going to gain, according to all present appearances, a very large number of Democratic votes. Many Democrats will vote for him for good reasons, and some, I must confess, for very bad ones. A lot of Populists will vote for him because they were turned down in the St. Louis Convention. Even a few Irish are showing a disposition that way. As the Spaniards say: "*El dinero es muy catolico*," and votes are good, no matter what their provenance. The *Sun* this morning comes out for Roosevelt.

———

[September 5th.]—I shall be here [Newbury, New Hampshire] for two or three weeks more. I have had an unsatisfactory summer, cut up by journeys and unexpected tasks. But everything has seemed to go in a fairly prosperous way. Tomorrow Vermont and Maine are to vote and we anticipate a comfortable majority. I see no reason to fear anything but an easy victory for Roosevelt in November. I think we shall have Congress also, though Babcock, pursuing his usual tactics, is scaring our people into harder work and more liberal contributions.

I was grieved the other day to see Henry Wolcott had come out for Parker. Not that he carries any weight, but the effect will be disastrous upon his brother, and will doubtless finish his chances for the Senate. The whole story has been deplorable—and so absolutely unnecessary.

I will say nothing about the war, as that active little devil of a Kuroki makes history faster than a letter can travel. Who could have dreamed last year that a Japanese army, with virtually equal forces, should have herded and driven like sheep the army of Russia from the Yalu to the Tai-tse?

Roosevelt was too busy to write as often as Hay, or at such length when he did write; but feeling that White was the ablest of the American representatives abroad, he was glad to maintain personal touch with him. Sometimes he threw out a mere hasty comment; sometimes he expressed some personal view with characteristic force. His notes of the spring and summer of 1904 to some extent supplement those of Hay. The first two are dated from the White House, the third from Oyster Bay:

[February 17th.]—Poor Hanna has just died. Thank heaven, before he became sick the whole opposition to me had collapsed. Hanna was a very strong personality, with many large and generous traits.

I am much obliged to you for your information about England's attitude toward the Yang-tse Valley. It is borne out by her recent action. Germany, I am bound to say, has acted very well. Was it not astonishing that the Russians should have shown themselves so utterly slack and unready?

———

[April 4th.]—Plunkett has already sent me that book, and I have been much interested in it. I appreciate your having taken the trouble to think of me in connection with it. He is a great deal of a fellow.

Do not take Cabot's over-sanguine view of matters. Nobody can tell how this fight will come out. I have been astonishingly successful in getting through the policies in which I believe, and in achieving results; but often the mere fact of having a good deal of a record is more against a man than for him, when the question is as to how people will vote; for my experience is that usually people are more apt to let their dislikes than their likings cause them to break away from their party ties in matters of voting. In other words, the people of the opposite party who like what I have done are less apt for that reason to leave their candidate than the people of my own party who dislike what I have done are apt to leave me. Politicians proverbially like a colorless candidate, and the very success of what I have done, the number of things I have accomplished, and the extent of my record, may prove to be against me. However, be that as it may, we now have a big sum of achievement to our credit.

[July 5th.]—Thanks for your interesting letter. I was pleased to know what Mitchell had said. It looks as if Parker will be nominated. As to what the result will be, I have not the slightest idea. I have long given up prophesying about the outcome of a political contest, especially one in which I am myself chiefly concerned. In such a political contest one sees almost exclusively the people who are friendly and zealous partisans; and accordingly all that is said is favorable.

McKim's visit must have been interesting. I am glad you had him see the King.

I am much pleased that Morley is coming to stay with us after election. Just before election it would have been almost impossible to have had any satisfaction out of his visit. I shall also be glad to see the Archbishop of Canterbury if he comes over. . . .

P. S.—We have just finished an old-fashioned Fourth of July. Here on the Neck, as you know, there are four families of us, and as the young people all have their special friends down as guests on the Fourth, we have walks, picnics, rows, dances, and fireworks. And the older people enjoy looking on about as much as the younger ones do in taking part.

Roosevelt's cordial reference to Hanna, who had been regarded in some quarters as a formidable aspirant for the presidential nomination in 1904, gives interest to Elihu Root's comment on his death. Writing to White at the end of February, Root said that everybody had been shocked and grieved by the loss of Hanna. "Many uninformed persons speak of it as being lucky for Roosevelt; I do not think so. I have never had the least doubt that Hanna would have proved an earnest supporter of Roosevelt when the time came, and that he would have been a great element in the campaign. The exchange of affectionate little notes between the two when Hanna was on his deathbed is a great consolation to anyone who was a friend of both of them, and the evidence of Hanna's affectionate feeling towards the President is very fortunate." Root added that "Whitney's death was a great misfortune for the Democratic Party.[9] Above all the other men in the party he had the breadth of view and commanding influence and persuasive power necessary to make its wild horses run together. He was beginning to exhibit renewed interest in the subject, and I think might have furnished the necessary leadership; it is very doubtful whether there is any man left capable of doing that."

Roosevelt and Hay together were doing far more than any previous President and Secretary of State to realize White's dream of a diplomatic and consular service founded on merit and kept to the highest professional standards; and a number of Hay's letters dealt with the subject. He and White wrote freely to one another upon the merits and demerits of members of the service all over Europe. None knew better than White where good work was being done, where a diplomatist was proving himself a misfit, and where neglect or ineptitude were being shown. He would report that in Brussels, or in Naples, a particularly able record was being made by the American consul; he reported once that the American *chargé* in a minor capital was often drunk and should be replaced as quickly as possible by a regular minister. As the century opened, he and Hay shared the opinion that Andrew D. White, a distinguished and very able man, was too far past his prime to make a really good representative in Berlin; while they and Roosevelt agreed that another distinguished and valuable man, George von Lengerke Meyer, was somehow not well adapted to his office of ambassador to Italy. Hay and White were in harmony in thinking that promising young men should be drawn into the service, that they should be advanced as rapidly as their experience and talents warranted, that the baser kind of politicians should be excluded, and that our diplomatic body should be lifted much nearer to the best European level.

Unfortunately, the spoils system was too deeply rooted to be greatly weakened even by President Roosevelt. After the election in 1904 there was a presidential shake-up of the service. Roosevelt asked for the resignation of all the ambassadors and ministers, and as Hay informed White in advance, he meant to accept many of them. "There will be things done between now and next April

[9] William C. Whitney, who did much in 1884 to organize Cleveland's victorious campaign and became Secretary of the Navy, died February 2, 1904.

in the diplomatic and consular service," wrote the Secretary of State, "that would appear absolutely incomprehensible to anyone who was not in the center of the spider's eye. Not an appointment nor a removal can be made without an instantaneous explosion of malice and selfishness on the part of leading Senators; yet the President has made up his mind to make a good many changes and to stand the resulting racket. The natural consequence is that whenever he—to use a Senatorial phrase—takes a place from a State, there is a row so furious and vehement that he generally ends up by giving them another place and sometimes two. The whole squabble and wrangle is so distasteful to me that I would gladly be out of it, and would certainly insist upon going were it not that the President has taken all consideration of personal appointments away from me, and makes appointments now directly, after consultation with Mr. Loomis as to the state of the private list." But despite political difficulties, Roosevelt's appointments were distinctly high in quality, and for this Hay deserves much and White at least a little credit.

White's personal habits in these years about the turn of the century continued to be much the same as in his earlier London residence. He still delighted in open-air exercise, riding constantly on horseback, bicycling a good deal—he brought a crack bicycle from America for Balfour, much to the latter's pleasure—shooting and deer-stalking, sometimes skating, and playing an enthusiastic but not brilliant game of golf. For sailing, racing, or such indoor games as billiards he cared little, but he liked to dance, and he was fond of the theater. He was never a man who greatly loved reading or study for itself, and at this time, as always, he was frankly indifferent to *belles lettres*—to novels, poetry, and essays. What reading he did was in history, memoirs, and biography, and ranged rather widely over both European and American subjects. But his favorite pastime at this period and throughout life was conversation. Like Johnson, he loved to cross his legs in a social circle and have his talk out, but unlike Johnson, he always emphasized the first syllable of the word "conversation." For him, talk was not good unless everybody participated with spirit and interest, and he disliked equally the person who remained silent in a lively group, and the person who cultivated monologue and a deliberate display of wit. A man of these tastes for outdoor sport and indoor society fitted perfectly into English life, and White continued to have more invitations to country houses than his work or his wife's health allowed him to accept.

During his last years in London White and his family were ideally housed in the attractive 4 Whitehall Gardens, with its lawn looking out over the Thames Embankment. Mrs. White's strength, after her critical illness of 1899, slowly improved. For a while she was much abroad—the Vosges, Spain, southern France— and even after her return her health was precarious; much of the time she could not entertain, her daughter Muriel acting as a charming and competent hostess. The closest friends of the family had felt her sudden prostration as a tremendous shock. They had rallied about her and her husband with the warmest expressions of sympathy. A letter from Henry James, dated December 8, 1899, and condoling with her over her absences on the Continent, is typical of many. Alas! he wrote:

Alas, alas, what weary pilgrimages—and what (you must feel) a weary pilgrim! What an endless bother, too, that the climate of this country is the one huge inconvenience in such a cluster of conveniences! However, I didn't mean to wail to you, but on the contrary, to try and make you see some bright and cheering sign. Cheer doesn't just now precisely abound anywhere; and I find this beastly Brummagem war a nightmare and a haunting—both actually and in its furthest possibilities, a direct and indirect dread. So I return—cravenly creeping into my own individual hole—to my little refuge on the south coast in a day or two; a little refuge which, I almost blush to say, has a semblance of a climate, sun and softness and brightness and quietness and out-of-doors growing things now; and above all, a remoteness from affairs. Affairs are awful —though I am horrid to remind you who live in the midst of them, of that. I am hoping that when you are almost on your back you may find yourself (even to yourself) so reduplicated in Muriel the Magnificent that you have moments of not, as it were, so missing yourself. All the same, I miss you all the same, even over the head of so many interesting things; for it is missing you to know that you suffer and don't fill, by standing upright, your beautiful indispensable niche; indispensable to the highest part of the whole human structure. But take time; don't be superficial. Throw everything and everyone overboard that doesn't directly and intimately enter into the scheme of your recovery. Everyone, that is, but *me*. If while you lie there it would help one tiny bit, to think you are thought of, are cherished, as one of the finest and most beneficent of images, memories, please truly associate that fidelity, dearest Mrs. White, with the name of yours ever so tenderly and constantly,

HENRY JAMES.

But though Mrs. White remained a semi-invalid, with but uncertain intervals of health, the family were on the whole exceedingly happy in their old London environment. It might have been supposed that White would feel an occasional twinge of restiveness over the fact that he was not promoted to the post of ambassador in one of the European capitals, but he did not. He knew that he could hardly do more useful or important work than fell to him in London. Hay had wished to appoint him to Rome when Ambassador Draper retired in 1900, but under political pressure from Senators Lodge and Hoar, McKinley felt that it was necessary to offer the place to George von L. Meyer of Massachusetts. White felt little if any disappointment. He sent a good-natured letter of expostulation to Lodge, who in reply explained, quite sincerely, that he had committed himself to Meyer before he knew that White would be inclined to accept the Italian embassy.[10] Beyond question it was a piece of good fortune that White was not removed to the relative inactivity of Rome in these years when so much was happening in Anglo-American affairs.

He continued during 1903 and 1904 to send Secretary Hay confidential letters on the political and diplomatic situation as he saw it, paying particular attention to relations between England and France.[11] In these years the *entente*, vigorously fostered by King

[10] Lodge to White, December 18, 1900.

[11] Once in 1903 White and his family went for a week-end at Lord Rosebery's country place, The Durdans, near Epsom. Muriel White's Diary tells us that he was "a delightful host and full of fun. He would not talk about politics and the tariff, rather to mother's disappointment, but he showed us all his quaint old books and curiosities, of which he has a great many. There is a very pleasant Austrian here who used to be in the embassy in London and who is now at St. Petersburg, Count Berchtold. He is said to be one of the cleverest men in Austria, but he impresses me as amiable and polite rather than remarkably intelligent." Berchtold's lack of intelligence was later to contribute mightily to one of the world's greatest catastrophes.

Edward, Delcassé, Paul Cambon, and others, was steadily being strengthened, and culminated on April 7, 1904, in the signing of the Anglo-French Agreement. White wrote on March 19th: "You have probably seen in the papers some allusion to an understanding which is said to have been arrived at between this country and France for the settlement of all their differences, and I have been making inquiries on the subject, with the result that the report would seem substantially correct. There is no doubt that an important agreement has been arrived at, as Sanderson of the Foreign Office, who lunched with me yesterday, admitted the fact. It will be a great feather in Lansdowne's cap." Already White knew that it dealt with the questions of Newfoundland, Morocco, and Egypt. George Wyndham had suggested to him that it would be an excellent idea to detach France from the rest of Europe and induce her to work in general partnership with England and America. On April 22nd White added more definite information:

The chief diplomatic event has of course been the Anglo-French agreement, which really does great credit to the principal negotiators, Lord Lansdowne, M. Cambon, and M. Delcassé. Curiously enough, it has been most cordially received on both sides of the Channel, and I have not come across any suggestion from responsible quarters that either country has been "done" by the other. It is doubtless particularly welcome in France as a guarantee that Russia can under no circumstances now expect France to join her against Japan, and for somewhat the same reason in this country, where nothing could have been more abhorrent to the national feeling than being obliged, under the Anglo-Japanese Treaty, to join Japan against France because France had joined Russia. But whatever the cause, the result is extreme satisfaction and relief on both sides of the Channel. According to the newspapers, there is a move in Russia to try to come to terms, in some such agreement as this, over the questions at issue between Russia and this country.

There can be no doubt that King Edward hoped that the Anglo-French *entente* would be supplemented by a close understanding with the United States. No little significance attaches to an interview between White and the astute monarch, in which the latter plainly revealed his feeling. Though he was about to leave for Washington, White wrote out a report of the conversation:

Although I hope to see you within the next few days, I think I had better transmit to you by letter a message which the King of England asked me to give you from him the night before I left London.

There was a "Court" at Buckingham Palace at which I arrived rather late and was somewhat surprised to be told by the officials that the King wanted particularly to see me privately and in fact was waiting to do so before proceeding to the throne room. I was at once ushered into the royal presence and the King said that having heard that I was leaving the next morning for America, he had sent for me to give me a message for the President. He first of all asked me to convey to you his very particular regards and his best wishes for the success of your second administration, and he went on to say that your election by such an overwhelming and unprecedented majority had given him great satisfaction and pleasure, and that he hopes you are aware of the admiration he has for your character and of the interest he takes in your welfare, which is of such great importance to the whole world.

The King then said, not, as I inferred, *necessarily* a part of his message, but it might or might not have been, that he hoped the President would never allow himself to be persuaded by any other Sovereign or Government—"I refrain," he said, "from mentioning any particular Sovereign or Government"—that they could be as good a friend to our country as His Majesty himself and Great Britain are to us; for in the case of the latter not only is the sovereign friendly but his *whole* people, whose interests and feelings are practically identical with ours, which is more than could be said of any other country. He wound up his remarks by saying that he intends shortly to write to you, though he did not say whether I was to tell you that or not, and he also expressed much regret at my departure from London, which was certainly not a part of his message to you.

It is a very unusual thing for anyone to be received in private audience by the King just before a Court, and his doing so to me was an indication of his desire to emphasize the importance attached by him to—and the friendliness of—the message he asked me to convey to you.

I think I have repeated it to you with accuracy. . . . I am sure I have not attributed to the King any sentiments which he did not express, my only doubt being whether I have given you an idea of the seriousness and earnestness with which he gave them utterance and of the interest he seemed to take in you.

From the time of Roosevelt's accession to the Presidency in 1901 it was understood that White would be sent to Italy at the earliest opportunity. The opportunity was long in coming, for Ambasador Meyer was unwilling to quit his post unless he were offered a promotion in diplomatic rank or saw a favorable opportunity to reënter Massachusetts politics. There was nothing to do but wait. "Cabot is in Massachusetts today," wrote Hay to White in the spring of 1902. "It is a great point gained if he and Hoar abstain from pressing upon the President a successor to Meyer if Meyer resigns. This is all I can say at present, except I have let the President understand that my dearest wish is to have the place given to you." White believed that there was a great opportunity in Italy for an ambassador who spoke the tongue as well as he did, who understood European diplomacy and the special conditions existing in Italy, and who earnestly wished to raise the prestige of the United States.

At last, in 1904, the moment came. Roosevelt, as we have noted, immediately after the election called for the resignations of all ministers and ambassadors, including that of Meyer. On December 27th, he wrote to White that "As you of course know, I intend to appoint you ambassador to Italy after March 4th. I need hardly tell you, my dear fellow, how glad I am to be able to do this." The nomination was at once announced, and February found White making preparations to transfer his family to Rome.

CHAPTER FIFTEEN

Ambassador to Italy: European Disarmament

IT WAS a characteristically thorough shake-up of the diplomatic service in which Roosevelt indulged at the beginning of his second term. In one day, March 6, 1905, he nominated no fewer than five ambassadors and eleven ministers to new posts. Whitelaw Reid, owner and editor of the *Tribune*, received the appointment he had so long desired—the ambassadorship to Great Britain. Robert S. McCormick was transferred from St. Petersburg to Paris with the understanding that he should stay for a year. W. W. Rockhill, with his veteran experience of the Far East and his knowledge of the Chinese language, succeeded E. H. Conger as minister to China, while Conger was promoted to the ambassadorship to Mexico. George von Lengerke Meyer was moved from Rome to St. Petersburg.[1]

The correspondent of the London *Times* interviewed several officials in Washington upon White's promotion. "If," said one, "we had ever had before Mr. Hay's time anything that could be called a diplomatic service, Mr. White's capacity would long since have been recognized and his great usefulness rewarded by promotion from the secretaryship in London to an independent post." "Yes," said another, "but to lose White from London is to lose much. Few ambassadors have ever sent home such full and illuminating reports. We have few, if any, better diplomatists."

White traveled alone to Rome in April, leaving Mrs. White be-

[1] Roosevelt had remarked of Meyer to newspapermen: "He holds his place neither by appointment by President McKinley, for that expired long ago, nor by my appointment, for I never selected him. He is virtually the appointee of Myron Herrick, and I wonder how long Mr. Herrick will think that holds good?" Nevertheless, Roosevelt rightly regarded Meyer as one of the two or three ablest men in the service. His work in St. Petersburg at the close of the Russo-Japanese War was invaluable.

hind in Switzerland while he took possession of the embassy offices and looked about for a residence. On the way he stopped at Nervi on the Italian Riviera, where Hay, now stricken with his last illness, was staying with his wife and Henry Adams on their way to Bad Nauheim. They had halted simply to break the journey with a rest, but Hay had so visibly improved that White urged Mrs. Hay to keep him there rather than hurry on to Germany. Indeed, as they all made a little holiday of White's arrival and ran into Genoa for a luncheon together, the "chief" seemed in as high spirits as ever. He said that there was nothing the matter with him except old age, the Senate, and two or three other mortal maladies; he chaffed Henry Adams as the Porcupinus Angelicus; and he doubtless repeated for White's benefit his little parody:

> Oh, Adams! in our hours of ease
> Rather inclined to growl and tease,
> When pain and anguish wring the brow,
> A ministering angel thou!

But Hay's imminent fate was all too plain, and it grieved White deeply to part from him. They were never to see each other again. On April 15th White was in Rome. On April 22nd Hay was in Bad Nauheim, whence he wrote White a letter that was plainly designed to reassure his friends. His physician had found his heart weak, but he hoped that after a few weeks' treatment he would be able to travel again.

White arrived in Rome at an interesting moment. In the background there were unrolling those great developments which were to lead Europe to the World War: the growth of Anglo-German naval rivalry, the strengthening of the Anglo-French entente, the appearance, shown by the exchange of visits in 1903-04 between Victor Emmanuel and President Loubet, of a definite rift in the Triple Alliance, and so on. Close under his eyes White could observe from Rome a series of rather disquieting events in Italy itself. The country was seething with agricultural and industrial discontent; socialism seemed to be growing apace; in the autumn before he reached Rome there had been a general strike, with riots in nearly all the large cities. A revolutionary movement was on foot, thrusting forward uncertainly but menacingly; as White traveled south in April, 1905, it was through the confusion of a railroad strike, which the government broke up by peremptory measures. Giolitti's Ministry had just given way to a feeble and colorless government headed by Signor Fortis, which was hanging on to office by its finger tips while the country waited for a stronger man to appear. The portfolio of foreign affairs was in the hands of Tittoni, a shrewder political leader than his chief, with whom White was glad to have an opportunity to deal.

It cannot be said that, apart from the Algeciras Conference, which we discuss elsewhere, Henry White's Italian service was marked by any event of great significance. It can be said that he was one of the best-liked representatives we have ever sent to Rome. Two days after his arrival he made his first call at the palace. The King and he sat down together. "There we talked for about twenty minutes about all sorts of things—the war, Italian politics, his own work and how he is unable ever to get far away, Rome, his little son about whom I asked. He spoke in a very friendly way of Meyer. . . . He has considerable charm of manner and has evidently softened since I saw him at Hatfield some years ago. He goes to bed at ten and gets up at five, and said he envied the President very much his getting away on so long a holiday. Altogether, the interview was very friendly and cordial." The King saw him frequently thereafter, and sometimes on an informal footing.

Though White had not been in Rome for thirty-seven years, he quickly found himself at home. It gave him a great thrill when, on entering the city, his train passed—and he instantly recognized —the old Protestant burial-ground outside the walls where Keats and Shelley lie; and he felt the same thrill again when within a few days he went to stand at the point where he had taken leave of the city when a youth. There was more ceremony about the court than he had been used to, and he wrote to his wife that "ambassadors are evidently much greater personages here than in England"; but he was at once welcomed by his associates as an old *diplomate de carrière*. The British ambassador, Sir Francis Egerton, whose lovely house and garden White thought the finest embassy in Rome, and M. Barrère, the French representative, were very cordial. White took a special fancy to the German ambassador, Count Monts, whom he described as "a bachelor about my age of the nice Seckendorffian type," and as "quite outspoken about the Emperor's impetuosity and the trouble he gives people by it." They all assured White that his ability to speak Italian was a great advantage, for Premier Fortis was reluctant to talk to the diplomatic corps in his bad French. These first busy days at his new post would have been perfectly happy but for the cloud thrown over them by Hay's illness. Hay wrote his last letter to White in May:

GRAND HOTEL KAISERHOF, BAD NAUHEIM,
May 14, 1905.

MY DEAR HARRY:

I have received all your good letters and have had much pleasure in reading them. My life here is so regular and dull that there is nothing to say about it. I sleep, I breakfast, I take my spindel bath, I rest, I lunch, I walk or drive, I loaf on the terrace and listen to music, I practise resistance movements, I dine, and sleep *da capo*.

Mrs. Hay has preceded me to Paris and is getting nicely through with her shopping. I shall be kept here a week longer than I calculated, as I left out of my count the "rest" days, and Dr. Groedel says I ought to have at least 24 baths, which will keep me here till about the 26th. I do not regret this, as I have little or nothing to do in Paris or in London, except to call on Delcassé and Lansdowne.

Jack Carter is as busy as a bee preparing for the joyous advent of Mr. Reid. He is overhauling Dorchester House, putting in a lift, fighting with Benson, and having no end of fun. Reid is expected there on the 3rd of June, and Carter expects to convey him from the station to his own house, as you did me on a similar occasion.

I shall always—the short "always" that is left me—remember that year with the keenest pleasure, the most important element of which is the recollection of your wise, intelligent, and ever-ready help, and your bright and cheery companionship. Happy is the ambassador who has such a counsellor! . . .

Poor Cassini! His head is in the basket. I sent him a kind message and received a grateful reply. It is cowardly business of them to sacrifice him for their own faults.

Most cordial regards to Mrs. White.

Yours affectionately,
JOHN HAY.

After the usual travail of search, disappointment, remodeling, and redecoration, White found a home in the Drago Palace, in the Via Quattro Fontane; and there Mrs. White joined him when the city awoke from its summer lethargy. For the first time since she had been taken critically ill in 1899, she was able—with the help of her daughter Muriel—to entertain largely. To her efforts was due no small part of the impression the new ambassador made upon the critical Roman world. Though her hair was now silvery gray, her commanding beauty was as striking as ever, and her gentle charm as appealing. She brought into Roman society a breath of reserve which was half English, and half reflected her ingrained Puritanism of character.

Two or three episodes in White's Italian service—the International Agricultural Conference of 1905, his much-discussed dinner to the cardinals, and his efforts in behalf of a limitation of armaments—may be singled out for brief mention. The Agricultural Conference was inspired by David Lubin of California, and brought representatives of thirty-eight nations to Rome. White always recalled it as an example of what good management could do at an international gathering. Most of the delegates arrived with a very vague idea of their objective and a strong conviction that no practical result would be obtained; but chiefly through the zeal and adroitness of the able Italian delegation, enthusiasm took the place of apathy. The result was that after sitting only ten days, the Conference agreed upon a convention creating the very useful International Institute of Agriculture. White was so genuinely interested in the Institute that when the United States hesitated to sign the convention, he pressed Root and Roosevelt for their support, and when favorable action was secured, the Italian Government sent Visconti Venosta to him with its special thanks.

The dinner to the cardinals was a very different matter. Archbishop Ireland, one of the men who had urged White's promotion, visited Rome in the spring of 1906, and White seized the occasion to take a bold step. No ambassador to the Italian Government was in any way recognized by the Pope, and all dignitaries of the Church were supposed to abstain rigidly from contact with the diplomatist accredited to the King. The hostility between the Vati-

can and the Quirinal was outwardly still keen.[2] White coura-
geously invited four cardinals to a dinner for Archbishop Ireland,
taking care to send his invitation on embassy paper. The Italian
Government was greatly pleased. So, also, as White had shrewdly
calculated, was the more liberal section of the clergy, while Pius X
himself let his approval be understood. When the Government
press took up the subject and interviewed the four cardinals, some
of the ultramontanists raised indignant protests regarding the dinner, and the aged and highly reactionary Cardinal Oreglia issued
a circular in which he called attention to the strict regulations
drawn up just after "the unhappy occupation of Rome," with regard to the houses that cardinals might visit. In short, there was
a little storm, but White was unperturbed. He wrote to President
Roosevelt after Oreglia's outburst:

The chief result of this circular has been indignation on the part of
many of the recipients thereof, who say that none but the Pope (who has
intimated privately to the cardinals who dined with me that it was all
right and to Ireland also) has the right to issue any instructions to
them, and one eminent cardinal whom I did not invite has sent me a
message since to express the hope that I will invite him to dine and
that he will consider it a high honor and gladly come. The longer I
remain here the more convinced I feel that whoever occupies the place
which I now fill, being the representative of the best and most enlightened Roman Catholics in the world, who contribute a very large portion
of the Holy See's income, should be received at the Vatican, and I have
no doubt that in the course of time—not mine here possibly, but before
very long—this will come to pass. We are unconnected with European
complications and cannot be expected (I mean our Roman Catholics,
who are also Americans and in favor of the government of other countries according to the will of the people thereof) to pretend to believe
in "the prisoner of the Vatican." There is not a member of the papal
party who would, if they could, get the Italian Government out of
Rome. Every time the Pope goes to St. Peter's the government is notified and sends members of its police in plain clothes to protect him,
and there are hundreds of ways in which the Vatican makes use of the
government. Many Roman Catholics who come to Rome are greatly
surprised that their Ambassador is not recognized at the Vatican, and I

[2] Society in Rome was divided between the "blacks," adhering to the Papal
Court, and the "whites," who went to the Quirinal; but this cleavage was not
felt so much among the younger people as their elders.

have no doubt, when it becomes generally known, that pressure will be brought to bear in the matter. . . . I also gave a dinner to the Methodist Bishop Burt, as I avail myself of every opportunity to emphasize the fact that I represent all in our country, and propose to do honor to any compatriot of distinction who visits Rome, whatever be his creed or politics.

More important were White's efforts, while in Rome, to promote an understanding between President Roosevelt and Mr. (later Lord) Haldane as to a possible limitation of armaments. Haldane, with whom White had been acquainted since the old days of the "Souls," was included in 1905 in Campbell-Bannerman's cabinet as Secretary for War. While carrying out his great reorganization of the British army, he was keenly interested not only in preparing England for war, but in preparing Europe to prevent war; and in the fall of 1906 he paid a visit to Germany, his aim being to contribute to cordial relations between the two countries. It happened that just previous to this, during the summer of 1906, White met him in London, and in the course of their conversation Haldane, who had spoken of his intense interest in peace and the reduction of armaments, suggested that possibly President Roosevelt might give valuable assistance. The Kaiser admired and respected Roosevelt; why should not Roosevelt use his influence with the Kaiser for partial disarmament? White did not know what Roosevelt's ideas on the subject might be, but he shared Haldane's fears that the vast armaments of Europe would yet lead to war; he therefore wrote to Roosevelt confidentially and urgently, and received a confidential reply. This reply is paraphrased in the following letter from White to the British War Minister:[3]

AMERICAN EMBASSY, ROME,
September 19, 1906.

MY DEAR HALDANE:
I recently sent you a line from north Italy which would have led you to expect a further communication from me, and I send it by the despatch bag from our embassy. . . .
First of all, the President considers that in such a matter as the limitation or reduction of armaments it is not possible for him to commit himself definitely without knowing what the conditions may be at the

[3] Roosevelt's reply to White is given entire in Appendix I.

Hague Conference next year. Therefore, the following suggestion of his views must be taken as tentative and suggestive, but not as in any way binding him, and still less the United States, definitely.

He agrees entirely with you as to the advisability of putting a check to the inordinate growth of armaments, and he also feels with you that in one sense we (the United States) are in a position to propose their limitation or reduction, but that in another sense we are not, because we have a small navy and an army so much smaller as to seem infinitesimal, compared with the armed forces of the other great powers which in point of population, extent of territory, wealth, and resources, can be placed in the same category with ourselves.

The President during his term of office has already reduced our army by twenty-five per cent. He considers it now to be at its lowest limit, and that to make a further reduction would be out of the question. But you can imagine what a similar percentage of reduction, which in our case involved only about twenty-five thousand men, would mean to the armies of Continental Europe!

With respect to the navy, the President feels that as regards the number of units it is just at the right point, but we should steadily though gradually replace inefficient with efficient units, which in his opinion would mean a program of building about a battleship a year, or occasionally omitting the battleship, a cruiser or a few torpedo boats instead.

Now would a program for Europe and Japan with which the foregoing program for ourselves should be compatible, be practicable in your opinion?

The President has a much less exalted idea than I have of his influence with the German Emperor, and he evidently has doubts as to his ability to accomplish anything in the proposed direction with him, but he is willing to try. He has no doubt that he can work with France and England, but he would like you and Edward Grey and the French to understand, if the attempt should be made, that in his opinion it is essential that there be a reasonable guarantee that a given policy will be carried out in good faith. He feels that it would be a great misfortune for the free peoples to disarm and leave the various military despotisms and military barbarisms armed—a view in which I am sure you will concur.

If China were civilized as Japan now is; if the Turkish Empire were no longer in existence and if all the uncivilized portions of Asia and Africa were held by England, France, Germany, or Russia, the President considers that he should be within reach of a genuine international agreement whereby armies and navies could be so reduced as to perform merely the requirements of internal and international police work. But as we are so far, as yet, from any such ideal possibility, he feels that "we can only accomplish good at all by not trying to accomplish the impossible good."

If I can be of any service to you in carrying this matter further either by letter or when I go to Washington, as I expect to do *via* England (where I shall hope to see you) early in November, I am at your service. You can write to me confidentially with perfect safety by the despatch bag or to the embassy here. I have not mentioned our conversation nor my communication to the President to my colleague in London nor to anyone else.

I have read with much interest of your recent visit in your official capacity to Germany, and I am wondering whether you had any opportunity of sounding the Emperor as to the possibilities in his opinion of accomplishing anything in the direction of disarmament.

Yours very sincerely,

HENRY WHITE.

Unfortunately for the world, now heading straight for the Great War, Haldane's efforts came to naught. When he visited Germany he was well received, but he quickly found there was little hope of inducing that empire to limit its navy in return for concessions from Great Britain. The Kaiser invited him to a review, and riding up to his carriage as the troops wheeled by, demanded: "A splendid machine I have in this army, Mr. Haldane; now isn't it so? And what could I do without it, situated as I am between the Russians and the French?" The time was unfavorable to a reduction of armaments; Haldane made no further approach to Roosevelt, and the subject lapsed. But we shall see that Roosevelt returned to it in his communications with White.

With the King of Italy White was soon on terms of friendship unusual between diplomatists and monarchs at European Courts. In later times American visitors found that the King spoke with especial cordiality of Henry White. He was dignified, he was efficient and tactful, he knew the traditions and methods of European diplomacy, but above all, he was *simpatico*. Years later, after the World War, the King was chatting with an American visitor. He spoke of the difference between diplomatists, some knowing how to smooth out difficulties, while others merely complicated them. "Now there was ——," he said. "He could not get on here and resigned in six months. I think the difficulty lay chiefly with his wife. You have lately had Draper, Meyer, Henry White, Leishmann, Griscom, O'Brien, and Thomas Nelson Page. Ah, Henry White! He was a man to be treasured as an ambassador and always kept in office!"

During the late summer of 1906 White paid the King a visit in the Piedmontese Alps, in order to shoot chamois and ibex. They talked without reserve, and stimulated by his recent conversation with Haldane and his knowledge of Roosevelt's interest in peace, White put to the King some frank questions as to the possibility of cutting down armies and navies. His account of their talk as well as of the sport is given in a letter to Roosevelt dated August 29, 1906:

I have paid the King of Italy a week's visit in the mountains, during which I had many long talks with him, and he spoke very frankly. I asked him particularly what his ideas are on the limitation or reduction of armaments, and he said that of course it would be a great boon to the finances of this country, were there a possibility of an international agreement on this question, which he thought might not be difficult in respect to navies. He fears, however, that it would be practically impossible to ensure the carrying out by the great European military powers of such an agreement in respect to their armies, as there are so many ways in which it might be evaded without the discovery of such an evasion on the part of a single power, by the others. In his opinion the most practical form which an international agreement for preventing the further increase of armaments could assume, would be an undertaking on the part of various nations not to alter or improve the weapons with which their armies are supplied. But he quite agreed with me that the very suggestion of such an arrangement would create an outburst of opposition on the part of the manufacturers of arms in all countries which could not be overcome, and notably in Germany, where the Emperor would never consent to such a clipping of the wings of the famous Krupp Works; and consequently that an agreement on these lines is out of the question. The King was anxious to know your views on the subject, which of course I was unable to tell him.

He has a great admiration for you, and says that he earnestly hopes that when you lay down your great office you will come to Italy and give him the pleasure of knowing you personally. He also asked me whether I thought you would like some good ibex and other heads, of which he has a large collection and would be glad to send you some choice specimens. I of course replied that I thought you would be glad to have some of them, but I did not revert to the subject again, thinking it best to inquire before consulting you. If therefore you would like the King to send you some heads I will tell him so the next time I see him. I enclose one of the little kodak pictures of the King and myself, which he had taken by his leader under a rock about 10,000 feet above sea-level, waiting for the ibex; also another which he took of me holding the horns of one of the five ibex that I killed during the week. I was fortunate to get the best head that was shot (but it is not the one in the photograph) and about fifteen chamois besides, the entire bag for the week being twenty-one ibex and sixty-one chamois, most of them killed by the King himself, who is a very good rifle-shot. The ibex exist nowhere else in the Alps, and were saved from extinction in the Piedmontese Alps by old King Victor Emmanuel.

We live in a curious little old house, four hours by mule-track from the nearest highroad, and we usually went up three or four hours more every morning, starting at four or five, before reaching the ibex region. The male ibex never go below the vegetation belt and a certain number die every winter from starvation rather than go down, as the females do, to a point at which they can find something to eat. They are very wild, with keen scent and sight, and are shot with a rifle, usually while running down precipitous rocky inclines, in the direction of which they are driven by beaters who go out the night before and scale the most inaccessible heights in a wonderful way.

The King is a very level-headed man, singularly devoid of prejudices, with plenty of character, decided views on most subjects, simple also in his tastes; and I need not say that on this occasion the trappings of royalty, which he always reduces to a minimum, were entirely absent. He has a theory that before long—possibly in his lifetime—the Poles in Austria, Germany, and Russia, in each of which countries they are very discontented, will come together and form the Polish nation again. He was very interesting on the relations of his government with the Vatican.

White added a paragraph referring to a visit which, following the Algeciras Conference, he had just made to England:

You were probably glad to see the recent meeting between the German Emperor and his uncle of England. I expressed to the latter when he asked me to come to see him recently in London the earnest hope that one of the most important results of the Conference would be an improvement in the relations between Germany and England, and that I hoped it would be possible for him and his nephew to meet before very long.

Roosevelt appreciated frequent personal letters from Rome. When White sent him a copy of Antonio Fogazzaro's famous novel of 1905, *Il Santo*, the picture of a monk inspired with a mission for reforming the Catholic Church according to the modernist creed, he devoured it and asked White to tell Fogazzaro that, although a Protestant, he agreed with him in all the fundamentals that he preached.[4] Now he replied to White, not omitting the disarmament question:

OYSTER BAY, N. Y.,
September 13, 1906.

DEAR WHITE:

By George! I do not think any Ambassador has a right to send photographs like that to an elderly President who used to hunt himself, and in whom such photographs excite a feeling of wild envy and revolt. Think of your having got five ibex, not to speak of the fifteen chamois! Why, I did not suppose that anybody but the King himself was allowed to kill those ibex. I congratulate you with all my heart.

If the King does not bring up the subject of the game heads do not say anything more to him about it, because my house is small and I prefer to have in it only heads of my own killing; and moreover I have not now any spare head I could send him in return. If, however, he brings it up and you feel that it would be a little awkward to refuse, why of course say that if he chose to send me an ibex head, or if he has no ibex head and can spare a chamois head, I would immensely appreciate it. Tell him at the same time how much I value the beautiful Dante and the twenty volumes of the reports, etc., of Eugene of Savoy which he sent me.

I doubt if I shall go abroad, at any rate for many years after I leave the Presidency. If I ever did I should particularly like to see him. I entirely agree with his position about disarmament. It would be an admirable thing if we could get the nations not to improve their arms. Ask the King if it would not be possible to get them to agree hereafter not to build any ships of more than a certain size. Of course the United States has not any army and can do nothing to decrease the size of armaments on land; but I will be glad to follow any practical suggestion as to putting a stop to the increase of armaments at sea. I think that the reduction in the size of ships as above outlined would be a practicable, though a small, step. . . .

Root has certainly had a wonderful time and I think he has accom-

[4] Roosevelt to White, Oyster Bay, September 24, 1906.

plished real good. Just at the moment I am so angry with that infernal little Cuban republic that I would like to wipe its people off the face of the earth. All that we have wanted from them was that they should behave themselves and be prosperous and happy so that we would not have to interfere. And now, lo and behold, they have started an utterly unjustifiable and pointless revolution and may get things into such a snarl that we have no alternative save to intervene—which will at once convince the suspicious idiots in South America that we do wish to interfere after all, and perhaps have some land-hunger!

Give my warm regards to Mrs. White. I have heard as golden accounts of her as of you.

Faithfully yours,
THEODORE ROOSEVELT.

I think it is a toss-up whether we do or do not win in the congressional election; there are many fools, and many good men who don't take the trouble to think deeply—and they all vote.

In the last two months of 1906 White, by arrangement with the Administration, visited the United States to use his influence in behalf of the ratification of the Algeciras Treaty. He found the treaty well regarded, and though he pressed his views upon wavering Senators and a few men who were invincibly hostile, like his friend Senator A. O. Bacon of Georgia, his efforts were hardly needed. While in Washington he stayed at the Lodges'. They, the Jusserands, Thomas Nelson Page, and others gave dinners for him; he saw his old friend Lord Curzon as he passed through Washington; Roosevelt asked him to dine at the White House on the occasion of the state dinner to the Cabinet, and he had a number of talks with Secretary Root and the President. As soon as he arrived he was told that in recognition of his services at Algeciras, the Government intended to advance him to the highest post available. If London had been open, he would have been sent thither, but Whitelaw Reid was not expected to retire before the end of the Administration; he was asked to accept Paris. It was a promotion which he deeply appreciated and his letters show that he was touched by the feeling that, simply by merit and hard work, he had advanced so near the top in the diplomatic service—to what Curzon told him was the "blue riband" post in diplomacy. Particularly was he pleased by Roosevelt's commendation. "I had a delightful walk of an hour and a half yesterday with the President, quite alone," he wrote to Mrs. White on December 11th. "He spoke of me in a much too flattering way. He said I had rendered him infinite service in many ways, and when I left him he sent his very particular remembrances to you, saying that he is extremely proud of you both as a woman and as an ambassadress. . . . He remembers perfectly well your talk with him about going on the Police Board of New York, and also, which I had forgotten, his visit to you in Stuyvesant Square to talk it all over."

The last weeks of White's Italian service were extremely busy. Returning to Rome, he wound up several matters of routine business at the embassy,[5] and (March 1, 1907) had the experience of a long audience with the Pope. White wrote in detail of it to Root, and repeated his frank conversation with the Pontiff. He told Pius X, whom he described as a man of charming simplicity, that he felt strongly that the American Ambassador to the King should be received occasionally by His Holiness, not in a diplomatic capacity, but as a distinguished foreigner who could give the Pope non-clerical information of value regarding the United States. When he first came to Rome, he added, he had supposed that the opposition to any visit to the Vatican came from the Italian Government, but two foreign ministers had told him that this was not the fact and that the impediment was offered by the rules of the Vatican itself. The Pope seemed a little surprised at the readiness of the Italian Government to let an Ambassador see him, and struck by the possible utility of White's proposal regarding frequent visits by the American representative, though his reply was guarded —he merely said that "one must hope" that it might come about.[6] White, at the special request of some cardinal who believed that Pius was misinformed regarding certain aspects of the dispute then raging between France and the Vatican, also spoke plainly on that subject, saying that the whole anti-clerical movement in France seemed to him to be the result of a popular determination not to

[5] White put a stop to the careless issuance of American passports at the consulates in southern Italy, and particularly Naples; many applicants, not citizens of the United States, obtaining them on payment of a dollar without real inquiry into their identity. White-Root correspondence, 1905-06.

[6] White to Root, Rome, March 7, 1907.

allow any foreign authority to intervene in French domestic affairs. At this the Pope protested that the Vatican was in no way interfering with political matters in France; to which White courteously assented, but pointed out that the support which the French clericals, including some Church officers, had given to the persecution of Dreyfus, had produced an opposite impression.

There ensued a flying visit to London, where White was commissioned by Secretary Root to ascertain confidentially the views of the British Government as to the discussion of disarmament at The Hague. The second Hague Conference was to begin in June, with Choate as the American delegate. It was to offer the world, as a few men dimly perceived, one of its best opportunities to arrest the fatal march of the great Powers to the catastrophe of 1914. Secretary Root and Sir Edward Grey were alike eager to raise the question of a limitation of armaments, and alike fearful that Germany and France would prove obstructive.[7] The British navy had just been reorganized by Sir John Fisher, and was still far more powerful than the German, so that in Berlin many regarded disarmament as a British or Anglo-American scheme to keep Germany in a subordinate position; while France, Russia, and Germany were all unwilling to reduce their armies. White was asked to find out through his English friends just what could be done. His observations, as he talked with British public men, gave him a startled sense that Europe might be approaching a general war. His old friend, Arthur Balfour, who had played a leading part in erecting the Permanent Committee of Imperial Defence, spoke with a frankness which surprised him. Clearly the former Prime Minister was not at all serious in what he said, but his tone as he referred to German naval expansion nevertheless indicated the sentiments of many. The colloquy, as it was overheard by White's daughter, ran substantially as follows:

BALFOUR (*somewhat lightly*): "We are probably fools not to find a reason for declaring war on Germany before she builds too many ships and takes away our trade."

WHITE: "You are a very high-minded man in private life. How can you possibly contemplate anything so politically immoral as

[7] The first Hague Conference had been held in the summer of 1899; the second was held June 15-October 18, 1907.

provoking a war against a harmless nation which has as good a right to a navy as you have? If you wish to compete with German trade, work harder."

BALFOUR: "That would mean lowering our standard of living. Perhaps it would be simpler for us to have a war."

WHITE: "I am shocked that you of all men should enunciate such principles."

BALFOUR (*again lightly*): "Is it a question of right or wrong? Maybe it is just a question of keeping our supremacy."[8]

White also had a talk with the Foreign Minister, and reported the gist of it to the Secretary of State.

WHITE TO ROOT, PARIS, MARCH 30, 1907

I saw Edward Grey shortly before I left London and his impression seemed to be that the French Government's reason for not favoring the discussion is the fear of pressure from their own people, many of whom are tired of the heavy taxation necessary to keep up and increase the heavy armaments, but Grey does not think the objection here is very deep-rooted. I hardly touched upon it with Pichon the first time I saw him, not knowing whether you wish me to urge it upon the Government here or not. I asked him how they feel about it and he answered that they have not made up their minds but are considering it.

Grey is distinctly against formulating any proposal in advance as suggested by Martens for reasons which you probably know and in which I imagine you concur. He told me that he always speaks and writes of the question as "expenditure upon armaments" and not "disarmament" or even "limitation of armaments." The British, Grey said, are determined to bring the question up at the Conference in any case. He told me of his correspondence with you through Bryce in reference to Martens's proposal as to mode of procedure—*i.e.*, that it should be referred to a committee of the great Powers at the Conference, and he was awaiting your reply when I left London.

In Paris White also saw the German ambassador, Prince Radolin, on the subject, and summarized his impressions in a cablegram to Secretary Root.

WHITE TO ROOT, PARIS, NO DATE

Very private. I have had confidential unofficial but frank conversation with German Ambassador whereof following is a summary. I said that

[8] Conversation recorded by the Countess Seherr-Thoss.

I came as a friend of his, without authority or inspiration from my government; that I feared by opposing, as I had good reason to believe, and endeavoring to influence Russian Government to oppose, the raising at the Conference of certain questions which nearly all other first-class powers wish to discuss, German Government would find itself in same position of isolation as last year and incur besides the obloquy of rapidly increasing lovers of peace everywhere, including Germany. German ambassador replied that he had no recent communication with Berlin on the subject, but practically admitted the probability of my conclusions if my information was correct, which he neither admitted nor denied.

I gathered from subsequent conversation, which lasted over an hour, that the Emperor is in a very difficult position, as the military and imperialist parties firmly believe that England's sole reason for raising the disarmament question is to compel Germany to disarm in order to attack her when weakened and to reduce her to impotence; that the Emperor is very much blamed for having yielded at Algeciras instead of fighting, and if he were to agree to discuss the disarmament question and find himself, as Germany must in the event of serious proposals to disarm being adopted at the Conference, not only in a minority there but in Germany also on that subject, there is no telling to what extremes the party aforesaid might resort; possibly even change of form of government, all of which very desirable to avoid. I intimated that the proposed discussion need not necessarily involve action, but would serve to demonstrate either impracticability thereof or what progress possible, whereas its suppression would greatly increase general feeling and leave public ignorant.

When the Hague Conference was held, Great Britain and the United States duly raised the subject of disarmament, and Germany, tacitly supported by France and Russia, refused to discuss it. The Germans were in a difficult position. Outmatched by England's navy, and knowing that Italy was a dubious partner in the Triple Alliance,[9] they felt it necessary to strengthen rather than

[9] White left Rome with one fixed conviction: that the Germans were much mistaken in believing that Italy, if a general European war occurred, would side with them and Austria. He believed that the tactless German treatment of Italy, the historic antagonism between Italy and Austria, and the immense influence of the French free-masons in Italy were sure to draw Italy to France and away from Germany. Count Monts, the German ambassador to Rome, was exceedingly tactless. He came up to Mrs. White at a large dinner party and said in the hearing of everyone, "Mrs. White, I pity you for coming to

weaken their armaments. But the continental Powers possibly missed a great opportunity, for an effort to delimit armed forces might have done much to avert the World War.

By the end of March, 1907, as the above communications show, White had taken up the duties of ambassador to France; he had been received cordially in Paris, and had exchanged speeches with the French President.

---

this village after London." At the opening of the Milan Exhibition he was conspicuous for his rudeness, falling into a rage because he and the other envoys were kept waiting for a time. The French, on the other hand, lost no opportunity to impress Italy with the fact that they held that nation in high regard.

CHAPTER SIXTEEN

At the Algeciras Conference

WHITE's promotion to the Italian embassy had come at a
moment when the relations of the great European Powers,
after a series of striking changes, were more interesting than at
any time since the Congress of Berlin. During the years 1903-05
a chain of events, involving a realignment of nations and a shifting
of the balance of power, had taken place under White's eyes.
Russia, humiliatingly defeated by Japan and threatened with revolution at home, was rendered temporarily impotent. Great Britain,
after the failure of Joseph Chamberlain's attempt to open negotiations with Germany leading to an alliance, swung toward a friendly
understanding with France, and in 1904, after an exchange of
visits by Edward VII and President Loubet, definitely concluded
the *entente cordiale*.[1] Italy, an ally of Germany and Austria, was
showing indications that under certain circumstances her loyalty
would be dubious. The year 1904 was the year in which Isvolski,
just transferred from Tokio to Copenhagen, had a talk with Edward VII and intimated to the British sovereign that Russia ought
to turn her back on the old Asiatic conflict with Great Britain
and seek her friendship. No one could guess whither all these
changes were tending, and with the blind optimism which marked
these years few worried about the catastrophe toward which Europe
was moving. White, better acquainted than nearly any other American with European affairs and personalities, was a keenly interested
observer of events.

He had scarcely taken his position in Rome when there burst
the first clap of thunder which preceded the World War—the
Moroccan crisis of 1905. It is a dramatic story, the more dramatic
because it might easily have ended in a conflict. Part of its secret

[1] Cf. Fay, Sidney B., *The Origins of the World War*, vol. i, p. 152 ff.

history may not yet be fully known, but one of its most striking elements, the intervention of President Roosevelt, now presents no mysteries.[2] In this intervention the President relied upon the discretion, tact, and adroitness of White, and the latter had his best opportunity to play a rôle of obvious and world-wide importance.

The Moroccan crisis possessed a large background, involving three continents and the chief developments of the new century in diplomatic affairs. Its underlying cause was the inveterate antagonism between Germany, which believed she was entitled to a larger voice in African affairs, and France, eager to thwart Germany at every possible turn; combined with the instinctive German dislike and apprehension of the new Anglo-French rapprochement. The direct cause was the action of M. Delcassé, the French Foreign Minister, in coolly buying off all the Moroccan claims of Italy and Great Britain by promising these countries a free hand in Tripoli and Egypt, while ignoring the special interests of Germany. The French convention with Great Britain, signed on April 8, 1904, included, as we now know, secret articles which contemplated the eventual partition of Morocco between France and Spain, and these articles were confirmed by secret clauses in a Franco-Spanish convention that autumn. Germany was not even consulted, though she had commercial interests which would be injured by France's "pacific penetration" of Morocco, and her consent could easily have been obtained by a *solatium*. The German Chancellor, Bülow, feeling that his government must assert itself, was ready to move with tactless abruptness; and he persuaded the Kaiser to act upon his views. The result was the Kaiser's visit to Tangier on March 31, 1905, a sharp strain thrown upon Franco-German relations, France's sudden realization that she was threatened with war when Russia was powerless, the fall of Delcassé, and the emergence of a situation

[2] Roosevelt's long memorandum on the secret history of the Algeciras Convention, of which copies were sent to Ambassador Reid in England and White in Italy, is published in Bishop, J. B., *Theodore Roosevelt and His Time*, vol. i, pp. 467-503. The greater part of it deals with the preliminaries of the Algeciras Conference; it contains important letters by Root, Jusserand, and Sternburg. An important feature is its evidence of Roosevelt's complete intimacy with Ambassador Jusserand throughout the affair.

in which the question of European peace or war seemed to hang in the balance.[3]

In this situation President Roosevelt hoped to play the rôle of peacemaker. German proposals were made for a conference, the Kaiser approaching Roosevelt on the subject in March, April, and May of 1905; Roosevelt, after some initial hesitation, vigorously seconded them; and it was agreed on September 28, 1905, that the Moroccan question should be submitted to an international congress. The President's feeling, as stated in a letter to Taft, was that the United States had no real interest in Morocco itself, and that he did not care to take sides between France and Germany; but that it was important to maintain the peace of the world, to prevent Germany from forcing war upon France, to safeguard neutral rights, and to bring about a better state of feeling between England and Germany. Insufficient emphasis has been given to Roosevelt's conviction that Anglo-German relations were really of more importance than Franco-German relations. As he wrote to Taft, who was then Acting Secretary of State:[4]

Each nation is working itself up to a condition of desperate hatred of the other, each from sheer fear of the other. The Kaiser is dead sure that England intends to attack him. The English Government and a large share of the English people are equally sure that Germany intends to attack England. Now, in my view this action of Germany in embroiling herself with France over Morocco is proof positive that she has not the slightest intention of attacking England. I am very clear in my belief that England utterly overestimates, as well as mis-estimates, Germany's singleness of purpose, by attributing to the German Foreign Office the kind of power of continuity of aim which it had from '64 to '71. I do not wish to suggest anything whatever as to England's attitude in Morocco, but if we can find out that attitude with propriety and inform the Kaiser

[3] It was long believed by many, including Lord Grey (see his *Twenty-Five Years*, vol. i, p. 51 ff.) that Germany wished to break up the *entente* while Russia was helpless; but this is not entirely true. The Kaiser and Bülow were hurt that the Anglo-French agreement ignored German interests; they suspected, and rightly, that there were secret clauses in this agreement. They disagreed on the course to be followed. The Kaiser wished to avoid offending the French. But Bülow forced him to land at Tangier as a spectacular diplomatic gesture, and thus precipitated the whole crisis. See *Grosse Politik*, vol. xix, p. 497 ff.; Fay, S. B., *The Origins of the World War*, vol. i, p. 168 ff.

[4] Roosevelt to Taft, April 20, 1905. See Bishop, *ut supra*.

of it, I shall be glad to do so. But I have to leave a large discretion in your hands in this matter, for if we find out that it will make the English suspicious—that is, will make them think we are acting as decoy ducks for Germany—we shall have to drop the business. Fortunately, you and I play the diplomatic game exactly alike, and I should advise your being absolutely frank with both Speck and the British people along the lines I have indicated, unless you have counter suggestions to make. Remember, however, that both parties are very suspicious. You remember the King's message to me through Harry White and his earnest warning to me that I should remember that England was our real friend and that Germany was only a make-believe friend. In just the same way the Germans are always insisting that England is really on the point of entering into a general coalition which would practically be inimical to us—an act which apart from moral considerations I regard the British Government as altogether too flabby to venture upon.

It was evident from the outset that the American rôle in the conference would be of the first importance. The European nations rapidly aligned themselves behind the two rival Powers. France was supported not only by Great Britain and Russia, but ultimately also by Italy, which broke away from the Triple Alliance for her famous *tour de valse*, while Germany was supported by Austria-Hungary, which the Kaiser later complimented as his "brilliant second" in the duel. Apart from both groups stood the United States, not wholly impartial, as we shall see, but certainly disinterested and unselfish. Roosevelt's aim of preventing an immediate conflict, preserving the integrity of Morocco, and contributing to a permanent understanding and friendliness in Europe, as Mr. Lewis Einstein has written,[5] "required tact, geniality, fairness, and poise, and no better selection could have been made to carry it out than that of Henry White."

As the date of the Conference approached at the beginning of 1906, the anxiety and tension in the chief European capitals increased. The French and British feared that the German Government might take an overbearing attitude, force a rupture of the

[5] Memorandum by Mr. Einstein for the author. The Italian *tour de valse* here mentioned was not strictly the first. Following the Franco-Italian rapprochement of 1900-01, Bülow had remarked that an extra *tour* need not worry the husband.

Conference, and precipitate war. The Germans feared that they would be overwhelmed in the gathering by a hostile combination of all the nations except Austria-Hungary. Some Germans also feared that England wished to provoke war in order that she might smash the German fleet while it was still weak. White heard much in Rome of the suspicion and dread which pervaded the European chancelleries. By Secretary Root he was kept confidentially informed of the observations of the American diplomatists in other countries. George von Lengerke Meyer wrote from St. Petersburg that the French were asking the Tsar to make a personal appeal to the Kaiser not to force hostilities.[6] "What they hope for," he cabled, "is the creation of a moral atmosphere making it impossible for the military part of Germany in extreme cases to precipitate war. French Government fears Germany taking advantage of present condition in Russia. In the event of certain circumstances, the President of the United States of all persons may have an opportunity to exercise moral influence with both France and Germany." From the Paris embassy Robert McCormick was sending the same news.

Paris, indeed, had nervously sounded the British Government to learn whether it would lend active support to France in the event of war. Mr. McCormick wrote [7] that Lord Lansdowne had not only told the French ambassador that England would come to the rescue of France if she were attacked, since public opinion would compel her to do so, but had offered to put this assurance in writing; an offer which was not accepted. On the resignation of Lansdowne, Sir Edward Grey took office on December 11, 1905. The French ambassador, Paul Cambon, naturally put to him the same question regarding British aid, but this time received an unsatisfactory answer. Grey, while willing to see military and naval conversations take place, would not pledge England to anything more than a benevolent neutrality. He did, however, tell Count Metternich, the German ambassador, that if Germany attacked France on any issue arising from the Moroccan agreement, public

[6] Cf. State Department, *Russian Dispatches,* vol. lxv, January 9, 1906.
[7] Robert McCormick to Root, Paris, December 15, 1905 (forwarded to White).

feeling in Great Britain would compel British intervention.[8] Naturally, this increased the uneasiness in Berlin.

McCormick in his dispatch offered some remarks indicating that he also thought the really dangerous antagonism in Europe was Anglo-German and not Franco-German. With all his admiration for France, he recognized that in material spheres Germany was her superior. "The German is the one strong, progressive, thorough people on the Continent, and William II in the acts which are so loudly condemned abroad is but the impersonation of these qualities; qualities . . . which find what to them is their natural ground of expansion everywhere forestalled by England, as England finds her commercial supremacy everywhere threatened by Germany."

Three nations thus looked with anxious eyes upon the course which Roosevelt would take at the Conference, France and England hoping for his support in checking any German aggression, and Germany, which was posing as the guardian of the Open Door in Morocco, hoping that he would assist in preventing the "Tunisification" of the country by France. Speck von Sternburg, the German ambassador, who was nearly as close to Roosevelt as Jusserand, told Secretary Root, who had now succeeded Hay, that the Germans desired no special privileges, and wished merely to maintain equal economic rights for all.[9] But Roosevelt believed that France was in the right, and assured Jusserand that if necessary he would take strong grounds against any step by Germany which seemed unjust or threatening. Next to the United States, Europe regarded Italy as a decisive factor. There was considerable rejoicing in France when the aged Marquis Visconti Venosta was substituted for Signor Silvestrelli as Italian delegate, Silvestrelli being regarded as under German influence, while Visconti Venosta was known to be friendly to the French.

Little hint of Roosevelt's intentions was evident in the formal instructions which he sent to White and his colleague, Samuel Gummere, the American minister to Morocco. These merely pointed out that the United States wished to secure equal rights in Morocco with other governments; that it wished an international agreement for an effective Moroccan police to furnish security, so that

[8] Dennis, A. L. P., *Adventures in American Diplomacy,* pp. 497, 498.
[9] *Idem,* 498. See also Harold Nicolson's *Lord Carnock.*

the door would not only stay open, but would lead somewhere; and that in dealing with financial reform, any discrimination in regard to foreign states should be avoided. "Fair play is what the United State asks, for Morocco and all the interested nations, and it confidently expects that outcome." Actually, however, the President's attitude was by no means reserved. While the Germans believed that his Open Door stand meant that he would take their side, his sympathies were firmly with France; and he indicated the fact in a letter which also deals with his efforts to end the Russo-Japanese War:

OYSTER BAY, N. Y.,
August 23, 1905.

(*Confidential*)

MY DEAR WHITE:

I was glad to get your letter and the interesting one from your boy. James had been telling me about the Fez matter. I shall send Choate to that conference. I want to keep on good terms with Germany, and if possible to prevent a rupture between Germany and France. But my sympathies have at bottom been with France and I suppose will continue so. Still I shall try to hold an even keel.

I am in the last throes of trying to get the Russians and Japanese to make a peace. The Russians are the worst, because they stand up with Chinese or Byzantine folly and insist, as Witte has just written me, that Russia will not admit herself vanquished—making it all I can do not to tell them some straightforward truths in uncomplimentary language. On the other hand, the Japanese have no business to continue the war merely for the sake of getting money, and they will defeat their own ends if they do so. The English Government has been foolishly reluctant to advise Japan to be reasonable, and in this respect has not shown well compared with the attitude of the German and French Governments in being willing to advise Russia. I have not much hope of a favorable result, but I will do what I can.

Sincerely yours,
THEODORE ROOSEVELT.

The President's letter was underlined by two "personal and confidential" notes which Secretary Root sent White, both dated November 28th. In one, after suggesting that White should try to ameliorate the condition of the Jews in Morocco, he remarked that France might have legitimate special interests there which needed a safeguard, and if this were true, he should not oppose their protection. In the other, after mentioning that the delegate Gummere was thought by some to be strongly pro-German, he continued: "This if true must not be allowed to throw us over into even apparent antagonism to the Anglo-French *entente* or to make us a means of breaking that up. It is useful to us as well as agreeable. Keep the American end of the business on an even keel. Keep friendly with all. Help France get what she ought to have, but don't take the fight on your shoulders. Help limit France where she ought to be limited, but don't take that fight on your shoulders. In the broader and really important part that the Conference is to play in the politics of Europe, keep the peace and make it as difficult as possible for any one to pick a quarrel. You are chosen because you know that broader field and how to act."

White arrived at the Andalusian port of Algeciras on the cruiser *Galveston*, and on January 16, 1906, the Conference opened. It was an interesting assemblage in the half-Spanish, half-Moorish town, where the delegates of the thirteen nations lived in the ornate Reina Cristina hotel together, and drove in carriages to the Conference hall a mile distant.[10] They sat in the gold-and-white dining-room at tables decorated by diminutive national flags, and at first treated each other with frigid politeness. For amusement there were drives, sightseeing, and golf; White dined often with the British chief, Sir Arthur Nicolson, who had a house; and he played bridge at the hotel. Half the newspaper correspondents of Europe seemed there, and the French journalists were especially troublesome, buttonholing delegates, putting their own opinions into the delegates' mouths, bringing out faked interviews, and irritating everybody.

To outward view, the Conference opened harmoniously. The senior Spanish delegate, the Duke of Almodovar, was unanimously elected president. In his speech upon taking the chair he declared that the Conference should base its work for the restoration of internal order and for financial reform upon three principles—the Sultan's sovereignty, the integrity of Morocco, and the Open Door; and to this the French and German delegates cordially agreed. But when it came to the interpretation of these smooth generalities,

[10] The best description of the Conference is André Tardieu, *The Algeciras Conference*; the best analysis is E. N. Anderson, *The First Moroccan Crisis*.

France and Germany were certain to be at swords' points. It was generally understood that if their delegates were to be brought together, White would bear the brunt of the task, and it would be accomplished by private rather than open negotiations. White's first effort, as he wrote Root, was to establish a cordial personal acquaintance with all the delegates, and especially the Germans and French. He had long known the British delegate, Sir Arthur Nicolson, at this time ambassador at Madrid, a quiet man whose reserve and shrewdness were invaluable; had he been less firm, he would have encouraged the Germans to hope for a rift in the Anglo-French *entente*, and had he been less tactful, he would have given the discussions the character of an open duel. White had also long known the venerable Marquis Visconti Venosta, the most commanding personality at the conference; a really grand old man, as White described him to Roosevelt, who had served with Cavour in his youth, had fought in the unsuccessful rising of 1849 against the Austrians, and seemed to embody the history of modern Italy. His desire was to act as a conciliator. White greatly enjoyed his talks with this "Nestor of the Conference," so full of memories; while the marquis, playing a difficult rôle, since the Triple Alliance bound him to Germany's chariot, and the Franco-Italian agreement upon Tripoli made it impossible to oppose France, thoroughly envied White's freedom of action. White was soon also on cordial terms with the two Spanish delegates, the Duke of Almodovar, who had thrice been Minister of State, and Señor Perez-Caballero. With the late war in mind, he showed them a special courtesy of attention, and the duke came to him just before the Conference ended with a word of gratitude. The Russian delegate, Count Arthur Cassini, White had previously met and neither liked nor trusted.

But it was the personalities of the French and German delegates which were the center of greatest interest. White had little difficulty in winning the confidence of both sides, which was fortunate, for to say that they distrusted each other is to put it mildly. Neither Paris nor Berlin had sent a man of first-rate ability, and the Conference would have gone off much more smoothly if such a Frenchman as Jules Cambon and such a German as Speck von Sternburg had been named. M. Paul Révoil, the Frenchman, had behind him a long official career—minister to Tangier, governor-general of Algeria, expert on foreign affairs in the Rouvier Ministry. He was a highly trained lawyer whose astonishing fluency of speech was more often used to conceal than explain his true meaning, and whose mind, as White complained, "ran too much on formulas." In argument he was excessively ingenious, subtle, and wordy. The French Government, having scant confidence in his abilities, rarely asked his opinion and sent him constant and explicit instructions. He would have made worse blunders than he did but for Sir Arthur Nicolson's advice. The two German delegates were Herr von Radowitz, ambassador in Madrid, an aging, feeble, and hesitant man, and Count Tattenbach, minister to Portugal, who was just the opposite—bustling, arrogant, and dogmatic. Though nominally second, Count Tattenbach quickly wrested the control of affairs from the nerveless hands of his associate. He was downright, ill-tempered, unable to see any point of view but his own, and profoundly convinced that the French could never be trusted. He never ceased to denounce the evil designs of the French to other members of the Conference.[11]

White saw that the rôle of conciliator would be difficult. But within a few days, by tact, energy, and candor, he had greatly improved the atmosphere, both in the conference hall and the hotel. In some ways it was an advantage to house the delegates together in the Reina Cristina, facilitating their discussions; in some it was a disadvantage. The place was the paradise of prying reporters. As one French journalist wrote, a delegate could not pass from room to room without being pursued by a pack of reporters famished for news and ready to herald to the world that a Frenchman had been talking with an American, and that a Russian had called on an Austrian. In the evening the correspondents feverishly roamed the parlors and smoking-room, pouncing with their questions on every hapless delegate. Rumors exploded on every hand; canards were being concocted in every corner. Cassini shook his fist at the journalists, and the feeble von Radowitz moaned over their iniquities. They heightened the feeling of nervousness that was in the air.

[11] Radowitz told White that if he alone had had the power to come to terms, the Conference would have terminated much earlier and more harmoniously. White to Root, Algeciras, April 14, 1906.

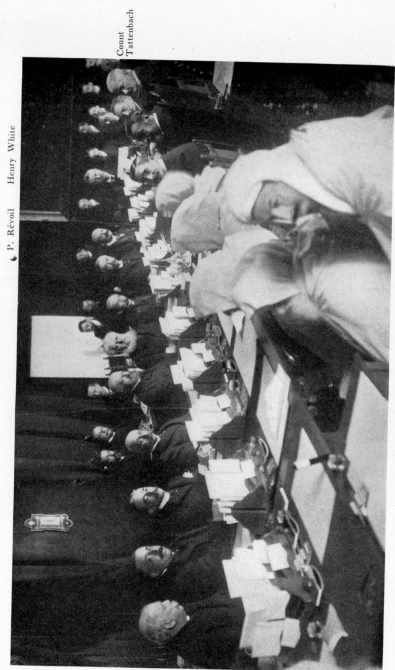

P. Révoil   Henry White

Count
Tattenbach

THE ALGECIRAS CONFERENCE

White did his best to calm the delegates. He utilized every opening, as he wrote Root, to "enter into private relations with such of them as might be concerned upon the more delicate matters," and lost no chance "to bring about private meetings between the two principals themselves with a view to friendly discussion."

The result of the Conference, as the world knows, was a diplomatic defeat for the Germans, and the interposition of President Roosevelt at the critical point was the main factor in this defeat. The two principal questions were the nature of the police control to be established in Morocco, and the character of the international bank to be set up for managing her finances. The police were the paramount issue. Early in the Conference Count Tattenbach came to White, and among other pleasant remarks said that the Germans wished neither *"vainqueurs ni vaincus."* [12] White replied that this was an excellent sentiment, but in his opinion the country which yielded its contention on the police question would be regarded as *vaincu*; and this proved to be the fact. The French wished the policing kept in their own hands, or at most shared with the Spaniards; the Germans began by insisting that it be confided to small neutral countries, such as Switzerland, Holland, or Denmark. White himself believed that if the police were kept entirely under French control, the Open Door would not last long.

The crisis upon the question of the police developed early in the sessions. On February 6th White telegraphed Secretary Root that the French would see the Conference go to smash before they would yield. They believed that their national dignity was involved; their officers and police instructors had been in Morocco for some time past, and the government resented any question of their fairness, while it argued that the French had seventy million francs invested in Morocco against Germany's five millions. [13] Yet Germany seemed also adamant. Count Tattenbach called on White on February 8th to say that he had instructions to stand fast for the selection of police officers from several minor Powers, the Conference to assign each Power a special port. Neither nation seemed likely to yield. France would go so far as to share her police control with Spain, but no further. Once France consented to do this,

[12] White to Root, January 12, 1906.
[13] White to Root, February 5, February 11, 1906.

White was satisfied that she was essentially right and fair in her stand, and intimated as much to the Germans. At the same time he was fearful that the Germans actually wished a rupture. He cabled Root on February 11:

> I am . . . satisfied Conference is likely to fail unless Germany can be got to accept French position in principle. There are indications that realizing she cannot get Conference to support her views, Germany beginning to think better terms obtainable by direct negotiations with France. If so, she should admit it and stop Conference.

The conduct of the Germans seemed to bear out White's fears. The tactless Count Tattenbach began trying to detach the astonished Sir Arthur Nicolson from the French, for he somehow imagined that since England's commercial interests were like Germany's, her support of France would be perfunctory, and she could easily be induced to abandon it.[14] "The damned Germans have had the audacity to offer us inducements to get us away from France!" Nicolson exploded when he saw White. His refusal was peremptory; and White wrote later to Roosevelt that it was "the greatest of all the German disappointments."[15] When M. Révoil heard of Count Tattenbach's efforts to woo the British delegate, he became stiffer than ever. Meanwhile, the president of the Reichstag made a highly injudicious and threatening speech, which caused a responsive outburst from the French press. The European skies seemed suddenly overcast with threatening clouds; hope of mutual concessions lessened, and no one knew what would happen. White came to the conclusion that bold steps were necessary and that Roosevelt should appeal direct to the Kaiser. He was pressing the French to admit the principle that a third Power, preferably Italy, might carry out some duties of police inspection. At the same time he

[14] The aggressive Tattenbach came to White when the latter had just arrived at Algeciras and remarked: "My government has empowered me to offer the British something which will make it worth their while to give up their friendship with France." White advised him not to commit the folly of seeming to offer the British a bribe unless he wished to cement the Anglo-French *entente*. On February 5 White wrote to Root in condemnation of Tattenbach's attempt to detach Nicolson from the French, calling it "very unfortunate from the German point of view."

[15] White to Roosevelt, April 8, 1906.

turned to Washington to bring pressure upon Germany. On February 13th he cabled Secretary Root, saying that the Germans had offered some unacceptable proposals, and suggesting that Roosevelt act forthwith: [16]

I have little doubt when foregoing German proposal is rejected, probably in two or three days, of which I shall immediately cable you, that a communication from the President to the Emperor will have great weight, and probably effect settlement. Meanwhile I hope to obtain French assent to third-power principle.

In effect, he was proposing that Roosevelt go over the heads of the Conference. He had cabled Root on the 11th that the Kaiser was probably ill-informed:

Recent conversations with Austrian Ambassador, and other reasons, confirm my impression that German representatives do not frankly inform Emperor as to situation.

Taking the cue, on February 13th Roosevelt cabled through Root, asking White's opinion of what would be a fair settlement of the issues. Here was White's great opportunity for usefulness—and he did not let it slip. At once he sounded the French as to the utmost limits to which they would go, while he approached the Germans on the subject of concessions. After long talks M. Révoil and von Radowitz both drew up memoranda for him. As a result, he cabled on February 16th a series of suggestions approved by the French and intended by White to form the basis of a proposal which Roosevelt should make to the Kaiser. These suggestions were (1) that the police should be organized in the Moorish ports by the Sultan, under his nominal authority, with a Moorish rank and file; (2) that the officers and non-commissioned officers should be French and Spanish, and "should be charged with instruction, management, pay, discipline, and assisting control"; (3) that the senior Spanish and French officers should make an annual report upon police operations "to the Sultan and to the Italian Government, which latter shall communicate it to the Powers"; and that (4) the international bank, which should furnish funds for paying the police, should be owned in substantially equal shares by all the

[16] Official despatches, White papers.

Powers, with a slight preference for France. White believed that by bringing in Italy as a third nation associated with police control, Germany could perhaps be satisfied. He concluded by cabling Roosevelt and Root that:

If Germany be quite resolved not to accept French and Spanish police, I think she ought to say so and break up the Conference, after sufficient discussion. . . . I am strongly opposed, for reasons known to you through my previous telegrams, to sitting several weeks longer and leaving the police question unsettled, as has been twice suggested to me by German Ambassador. I have great hopes of result from proposed communication to Berlin at this moment.

This was enough to furnish Roosevelt the ground he required for approaching the Kaiser. He adopted, with a few alterations, the plan suggested by White for settling the police and bank questions together, and on February 19th, through Root, proposed it to Speck von Sternburg for reference to his sovereign. Four days later Germany replied with a substantial refusal. That is, while accepting three of the four points listed above in White's plan, and approving Roosevelt's additional suggestion that the open door, in accordance with previous French pledges, be guaranteed, she still rejected the plan for limiting the control to French and Spanish officers. The deadlock continued, with all the European capitals breathlessly watching the situation.

In the next two weeks White was busy day and night, trying desperately to bring the French and German delegates nearer together, and sending long reports to Root and Roosevelt. "It is very amusing," he wrote his wife, "how most of the members of the Conference don't in the least know what is going on." On February 20th he telegraphed Root that while the position was decidedly unfavorable, he did not despair of a settlement. On the 22nd he added that Count Witte had addressed a strong personal appeal to the Kaiser not to let the Conference fail. A little later he sent news that Germany had informed Russia that she could not give way on the police question, and that while this hung fire, France would make no concession regarding the bank. It seemed a hopeless tangle. When on March 2nd Root telegraphed White that "Emperor has refused assent to essential features of arrangement stated in my cable to you of the 20th of February, and we do not think it advisable to make any proposal to the conference on the questions involved therein," he must have felt that the game was almost lost.[17] But he worked on undauntedly, and cabled Root on March 5th:

After meeting last Saturday on bank which was harmonious, though little progress made, I had long private talks with French and German delegates; told them that we can make no more proposals, and that I consider rupture imminent; urged deplorable consequences thereof, and responsibility of those two Powers. Result visit of second German delegate to French Ambassador to urge their coming to terms; latter sought me early yesterday to say he thought agreement on bank not impossible, that French public opinion would not admit his discussing it further with German delegate privately himself, but if Italian Ambassador and I would try to bring French and German views together he thought we might succeed. We are now trying, of course unofficially, and making no proposals, to harmonize few remaining differences before official meeting on bank next Thursday. It is evident that neither country wishes to assume the responsibility of rupture, especially on bank. . . .

Meanwhile, President Roosevelt was still ready to act energetically to terminate the dispute. White had felt that the first efforts at Berlin should be energetically followed up, and had repeatedly said so. For example, he wrote on the last day of February that "Perhaps if opportunity offers a hint to Berlin that our government deprecates delay on general principles might be efficacious." On March 7th Roosevelt sent another message to the Kaiser. He said he could ask France for no more concessions. The Kaiser, in a letter of the previous June, had promised that if difficulties developed in the Conference, "I will in every case be ready to back up the decision which you [Roosevelt] consider to be the most fair and most practicable." Now the President made it clear that he expected the Kaiser to redeem this promise. If Germany rejected the plan proposed by the United States, he wrote, the response of public opinion throughout the world would be so unfavorable that the German Government would lose far more in credit and moral power than it could possibly gain at Algeciras; it might be held

[17] For the perturbation throughout Europe, see Dennis, *ut supra*, p. 502.

responsible, even to an unreasonable degree, "for all the evils that may come in the train of a disturbed condition of affairs in Europe."

It was a blunt and positive letter, but for the moment the Kaiser still refused to yield. Instead, his Government instigated Austria to bring forward another proposal with regard to the police—a plan under which the French should officer the police in four ports, the Spaniards in three, and the Dutch or Swiss should choose the highest officer in the port of Casablanca, who should also be inspector-general of the police in all the other ports. White, cabling a summary of this plan on March 8th, declared that the French would agree to a Swiss or Dutch inspector-general, but never to his having command in any port. Moreover, he added, the French were greatly stiffened at Algeciras by confidential news from Jusserand in Washington that President Roosevelt had addressed a vigorous personal communication to the Kaiser. Throughout the negotiations, Roosevelt had been taking Jusserand into his confidence.

The Kaiser had played his last card, and for the moment he had reason to hope that it would prove to be trumps. Casablanca was the one port in which German commercial interests predominated. Even the Russian and British delegates thought, as White reported, that the French might consent to a Dutch or Swiss commander of police there, and that they could not afford to break up the Conference by rejecting the scheme. If Roosevelt had yielded, this would doubtless have been the basis of the settlement. But he did not yield. Stepping in vigorously once more, he saw Speck von Sternburg, who at once cabled Berlin the following report of his views— views which were simultaneously made known to Jusserand, were cabled by him to Paris, and were relayed to M. Révoil in Algeciras: [18]

The Austrian proposal in my [Roosevelt's] mind is absurd, because it favors the very ideas the Conference has been trying to eliminate, namely, partition and spheres of influence. Placing French and Spanish officers in the same ports gives according to my views a safer guarantee than placing them separately in single ports. This has distinctly the flavor of a French, a Spanish, and a Dutch or Swiss sphere of influence. I also

[18] March 14, 1906; Bishop, J. B., *Theodore Roosevelt and His Time*, vol. i, p. 497 ff.

do not see how the duties of the police inspector can be made compatible with military discipline. Austria wants an officer, who performs the same duties in the port of Casablanca as his French and Spanish comrades do, to act in all ports as their superior and inspector. This would bring friction at the start. The proposal I suggested is the better and safer and the only one I can support.

This statement of Roosevelt's to Berlin was somewhat amplified in a later cable to White, which Secretary Root authorized him to show to the British and French delegates to strengthen their stand. Roosevelt and Root in this wrote of the Austrian plan: [19]

This seems to us to provide for a potential partition of the territory in violation of the principle upon which we have agreed with Germany. From our point of view all the reasons which existed against leaving to France the control of all the ports exist against leaving to France the control of some, to Spain the control of some, and to Switzerland either in its own interest, or in the interests of some other Power, the control of one. The very fact of the division of the ports implies existence of a special right on the part of the three countries in the ports assigned to them respectively. The immediate effect can only be the creation of three separate spheres of influence, with inferior right and opportunity on the part of all other Powers. And the nations to whom these spheres are assigned may be expected in the ordinary course of events to enter into complete control.

Roosevelt was of course entirely right, the Kaiser's scheme being one that would have led directly to the creation of French, Spanish, and German protectorates. Covering his retreat as gracefully as possible, the Kaiser now surrendered. He indicated that he would accept Roosevelt's plan, stipulating merely that there be a Swiss inspector-general, without a port, who should make annual reports on police administration to the Diplomatic Corps in Morocco. Roosevelt and Root replied that they would regard this arrangement with favor, and at the same time White ascertained that France would accept it.

M. Révoil told him that it was impossible to concede the command of one port to the inspector, "but if Germany will give up port and accept inspector-general, to reside at Tangier with real authority to inspect and report to Powers on police at all the ports,

[19] Root to White, Washington, March 17, 1906.

he will take upon himself to yield extra bank share claimed by France . . . and conclude settlement immediately." Meanwhile Roosevelt, in a talk with Speck von Sternburg, explained that the American people were rapidly taking sides with France against Germany, a fact which was obvious and which Sternburg had noted in his dispatches to Berlin. The Kaiser not only gave way completely, but he commanded Sternburg to say, in a letter which the ambassador sent to the President, that "Sincere regret is expressed that the attitude of Germany should have led to certain misunderstandings. . . . The immediate removal of all misunderstandings is more important to Germany than the whole Morocco affair." This practically ended the matter. Late in March there was a flurry over the exact phraseology defining the supervision to be exercised by the diplomatic body, but by hectic efforts on March 27th White obtained an agreement.

The French, with Roosevelt's support and thanks in part to White's timely outline of a proper plan of settlement, thus scored a victory, a much greater victory, beyond doubt, than Roosevelt realized or intended. He did not wish to promote the "Tunisification" or peaceful penetration of Morocco, but instead desired it to remain an autonomous country, with no European power in sovereign control. This is evident from the emphasis in Root's dispatches upon the undesirability of any spheres of influence, and from Root's insistence that the Franco-Spanish police control should be truly joint and not several. White knew that there was a secret agreement between France and Spain regarding Morocco, while he guessed, though he did not know, that it divided the country into spheres in which each was ultimately to have a free hand; and these suspicions he divulged to Root on March 20, 1906. If Jusserand knew of the secret clauses in the Franco-Spanish and Anglo-French treaties, he took good care not to hint anything of the fact to Roosevelt.

Within a few years Morocco was destined, except for a small portion under Spanish sway, to pass completely into the control of France. The German press congratulated the Government upon its brilliant diplomacy in forcing the fall of Delcassé, the calling of the Algeciras Conference, and the formal recognition of Morocco's independent status. On April 1st White cabled from the Conference: "German Emperor has telegraphed German Ambassador following words, in English: 'Bravo! Well done!' Ambassador does not want this known." But the best-informed Germans realized that France had won. In the United States Roosevelt made a tactful effort to cloak the German defeat, and at a meeting of German-American veterans on March 12th, in a speech which both Sternburg and Jusserand had previously read, he gave warm praise to the Kaiser for the triumph of Germany's commendable aims at Algeciras.

In retrospect White, who wrote a long letter to Root [20] reviewing the Conference, pointed out that the Germans had made a series of errors. Their first blunder was in sending the stiff and tactless Count Tattenbach, who was better than M. Révoil but not good enough. Their second was in failing to perceive that the French would never yield the main point on the police question. "From the time my letter of February 5th was written until the settlement was reached," he wrote, "I never ceased to tell our German colleagues that no settlement would be possible which did not recognize the principle of superintendence of police by French and Spanish officers only, with an inspector of a third nationality; and I always refused to have anything to do with the attempts they made to get me to negotiate for them with the French on any other basis." The third blunder occurred when they had nearly maneuvered the French into accepting a Swiss commander of the police in Casablanca.

Both the British and Russian delegates, to White's certain knowledge, advised M. Révoil to accept this Austrian proposal, saying that France could not possibly break up the Conference on this one port, and their governments gave similar advice privately at Paris. Opinion at Algeciras was almost unanimous in favor of the Austrian plan. But the Germans, unable to keep their success to themselves, privately circulated a report at the leading capitals, through their ambassadors, that the British and Russians were acquiescing in the Austrian proposals. This the British and Russian Governments, being bound to support France, promptly denied, thus strengthening France's hand; and then Jusserand cabled his timely hint from Paris that Roosevelt was again approaching the Kaiser. "This," White writes to Root, "was one of the most curious episodes of the Conference, and there is no doubt that the eighth port was saved to the French and Spanish police superintendence entirely through

[20] White to Root, April 14, 1906.

the President's action and your admirable note of March the 17th, which placed the police question on clear and indisputable ground —the only ground, in fact, upon which France and Spain could legitimately claim the position eventually assigned to them."

White, in sending President Roosevelt a long review of the Conference,[21] spoke even more frankly upon some points. Both the French and German delegates came to Algeciras, he thought, under a misapprehension; Count Tattenbach thinking that as Germany professed to be advocating an Open Door principle advantageous to all the Powers, the latter would take the side of Berlin, while M. Révoil fondly believed that if he could make one of the whirlwind legal arguments which he was wont to use in the French courts, he could sweep the delegates off their feet. He pointed out that Italo-German relations had been under a heavy strain at the Conference, and that their friendship emerged badly battered. The aged Marquis Visconti Venosta had found his course difficult to chart, and at one time a formal complaint was quite unjustly made of his leaning toward France by the German ambassador in Rome, to which Visconti Venosta replied by a sharp message to the German Chancellor, Prince Bülow, who thereupon closed the incident by making an apology. As for Anglo-German relations, White believed that the Conference had perhaps improved them. At first the Germans had been indignant at the tenacity with which the British delegate supported the French, and had hoped to win him away:

[21] White to Roosevelt, April 8, 1906. Roosevelt replied almost immediately, sending his long memorandum on the Conference, and thanking White. "You have added to the reputation of your country and you have filled to perfection a difficult and trying position. . . . I may add that Jusserand, who is a trump, toward the end became very much disgusted with what he evidently regarded as a certain furtiveness and lack of frankness in the French in handling their case. I gained just the opinion you did of both the French and German diplomats. Until the Conference met I felt that France was behaving better than Germany, but toward the end it seemed to me that neither one was straightforward. It must have been delightful meeting Venosta. What a wonderful old man he must be! If you see him I wish you would convey to him the very high regard of the present President of the United States, who was not born until ten years after he had taken part in the first desperate effort in behalf of United Italy, and who was a baby in arms when, in 1859, Cavour's plans at last blossomed into their long fruition."—Roosevelt to White, Washington, April 30, 1906.

When they found the real state of the case, the Germans went to the other extreme and imagined that England intended breaking up the Conference in the hope of driving France into war, the result of which would be the destruction by England of the German fleet, and it took some time to disabuse the Germans of this idea. I stoutly combated it every time the German delegates mentioned it to me, which was quite frequently for a time, and I am glad to say that before the Conference ended they were convinced that I was right and that the rôle played by England was a useful one. I am therefore not without hopes that one of the results of the Conference may be an improvement in the relations between Germany and England; and Nicolson seemed rather disposed to agree with me. The Germans would now like this, having ascertained that they have been unable to insert a wedge—much less make anything like a cleavage—in the Anglo-French understanding which at this Conference had all the effect of an alliance. And it is all the more desirable that Germany, for her own sake, should improve her relations with England, as another prospect of the near future is, I have little doubt, and partly as a result of—or rather somewhat accelerated by—the Conference, an Anglo-Russian rapprochement. Nicolson, who is going to St. Petersburg as ambassador, is full of it, and there could not be a better man to help it along.

Altogether, White felt that American participation in the gathering, which had been severely criticized by such men as Senator Morgan, had been justified. He wrote to Roosevelt:

I hope you feel that I have carried out the spirit as well as the letter of the Secretary of State's instructions and that the critics in the Senate of your policy in causing the United States to be represented at the Conference at all, must now admit that it is possible for us to take an important part in a European assemblage of this kind, and fully to assert our right to equality of rights, commercial and economic, with any other nation, in a country such as Morocco, and yet in no wise to take sides in any of the political questions at issue between certain of the nations there gathered together. There is no doubt that the presence of the United States was exceedingly welcome to France and Germany as well as to all the other Powers; that any opinion we expressed (which I did privately very often) was listened to with serious attention, and often adopted, and that there were many occasions during the three months just ended on which my influence privately exercised, with both French and German delegates, has brought about pacific terminations to crises which seemed on the point of becoming acute.

Algeciras was one of the preludes to the World War, and its chief importance lies in its relation to the great conflict. It averted the struggle at a time when Russia was helpless and the French army unprepared and torn by internal dissension. It strengthened, as White had said, the Anglo-French *entente*. After all, French policy had proceeded so far in Morocco that the "Tunisification" of the land could be stopped only by war, and this fact Germany found out at Algeciras. As a German there told Mr. Lewis Einstein, who assisted White and Gummere during the Conference, "We have spit in their soup, but that is not diplomacy." If formally the Conference did not seem very constructive, actually it did much. It gave France a breathing-spell, and Russia a period in which to recover; it showed that the United States could intervene with effect in Old World affairs, and it allowed the Powers a few more years in which to avert the great conflagration—years and opportunities which they threw away.

CHAPTER SEVENTEEN

The French Embassy: Roosevelt in Europe

THE last two years of Roosevelt's second Administration witnessed several interesting events in home affairs—the panic
of 1907, the round-the-world trip of the battleship fleet, and the
Bryan-Taft campaign—but few of importance in our European relations. The second Hague Conference, held in the summer of 1907
with Choate as the principal American delegate, presented the
encouraging spectacle of forty-four nations in conference upon
means for preserving peace, but as we have seen, its visible accomplishments were meager. After its close Secretary Root turned his
energies to Latin-American affairs, and in the last weeks of the
year was busy directing a conference of Central American republics
which met in Washington. Meanwhile Roosevelt's attention was
being more and more drawn toward Japan, which was showing
resentment at the discriminations against her citizens in the Pacific
coast states. But in Europe there was little that stirred officials in
Washington; there were no dramatic episodes involving our interests, no more Venezuelan affairs or Open Door negotiations, not
even an important claim to press. The best our diplomatists in
Europe could do was to observe carefully the many European rival-
ries, intrigues, and apprehensions, and wait for more eventful days.
White went to Paris, hoping that it would prove a larger sphere,
but in his two years there he found opportunities as an onlooker
and little more.

Once more it was necessary to make a long and irritating search
for a suitable embassy, and to put up with the exactions of those
who owned the few eligible buildings. A satisfactory house, which
White later wrote President Taft was perhaps the most suitable
that any American representative in Paris had obtained within fifty
years,[1] was at length found at No. 5 Rue François-Premier: a roomy

[1] White to Taft, Paris, April 17, 1909. The rent was 30,000 francs a year,
and White had to spend 177,000 francs, or more than $35,000, in remodeling

hôtel of gray stone near the Grand Palais and Pont Alexandre III, with a garden terrace at the rear overlooking the Cours-la-Reine. Despite the difficulties of getting settled, White's arrival in Paris was in many ways like a home-coming; here he had spent his youth, here he had brought his bride, here he had been in most subsequent years of his life, and here his brother Julian now lived. He knew more prominent people at the outset than most of his predecessors had known at the close of their service; he was familiar not merely with the language, but with the national character and ways of thought. He found that his reputation had preceded him, for his work at Algeciras was well known. The principal ambassadors in Paris were Sir Francis Bertie, Count Khevenhüller of Austria, A. I. Nelidov, who when Russian ambassador in Constantinople in 1896 had laid audacious plans for the seizure of that city by a *coup de main*, and Prince Radolin, the able German ambassador; he had met them all before, and Bertie he knew fairly well.

The French political scene was one of normal confusion and uncertainty. Shortly after White's arrival, in the autumn of 1907, the Clemenceau-Caillaux Ministry came into power and remained there, but its two leaders were inharmonious. Clemenceau was intent upon cementing the alliance with Great Britain, while Caillaux preferred a rapprochement with Germany; at home Clemenceau wished above all else to continue the work of separating church and state, while Caillaux's chief aim was to impose a new system of taxation, including an income tax. The same unrest among the workers and the same rising tide of socialist sentiment which White had marked in Italy were to be observed in France; the General Confederation of Labor was busy, and strike followed strike, with the power of Jaurès steadily increasing. Foreign affairs under Clemenceau were in the hands of M. Pichon, who had to deal with the simmering situation in Morocco and the Balkans.

White, who was destined to meet Clemenceau again at the Paris Peace Conference, had an opportunity to study at close range the most realistic and astute of French statesmen. He and the Premier had common ground, for Clemenceau knew America by three years' residence. The notes they exchanged point to a friendship

it—which helps explain why the foreign service in these years was not for poor men.

that was easy and informal. "Won't you and Mrs. White excuse me," writes Clemenceau in the spring of 1909,[2] "from attending your dinner on Tuesday? I break my rule by asking this because of my luncheon the other day with the President of the Republic and the King of England. Since then I have suffered from incessant cramps in the stomach. If you wish to make me a sicker man, I shall accept your invitation; I don't want President Taft declaring war on us at the beginning of his term. But if you will listen to the voice of misery and give me permission to go to bed on Tuesday at nine o'clock with a hot-water bag, I shall be everlastingly grateful." Clemenceau talked with the utmost frankness, and White gradually came to estimate him as one of the ablest and strongest men in Europe—and incidentally as one of the most dangerous opponents that any other statesman could find.

The chief questions between France and the United States, which need not detain us long, were of a commercial character. Certain French interests were decidedly irritated, when White took over the embassy from Mr. McCormick, by features of the American application of the Pure Food Act passed in 1906. White could do nothing but give his assurances that the Government would try to administer the strict terms of the law with due reasonableness, and to point out how inevitable it was that at the beginning some subordinate officials would be technical and arbitrary. He found also, when he arrived, that the French were preparing to discontinue the benefits of the minimum tariff to importations of coffee from Porto Rico, and were likely to follow this with similar action on other imports from America. There was a commercial treaty between the two countries, dating back to 1898, which provided for reciprocally low rates on various exports from both; but the French complained that their whole tariff was much lower than our high Dingley tariff, and that the situation was unfair to them. The French had signed a supplementary convention on August 20, 1902, to apply minimum tariff rates to Porto Rican coffee until February 23, 1903; they had generously kept the low rate effective, but now they wished to raise it. White succeeded in arranging a new commercial agreement by which our coffee was kept on the old basis in return for an American reduction of duties on French cham-

[2] Clemenceau to White, Paris, March 7, 1909.

pagne and other sparkling wines. Hardly had this question been settled before the new Payne-Aldrich tariff bill raised a storm in France which White found it difficult to allay.[3]

Legally, White was now a resident of Newport, R. I., and one of Senator Aldrich's constituents. He believed in the protective principle and felt a certain sympathy for Aldrich's position; and while he condemned the excesses of that tariff measure, which was to prove so disastrous to the Republican party, he did what he could to mollify French opinion. Every step in the progress of the bill during 1909 was watched with indignation in France. Jusserand came home from Washington in July in an unhappy frame of mind over it. When White saw him he was full of resentment and was talking angrily of reprisals or an open tariff war. Various parliamentary leaders, including the chairman of the customs committee of the Chamber of Deputies, were equally hostile; and as soon as the law went into effect, the irritation was increased by vexatious questions regarding the interpretation of the administrative provisions.

It happened that Senator Aldrich visited Europe after the passage of the bill in pursuance of his old work of studying state banks in the leading countries; and White thought it advisable to show leading Frenchmen that he was not such an ogre as they imagined him, and to let him offer his own explanations of the disputed sections. He accordingly arranged to have the governor of the Bank of France invite the Minister of Finance, the Director of the Mint, White, and Aldrich to a dinner at the Bank. "We curse you in France, Mr. Aldrich," the Finance Minister remarked genially, "but we are delighted to welcome you and have a talk with you regarding these new tariff barriers." A little later White arranged another dinner at which the Ministers of Finance, Foreign Affairs, and Commerce, with other personages, heard Aldrich's explanation of his short-lived tariff law. Nevertheless, while Aldrich was in Europe White wrote to the Assistant Secretary of the Treasury, James B. Reynolds, that there was "a general feeling of soreness on the tariff question," which was aggravated by a clause continuing the old commercial agreements with Germany for nearly six months longer than those with France. He had been compelled to labor hard, he

[3] *Foreign Relations*, 1908, pp. 289-331.

declared, to convince "the official mind here that any idea of tariff war or retaliation, etc., would be suicidal for this country besides being utterly useless." White thought highly of the reasonableness of M. Pichon and of the Minister of Commerce. But protectionism was growing rampant in French industrial circles as it had long been in the United States, and the Ministry was so dependent upon the harmony of diverse groups in the Chamber that it could not take an independent stand. French indignation remained warm. The State Department having asked White on October 16, 1909, to induce the French to keep petroleum imports on the minimum tariff basis, White replied that any such request would only meet a brusque and humiliating refusal "in view of the generally hostile feeling to our new tariff, especially without a possibility of corresponding concessions on our part." Washington thereupon directed him to press the matter as far as he felt it safe, and as a last resort to threaten retaliatory action.[4] Thus the wrangle continued until White left office.

The two most alarming episodes in European affairs during White's service in Paris were the Casablanca troubles and the annexation of Bosnia-Herzegovina by Austria. The former amounted to little. A number of Europeans having been killed by the Moors at Casablanca and Marrakesh, in the summer of 1907 the French landed large forces of troops and occupied the whole Casablanca area. For a time the weather looked squally, but the trouble blew over. "Clemenceau is here," White wrote to Root from Carlsbad on August 7th, "and I have seen him several times. He feared that the Casablanca incident might have taken him back to Paris, but fortunately the Germans have given no trouble this time, and the French minister to Morocco, whom Clemenceau summoned hither and who has been breakfasting *tête-à-tête* with me today, says that Germany in reply to the intimations conveyed by the French Government as to what they were about to do, gave the latter to understand that Germany is *solidaire* with the French in the matter. As a matter of fact the Casablanca rising is rather a blessing in disguise, as it will enable the French to organize the police more promptly, backed by their own military force."

The sudden annexation of Bosnia and Herzegovina at the begin-

[4] Huntington Wilson to White, Washington, October 29, 1909.

ning of October, 1908, and the simultaneous proclamation of Bulgaria's independence, were much more serious events. White's first impressions as cabled to Root reflected the confusion in Europe.[5] France and Britain were taken aback and annoyed; Russia denied (quite falsely) that she had given her approval in advance to annexation, but admitted that she had furnished Austria assurances that she would not go to war over the *coup*; it was generally believed that she had been squared by the promise of access to the Dardanelles in the near future. As a matter of fact, the Austrian Foreign Minister, Baron Aehrenthal, and the Russian Foreign Minister, Isvolski, had acted in close coöperation, both thinking that the Turkish Empire might be approaching liquidation, and finding in the Young Turk revolution of July, 1908, an excuse for action. They had laid their plans in what is now known as the "Buchlau bargain," though Aehrenthal had acted more precipitately than Isvolski liked. White added that many thought Germany had instigated the whole transaction, because of her annoyance over the recent Turkish revolution and her wish to isolate England and France, but that in reality he believed the annexation was distasteful to her. His fuller impressions were given to Root three days later.[6]

In this later dispatch, White pointed out that neither the annexation of Bosnia-Herzegovina nor the simultaneous proclamation by Bulgaria of her independence really changed the status of the two lands. No one ever believed that Bulgaria would become Turkish again, or that Austria, supported as she was by Germany, would ever give up Bosnia-Herzegovina. It was the time and the manner in which the changes had been effected that were seriously agitating European opinion—making France and England indignant at the breach of the Treaty of Berlin, and causing Serbia to arm. The bloodless Young Turk revolution, which had forced Abdul Hamid to restore constitutional government, had been regarded as a blow to German prestige in Constantinople and an indication of the probable return of British influence, while the new liberal ideas in Turkey were naturally repugnant to Russia on general principles. As the Young Turks loudly proclaimed their intention to maintain Turkish territory intact, wrote White, "I imagine that Austria and

[5] White to Root, Paris, October 6, 1908.
[6] White to Root, Paris, October 9, 1908; "personal and confidential."

Bulgaria have both thought it wiser to confirm the *fait accompli* while the Turkish Government is in a comparatively weak period of transition, than to wait for the Turkish Government to be strong enough and to show sufficient ability for self-government to cause complications by suggesting the return of Bosnia-Herzegovina and possibly Eastern Rumelia to Turkish rule." The double coup was obviously the result of Austro-Russian consultation, ignoring England and France, and obviously the most interesting question was whether Germany was pleased or displeased by it.

On this subject White maintained his first view that Germany disliked the two steps. She had been negotiating with the Young Turk government for the retention of her military instructors and other officers in Constantinople, and now her negotiations were likely to be frustrated by Austria's acts. "I am informed on pretty good authority," he added, "that Germany had spent a good many million marks in bribing the late corrupt Turkish officials and that she naturally felt that all this money will have been wasted unless in some other way arrangements could be made with the new Government for the maintenance of her influence." White also noted that these Balkan events were a blow to the diplomatic prestige of Edward VII, who was supposed to have straightened out European affairs generally with his friend the Austrian Emperor that summer at Ischl—a friend who promptly turned around and violated a common European treaty! Talking with the new Turkish ambassador, "a fine old fellow," White learned that Turkey would throw herself upon the hands of Europe rather than fight for her nominal possessions, for the sad experience of the Greco-Turkish war had shown her that even when victorious the fruits of victory were taken away from her. As for Italy, her national feeling was antagonistic to Austria and White perceived evidence that public sentiment would call Signor Tittoni and the Government to sharp account for acquiescing in a new Balkan arrangement without securing any advantages for herself. Serbia was bristling up in warlike fashion, but her weakness made any belligerent action impossible. While thinking that a general European conference was possible, White recognized that there was the strongest opposition to this on the part of some nations which did not wish the whole Balkan question, and particularly the question of the

Dardanelles, reopened lest it prove impossible to close it again without war.

It was while the European situation was still tense that White received a letter from Roosevelt which presumably touched upon some delicate international question. We can only conjecture what it contained, who wrote it, or why the President wished it sent to Arthur Lee (later Lord Lee of Fareham), whom Roosevelt had known well as British military *attaché* in Cuba in 1898, who was an honorary member of the Rough Riders and had recently been civil lord of the admiralty:

> THE WHITE HOUSE, WASHINGTON,
> October 17, 1908.

Strictly Confidential
DEAR WHITE:

The enclosed letter explains itself. Of all the people in Europe you are the man in whom I have the most implicit trust, taking into consideration your experience, training, judgment, and good faith combined. Accordingly I ask you to read the enclosed. Then when you get the opportunity take it to London, give it to Arthur Lee, let him read it as often as he likes, but yourself see that it is destroyed immediately thereafter and that no copy is kept of it. I have entire faith in Lee's honor, but it is well to run no risk about leaving such a letter where it could by any possibility be seen. When I come out of Africa in the spring of 1910 I shall stop in Paris to deliver a lecture at the Sorbonne as Jusserand has just delivered an invitation to me to do so. I think I wrote you that I was to deliver the Romanes Lecture at Oxford also.

With warm regards to Mrs. White, believe me,

> Faithfully yours,
> THEODORE ROOSEVELT.

White found an early opportunity to take the trip to London, gave the letter to Arthur Lee to read, and destroyed it on November 28th.

The usual multitude of small duties pressed upon White in his Paris office. He had extradition cases to look after; he labored hard to induce the American Government to let the fleet stop at a French port in 1908 on the way home from its round-the-world cruise; and he made speeches on the Fourth of July, on Thanksgiving Day, and many other occasions. Though the Franco-American arbitration treaty of March, 1908, was mainly negotiated in Washington, he did what he could to facilitate it.[7] Finding the permanent embassy staff deficient in various respects, White labored to effect a number of changes—against difficulties, for Washington was slow to move. None of the three secretaries belonged to any French clubs or moved in political circles, so that he was without the confidential information as to French opinion which he felt useful. The first secretary, Henry Vignaud, was a man of intellectual distinction, the owner of a fine library on Hispanic-American exploration and an authority on the life of Columbus; he was active, clear-headed, and of great experience. But he was seventy-six when White arrived, and had made a point of keeping the second and third secretaries in rather imperfect tutelage lest they learn the embassy business so well as to displace him. His system of arranging the embassy archives was excellent in all respects except one—he understood it, but nobody else did or could. But by the time White left Paris, the official work was being done much more smoothly and efficiently.

Though he did not write to Secretary Root so frequently or intimately as he had done to Hay, White did correspond constantly with Roosevelt. In the fall of 1908 he was in Washington, dined at the White House, had some long talks with the President and escorted Mrs. Roosevelt one day to visit his Ridgely cousins at Hampton. "The President," he wrote his wife,[8] "in speaking of his likes and dislikes the other night, said to me that women interest him as a rule very little, but that there are three or four in the world whom he really cares to see much of besides Mrs. Roosevelt; and he said that you and Mrs. Lodge are the two foremost of that category." He found Roosevelt already immersed in plans for his hunting trip to Africa and subsequent visit to Europe; Jusserand had made all the arrangements for his lecture at the Sorbonne —which Roosevelt told White he had already written in full! Some of Roosevelt's letters during these Paris years illustrate the way in which he tried to keep White informed of his views on foreign and domestic affairs. He was writing, for example, in the fall of 1907

[7] *Foreign Relations,* 1908, pp. 331-333.

[8] White to Mrs. White, Washington, November 23, 1908. White enjoyed this visit a great deal. He wrote that "Old Henry Adams is excellent company and the best of hosts."

and the spring of 1908 about the results of the panic of 1907, the Japanese situation, and the voyage of the battleship fleet:

Thanks for your interesting letter. I received word from the French Foreign Office through the Ambassador after the Rochambeau celebration. I much appreciate what they said of me. I am also interested in your account of the visit of the Norwegian King. I am so glad you liked O'Brien's promotion.

I am concerned about the Japanese-California situation and I see no prospect of its growing better. The San Francisco mob has behaved atrociously; and as, in my judgment, there will be much suffering in that city in the near future and great multitudes of men out of work, I fear a recurrence of trouble at any time. Between ourselves, I have arranged to keep plenty of troops in the neighborhood. One trouble, of course, is that I must be very certain that the provocation completely justifies my sending troops, or else the action will merely do harm; for in a democracy like ours a public servant must continually keep in mind not only what the letter of the law permits, but how far he can arouse and guide public sentiment so that it will justify him. Moreover, the utterances of the extremists in Japan have begun to make an unpleasant feeling in this country. The Japanese are absolutely right in contending for their treaty rights and for the proper treatment of the Japanese here; but it is quite out of the question for us to permit any foreign country to say that we must receive their people in mass as immigrants, or must permit them to be naturalized if they so desire. Every nation has, of course, the right to limit immigration and naturalization according to its own view of public policy.

Douglas and Corinne have been sounding the praises of Mrs. White and yourself—and with all that they said I was more than prepared to agree.

Many thanks for your letter and the clippings. I am glad of what you were able to do for Admiral Stockton and his ships. I trust Stockton was able to entertain the Japanese officers, as he proposed.

I am sorry to say that the Japanese yellow press is showing itself to be quite as obnoxious as our yellow press at its worst, and I think it is high time for our fleet to visit the Pacific. I am exceedingly anxious to impress upon the Japanese that I have nothing but the friendliest possible intentions toward them, but I am none the less anxious that they should realize that I am not afraid of them and that the United States will no more submit to bullying than it will bully.

I wish Congress would provide suitable houses for our Ambassadors. As you know, Nick Longworth introduced such a bill, but I am afraid it will take considerable time before we succeed in securing the passage of such a measure.

ROOSEVELT TO WHITE, THE WHITE HOUSE, NOVEMBER 18, 1907

I have your letter of the 5th instant, with enclosure from Mr. Brunner. I will at once put the plan before Cortelyou. I wish we could better our system, and I shall do my best to bring about a bettering of it; but mind you, no small part of the trouble comes from the fact that we are a young and vigorous as well as a crude community. There are no such violent oscillations in the business communities of the Old World, because there is not the chance for them. This is something that ought to be remembered.

ROOSEVELT TO WHITE, THE WHITE HOUSE, NOVEMBER 27, 1907

Many thanks for your interesting letter and the enclosed clipping. I quite agree with you that foreigners as well as ourselves always mistake the evanescent for the permanent, and always forget that they made the very same mistake the last time the same conditions were present. They will get over the effects of this panic in time both at home and abroad, just as they have got over the effects of previous panics; and during the continuance of the panic there will be the same fear, and distrust, and folly, and bitter denunciation of the man most prominent at the moment in public life, that we saw in previous panics. Our fiscal system is not good from the purely fiscal side. I am inclined to think that from this side, a central bank would be a good thing. Certainly I believe that at least a central bank, with branch banks in each of the States (I mean national banks, of course) would be good; but I doubt whether our people would support either scheme at present; and there is this grave objection, at least to the first, that the inevitable popular distrust of big financial men might result very dangerously if it were concentrated upon the officials of one huge bank. Sooner or later there would be in that bank some insolent man whose head would be turned by his own power and ability, who would fail to realize other types of ability and the limitations upon his power, and would by his actions awaken the slumbering popular distrust and cause a storm in which he would be as helpless as a child, and which would overwhelm not only him but other men and other things of far more importance. (There! that sentence is as long and involved as if I were a Populist Senator; but I hope it conveys my idea.) One difficulty is that on this continent we are as naturally insular, or parochial, as ever the English were in the old days when compared with the rest of Europe. The same feeling that made England believe that it did not have to take part in any European concert of any kind makes this country feel that it can be a law for itself in many different matters. As yet our people do not fully realize the modern inter-dependence in financial and business relations. I believe that there will be an awakening, but it will be gradual.

Of course as yet it is impossible to say how long this depression will last, or how severe it will be. Naturally and inevitably I shall be held accountable for it, at first by those who wish to hold me accountable for everything, and gradually by honest men who suffer and who cannot be expected while suffering to keep their sanity of judgment. The business community of New York (by which I mean the New York plutocracy and those who are in the pay of or led by the plutocracy) is a rather preposterous body when judged by anything but its own peculiar, and not always healthy, work. In private conversation these business men will themselves tell you how much they suffer from the scoundrelism of the ——s and ——s and Morses and Heinzes and Barneys, the insurance crowd and the rest of those who represent simply a sublimated type of sand-the-sugar deacon in a country store; but the minute that any action is taken to get rid of the rascality, they fall into a perfect panic and say that business conditions must not be jeopardized; and they are blind to the fact that sooner or later the rascality must be found out and that then honest men will suffer for the deeds of the rascals.

In my message I think I have brought out pretty clearly the fundamental soundness of our position.

That must have been a very interesting experience you had in England. Poor Chamberlain! I suppose his work as a public leader is over. What an extraordinary public career he has had! I suppose he cannot help feeling a sense of incompleteness in the fact that he has never been Prime Minister, although the ablest man in English politics, with the exception of Gladstone, since the death of Beaconsfield.

ROOSEVELT TO WHITE, THE WHITE HOUSE, JANUARY 13, 1908

Allow me to say that you have with extraordinary keenness struck the exact situation about the central bank when you say that our big financiers are for the most part speculators, which is not true of the European big financiers. This is the keynote to our troubles; that is, we have to contend with the men who are in speculative, and not in legitimate business; or the men who, while in legitimate business, make illegitimate or speculative proceedings one main branch of their business. The legislation proposed in Congress is merely palliative.

As the correspondence just quoted shows, White had sent the President some comments of leading French financiers on the economic situation after the panic of 1907. Through his acquaintance with André Tardieu, who at this time was foreign news editor of *Le Temps*, and with other Frenchmen whose knowledge extended behind the political scene, he was able to tell Roosevelt something of the general effect, which he regarded as salutary, of the cruise of the battleship fleet.[9] It was not possible for it to pay a formal visit to a French port, for such a call of courtesy had been refused to the British, and would have irritated the Germans; but it directed the attention of Europe to the rising naval strength of the United States. White also wrote a good deal to the President about English politics, and when Campbell-Bannerman resigned, in 1908, and H. H. Asquith succeeded him, they both agreed in admiring the new Prime Minister even more than the old. In the campaign of 1908 White wrote that, as a representative of the whole people without respect to party, he did not think he ought to take any part in the contest, to which Roosevelt of course assented. It was going to be a real fight, added Roosevelt. "The times are hard, and this of course means that the battle will be difficult, especially as the more idiotic type of plutocrat thinks Bryan not much worse than me or Taft; in other words, is willing to risk socialism rather than to submit to a régime of fair play."

A little later the tragically early death of Speck von Sternburg evoked a letter from White to the President on the high qualities of the German diplomatist, who by blood was half English. Roose-

[9] Apropos of the expanding American navy, Roosevelt wrote: "Congress will not stand for the four battleships. To be frank, I did not suppose that they would; but I knew I would not get through two and have those two hurried up unless I made a violent effort for four."—Roosevelt to White, Oyster Bay, June 30, 1908.

velt replied with some interesting information about his prospective trip.

OYSTER BAY, N. Y.,
September 10, 1908.

MY DEAR WHITE:

Yes, I sincerely mourn Speck's loss, tho I can not be sorry for the gallant little fellow himself, for life was one long torture for him. I have never met a man for whom I had a higher respect or regard. It is very hard on the Baroness.

Moreover, as you say, it is a real loss for the two countries. I shall keep Lancken in mind in the very improbable event I am given any chance to say anything in the matter.

I intend to come out from East Africa by Khartoum, and have been in communication with Wingate, who has been more than nice about everything. I only hope the British East African people will be as pleasant as he has been. Curzon has written me, on behalf of the authorities at Oxford, to ask me to deliver the Romanes lectures there and to get the same kind of degree, whatever it was, that they gave the Kaiser. I have accepted for some time in May, 1910, which will be a month or six weeks after I have left Africa. When I am in England I suppose I shall be informally presented to the King. I shall be a private citizen then, and of course can only meet him as a private citizen—and in addition, I should greatly resent being treated as anything else, for I am no hanger-on to the shreds of departing greatness, and when I leave the office I leave it completely and entirely. Now, I shall probably spend a few weeks in Europe before I reach England. I wish to travel as quietly as possible, and simply see, for instance, the hill towns of Italy, certain country districts of France, and the like. If I could avoid seeing any sovereign I should like to do so, but if this would make me look churlish, or cause trouble in any way, why of course I shall be presented, trusting that the presentation will be informal and that under no circumstances will I be given a formal entertainment such as a dinner, etc. Now I have been puzzled about the Kaiser. I have had a pleasant correspondence with him at times, and there is much about him that I admire. On the other hand, I would not of my own accord care to go to see him, for Berlin is out of my way, and I will not put myself in an attitude of going to any place for the sake of being received by the man in authority. If he should wish to see me and should express that wish, I would go to Berlin and see him, but not otherwise; and the thing that puzzles me is how to avoid hurting his feelings by seeing the King of England

and not him, and on the other hand not give him the erroneous impression that I would like to have him, as a favor to me, allow me to come to Berlin to pay him my respects.

Sincerely yours,
THEODORE ROOSEVELT.

White made the common-sense reply that it was absolutely certain the Germans would invite Roosevelt to their country just as the British had invited him to Oxford and the French to Paris; and this was precisely what happened, the German ambassador transmitting a request from the Kaiser that Roosevelt should speak at the University of Berlin.

When Taft was elected President, it was assumed by White and all his friends that as a matter of course he would be either retained at Paris or transferred to the London Embassy. He was the best-trained member of our diplomatic service; he embodied as did no other man the principle that diplomacy should be a profession, and this principle was steadily gaining public support. The most influential men in Washington were his friends and supporters—Roosevelt, Root, Lodge, and Aldrich. An additional consideration was the friendship which had subsisted between White and Mr. Taft's father, Alphonso Taft, from the time of their association together in the Vienna legation. In all the gossip which emanated from Washington as the Taft Administration began it was taken for granted that White would be retained in the service. When Mr. Taft came to Washington in December, 1908, Lodge had a walk and a long talk with him, and emphasized the importance of retaining White; while he also talked with the man who was to be the next Secretary of State, Philander C. Knox. Lodge was head of the Foreign Relations Committee, and while Root had been Mr. Taft's first choice for Secretary of State, Lodge had been his second; it was only when Lodge declined that Knox was chosen. The Senator reported that Mr. Taft and Knox were both for keeping White in Paris.[10] The crowning assurance was a letter from Roosevelt dated April 9, 1909. "Taft told Lodge and me both that he intended to keep you. It was not a promise, but it was an unqualified declara-

[10] Lodge to White, Washington, January 12, 1909.

tion of intention; and I cannot imagine his being so unwise as to let you go. I most earnestly hope I shall find you in France next year." [11]

Yet before this letter reached White, the harshest blow of his career had fallen. At the beginning of April he received a letter from the Assistant Secretary of State, dated March 25th, saying that his resignation would be accepted to take effect January 1, 1910. No successor would be appointed until near that time, but President Taft wished him informed at once out of consideration for his personal convenience and plans. Under this blow, keenly felt though it was, White never winced. He wrote to President Taft at once, begging that he might be relieved from duty and his successor appointed as soon as possible; and without a word of complaint to anyone began making preparations for departure. But the indignation of his friends and associates blazed up at once. As soon as the change became known the press was outspoken in comment. When Robert Bacon was told that he would be nominated as ambassador, he protested vigorously, declared he would rather not have the place than take it at White's expense, and accepted only when it was made clear that White would be ousted in any event. Aldrich, writing to White, gave vent to his disappointment and irritation. So did Choate; he had gone to Washington and learned all about the matter from Root himself, who was much distressed.[12] He wrote that the worst feature of the incident "is the utter lack of appreciation of the value of continuity in the diplomatic service, and the treatment of appointments in it as political spoils. I hoped this Administration would rise above that, and at least in a case so unique as yours, avail itself of your thirty years of service, which has put you in the very front rank of the world's diplomatists." But the most important letters were from Roosevelt and Lodge. When news of White's virtual dismissal reached Roosevelt, he was in the depths of British East Africa, but he hastened to write in indignant sympathy. This was the first official act of Taft's of which he strongly disapproved:

[11] Taft offered the London post to Charles W. Eliot.—Lodge to White, April 3, 1909.

[12] Choate to White, Stockbridge, July 9, 1909.

LAKE NAIVASHA,
July 21, 1909.

DEAR WHITE:

This letter must be personal, for the last thing I must do is in any way to criticize my successor. But if as I hear to be the case you are to be displaced, I wish you to know that everything I could do was done on your behalf, not because of my affection for you, great though that is, but because as I told Taft I regard you as without exception the very best man in our diplomatic service. I told Taft that I had no personal request whatever to make of him, but there were certain men whose qualifications for the public service were of so high an order that I felt I ought to dwell on them, and that conspicuous among these was yourself. To me as well as to Cabot Lodge he said without any qualification that he intended to keep you. It was, of course, not a promise any more than my statement that I would not run again for President was a promise. But it was an expression of intention which I was at entire liberty to repeat. I feel that your loss will be very greatly felt, and I am sure that you will come back into the diplomatic service in the end.

Give my love to Mrs. White, and tell Jack how pleased I am whenever I think of the way he has gone to work. Remember me warmly to your daughter. I know you will be glad to hear that Kermit has really done very well, and we have had a most successful trip.

Always yours,

THEODORE ROOSEVELT.

Lodge wrote at greater length, and with caustic frankness upon the motives behind the dismissal, which he vigorously arraigned. The reason for the dismissal lay in a trifling incident of White's earlier career. When Taft had visited London on his honeymoon in 1886—twenty-five years earlier!—he had asked White to procure him seats for a notable debate in Parliament. This proved to be impossible, and White instead sent the Tafts some tickets to view the royal mews, then a privilege of value. His well-meant act was misunderstood, and the Tafts never forgot the incident. But White felt no rancor; he recognized that Taft had a perfect right to drop him; he always expressed a warm admiration for Taft's general regard for the merit principle in the diplomatic service, and he willingly accepted office under Taft. Nor did he lose much, if anything, in failing to retain the Paris position for a year or two longer.

White's labors in Europe for nearly a decade to come ended with his share in arranging for the reception of ex-President Roosevelt. He heard from Roosevelt during the autumn of 1909. A letter written "on safari," in East Africa, October 16, spoke of a variety of topics. These included Robert Bacon's fine spirit, the Kaiser ("I have grown really to look forward to seeing him. He is one of the most interesting and powerful figures we have seen in the public life of our day"), the joys of lion-hunting, and his pity for all childless people. "The compliment which the French people, Government, and press have paid you," he wrote, "is unprecedented in our diplomatic history." And he closed by saying: "Of course you can't be in Paris next spring; but I do wish you could be either in Berlin or London." White, writing to Secretary Knox in September, when he was busiest trying to reconcile Frenchmen to the new Aldrich tariff, insisted that he must be relieved from duty in November at the latest, and his request was granted. The spring of 1910 found him in Europe at last a free man, and he was able to be with Roosevelt, at the latter's request, at three capitals—Vienna, Berlin, and London.

He heard from the Colonel as he emerged from Africa; a characteristic letter, for example, dealt with British colonial administration.[13] "I had a most interesting time in the Soudan and Egypt, and I must say I have come away with rather a contempt for the British attitude in Egypt. I don't believe for a moment that it is any worse than we would take if at this time we had, what the *Evening Post* desires, a mixture of mugwumps, ultra peace advocates, and maudlin, hysterical sentimentalists, plus Bryanites, to dominate our foreign affairs. But it certainly makes the English look flabby. Both the Sirdar and Gorst, who is Cromer's successor, wrote me most enthusiastic letters of thanks for the way I had met the situation; but what I said will be small good, unless they have the nerve to back it up by deeds. The Sirdar is a fine fellow." From Egypt the ex-President went to Italy, and thence northward.

Of the events of Roosevelt's visits to Vienna and Berlin White has left but a scanty record. He was waiting at the hotel set aside for Roosevelt when the latter arrived in Vienna early on the morning of April 15, 1910. "When he saw me he bounded with joy,"

[13] Roosevelt to White, Naples, April 2, 1910.

White wrote to his wife,[14] "and I have been constantly with him ever since. He made me breakfast with him alone, and talked most freely on matters political, whereof full particulars when we meet. It is wonderful how he understands the limitations of Cabot and his best friends, and how he understands the public at home. He is now having his audience with the Emperor and I am availing myself of his absence to write to you. This morning he had a long talk with Aehrenthal, of whom he thinks highly as a man of strength and ability. Theodore also made me lunch with him in company with two African hunters and I am shortly going off to a place called the Spanish Riding School to see some historic *haute école*. I may say that his political views and intentions will meet absolutely with our approval. The German Emperor has now asked Mrs. Roosevelt also to stay at the castle. Theodore refused until he did so; a rather interesting episode whereof further particulars also." It is a pity that we do not have some of these "further particulars." The mention of Roosevelt's political views is partly explained by a reference later in the same letter to a talk with Mr. Lawrence Abbott, who was of the ex-President's party. Roosevelt was becoming decidedly irritated over the course taken by the Taft Administration in dealing with the tariff, in the recent dismissal of Gifford Pinchot, and other matters; in fact, irritation is too mild a word. Mr. Abbott said, wrote White, "that Theodore has particularly resented the President's action regarding me after his promise before assuming office, and seems quite unable to get over it."

In Berlin White accompanied the ex-President when, on the day of his arrival, he lunched with the Kaiser and von Bethmann-Hollweg at the "Neues Palais" in Potsdam. The following day the Kaiser invited Roosevelt and White to go with him to some striking army manœuvres, where five hours were spent in the saddle, they and Kermit Roosevelt being the only civilians present. White wore tweeds and Roosevelt khaki; the Kaiser was of course resplendent in uniform. The scene was impressive, the helmeted troops wheeling past in long files, the Kaiser stiffly saluting, while the ex-President raised his hat from time to time. At the beginning of the review William II, surrounded by his officers, said with

[14] White to Mrs. White, Vienna, April 15, 1910.

impressive formality, in German: "Roosevelt, *mein Freund,* I wish
to welcome you in the presence of my Guards; I ask you to remember that you are the only private citizen who has ever joined
the Emperor in reviewing the troops of Germany." As White later
said, the Kaiser's speech and his emphatic use of the phrase "mein
Freund," seemed to those who knew the strict military discipline
of Germany a signal act of homage.

White, leaving Germany, went to London at the end of April,
spent a fortnight with old friends, and was at Dorchester House
to greet Roosevelt when he reached England the middle of May.
Before his arrival, Edward VII died on May 6th, 1910, and Roosevelt attended the funeral as President Taft's special ambassador.
White's letters to his wife describe the lying-in-state of the dead
sovereign in Westminster Hall, and the burial on May 20th at
Windsor, the coffin being followed by the new king, George V,
the Kaiser, seven other European sovereigns, and Roosevelt. It was
such a scene as since the World War can never be duplicated.

More interesting than the funeral to White, as to the American
public, were the meetings between Roosevelt and the various sovereigns.[15] On May 19th, the day before the funeral, White breakfasted with Roosevelt at 8:30, and with the exception of a few hours
in the morning, when he went to Eton with Mrs. Roosevelt, Ethel
and Kermit Roosevelt, and Sir Cecil Spring-Rice, he was constantly
with the ex-President. Roosevelt lunched with Lord Cromer, and
told White that Cromer was "the most wonderful personality he
had ever met." After luncheon a number of well-known Englishmen called at Dorchester House to pay their respects, while the
kings of Denmark and Greece came by special appointment; the
last-named, White noted, looking rather the worse for wear after
the stormy events of the preceding few years. The two sovereigns
were shown in while other visitors were kept waiting in an adjoining room. They were so much interested by Roosevelt's vigorous
personality and conversation that they stayed a good deal longer
than he had expected; and it became evident to White, who was

[15] White wrote for Mrs. Roosevelt, November 25, 1912, a rather long and
careful account of Roosevelt's visit in London as he observed it; a copy is
in the White papers in the Library of Congress.

Henry White   The Kaiser   Roosevelt

ROOSEVELT, THE KAISER, AND HENRY WHITE

watching the scene, that he was seeking some way to bring about their departure, when fortunately Prince Henry of Prussia entered the room. Roosevelt promptly seized his opportunity. Greeting the prince warmly, he said: "My dear Prince Henry, I am delighted to see you and I only wish I could ask you to sit down and have a good talk. But, unfortunately, I am obliged to go out and make a number of official calls, among others upon your brother the Emperor, who was kind enough to come here yesterday to see me before my arrival." Of course the two kings took the hint, and after Prince Henry had exchanged a few friendly words with Roosevelt, all three departed together. Thereupon Roosevelt passed into the other room, shooks hands with the visitors who had been waiting to see him, among them the Lord Chancellor, Lord Clarendon, and eight or ten others, explained that he was sorry not to be able to remain, but was obliged to go at once to keep several appointments, and, with White accompanying him, left the embassy.

Roosevelt and White then drove to Buckingham Palace, where the Kaiser was staying. To their considerable relief, for Roosevelt had seen a great deal of the Emperor in Berlin, they found he was out; and the Colonel thereupon left his card, scribbling on it a note to the effect that he was sorry not to see His Majesty, but was looking forward to meeting him that same evening at a state reception.

But just as Roosevelt and White were reëntering their car at the palace door, the Kaiser drove up in one of the state carriages. Espying Roosevelt, he thrust his head out of the window and exclaimed, "My dear friend, I am so glad to have arrived in time to see you, and should have felt greatly distressed if I had missed your visit." He leaped out of the carriage, rushed up to Roosevelt with characteristic animation, and shook his hand warmly. "It is a great piece of luck," he said. "I have an hour to spare, and we can have a good talk together." "Oh," demurred Roosevelt, "I am sorry to say I have not an hour to spare nor anything like it, for I have a great deal to do this morning." To which the Emperor replied, "How much time can you give me?" Roosevelt gave his watch a hurried glance, and with his usual quick way of snapping out answers, replied: "I'll give you twenty minutes." "All right," said the Kaiser. "I'm very glad to get that much of your time. Let's go off and have a talk together." And this they did, the Colonel returning to join White within the twenty-minute period. Then White and he drove off together to continue their round of calls.

At the reception that evening, to which White accompanied Roosevelt, there were again some amusing incidents. Roosevelt had no sooner been ushered into the reception-room at Buckingham Palace than he was surrounded by all the kings and hereditary princes present, except George V, who was of course obliged to receive his other guests; and he remained thus surrounded the entire evening, answering questions put to him by one sovereign after another to elicit his opinion on public questions connected with their respective countries. White observed him at one moment clenching his fist emphatically and saying to a ruler, "Oh, I would never have taken that step at all if I had been in your place, Your Majesty." A few minutes later, clapping the back of his right hand into the hollow of his left in a characteristic gesture, he assured another sovereign: "That is *just* what I would have done; quite right!" This animated talk continued till the end of the evening, and he was accompanied to the door of the palace, on his departure, by three of the sovereigns, including the King of Norway, who had conceived a particularly strong admiration for him. Indeed, he was the lion of the evening.[16] White also recalled that during the reception the Kaiser, seeing Roosevelt in conversation with the Tsar Ferdinand of Bulgaria, took him by the arm and drew him away, saying: "That man is entirely unworthy of your acquaintance. I should not spend any time talking to him. He is a poor creature." This word of caution is not the less interesting now because of the rôle the Bulgarian Tsar afterward played in supporting the Kaiser during the war.

A few weeks later, and both Roosevelt and White were at home

[16] White wrote to his wife at midnight on May 19th: "The kings have been fairly scrambling for a share in his conversation and to confide in him their views and ascertain his, the Emperor being particularly eager to introduce him to brother sovereigns. He likes the King of Spain, some of whose frank statements, which he said he particularly wanted Theodore to hear, regarding his difficulties and touching his views respecting the clericals in his country, I don't quite like to quote."

again in the United States; both out of office, but both still connected with public affairs, for Roosevelt was about to plunge into the attempt, against bitter opposition in the Republican party, to elect Henry L. Stimson governor of New York, while White was about to undertake a special diplomatic mission to South America. They were now closer in feeling than ever. Roosevelt never forgot and never quite forgave President Taft's treatment of White. In the summer of 1913, when he was a member of the staff of the *Outlook,* he was contributing chapters of his autobiography to its pages.[17] One July day he wrote from Sagamore Hill to Mr. Lawrence Abbott asking him to insert a paragraph saying that the American public rarely appreciated the work done by its diplomats, and concluding: "The most useful man in the entire diplomatic service, during my own Presidency, and for many years before, was Harry White. When I left the Presidency he was Ambassador to France; he was removed shortly afterward by Mr. Taft, for reasons unconnected with the good of the service, and to the serious detriment of the service." To this paragraph Mr. Abbott made two objections. He proposed that Roosevelt should write that White was "one of the most useful men" in the entire diplomatic service, instead of "the most useful man," and that Roosevelt should omit the final phrase declaring that White's removal was "to the serious detriment of the service," for he regarded this as an anticlimax. Before Roosevelt had received this letter, he had gone away on one of his Western trips; but a fortnight later he wrote back from the Grand Canyon, saying:

Now for the Harry White matter. I wish to adopt most of your suggestion; but to keep the statement that he was the best man in the service because that is the truth. How would it do to have it read as follows?:

"The most useful man in the entire diplomatic service, during my Presidency and for many years before, was Harry White; and I say this having in mind the high quality of work done by such admirable ambassadors and ministers as Bacon, Meyer, Straus, O'Brien, Rockhill, and Egan, to name only a few among many. When I left the Presidency, White was ambassador to France; shortly afterwards he was removed by Mr. Taft, for reasons unconnected with the good of the service."

[17] Memorandum by Lawrence F. Abbott, March 13, 1928.

It is in this form that the passage stands in Roosevelt's published biography. It is an example of his lasting indignation over anything that he regarded as an injustice; no other President has ever rebuked his successor for failing to retain a diplomatist in office. We know now that Roosevelt deeply resented the fact that Taft did not keep James R. Garfield in office as Secretary of the Interior, and did not promote William Loeb, Jr., to the Cabinet; he felt just as warmly about White.

CHAPTER EIGHTEEN

Taft, Roosevelt, Wilson: The World in Arms

To HENRY WHITE, as to nearly everyone else of international contacts and broad interests, the bursting of the World War seemed to shut down a steel curtain between two periods of life. It closed one era of Western civilization and opened another. He instinctively felt that his world—the world of constant travel, cosmopolitan intercourse, secure comfort and culture—would never be the same again. The war was to bring him one last and largest opportunity for service to his country, and place him in a position of greater prominence than he had before occupied; but of this he could divine nothing in the first years of the conflict, while the United States still strove to keep apart from it. He knew only that the future for some of the nations he knew and loved best was full of dark uncertainties and hazards, that his own life had lost some of its safety and ease, and that he had personal anxieties of a painful sort connected with the war; his daughter was now a German subject, his son-in-law, Count Hermann Seherr-Thoss, was a German officer, and he had grandchildren in Germany.

The years between his retirement from the French Embassy and the outbreak of the war had been busy and well occupied. He had settled in Washington and begun the building of a house on Crescent Place, in one of the newer parts of the city. He had gone much into society there and in New York. He kept up his friendship with Roosevelt, Lodge, Root, Choate, Jusserand, and Bernstorff, while he formed a new and fairly close friendship with a man who previously had been only an acquaintance—James Bryce, the British ambassador in Washington. Though he never cared for public speaking and did not excel in it, he made a good many appearances on the platform. He also gave conscientious service to several civic, cultural, and religious organizations; he was a member of the executive committee of the Carnegie Institution, he paid some attention to the affairs of Johns Hopkins University, which in

307

1914 gave him the degree of LL.D., and he was one of the most active of the Episcopalian laymen in Washington, taking a keen interest in plans for the Washington Cathedral at St. Albans. Once and only once, in the spring of 1910, he accepted from Mr. Taft a quasi-diplomatic appointment, heading the American delegation to the Fourth Pan-American Conference, which was held in Buenos Aires in the summer of that year.

This mission to South America, which included service as special ambassador to the centenary celebration of Chilean independence, offered a number of pleasing experiences and a notable opportunity to enhance the respect and friendship felt for the United States. The last previous conference, that in Rio Janeiro in 1905, had been attended by Secretary Root himself. White felt on his mettle to make this conference equally harmonious and fruitful, and to deepen the telling impression which had been made in South America by Root's noble series of addresses. American exertion was needed, for Secretary Knox's handling of Latin-American affairs had not been happy; his "dollar diplomacy" had produced a bad impression, and former Secretary Root's concern over the consequent resentment had been communicated to White. In Chile particularly there was a feeling of irritation due to Knox's brusque handling of the so-called Alsop claim.[1] White realized that the atmosphere and spirit of the conference would be more important than its measures, and that his most important achievements would be of an intangible sort.

His delegation was an able and congenial body of men, comprehending John Bassett Moore, later counselor of the State Department, General Enoch H. Crowder, who had been one of the guiding American agents in the management of Cuba, Paul S. Reinsch of the University of Wisconsin, later minister to China, and David Kinley, then professor in and later president of the University of Illinois. It need not be said that all four contributed much to the successful labors of the American Mission. The whole party, including White's son and secretary, John Campbell White, Professor W. R. Shepherd of Columbia as general secretary, and a body of correspondents, was taken down on the transport

[1] Cf. Bemis, S. F., *American Secretaries of State and Their Diplomacy*, vol. ix, p. 308 ff.

Sumner, which proved a cramped and uncomfortable vessel. Diversion was afforded by a young Argentinian who masqueraded as correspondent of the *Prensa* of Buenos Aires, but turned out to be simply a sharper beating his passage to Argentina; and by a reporter for the New York *Herald,* who twice went on sprees lasting for a week.[2]

In Buenos Aires White found the Argentinians and South Americans generally much pleased by the arrival of his mission, extremely courteous, and anxious to outvie one another for American favor. He had to be careful not to show more cordiality to the Chileans than the Argentinians, or to the Brazilians than either. In the conference itself he was the most important single figure, and discovered that the deference to American wishes was almost excessive. The chairmen of the different delegations told him at once that, forgetting past unpleasantnesses, they wished to work in close relations with him. Theoretically the order in which the different countries voted was determined by lot, but it happened that "America" (as the United States was always called) came first, followed by Argentina, Brazil, and Chile, with the others in irregular order. On the various questions which came up—compulsory arbitration of money claims, sanitation of ports, trademarks, patents, copyright, steamship service, and intellectual exchanges—the greater Powers, excepting sometimes Mexico, lined up together as if automatically, most of the others followed, and the minority seldom exceeded two or three out of a total of twenty nations.[3]

Whenever any conflict of moment threatened to develop between the United States and other leading nations, the latter gave way. White and his delegation adopted the policy of saying very little and encouraging others to talk, a policy which cost nothing, for there were always nations eager to voice the opinions of the United

[2] Memoranda for the author by President Kinley and John Campbell White.

[3] White's very full report on the Conference was embodied in a letter, "Personal and Confidential," to Secretary Knox dated October 22, 1910. White's good offices were sought in a number of directions. Thus he was approached in Buenos Aires by representatives of Chile and Peru on the question of Tacna-Arica, while in Santiago the Minister of Foreign Affairs brought up the subject. White tried to quiet the feeling on the dispute, but thought nothing more important could yet be done.

States. The Venezuelans and Dominicans alone showed hostility, and the Americans kept on good terms with them, White jocularly calling them "conspirators" to their faces. When at one point Señor Lugo of Santo Domingo rose and made a speech breathing covert enmity to the United States, White went up to him, shook him warmly by the hand, and congratulated him on his eloquence.

At one of the first receptions he attended in Buenos Aires, White lighted upon Clemenceau, who had just arrived on a lecture tour. The Frenchman gave a whoop of delight when he saw him—he had not known of White's presence in the city. As White wrote to his wife, Clemenceau was making a pretty penny out of his lectures, for seats were fifty pesos each for a series of twelve, and the opera house, which held more people than that in Paris, was always packed. White attended the first lecture. "He spoke without a single note for an hour and forty minutes, walking up and down the stage and thinking aloud on democracy, which he made out to have originated with the Greeks, to have been crushed out by the Romans, and save for being kept faintly alive during the dark ages by the monks in their monasteries, to have disappeared completely from the fall of the Roman democracy until its reappearance in America. Several times during his allusions to the latter he turned to me and once addressed me by name."

White and Clemenceau spent a morning together viewing the city institutions under the guidance of the mayor. He and his son made a delightful trip to one of the great ranches owned by Señor Martinez de Hoz, a holding nearly thirty miles square near Mar del Plata, to which they went by special train. They attended the opera, were dined by the American minister, Charles H. Sherrill, who had won an excellent place for himself, and made a pilgrimage to hunt up the grave of Cæsar Rodney, once Attorney-General and Senator, who had died while minister to Argentina. On arriving in Chile, White delivered several public speeches in connection with the centenary celebration, while in private he did what he could to lessen the irritation caused a year earlier by what the resentful Chileans called Secretary Knox's "ultimatum" on the Alsop claim. He also continued in Santiago the efforts he had made in Buenos Aires to increase the mutual good-will of Argentina, Brazil, and Chile, of which there had been a plentiful lack. The President of the republic died on the day the American delegation arrived, and immediately afterward a convention of seven hundred members met in Santiago to nominate a successor. White greatly pleased the Chileans by his constant attendance at the convention; he went because it interested him, but the Chileans considered his presence a proof of American concern for their political welfare. "It is marvelous," wrote White to Secretary Knox, "how much a slight exhibition of personal interest and sympathy will accomplish with Latin-Americans."

Indeed, White made vigorous use of his letters and reports to impress on Knox the desirability of showing the Latin-Americans a good deal more tactful consideration. The Secretary of State had no such interest in the other nations of the Americas as his predecessor, Mr. Root, had shown. He had treated some of them with marked chilliness. When their ministers visited the State Department they were almost invariably received by subordinate officials. In repeated passages, some of them almost admonitory in tone, White urged Knox to take time to see the South American diplomatists,[4] to keep himself informed on Latin-American affairs, and to attend in person some of the meetings of the Pan-American Union, as it was decided in Buenos Aires to style the old International Bureau of the American Republics. He wished the Secretary to apply seriously his own statements that Pan-Americanism should "take first place" and be "by far the most active sphere in our diplomacy."[5]

In the fall of 1911 the walls of White's new house at 1624 Crescent Place had been erected, and one pleasant occupation of the

[4] White's report, *ut supra*. "May I add," he wrote, in speaking of the desire of the Latin-American Ministers to see Knox personally, "that I appreciate to a considerable extent their feelings, having always declined when *chargé* off and on for twenty years in London to transact business of importance with anyone but the Minister for Foreign Affairs himself?"

[5] White summed up the work of the Conference in a private letter: "A great deal of useful work has been done of a practical kind: a treaty for the settlement of pecuniary claims, another for the enforcement of sanitary regulations in different ports, and several agreements for rendering uniform consular documents, trademarks, and copyrights; and the question of improved steamship communication has been very seriously discussed."—White to Mrs. White, Buenos Aires, August 19, 1910.

winter and spring was supervising its completion—one of the most artistic mansions of Washington, commandingly placed in that northwestern part of the city whither many of the embassies and legations were now being transferred. Mrs. White had returned in improved health from Marienbad, where she had spent the summer, and was able to share cautiously with him in the social life of the capital. White's diary is full of brief jottings of his engagements—dinners with the Lodges, the Bryces, the Jusserands, with Charles Francis Adams, or with Henry Adams and his niece; a call to congratulate Alice Longworth on the fifth anniversary of her marriage; lunch with John Hays Hammond, and so on. He mentions a ball given by Mrs. Franklin Mac Veagh, where the lights suddenly went out. Mrs. John B. Henderson headed a bold marauding expedition which brought candles from the French Embassy and other places in the neighborhood. Frank Millet and others stuck them in bottles to give a faint illumination, and the guests joined President Taft and his partner, Miss Mabel Boardman, in dancing on as if nothing had happened.[6] Henry Adams pretended that Washington, always a wretched place, had become more hopeless than ever. He wrote to Mrs. White, in his characteristic vein of cynicism, that it had become a perfectly blind chaos, and he found nobody to guide him through it; that the Senators sputtered with fury and conservatism, understanding less than he did and becoming much angrier about it; that the army was in a muddle and the State Department no longer existed; and that mental paralysis had crept over society. But the Whites found both New York and Washington delightful.

Factional politics in the Republican party were beginning to become acrid, and the letters exchanged between Roosevelt and White throw light upon the bitter cleavage which was developing. At the request of Charles E. Hughes, then governor of New York, Roosevelt had plunged into the 1910 campaign in the state to elect Henry L. Stimson as Hughes's successor. Because of the rising discontent with the Taft Administration and Aldrich Tariff, he wrote to White in advance of the election that he feared a landslide against the Republicans. Lodge feared a similar landslide in Massachusetts. It came there, and in other states as well. Stimson was defeated, Demo-

[6] White to Mrs. White, Washington, February 11, 1911.

crats were chosen for governors of New York and Massachusetts, and the Republican majority in the Massachusetts legislature was cut so heavily that Lodge's reëlection was uncertain. He wrote that the margin was sufficient to reinstate him under ordinary conditions, but that the fight had been concentrated against him with "absolute ferocity," and his fate was dubious.[7] Roosevelt showed even greater chagrin. "The people this year," he wrote to White, "or at least a considerable section of them, have gotten into the frame of mind where they are against anyone who is of sufficient prominence, and about whom they have heard too often. They are against me, Cabot, Taft, all of us. I never saw a greater exhibition of folly, mixed with sordid baseness, than the exhibition made of themselves by the respectable classes, especially the leaders of the financial, social, and intellectual worlds, in New York city and the neighborhood." He added that the election had saved him from one uncomfortable predicament. "I can now see what I did not at the time see, *viz.*, that if we had carried New York, either there would have been a great movement to put Harry Stimson in as President, or else I should have been faced with the disagreeable question of saying whether or not I would take it myself. Now in all human probability no such question will arise. Whether we can elect Taft or not I do not know, but at present it looks as if it would either be Taft or a Democrat."[8]

This was one of the last letters in which his reference to Mr. Taft was tolerant. Eleven months later he thanked White for a sympathetic note on his fight for the "new nationalism," saying that it was hard work dealing with either the Progressives or Conservatives, and that if one associated with either exclusively he grew to long for the others! Soon after, on November 22, 1911, he acknowledged another sympathetic letter in which White had expressed approval of an article in the *Outlook*. "Poor Taft!" exclaimed Roosevelt. "When he was in my Cabinet four years ago he was heartily approving my utterances, which were then exactly what they are in this article; but he wabbles so, and so lacks the gift of leadership, that he has not been able to impress these views upon the public. I think it is delightfully comic that he should now

[7] Lodge to White, Hotel Belmont, New York, November 18, 1910.
[8] Roosevelt to White, New York, November 28, 1910.

endeavor to say that he was the man who really discovered the proposal." Thenceforward his comments upon the President were increasingly sharp. He discussed at some length with White the arbitration treaties which the Taft Administration drafted with Great
Britain and France in 1911, calling them "preposterous" and declaring that "the President handled the business poorly." He disapproved of much of the foreign policy of the Government.

At the beginning of 1912 Roosevelt was still uncertain of his
course. White wrote to him in January about the Jackson Day dinner, suggesting that the Democrats were likely to nominate Woodrow Wilson and John W. Kern. Roosevelt replied that he thought
Marshall a more likely nominee than Kern, but that the ticket
suggested was very likely because it would be very strong.[9] "Of
course," he continued, "I am being bedeviled on all sides either to
say I will run if nominated, or that I will not run if nominated. *At
present* my feeling is that it would be very foolish to say anything
publicly at all; but the situation changes so that I may *have* to
speak out. But, my dear fellow, do not make any mistake; I think
this is only a flurry, and that Taft will in all human probability be
nominated." Within a few weeks Roosevelt's determination became
fixed. On February 24th he tossed his hat into the ring. White wrote
to him at once pledging his affection and support, and the Colonel
replied confidentially on March 5th. He had not said anything
against Mr. Taft, he declared, and so far as he knew, the President
had always *spoken* favorably of him. For that he cared little.
"What I do care for is the fact that he has tried to reverse the
policies for which I stood and for which he stood while he was
my lieutenant. Moreover, ——, ——, and the other people responsible for his canvass have been consistently occupied with, and are
now engaged in, a perfectly dastardly campaign of slander and
mendacity against me—a campaign which the President, of course,
could have stopped at once. But he has never raised his finger to
stop it." [10]

White, having occasion at the same time to call upon Mr. Taft
regarding a dinner of the Pan-American Society, appealed to him to

[9] Roosevelt to White, New York, January 16, 1912.
[10] White to Roosevelt, Washington, March 3, 1912; Roosevelt to White,
New York, March 5.

keep wrangling and abuse out of the contest; and the President revealed feelings which did him credit. He remarked that nothing would induce him to say anything against Roosevelt personally; that he had never ceased to feel grateful for all that his predecessor had done for him; that Roosevelt had made him President, and he could never forget the old happy relations of intimacy. He was plainly moved. White replied that, since they were talking frankly, he could not help expressing his regret that the President had not made it clearer, just before and after his election, that he really regarded Roosevelt in this way, for certain of his acts at that time had been decidedly unfortunate. Without making any direct reply, Taft said that when all this political turmoil had passed he trusted that he and Theodore would come together and be as of old. White genuinely admired both men, but he was completely behind Roosevelt. The mass of the people, he believed, were convinced that they were not getting a square deal, as many were not, and were growing desperate; they trusted Roosevelt to attack the predatory interests and get it for them; "and you," he wrote to the Colonel, "are in a position, and have strength of character, to keep the progressive movement within bounds, and to guide it toward the attainment of its legitimate aspirations without going too far, and you have my best wishes for success in this great work."

In the campaign White, as a retired diplomatist, played no active part. Roosevelt wrote him but once after it began,[11] saying merely that he was in the fight to the end, for "The old parties mean absolutely nothing, and the Republican party is seething with corruption." White regarded Roosevelt's tremendous vote as a personal triumph for the Colonel, and wrote him to that effect, receiving in reply a letter that bespoke no crushed spirit. "It was a phenomenal thing," stated the Colonel, "to bring the new party into second place and to beat out the Republicans. The Democrats nominated their strongest man, and yet we reduced his vote to less than that of Bryan four years ago. My own view is that if Wilson behaves himself, the Democrats will continue in power for some time; but of course nobody can tell, and our business is to keep the Progressive Party in such shape that it will be ready to serve the nation in any way that the nation's needs demand."

[11] Roosevelt to White, July 1, 1912.

It was natural that in 1913-14, with White residing in Washington and Roosevelt in New York, the two should exchange ideas and information, particularly on diplomatic affairs. Since White saw all the foreign representatives frequently, he knew more of what was going on than Roosevelt, and the two could often collaborate to advantage. The most important example of their partnership was their effort to do something, in these two years, to ease the irritation of the Japanese over the treatment of their subjects in the United States. When Roosevelt was writing the chapter in his autobiography which dealt with the Russo-Japanese War and the Treaty of Portsmouth he asked White to read a copy of it to Baron Chinda, the Japanese ambassador, allowing the latter to make notes but not to keep the chapter. Two days later he fired a new note at White, saying he had just learned that some of the Japanese were alleging they had a grievance, in that by bringing about the Peace of Portsmouth on his own initiative, Roosevelt had deprived them of the chance of getting an indemnity from Russia. He asked that Baron Chinda be warned that if this sort of talk went on, he would publish in full the note of the Japanese Government requesting him to bring about the conference, for he would not submit to Japanese complaints when he had only done as the Japanese themselves had suggested. Naturally Chinda was somewhat hurt; but White felt, when he had straightened out the misunderstanding, that he was in a position to bring the two men together on more important subjects.

The little storm which blew up in the spring of 1913 over the new California land bill, prohibiting the holding or leasing of farm land by Japanese, was for a time a cause of marked anxiety to the Wilson Administration. Baron Chinda called the attention of the State Department to the pending bill on April 4th, President Wilson telegraphed a protest to Governor Hiram Johnson on April 22nd, and Secretary Bryan immediately hurried to Sacramento. White thought it a great pity that the Californians should act so unfairly, and at the beginning of April, after a long talk with Chinda, appealed to Roosevelt to use his influence in restraining California. Roosevelt did indeed act in the crisis. He telegraphed to Hiram Johnson on April 20th and again on April 28th, setting forth his views at length. Pointing out in the first telegram that any State legislation which has an international character necessarily raises questions with which it is the right and duty of the national government to deal, he continued: "All the States have the right to pass land laws which do not discriminate between foreign nations or take any other position inconsistent with our treaty obligations, but if there is a question as to whether the proposed laws do violate a treaty, surely the proper course to follow is to have the California Senators and Congressmen bring the matter promptly before the Administration and insist on whatever measure of relief the needs of California's people demand. This was the course I successfully urged on California six years ago, and I then as President kept friendly relations with Japan and yet secured the exclusion of the Japanese laborers as the people of California requested and met completely the then needs of California." He sent a copy of this telegram to White, to be shown "discreetly around among one or two of your friends"—which probably included Baron Chinda.

With it he sent a copy of a crisp telegram to Baron Kaneko in Japan: "Am doing all I can but Japanese war threat for such inadequate reasons embarrasses Japan's best friends. Theodore Roosevelt." In his second telegram to Governor Johnson, sent on the very day that Bryan arrived in Sacramento, Roosevelt criticized the Wilson Administration for trying to restrain California without itself providing any adequate remedy. The Federal Administration, he declared, had the power and duty "to secure what California needs while behaving to Japan with entire and reciprocal justice, consideration, and courtesy, and surely it will take this attitude on California's request and will not by its inaction or refusal to exercise its powers and perform its duties oblige California itself to act." This criticism was underlined by a letter which he wrote to White from the office of the *Outlook*:

ROOSEVELT TO WHITE, MAY 2, 1913

I enclose you copies of my two last telegrams to Johnson. I shall not publish any of them, for this reason: the attitude of President Wilson and Mr. Bryan has been hopelessly weak, so as to render it quite impossible to stand up for them. Wilson's duty, according to my view, was perfectly clear. He should in the first place have asserted the power of the Federal Government to act as regards all treaties, and in the next place acknowledged its duty to safeguard California's interests. The Californian position is fundamentally right. The Japanese must not, as a class, own agricultural land. Moreover, they ought not to be here in any numbers, either as small clerks and tradesmen or as agricultural and industrial laborers. This was clearly understood under my agreement with them five years ago. With their usual fatuity, Taft and Knox surrendered the proper position by the treaty two and a half years ago. Their act in making this treaty was unpardonable, for they abandoned our right to keep out Japanese laborers. They excused themselves on the ground that they retained the right to abrogate the treaty. I need not point out to you that it is an infinitely more serious thing to abrogate a treaty in order to do what that treaty forbids than it is to exercise a right reserved under a treaty. One carries out a treaty; the other breaks it in order to do what the treaty forbids. Yet not only Taft and Knox, but the Californians themselves, paid no heed to this matter. I wrote to Taft about it, and to the Californians about it, and in the *Outlook* we had an editorial taking the proper view of the situation. But as usual with our people there was no protest against making the treaty, the people interested apparently thinking it sufficient to retain the right not to carry it out! Wilson's position was rendered a little more difficult by this treaty of Taft's, but it was fundamentally the same as mine was, and his action should have been fundamentally like mine instead of the reverse. I told California that it was for the nation and not the State to act, but that I would adequately safeguard California's rights, and I did. That is, I asserted the national right, and I offered an adequate remedy. Wilson has told California that it was all right, but tried to coax it not to exercise its rights, and offered no adequate remedy. Under the circumstances all that Johnson could do was what he did, that is, pass the law demanded by the situation and try to see that it did not violate the treaty. Of course my view is that it is for the nation and the State to see that the treaty is not violated. . . . Well! grape juice diplomacy under Wilson does not bid fair to be much better than dollar diplomacy under Taft. And apparently he is about to take the same preposterous view of arbitrating the canal question.

While recognizing the logic of all this, White was not fully satisfied with Roosevelt's position. Roosevelt had said in another letter to White that any mass-settlement by either Japanese or Americans in the country of the other was highly undesirable, and that he would not for a moment admit that any foreigner had the right to say what immigrants should be received in the United States, or on what terms. This was correct, but White would have liked him to take a sterner attitude toward California, which in May passed a modified but still objectionable land bill. However, some of the seed which White had sown bore fruit later. In the fall of 1914 the Californians again seemed on the point of passing objectionable legislation, and Chinda again protested to White as the friend of Roosevelt. On taking the matter up with the Colonel, White found that he had written to Governor Johnson three weeks earlier, urging him to prevent the passage of the bill which was worrying Chinda. Johnson shortly replied, saying that he expected no more trouble with the anti-Japanese agitators—and there was none.[12]

In the letter in which he described his protest to Johnson, Roosevelt loosed a few more wrathful thunderbolts at the Wilson Administration. It was hard to deal with, he wrote:[13] "I don't think we have ever had a President, a Secretary of State, and a Secretary of the Navy so unfit from every standpoint to deal with international affairs. It is a veritable calamity. The trouble is they never think of international affairs in any proper sense of the word at all. Here is this matter about which you write me, I had already acted over two weeks before the Japanese Ambassador came to you with the request that you communicate with me. This was because my training has been such that I look out for these things; and in similar ways I would have looked out in advance as to what was to be done in Belgium."

White had a more tolerant estimate of the diplomacy of the new Administration, and so, as we shall see, did Lord Bryce. In one of its diplomatic problems he intervened more directly. This was the question of the Panama tolls, where he could speak with expert knowledge in support of President Wilson's appeal for repeal of the law exempting our coastwise shipping from the canal charges. White wrote to Senator McCumber that he had initiated the negotiations for the Hay-Pauncefote treaty, and believed that he knew what was in the minds of the British and American leaders when it was signed. He was certain that American exemption from the

[12] Roosevelt to White, New York, December 8, 1914.
[13] Roosevelt to White, New York, November 30, 1914.

tolls for coastal shipping had never been suggested, and that any such idea was in flat conflict with the wording of the treaty as to "equal terms" in the use of the canal. He also wrote to President Wilson that Lord Salisbury had been emphatic that the one British condition for abrogating the Clayton-Bulwer Treaty was that the canal should be opened to the vessels of all nations on an absolutely equal footing; and that when he came to the United States to win leading Americans over to the Hay-Pauncefote agreement, this had been everywhere assumed. White's declaration was used with effect by Senators Lodge and McCumber in the Panama tolls debate.

Henry James was in America in 1910 and 1911, having brought his brother William back from Bad Nauheim the summer of the former year to die at his home in Chocorua, New Hampshire. From that town he wrote in lonely and sorrowful accents to the Whites. It had been an *année terrible* for him, he said, for there was first an interminable and distressing illness of his own, and as he emerged from that his brother fell a prey to an old and long dormant malady of heart disease. "His extinction is for me an unutterable loss; he was not only my dearest brother, but my best and most distinguished and most supremely interesting of friends. It makes me feel old and ended and utterly stricken. But I shall struggle against this. I shall stay in America to be near my sister-in-law and his children—to whom I cling and who cling to me and are delightful and interesting in a remarkable degree. Stay this winter, I mean, and then return to England, not again, I hope, to revisit these shores." He spoke of the charm of Chocorua. "My brother made this intensely rural or woodland refuge, and liked it for quiet summers, and his shade abides much for me here."

James did plan to visit them in Washington in the spring of 1911, bringing his model English servant—"so diminutive that he takes up little room, but also so athletic that he yearns to make himself generally useful; in short, an intensely modest pearl." [14] But circumstances prevented his trip. A niece fell ill of appendicitis; he feared also the heat of the subtropic zone, as he called Washington. "I have a constitutional terror of hot weather—and the nature of the American summer had much to do with my flight from these shores long years ago. I shouldn't be a graceful guest or a crisp and finely

[14] Henry James to White, Cambridge, May 1, 1911.

starched ornament to your circle at all." The Whites, for their part, were about to pay a flying visit to New York, and to go on north to Ottawa, to visit Lord Grey, the Governor-General of Canada; on May 9th they attended the state ball at Government House in Ottawa. They therefore missed Henry James entirely. To Mrs. White came a characteristically affectionate letter from him, written at Salisbury, Connecticut:

All thanks for your gentle letter—letting me down so easily from my pusillanimous failure to brave the fiery furnace for your gracious and generous sake. I feel this now though the subsequent days only confirmed and consecrated my poor prudence. I motored over here (eighty wondrous miles) from Farmington three days ago, after suffering at the latter place such an experience of sweltering heat, during the previous week, as made me ask myself what your latitude would then be treating you to. What an ungracious pity, that our national capital and the pleasantest city should be in the torrid zone. But we have truly an unspeakable and incalculable country—a land and clime of such violence and yet in some ways of such harmony. All this Connecticut beauty is harmonious even to the romantic degree in its profusion and grace, and the motor helping (it is really the consolation of my declining years), I am enjoying the large free Arcadian side of it without limit. I am staying here most agreeably with my cousin and her mother. . . . But after August 12th I shall be in England and anxiously watching, yearning, for your advent. I wish indeed I might have seen the Washington creation.
I am still your faithfully fond old
HENRY JAMES.[15]

A special word should be said of the friendship which sprang up between White and James Bryce in the years 1909-1913, when they were thrown much together in Washington, and which was continued afterward by correspondence. Though White's tastes were less intellectual and scholarly than Bryce's, their cosmopolitan experience and similarity of outlook, with their deep interest in Anglo-American friendship, made them highly congenial souls. Bryce was often at 1624 Crescent Place, and White was often at the British Embassy. When in 1912 Bryce decided to leave the United States he wrote White that he regretted nothing more than

[15] A later letter by Henry James to White, too long for inclusion here (February 23, 1913), describes his Cheyne Walk home, or "Thames-side perch," and a serious illness. See Appendix IV.

parting from him and Mrs. White, "who are among the five or six oldest and best friends we have in the United States"; he departed only because he wished to complete two big books begun many years before, and to drop the responsibilities of office before he grew old and feeble.

Bryce wrote frequently to White from the House of Lords or from his home "Hindleap" at Forest Row in Sussex. He longed for news of the family, he said in the fall of 1913, for it was sad to be cut off from friends to whom they had been attached by an.intimacy growing ever closer. He wished also for some confidential information regarding American politics—whether President Wilson's success with the Underwood tariff would give him a hold on the Senate sufficient "to guide it back into the path of unemotional righteousness whence it strayed under the feeble management of the last Administration"—whether he would be able to get it to renew the Colombian treaty and deal justly with the Panama tolls question. "It is a pity," he added, "that Bryan has given so much occasion for Europe to ridicule the State Department. He has, after all, attended to business more in the intervals of his lecturing and golf than Knox did in the intervals of his touring and golf; and I have a certain weakness for Bryan personally which makes me repel these criticisms." He had lately been in Russia, where he reported reaction to be in the ascendency, and in Berlin, where he rejoiced to find that Anglo-German relations were really better.

Later in 1913, and again in 1914, Bryce wrote White letters which were full of anxiety upon the situation in Ireland, and upon nothing else. It was painful in London, he said, to see what a sharpness had crept into the social air, how *acharnés* the partisans had become, and how much the sense of duty to law and order had been weakened. It was almost impossible to believe oneself in the old England when the leading statesmen talked lightly about civil war in Ireland, and suffragists continued to burn down houses with impunity. Fortunately, he wrote later, "Asquith's speeches have been admirable, and his hold on the party equal to that which the G. O. M. used to exercise. *O si sic omnes!*" White had paid his daughter in Germany a visit in the summer of 1911. He and Mrs. White went back to visit her family at their estate in Upper Silesia in the summer of 1914, but they did not see the Bryces on their way. They were at the Rosnochau estate during the fateful July of the Sarajevo assassinations.

It was upon this life of travel, friendships, and minor political or diplomatic preoccupations that the storm of August, 1914, suddenly burst. The suddenness with which it descended was as startling in that part of Germany as everywhere else. On Thursday, August 1st, White had left Rosnochau and gone to Breslau, about a hundred kilometers distant, to cash some drafts; there was not the slightest symptom of apprehension or of unusual troop movements. A number of German officers were expected that night at the castle on their way to manœuvres in the neighborhood. During the day telegrams arrived saying that the manœuvres had been postponed and the officers would not arrive—the first notice that trouble was imminent. So sudden was the postponement that the orderlies who always preceded their officers had actually arrived at the castle. The next day was one of excitement. On Saturday, the 3rd, the authorities of Silesia issued a proclamation that war had been declared and requested all foreigners to proceed as rapidly as possible to Berlin; and White, Mrs. White, and their daughter with her two children departed for the capital the following day. For more than two weeks they were kept in Berlin, till the American Embassy arranged for special trains to Holland. Meanwhile, White's son-in-law, Count Seherr-Thoss, was compelled to return from the Russian front to undergo a severe operation, and when White and Mrs. White left for The Hague and home, they took— at the parents' wish—the two children.

This fortnight in Berlin was one of considerable anxiety but also of intense interest. The hotel where the Whites stayed, the Adlon, was jammed with distressed Americans and Britons; the American Embassy day after day was besieged by crowds who filled the courtyard and main floor, clamoring for protection, passports, or money. At midnight on August 4th, after German troops had entered Belgium, Great Britain declared war. White never forgot the effect of the news of this British step upon the enormous crowd which had collected in the Pariser Platz and Unter den Linden in front of the Hotel Adlon. "It was as though a thunderclap had fallen upon them," he later wrote. "First of all almost silence, as though the crowd were stunned; then murmurs, followed by something resembling a deep growl; and eventually shouts of indignation and the swaying of the crowd, with demonstrations more or less hostile, toward the hotel, in which British newspaper correspondents and others of that nationality, as well as certain diplomatists belonging to the Allied countries, were supposed to be staying."

During the fortnight he was invited by General von Falkenhayn, who within two months was destined to succeed General von Moltke as chief of the General Staff, to a dinner at the War Office.[16] He had not known Falkenhayn, but the German Government was anxious to enlist the sympathies of prominent Americans. There were about a dozen guests, the conversation was general and non-political, and no one at the table would have imagined that a great war was under way. After dinner Falkenhayn led White into a quiet corner of the garden for a talk. White remarked on the fact that for two hours the general, who was responsible for the movement of such vast numbers of troops to both the eastern and western frontiers, had received no telegram or other message. To this Falkenhayn replied that he and the former heads of the War Office had for years been laboring to make the military machine as nearly perfect as possible; though the troop trains were allowed a margin of four hours to reach their destinations, he was to be notified when any happened to be over ten minutes late—and as yet he had received no such notification.[17]

The general then remarked that the war was "a very serious

[16] White's experiences in Berlin and interview with Falkenhayn are described in a memorandum of nine typed pages, undated, deposited with the White papers in the Library of Congress. Admiral Mark Kerr in his book, *Land, Sea, and Air*, gives a garbled report of White's experiences. An excerpt from the memorandum is printed as Appendix II of this volume.

[17] It may be noted here, as bearing on the question of war preparations, that in August, 1912, White and his wife were staying with their daughter at Rosnochau for the army manœuvres held that year in Upper Silesia. A number of generals came to stay at the countess's house, among them General von Pritzewitz. He made a remark which White thought decidedly sinister. "Our Emperor," he said, "has made us twice ridiculous in the eyes of Europe by giving way at Algeciras and Agadir. The next time we generals shall not permit him to give way and he will have to fight whether he likes it or not."—Diary of Countess Seherr-Thoss, Rosnochau, August 11, 1912.

business." He went on to say that they had not for a moment expected Great Britain to enter the conflict, both in view of the threat of civil dissension in Ireland and because the German intelligence department had told them that certain members of the Cabinet and the great majority of the British people were opposed to joining in any war, and that the coming in of England had made all the difference in the world, both as to the duration of the war and the certainty of its outcome. "Not," he said, "that the British army is large, or likely to weigh very heavily in the balance, but what there is of it is composed of extraordinarily good material. What is of far greater importance, however, in connection with England, is, from our point of view, the bulldog tenacity of that nation, which will make them hold on to the bitter end in spite of obstacles which would be insurmountable to any other army." Somewhat taken aback, White asked if Falkenhayn felt any real doubt as to the eventual German victory. He replied that he would not like to confess any positive doubt, but he was certain of one fact —that it was nonsense to talk of the war's being over in two or three months, as most people in Germany were saying at the time, and that he thought it was likely to last three or four years. He also said that "those peace people at the palace" (meaning the Emperor and the men about him) had held back the mobilization of the German army for nearly forty-eight hours after he himself had thought it necessary, because of the Russian mobilization, of which he was aware several days before it was generally known. The general was in a frank mood about the government. He remarked that it had always been Bismarck's policy to divide the Powers of Europe and have some of them on Germany's side when any great international question threatened a war; but in this instance they had succeeded, as he put it, "in getting the whole world united against Germany," and it remained to be seen whether she could hold her own, in the long run, against so fearful a combination. And he added again that the entrance of Great Britain had completely upset Germany's calculations and might make the whole difference in the result of the war.

In later years, White often thought over that quiet evening in the attractive garden of the War Office in Berlin, he and his companion strolling through the summer night while hundreds of thousands of men were being borne in troop trains to their death and all Europe was being turned into an armed camp. His conversation with the frank general, who spoke in fluent English, left several impressions firmly fixed in his mind. One was that it had been fear of Russia, as to the strength and condition of which the German General Staff was badly informed, which was the immediate cause of Germany's entrance upon war—not a desire to crush France. Falkenhayn's remark as to the "peace people at the palace" again confirmed his impression that the Kaiser was very loath to declare war, and had probably done so under extreme pressure from Moltke, Tirpitz, and others. Finally, he was struck by the evident foreboding of final defeat which came over the head of the German War Office as he reflected upon the strength of the British Empire and the tenacity of British purpose. "When they begin," Falkenhayn said, reflectively—"when they begin, by God! they never quit."

As quickly as possible, White, his wife, and his little grandchildren, Hans Christoph and Margaret, returned to the United States. Various of his friends had been abroad that summer. One was Senator Lodge, who was in England. One was Cecil Spring-Rice, who wrote on July 29th—of all days—to White describing his peaceful vacation on the English coast and rejoicing that his leave might be extended for another month, for all was quiet! Another was Roosevelt, who had been traveling about Europe seeking to regain the strength lost in his Amazonian explorations. Bryce wrote that he had had some long conversations with him and found him full of vivacity and mentally fit, though looking unwell; Spring-Rice thought that he grew tired easily. Still others scurried home as the hurricane broke. From his old friends in England—from St. John Brodrick, Curzon, Bryce, and others—a series of letters came to White in all possible tones, Brodrick stoical, Curzon resentful, Bryce philosophic. Curzon indulged in a dignified but bitter arraignment of Germany. Bryce, in comparison, brought to the questions of the war a singularly unprejudiced mind. Most Englishmen, he wrote on August 12th, assumed that Germany had planned the whole war, and incited Austria to bully little Serbia. Personally he doubted this, or rather held that both Germany and Austria had thought Russia would not fight and presumed too far on their own strength. He blamed the guilty folly of Austria and the criminal conduct of Russia, but he reserved judgment as to Germany.

Naturally the war was a source of great anguish to White. He had some close friends in France and many in England, while he loved the people of both countries; and on the other side of the Rhine was his daughter, intensely loyal to her adopted country. The winter of 1914-15 he and Mrs. White spent at Crescent Place, her health now being increasingly bad and at times almost alarming. His letters give an attractive picture of their life there: their joy in the grandchildren, their contacts with old friends, his interested scrutiny of world affairs. But he was often anxious about his wife and always sorrowful about Europe. Frequently he met the ambassadors of the three principal warring powers, Spring-Rice, Bernstorff, and Jusserand. They did not confide in him, and since he had such close connections on both sides, and was constantly writing to England and to Germany, he did not ask or invite any confidences. He tried to be neutral in thought and feeling, as President Wilson urged all Americans to be. But this did not preclude his forming decided opinions on events of the war. He thoroughly condemned the German invasion of Belgium. When Nurse Edith Cavell was shot, he wrote indignantly of the deed as atrocious not merely in itself but even more in its circumstances— done so hastily, at dead of night, by officers who acted as if they feared a little delay would result in a reprieve. He was horrified by the sinking of the *Lusitania*, and he approved entirely of the vigorous but pacific way in which President Wilson handled the resulting situation.

In this effort to be neutral he moved more and more toward alignment with the foreign policy of the Administration, and diverged more and more from the position of Roosevelt, who would have intervened sternly against Germany in Belgium and wished threatening measures taken after the *Lusitania* incident. Several times he talked the situation over with Roosevelt, and once, visiting at Oyster Bay, showed the Colonel a letter from his daughter in which she stated the German point of view upon diverse aspects of the war; he was more patient and tolerant than Roosevelt. In this he was supported by Bryce, who was also tolerant and who understood America's neutrality, and by the expert and liberal counsel of his half-brother, William Buckler, who from December, 1914, to December, 1918, was attached to the American embassy in London. From Mr. Buckler he received constant letters reflecting the sanest British opinion, and containing much first-hand information from contacts with British political leaders. Like Buckler, White longed ardently for a peace by negotiation; it seemed to him impossible for the Allies to crush Germany, or Germany the Allies, and he deemed it horrible for two great military machines to go on destroying hundreds of thousands of young men without result.

Bryce, as we have said, bore him out in his general attitude. "There is unfortunately," he wrote on Christmas Eve of 1914, "a good deal of feeling against the German nation as a whole, and tuned up by part of our press, but no such personal hatred as seems to be felt and preached in Germany against England. Acts of humanity or chivalry by German soldiers are published in the newspapers and gladly welcomed. Recruiting goes on fast enough; *i.e.*, as fast as preparations can be made to receive the recruits." Six months later, in July of 1915, he was still moderate in his expressions about the Germans, still sure that the time for mediation had not yet come, and still preoccupied with the idea of peace. He spoke of the sinking of the *Lusitania*, but without passion. The Germans had gone too far and would probably draw back, he believed. Their view of the war was fundamentally different from the British view, for with them state interest justified everything— that was all. He agreed with White's opinion that Bryan united high but vague intentions with a mediocre intellect. "Although, of course, vanity plays some part in his action, I think he is quite sincere and probably conscientious in his feeling that he must take no part in any action which might lead to war; but is this feeling shared by any large part of your population? It does not look to me as if pacificism and the doctrines of Tolstoy, of which Bryan is a follower, have any hold upon the mind of the people who have hitherto supported Bryan in the Middle West, and I fear that his simplicity or vanity, or both, may lead him to welcome from those who are really German sympathizers that support which they give for their own ends. He struck me, when I had dealings with him, as almost unable to *think* in the sense in which you and I would use that word. Vague ideas floated through his mind but did not unite to form any system or crystallize into a definite practical proposition. He is, however, a clever politician, and even a skillful tactician, as his action in the Baltimore Convention showed. His wife has much more practical sense and capacity for understanding an argument than he has, and I sometimes wished that she had been Secretary of State."

White's daughter described the anxiety, the privations, and the sorrow which pervaded Germany, while more than one person wrote to him of the same facts in England. Perhaps the most touching letter was one from Henry James in the early weeks of the war (October 26, 1914), in which the anguished novelist poured out his feelings to "Dearest, dearest Harry and Daisy," through four typewritten sheets. The war had nearly overwhelmed him, he wrote, and he had received their letter with joy and gratitude; he deeply appreciated the sweetness of old fidelities and loyalties, pushing through "the dark thick envelope" of anxieties and oppressions, of lacerations and bereavements and mournings. He felt alone in the world, though "dear old Henry Adams and his somewhat austere seraglio I communed with a few days since." It had soothed him that summer to think of his old friends in their umbrageous harbor of security at Stockbridge. He wished he might sit for an hour with them in Washington, under the Sargent portrait, and not too far from "the incomparable original." But England was filled with distresses:

We live mainly in the one sort here—that is, so far as the intimately personal sort is concerned; I mean the constant shock of all the bereavements and losses suffered around us, or the more and more quickened apprehension of the same—everyone one knows with any family belongings at all having husbands, sons and brothers deeply engaged, these latter often to a great multiplicity. A friend has just told me of a near country neighbor of his, a wonderful gallant widowed lady, who has six sons and every one of them at the front. It's a different enough world, you see, from the old utterly golden one (in comparison) which your charming allusion to the far-away Ramslade days brings to me in a way that makes the whole stretch of the past, of *all* the past, as I knew it but three months ago, seem a dim antediluvian thing, prehistoric, fabulous, incredible for felicity by the mere fact of *not* having had in it such things, for instance, as the huge Belgian horror, brought home to us by the way that England is really taking almost a whole nation to her so-far-as-possible consoling breast. There is scarce a village here that isn't peopled with the ruined refugees or transported wounded of all that infamy—of which the history will come forth into the glare of day at the due settling time. It's the element in one's whole consciousness that haunts, and from the first has haunted, me most—but when I talk of it at all I can talk of nothing else; and that's not what I want to do with you. I do remember the sweet old episode of my dreadful delinquency over the Ramslade pup, which you draw forth so tenderly from the night of time, every pang of guilt in my having been so false to my charge reviving for me as I brood over it.

During the summer of 1915 the Whites were at Dublin, New Hampshire, with the grandchildren and "little society save old Henry Adams," as White put it. As the next summer opened Mrs. White was worse.[18] They took up their residence at Lenox; their

[18] White's anxiety for his wife kept him out of public life. In the summer of 1914 Bryan wished to appoint him a delegate to the Pan-American Conference planned for that autumn (and later postponed), but White refused. In the following spring he again declined an invitation from Bryan to serve on the permanent commission appointed under the new "cooling-off" treaty between England and the United States—these treaties being the pride of Bryan's heart, and having White's warm approval. White saw a good deal of the State Department under Bryan, and has left us his impressions of it. "Bryan was the same kindly, good-natured man; highly appreciative of the position to which he had been appointed, but absolutely ignorant of the duties and responsibilities thereof, or even of the line of conduct necessary to maintain the dignity of that high office in the eyes of our fellow countrymen. He was the despair of the foreign ambassadors and ministers, who had great difficulty in securing his attention for the discussion of the questions which they brought before him, although they always found him exceedingly friendly. Moreover, Mr. Bryan had a theory that he should be easily reached by anyone who wanted to see him, and with that in view, kept the door of his room in the Department of State open; the result being that it was always crowded with people. . . . As far as I can remember, the floor of the Department on which Mr. Bryan's room was situated was a sort of pandemonium through which one had to push one's way." Bryan also, amid circumstances of considerable secrecy, offered White the position of minister to Haiti, believing that with his experience and knowledge of French he could do much to restore order there, but White

daughter was hastily called home from Germany; and after great suffering, on Saturday, September 2, 1916, she died. White, sorely stricken, wrote a few days afterward to his half-brother in terms of characteristic dignity. *"Elle avait une rare nature, grande et sans petitesses quelconques, surtout sans sentiments de jalousie, et un très-grand cœur. Pendant les trente-six années de notre vie ensemble nous n'avons point eu de querelle—quelque petite que ce fût—ni même de malentendu—jamais rien à 'expliquer'; car nous nous sommes parfaitement entendus depuis le commencement."* His daughter stayed to console him until October 12th, when she returned to her husband and baby in Germany, taking the two older children with her; and White was left more alone and lonely than ever before in his life. There was nothing to do but to return to Washington, and lose himself so far as he could in public affairs—affairs that were now fast carrying the United States toward war with Germany.

When we say that White made an earnest effort to be neutral in thought and feeling, we do not imply that he succeeded. His sympathies, like those of nearly every one about him, inclined toward the side of the Allies, or at least the great democracies of Britain and France. He never thought it in good taste, as he wrote Mr. Buckler, to express himself with vigor against a country of which his daughter and grandchildren were subjects, nor good Americanism to take sides intemperately in any foreign war. But nobody detested more than he all that was signified by the phrase "German militarism," or wished more earnestly to see it extirpated before his grandchildren grew up. After the sinking of the *Lusitania*, moreover, he was constantly fearful that a combination of German arrogance and blundering might force the United States into the war. Repeatedly he wrote in a warning tone to his daughter, who was in a position to bring ideas and information before even the highest German authority. Berlin must never think, he said, that the German-Americans would fail the republic of their adoption; if war came, with few exceptions they would stand by the United States. It was unfortunate, he added, that Germany did not realize how defective was her diplomacy, the weakest spot in her armor.

declined. See letters of Bryan to White, Washington, May 5, August 3, 1914; White's memorandum on Bryan.

The qualities required for successful diplomatic work he described as innate, and dependent on personality, sympathy, and ability to understand the point of view of others. These qualities the Germans lacked, and no amount of mere drill could take their place. He could name only two or three good German diplomatists, his old Paris colleague Prince Radolin being one of the best—perhaps because he was a Pole.

In one letter written after the sinking of the *Sussex*, White warned his daughter that if Germany continued destroying American ships and breaking her promises, the United States would inevitably be forced into the war and would make a German defeat certain. This letter Count Seherr-Thoss at once translated and sent in the form of a report to General Ludendorff, who returned it with some rudely skeptical remarks in the margin. The count then took it to headquarters to show it to the Emperor, but was refused an audience by the Kaiser's aide-de-camp, on the ground that "We know the kind of reports you send to General Ludendorff about America. We don't wish the Emperor to hear them." After dinner at headquarters that night the count approached the Kaiser, saying that he had a very interesting and important letter from his father-in-law in Washington; but the Emperor, visibly embarrassed by the presence of his *entourage*, replied coldly: "I would rather you told me about your father's pheasant-shooting in Silesia." [19]

White's daughter wrote that in the opinion of most Germans, the American Government was Anglophile. There was no ground for that view, White replied. When in the fall of 1915 he mentioned to Henry Adams her report that the State Department was believed to be under the sway of Sir Cecil Spring-Rice, Adams humorously replied: "I wish you would tell Spring-Rice that the Germans think so, for he has just been complaining to me that he has no influence whatever with the Wilson Administration." The real reason why Germany came off second best, White wrote, was that the British knew so much better how to handle American opinion. He was particularly struck by the weakness of Bernstorff's note of April, 1915, protesting against American arms shipments, for he recalled how Germany had exported arms to Mexico after

[19] Memorandum for the author by the Countess Seherr-Thoss.

President Wilson had laid an embargo on American shipments. Apart from the fact that our dispute with Germany involved life while that in England involved property alone, England was much more tactful. Every time a note was nearly ready to be sent to England, the British Government made some important concessions which necessitated redrafting it—this had happened four times within a few months—while it was only after the sinking of the *Arabic* that Germany showed any real disposition to meet the demands made by the United States in its *Lusitania* notes.

Feeling that war might come, White believed in getting ready for it. Twice during 1915 he made speeches in favor of "preparedness," advocating compulsory military training not because he strongly believed in it, but because he thought that pressure for such an extreme demand might force Congress to take at least partial measures. He had occasional meetings not only with Roosevelt, but also with General Leonard Wood, and was influenced by his views. As yet he was not sympathetic to the most advanced proposals for another form of "preparedness"—preparedness by international organization to avert or stop future wars. When he was invited in the fall of 1915 to join the League to Enforce Peace, of which ex-President Taft, Alton B. Parker, Herbert S. Houston, and A. Lawrence Lowell were the active heads, he refused, saying that he was "utterly opposed to this country's entering into alliances with others for any purpose whatever, particularly for that of going to war or having war made upon itself in the event of its being considered by other Powers to have violated the rules of the League." He did not believe that the original proposals of the League to Enforce Peace would attain the desired end; and Joseph H. Choate, whom he consulted on the matter, agreed with him, writing that he considered the League to be "only another term for a league to make war." It is evident that White in 1916 took no such extreme stand in hostility to most schemes of international organization, and showed no such exaggerated nationalism, as did his friend Roosevelt. But it is also evident that he thought there was something fundamentally wrong with a league for peace which committed itself at the outset to a program of possible war. Choate wrote to him that he felt more belief in the National Security League—toward which White's own attitude was decidedly distrustful. In the campaign of 1916 White could play no active part, but he gave Hughes what support he could, chiefly because of party loyalty, but partly because he thought Republican leadership would be safer amid the stormy international events of the future.

The war came closer and closer to America. White hoped to the last that some means might be found to draw the two sides to peace before the United States plunged in, and he gave the heartiest approval to President Wilson's efforts to induce the combatants to define their aims. Through Mr. Buckler's letters he gained some knowledge of what Colonel House was attempting to do in Europe, and like Buckler, he hoped for the success of these efforts. Bryce wrote to him that he would like to see a peaceable adjustment, but a letter from Curzon in the summer of 1916 contained a sharp condemnation of Wilson's moves. The attitude of America generally has been a great disappointment to us, Curzon stated. Most Britons, he went on, looked with great contempt upon Wilson, and had not the least intention of letting him come in as a glorious peacemaker to facilitate his election. It became evident that the war would go on, that it was assuming a more desperate character, and that the moment was at hand when America would be forced to fight. When in the first days of 1917 the German Government proclaimed its intention of waging unrestricted submarine warfare, White knew instantly that this meant war. His feeling on the subject of American rights at sea was as stern as Roosevelt's. His one thought, as the United States prepared to enter the conflict, was of making himself useful to the country.

CHAPTER NINETEEN

America at War: The Foundations of Peace

ON DECEMBER 4, 1918, the *George Washington* passed majestically out of New York bay with the battleship *Pennsylvania* just ahead and destroyers on each side, carrying President Wilson to the war-torn continent where every nation, victor and vanquished, awaited him as the bearer of peace. With him went two of the four peace commissioners whom he had chosen to assist him, Secretary Lansing and Henry White. The other two, Colonel House and General Bliss, were already in Europe. Facing the culminating responsibility of his career, White accompanied the President as the one Republican and the one experienced diplomatist in the group. More than once later, both publicly and in private letters, he frankly confessed that nothing in his long life had surprised him so much as his appointment to the Peace Commission. He had not sought the post, and he understood what labors, difficulties, and attacks it might entail; but he took it gladly. When the *George Washington* was met by the American squadron off Brest and entered the roadstead between lines of American battleships, a sense of wonderment still clung to him. But he had certain definite ideas as to his duty to both his party and country, and he welcomed the opportunity to apply them.

The reasons for his selection by the President, a selection which surprised the country no less than himself, are by no means difficult to explain, though at the time they were guessed by few. The public had expected that a more prominent Republican and more pronounced party-man, such as Mr. Root or Mr. Taft, would be chosen. Colonel House then and later believed that Wilson should have named a man of greater eminence and activity in Republican councils. So did Secretary Houston, who feared that Mr. White would not satisfy the regular Republicans in the Senate or elsewhere. As a matter of fact, the choice pleased Senator Lodge and more than pleased Roosevelt. "I am simply overjoyed that Harry

White is to be on the Peace Commission," Roosevelt wrote Lodge.
"If —— had been appointed, I would have felt that we had reached
a lower point of infamy than has yet been attained."[1] It was understood in Washington that Secretary Lansing was chiefly responsible for White's nomination.[2] But if we review some of White's
activities during the year and a half of America's participation in
the war, we shall see that he was commended to the President
not only by his training and experience, but by his ideas and
opinions on the subject of peace.

It may indeed be said that the popular view of the time, that
White was a neutral Republican, almost devoid of party attachment,
and that he represented the conservative old-school diplomacy,
was upon both heads totally in error. He went to Paris as a loyal
Republican, whose allegiance to his party had never wavered, who
since 1896 had been in touch with its principal leaders, and who
was now in very close relations with its most redoubtable
chieftains—relations which, as we shall see, he maintained by a constant and detailed correspondence, throughout the Peace Conference, with Senator Lodge, ex-Secretary Root, and others. As for
his opinions upon international affairs, they were distinctly progressive and liberal, the very antithesis of those held by the old-
school diplomatists of the day. His Republicanism was always
stanch. His liberalism had grown with every month of the war.
Torn between his affection for England and France, and his regard for the Germany of his daughter and grandchildren, he had
come to see plainly the desirability of an early and just peace,
the folly of revenge, and the urgent necessity for a new world
order to prevent such hideous conflicts. The growth of these ideas
appears most clearly in his correspondence with his half-brother in
London, William H. Buckler.

In the end, White's liberalism was destined to outweigh his
partisanship. He was to uphold President Wilson's principal ideas,
though deploring his mistakes, and regretfully but firmly to oppose
the stand taken by Senator Lodge and other critics of the League.
Dissenting completely from the position of the Irreconcilables, he

[1] *Letters of Theodore Roosevelt and Henry Cabot Lodge*, vol. ii, p. 548.
[2] David F. Houston, *Eight Years With Wilson's Cabinet*, vol. i, pp. 348,

was to be as strongly in favor of the League as Mr. Taft, Mr. Hughes, and Mr. Wickersham. It is not necessary to maintain that White in 1917-18 was gifted with unusual insight into the dark and intricate international situation of the period. He had no such acquaintance with currents of war-time policy as General Bliss had gained through his membership in the Allied Conference and the Supreme War Council; much less the familiarity possessed by Colonel House. The vision of a new international organization which had seized President Wilson was one which he imperfectly apprehended when he went to Paris, and which became clear to him only by degrees. But in the end he had the imagination to appreciate the President's central aim, which was more than Lansing did, and the liberalism to support it consistently, which is more than could be said of some intimate party associates. In the world's crisis he was not one of those who failed through blindness or partisan narrowness.

To understand all this, to understand why President Wilson found it so natural to appoint White to the Peace Commission, we must go back to the early months of 1917.

When the President asked for a declaration of war against Germany, White hoped that American entrance into the conflict would shorten it and abridge its horrors. He had fervently approved of Wilson's note of December, 1916, to all the belligerent powers, asking them to state their view of the terms on which the war might be concluded. The time, he thought, coming just after the Kaiser's "peace drive," was unfortunate.[3] But unlike those sympathizers with the Allies who objected to Wilson's disclaimer of judgment between the respective claims of the belligerents, he held that the note had done much to advance the cause of peace. He approved warmly, again, of Wilson's address before the Senate on January 22, 1917, in which he declared for "peace without victory." He was totally at a loss to understand why the Germans made their announcement of unrestricted submarine warfare at the moment when the President was thus pushing the question of peace to the front.[4] From Count Bernstorff he learned that Colonel House had conveyed an offer to act as meditator in effecting a negotiated peace,

[3] White to Buckler, Washington, January 19, 1917.
[4] White to Buckler, Washington, February 23, 1917.

and that Bernstorff had fruitlessly appealed to Berlin to postpone the decision for unrestrained use of the submarines. When relations were broken off, White saw Bernstorff on the eve of his departure from Washington. The German ambassador told him that Wilson could not have followed any other course than he had taken, and that he himself would have given anything to stop his superiors in Berlin.[5] "Sad it is to think," White wrote to Buckler when war came, "how different events might have been with a little more wisdom on the part of a nation which seems capable of everything except that clear perception of the sentiment of other peoples which is so indispensable to success in international affairs."

Repeatedly during the next few months White wrote to Mr. Buckler in London regarding their common hopes for a peace without vindictiveness, on a just and durable basis. He hoped the Russian revolution "*aurait eu pour effet le raccourcissement de la guerre.*" [6] He was pleased that American counsels would now have much weight in the discussion of preliminaries of the peace, and that President Wilson would certainly not consent to the "impossible conditions" proposed by the Allies in their last peace note. He did not believe that there was real enthusiasm for the war among the mass of the American people, and fearing that the first casualty lists would have a depressing effect upon national morale, he hoped for a peace before the losses became heavy. Mr. Buckler being, as we have seen, a special assistant at the American Embassy in London, White encouraged him to gather confidential information as to the feeling in England upon peace, and to transmit to him special reports to be handed to Colonel House and thus perhaps reach President Wilson himself.

The British and French missions sent to the United States just after the declaration of war, headed by Mr. Balfour, M. Viviani, and Marshal Joffre, received an enthusiastic popular welcome in New York, Philadelphia, and Washington, and an ovation in Congress. At the request of the State Department, White welcomed the Frenchmen to his Crescent Place house as their headquarters. For a fortnight Joffre, Viviani, and their staff were there, the great flags of the mission flying at each side of the house during the day, four

[5] White to Buckler, New York, March 15, 1917.
[6] White to Buckler, Washington, April 11, 1917.

THE FRENCH MISSION ARRIVING AT HENRY WHITE'S HOUSE

searchlights at the corners lighting up the grounds at night, and a
guard of police constantly patrolling the vicinity. White asked some
prominent members of Congress to dine with the mission, and
accompanied it when it visited Baltimore. But his chief interest was
in talking with Joffre and Viviani upon questions not of war, but
of peace. The latter told him that if Germany would only cede
Alsace-Lorraine and adopt a more democratic form of government,
France would be willing to end the war; for Russia no longer
wished to acquire Constantinople, and the other questions would
present no great difficulty.[7]

As the summer passed, with the formidable new American army
beginning to take shape and the war spirit rising, White's interest
in peace did not slacken. The death of Joseph H. Choate, who had
become one of his closest friends, was a sore blow; he went immediately to the family home in New York, spent part of every day
with Mrs. and Miss Choate, and accompanied them to the funeral
at Stockbridge. Roosevelt he saw when the Colonel came to Washington in his fruitless attempt to obtain permission to raise a
division for service in France; despite his rebuff the Colonel was in
good spirits, and much amused by Joseph Tumulty's efforts to
impress upon him that he must be very guarded in his statements
to the press about his interview with Wilson. In June Harvard gave
White, together with Spring-Rice, the degree of LL.D., an honor
which he valued the more because Mrs. White had once hoped it
would come to him. He worked with the Navy League and the
War Service Commission, he helped receive the Italian war mission, and in September he took charge of the Potomac division of
the Red Cross, comprising Virginia, West Virginia, Maryland, and
the Federal District. But despite these occupations, he kept in touch
with those who looked forward to the end of the war. In August,
when he visited Mr. Hugh Wallace at Manchester-by-the-sea, Colo-

[7] White to Buckler, Washington, May 4, 1917. Marshal Joffre, in a letter
of March 8, 1928, recalled how useful White had been to him on this visit.
"I can affirm," he wrote, "that it was in Henry White's house that were sown
the seeds of the military and naval coöperation which bore fruit several
months later on the battlefront. I particularly remember two dinners to which
he invited some of the most influential persons in America, and where I was
able to speak frankly and fully of the ways in which I thought American
military assistance might best be given."

nel House motored over from Magnolia to see him. They had a long conversation about the military party in Germany, the chances of its early overthrow, the progress there toward a democratic form of government, and the hopes for peace under the new Foreign Minister, Kühlmann.[7a]

There were a good many reasons why White, whose confidence in American and Allied victory was complete, should take a realistic view of the issues bound up with the war. He knew European politics, and the tortuous and selfish mazes of continental diplomacy. He heard occasionally from his daughter and his son-in-law, Count Seherr-Thoss. He had frequent letters from his son, now connected with the American legation in Athens, and conversant with all the news of European intrigue current there. From Mr. Buckler in London, a Cambridge graduate, married to an Englishwoman, and devoted to the Allied cause, but also a man of signally cool and liberal outlook, he received a steady stream of information quite different from that supplied by propagandist agencies.

Indeed, though heart and soul in the war, White distrusted some aspects of British, French, and Italian policy with what now seems remarkable shrewdness. His letters show that he had a very measured regard for Walter Hines Page. When Colonel House returned to Europe late in 1917, White took a half-malicious joy in imagining the effect of this visit upon Mr. Page, who had been decidedly chilly toward Mr. House's previous activities. He had confidence in the detachment of Colonel House, while he distrusted Page's strong Anglophilism. "It is almost disastrous at this moment," he wrote, "to have some one in London who is afraid of crossing our English cousins, and who says 'yes' to everything they demand, which (between ourselves) is a great deal indeed. You will have seen the letter of Lord Northcliffe, who speaks of five hundred officers and ten thousand workers under their orders in this country! The more I see of Colonel House the more I feel that he is a good and prudent counselor of the head of the nation, who does not lack the courage of his convictions and stands by them when occasion de-

[7a] "I am very glad to know," White wrote of House, "that he makes the important distinction between the military party and the Emperor, and that he has counselled the President not to denounce the latter."—White to Buckler, Lenox, August 8, 1917.

mands it." [8] Again, when Clemenceau came into power, White felt that France was dominated by a leader who was, as he wrote, imperious of temper, extremely able, lacking in imagination or constructive ideas, and *"capable de tout"*—in short, a man who under some circumstances would be extremely dangerous.[9]

It happened that there appeared in the Washington *Post* of November, 1917, an anonymous article which suggested that the American Government was already converted to the idea of associating itself with the Allies' agreement never to make peace except in conjunction with one another. "On reading that I leaped from my bed," wrote White, "electrified at the very idea of such an idiotic step on our part, which would renounce at one stroke our dominating position and place all our resources at the disposal of the Allies." He hastened to speak of the subject to Rear-Admiral Grayson. The latter told him that the article had made the President furious, disturbing him to a very unusual degree, and he assured White that Wilson thoroughly appreciated the commanding position which he held so long as he remained independent, and had no intention of renouncing it.[10]

Apart from the press and the news received through diplomatic friends and his son, White's main source of foreign information during 1917-18 continued to be his half-brother, Mr. Buckler. Many facts, mostly confidential, were reported or discussed in Buckler's letters, and when Colonel House returned from Europe numerous brief memoranda came from Buckler for House's use. These memoranda had a peculiar value, for Buckler maintained close relations with a large number of prominent Liberals and Labor representatives—his old Cambridge friends Charles Trevelyan and Noel Buxton, and others like H. N. Brailsford, H. W. Massingham, and Henry W. Nevinson; while he was sympathetic with many of the ideas of Lord Lansdowne, Lord Haldane, and Mr. Ramsay MacDonald.[11] He was out of sympathy with those who insisted on a

[8] White to Buckler, Washington, November 2, 1917.
[9] White to Buckler, Washington, November 16, 1917.
[10] *Idem.* White, who usually wrote to Buckler in French, calls Grayson *"un très-brave garçon."*
[11] In December, 1917, White went to the White House and placed in Wilson's own hands a memorandum from Buckler on the famous "peace

dictated peace and an imperialistic division of spoils. He took a much more incisive and critical view of Allied policies than Ambassador Page ever took. White was thus kept informed of the very latest trends of Liberal and Labor opinion as the war drew to a close. The mere transmission of Buckler's memoranda meanwhile demonstrated to Colonel House, and indirectly to Wilson, that on questions of peace White was entirely open-minded.

Some examples of the information which passed through White's hands may be of interest. From the moment of American entrance into the war, and even earlier, Buckler was anxious that our Government should understand the point of view of the "negotiation group" in general and of the Labor Party in particular. He met Lord Robert Cecil as the United States plunged into the conflict. "Lord Robert's own views are very moderate," he wrote, "and he welcomes our influence as having that same tendency. He even strongly expressed the view that it would be a mistake to annex German territory or impose punitive terms even if it were possible to do so. I asked: 'Then are you not in favor of peace without victory?' 'Perhaps I am,' he said, 'but though that phrase is doubtless suited to an American audience, it would not be understood by our people.' A very tactful answer and an amusing admission!" [12] Buckler reported at the same time the first great public meeting in London at which peace terms were seriously discussed and the "knock-out policy" of the Lloyd George Government harshly criticized, Lord

letter" which Lord Lansdowne had published in the London *Daily Telegraph* of November 29th, asking for a precise statement of the Allied peace terms in order to hasten the termination of the war. The letter aroused fierce dissent, but both Buckler and White thought highly of it.—White to Buckler, Washingon, December 19, 1917.

[12] Buckler's memorandum for White and House, June 29, 1917. Buckler early saw that White was informed of the gist of the secret treaties among the Allies. He sent him copies of the London *Nation* and other periodicals dealing with these treaties, upon which White commented with interest. But White also heard something of the treaties from Viviani and Joffre, who discussed with him the proposed division of Mesopotamia and Syria between England and France.—White to Buckler, Washington, November 2, 1917. All this is of interest in view of Wilson's later statement that he did not learn of the secret treaties until he had reached Paris.

Parmoor and Noel Buxton making the principal speeches. He also saw Lord Lansdowne: [13]

On Sunday I called on Lord Lansdowne to see what confirmation I could get from him of the attitude toward peace negotiations which he assumed last November. He was most friendly, began asking after you [Colonel House], and said he hoped your good work would some day bear fruit in producing terms which could be discussed. Personally he was in favor of considering any offer or proposal and was against banging or bolting any door, but as to his attitude while in the Cabinet his lips were sealed by the pledge of Cabinet secrecy. He had been disappointed by the failure of the Germans to produce an outline of their demands such as the Allies had given of their own. When, however, I reminded him that this very *Entente* statement had smashed the German moderates and directly led to the U-boat crisis, he did not attempt to justify the *Entente* terms.

At a breakfast arranged by Noel Buxton to discuss with Lloyd George the possibility of detaching Bulgaria from the enemy side, Buckler ascertained something of the Prime Minister's views. They were a strange mixture of jingoism and radicalism. He thought the knock-out blow to Germany absolutely indispensable, but professed to be glad the United States had come in, so that at the final settlement it might moderate the demands of Great Britain's Allies, who were far more grasping than she. That is, as Buckler put it, Lloyd George wished to stimulate jingo greed by a crushing victory and then to apply an American sedative.

With Mr. Ramsay MacDonald, Buckler conversed more frequently, and Mr. MacDonald took time to write out, for the benefit of Colonel House and the President, a statement regarding the effect in Great Britain of America's entry into the war. It read: [14]

1—The majority of our people welcomed America's entry into the war, but a minority, much larger than newspapers or vociferous opinion indicates, regard it not with any hostile feelings but with regret. They come to that view because (a) they do not think that American military help was required in order to compel any of the Powers to make a reasonable peace; and (b) they think that America, out of the war, would have done

[13] Buckler's memorandum for White and House, London, June 29, 1917.
[14] Ramsay MacDonald to Buckler, London, August 17, 1917. The Russian revolution here mentioned was of course the first revolution, not the Bolshevik revolution.

more for peace and good feeling than in the war, and would also have had a better influence on the peace settlement.

2—The majority is composed of (a) what I would call the war emotionalists who have no policy and do not think things out, and also (b) of those who have a very distinct policy in their mind.

3—Most of the latter regard the Russian revolution as a calamity. Some think it necessary, others believe it to be a mere sinister move. Others again welcome America for the moral support it gives the Allies, because it completes the league of democracies against Germany, and strengthens enormously the cause of the Allies.

4—The view of this 2b section is that America has come in at an opportune moment to readjust the balance tilted against us by the Russian revolution. They consider that we can now prolong the war until America has become an effective partner in it, and that if Russia is crushed and compelled to make peace, the Allies can still refuse all overtures, negotiations, or political approaches of any kind and pursue a program of a complete military issue.

5—In consequence of this there has been a decided hardening in the dominating opinion of this country, and I look forward to more troublous times rather than easier ones for my friends and myself in consequence. Russian opinions and interests are also more neglected than they would otherwise be.

6—Amongst political sections miscalled "pacifist," President Wilson's recent pronouncements have been regarded with disappointment, and they are interpreted here by all sections as marking a complete reversal of his old views regarding the war and its settlement, and also regarding the whole European problem.

7—On the whole, these people still take the view that whether America came in or kept out, a real decisive victory after the style of Waterloo is out of the question, and that all that America's aid can do is to encourage and enable the European Powers to continue a war of attrition much further than would otherwise have been possible without in any way producing definite results.

8—They look in vain for indications that Mr. Wilson is still aware that this war will have to be settled by political agreement, however long it is fought, and are in consequence driven to the conclusion that the effect upon Europe of America's entry into the war has been to strengthen aggressive Jingoism and to set back the moral and political movements that had become strong in consequence of the Russian revolution.

9—They are amazed at the attitude taken by your government regarding the Stockholm Conference, as they expected that America with its republican and democratic traditions would have stood for the rights of the peoples, and would have facilitated the clearing up of the issues and the removal of misunderstandings by direct democratic contact and exchange of opinions. A pronouncement to that effect by America would have had a tremendous influence for good on this side. . . .

Mr. MacDonald thought this a fair summary of the existing situation. He added that if he were an American he would wish his government, now that it was at war, to take several precautionary steps. Undoubtedly he hoped that Wilson would see these recommendations:

1—It should renew its declaration that the utility of war was severely limited by the political objects which it could gain, and that whilst you can have peace without victory, history shows that as a rule nations have had victory without peace. That would prevent Europe from thinking of the war as being simply of the nature of a dog-fight—a view which, I am afraid, too many of our people are taking. It would also compel them to welcome political activities parallel with military activities.

2—The policy of refusing passports to representatives of both majority and minority sections of the international movement should be reversed.

3—Something should be stated clearly indicating that, in the view of America, the countries fighting in the cause of the Allies should maintain within their own borders liberty of honest discussion, and freedom for minorities to contribute to the solution of the tremendous problems over which this war has arisen and which in so many respects it has hitherto only intensified.

This was wise and honest counsel, and as White well knew, the United States had need for it. A somewhat sharper warning to President Wilson was forwarded from Charles Trevelyan in the early summer of 1917. He wrote to Buckler that it was probably impossible as yet to obtain liberal and fair terms of peace from Germany, for the submarine campaign was not wholly discredited. But the Allies, he added, were just as unfair: [15]

Russia and the United States alone are seeking for a democratic and international peace. Great Britain, with its intention to keep the German

[15] Charles Trevelyan to Buckler, London, June 28, 1917.

colonies and Mesopotamia by right of conquest, France, with its intention to get Alsace and Lorraine by right of reconquest and not the
decision of the population, Italy, with her imperialist demand to control
the Adriatic by annexing non-Italian populations, are as responsible for
continuing the war as the German Government which refuses to repu-
diate its imperialist designs on Belgium, France, etc. I have no doubt
that President Wilson realizes this. It may be true still that he can't
force Germany to reason except by fighting. But by placing himself
beside Russia and demanding that the Western European Allies should
openly disavow all ideas of conquest and should accept his policy he can
compel *their* acquiescence in a proper kind of peace. The reaction on
Germany would be decisive. . . .

Personally I maintain a deep-seated confidence in President Wilson.
But I see a danger of one of the most tragic reverses of history if he
finds himself isolated with the Western European powers who have not
adopted his policy, and sees Russia, which has adopted it, forced into
anarchy or a separate peace by its inability to get more than insincere
phrases from the other Allies.

In the months which followed Buckler steadily chronicled everything that bore on the progress or retrocession of the "moderate"
movement. In January of 1918, for example, he wrote that the
tendency toward a negotiated peace seemed to be growing apace.
He cited the approval by the British press of Lloyd George's conciliatory speech to the Labor Conference, and the chorus of praise
which greeted President Wilson's speech of January 8th containing
the famous Fourteen Points; and he noted that Ramsay MacDonald
and George Lansbury had been asked at different times to breakfast
with Lloyd George.

During 1917-18 White was an interested but passive observer of
the political scene, coming into frequent contact with Lodge and
other Republican leaders. Approving with few if any reservations
of the President's foreign policy, he disapproved of a good deal in
the home administration. It seemed to him that Wilson did not
surround himself with sufficiently able men, or make effective use
of the immense reservoir of business and political capacity which
drained into Washington in the war years. He saw Roosevelt several times in the capital, and found that the party chiefs all looked
forward to making him their candidate for President in 1920. But
White's work as regional director of the Red Cross and president

of the War Camp Community Service forbade his sharing in the congressional campaign of 1918.

More than once during 1918 Colonel House thanked White and Buckler for some particular bit of information. He was pleased, for example, with some packets sent during March, and which he showed President Wilson; one of them related to Bertrand Russell, who was in trouble in England for his pacifist utterances. White himself was aroused in behalf of the philosopher. "Certainly the observations of Russell do not merit the punishment which has been inflicted on him," he wrote, "and you are right in believing that his enemies have simply seized the opportunity to vent their spite. I could do nothing more than call Colonel House's attention to the matter. Everything here is now in the hands of the President, and there are only two or three persons to whom he listens, the Colonel being one." [16]

As the summer wore on, it became evident that the successive Allied blows were bringing the war to an end. At the close of August White was confident that the struggle was nearly over. He was calculating, he wrote, that the German people would be disheartened by the discovery that their Government had been lying on the subject of the American troops in Europe, the accomplishments of the submarines, and other subjects. "How they ever had the folly to make us enter the war I have never been able to understand. And our activity has been so much more vigorous and effective than we ourselves had expected. Sentiment is almost unanimous, so far as I can learn, for pursuing the war to the end, and the new call for all those between the ages of 18 and 45 seems not to have excited the least opposition. Altogether, the transformation of a democracy like this into an autocracy to make war is one of the most remarkable phenomena in history." [17] But he still hoped for a mild and liberal peace.

It will be seen from all this that in appointing Henry White President Wilson had much more in mind than the mere fact that White was an experienced diplomatist and a Republican of not too pronouncedly partisan type. The President required more than that of an associate on the Peace Commission. He knew from Colonel

[16] White to Buckler, Washington, March 6, 1918.
[17] White to Buckler, Washington, August 31, 1918.

House and to some extent from personal contact that White was a man of liberal views, in close touch with events in Europe and holding advanced ideas regarding peace. He was appointed not as a conservative, as Mr. Root would have been, but as a moderate who had intimate connections in the Central Powers as well as the Allied countries, who would favor a just instead of a vengeful peace, and who would be eager to extirpate the causes of war. President Wilson knew that he was a friend of Roosevelt and Lodge, and that while the former would be angered by the appointment of Mr. Taft, he could have no objection to White. Finally, he was aware that White's long acquaintance with European leaders—with Balfour, Curzon, Clemenceau, Sonnino—might be valuable, while no other American was so well versed in diplomatic forms and precedents.

Nevertheless, the appointment was a complete surprise to White. The President offered it to him through Secretary Lansing, confirming the offer by a brief letter; and after telephone conversations with Roosevelt and Lodge he accepted. He wrote to Mr. Buckler (November 24):

As I learn that a mail will leave tomorrow morning, I hasten to write a few words this evening to tell you what you will presently learn through the press, that I have been chosen a member of the delegation which is to represent this country at the Peace Conference. I have never been more surprised in my life than when Lansing sent for me last Tuesday (the 19th) toward the dinner hour, and offered me this post on the part of the President. I was not aware that they were even dreaming of me. After asking until yesterday morning to give my decision, and having consulted Jusserand and been assured by him that my relationship with Muriel would constitute no bar to the services I might render the two nations, I accepted; but not until I had insisted that Lansing should explain the significance of the President's points upon the League of Nations, the question of economic barriers, and the freedom of the seas.

Nobody appears to have suggested my name, and of course I never dreamed of suggesting it myself. It seems that Lansing and the President hit upon me themselves as the representative of the Republican party. I am not sure just how the leaders of the party will actually take my appointment. I have never been a politician, and in fact have always refused to be anything but a simple diplomatist, ready to serve the nation no matter which party had charge of the Government. It seems that Labor could not bear Root, so that his name was never seriously considered. It is evidently an honor conferred simply on the basis of my diplomatic experience, and especially because I have been a member of other international conferences; while it must be remembered that I have never made any public statement hostile to the President.

I fully appreciate the enormous difficulties of the undertaking, some of which I shall explain when I see you presently.

Adding that he thoroughly approved of the President's plan of going to Europe in person, for only by so doing could Wilson fully understand the tremendous obstacles that must be beaten down before an agreement could be reached on the principal questions, White expressed the hope that this visit would prove of short duration. It would be well for Wilson to open the conference in Paris; it would also be well if he found that he did not have time to stay long. Mr. Buckler had written with regretful condemnation of the feeling in Europe that the President would be too lenient to Germany, and White expressed the same regret over American feeling; "here also the President is suspected of not feeling sufficient severity for the Germans."

Of White's consultation with Colonel Roosevelt, Senator Lodge, and Mr. Root before he sailed we shall say something in the next chapter. On December 14, 1918, the President, Secretary Lansing, and he arrived together in Paris. From the Hotel Crillon a few days later he wrote Mr. Buckler of their tremendous reception, the enthusiasm of the populace bursting all bounds, and of his hope that it would have a favorable political effect. The great adventure had begun.

CHAPTER TWENTY

The Peace Conference: The Council of Ten

IT WAS a groping world which waited for peace in the last weeks
of 1918; and public opinion in the United States was groping
as much as Allied opinion or German opinion. Where were the
decisive leadership, the far-sighted vision, the bold practical plan,
which should relieve the planet from it almost intolerable agonies,
fears, and hatreds? Multitudes turned to President Wilson for this
vision and leadership. He had projected his policy, in the famous
Fourteen Points, along a line which had caught the imagination of
the world—a line which seemed to leave the past behind and carry
mankind into a new and brighter future. But for the moment Europe
trusted him more than did America. Behind him there did not stand
a united and confident country. With the signing of the armistice
the forced unity of the war-time period had collapsed, while the
almost simultaneous elections had revealed a deep division in the
nation. The great body of Republicans were antagonistic, many
Democrats were restive, and an influential array of independent voters were hurt and apprehensive as they reviewed his autocratic
domestic policies. The majority of his countrymen, while thrilling
temporarily to his idealistic utterances, had not fully understood his
aims in foreign affairs. He had not succeeded in building up a great
mass of public opinion which comprehended the importance of his
proposed League of Nations, or was ready to insist upon a liberal
peace.[1]

White felt that it was imperative for him, before he departed
with the President, to consult the principal Republican leaders upon
the task before the Peace Commission. He would be the sole representative of the party in this momentous conference. After the
election, Roosevelt had roughly proclaimed that "Our Allies and

[1] Cf. *New Republic*, November 30, 1918, on Wilson's "partial loss of
popular confidence."

our enemies and Mr. Wilson himself should all understand that Mr. Wilson has no authority whatever to speak for the American people at this time." As yet White felt uncertain either of what Wilson really desired or of the Republican views. By finding out both, he might do something to effect the harmony which he instinctively felt would be badly needed.

On November 26, 1918, he and Elihu Root sat together at Roosevelt's bedside in Roosevelt Hospital in New York, talking of the peace terms to be fixed in Paris.[2] Roosevelt himself, now within six weeks of his death, was too ill to say much. Mr. Root did most of the talking. The subject was one on which he had spent much thought; indeed, he had written a memorandum on it for Colonel House the previous August, and what he now said chiefly followed that memorandum.[3] The gist of his discourse, which White hurriedly jotted down in pencil notes, was that the peace must be fair to all oppressed peoples, and that above all there must be an international organization to prevent future wars.

Root believed, he said, that there must be a community of nations; that in the future all international wars, instead of being regarded merely as the affair of the peoples engaged in them, must be looked upon as breaches of the peace which offend and injure all nations; and that the world community must take steps to outlaw and prevent national wars just as local communities have done away with private war. For this purpose, he went on, suitable institutions must be developed. There must be an agreement by the world upon some agency which could speak for the whole community in calling any two disputing nations to take their quarrel to a world court, or an international conference. But it was important, he added, to make no agreement for a league of peace, or other international organization, which would not be kept when the time came for action. "Nothing," he said, "can be worse in international affairs than to make agreements and break them."

In brief, Mr. Root was interested chiefly in preventives of future war, and he made this interest plain in Roosevelt's presence. He alluded incidentally to the right of the Jugo-Slavs to a broad win-

[2] Memorandum made by White, November 26, 1918.

[3] Root gave White a copy of this memorandum; it is published in full in Seymour, Charles, *The Intimate Papers of Colonel House*, vol. iv, pp. 43-47.

dow on the Adriatic, to the right of Italy to Trieste, and to the claims of the Lithuanians to nationhood. But his most important remarks, which White noted roughly on some cards, had to do with a machinery for peace. "Anything attempted," ran one of White's quotations, "must be based on community of nations." He spoke of "an international agreement with fundamental objects (1) to unite in conferring and (2) in discouraging and opposing any country violating peace." But he would limit this by "leaving to each country to determine what it is to do. The United States would not fight about Belgium." White's cards contain no quotation from Roosevelt. But he said later, in a public address, that at this meeting Roosevelt had unequivocally indorsed the general idea of a League of Nations.

Very different was the conversation which White had in Washington, in the hurried intervals of packing, with Senator Lodge. The chairman of the Senate minority cared little about pressing an international organization for peace; that could wait. Like Root, he had made a statement in August of his views. Standing in the Senate and shaking his finger like another Cato, he had appealed for dictating the harshest terms of peace to Germany. His speech resounded with demands for an utter and crushing victory, for marching to Berlin and there imposing peace, for beating Germany to her knees; no peace that satisfied Germany in any degree, he declared, could ever satisfy us. He denounced Lord Lansdowne. He laid down a number of the fairly evident essentials of peace—the restoration of Belgium, the cession of Alsace-Lorraine, the establishment of Poland, Czechoslovakia, and Jugo-Slavia in full independence, and the redemption of Italia irredenta; but in his speech he said nothing about a League. In conversation with White he spoke of it, but only to warn him against placing our army and navy at the disposal of any such body, and against bothering with any League at all until peace was signed. Immediately after their talk, in the last hours before White sailed, he wrote out a nine-page memorandum for White's guidance.[5] Confidently asserting that this represented the views not only of the Republican party, but of

---

[4] *Congressional Record,* August 23, 1918.

[5] Lodge to White, Washington, December 2, 1918. "This," said Lodge, "is the memorandum of which we talked." The italics below are the author's.

America in general, he proposed that White should show it in strict confidence to Balfour, Clemenceau, and Nitti, all of whom Lodge knew personally.

His motive in this Lodge stated to White with his usual candor. The memorandum should be shown to these European statesmen, he wrote, not as an attempt to enlighten them upon the terms of peace, but to inform them "what I believe to be the real feeling of the people of the United States and certainly the Senate of the United States. *This knowledge may in certain contingencies be very important to them in strengthening their position.*" That is, Lodge believed that Wilson's ideas misrepresented the United States. He believed it so firmly that he wished to assist the European leaders in impeding and thwarting Wilson. White never thought of showing the paper to any representative of the Allies, and kept it wholly secret.

It was an important paper, this outline of Lodge's suggested terms of peace. It represented the earnest beliefs of one of the principal Republican statesmen, who as head of the Foreign Relations Committee would wield the greatest influence and power. When he wrote it, feeling against Germany had been aroused to the highest pitch. This fact in part accounted for the fierce emphasis which Lodge placed upon his leading premise that it was necessary in every way to cripple Germany in order to prevent future war. He began his memorandum with three cardinal points:

MEMORANDUM: LODGE TO WHITE, DECEMBER 2, 1918

1—It is absolutely vital that the terms of peace should be determined by the United States and the Allies first and when those terms are agreed upon by the Allies and the United States they must be imposed upon Germany. Germany must not have opportunity for discussion but must accept the terms we impose. This is believed to be substantially settled already. . . .

2—The first and controlling purpose of the peace must be to put Germany in such a position that it will be physically impossible for her to break out again upon other nations with a war for world conquest. The following points are suggested because it is believed that they will effect this result.

3—Belgium must be completely restored and her entire independence assured. This it is assumed may already be regarded as settled by the armistice.

From this Lodge went on to suggest a number of territorial arrangements, following in the main his Senate speech but at some points going into greater detail. A notable feature of his memorandum was his willingness to make the United States a part-guarantor of many elements of the European settlement. In addition to what he had already said of Alsace-Lorraine, Poland, Jugo-Slavia, and Czechoslovakia, he mentioned other countries. Greece, he wrote, should have the Aegean Islands and "all that northwestern part of Asia Minor where the Greeks are predominant." The Turkish Government should be removed from Europe, and "Constantinople and the Straits should be neutralized and made free under the guardianship of the United States and the Allies." Rumania should be given the Rumanian population of Transylvania. "How Russia is to be dealt with and whether an independent state shall be formed in the Ukraine are questions which can only be determined by the Allies and the United States after full conference and examination." The Poles should be given Danzig and both banks of the Vistula; and "for the peace of the world it would be very desirable to add East Prussia to Poland." Lithuania, Livonia, and Esthonia should be made independent "under the protection of the Allies and the United States." Danish Schleswig should be restored to Denmark, and "the Kiel Canal should be internationalized and neutralized and made free to the world." The German colonies should under no circumstances be returned to German ownership. The independence of Czechoslovakia "must be made secure and sustained by the Allies and the United States in every way."

Lodge included a section upon indemnities, which he wished to be made very large. Germany, he wrote, must pay for the ruin she had wrought in Belgium and northern France, for her injuries to the commerce of all other nations, and for the injuries inflicted upon civilian populations everywhere. "There is a strong argument for making her pay at least a portion of the cost of the war which she precipitated and for which she alone is responsible. Heavy indemnities must therefore be exacted. They will be so large that they cannot be paid immediately, but the ultimate payment must be secured beyond any question and cautionary towns or provinces must be held as a part of that security . . ." Still more harshly, Lodge added an

ADDITIONAL MEMORANDUM: LODGE TO WHITE, DECEMBER 2, 1918

Nothing would so protect us from war in the future as the separation of the German Empire into its chief component parts. I do not know how far this will go; but if Bavaria, for example, should wish to treat separately or have a separate treaty to sign, I think it ought to be encouraged. The reports about Turkey turning to us for protection and help are mischievous. This country cannot afford to appear as the protector of Turkey. The American people would like to see the Turkish Government entirely out of Europe and all the oppressed peoples which Turkey has been tyrannizing over and subjecting to massacre freed from her once for all. I think this is a point on which not only the Senate but the American people feel very strongly.

Senator Lodge filed a caveat against the third of Wilson's Fourteen Points, saying that his general interdiction of economic barriers must never be so interpreted as to interfere with discriminating tariffs or reciprocity treaties. He objected also to President Wilson's point regarding the freedom of the seas, saying that none of the great naval Powers wished needless armaments, "but they cannot permit any other nation or any agreement of nations to dictate what the necessities of their own defense require or deprive them of the power of blockade." On the League he was equally emphatic, and indulged in words of significant prophecy:

The League of Nations to preserve and enforce peace presents a conception which must appeal to every right-thinking man, but like many other general ideas when we pass from theory to practise the terms and details are vital. It need only be said here that under no circumstances must provisions for such a league be made a part of the peace treaty which concludes the war with Germany. Any attempt to do this would not only long delay the signature of the treaty of peace, which should not be unduly postponed, but it would make the adoption of the treaty, unamended, by the Senate of the United States and other ratifying bodies, extremely doubtful.

Roosevelt lay dying; Root was for a moderate peace, and for international institutions guaranteeing a new world order; Lodge was for a harsh peace, and impatiently suspicious of international institutions; Taft was for the League; nobody was certain just where Mr. Hughes stood—and so White sailed away to Europe. He left behind a confused party and confused country, and approached a continent where confusion was worse confounded. It is unnecessary to say that White disagreed completely with Lodge's major premise that it was necessary to cripple Germany in every possible way before peace could be secure. He knew from his daughter how complete was Germany's collapse, how bitter was the German feeling against militarism, and how deep was the desire for democracy and peace.

On the question of the League he had not yet made up his mind. He was aware that there was no real consensus of Republican, of Democratic, or of American feeling on this and on some other important issues before the peacemakers. There was certainly yet no definite party view that he could be asked to represent. But he divined that there would shortly be a deep gulf between the opinions of President Wilson in Paris and Senator Lodge and his associates in Washington; and from the beginning he cherished a hope that whatever might be his part in writing the treaty, he could serve a large purpose in his old diplomatic rôle of mediator, and in bringing discordant American minds together.

It is in this special hope of White's that we find the key to his most significant activities during the first three months of the Peace Conference. He believed that as the only Republican on the Commission and the friend of Roosevelt, Root and Lodge, as well as the friendly associate of Wilson, House, and Lansing, he could do much to enlighten both sides. He could act to moderate any clash of views. This ambition explains why, in the interval between the President's arrival in Europe and his return for a brief visit late in February to the United States, White took such assiduous pains to correspond with Senator Lodge, Mr. Root, and John Jacob Rogers of the House of Representatives.[6] It explains the earnest, sometimes desperate efforts he made in these letters to set forth the President's point of view and the necessities of the European situation. To Lodge in particular he sent frequent and intimate reports of the Conference, headed "personal and confidential," addressed to "Dear

[6] In White's papers in the Library of Congress are preserved full files of this correspondence.

Cabot," and signed, as Lodge usually signed his replies, "Affectionately yours." He felt the great opportunity which lay before
him, and rose to meet it in these weeks with characteristic disregard
of merely personal or party considerations—wishing to serve what
he deemed the best interests of the Republic and nothing else.
Even for those who, like White, Lansing, and Bliss, were seldom
allowed any large share in the central work of the Conference, the
days were crowded, difficult, and exhausting. Yet at midnight
White would be still sitting at his desk in the Crillon, dictating to
his indefatigable secretary the letters which he hoped would convey
needed information to the party leaders, modify some of the views
of Senator Lodge, and make the peace acceptable.

It is important to realize that White's own position developed
steadily, and that more than one of the arguments incorporated
in his letters represented facts and ideas which, through his contact
with the terrible realities of Europe, had wrought a transformation
in his own mind. At first he looked askance upon the President's
decision to attend the Conference in person. He liked the plan of a
state visit, which pleased his diplomatic instincts; he approved of
an effort by the President to feel out for himself the difficulties of
the situation; but he did not wish the President to sit long in the
Conference, and hoped he would soon return home. His first idea
was that Wilson should open the Conference and then retire, to
exercise his enormous influence from Washington. He always believed that when Wilson went home in February he should have
stayed; but he became convinced that Wilson's first two months in
Paris were for the good of the world. So, also, his opinion of the
League of Nations changed. At the outset White, like most Americans, had little enthusiasm for the League project, and preferred
to have it thrust over for more deliberate consideration after the
conclusion of peace. He had no mercurial temperament or intellect,
but his mind was remarkably open; his long training had made
him willing to listen sympathetically to both sides of any issue and
weigh them judicially. He did not easily fall under the influence
of personalities. For that matter, there was little in Wilson's personality to captivate him, and his relations with the President,
though cordial, were never close. But he did fall under the influence
of facts as he saw them, and the impact of facts led him to alter

his opinion on some of the cardinal points he had discussed with
Lodge.

Secretary Lansing believed to the end, and emphatically affirmed
in his later writings, that it was a disastrous error for Wilson to go
to Paris.[7] He believed and vehemently declared in his volumes on
the Conference that the League was a mistake and the Covenant
should never have been incorporated in the treaty. Lansing was a
Democrat, and had been close to Wilson for three years. White was
a Republican who had never been close to the President. Yet White,
who agreed with the Secretary of State and disagreed with Wilson
on minor points, came to the conclusion that in the initial stages
of the Conference, Wilson gained decided advantages by going to
Paris. If he was far from an ideal negotiator, his keenness, skill in
argument, and inflexible insistence on a few great central aims
made him the best negotiator available; while his presence saved
time when time was indispensable to the rescue of Europe. As for
the League, White always realized that it was an experiment. Yet
he quickly became convinced that it was a most hopeful experiment,
and that the only way of getting it was to put it into the treaty.
There was much in Wilson's conduct at the Conference which
displeased him; but it is a striking fact that on these two great
salient considerations the one Republican delegate agreed with
Wilson, while the one Democratic official did not.

The voyage of the American delegation to Europe on the *George
Washington* was uneventful. White had a number of informal chats
with the President. He heard from those who were present at it the
details of the often-described meeting in the cabin three days before
landing, where Wilson spoke on the nature of the peace to be made
and the probable character of the League, concluding with his fine
appeal to the experts of the delegation: "Tell me what's right and
I'll fight for it; give me a guaranteed position." On December 8th
Wilson called White and Lansing into a more confidential meeting.
The President had just received a wireless message from Colonel
House in Paris saying that the Allied Conference had reached certain conclusions subject to his approval, most of which were of no
moment, but of which one or two disturbed him. For one thing,
the conferees had decided to make an investigation as to the amount

[7] Lansing, Robert, *The Peace Negotiations: A Personal Narrative,* p. 14 ff.

of indemnity which Germany could possibly pay, before formulating the Allied bill of damages, the plan being to assess the latter in proportion to the former. Wilson condemned this as getting the cart before the horse, and as a repetition of the selfish Allied procedure after the Boxer Rebellion. From this, as White states in a memorandum written that same day, he turned to the League idea:

He then alluded to Mr. Taft's speech on the League to Enforce Peace, as reported in today's wireless news, to which he objected as unfair to himself (*i.e.,* Mr. Taft's statement that the President had been in favor of the League, then had cooled off toward it, and had now come back to his original position; and also the statement that he had ever adhered to Mr. Taft's ideas on the subject, which he considers impracticable). I was much relieved to find that the President's idea as to the League is a rather general one—*i.e.,* that it should be composed of the representatives, in the capital fixed upon as its headquarters, of the Powers forming part of it, whose duties would be to report to their respective government's tendencies on the part of any Power to break the world's peace. Those governments would then, if they should agree to do so, make representations in the matter to the Power in question, and if no attention were paid thereto the Powers making them would be empowered and even compelled (if they all agreed in the League of Nations treaty to do so) to institute a general economic boycott against the offending Power. If the latter were to fail and the offending Power should persist in going to war, there would be no authority, under the League of Nations agreement, for the other Powers to take any further joint action of a punitive character, but each of them would be free to decide for itself, either in consultation with each other or singly, what additional steps, if any, should be taken to prevent the Power threatening to break the world's peace from doing so.

This statement on the League closely resembled that which Wilson made to the meeting of experts in the cabin, except that there he spoke of a League Council to be set up at the chosen capital of the organization. The President's ideas on the subject were as yet vague and elementary.

Paris had made itself resplendent for the reception of the Americans. Although White had seen many impressive and enthusiastic demonstrations there, beginning with the Second Empire and the homage of many crowned heads to Napoleon III in 1867, he had never witnessed anything which approached the exaltation of the

crowds that filled the avenues and all their approaches as President
Wilson made his entrance. The following day these scenes were
repeated with an even wilder fervor natural to the Faubourg St.-
Antoine as its population turned out to see President Wilson drive
from the Hôtel Murat to the Hôtel de Ville. At the Sorbonne White
was struck by the effect Wilson produced when he appeared at that
ancient seat to be received by the faculties, glowing in their mediæval costumes of yellow, scarlet, and blue; the President's de-
meanor was of perfect simplicity and dignity and made a telling
impression. At his various public appearances, while the Frenchmen
used notes or manuscripts, Wilson spoke without a written line.
Then, just before Christmas, the President departed for England.
White had been talking meanwhile with Clemenceau, Pichon, and
other French leaders and catching an undertone very different from
the cheers of the Parisian populace. He felt sure, despite the campaign speeches that Lloyd George had been making, that it was
not from Great Britain but France that Wilson would encounter
his most serious opposition.

While the Americans were thus nervously marking time—for
the French pleas of unreadiness to begin the Conference and the
British general elections made a vexatious delay unavoidable—White
read with consternation in the Paris press a summary of Lodge's
Senate speech of December 21, 1918.[8] In this speech Lodge again
called for a hard peace, a peace which should leave Germany disabled and helpless; for the exaction of heavy indemnities; and for a
total postponement of all plans for a world league until after peace
had been made, relying in the meantime on a league of victors.
The Senator believed that Wilson, then occupying the most powerful and commanding position held by any man in modern times,
was on the verge of an appalling blunder. In Lodge's opinion, he
should have said to the Allies that the boundaries to be fixed in
Europe were nothing to us; that we wished a treaty which would
put it beyond Germany's power for many years to destroy the
peace of the world, and wished the Allies to make it at once; and
that we would agree to such a treaty as rapidly as possible. By this
gesture of turning Germany over to her foes, the President could

[8] *Congressional Globe*, December 21, 1918.

WOODROW WILSON, 1918-1919
(On the *George Washington*; with President
Poincaré; with General Pershing)

bring back a satisfactory peace at once and, in Lodge's words, render "an unrivaled service to humanity." He held that to try to attach the provisions for a League of Nations to the treaty would launch the opponents of Germany on a sea of boundless discussion, which Lodge felt was the very thing Germany most desired. It would produce long delays in Paris, and when the treaty came before the Senate still further delays in Washington.

White did not believe at all in callously turning the Central Powers over to their European enemies and leaving the rearrangement of the world generally to the heads of the Allied states. He had heard enough in Paris to know there was little mercy there, and little desire to avoid sowing the seeds of future wars. He did not greatly fear Germany; he began to see reasons for the League. The letter which he wrote to Lodge under these circumstances was characterized by signal tact.[9] He spoke of the Christmas lull which had descended with Wilson's departure for London, and of the felicitous impression the President was making everywhere, even on the politicians. "Curiously enough, the President's reception appears to have had some effect, according to statements made to me by those who know, upon the political situation here, which now seems to be that any Ministry, in respect to which the people has doubts of its being in agreement with the President, is likely to be overturned. As bearing out this theory, a very significant article appeared in the *Temps* newspaper on Sunday the 14th, the purport of which was that, while until now not much had been thought of the League of Nations and other presidential policies, it would be well for France to get into line in that respect; and as you know, the *Temps* is inspired by the Quai d'Orsay."

From this mild beginning he went on to intimate that the Senator might consider other points of view regarding the League. He spoke of Lodge's speech in respectful terms, saying that so far as he knew no members of the delegation opposed in principle his views on the conditions of peace. "I talked during the voyage with the President about the League of Nations, and you may be perfectly sure that he will not assent to any organization of that League whereby our army and navy would be placed under the

[9] White to Lodge, Paris, December 24, 1918.

orders of a combination of Powers, or any orders but our own. I think, moreover, that people will be surprised, if his views should be adopted by the Conference, at the very slender organization which is contemplated as a first start for that proposed League. The opinion, however, appears to be growing over here, and I understand in England also, that unless whatever League of Nations is to be formed should be one of the first subjects considered at the Peace Conference, it will never be founded at all; on the ground that, the moment peace is made and the various European nations have got what they want in the way of territories and indemnities, they will take very little interest in the founding of a League of Nations. I am bound to say there is a good deal to be said for this latter point of view, although I am still inclined to that which I expressed to you before leaving home."

"A good deal to be said"—so much for White's observations in his first ten days in Europe. He had not been influenced by Wilson, of whom he had seen singularly little; indeed, he had seen far more of Lansing, who took Lodge's view. He had not seen Robert Cecil or Léon Bourgeois. It was the hard facts of the situation which he had in mind when he wrote that "much is to be said." Lodge's reply was chilling. He was delayed in writing by Roosevelt's death and funeral, but when he did write he was positive of his old opinions. He did not believe that the French or British Ministers would be compelled by public opinion to yield to Wilson, for they had already disagreed a good deal with him. He stood for making peace at once, after which they might take up the League "and see what they can do with it." Distrusting the League idea, he rejected White's assurances about the army and navy. "The trouble with the League of Nations is that nobody knows what it means. When the terms to which we are to be asked to agree are stated there will be an opportunity then for intelligent criticism. I am very sure, however, that neither the Senate nor the country will ever agree to allow their army and their navy to be ordered about by any international body; nor could you get this country, in my judgment, to abandon the Monroe Doctrine." Senator Wadsworth had just returned from Paris and had stated opinions as hostile to the League as Lodge's own. Nor had Lodge's feeling against Germany abated.

While the French and British still delayed the Conference and Wilson paid a visit to Rome, ominous news came from central and eastern Europe. The calamities of war had been replaced over a great part of the continent by the perils and agonies of economic collapse. More than 160,000,000 people in enemy and liberated countries were facing the most terrible famine since the Thirty Years War.[10] Four once great empires had been passing through the throes of revolution, and the fourteen nations which had emerged were unstable, half organized, and trembling with weakness. Economic and military barriers had been erected everywhere; a passion of food-hoarding was sweeping the countrysides; strikes, business failures, and disorder were suddenly epidemic in all these countries. With winter sweeping down, coal production had failed. The Bolshevism which had conquered Russia seemed about to overrun the neighboring countries to the west. It was imperative that the United States come to the rescue, and President Wilson and Mr. Hoover urged Congress to appropriate $100,000,000 for relief. White seconded their appeal:

CABLEGRAM: WHITE TO LODGE, JANUARY 8, 1919

Feel I should no longer delay laying before you condition which has been gradually forcing itself upon our delegation and which now dominates entire European situation above all else, namely, steady westward advance of Bolshevism. It now completely controls Russia and Poland and is spreading through Germany. Only effective barrier now apparently possible against it is food relief, as Bolshevism thrives only on starvation and disorder. Consensus of opinion is that joint military occupation which has been suggested by France for Poland even if practical would not solve problem. Confidentially Paderewski has sent us a most urgent appeal for assistance in Poland where conditions he says are desperate. I consider it therefore of utmost importance that President's request for hundred million appropriation for relief be granted at once. Impossible to inaugurate Peace Conference under proper auspices without previous adequate provision to cope with situation. . . . I cannot too strongly impress upon you urgency of meeting situation herein described, Please communicate this to John Rogers, Gillett, and Root as a confidential message from me. . . .

[10] Herbert Hoover in E. M. House and Charles Seymour, editors, *What Really Happened in Paris*, 336.

To this message Lodge replied by mail in somewhat cool fashion. White had expressly said in his cablegram that Germany would pay cash for food, but Lodge wrote him:

LODGE TO WHITE

The bill for the hundred millions has passed the House and is now in the Senate. It will go through; but there is a general determination that it shall be carefully guarded, and that the expenditure of the money should be in the hands of officers of the government who shall be responsible to Congress for the use of the money. I think there is also a very strong feeling in this country against giving food or money to the Germans. Reports from all the soldiers who are occupying German territory and from our naval officers who are on the inter-allied commissions to take hold of the ships and have been in the German seaports, all say that the Germans have a sufficiency of food, and are better shod and on the whole better clothed than they are in France or England. I believe our expenditure will be carefully limited to those people who were either our allies or our friends.

The delay in making peace, Lodge added, was serious, for "the situation is not improved and delay helps the Germans." The Germans, as White knew from his daughter, cursed every day of waiting on the ground that delay and the continued food blockade were starving their children, killing their aged, and leaving the whole people bloodless and exhausted.

Before Lodge's reply reached Europe, the Conference had buckled down to work. The first plenary session was held January 18th, and had been preceded by some sympathetic work on the part of the American delegation. White, indeed, had fruitlessly pressed Wilson on the voyage over to draft a careful plan, elaborating the Fourteen Points and making some of them clearer. On January 8th, Wilson asked his four American associates to list the subjects which should be taken up first, and they named, in order, Representation, the League of Nations, Reparations, New States, Territorial Adjustments, and Colonial Possessions. Two days later Wilson had a meeting with the Americans (House was ill), and representation having been settled by the adoption of the plan for the Council of Ten, took up the League. An electric tension was in the air, and the discussion resulted in a breach, concealed but practically total, between Wilson and Lansing.[11] The President distributed copies of his original plan for the Covenant of the League, as he had hastily rewritten it since his return from Italy, and pointed out the features which he regarded as essential to any final scheme. At once Lansing began proposing objections, and mentioned that he had requested the legal advisers of the American delegation to draw up an outline or skeleton of a treaty. Wilson flared up angrily. With what Lansing calls great candor and emphasis, he declared that he did not intend to have lawyers drafting the peace. Lansing was the only lawyer on the delegation, and he took the hint to his very hurt bosom. After placing these initial criticisms before Wilson, he refused thereafter to bear any part in the revision of the Covenant, of which he unostentatiously washed his hands.

By the end of January three of the American delegates, Lansing, Bliss, and White, knew that they would play a minor rôle in the making of the treaty. The peace passed into the hands of two men from each of the five great Powers, ordinarily the head of the delegation and his foreign secretary. Wilson usually took Lansing to meetings of the Council of Ten, but it was Colonel House in the background who really counted.[12] Observers noted that the American and British leaders, Wilson and Lloyd George, seemed in fact less open to suggestions from their Foreign Ministers, Lansing and Balfour, than from any other source. But the other American delegates, as White makes clear, were frequently consulted by the President. A letter to the Assistant Secretary of State describes the situation:

WHITE TO WILLIAM PHILLIPS, JANUARY 24, 1919

The President himself is really a wonderful man, and the more I see of him the more I am impressed with that circumstance. He has absolutely established the combination of President and Prime Minister to an extent that I should never have believed possible, and he passes from one to the other in the most natural way in the world.

You are probably aware that your idea of a diplomatic secretary or

[11] Lansing, Robert, *The Peace Negotiations: A Personal Narrative*, p. 107.
[12] Cf. Baker, Ray Stannard, *Woodrow Wilson and World Settlement*, vol. i, p. 97 ff.; Seymour, Charles, *Intimate Papers of Colonel House*, vol. iv, p. 250 ff.

attaché did not work, and the Hôtel Murat is conducted on much the very same basis as the White House. The excellent Hoover [13] (happily now in a cutaway coat instead of the usual jacket) is in the anteroom and watches carefully all who approach, and at no time, from the beginning, has he had any idea that French generals or *attachés* of any kind should take his place in guarding the approach to the President. And really it seems to have gone off pretty well. . . . Miss Benham issues invitations to tea with Mrs. Wilson just as she did at Washington, and all seems as happy and serene as a marriage bell.

You have seen that the Conference was duly opened with considerable ceremony, and with that exception most of the business transacted among the delegates has so far been by the Prime Ministers of the various countries (of whom the President is proud to consider himself one) and Foreign Ministers, while our delegation has meetings with the President every day, to discuss what has taken place and what is coming on the next day. I am not at all sure that this is not a more expeditious way of getting through business than if all the members of each delegation were sitting around the table. I am glad to say so far things have gone well with our delegation. Possibly our people at home may have been somewhat astonished at the decision taken yesterday about Russia; that is to say, to summon the various contending parties, provided they proclaim a truce among themselves, to Prince's Isle in the Sea of Marmora, whither the Great Powers are each sending two delegates to meet them in the hope of effecting a reconciliation. If anyone suggests the horror, as no doubt some one will, of meeting the Bolsheviks for any purpose whatever, it may interest you to know that the only alternative (when the President brought the French finally to the point) was that a large military expedition should be sent into Russia, the greater part of which should be composed of our troops. You can easily imagine what sort of reception that project would have met with in our country, and the moment the President gave them to understand that it was impossible for us to fulfill our share of the proposal, it collapsed. The fact is that neither the British nor the French can send troops anywhere at present to fight out of their respective countries, for the simple reason that they are all tired out and will not go, as the Governments of these countries know very well.

The meetings of the Council of Ten, which White occasionally visited, were held under circumstances of the greatest dignity. In

[13] White of course refers to Irwin H. Hoover, the veteran chief usher of the White House.

the spacious study of the palace on the Quai d'Orsay, where high windows looked out on a formal lawn, with the winter snow or drizzle falling on the lazy Seine, the delegates gathered. At one end, seated with his colleague Pichon at a little table, with his back to a blazing fire of logs, was Clemenceau, the presiding officer; at his right were seated the other delegates, behind little tables facing him; at his left were the secretaries of the gathering. Officials of the smaller states and representatives of various interests, when called into the room to present their arguments and facts, stood with the secretaries facing the fireplace and Clemenceau, Lloyd George, Orlando, Makino, and Wilson. The Council of Ten, in its seventy-two sessions, did most of the preliminary work of the Conference; then it disappeared, the Council of Four emerged, and in the final period when the important decisions were made, the Four dominated the situation.

January was for White, as for everyone else, a month of endless conferences, inquiry, and exploration of international feeling and demands. He paid a short visit to the front, seeing Château Thierry, Belleau Wood, the vast area of devastation between the Argonne and Verdun, and Rheims. The desolation and horror of the spectacle affected him deeply, while he was left full of admiration for the fighting qualities the American troops had displayed. In Paris he saw Kermit and Theodore Roosevelt, saddened by their father's death. From day to day he had many talks with public men, including Clemenceau, Venizelos, Premier Huysmans of Belgium, and Signor Sonnino; and all the representatives of minor nations began calling to advocate their own particular views. Some of these men jarred upon him—Sonnino, for example, whom he regarded as the very embodiment of the extravagance of the Italian claims. Others, like Venizelos, who had an exceptionally attractive way of presenting his case, he liked to hear. But as he listened to one European spokesman after another, his feeling of distrust and suspicion increased. He wrote to Lodge in the busy hours when the Conference was just beginning:

WHITE TO LODGE, PARIS, JANUARY 14, 1919

I am sorry to say that, whether because of the fact that France now realizes that she is the only great military Power in Europe, or for some other reason—possibly the time given to the various political groups during the past month for reflection as to what they might compete with each other in asking for—the expectations of this country would seem to be considerably in excess of what they originally were: to wit, Alsace-Lorraine, plus of course the heaviest possible indemnities by way of reparation and restoration. One now hears a good deal about the whole of this side of the Rhine, and a very extensive and I cannot help think impolitic propaganda is being made in Luxembourg for its annexation to France rather than to Belgium, which has been counting upon that addition to her territory.

Then the idea has unfortunately been spread abroad by those in authority—notably Klotz, the Minister of Finances—that the indemnities to be received from Germany will be sufficient to prevent any increase in the taxation of this country (which as you know has not been made in the frank and practical way that the British and American increased taxation has been), and that not impossibly taxation will be lowered rather than raised, as a result of the German payments through a long series of years; which of course, the more one looks into it, the more one realizes to be an impossibility; but as the public has been led to believe the reverse, it will not be an easy thing for it to realize actual conditions when they are settled by the Conference. An emissary in the shape of an old friend of mine, long connected with public affairs here, actually came the other day to see me for the purpose of explaining that unless the Conference could secure a sufficient indemnity to prevent any increase in taxation, there would be a revolution in France. All of which I mention for your private information, and that you may realize how numerous and very real and complicated the problems are that we are likely to have to face.

Italy, as you probably know, wants everything; not only the Italian Irredenta which is traced in the interesting guide memorandum which you furnished me on the 2d of December and which I keep before me and have frequently read over since; but also Fiume, the greater part of Dalmatia, Dodecanese Islands, and much else besides; and, unfortunately, they are endeavoring to forestall the situation by a military penetration into those regions, whereby much local irritation and occasionally armed contests are caused, of which we hear through our military and naval intelligence.

The reparations problem was handed over to an expert commission, which included Thomas Lamont, Norman Davis, Bernard Baruch, and Vance McCormick. No one as yet had more than a vague idea of what it was possible for Germany to pay, but White did know that excessive indemnities would defeat their own purpose. On the League of Nations he was now definitely swinging over to the Wilsonian position; he added in his letter to Lodge:

In my last letter I mentioned a growing opinion that unless the League of Nations should be taken up almost if not actually as the first subject of discussion at the Conference, it would not be likely to materialize. That view has crystallized very materially during the past two or three weeks, and indeed, the general opinion now seems to be, as far as I can get at it, that as so many decisions of the Conference are likely to be affected by the existence of a League of Nations, it is of great importance to have that subject taken up and settled if possible as soon as may be.

I should be afraid of misleading you if I were to attempt to outline accurately the exact form which the League of Nations is likely to assume; there are various projects under consideration, and even our delegation has not quite settled the exact phraseology which we are prepared to advocate; but I have no reason to modify what I said on the subject in my last letter, and I have decided that, in view of the consensus of opinion previously referred to, it would be useless for me to make a point of the postponement of the question until after the other matters with which the Peace Conference will have to deal have been settled. . . .

I have not said anything about the President's reception in Italy, as it must have been so fully described by the many correspondents who accompanied him, but I am told, and have no reason to doubt, that nothing was ever seen like it and that in Milan and Turin particularly the demonstrations of enthusiasm were of a wonderful nature. So far he has shown himself quite equal in argument and clearness of statement to the statesmen of this and other countries whom he has had to deal with; although, up to the present time, I am not sure that he has produced any impression upon Sonnino, who is the embodiment of the extravagances of Italian claims, and appears to be staking his reputation upon his capacity for maintaining them, which of course he cannot do in the long run.

As the work of peacemaking really began, a multitude of duties devolved upon White. Commission after commission was created to deal with special problems, until more than fifty had been established; and upon one of the chief, which we shall describe later, he had to pull a steering oar. The American newspaper men fell into the habit of coming to him more frequently than to the other delegates, and by February 1st he was tacitly charged with the duty of holding a press conference each morning. He tried to make it as informative and satisfactory as possible. But the correspondents were clamorous for a precise statement of the "American plan," by which they meant the program of the American commissioners upon the League, the division of territory, the reparations, and other points; while the view of the delegates, and particularly of White, as an old diplomatist, was that the American group should keep its hand hidden till they learned what the other nations desired—first, because it would put the Allies in a good humor to have some of their suggestions accepted, and second, because the United States, holding in some respects a dominant position at the Conference, ought not to antagonize the other nations by taking a dictatorial stand and insisting on its own fixed terms at the outset. The Americans could lay down their stipulations when "it becomes absolutely necessary to do so, as of course it will sooner or later," White wrote his son. After seeing the newspaper men, he faced an incessant stream of callers. Each representative of a minor nation who could not get at Wilson's ear, or failing that, at Colonel House, used every device within reach to obtain an interview with White, Lansing, or Bliss.

White wrote with mingled humor and impatience of these besieging hosts, who devoured every possible moment of his time. He would sit down at his desk for a study of documents, and in rapid succession (we take a typical day) would come the representatives of the Aland Islands, to urge their union with Sweden; the representatives of the still unrecognized Esthonian Republic, to talk of the proposed conference of the various Russian factions at Prinkipo; the self-styled president of the Government of North Russia, a fine old gentleman from Archangel named Tchafkowsky, who brought the brilliant suggestion that if the Allies and the United States would not send an army against the Bolsheviki, then the League of Nations should enlist a great international force and dispatch it to Russia; a procession of Albanians, Siamese, Finns, Chinese, and others of every clime and race, with a sprinkling of American soldiers or Congressmen or mere visitors eager to learn something about the "inside" of the Conference—of which White still did not know a great deal more than they. As yet, in January and early February, there was a very little "inside" knowledge anywhere, and what existed was almost a monopoly of the favored members of the Council of Ten.

A plenary session of the Conference on January 25, 1919, with White concurring, adopted a resolution declaring that a League of Nations should be formed, that its constitution should be an integral part of the peace treaty, and that the work of drafting this constitution should be intrusted to a commission. This commission, over which President Wilson himself presided, set about its labors on February 2nd. White had little connection with its work, the American members being Wilson and House, but he heard much of its progress. At the same time, on January 25th, a Commission on the International Régime of Ports, Waterways, and Railways was established, with White, David Hunter Miller, and Manley O. Hudson as the American members. This body, as Mr. Ray Stannard Baker says, was one of the hardest-working groups in Paris, holding no fewer than forty-three meetings and publishing in the end a report of 400 printed pages which was a model of thoroughness in the discussion of intricate politico-economic questions.[14] While these and other commissions—on financial arrangements, on war criminals, on the economic clauses, on the former German colonies, on the protection of minorities, and so on— were busy, the Council of Ten was trying to thrash out some of the major issues of the Conference. There commenced a series of struggles, a clash of determined and persistent wills.

From behind the double doors where this Council sat there drifted out to White, to Bliss, and to the world in general rumors of the contests in which President Wilson was engaging as he met the Prime Ministers of France, Great Britain, and Italy. The last week in January was largely given up by the Council to the debate upon annexations. The French, the British, and the British Dominions demanded the right to take over the German colonies and the greater part of the Turkish Empire in full sovereignty; President Wilson refused to consent to the principle of such annexations, and insisted that these areas should pass under the control

[14] *Report*, Commission on the International Régime of Ports, Waterways, and Railways.

of the League. White heard of the dramatic scene when Lloyd
George, to reinforce his arguments, brought the Prime Ministers
of the young English-speaking democracies, Canada, South Africa,
New Zealand, and Australia, into the great room on the Quai
d'Orsay. The dominions declared that they meant to keep the
colonies which they had conquered. "Do you mean, Mr. Hughes,"
said President Wilson to the Australian leader, "that in certain circumstances you would place yourselves in opposition to the opinion
of the whole civilized world?" "That's about it, Mr. President,"
rejoined Hughes. White heard much of the campaign of propaganda which the French launched against Wilson's "impracticable
ideals" regarding the colonies and other questions; he saw the
French newspapers which contained vitriolic attacks on the President. The question of security was also coming up in the Council
of Ten. President Wilson advocated not only the disarmament of
Germany, but the serious limitation of armaments by all other
countries; but France was demanding protection either by
enormous military preparations or by military alliances—if possible, by both. M. Klotz continued to press his claims for the last
mark in reparations.

Meanwhile, the blockade of Germany, against which the Americans were all raising voices of protest, continued. Conditions in all
central, eastern, and southeastern Europe grew worse rather than
better. President Wilson had seen to it that economic experts had
been sent to Europe immediately after the armistice to deal with
feeding and general relief—Herbert Hoover, E. N. Hurley, Norman H. Davis, and others. In December there had been created an
Inter-Allied Supreme Council for Supply and Relief, with Mr.
Hoover as director-general; a body which developed in a short time
into the Supreme Economic Council. Again and again the President appealed for a free exportation of foodstuffs to the half-
starving populations of Central Europe, but always the French
Government thwarted him. This French policy filled White, who
had small grandchildren in Germany and heard much from his
daughter of the desperate plight of the people, with futile
indignation.[15]

[15] The food problem and its solution is most fully discussed in Temperley,
H. W. V., editor, *A History of the Peace Conference,* vol. v.

To do what he could in helping to find food for Europe, White cabled to Lodge again on January 19, 1919, protesting against the Senator's amendment to the Food bill excluding Bulgaria, Turkey, and German Austria from its provisions. He pointed out that a revolution in Bulgaria had placed a pro-Ally government in office, and that General Franchet d'Esperey had just urged immediate relief for the Bulgarians on the ground that if it were refused the government would fall and military operations recommence. As for Turkey, White cabled, the Christian population was so intermixed with the Moslems that the former would starve with the latter unless food arrived; while the position of Austria was tragic, and the Allies were actually furnishing her with the most important staples because they wished to save the new republican government. In a letter a few days later White added a few more arguments and spoke of a variety of matters—the uneasiness of the French over their Russian investments, a luncheon with Sazonov, the "general desire to get us into European affairs more and more, both for financial and other reasons," the emphatic refusal of the French and British peoples to send their troops to Russia or any other place for more fighting, and the check to Bolshevism in the German elections, with the more hopeful outlook for German unity.

The United States, cut off from any really reliable information of the developments at Paris, receiving a good deal of news from French and other sources hostile to Wilson, and falling into the backwash of the war, was beginning to survey the Peace Conference in a chilly mood. White's first sharp warning of this came in a letter from Senator Lodge dated February 1st. The hundred-million-dollar food bill, wrote Lodge, had been passed with great reluctance, amid much criticism in the Senate and outside; there was a feeling, particularly in the Senate, that Mr. Hoover would be likely to spend the money without much regard to the limitations imposed by Congress. There was also, he added, a great deal of irritation in the United States over the delay in making peace with Germany, and the country was finding it hard to understand the amount of time that had been taken up in discussing matters not essential to the treaty. He had himself read with interest and anxiety what White said in criticisim of France, and questioned White's opinion, saying that it might rest on exaggerated stories from selfish sources. It was plain that Lodge rather approved the French attitude; he spoke of France as the one nation which possessed a clear idea of what she wished to do in obtaining an early and effective peace. As for the German colonies, he believed that the United States had no interest in them. For evident reasons, there was a good deal of American concern over the Christians in Turkey and the right treatment of Greece, but the United States had no desire to meddle with African territory. The Senator threw out one more brief but ominous reference to the League. "It seems here pretty clear that the League of Nations is going to be a voluntary association, and the idea of putting force behind it is abandoned. If they do put force behind it, I think it will be ill received here by the country generally and I do not believe it could pass the Senate."

It was not until the second week in February that White could write to Lodge again; and when he did so, it was in a somewhat stiffer temper. The striking feature of his long rejoinder was the warmth with which he now espoused the League of Nations. He began with a paragraph on the preposterous claims of the Italians, who were asking for almost everything in sight—Fiume, Sebenico, Zara, Pola, the Dodecanese, and a large slice of Dalmatia. The question of Fiume, indeed, was now giving White anxiety, for he regarded it as the one good outlet to the sea for the Jugo-Slavs. An Italian agent had told him confidentially that Italy would quit the Conference before it would give up the port. "I ventured to suggest," wrote White, "that it did not seem to me that the sympathies of the world, and particularly of our country, would be aroused by the adoption of that course." But he gave special attention to the League, seeking to reassure and enlighten Senator Lodge.

WHITE TO LODGE, PARIS, FEBRUARY 10, 1919

Since my last letter the Conference has got down pretty steadily to work. The various committees have been formed, and that of the League of Nations is working every night in this hotel, with the President in the chair, from about half-past eight until nearly midnight, as well as in the daytime when possible. The proceedings have been, on the whole, harmonious, and the draft is practically agreed upon, and will be laid before the Conference this afternoon.

With regard to what you say in your letter on that subject, I can only repeat once more than no member of this Commission has the slightest intention, or ever has had, of allowing our army and navy to be placed in a position in which it can be subject to the orders of any international body; nor, so far as I have heard on the part of anyone, of abandoning or modifying the Monroe Doctrine. I entirely agree with you in what you say as to the difficulty of expressing an opinion about the League of Nations until there is a full knowledge of what it means; that is, until the draft of the committee of the Conference is finally adopted and brought before that body. Its cardinal principle, as I understand it, is that the invasion of any country by another, as for instance, Belgium and France in the late war, will be *ipso facto* an act of war not only against the nation invaded, but against the other nations forming part of the League, and indeed, against any others not members thereof who choose so to consider it. Of course, an act of war on one side does not absolutely require its being accepted as such by the other, but there is no doubt that if the Germans had been sure that their invasion of Belgium would have actually been an act of war against England, they would not have attempted it.

You are reported by the papers as having spoken in the Senate against the mandatory principle as one of the probable features of the League of Nations; but I have nowhere seen as yet what you actually said upon that subject. Personally, I cannot but feel, from what I have already seen at the Conference of the tendency of every nation, excepting perhaps Great Britain, to grab all that it can get, that the only way to stop that tendency is the proposed mandate of the League of Nations which, while giving the government of colonies or backward countries into the charge under such mandate of a nation which would otherwise have annexed them, is the only way to stop the tendency to which I have referred. I think we shall find that principle exceedingly useful when the claims of Japan come to be considered, which, as you foreshadowed in your memorandum, include Kiau-chau and the Caroline Islands. A mandate to Japan under the League of Nations to administer the islands in question would be a very different thing from their annexation to that Empire, and the principle of no annexations will make it less difficult to convey to Japan the idea that China's lease of Kiau-chau to Germany came to an end when those two countries went to war with each other, and consequently that Japan has no claim to that port and its hinterland under that lease, which I have reason to believe is what she is likely to claim. . . .

I am greatly interested in what you say as to the possibility of our people's being willing to accept a mandate from the League of Nations to administer Constantinople and the Bosporus. Suggestions to that effect —also in respect to our doing likewise for Armenia and others—have been made to me and others of our delegation from many different sources. Our acceptance would simplify many of the difficulties now attending any arrangement for the government of that part of the world. I had a sort of feeling myself that, with time to educate public opinion up to the idea that our so doing would be for the world's good and the promotion of peace, our people might possibly not be unwilling to assume that amount of responsibility, and I am exceedingly glad to know that you are inclined to that opinion.

There followed in White's letter some remarks upon Armenia, for which he felt then and later that the United States should accept a mandate; the mandate which might have saved the Armenian people, but which the United States was too cautious, too fearful of international entanglements, to assume. White still hoped that the interest of the Protestant churches in the fate of the Christian Armenians would create a favorable public feeling. He recognized that without this public feeling it would be impossible to undertake anything, and that the Peace Commission could never pledge the country without fairly definite assurance of the pledge being redeemed; and he asked Lodge if he could not obtain an expression of opinion in the Senate by taking up the subject in one of his speeches. He continued:

I do not think it will be possible to make Greece the mandatary for Constantinople as suggested in your memorandum, although Venizelos greatly desires it; as such an arrangement would be unacceptable to France, and still more to Italy, which latter would absolutely object to it.

I am telling you all this not with a view to giving an idea that I consider the questions with which we have to deal insoluble, but merely to show you how many difficulties and how many points of view there are in the way of a satisfactory settlement. I entirely agree with you as to the importance of making peace as quickly as possible, but the delay is no fault of ours. We expected to get to work with the representatives of the other great Powers on the 21st of December, and it was a great disappointment to the President and to the rest of the delegation that neither France nor England, for various reasons, were disposed to take that view. For one reason, they were not ready with their bills for damages and indemnities, and, of course, the British election did come about that time; and then it seemed important, as indeed I think it was, that the President should visit Great Britain and Italy, both of which countries were clamoring for him to go to see them. . . .

The situation of France, in regard to taxation during the war, is exceedingly curious, and I am more and more impressed with that view as I become better acquainted with the course pursued.

Although the income tax was voted, it was only partly collected, and from persons who had made a return of such an amount of their income, I am told, as their *notaire* or *homme d'affaires* thought reasonable and proper; but I am inclined to think that it was not considered necessary to pay the full amount of one's income. . . . I have made inquiry on this subject of a considerable number of my friends who have a goodly share of this world's possessions, and the answer is invariably the same; that in no case has any income tax been applied for, much less collected, from a full return; and in reply to an inquiry of mine for an explanation of this circumstance, an official of the Ministry of Finance said very frankly that the government was afraid that if they attempted to collect any serious increase in the taxes the people would not have been disposed to go on with the war.

The French, said this official somewhat brutally, "will give their blood, but not their francs." [16] After some remarks upon French unreasonableness with regard to indemnities, and the very bad qualities of Marshal Foch as a politician, "a rôle which he seems somewhat tempted to assume since the realization that France has changed places with Germany in becoming the great military Power of Europe," White reverted to Wilson. His letter continued:

It is probable that before another letter from me can reach you, the President will have returned to Washington, and I feel that, in justice to him, I ought to say that our national dignity has not only not suffered by reason of his trip abroad, but that it has been materially enhanced by his presence in Europe, and in saying this I ought to add

[16] White wrote in another memorandum that he had asked M. Klotz: "Why didn't you make the people pay heavy income taxes during the war, as the British and Americans did?" To which M. Klotz replied: "If we had, the war would have been over in a few months. The French peasant will give up his sons, but he will not give up his money."

that, while approving of the principle of our Presidents exchanging visits occasionally with other chiefs of state, I was, before leaving home and for some little time after arriving here, exceedingly uneasy at the idea of his attending the Peace Conference, for reasons which I think I mentioned to you; but my anxiety in that respect has entirely disappeared. It may be that many of the delegates, as you suggest, are not entirely in sympathy with his views, but you may have observed that not one of them has yet deemed it wise to place himself before the public in opposition to the President.

His reception by the Chamber of Deputies was an exceedingly impressive event. Deschanel's speech was a real work of art from every point of view; admirably delivered by a man of marked personal distinction and exceptional gifts as an orator, who laid exactly the right emphasis on every word; and the President's reply, which has doubtless been cabled to our newspapers, delivered with equal dignity, was at times received with great enthusiasm, and was listened to by the members, as well as the President of the Chamber, all standing.

All of which is not meant to convey the idea of agreement, on my part, with all of the President's views, but I am merely stating, for your information before his return home, what I believe to be his due as to the dignity and distinction which have characterized everything which he has done in Europe, and particularly every occasion on which he has come in contact either with the public or with private indviduals. I have seen nothing but courtesy on his part to the various members of our own delegation; and in my own case he has always been ready to listen, and in several cases to accept suggestions, particularly in the phraseology of his draft of the constitution of the League of Nations. And there is no doubt that he has dealt with other leading members of the Conference with great tact.

It grieved White, a life-long admirer of France, to be compelled to condemn the methods and aims of the French leaders—of Poincaré, Foch, Klotz, and to a lesser extent Clemenceau. The insistence of these Frenchmen upon the continued blockade of Germany seemed to him inhuman and short-sighted. The unconcealed desire of Foch and Poincaré to wrest the Rhineland from Germany impressed him as a violation of the principles announced by the United States, a gross injustice, and if carried into effect, a certain cause of future war. He had no use for M. Klotz's mixture of greediness and timidity in approaching the problems of reparations and taxes. An additional irritant was the demand of Marshal Foch that at each renewal of the armistice, harsher terms should be imposed upon Germany. White and General Bliss repeatedly talked of the subject. Bliss had wished one armistice agreement and only one, which in his opinion should have been definitive. White entirely shared the views which Bliss was expressing in the Supreme War Council; and in closing this letter of February 10th, he included some plain words about France:

There are many undercurrents here of political intrigue, which bear more or less upon the Conference, and that circumstance is perhaps one of the unavoidable objections to its having been held in France. But it is difficult, in a country such as this, or indeed in almost any country, in these days, to get men in public life to look beyond their own immediate interests or what they conceive to be those of their country, irrespective of any other. I shall be able to tell you more of this when we again meet. One of the reasons why I think they were not in a great hurry to get under way with the peace negotiations is that they hoped by these monthly renewals of the Armistice to realize more fully what they think will be needed in the Peace Treaty, and meanwhile to enforce at each renewal of the former, new conditions not originally contemplated. As I understood the Armistice, it was to be renewed as originally agreed upon until the Peace Treaty should be signed, and I cannot help thinking that these periodical renewals, which cause a good deal of agitation once a month, with suggestions from all sides as to what new conditions should be made, are undesirable and hardly straightforward; besides giving the Germans something to object to each time on the ground that it was not originally contemplated and also an increasing amount of knowledge beforehand as to restrictions likely to be imposed upon them in the Peace Treaty, instead of having them discover all that for the first time upon their arrival there.

As much as his limited time allowed, White received and talked with members of the French Chamber, who were only too glad to discuss the Conference with him and learn his views. They thought of little, most of them, but of the means of protecting France against Germany; as White said, repeating a phrase current among the Americans and British in Paris, the whole people seemed a little shell-shocked. They honestly feared, he discovered, that within a few years Germany would once more fall upon them. It was a fear which struck White as quite illusory, for he was certain the Germans had had enough of war and would be very slow indeed to resume that method of extending their power and wealth. Various Frenchmen told him that there seemed to be no guaranty in the League of Nations plan for the protection of France. To this his invariable reply was that they were thinking of the old protection of armies and strategic frontiers, and that the League offered a new-style protection in world-wide sentiment for peace, supported by economic sanctions and perhaps in any really desperate crisis by still other and stronger weapons.

During the first fortnight of February interest centered almost entirely in the Council of Ten and the greatest of the commissions, that on the League of Nations, though in the background a number of the other commissions were busy upon highly important problems. The President and his helpers were bending every effort to get their essential work done before Wilson was compelled to leave for Washington to be present at the adjournment of Congress on March 4th. By tremendous efforts they succeeded. On February 12th Wilson and Clemenceau met in the Council of Ten in a final direct clash over the renewal of the Armistice, and the President, supported by Balfour, was victorious. Clemenceau's demands for new terms and for limiting the renewal to one month were defeated. Instead, the renewal was made on practically the former terms, and was for an indefinite period, while it was provided that the final military and naval terms should be drafted immediately in the form of a preliminary treaty, and offered to the Germans. Two days later, on February 14th, in one of the most interesting and momentous of all sessions of the full Peace Conference, President Wilson presented the finished Covenant of the League, and read it to the assembled representatives of half the peoples of the globe. "A living thing is born," he declared. "While it is elastic, while it is general in its terms, it is definite in one thing that we are called upon to make definite. It is a definite guaranty of peace. It is a definite guaranty by word against aggression." [17]

Among the members and advisers of the American Commission, in these days, there was something like a feeling of exultation. The Conference had opened under threatening auspices, with every

[17] Wilson's address is published in a large number of printed collections of his addresses;—*e.g.*, Shaw, Albert, editor, *The Messages and Papers of Woodrow Wilson*, vol. ii, p. 623 ff.

prospect uncertain; now, after a month, it had made the most encouraging progress along the lines the Americans had marked out. The League had been made an integral part of the peace, and the work of drafting its constitution had been given due precedence. The principle of outright annexations and a division of booty had been refused application to the German colonies. Foch's attempt to impose still harsher military conditions upon the German Republic had been frustrated. Europe was still seething with discontent and change, still racked by misery and starvation, but beginning here and there to show evidences of recuperation. There was a feeling in the air, which White felt but did not wholly trust, that the worst might already be over. Actually the worst of the fighting in Paris, and of bickering over the treaty terms in both Europe and America, was still to come.

It was in these seemingly brighter hours, as he read the accounts of the President's departure westward from the harbor of Brest, and took up the task of attending the Council of Ten in alternation with Colonel House, that White found time to write another exceedingly long letter. That of February 10th had filled thirteen typewritten pages; this of a week later filled seven. He began by explaining again to Senator Lodge the long delays:

WHITE TO LODGE, PARIS, FEBRUARY 17, 1919

The fact is, the cessation of the war came too suddenly and found everyone over here—and particularly in France—unprepared to deal with it, and since I have seen during the last few weeks the elaborate and deliberate way in which they work up all these various questions in the respective ministries concerned, I see how impossible it was from their point of view for us to get to work when we arrived in December, and how it is only now becoming possible for them to face the serious issues, after having given them a sufficient amount of study in the different ministries. But even now we have not yet succeeded in getting definite figures in respect to the claims for indemnities against Germany. The lowest figure I have heard mentioned is one hundred billions, and the highest one hundred and twenty billions of dollars. But until the actual statement is produced at the Conference by the various Powers concerned, it is, of course, impossible to tell you what the exact figure is; nor have our banking and treasury experts yet told us what they think approximately Germany will be able to pay. It may interest you to know that, as the idea seems now pretty general that "an international arrangement" is to be made for paying the expenses of the war (an idea which, let me say, we have not given the slightest encouragement, as, under that arrangement, we are expected to pay by far the largest share and possibly to advance as a loan the share of most of the other Powers), there is no particular interest in keeping the amount down. The latest news is that Germany will be expected to pay all the costs of the war of every nation of every sort and kind.

Hughes, of Australia, has stated plainly that he considers the man in Australia, who had to mortgage his house to pay taxes or other expenses connected with sending Australian troops to the war, is in exactly the same position as the unfortunate inhabitant of the towns of Belgium and France which have been annihilated and whose industries have been systematically destroyed by the Germans; and so it goes merrily on.

White, as he explained, had warned the French against entertaining any hope that the American people would be inclined to foot the war bills:

We are waiting until our experts furnish us with figures as to the possibilities before making our position known, but confidentially, when Pichon yesterday suggested to me in a private talk, and, of course, unofficially, this idea of a combined Allied financial arrangement, I asked him where he thought the money was coming from, and, upon his hesitating, I suggested whether he thought there was much money anywhere except in the United States and upon his assenting to that proposition, I had no hesitancy in telling him that I had not the slightest idea that our people would consent to anything of the kind. Of course, it may be that general bankruptcy in Europe, which I suppose is conceivable if Germany cannot pay all the debts and we are unwilling to advance the rest of them, may be a worse situation for the world at large than for us to have to do something of this kind. But I am bound to say, after reading as I have today in one of the papers, that in making up our accounts it is found that the war has cost us twenty-six billions and a considerable number more of millions, I do not feel very much inclined to assume further financial responsibilities on a very large scale.

From this subject he returned to the League of Nations and its connection with the delay of the Conference:

It may interest you to know that Wickersham is favorably impressed by the draft for the League of Nations, and says that much more has been obtained of a substantial character than he ever believed possible, and while of course perfection is not obtainable—certainly not in the first draft of such a far-reaching plan—nevertheless it is an exceedingly good start. He was present at the Conference and heard the President read the draft and make the speech before laying it on the table.

Before you receive this the President will have had the opportunity he has arranged for explaining to you and the other members of the Foreign Affairs Committee the answers, as he conceives them, to such objections as may be raised (and of course a number must be) by the members of these bodies. I shall be curious to know your impressions of the document.

In reply to the criticism that time has been wasted by placing the League of Nations before other matters at the Conference, you will see from what I have already said in respect to the financial and other questions that such time has not been wasted, by us at least, and moreover there have been constant meetings between the various Delegates and exchanges of views and endeavors to come together all the time since the Conference met, in respect to most, if not all, matters of importance which are to come before us. We are very strongly desirous of getting the preliminaries of peace with Germany signed on the three or four main questions—abandonment of her colonies, limitation of her boundaries, the financial payments, and one or two other matters—and propose making every effort to bring that about.

With President Wilson's temporary absence on his trip to the United States, the first phase of the Peace Conference came to an end. There was, indeed, a lull or interim period in which the Triumvirate who really controlled the Conference were all absent; for Clemenceau was shot on February 19th, while Lloyd George returned to London to attend to pressing domestic problems. There ensued a period in which for three weeks Balfour and Colonel House exercised an ascendency over the Conference, and in which the center of interest was no longer the Council of Ten, but the work of the commissions, which these two men pushed forward with all possible speed. Five days after White's letter of February 17th, Balfour took up with energy the task of expediting the general labors of the Conference. He presented a motion in the Council of Ten that it was desirable to consider immediately certain "Preliminary Peace Terms with Germany," without prejudice to the decision of the Supreme War Council to present naval, military, and air conditions at an early date; and to press the necessary investigations with all speed. The Council of Ten acted favorably on this motion.[18] He also obtained a decision that the work of the territorial commissions should be presented, in finished form, by March 8th. The road to the great final decisions was to be opened rapidly. For this some of the conditions were favorable. A saner view, as White noted, was beginning to be taken by Frenchmen.

WHITE TO LODGE, PARIS, FEBRUARY 20, 1919

I am glad to tell you, of course very confidentially, that I understand Foch (since his last return from Treves to meet the Germans about the renewal of the armistice) has expressed himself as being much impressed with the necessity of losing no further time in arranging peace terms with Germany, which is what we have been advocating all along, and particularly with the fact that if they are not concluded before long, the difficulties in bringing about such conclusion may be greatly increased; because, if a very large number of men in that country who are being gradually demobilized are not soon afforded the means of going to work, there is little doubt that Bolshevism will resume its sway—a prospect which, I need scarcely say, is not pleasing to authorities of this country. That circumstance and the attack on Clemenceau's life, one of the features of which is an evidence of the unrest and discontent prevailing here and elsewhere among the people, will, I hope, lend weight to our constantly repeated views on the subject; and perhaps you may hear before long of very material progress towards the conclusion of peace between the Allies and Germany, as Foch has at last adopted, I understand, our idea as to the fixing of a lump sum to be paid by Germany, the division of which can be arranged between the different Powers afterwards.

I do not think you need be in any fear of a recrudescence of the old Prussian Government. From all that we hear, the contempt for the late military system goes so far that uniforms are at a distinct discount at present. . . .

I agree absolutely with you in the feeling that "we have got to take our share in carrying out the peace, which is really a part of the war"; though I apprehend a great deal of difficulty in making our people take that view of our future responsibilities.

[18] This subject is fully discussed in Seymour, Charles, editor, *The Intimate Papers of Colonel House,* vol. iv, p. 321 ff.; Mr. Seymour emphasizes the argument for compromise arrangements during Wilson's absence. But White came to believe that House's genius for conciliation led him astray.

But not all was well. President Wilson was kept informed of the plans which Balfour and House had laid in concert for clearing the ground, and of their hopes for expediting the general terms of peace while safeguarding the League; and busy with his problems in the United States, he signified no disapproval. Early in March reports from the commissions began to be turned in. Steady progress was made before President Wilson returned to Paris, after an absence of almost precisely a month, on March 14th. For this Colonel House deserves credit; but at the same time Colonel House evinced a tendency to make concessions, to compromise on important points, which deeply disturbed both White and General Bliss. They shortly had an uneasy feeling that he was surrendering too much. White tells us that a tension developed between House and Bliss which made it necessary for him to use his calming influence. For himself, he gradually lost confidence in House's strength or willingness to fight for a principle. When President Wilson returned, he at first seemed to accept what had been done and what was going forward. But there quickly supervened, in the later phase of the Conference, a significant change in his attitude toward Colonel House, and White and others who knew the inside of affairs marked a growing coldness. There was no doubt in White's mind, as we shall see later, that President Wilson was seized by the same distrust of House that he himself felt, and that it had precisely the same cause.

Meanwhile, events of the greatest importance were taking place in the United States. Wilson's principal objects in returning to America were two: to sign the bills of the expiring Sixty-fifth Congress, and to discuss both publicly before the country, and privately with the leaders of Congress, the proposed Covenant of the League of Nations. Word had come from the United States that public sentiment was dubious and in part hostile. White thought that Wilson ought to return and stay to deal with this public feeling, guiding the final Paris negotiations by cable. On Colonel House's advice, the President before sailing cabled a request to the Senate and House Committees on Foreign Affairs to dine with him at the White House on February 26th, asking that Congress should meanwhile refrain from making the League a subject of debate. He wished to go over the Covenant with the two committees "article by article." The eyes of a great part of the world, which had been fixed upon President Wilson's attempted leadership in Paris, now swung to his attempted leadership in Washington. White's interests also partly turned to Washington, and he endeavored more vigorously than any other American delegate to take a share in the American discussion. To his attempted coöperation with President Wilson we shall now turn.

CHAPTER TWENTY-ONE

The Peace Conference: Wilson and Lodge

ON FEBRUARY 20, 1919, President Wilson's ship was in mid-Atlantic, heading toward Boston; he was to land there on the 25th and speak on the League. White had been up late the previous evening at a large dinner at the British Embassy in honor of the Prince of Wales. He had chatted with the prince, telling him how well he had known his grandfather and great-grandmother when they were sovereigns, and how Mrs. White had been asked to see the Prince when he was a baby two weeks old. That morning he, Lansing, Bliss, and Mr. John Foster Dulles had sat in a meeting of the Peace Commissioners. They had taken up the usual round of more or less important matters: a report from Mr. Hoover on the food situation, the work of Archibald Cary Coolidge on the Carinthian boundary, a violation of the President's confidence by a reporter for the Paris *Herald*, the security for the proposed food loan of $60,000,000 to Austria, a memorandum from the Danish Red Cross on Bolshevik atrocities, and so on. These meetings were ordinarily dull affairs, and White was glad to conclude this one; on returning from it, he found much to concern him in a letter from Lodge and in some Washington dispatches.

Atlantic mail communications were still in confusion, and Lodge's letter of February 1st had taken twenty days to arrive. We have already sketched its contents—its objections to the delay in Paris, its espousal of the French views, its comment on the impossibility of inducing the United States to take charge of any Germany colonies in Africa. The news dispatches supplemented it by speaking of the growing irritation in the Senate against the League, the preparations for giving Wilson a rough reception, and the feeling of some Senators that Wilson had been unfair in promising a Boston speech when he had requested them to refrain from any public discussion. Senator Borah had attacked the Covenant the day Wilson sailed, as "a renunciation of the Monroe Doctrine" and as wiping out "all distinction between European and American affairs." Senator Frelinghuysen had defiantly announced, "I still stand for American independence." [1] White's sensitiveness to the situation is shown by the fact that he immediately sat down and answered Lodge in a cablegram:

WHITE TO LODGE, PARIS, FEBRUARY 20, 1919

Respecting irritation at delay in concluding peace, mentioned second page your letter February 1, I sent you yesterday by courier document containing military peace terms urged by General Bliss on Supreme War Council with President's approval for original armistice November eleventh which Foch declined to accept. They involved complete disarmament and demobilization of German army. Have reason to hope efforts we have been steadily making to push settlement of peace terms with Germany may before long be successful. Delay not our fault. President landing Boston because Mayor Peters urging him to come there for more than a year and certain reasons render landing New York undesirable. Papers announce he will speak Boston, which I believe erroneous. When leaving he had no such intention at Boston or elsewhere before meeting Foreign Relations Committees. Condition Clemenceau precarious next few days, owing advanced age. His absence from Conference even short time very unfortunate just now. Attack symptomatic of unrest, general uneasiness, and discontent. Lieutenant Condon, my military secretary, intelligent and discreet, arriving and returning with President, will visit you at my request for impressions you may confide to him.[2]

With this cablegram went another long letter, from which it is unnecessary to quote again in any detail. White was much grieved by the attack on Clemenceau, and afraid that M. Pichon, a man of very different caliber, would try to manœuvre Balfour out of the principal position. Moreover, Foch had just been brought to reason on the question of the armistice, and White had trusted to Clemenceau to keep him in that frame of mind—for he recognized that Clemenceau, despite his hatred of Germany and whole-souled devo-

[1] New York *Times*, February 16, 1919.

[2] On February 16th the Germans had signed a renewal of the Armistice, its terms restricting the German operations against Poland. The Germans called the new terms oppressive; they also bitterly attacked the continuance of the food blockade, and Herr Erzberger said that many Germans were starving. The action of Congress in so drafting the hundred-million-dollar food bill as to deny Germany its benefits was deeply resented.

tion to France's interests alone, was essentially far more moderate than Foch or Poincaré. He discouraged the idea of our ever taking over any of the African colonies; suggested that Lodge would do well to talk with George Wickersham when the latter arrived from Paris, for he understood many of the difficulties under which the Peace Conference was laboring; and wrote reassuringly of Germany's new hatred of militarism. It was a tactful letter, and mentioned Wilson only once. "I am eagerly looking forward to your next letter and especially to your views after having seen the President," concluded White. "Yours affectionately . . ."

For the position which Senator Lodge and others were taking in criticism of the League of Nations plan there was a very real measure of justification. The League Covenant, as it had been tentatively accepted on February 14th and published to the world, was full of faults. In the form it then had it showed hasty preparation, with various rough edges, loose phrasing, and a number of lacunæ. Nothing whatever was said of the possibility of any member state withdrawing from the League. There was no reference to the Monroe Doctrine. It was not clear that the decisions of the League Council must be unanimous, that being left to inference, nor was it clear that purely domestic questions, such as a nation's control of its own immigration policies, were beyond the jurisdiction of the League. There were minor defects which to careful students seemed regrettable and even dangerous. It was of course untrue, as White had repeatedly said, that the preparation of the League Covenant had slowed up the general work of peacemaking; on the contrary, it had expedited that work. But the principal reason why this fact was not understood by many American critics was that President Wilson, despite the pleadings of Ray Stannard Baker and others, had provided no proper machinery of publicity. White had taken a keen interest in the framing of the Covenant, and was responsible for the clear exclusion of any idea of the League ever controlling any national army or navy, on which he had several times spoken to Wilson. He believed with Lord Robert Cecil that the League was an eminently practical scheme which would minimize the danger of any great international conflict. But he felt that there were flaws in the instrument.

Wilson's speech in Boston was delivered to a nation tense with interest. The Senate had paid no attention to the President's request for a postponement of discussion. It had begun debate on the Covenant February 18th, Poindexter and Fess attacking the League. Mr. Taft answered in San Francisco, saying that "most of the men who are sitting up with the Constitution to defeat the League are men whom I would not trust overnight." [3] White, like others, was somewhat disappointed in Wilson's address, which he thought offered an inspiring picture of his ideal of a society of peace, but which seemed to him to deal too much in generalities and too little in specific explanations and arguments. Then the President went direct from Boston to Washington for his dinner of February 26th to the two Congressional committees. Mr. Borah had ostentatiously refused the President's invitation, writing that nothing Wilson could say would cause him to change his mind, while Senator Fall did the President the favor of also staying at home.

It was a historic dinner, and White was fortunate in having reports of it from two friends, Senator Lodge and Representative Rogers. Covers were laid in the state dining-room for thirty-six. Lodge escorted Mrs. Wilson from the table. The guests retired to the East Room, where they seated themselves in an oval, at the apex of which was President Wilson. The frame of mind in which Lodge had approached the dinner was revealed in a letter he mailed to White five days before it occurred. Again he declared his impatience with the delay in Paris, which was due only to one thing, the discussion of the League; again, in referring to the armistice, he declared his faith in France—"I have absolute confidence in Marshal Foch. I am certain that nothing he demands or agrees to would be for the benefit of Germany." (White indorsed that last sentence!) He spoke briefly of Wilson's invitation. "As he is the President of the United States, of course I accepted the invitation to the dinner. I should not have thought of doing otherwise. I also felt, as a gentleman and man of honor, that having accepted the invitation to dinner I should comply with his request not to discuss the terms of the League as set forth in the draft of the committee, until after the dinner. The President, however, does not seem to look at it in the same way, and is going to land in Boston, my own

[3] Senator Reed of Missouri distinguished himself by calling the League "infamous."—New York *Times*, February 19-24, 1919.

city, and there address a great mass meeting which is all arranged for while I am reduced to silence because I wish to observe what I think is required of an honorable man." Ten days later Lodge incorporated in a long letter a paragraph on his meeting with Wilson.

LODGE TO WHITE, WASHINGTON, MARCH 5, 1919

If George Wickersham likes that League as now presented, he is easily pleased. It is one of the worst-drawn documents I have ever read. The drafting clerk of the Committee on Appropriations could have drawn a better instrument. It is full of doubtful points about which there would be discussion in the League itself before a year had been passed. There is a majority against that League in the Senate today. The 39 signers of the resolution, saying they could not accept it, represent more than a majority. A point had been reached where the Senate made up its mind that it was time the Peace Conference knew that the President was not the only part of the government necessary to the making of a treaty and that there were other views to be considered. Nobody is against a League which will make for the peace of the world, but there is a strong body of opinion, which seems to be constantly growing, that this League will not make for the peace of the world and there is great hostility to the abandonment of the Monroe Doctrine, to bringing immigration and similar questions within the jurisdiction of the League, and to Article 10 with its guarantees of the political independence and territorial integrity of every nation on the face of the earth. A guarantee by the United States will have to be carried out absolutely and many people hesitate about such an enormous pledge, put into a League which is indissoluble and where no right of withdrawal is provided.

If General Bliss's scheme had been adopted it might have expedited matters, but the fact remains that the time of the Conference has been largely taken up by the League and that substantially little progress has been made on the peace with Germany, which ought to have been made first. The demand for the complete return of our soldiers, which can only follow on the proclamation of the German peace, is constantly rising more loudly and strongly.

I cannot imagine that the United States would ever think of entering into an agreement to pool all the debts of the war and pay the lion's share; in fact, I do not believe the United States would enter into any such agreement at all and justice does not demand it. I hope they will make the indemnities to be paid by Germany as heavy as is consistent with their being paid and will take due security for their payment.

For obvious reasons I will not go into the question of the dinner at the White House. The President was very civil and answered questions, but we got no information that we did not have before, and his explanations, like those of everybody else, were based largely upon necessary inferences. The only way to answer the questions which arise and upon which men differ, in regard to the interpretation of the articles, is in the instrument itself. The constitution of the League must be so precisely and well drawn that it will answer all questions or else raise none.

There can be no doubt that these last two sentences of Lodge's stated a valid criticism. He wrote later in his book on the Senate and the League that Wilson's performance under Senator Brandegee's searching cross-examination was anything but good, and that the Congressmen went away as wise as they came. But there is equally little doubt that the President made an earnest effort to be informative. Senator Pittman justly spoke of "the clear, frank, and cordial manner in which the President invited and answered all questions." John Jacob Rogers took a favorable view of the meeting, and wrote to White:

JOHN JACOB ROGERS TO WHITE, WASHINGTON, MARCH 3, 1919

The White House dinner a week ago tonight was a most interesting one and in most respects a memorable one. I thought the President appeared extremely well. He submitted himself to quite rigorous cross-examination for two hours, answering every question, easy or difficult, as fully as possible and with apparent candor. He showed not the slightest vexation, even when Senator Brandegee was pressing him rather closely on certain of the difficulties which to his mind were of importance. I never saw Mr. Wilson appear so human or so attractive as that night. There was no suggestion of a feeling of militant arrogance about him. He apparently tried to give the impression that he was really one of the circle in the East Room, who was answering rather than asking questions only because he had been so recently in Paris, and had been a factor in the preparation of the instrument under discussion. He showed a good general familiarity with the document itself—of which, by the way, he did not have a copy at any time before him during the two hours—but I think scarcely had a letter-perfect knowledge of some of the minor details. I do not say this in criticism, for my own impression was that he was as thoroughly versed as he need have been, or indeed could reasonably have been expected to be. But some of the Senators there that night thought that he was not at all adequately informed. As I said, my own impression was quite the opposite.[4]

It was inevitable that, with so much misunderstanding on both sides and so little flexibility of temper on either, the President and his senatorial critics should not only drift far apart, but should commit themselves to antagonistic positions. It was this *committing* of the two sides, this taking up of an unchangeable stand, which White and other sober onlookers dreaded. He was willing to see the two sides differ if only the situation were kept fluid, if only a subsequent agreement remained possible. But the die was now cast by both. The greatest bitterness was becoming evident. Immediately after the White House dinner Senators Lodge and Knox assailed the Covenant and again demanded that peace be put first and a possible League left till later. Lodge declared that the United States must not be drawn "by any glittering delusions, through specious devices of supernational government, within the toils of international socialism and anarchy."[5] Knox a day later called the League proposal "a betrayal of the people." On March 2nd Senator Brandegee proposed the famous round-robin which Knox drafted and thirty-nine Senators and Senators-elect promptly signed; a round-robin which declared that it was the sense of the Senate that negotiations should immediately be directed to making peace, and that only when this was done should tne League be taken up. Just before midnight on March 3rd Lodge arose in the Senate and read this declaration and the signatures. Senator Swanson instantly objected to consideration of the subject, but Lodge's purpose had been served; the declaration had gone into the *Congressional Record* and had been flashed all over the United States and the world.

It was a defiance to which President Wilson lost no time in making defiant answer. The following evening, March 4th, he was in New York on his way back to Paris. Congress had adjourned at noon, after a heated filibuster which had killed indispensable appropriation bills and made an extra session unescapable. The President rode to the Metropolitan Opera House through one of

[4] See the *Congressional Record*, February 28, 1919, for discussion of the New York *Sun's* caustic article on the dinner.

[5] *Congressional Record*, February 28, 1919.

the greatest demonstrations ever seen in the city. Caruso sang "The Star-spangled Banner"; Taft and Wilson emerged on the stage arm-in-arm; Governor Smith introduced them. To his applauding audience, Wilson declared that when the treaty came back, "gentlemen on this side will find the Covenant not only tied in it, but so many threads of the Treaty tied to the Covenant that you cannot dissect the Covenant from the Treaty without destroying the whole vital structure." Immediately afterward he went aboard his ship and sailed again for Europe.

To White the heated Senate attacks seemed extravagant and absurd; the President's defiance seemed impolitic. He thought that Wilson should never have returned to Paris. He should have stayed in Washington, called his extra session at once and faced his Senate opponents, and appealed to the still ill-informed sentiment of the country to support him. His work in Paris he should have deputed to others, keeping the final decisions in his own hands. In White's opinion, affairs in both Paris and Washington would then have gone far better.

In the Paris *Herald* of March 6th White read the headlines which announced, "World League imperiled by Senators' Action." The dispatches told of the round robin, the senatorial filibuster on the finance bills, and the certainty that the League Covenant could not be ratified unless amended. Though two days earlier he had read the reports of Lodge's speech, White was taken aback by this news. He had gone a few days before to the Council of Ten, and, behold! there was Clemenceau, risen from what many had fancied would be his death-bed, as fresh, alert, and high-spirited as ever. The "Grand Young Man," as Lloyd George called him, had been hurriedly packed off by his uneasy friends, but his return had cheered up the Conference immensely. White had talked with Foch, who now seemed much more reasonable, assuring him that it was important to lose no more time in making peace with Germany. The efforts of Balfour and House had accelerated the work of the Commissions, which had begun to make their complete reports and were expected to have the last of them in by March 8th. Altogether, White thought it probable that, if all went well when Wilson returned, the treaty might be finished and the Germans brought to Paris early in April. But now, at just the moment when all looked bright in the Conference, a storm was gathering in Washington. It was a storm which gave White the deepest concern.

White wrote letters to Lodge on March 1st and March 7th; Lodge wrote letters to White on March 4th and March 5th. The first of White's letters, composed before the most disquieting news had come from Washington, was merely a casual budget of intelligence. He forwarded some clippings from the British press, told of his meetings with Clemenceau, Foch, and Venizelos, alluded to the danger from Bolshevism, and threw out a passing word on the League. Venizelos had said that it was essential if the world was to avoid a whole epidemic of wars for decades to come. "I am afraid," wrote White for himself, "I shall not agree with your views on the League of Nations, and I rather imagine that if you had been on the spot as I have, they might perhaps have been somewhat modified." But his second letter expressed the keen anxiety which possessed him after reading of the clash between Senators and President. Filling nine typewritten pages, it was in part a plea for the high aims of the League, in part an argument on some practical points in the Covenant, and in part a request that Lodge would advise him promptly and fully as to the changes needed to make the Covenant acceptable.

Lodge in his speech had stated a number of reasons why he believed the League would, as he put it, contravene the Monroe Doctrine, strike at American sovereignty, involve America in all foreign disputes, substitute internationalism for nationalism, and be a benefit chiefly to Europe.[6] He had reviewed the Covenant articles ably and fully. As general suggestions, he had proposed that the Monroe Doctrine be specifically recognized; that immigration and other questions vital to national existence be exempted from League control; that provision be made for withdrawal from the League; and that a definite statement be made as to whether the League should have an international force of its own. White undertook to argue some of these points. He feared a statement on the Monroe Doctrine as likely to give Japan a handle for demanding

[6] Lodge's side of the whole controversy is given in his *The Senate and the League of Nations* (1925).

recognition of her privileged position in China, and exceptions of other kinds for other nations as a matter of mere selfishness and *amour propre*. He thought that the Covenant gave the League no authority whatever over immigration and other purely domestic questions, and that it was needless to worry about its interference therein. Every other member of the Conference with whom he had talked, he said, took the same view. As for the international force, he particularly prided himself upon having seen to a clear understanding that there was to be nothing of the kind, and no possibility of the League summoning the forces of the different members. He did not see how any other meaning could be read into the instrument, nor did those about him. Above all, he emphasized the fact that it would be valuable "for me to know the actual phraseology which you would propose to cover all the points apparently made in your speech."

White objected vigorously to some of the statements Lodge was making in both his letters and speeches; statements which, as he intimated, revealed marked ignorance of the actualities in Europe. Lodge was afraid of a revival of Germany's warlike spirit; yet White and the other Americans in Paris were afraid of her political and economic collapse. No one at the Peace Conference at the beginning of March felt sure there would be a responsible government to deal with in Berlin when the time came for signing the treaty. Lodge, again, thought that France was the one country with a clear conception of what she wanted. "You never were under a greater misconception," wrote White. France, he explained, knew so little what she wanted that it was totally impossible to get a bill for damages from her, while in discussing the Rhine in his own Commission on Ports, Waterways, and Railways a few days earlier, her representatives had asked Germany for a blank check for the next five years, including free use of the right bank, "for the reason that France does not know what she may want and is afraid she will forget something." For a mild man, White was growing almost scornful in repelling the accusation that the Commissioners had delayed the peace by their work on the League Covenant. There was a note of eloquent reproach in what he wrote of the League's purposes.

WHITE TO LODGE, PARIS, MARCH 7, 1919

I shall be particularly grateful for the exact phraseology you would propose "for excluding the Monroe Doctrine from the League's purview," and for the other amendments you think necessary. You scarcely, I think, contemplate a statement of that kind in so many words, because the effect of that would be the introduction by Japan of exceptions in her behalf in respect to her special interests in China and elsewhere in the East, and probably a suggestion for an international force by France in the Rhine Provinces, and exceptions of all kinds for different nations as a matter of national pride and prestige. . . .

I agree with you that if we enter upon any League of Nations it will be more for the benefit of the world at large than for ourselves, and also that "it must be with a view to maintaining the peace of Europe." But surely that is why we went into the war, and no one advocated more earnestly our doing so than you. We certainly did not go into the war for any material gain of our own, and I have not the slightest doubt on two points—first of all, that unless we form part of any League of Nations which may be set up, there will be none; and, second, that if no agreement for a League of Nations can be arrived at, we can only revert to the old and only final method of settling international disputes, namely, war, for which I am inclined to think the soil is not devoid of fertility in various parts of Europe, and in saying this I do not refer to Germany, except in respect to civil war.

In view of the fact that more than seven million, two hundred and forty-odd thousand men have been killed in this war; that five million more men have been entirely incapacitated for any sort of usefulness during the rest of their lives, either by blindness or the loss of both arms or legs or one of the innumerable reasons which you can imagine, I cannot but feel that a strenuous effort must be made to try to prevent a return to the barbarous methods hitherto prevailing, which will, of course, be even more barbarous hereafter in view of the constant scientific improvements in weapons for the destruction of human life.

He was pleading in this letter that Senator Lodge should send him material, in the form of precise phraseology for the Covenant, which would enable him to bring the President and the Senate closer together. He made this explicit by continuing:

I am far from maintaining that the Covenant, as drawn, is perfect, nor do I believe that anyone who had to do with its preparation is of that opinion, but I remember that our late dear and lamented friend, Theodore Roosevelt, used to say that he always tried to get the best that he could obtain in respect to a measure of importance, instead of holding out for perfection, which, in matters requiring the assent of a great many persons of different ways of thinking, is practically impossible to obtain.

I need scarcely say that my suggestion as to your sending me the phraseology of what you would suggest for the League, is for my private information, and not for communication to, or discussion by, my colleagues on the Peace Commission, unless you wish otherwise, in which case I shall be only too delighted to show what you write me to them and endeavor to get it through if I agree therewith.

Your suggestion that the League "be made up by the European nations, whose interests are chiefly concerned," is impossible to carry out, for the reason that none of them will be willing to form any such League unless we are parties thereto. . . .

We of the Commission have just been holding a meeting with our financial and economic experts, whose opinion is unanimous to the effect that we are now on a volcano which may explode at any time, unless food can be got into Germany and other parts of Europe in which the population is starving or progressing rapidly toward that condition.

In writing this letter, White of course consulted no one. President Wilson was on the Atlantic, halfway back to Paris; Lansing was out of sympathy with White's opinions; White did not care to have Colonel House or General Bliss know the details of his correspondence with Senator Lodge and the other Republicans. He was playing an isolated hand. The convictions under which he wrote oppressed him all the evening of March 7th, and all day on the 8th. The French newspapers were full of Washington news and gossip on the contest between Wilson and the Senate, which they garnished with malicious comment. White realized that his letter would not be in America for ten days, and that a reply would not reach France for at least ten more. Meanwhile, ability to act promptly might be essential. Finally his anxiety impelled him to a bold step—yet a step which, in view of his long friendship with Lodge, his consultation with him before leaving for Paris, and their correspondence since, was natural and proper. He telegraphed to the Senator in code, by way of the State Department:

Should be grateful if you would cable me in cipher, through State Department, exact phraseology of amendments modifying League of Nations Covenant which Senate considers important. Our desire is to meet Senate's views as closely as it is possible to obtain acquiescence therein of other nations anxious for recognition of their own special interests which they will immediately insist upon in the Covenant if we demand exceptions in favor of ours. Wrote you fully two days ago but feel use of cable desirable, time being so important. Please send by next courier full reports your and Knox speeches.

And what of Lodge, thus invited to help in amending the Covenant? Exhausted by the day-and-night sessions before adjournment, he had gone back to Boston for rest and to prepare for his debate on the League with President Lowell of Harvard, which was to be held on March 19th. His frame of mind is clearly indicated by his letters of March 4th and 5th, sent to White just before he left Washington. The greater part of one of these letters has already been quoted, and the other was much like it. He still believed that attention to the League had greatly delayed the peace. He was convinced that the Covenant was "a loose, dangerous document," which "must be redrafted if it is to get through here." Feeling against the League, he thought, was growing rapidly. "When the League was first talked of all the letters I received on the subject were favorable to the League, without going into details; then the letters against it began to come in, and rose steadily to 4 to 1, 6 to 1, and now 10 to 1 against it. This merely shows that people are beginning to think. I have a very large mail, so that in its way it is something of an index." Lodge honestly believed that the League would lead to dissension rather than peace, and he knew that many Americans believed so.

As to the fate of the Covenant, the Senator was determined that it should be drastically revised or discarded. He anticipated a clear majority in the Senate against it. He did not object to a sound League—"people generally want a League of Nations to promote peace." But he objected strongly to this League, and so did the thirty-eight other Senators who signed the round robin. "In addition there are some fourteen or fifteen more Senators, Republican and Democratic, who did not sign it but who would vote against the League, so that the 'group' (as Mr. Wilson calls them) represent a decided majority of the Senate; but 39 are far more than a third. We took this course because the news from this country has been so rapidly suppressed—which is very clear from letters we have got here—that the people in Paris and elsewhere abroad have no idea of the real attitude of this country and it seemed the only way to make them understand that Mr. Wilson had against him an opposition of extreme seriousness and that he could not hope to pass through the Senate the League as now proposed." Lodge's statement of his position was entirely moderate. As to the character of the revision he asked, he said nothing in his letters.

It was natural for Lodge and his associates to leap to the erroneous conclusion that White had consulted the President before sending his cable of inquiry. Wilson was in constant wireless communication with Paris and Washington; might he not even have instigated White? Lodge was mistakenly sure that there existed a close presidential censorship of all dispatches to and from Paris. The Commissioners actually sent cablegrams freely, with no censorship or check by anyone. The cipher protected any confidential message. Lodge was also suspicious of a message which had passed through the State Department, though the secrecy of such messages as this was scrupulously observed. The Acting Secretary in charge of the Department was Frank L. Polk, and he never heard of White's cablegram—as he stated several years later—till White himself mentioned it in the following August.

Lodge at once laid the cablegram before Messrs. Brandegee, Knox, and Root, and all three echoed his suspicions. Root wrote to him that his relations to the Covenant should continue to be direct relations, and that he should avoid back-door methods. In the first place, argued Root, if he acted through White he would be committing himself as an independent officer of the government, while the President would not be committed at all by what his subordinate might do or say. In the second place, if the Senate's views were to be effective they must reach the President not as an appeal to his judgment by a subordinate, but as the demand of a co-equal power to which, under penalty of failure, he must yield. It should be said that neither of these reasons was sound. Lodge could easily have made constructive suggestions to White on a confidential basis, and in such a way as not to commit himself at all. For that matter, he had committed himself pretty definitely in his speeches. As for reaching the President, there was every reason for using a variety of methods, and Wilson's temperament responded better to conciliation than to threats.

But Lodge never for a moment considered responding to White's request in the spirit in which it was made—a request for open diplomacy in dealing with the Covenant in Washington as in Paris. White might well have been more explicit in phrasing his telegram. His word "our" was unfortunate—it seemed to associate the other Commissioners with him. He did not make it clear that he would not show Lodge's information to the President; that instead he would use it in an effort of his own to change the phraseology of the Covenant when it came up for discussion in the proper Commission of the Conference. It was later a shock to him to learn that his innocently-meant passage had caused so much Republican excitement and consultation. He explained, when Lodge published his book on the Senate and the League in 1925, that his object was simply to obtain private information from an old friend and Senate leader which would enable him, and not President Wilson, to make an effort to change the phraseology of the Covenant. But even if he had been more explicit, Lodge would have refused. Lodge cabled:

CABLEGRAM, LODGE TO WHITE, WASHINGTON, MARCH 15, 1919

Have considered your cable March 9th. The President expressed no willingness to receive any communication from the Senate while that body was in session. If he now wishes to have amendments drafted which the Senate will consent to, the natural and necessary course is to assemble the Senate in the customary way. Manifestly I cannot now speak for the Senate or consult its members, nor can they consult with each other, nor can the President consult them while they are at their homes in 48 States.

Four days later he was debating with President Lowell of Harvard in Boston, and Lowell was reproaching him for giving the League destructive without constructive criticism.

White's gallant effort to smooth the path for the League Covenant thus failed. It was a pity that it did so. When he sent his cablegram, the Covenant was still but a tentative draft, subject to correction. The very fact that it was given to the public at this stage, instead of being held secret until the time for ratification, showed that it was regarded as unfinished and that discussion was invited. President Wilson and everyone else knew that it was defective. Wilson and the other sponsors of the Covenant were experimenting in open diplomacy, and they wished just such assistance as Mr. Taft and Mr. Root later gave when they offered suggestions which were incorporated in the Covenant. What was needed was criticism of a friendly, not a hostile, kind. The men who, like Senators Borah and Moses, opposed a League of any sort, could be counted upon to furnish plenty of the destructive criticism; it was for men like Lodge, who avowed themselves in favor of the proper kind of League, to make it possible by constructive suggestions. The sooner such suggestions were made, the better. While the draft Covenant was merely tentative and still before the Peace Conference, changes would be easy.

The fact was that White and Lodge were moving in such different spheres that they could understand each other but imperfectly. Lodge was partly right in thinking that the delegates in Paris were cut off from American opinion and feeling. White did not and could not realize that public sentiment in the United States was growing steadily chillier toward the League; we find him making the surprising comment in one letter that Mr. Taft, as the League champion, seemed to have a good chance of the Republican nomination in 1920. Nor could he understand how bitter was the feeling among many Republican Senators against Wilson. They felt that the President was ignoring and trying to ride rough-shod over a department of the Government that had equal authority over foreign relations. "I hardly think," wrote Root to Lodge, "that White appreciates the attitude which the President has assumed towards the Senate." Lodge commented resentfully, in his debate with Lowell, upon the fact that Wilson had not consulted the Senate prior to or during negotiations, though Washington, Jackson, Lincoln, and Grant had all done so. On the other hand, Lodge was utterly incapacitated for understanding a great deal in the situation of Europe and the world which White, from his vantage point in Paris, comprehended perfectly. Naturally a man of narrow vision, strong in national feeling and weak in international instincts, Lodge had little perception of the vital need for the League, little knowledge of the tremendous difficulties of making peace, little sense of the unavoidability of compromise and give-and-take in Paris. He did not see, as White did, that the old nationalist fears, the traditional arrangements for defense and offense, the habit of looking suspiciously at every international agreement, must be given up. The old road had led to disaster. A new one must be found—and it would require courage, imagination, and generosity.

It speaks well for the friendship of years between White and Lodge that after the exchange of cablegrams neither showed resentment toward the other. From their different standpoints they lectured each other a little more vigorously, that was all. Neither stood much chance of converting his friend, but each tried hard, none the less. Particularly did White employ his best arguments.

White's three final letters to Lodge in March, on the 11th, the 19th, and the 25th, have three aspects of particular interest: his growing resentment toward the French, his fears for German stability, and his continued concern for the League. It cannot be imagined that White had any prepossessions hostile to the French. He had learned to love them as a boy, and his years as ambassador had strengthened his sympathy. But their course in Europe in these early months of 1919 dismayed and shocked him. He spoke of the incident at Spa early in March, when the Germans refused to give up their merchant ships because Foch would not offer full assurances as to the provisioning of Germany. There was genuine fear at this time that Germany would simply refuse to sign the peace and invite the Allies to come in and do their worst; and White felt that if such a calamity actually ensued, the blame for it would rest largely upon Foch. Many American army officers disliked the French; American political observers were constantly bringing back unfavorable reports. White wrote:

I have refrained, up until now, from telling you of the way in which the French are giving evidence of an intention to assume the position in Europe and elsewhere of which Germany has been deprived by the war. All our members of the Allied commissions report that wherever they go the French member always takes the lead and puts himself forward and ours have little or nothing to say. This is particularly the case in Poland, where it appears M. Noulens, the chief French representative, always takes the lead. At Spa it appears that the Assembly of the Allied Council is, so far as our people are concerned, a farce, as the French general simply comes in, calls the meeting to order, turns over a certain number of sheets of paper, and states "The Marshal orders this or that," and that "such and such is the case," and the meeting then adjourns. In other places the situation is quite similar and is not discouraged by our British friends, who are perfectly willing that French vanity should be gratified in the way I have described, while they are making hay for themselves in the way of commercial advantages by looking into the situation closely wherever they go, and paving the way for the resumption of commerce after the war. I am not blaming them for this, but merely mentioning it as an interesting circumstance. . . .

I cannot see that the League of Nations has had anything whatever to do with the sending of our troops home. All the members of the Commission are heart and soul with you in the desire that they shall be got home as soon as possible, both because we know the country wants them sent back, and because we feel that efforts are being made to get us in some way or other committed to projects which may, and almost certainly will, necessitate military coöperation if we are not extremely careful to protect ourselves; also for the further reason that the longer our troops stay in France the stronger becomes their feeling of antagonism to the French, who they think—no doubt in many cases unjustly—are endeavoring to fleece them, notwithstanding the fact that they risked their lives to come over here and save France from destruction, which they did. Of the extent to which this feeling prevails, I have heard from Piatt Andrew, whom you know and who is and has been as devoted throughout the war as any man in all America to the Allied cause. Well, he recently came to see me and said very sadly: 'It is tragic to feel how all the idealism connected with the war has gone; how things have come down to the old sordid basis prevailing before the war, and particularly how sad it is that the tremendous feeling in favor of the French, which our troops had, has disappeared and they will go home not only without those feelings, but probably with a sense of antagonism in place thereof.' "

There was much indignation at the time among American newspaper men at the manner in which the French, and to some extent the British also, manipulated the news. This feeling White shared.

There were constant petty leaks from the supposedly secret meetings of the various commissions, especially when anything occurred likely to put the Americans in an unfavorable light. For example, when the American expert in the commission dealing with Greek claims remarked that he doubted whether a majority of the Hellenic inhabitants of Asia Minor were desirous of being united to Greece, all the French papers the following morning contained notices that the American delegate was the only one opposing the reunion of western Asia Minor with the Motherland. Then came a flood of telegrams from Greeks all over Europe, while White suffered a series of reproachful visits from Venizelos, Coromilas, and other Greek representatives in Paris. The French Ministry of Finance took very hard the emphatic decision of the Americans that the proposed pool for the payment of war debts was out of the question; and when Clemenceau brought forward his scheme for Anglo-American protection of France, White felt that altogether too many efforts were being made to impose on the United States. He wished the proposal dismissed forthwith.

White hoped that his observations would weaken Lodge's regard for the French, especially upon points which became subjects of contention between Wilson and the French leaders; but he was disappointed. Lodge's outlook was too much like that of the French to permit him to criticize them. He thought that there was both a German propaganda and a still stronger Wilsonian propaganda against France, and that the American people saw through it all. They would never "approve abandoning France or crowding her in any way," he stated; they looked upon France as their own barrier and outpost against Germany, and wished to strengthen her. Not at all important in itself, this difference between White and Lodge on the French claims was decidedly important as a symptom of their general divergence. While Lodge of course opposed American aid to France through a financial pool or a special alliance, he was willing to give her a free hand against Germany —which White was not.

White's impressions of the situation in Germany were gained partly through the Peace Commission's observers there, and especially General Harries, whose report early in March—a decidedly gloomy one—he transmitted to Lodge; partly through the press;

and partly through his daughter and her family. At the beginning of March there was a general strike in Berlin, with hundreds killed in street-fighting; in April there was a revolution in Bavaria and a short-lived Communist Republic was proclaimed in Munich, while a revolt of discharged soldiers occurred in Dresden. White's daughter was in Berlin when the strike began, and saw blood flowing in the gutters. Immediately afterward, sending her children to join their father at The Hague, she herself went to Lucerne to recuperate. From there she sent piteous accounts of the suffering among the German and Austrian people, and of the dark and uncertain outlook. White had been in a fever of anxiety about her ever since the collapse of the German armies and Government, had sent constant letters and messages to her, often by roundabout ways, and was enormously relieved when she reached Switzerland. Once he wrote to her in Germany that he sometimes felt thankful that her beloved mother was dead, for the turmoil and trouble of the world, the anxiety over her child and grandchildren, would have been an almost intolerable strain upon her.

His feelings upon Germany were mixed. Of course he had a profound sympathy for the poor German people, a deep conviction that they were entitled to immediate peace. But he had an equally deep indignation at some of the things the Germans had done in France, including their systematic destruction of farms and factories. He and his daughter agreed upon the criminality of the German leaders; "gambling away," White wrote, "such a wonderful heritage, which in patriotic, reasonable, and far-seeing hands might have been productive of so much good in the world." He believed that the Germans had little idea of the unnecessarily cruel and wanton acts committed in their behalf by orders of their late rulers. People east of the Rhine, he felt, were as biased judges of what was just and right in the way of peace terms as were the French west of the Rhine; and in fact, it was almost impossible for the most detached observer to say what penalties were just and what were not. The facts of which he was certain were that German recovery and unity were vital to European civilization, and that a lapse into chaos in Prussia, Bavaria, and Saxony would be only less injurious to the Allies than to the Germans themselves. Hence his anger at the French impediments to the feeding of

Germany by Mr. Hoover's organization, and his irritation at the delays to peace. As late as March 23rd he was writing to his daughter:

Answering your letter of March 2nd, food is going in, I hope. The fault is not ours; it is no more that of any of our colleagues on this commission than of mine, and still less is it Hoover's. The details I will tell you some day. I cannot write them now. I hope "they" are waking up to the dangers of Bolshevism. But curiously enough they are foolish enough in this country to believe it is safe from that curse, whatever may be the case in any other, whereas I have every reason to believe the reverse.

And later in the same letter:

I share your feelings most fully in respect to your poor sister-in-law and her little girls. I hoped they might perhaps have been with her parents, and wish I could help you in getting them out of Hungary or suggest a way to do so. As regards the food I certainly understand that it is going in and that Hoover's agents are at certain courts attending to it. He has been loud in his denunciation of the starving of women and children, and if he could have prevented it, there would have been no prohibition in the act of Congress upon giving food when necessary to enemy countries. . . .

Try to get it out of your mind that I am not fully alive to what is going on and doing the best that I can under the circumstances to alleviate conditions and get on to peace conditions, as is everyone with whom I am associated in this Hotel. Some day you will know particulars. I cannot possibly write them, as you must understand.

On the League, White, after the rebuff from Senator Lodge, wrote much more frankly to John Jacob Rogers than he did to the Massachusetts Senator. Rogers, a graduate of Harvard who had been in Congress since 1913, was sympathetic to the League. White described to him some of the innumerable difficulties of making an effective League amid all the susceptibilities, fears, and jealousies of Paris. He thought that Lodge's apprehensions were mainly of imaginary evils. He saw nothing in the Covenant to contravene the Monroe Doctrine, and he feared the result of a special American reservation on that point—Japan would wish a reservation on the Near East, and France on the Rhineland.

As for Lodge's demand that there be a clearer interpretation of the clause relating to the use of troops, White remarked that Article XVI was surely clear enough; the words "recommend what effective military or naval force the members of the League shall severally contribute" were perfectly explicit, and "recommend" assuredly meant to recommend—not to order. If this Article were strengthened, then the French would be demanding an international force to police the Rhine provinces. If it were weakened by inserting a blunt statement that under no circumstances should any Power furnish troops unless it was perfectly willing to do so, which was what the Article really meant, this would cause unnecessary alarm, and France would feel that the United States had no intention of ever carrying out the provisions of the Covenant.

In short, we find White early in March analyzing Lodge's speeches in some detail, and expressing to Congressman Rogers his belief that they were hypercritical and wrong-headed. "Of course, all such documents have to be matters of compromise," he wrote; "and if you knew the difficulties which existed in bringing the various nations concerned to an agreement, you would realize what a great feat has been accomplished in bringing about the acceptance of the Covenant as it stands." He frankly said that there was one conclusion to which he had come only since his experience in Paris. This was that unless they were able to secure a League of Nations more or less closely resembling that in hand, the world would be faced with the certainty of early wars more horrible than any which had been seen before; for the continuous scientific improvement in lethal weapons, some of them perfected though not used just as the war was ending, presaged deadlier and more relentless conflicts than ever. White wrote of the subject with burning earnestness. "It seems to me," he concluded a letter of March 5th, "that a frightful responsibility will rest upon any set of men who are instrumental in preventing the trial, at least, of an experiment to settle international differences in some other way than by methods involving such frightful sacrifice of human life and tending toward the destruction of civilization."

Wilson was back in Paris, as we have said, on March 14th. White saw him almost at once, and had a talk with him about the White

House dinner, the Covenant, and the Senate. He found Wilson not at all stiff or impracticable in temper. The President spoke of the Covenant as something still malleable and subject to even extensive changes. As a matter of fact, it was a constitution in the making, and an immense body of suggestions for additions and changes was being brought forward. Neutral powers submitted their views at great length; Mr. Taft and Mr. Root had proposals to make; the French were still pressing for an international force to serve the League, some League military staff, or at least some League supervision of national forces; the Japanese supported a series of amendments guaranteeing racial equality; the Swiss wished to include a special clause recognizing their neutrality; and so on. At this stage, if Senator Lodge had sent White the suggested amendments for which the latter asked, he could have made effective use of them. President Wilson expressly invited White to offer any suggestions of his own, and would gladly have listened to any ideas he presented. White wrote of the President's receptiveness and open-mindedness in the matter:

WHITE TO REPRESENTATIVE ROGERS, PARIS, APRIL 7, 1919

There is not the slightest doubt that the President's intention was to meet the Senate and House committees in the spirit which you describe. I have discovered since knowing him that he is really shy, and, in an atmosphere which he does not feel to be entirely sympathetic, much more in one which is antagonistic (as I think he felt that on the occasion in question it was in the main), his reserve increases in proportion to the absence of sympathy. That he has a very human side to him there is no doubt, and I also have found him at various times attractive, as you did on the night of the famous dinner. I have also noted that he is much more "get-at-able" in conversation with one other person; whether on account of his natural shyness or what, I do not know. But certainly when we talk to him as a Delegation, he is apt to do most of the talking, whereas when I see him alone, as I sometimes do—and certainly I am always able to do so when I seek an interview—I have found him a very good listener, and apparently appreciative of what is said to him. I suppose it is for that reason that he deals so much with and through Colonel House rather than taking advantage of the collective information of all those by whom he is immediately surrounded; whether it be the Peace Conference or his own Cabinet at home.

In the same vein White wrote to Root, whom he knew to be a man of liberal outlook. He emphasized the arguments for the League, and the still plastic nature of the Covenant.

There is a great deal to be said for the point of view that, unless a League of Nations is promptly set up and put into operation, the danger of war's breaking out somewhere, soon after the adjournment of this Conference, will be greatly enhanced. The soil is fertile in many directions—by which I do not mean Germany—for another outbreak; so strong are the animosities of certain countries against others. . . . There is the further objection to the postponement of the establishment of a League of Nations that, if peace is made without it, and the various Powers separate, some of them satisfied with what they have obtained and most of them the reverse, there will be very little chance of getting them together again within a short period in a frame of mind adapted to making an agreement with each other in respect to such a League.

There is another and very potent argument for embodying a League of Nations Covenant in the Peace Treaty; namely, the necessity of getting Germany's adherence thereto, which will certainly not be possible within the near future after the signature of the Peace Treaty, unless her entry into the League should be made much more easy than it is in the existing Covenant.

On the other hand, there is a good deal to be said for the claims of certain members of the Senate that a measure of such far-reaching importance and intended to remain in operation for an indefinite period, should not go into effect without ample time for a full discussion thereof.

Confidentially, the President is not in the least averse to amending the Covenant, as our home telegrams seem to imply. On the contrary, he, Clemenceau, and Lloyd George have been in close conference on that very point for a goodly number of hours since his return, and that is one of the reasons why I regret Cabot has not been able to send me his—or what he conceives to be the Senate's—views as to amendments. Frank Hitchcock, who is here and has become deeply interested in the League, has, as a representative Republican, furnished us with four or five amendments which he thinks likely to meet the views of the Senate. The latter have all been carefully considered by the three leaders above mentioned; but, after much time devoted to the subject, it has appeared very difficult, if not impossible, to get any of these amendments adopted without having to accede to claims for exceptions on the part of other countries which the Senate would not accept for a moment.

Since I began my letter House tells me that Clemenceau has informed him that the general guarantees in the Covenant of the League of Nations against aggression by one Power upon another are not considered sufficient to satisfy the anxiety felt by the people of this country against the possibility of a sudden attack by Germany, and that he must insist on the insertion in the Peace Treaty of a clause guaranteeing that the United States and Great Britain will immediately come to the assistance of France with armies in the event of a repetition of a sudden attack such as occurred in 1914. Clemenceau was induced to modify this suggestion to the extent of agreeing that if a paragraph can be inserted in the Covenant of the League of Nations covering this special guarantee on the part of Great Britain and the United States, he would be satisfied therewith. This has introduced a new complication for us; as, after a brief discussion of the matter among ourselves, we do not see how it is possible to insert in the Treaty or the League of Nations Covenant any such guarantee on our part which the Senate will, or ought to, accept. Lloyd George, however, has already said that he will give the French a written guarantee to that effect in respect to England. We are all turning our minds to the subject today to see if we can devise anything to meet the situation, and particularly the very natural objections of the Senate to any such guarantee; I am bound to say not with much prospect of success, as far as I can see.

White added that Lloyd George's promises did not inspire much confidence in the French, and that Clemenceau therefore wished an American endorsement of them. The persistence of the French in trying to tie America by treaty to some form of virtual alliance was quite extraordinary; they were no sooner rejected at one point than they turned to another:

In view of the fact that Germany is to be disarmed; that her army is to be limited to 100,000 men; that she is to be bound not to manufacture or obtain arms and ammunition for an army any larger than the number aforesaid; that she is to surrender all her ships of war and all her merchant ships; it is impossible to comprehend the extraordinary obsession felt in this country lest Germany within the next few years repeat the action which she took in 1914. It is probably based somewhat upon the realization by the French that the terms they want imposed upon Germany are likely to involve a desire for revenge on her part as soon as it may become practicable, and also upon the fact that the German population is likely to be increasing regularly while that of France will probably decrease, especially in view of the death in the war of fifteen hundred thousand probable fathers. But whatever be the cause, it exists to an extent which those who have not been in close touch with French representative men as we of this Commission have (and I particularly, who alone of the five speak French and have been meeting Frenchmen at small luncheons and dinners almost every day since my arrival), cannot possibly appreciate.

It is well known that little of the final Covenant of the League —not a single leading idea—originated with President Wilson. As his biographer, Mr. Baker, says, he was simply the compiler or editor of the great document, piecing together the projects which came to him from other sources; from the Pan-American scheme of 1916, from the American League to Enforce Peace, from the British League of Nations Societies, from Elihu Root, House, Taft, Lord Phillimore, Lord Robert Cecil, and General Smuts. It was not until March 18th that Taft cabled his suggestions regarding the Monroe Doctrine, withdrawal from the League, unanimity in the Council, and the exclusion of domestic questions from League jurisdiction. At the same time Root suggested six amendments for the Covenant, seeing that a copy of his proposals went to White direct. The work of amendment went on until the close of March.

Unquestionably President Wilson's great achievement in Paris lay in making the League of Nations idea his own, and with invincible determination, against selfish obstruction and fierce criticism, compelling the world to accept it. The blundering and meanness of the Conference and the errors of the Treaty will be forgotten, but his name will be enshrined in this charter of a new international régime. Doubtless also much of White's best work in Paris lay in the stanch support which he gave to this central object of the President. A veteran of pre-war diplomacy, he renounced it to demand a new world order. "If some new means are not devised for the settling of international questions other than by war," he wrote to his son, "we are unquestionably on the road to the disappearance of what we believed to be a wonderful civilization, built up during the centuries which have elapsed since the fall of Rome, and the introduction of barbarism. It is a horrible idea to face, and I have been deeply impressed therewith since my arrival here and the months I have already spent looking over the situation and realizing that the public men of this part of the world are still thinking as their predecessors thought in the days of the Treaty of Vienna. . . ."

Yet while the League Covenant was being brought into shape in Paris, American distrust and opposition were increasing. Lodge's continued letters to White embodied a generally accurate view of the complex situation. He wrote emphatically and unyieldingly, reiterating his belief in the League and his conviction that strong amendments were needed. One interesting letter followed his absence in Boston.

LODGE TO WHITE, WASHINGTON, APRIL 8, 1919

You need have no apprehensions about Mr. Taft being the Republican candidate for the Presidency. He never had any chance, and if he ever did have it would now be less than it was. He has supported the League in his own fashion. On the 7th of March he came out with a statement in which he accepted practically every amendment I suggested in my speech of the 27th of February. Then he revolved again and said the draft might be improved but that it was worth ratifying anyway. These oscillations have not strengthened him with the country. The same thing was true of the Lowell debate, although Lowell appeared very well and has a much cleverer and more accurate mind than Taft. Lowell admitted and agreed with practically all my amendments and made some additional criticisms of his own. My purpose in that debate was not to try to score points with my friend Lowell but to try to get my views before the country, which happened to give a great deal of attention to the discussion. I desire to have people think about what they are doing, and the thought and the discussion are both increasing. I think a majority of the people of the country desire a League, but there is an active minority against any League and I think the majority of the people today, in the course of the discussion, although they want a League, will insist on some very vital amendments covering particularly the Monroe Doctrine and the question of immigration. The draft as originally put forward had a majority against it in the Senate. It could not be ratified. Of course, it is impossible to offer an opinion on what will finally be submitted to us, because that is not known. I am not opposed to any League; on the contrary, I should like to see a League among the nations with whom we have been associated in the war which would tend to promote and secure the future peace of the world, without impairing certain rights and policies of the United States which do not in the least concern or trouble Europe. You speak of amendments in our favor requiring that we should make amendments to oblige other countries. It appears to me, if you will permit me to say so, that you misapprehend the situation. Unless we join there will be no League and my information—which comes from the best authority at the Conference outside our own delegation—is that the other nations would be only too glad to make any amendments that we desire, and we should ask no amendment which would in the least interfere with Europe, or which would not in its effect be common to all nations. The only gain that we can make from a League is promoting and securing the peace of the world. We are not there with any selfish interests of any kind. We can get along without guarantees. We have no boundaries to settle. There is no territory on earth that we wish to acquire. We are entirely unselfish in the matter, and therefore we must have a different sort of consideration in regard to our rights and policies, which do not interfere with other people.

You say in your letter of March 7th that the only final method of settling international disputes is what we shall be drawn back upon if the League fails, and that is war. Why the whole League of Nations as proposed contemplates war. Its intent is to use war to enforce peace. . . . Two weeks before his death I had two long talks with Theodore. The draft that Mr. Wilson finally produced was not then in our hands, but Theodore and I discussed the whole question with the greatest thoroughness and we were in full agreement. I am following precisely the line that he wished me to follow and that he mapped out as the true line to be followed in dealing with the League whenever it came before us.

When Wilson returned, White had high hopes that the labors of the Peace Conference could be pushed forward to an early conclusion. He himself had worked day and night. He thought that early in April it should be possible to summon the Germans to Paris and present the treaty for signature. Under Balfour's guidance all had gone smoothly, the commissions had submitted their various reports, and it was necessary only to make the final decisions in the light of these expert findings. But White did not fully realize that it was precisely because the Conference and its commissions had dealt only with preliminary work, and had deferred the great decisions until Wilson, Clemenceau, and Lloyd George were all back together, that everything had gone so smoothly.

HENRY WHITE AT THE PEACE CONFERENCE
(With General Bliss; leaving the Crillon)

Even as it was, he had been distinctly perplexed and irritated by the attitude of leading Frenchmen, and filled with a sense of still deeper disquiet as he talked with the Italian leaders regarding their demands. From the moment that Wilson landed at Brest on March 14th there was a feeling of tension in the air. The Rhineland, reparations, Fiume, racial equity, Shantung, Silesia, the Saar—in these and a dozen other issues there was dynamite. White could only hope for the best.

There was distinct optimism in the letters White sent to Rogers and Lodge just before and after Wilson's arrival, but it was guarded. He felt that the air was being cleared and the foundations of peace were being securely laid; yet he knew that something might go wrong. The French demand for a security treaty was ominous. "This last French suggestion," he wrote to Lodge on March 19th, "has only been made since our financial experts have made it perfectly clear to those of the French Ministry of Finances that our becoming a party to the proposed pool for the payment of war debts is absolutely out of the question. I do not see any way of getting around this last suggestion except by an emphatic repudiation of it, which, however, may lead to unfortunate consequences." He used the pertinacity of the French as an argument for the League. "If the privilege of retiring from the League at any time that it may suit any nation to do so is clearly set forth in the Covenant," he continued, "I do not believe France will think the agreement worth the paper on which it is written, as our membership in the League will be its mainstay, and France will feel, if we are likely to retire during the first few years after the creation of the League, there will be no guarantee of protection left to her, except the impossible one which she has just suggested. . . . People over here are rather taken aback, I find, by the form assumed by the Senate's opposition to the President, the tendency of which is a desire to prevent our getting involved in European affairs, whereas they appear to have hoped—why I cannot imagine, except that the wish was father to the thought—that the love of our country for France would have caused us to agree to what is *practically* an alliance for her protection. But do not imagine from what I have written that I consider the League of Nations Covenant a perfect document or anything like it, which I certainly do not." The French and Italian demands plainly worried him.

It is therefore not surprising to find that on March 21st, less than a week after Wilson had resumed his labors, White was writing to Rogers in hot indignation. The situation had become almost intolerable. He had made up his mind to see the President within a day or two and urge him strongly to bring affairs to a head with Clemenceau and Orlando. He would advise the President to present an ultimatum—to say just what the United States would do and would not do, and to say that unless an agreement were reached the American delegation would stand ready to appeal to their nation and advise a separate peace with Germany. The ultimatum might fail. "In that case," continued White, "I should advise the President to go home promptly, call Congress together, and lay the situation before it. It is very necessary to give a great deal of scope to the Latins in the way of talk, but this we have done and, according to my experience, there comes a moment when it becomes necessary to put one's foot down, take a decided stand, and bring things to a head." A few days later White had an interview with Wilson and gave him precisely this advice. What were the events which had brought the Peace Conference to this unhappy pass?

CHAPTER TWENTY-TWO

The Peace Conference: The Crucial Phase

FOLLOWING President Wilson's return to Paris on March 14th, the Peace Conference passed through a stormy month. During these weeks the disputes of the chiefs of the four principal nations rose sometimes to an alarming pitch, and twice or thrice hope for an amicable agreement was almost lost. The brutal fact was that in the end they simply had to agree. Woodrow Wilson alone was in a position to leave the Conference and advise his country to make a separate peace, and even for him the act would have had the most dangerous consequences. But the exaggerated demands of France, Italy, and Poland, the stern resistance which Wilson gave to them at most points, the vacillating opposition of Lloyd George on some, and the vehemence with which the European press, the politicians, and some of the minor delegations took up the controversies, for a time made the outcome of the complex set of negotiations difficult to predict. On some issues it was hard to pronounce with certainty what was the right course; such questions as Memel, Danzig, the Polish corridor, and Asia Minor offered were baffling almost beyond precedent. On other issues, like Shantung, the Rhineland, the Saar, and Fiume, the right position was fairly clear, but powerful interests were ready to battle against it. Crisis led to crisis, till the growing conflict culminated in Wilson's cablegram of April 7th summoning the *George Washington* back to France.

It was Lloyd George who, with President Wilson reluctantly acquiescing, brought about the substitution of the Council of Four for the Council of Ten. When Wilson came back it was evident that as the work of the Conference grew more intense and the great decisions became pressing, he, Lloyd George, Clemenceau, and Orlando would often have to act alone. Private meetings of the three first-named men were held on several days. Meanwhile the Ten continued to sit as usual. But in the Ten it was impossible

to keep secret the seriousness of the dissensions; while with no settlement sometimes possible except by mutual concessions, ten men
could not transact business rapidly. A sharp break soon occurred.
The Poles, demanding that all Upper Silesia, Danzig, and the Polish
Corridor be assigned them, were supported by the French and
opposed by Lloyd George. There was a leak of information from
the acrimonious debates in the Council of Ten. The French press
one morning, to the astonishment of the British and Americans,
appeared with a summary of the secret committee findings, secret
maps, and a slightly garbled account of what Lloyd George had
said, enabling the Paris *Daily Mail*, controlled by Lord Northcliffe, to deliver a bitter attack on the Prime Minister. In justified
anger, Lloyd George declared on March 21st that the disclosures
which were daily appearing in the press were doing much harm
in Germany and producing a world-wide impression that the Allies
were only fighting for individual advantages.[1] He asserted that
"such incidents must be put a stop to."

They were put a stop to. The Council of Ten disappeared, leaving as a vestige the Council of Ministers of Foreign Affairs, or
Council of Five; and the real work of the Conference passed into
the hands of the Four, who carried on in English, and usually in
an atmosphere of privacy, their arguments and their search for
adjustments.

White, like everyone else, realized that at this stage the assumption of all decisions by the central group of Four was perhaps unavoidable. But, by virtue of his diplomatic experience, he was
acutely aware of the disadvantages of the method, and he regarded
its adoption as regrettable. It terminated the leakage of information. But he doubted if it greatly accelerated the work, and felt
certain that it opened a way for grave errors of judgment.[2] As he

[1] The creation of the Council of Four and its methods of work are well
described by Clive Day in House, E. M., and Seymour, Charles, editors,
What Really Happened at Paris, p. 31 ff. As he says, it must not be assumed
that the Four arrogated all authority to themselves. "Most of the articles in
the treaties were taken bodily without change from the reports of
commissions."

[2] Colonel House approved of the transfer of negotiations to the Council
of Four, and encouraged it; Seymour, *Intimate Papers of Colonel House,*

wrote to his son, he had never approved in principle of the heads of states sitting in person to negotiate a treaty, and he thought that in practise it was now proving unhappy.

WHITE TO JOHN CAMPBELL WHITE, PARIS, APRIL 2, 1919

It is unfortunate for the reason that when suggestions are made, suddenly, for which time should be taken for consideration, there is no one for the Four to refer to, as they are the final factors in the situation. Whereas, if Ministers of Foreign Affairs or Ambassadors were sitting at the Conference, they are much more free to make proposals to each other *ad referendum* or suggestions whereby concessions on one side might bring about similar concessions on the other. The die, however, is cast along the present lines, and I do not see how they can now be modified.

There is another consequence of the present arrangement which I do not like, to wit, the President sitting alone instead of having Lansing by his side. As far as my experience goes, nothing escaped the latter when I was sitting with him at the Quai d'Orsay during the absence of the President in the United States; on the contrary, he was extremely acute in detecting every manœuvre, and in exposing it by asking some very straight question in a very courteous and often apparently innocent way, the result of which often caused the proposal to be abandoned without further effort to keep it going, for the reason that it would not stand the light of day. It is almost impossible for one mind to keep before it every question which is brought up and the way it should be dealt with, especially after many weeks of close application to such subjects.

In a letter to John Jacob Rogers he pointed out another drawback:

WHITE TO ROGERS, PARIS, APRIL 7, 1919

There is a further objection to the present system in connection with the four eminent statesmen engaged, in that of the three who speak English, only one can speak French, thereby leaving it to the single member of the four who speaks French and English, namely Clemenceau, to do the translating for two of them to the third, and *vice versa*; neither of the three having any understanding or control over what is

---

vol. iv, p. 387. Lansing vehemently disapproved and attacked the procedure; Lansing, *The Peace Negotiations: A Personal Narrative*, p. 220 ff.

being said in his behalf in the language he does not understand. It is
now being freely said—and I must admit truly—that the present system
is the *revanche de la diplomatie.* Curiously enough also, none of these
eminent gentlemen appears to have the faculty of mobilizing his coad-
jutors and devolving some of the negotiations upon the latter, the result
being that they are unequal to regulating affairs involving the greater
part of the world by themselves, I fear.

At a later date White more than suspected the European statesmen of wishing to isolate Wilson in the Council of Four in the
hope that they might handle him more easily. Early in April he
tried to encourage Wilson's growing disgust with the Four, and
his disposition to call for a renewal of plenary sessions. Incidentally,
White felt that Clemenceau during April and May was not the
same man mentally that he had been before the attack on his life;
that he did not possess the quickness, openness of mind, and decision that he had shown before. The old statesman dozed off to
sleep sometimes during the more tiresome hearings, though he
roused himself like a tiger whenever France's interests came up.
His convalescent state was unfortunate, for it placed him more distinctly under the influence of Foch. As for Foch himself, he seemed
very much under the sway of a man whom White, Bliss, and
Lansing regarded as dangerous in his ideas and temper—General
Weygand.

Among the hasty decisions by the Four which White deplored
were the fatal commitments of May with regard to Russia and
Turkey. As a result largely of the sending of White's brother, Mr.
Buckler, in January to interview M. Litvinof at Stockholm, the
Powers invited the various Russian factions to meet in a peace conference on the island of Prinkipo in the Sea of Marmora. The Bolsheviks accepted in rather ambiguous terms; various anti-Bolshevik
factions contemptuously refused. White always felt that it was a
pity the Prinkipo Conference fell through, since he had hoped it
would stop the futile wars which tormented Russia. He thought
also that the Four were ill-advised in their note of May 26th to
Admiral Kolchak, promising further American and Allied assistance
under certain conditions; in his opinion the whole Russian venture

should have been liquidated as quickly as possible.[3] Again, he regretted the hasty decision of the Four on May 12th in authorizing the Greek landing at Smyrna, which began a bloody three years' war in Asia Minor. Venizelos went far beyond the necessities of the situation in his use of this authority, but the responsibility of the Four for one of the dark pages of the time is ineffaceable.[4] If there had been more discussion, if the immediate conferrees on any question had always found it necessary to refer to higher authority, such blunders might have been avoided.

But the three European questions which most directly and fully interested White were Poland's demands for territory, ports, and security, Italy's demands for land at the expense of Austria and Jugo-Slavia, and France's demands for new boundaries, security, and monetary advantages. On all three questions, even where Wilson was slow to move, White took an atttitude of opposition to extreme claims. On the Silesian question, the Italian efforts to grab Fiume, and the French attempt to secure an American alliance, he felt intensely. At the cost of some violence in chronology, we may isolate these three subjects and take them up one by one, quoting White's most vigorous expressions of opinion. He wrote a good deal about Italy and the French, and at times his language was scorching.

Upon the reëstablishment of Poland no one disagreed. Everyone assumed that the proud and headstrong nation which had been imprisoned for so many generations by a league of neighbors should be released, and should have her rightful possessions restored to her. One of Wilson's Fourteen Points provided that there should be "an independent Poland, with secure access to the sea, embracing all territories inhabited by indisputably Polish populations." The French, anticipating alliance with the new nation, wished a Poland "*Grande et forte, très-forte*," as M. Pichon put it. Lloyd

[3] Winston Churchill gives an able if partisan review of Russian events in *The Aftermath*, chap. ix. He prints the note of the Four (together with the Japanese delegate, Saionji) to Admiral Kolchak on pp. 182-185.

[4] Tragedy sprang immediately from this Smyrna business. Within a few weeks, "it is a moderate estimate that over 2,000 Turks, men, women, and children, were done to death unnecessarily by this decision of the War Council, and the Council of Four"; Westermann, W. L., in House, E. M., and Seymour, Charles, editors, *What Really Happened at Paris*, p. 195.

George, on the contrary, felt little enthusiasm for a strong Poland.[5] The American position, which White indorsed, was that Poland should have what an impartial investigation determined to be properly hers, and no more. Since the German and Polish populations had at many points become inextricably mixed and the ethnographic maps looked like an incomprehensible mosaic, the investigation presented immense difficulties.

Unfortunately, the Commission which the Conference appointed on Polish affairs, headed by M. Jules Cambon, leaned strongly toward the Franco-Polish view on disputed points. In the report which it submitted to the Supreme Council toward the end of March, it recommended that Poland be given the greater part of Posen and Upper Silesia, a broad corridor to the sea along both banks of the Vistula, and the city of Danzig. The corridor, as originally outlined, was larger than ethnographic considerations should have permitted, while everyone knew that the Danzig district was overwhelmingly German. Lloyd George felt that the arrangement was dangerous, in that it gave Poland more Germans than she could digest, and made the risk of a German-Polish war too heavy. He therefore insisted upon a plebiscite in the Marienwerder district east of the Vistula, and upon making Danzig a free city under the protection of the League. President Wilson agreed to these suggestions, and Clemenceau was forced, very unwillingly, to consent. As yet the arrangement called for giving Poland most of Upper Silesia. When this became known in Germany early in May, the German nation protested in strong terms. So also did the British Labor Party; so did various liberal groups in England and America. Once more Lloyd George intervened, again President Wilson followed his leadership, and it was finally determined that the fate of Upper Silesia should be decided by a plebiscite.[6]

Throughout all these shifts in the German-Polish terms White

[5] Wilson sympathized strongly with Polish aspirations. But he told Ray Stannard Baker on April 7th that "the only real interest of France in Poland is in weakening Germany by giving Poland territory to which she has no right." Baker, *Woodrow Wilson and World Settlement,* vol. ii, p. 60.

[6] For the partition of Upper Silesia the best account is Temperley, H. W. V., *A History of the Peace Conference,* vol. ii.

was more concerned than any other American delegate in finding a just solution. He wished full justice done to the Germans of Danzig, the Marienwerder district, and above all, Upper Silesia. He was the only peace delegate of a great Power who had ever stayed for some time in Silesia. His visits to his daughter had given him a substantial knowledge of the region, and she took pains to send him information. The comparative ease with which Wilson was brought to support the plebiscite was due to the efforts White had been making long before Lloyd George's appeal in May.

He had seen Wilson repeatedly on the subject, explaining the injustice of the wholesale cession of Upper Silesia to Poland. The President at first questioned the impartiality of White's arguments and figures. "I have heard from the French and the Poles," he objected at one meeting, "that you have a son-in-law in Upper Silesia who belongs to the class of German landlords who have been grinding the faces of the Polish peasantry for centuries." White explained that the peasants had been independent proprietors ever since the revolution of 1848, and were on the best of terms with the great landowners, who could not possibly oppress them even if they would. He said also that he knew from personal observation that many peasants who spoke both languages were German in feeling, and prized the higher degree of civilization which they felt they enjoyed under the German flag. At least it was unfair, he suggested, to place a whole province upon what might prove a lower level of culture without consulting its people.

White's words had the influence for which he hoped. It may be noted here that a year before Wilson died, White and his daughter called on him in his Washington home. As he limped into the room Wilson was an affecting sight. He attempted a pathetic little pleasantry. "My friend Mr. White's lameness," he said, "becomes him so well that I have taken a leaf out of his book." Before they left he remarked to Countess Seherr-Thoss: "But for your father I should never have known the truth about Upper Silesia; the French and the Poles had entirely misled me." [7]

For that part of the Italian claims represented by the great battle-cry "Trent and Trieste!" all the Americans had sympathy and re-

[7] Memorandum by the Countess Seherr-Thoss.

spect. In the Trentino region on the north and in the Isonzo region on the east Italy had always possessed frontiers which left large numbers of Italians under a foreign flag, and which were geographically and strategically unsound. The Fourteen Points had promised to Italy a readjustment of frontiers along clearly recognizable lines of nationality. Everyone on the Allied and American side wished to make this readjustment in a generous spirit. It was early agreed by President Wilson, for example, that Italy should be given all three of the main keys to the Adriatic: Pola at the north, Valona guarding the southern entrance, and Lissa in the middle. But Italy, exalted by her tremendous final victories under Diaz against the Austrians, and determined to bring all Italians behind secure frontiers, made claims of the most unjustifiable sort. The Treaty of London, which had brought her into the war, had promised her on the north everything up to the Brenner Pass, and on the east had assigned to her not only the Italian-speaking areas around Gorizia and Trieste, but a great stretch of almost pure Slavonic territory around the head of the Adriatic and down the eastern shore of that sea. This last territory was, of course, and with justice, now claimed by Jugo-Slavia. The American Government took the position that the secret Treaty of London was null and void, and that the problem of the Adriatic should be decided, as the Fourteen Points indicated, on a basis of strict racial justice. The Italians took the position that the Treaty of London was still entirely valid.[8]

At one point, indeed, the majority of Italians went beyond even the Treaty of London. Not only the Nationalists, who claimed nearly everything in sight, but the so-called *Rinunciatori*, who wished to conciliate Jugo-Slavia and were hence ready to give up Dalmatia, part of Istria, and the Trieste hinterland to the Serbs and Croats, demanded the cession of Fiume to Italy. In the Treaty of London, made at a time when the Allies were carrying through some rather tortuous negotiations with Serbia and Bulgaria in an

[8] Asquith excused the Treaty of London in his Paisley speech, February 5, 1920, on the ground that "the French and ourselves were fighting for our lives on the western front."—Temperley, H. W. V., *A History of the Peace Conference*, vol. i, p. 191.

effort to bring the latter nation into the war, Fiume had been expressly reserved for the Jugo-Slavs. This was mere justice. Though the city contained a few tens of thousands of Italians, it was cut off from Italy by territory which contained almost half a million Jugo-Slavs, while it was the only port which could readily meet the economic needs of the new Jugo-Slav state. It was of slight value to Italy, but almost essential to her weak neighbor. Only a little study was needed to show that it would be an outrage upon every principle of right and fairness to give the Fiume district to the Italians. Some Italians were just enough to see this, and Sonnino was ready to surrender the city, but the nation as a whole, led by Orlando, insisted upon its pound of flesh.[9]

It was upon this issue that White most sharply condemned Colonel House's tendency to improper compromises. Debate upon the Adriatic question had begun in the Council of Ten two days after Wilson left for the United States, on February 17th; the Jugo-Slavs next day were allowed to air their case in full; the Italians, guided by the cold, shrewd Sonnino, refused to permit the subject to be referred to an expert commission, as the Polish question had been, and a deadlock promptly developed. That deadlock was as complete as ever when the President returned in the middle of March. No progress had been made. Much earlier, a number of American experts, including W. E. Lunt, Charles Seymour, Clive Day, and Douglas Johnson, had given the subject thorough study and presented on January 21st a report which exposed the flimsy nature of many of the Italian claims. It took into consideration not merely lines of nationality, but strategic, economic, and political lines as well, and treated the Italians generously. Every mile of its recommended frontier, from Switzerland down to the farthest point on the eastern Adriatic, lay well within alien territory containing few or no Italians. But the report flatly denied their right to Dalmatia, to a number of islands which they claimed off its coast, and to Fiume. The line traced by this group became known

[9] Susmel, E., *La Città di Passione, Fiume 1914-20*. Late in 1918 there had been a dual occupation of Fiume by Italian and Serbian troops; but the city was shortly placed under the supervision of an inter-Allied force pending a decision by the Peace Conference.

as the "American line" or "Wilson line," and White thought that not one inch of it should be yielded.[10]

Unfortunately, Colonel House took a different view. The Italians brought heavy pressure to bear on Colonel House, on Dr. Mezes, the head of the technical experts, and on not merely the four men who had signed the report of January 21st, but other experts as well. The four experts on the Adriatic problem stood adamant; Colonel House, Dr. Mezes, and some other experts did not. With the approval of Colonel House and Dr. Mezes, a separate group of experts, who had no real responsibility for Italian frontier questions, met with the Italians and worked out a set of compromises. These proposals, as submitted to the President, offered far-reaching and as White believed quite unjustified concessions to Italy upon Fiume and Dalmatia. White later expressed warm resentment at the attitude of Colonel House toward the four authorized experts, and at House's treatment of himself and Bliss; while it is clear that he even came to believe that a deliberate effort was made to mislead Wilson.[11] In April Colonel House proposed a compromise which would give eastern Istria to Italy and place Fiume and northern Dalmatia under a temporary League administration until their sovereignty was determined; a proposal which filled White with indignation.

It was Wilson's duty, in White's opinion, to stand firm on the "American line." The four authorized experts made a supplementary report on March 18th reiterating that Fiume and all Dalmatia should go to the Jugo-Slavs; and on April 4th, joined by Allyn A. Young, they again stood to their guns, informing the President that Fiume should never be a free port, but should be Jugo-Slavia's "without restriction." They objected to a League administration as unfair both to the new monarchy and to the League. For a time the decision hung in the balance. Wilson, till he could make a

[10] On this whole matter, see Seymour, Charles, *The Intimate Papers of Colonel House,* vol. iv, p. 433 ff.—with much to be read between the lines; Baker, R. S., *Woodrow Wilson and World Settlement,* vol. ii, p. 127 ff.— still more between the lines; Miller, D. H., *Atlantic Monthly,* August, 1921. p. 272 ff.

[11] A "Memorandum on the Question of Fiume," prepared by those who wished to make what White regarded as improper concessions to Italy, is printed for the first time, in Appendix III of this book.

thorough study, was sufficiently under House's influence to hesitate. Already he had made one serious error. At an early stage of the conference he had committed himself to an unfair line between Italy and Austria, promising Orlando that Italy should have the Brenner Pass boundary though this meant handing 240,000 Tyrolese Germans over to Italian rule. The American experts pointed out this blunder and he deeply regretted it, but he had fairly bound his own hands. Should he make another mistake? White and Bliss pleaded with him. On April 17th, for the third time, six experts (for Isaiah Bowman now joined the other five) laid before Wilson an irrefutable plea for giving Fiume to Jugo-Slavia, attacking at the same time Colonel House's pet argument that Italy's support of the League must not be endangered. Her support, they declared, must not be bought by a rank injustice. General Bliss, Secretary Lansing, and White rallied behind the six in a special letter to the President. As a result, on April 18th Wilson declared that he would never give Fiume to Italy. Colonel House, receding, drew up a new proposal by which Fiume was to be held in trust by the Five Powers under the League until such time as the Italian leaders could save their faces on the matter—and the Italians promptly rejected it.

These negotiations took place in an atmosphere of excitement, and when the smoke blew away it seemed clear that Wilson's trust in Colonel House, like White's, was permanently impaired. White always believed that the Fiume issue would have been settled promptly and justly if Colonel House had stood firm instead of compromising. He strongly condemned Colonel House's manœuvres in dividing the experts. [12] This episode unquestionably explains much of Wilson's breach with House. White was in the thick of the matter, for Sonnino and Orlando, remembering his service in Italy, had naturally made a special effort to enlist his help. His letters contain frequent mention of conferences with them. In common with everybody else, he liked the Prime Minister, Orlando, the better, but he felt more respect for the Foreign Minister's abilities. Sonnino, in fact, the son of a Jewish father and a Scottish mother, was a man of exceptionally strong character, cold tempera-

[12] See White's letter to Lansing, November 8, 1919, quoted on page 475. Cf. Lansing's *The Peace Negotiations*, p. 233 ff.

ment, and shrewd mind; Orlando, a Sicilian, was warm and impulsive. In one of his notes White contrasted the two. "Orlando sheds tears copiously from time to time in the Committee of Four when things are not going his way," he wrote, "and is generally a sympathetic type of Latin; much more so than Sonnino, who is more or less a sphinx and very uncommunicative. The two have divided the Italian question between them, Orlando insisting upon Fiume, which was not provided for in the Pact of London, and Sonnino sticking to the Pact of London, saying he has no particular concern for Fiume." From time to time other Italians were detailed to work upon White. "I had three Italian ambassadors discharging their volleys at me for more than an hour yesterday evening," he wrote to his friend, Representative Rogers, upon one occasion; [13] "getting themselves into a state of the most exalted heat and reacting upon each other lustily—I almost felt not without enjoyment." But he was too well informed to listen credulously to their arguments. Like the other American delegates, with the exception of the too-conciliatory Colonel House, he never lost a chance to urge Wilson to stand fast.

In seeking a just solution of the Fiume question White did not confine his attention to Paris circles. As always, he felt it was urgently important that Congress and the American people be well informed. He wrote at great length on the subject to Senator Lodge, Representative Rogers, and Mr. Root. Particularly did he grow indignant when he found that Lodge was taking precisely the wrong stand and was encouraging the Italians to hold out for a cession of Fiume and Dalmatia.

In writing to Lodge on April 3rd, White was hopeful that the treaty would soon be completed; the great obstacles were the indemnity question, French security, and the Italian claims. In writing again on the 14th he showed more impatience. An agreement of a kind had been reached on reparations, and the Saar problem was being solved. But the questions of the Rhineland and the Adriatic remained, and were becoming more irritating. He was disappointed with the Italians. He did not say so to Lodge, but to Rogers he wrote that it was amazing to hear them talk of the great services they had rendered in the war, when all the world knew

[13] White to Rogers, Paris, April 17, 191

how troops had had to be rushed from France and England to their aid. They even had the nerve to declare that they had saved the Allies "five times," the first time being when they had refused to attack France at the beginning of the war! But in his letter of April 22nd to Lodge he spoke in blunt language:

Meanwhile, as I suppose you may have seen by the papers, the Italian question has become acute—that is to say, the state of excitement into which the Italians have got themselves at the instigation, I do not doubt, of their government, in respect to Fiume and the Dalmatian coast, for which they appear to have bargained themselves into the war. We have all given much consideration to this question and have even had maps in relief made in order to study it in all its bearings, and there can be no doubt in the mind of any unprejudiced person that, to give Fiume to the Italians when they already have Trieste as a commercial and Pola as a military port, would be extremely unfair to the new Jugo-Slav nation, and place its access to the Adriatic, as well as that of Hungary and other parts of the hinterland, at the mercy of the Italians. Lloyd George and Clemenceau are with the President in refusing to give up Fiume to the Italians, who say, however, that if they do not get it Orlando's Ministry will be overthrown and a revolution will ensue. Our delegation is united in the opinion that the President should not give way in this matter, nor acknowledge the Pact of London. . . .

There is another reason for holding out about Fiume, because if we give way on that point, we shall not have much of a leg to stand on in opposing the appropriation by the Japanese of Kiau-chau, which they are claiming, notwithstanding their promise, when they took it, to give it back to China. I understand also that they are likely to insist upon some paragraph recognizing "the equality of nations as to race and creed," or other words to the same effect, either in the treaty or as a resolution passed at a plenary session of the Conference, and I know that they are pressing for the latter as an offset to the Monroe Doctrine. So that our difficulties are not yet ended; and there is also a possibility that the Germans may not sign the treaty, with every chance in that event of further complications.

With his letter of April 14th, White sent to Lodge the memorandum of Rear Admiral Niblack of the United States Navy on Fiume, Dalmatia, and the Italian policy in the Adriatic. This denunciatory document showed that the Italians had no real economic stake in either Dalmatia or Fiume; that in occupying Fiume they had violated the terms of the Armistice by trying to Italianize the city, establishing their own police, overthrowing the local provincial governments, changing business signs and street names, and arresting and deporting or interning great numbers of Jugo-Slav subjects; and that in northern Dalmatia their occupation was "repressive, relentless, reactionary, and malevolent." Admiral Niblack flatly charged that Italy's intention in Fiume was to destroy its business possibilities so that it might not compete with Trieste, Genoa, or Naples.

The whole Eastern Adriatic crisis came to a head in the third week of April. We have seen that in the clash of the experts, the advocates of extreme concessions were decisively worsted. White reminded Wilson of the error he had made in dealing with the Tyrol; he told him that if he knew anything of the Italians and their character, in the end they would give in. The result was that the President did stand firm. In a dramatic meeting of the Four on April 19th, with Lloyd George and Clemenceau supporting him, he faced Orlando and Sonnino, rebutted their arguments, appealed to the new order in world affairs, and told them that by trying to save the Jugo-Slavs, Austrians, and Hungarians from being left with a rankling sense of injustice, which would bring on new wars, he was proving himself a better friend of Italy than they. They persisted in their stand. Orlando threatened to leave the Conference. On April 23rd Wilson suddenly appeared with his famous statement to the Italian people and the world.[14] The next day Orlando and Sonnino, as a gesture of complete defiance, left for Rome; and as they caught their train Balfour handed them a secret memorandum which asserted the opposition of France and Great Britain to the cession of Fiume. Italy was left isolated.

Amid the world-wide controversy which all this created, Lodge appeared on April 30th with a message to the Italians of Boston. He declared that Italy should have naval and military control of the Adriatic; that though the Treaty of London provided for the return of Fiume to Croatia, the dissolution of the Austrian Empire

[14] White wrote his son on April 23rd that Orlando and Sonnino had aroused Italian feeling, "thinking they could bluff it through," and were now frightened by their predicament.—White to J. C. White, Paris, April 23, 1919.

had radically changed the situation contemplated by that treaty; and that if Italy believed Fiume necessary to her protection, it should be hers. The Italians might well regard Fiume, he said, as the founders of the United States regarded the mouth of the Mississippi when they said that any nation which held that mouth was a natural enemy. The news of this utterance was promptly cabled around the globe. When White saw it his irritation with Lodge mounted again. As the first summary came over the cables he sat down to write to the Senator. He was glad, he stated, that in speaking of Fiume Lodge had said that Italy ought to have it *if it were necessary to her protection*; for Italy had not made that claim and could not do so. "I cannot help feeling, moreover, that your comparison of Fiume to the mouth of the Mississippi applies to the Jugo-Slavs and other countries of the hinterland of that port rather than to the Italians, who with the great naval port of Pola at one end of the Adriatic and Avlona at the other, will have complete control of that sea, as it is not intended that the Jugo-Slavs shall have any navy beyond a few small gunboats." A few hours later Lodge's complete letter had been cabled over and was at hand. White sat down again and completed his rejoinder to the Senator:

WHITE TO LODGE, PARIS, MAY 1, 1919

At this stage (four p.m.) the full text of your letter to the Italians in Boston has been brought to me, having been cabled this morning from Washington by the American Radio News Service, and I cannot help feeling, after reading it, that my efforts to keep you accurately informed in respect to the situation have failed signally or you would have worded your letter somewhat differently, if indeed you had written it at all.

Had you been able to study the question as I have here for several months past, you would have realized that the alleged good ports to which you refer and which Italy is willing to leave to the Jugo-Slavs on the Dalmatian coast, turn out not to be good ports at all from any point of view; especially that of commercial access for Jugo-Slavia to the Adriatic. . . . Fiume cannot possibly be considered necessary for the safety and protection of Italy, if Pola, with immediate access to the Adriatic and somewhat further south, be in her hands. It is perfectly well understood that Italy's object in wanting Fiume is that she dreads its becoming a successful rival of Trieste. If it should become an internationalized port many fear the probable removal in that event of the large number of Croatian business houses now in Trieste to Fiume, whereas if under Italian control, Fiume can be successfully used to hamper and if necessary even to prevent the outlet to the Adriatic of the various nationalities of the hinterland.

I have no personal feeling in the matter at all; but a sense of fairness, based on a careful study of the situation and a constant hearing of the arguments on both sides—though much more on the Italian than on the Jugo-Slav—have convinced me of the impropriety, from the point of view of the maintenance of peace in that region, of allowing Fiume to pass under the domination of Italy. The latter has been deporting Croatians and others in considerable numbers from Pola, Fiume, and other parts of the Dalmatian coast without waiting for action to be taken by the Conference, and has also had, for a number of months past, a large and increasing military force in Fiume which has used various means, not difficult for those in authority to bring to bear, if necessary, for the forcing of the Croatian inhabitants to express themselves as favorable to Italian sovereignty.

I understand that what the leading merchants of Fiume really want is that it shall be free from the control of either the Italians or the Jugo-Slavs, and it is just that particular arrangement to which Italy absolutely objects. In spite of what has been said to the contrary, Clemenceau and Lloyd George are just as determined as is the President that Fiume shall not be given to Italy, although they say that if driven into a corner they will be obliged to acknowledge the signatures of their respective governments to the Treaty of London.

But it was impossible to convince Lodge or even to induce him to modify his position. He continued speaking in behalf of the Italian claim. There was an ill-informed opinion in America that Wilson's decisions on Danzig and Fiume had been grossly unfair to the Poles and Italians, and as soon as the Senate met again not only Lodge, but such men as Laurence Y. Sherman of Illinois made vigorous assertions to this effect. In his first two letters in May Lodge assured White, with some heat, that he had made a special study of the Adriatic question, had read histories of Dalmatia, and knew perfectly well what he was talking about. To give Fiume to Croatia, he wrote, would be carrying out the provisions of the evil secret treaty; the population of Fiume was mainly Italian; its principal importance was not economic, but military and naval; there were plenty of good usable ports scattered along Dalmatia which the Jugo-Slavs might have. Wilson, according to Lodge, was pretty well wrong in all his territorial decisions. "Self-determination is refused to Fiume and the hinterland governs, and to Danzig self-determination is allowed and the hinterland has no rights at all. I am not interested in questions of consistency, but I am strongly of the opinion that Danzig ought to go to the Poles and Fiume to the Italians."

White wrote to Lord Bryce that with the world fast losing faith in the Peace Conference, it was deplorable that the loose incitements of Sonnino and Orlando should be raising the threat of a revolutionary uprising in Italy; but he wished to stand firm. He was scornful of Italy in his letters to Representative Rogers. They had sold themselves to the highest bidder in 1915; they had pointed a pistol at the Allies and obtained half of the German-populated Tyrol; "they willingly absorbed these 239,000 Germans, and yet are prepared to bring on a war for the sake of 24,000 Italians representing only 54 per cent of the actual population of the town of Fiume." [15] Wilson's action in issuing his statement on the subject was advised by the entire American delegation. Now, on May 5th, the Italian delegates who had so ostentatiously left Paris were about to come back, "as I felt sure they would, knowing them from long experience. I knew it was more than they could bear to be left out of a Conference such as this, with all their claims to be a great Power; but I find there is even more to their coming than I had suspected, and that is that the Ministry would probably have fallen unless they had come, and promptly come." The Italians did return, crestfallen. "None of the delegates expressed surprise or exceptional delight at their reappearance," wrote White to James Ford Rhodes, "and one or two of them, in saying good morning to their Italian colleagues, remarked upon the quality of the weather; the result being that their influence is less now than before they left." The American leader had emerged triumphant.

In the end the Treaty of St.-Germain left the Adriatic question unsettled, and the most important points had to be determined later by direct negotiation between Italy and Jugo-Slavia. Even after D'Annunzio had intervened with his violent seizure, Italy gained little. The port of Fiume was divided, Jugo-Slavia getting what has

[15] White to Bryce, Paris, April 8, 1919; White to Rogers, May 5, 1919.

since become much the more important part of it, while the Italians were left with a mere foothold in Dalmatia. President Wilson had, in the great essentials, prevented a dangerous injustice from being done to the Jugo-Slav nation.

But it was not the Polish and Italian questions that presented the most danger and threatened a real breakdown of the Peace Conference; it was the general French problem. White's emotions were more deeply involved in this than in anything else. Danzig, Upper Silesia, and Dalmatia sank into insignificance when compared with the questions of the Rhineland, the German reparations, and French security. Under the word "security," indeed, some Frenchmen wished to justify a wholesale mutilation of both Central Powers and their allies. Germany was to lose the Rhineland, Upper Silesia, Danzig, the Saar, and so on; the neighbors of Austria and Hungary were to be presented with great slices of their territory, so that there would be German and Magyar "irredentas" scattered all over Europe. To avoid any possibility of fixing the reparations totals too low, they were to be left indefinite. When Wilson came back in the middle of March it was to find that Germany was still in a semi-starving condition because the French had refused to let her be fed. Herbert Hoover had complained that French representatives obstructed every financial measure that the Americans proposed for assisting the peoples of Central Europe. Not until March 13th was a food agreement for Germany finally reached at Brussels.[16] Hungary early in April fell into the hands of the Communists under Bela Kun, and on April 22nd a Rumanian invasion of eastern Hungary began. In many lands, as Lloyd George later put it, the foundations of society seemed to be crumbling into dust. It was necessary for the Conference to move rapidly, and the French claims stood in the way of all Wilson's liberal designs.

When April opened the issue was drawn so clearly between Wilson and Clemenceau that the latter threatened to resign as Premier. He was confronted on one side by Wilson's immovable commitments to a new world order; on the other side he was fiercely attacked by Foch and Poincaré. Wilson knew that the out-

[16] The provisioning of Europe in these bitter months is ably treated by Herbert Hoover in House, E. M., and Seymour, Charles, editors, *What Really Happened at Paris*, p. 336 ff.

look was gloomy. "A new Premier," he told Ray Stannard Baker, on April 2nd, "would probably be no better than Clemenceau." Some one like the utterly impracticable Poincaré himself might come in. Hungary was collapsing, Germany might follow any day, Russia threatened to overwhelm all eastern Europe; yet still the French held out for the erection of a separate Rhineland state, for the Saar, and for an impossible reparations settlement. "The President," wrote Baker in his dairy, "said that it could not go on many days longer; that if some decision could not be reached by the middle of next week, he might have to make a positive break."

Upon this situation also White wished to keep his friend Lodge thoroughly informed. He pointed out on March 25th that some French leaders wished to invade Germany, dragging America with them. "I am afraid that the French military party here feels that while it will be almost impossible for this nation to consent to their invading Germany unassisted by any other Power, we might be persuaded to accompany them, whereby the object they have had in mind of getting us permanently involved, especially in a military way, in their support in European affairs, would be attained." He added on April 3rd that there was grave danger the President would have to confess a deadlock, leave the Conference, and lay the subject before Congress. The reason, he told Lodge, lay in "the realization during the last few days that Marshal Foch absolutely demands for the protection of France (1) the establishment of an independent state in the Rhine Province under the control of a government not connected in any way with the German National Government; (2) an inter-allied army permanently stationed there for all time to come, to which we should contribute a contingent of about 100,000 men; (3) as a further protection to France, that we should join with England in agreeing to come to the rescue of France in case she should again be attacked by Germany, the latter agreement being in the form, not of an article in the League of Nations, but of a short treaty which of course would have also to be submitted to the Senate." [18] It seemed impossible, he continued, for the Americans to make their French friends understand that the President had neither wish nor power to

[17] Baker, R. S., *Woodrow Wilson and World Settlement,* vol. ii, p. 41.
[18] White to Lodge, Paris, April 3, 1919.

engage in a permanent occupation of any part of Europe, and that
Congress would never give him any such power. He thought sometimes that the French military party did not really wish the Conference to result in peace with Germany; but he felt sure that the
French people, who were very anti-military in their views, wanted
peace at once. For himself, White was emphatically for delivering
an ultimatum to the Quai d'Orsay. He had told Wilson so on March
30th. As he wrote to Lodge in his letter of April 3rd:

I ought to add, realizing as I do the capacity of the Latins to protract
discussion to an unlimited extent, that I have felt that the time has
pretty well come for us to put down our foot and come to an understanding, telling them quite frankly what we are willing to agree to,
and what will be impossible of our assent; adding that we have only
come here to assist in bringing about a Peace; that we have no interests
of our own to satisfy and still less have we any desire to compel them
to agree to any conditions which they consider undesirable or unfavorable from a strategic or any other point of view. On the other hand, that
it is impossible for us to affix our signatures to conditions which we consider likely to lead to war in the very near future, and that if an agreement be impossible, our only course is to retire from the Conference and
for the President to lay the situation before the Congress of the United
States, which, of course, he would immediately call together for that
purpose. Having this in mind, I had a long talk with the President four
days ago and laid my views before him, urging upon him strongly the
necessity, especially in consideration of the unrest and agitation caused
by the delay of the Conference in coming to any decision, for him to
take the line I suggested. He seemed to be favorably impressed with
what I said, and I am inclined to think will put the ideas I presented
to him into effect before very long.

In an effort to facilitate an agreement on one disputed subject,
reparations, White arranged a meeting between some of the American financial experts and two members of the budget committee of the Chamber of Deputies. They sat down at luncheon in his
rooms at the Crillon. But after a talk of two hours nothing was
accomplished.[19] The French realized the impossibility of getting
enough from Germany to balance their budgets, but as yet they
were unwilling to face the French taxpayers with this fact. The
two Deputies suggested that no fixed sum be named in the treaty,

[19] *Idem.*

and the matter be left to an international commission which should meet annually and decide what Germany could pay for the ensuing twelvemonth, a procedure of which White thoroughly disapproved. A few days later White sat again at a meeting of the French and American financial experts. The situation had not materially improved, except that the French had now withdrawn their proposal for an inter-allied army in the Rhineland and were insisting upon being allowed to occupy the Rhine provinces alone if the United States and England would not join them. By this time White was thoroughly aroused. He was letting it be known on all sides that he thought the American delegation should either obtain French consent to its program or leave forthwith. He wrote to John Jacob Rogers:[20]

I had another meeting at lunch Saturday . . . between the French and American financial experts, and I think we have succeeded in making it plain to them that no assistance can be rendered in the way of credits granted by the nation or loans or anything of that kind without the authority of Congress, and that unless peace is made quickly, and a peace of which the American nation will approve, based on the Fourteen Points, our country is unlikely to look with favor upon the rendering of further financial assistance to Europe. On the other hand, that if such a peace be quickly made and thereafter the deplorable situation of France from a financial point of view be explained to Congress and to our people, they might not be indisposed to grant further assistance, although, of course, we cannot guarantee anything of the kind.

I also stated that the time, in my opinion, had arrived when we would have to decide whether it be worth our while to remain here any longer, and that it might not be unlikely, if no decision seemed possible, that the President would go home and inform Congress thereof. That body might thereupon not impossibly simply pass a brief act stating that peace exists between the United States and Germany. Everyone to whom I have suggested this idea seems horrified at the possible consequence of putting it into operation, and is hoping that it may not be necessary to do so. I am afraid that Lloyd George makes a certain amount of mischief by telling the French that he is always ready to support them and that we are not; whereas he frequently talks to us in the same way about the French. Altogether, the situation is still critical, but in my opinion by no means hopeless.

[20] White to Rogers, Paris, April 7, 1919.

In the midst of these critical difficulties, President Wilson fell sick of influenza in his house in the Place des États-Unis, and for several days was confined to his bed with a congested chest and high fever. Colonel House took his place in the Council of Four, showing, some observers thought, an excessive desire to conciliate the French; but as his proposals were brought in to Wilson, the President answered "No." When Wilson rose from his sickbed, it was to send his famous cablegram to the Navy Department ordering the *George Washington* to sail at once for France. This stroke, at once made public (April 7th), did much to clear the air.[21] Clemenceau prepared to give way at the principal points of contention. After all, he realized that the withdrawal of the American delegation would have profound political consequences in France, and that it would have profound political consequences in France, and that it and America to preserve French security. The next week was spent in arriving at a series or compromises between the Americans and French. Only Marshal Foch and the military group continued to demand the old terms. White wrote to Lodge on April 14th:

In my last letter I think I said something about its sometimes occurring to me to doubt whether the military party really wants this Conference to result in peace. Since then Marshal Foch has stated distinctly in the presence of General Bliss that nothing would give him more satisfaction than the refusal of the Germans to sign the treaty, as in that case he would be able to enter Germany at the head of an allied army, to overrun the country completely, to take possession of the financial centres, and to squeeze out every bit of money obtainable anywhere throughout the land. I cannot but feel that our people would not approve of our troops remaining abroad for an indefinite period to assist in carrying out the Marshal's wishes, unless, of course, the Germans should resume fighting,

[21] R. S. Baker treats the sending for the *George Washington* as an effective threat—*Woodrow Wilson and World Settlement*, vol. ii, p. 61. Charles Seymour regards it as an incident of small importance—*Intimate Papers of Colonel House*, vol. iv, p. 404. White, who was in an excellent position for judging, emphatically took the same view as Mr. Baker. He thought that the President summoned the ship in order to be prepared for any eventuality, including his early departure from the Conference. And he says repeatedly in his letters of the time that the threat that the Americans might withdraw filled the French and others with consternation.

of which there is no prospect or danger whatever, according to our military sources of information in Germany.

White inclosed with this letter to Lodge a report which Major-General Kernan of the American army had made after spending two months in Poland as a member of the Noulens Mission. He had found the French uniform everywhere throughout Central Europe, and a concerted effort going forward on the part of French agents to foster the military spirit in Poland and Czechoslovakia— he believed also in Rumania. An imperialistic idea had seized many Frenchmen, and they were making overt attempts to create a chain of highly militarized states under French tutelage. Poland was trying to raise an army of approximately 600,000, and the Czechs of about 250,000. Their claim that this was for defense Kernan regarded as largely pretense. Each of the three states named had aggressive designs upon the surrounding territory, and each was determined to get by force as large an area as possible. General Kernan's report, as White said, was borne out by news from other American travelers. "I suppose a certain amount of all this," he wrote to Lodge, "is due to a feeling of exuberance at France's being once more the great military power of Europe, but it renders her somewhat difficult to deal with from many points of view, as you can easily understand." He advised Lodge that the United States ought to show decided reluctance in its grants of money either to France or to these satellite nations.

But one by one, as the April days passed, compromises were made with at least a show of agreement between the French and Americans. The Saar was placed under the League, with a plebiscite in fifteen years; the reparations total was left unsettled; and it was decided that the left bank of the Rhine should be occupied for a maximum period of fifteen years, while a separate treaty was to be drafted for Anglo-American assistance to France if she were attacked by Germany. White deplored the American concessions on the reparations question, and condemned the treaty guaranteeing France against unprovoked attack. But he saw that compromise was unescapable, and was relieved by the slackening of the tension. By the middle of April he was fairly satisfied that there would be no rupture with France, and had transferred his principal concern to the Italian demands and the Japanese claims upon Kiau-chau. His letter to Representative Rogers on April 17th breathed a spirit of relief after all the anxieties of the preceding three weeks.

Even on the 14th he had been able to inform Lodge that the outlook was generally hopeful, and to take up again the question of the League of Nations, setting forth his satisfaction with the amendments just adopted. That was the day on which the Germans were finally invited to send their representatives to Versailles. The great work was nearing its conclusion. White felt free to leave Paris for a tour of the devastated regions with a party of other Americans, including the Houses, the Lansings, Ambassador Wallace and his wife, and General Bliss; the Jusserands accompanied them. A special train was put at their disposal, and they traveled north to Arras, Noyon, Péronne, and other ruined or half-ruined towns. When they returned, still more had been done by the Council of Four to whip the treaty into shape, and the time was at hand for the arrival of the Germans on April 28th. The treaty was to be delivered to them on May 7th.

White's own special Commission, that on the International Régime of Ports, Waterways, and Railways, had done a large work. It was the creation primarily of the British, who with their large export trade wished to sweep away as many as possible of the vexatious restrictions upon the use of harbors, rivers, canals, and other means of transit. Signor Crespi of Italy was chairman. The British were insistent that the Commission should draw up a sweeping convention on freedom of transit, to be included in the treaty. The French, on the other hand, wished to insure freedom of transit for the Allies, particularly in Central Europe, without yielding any reciprocal advantages to the Germans. White was in a position to exercise a dominating influence. He opposed the French effort to ostracize the Germans and to build a one-sided settlement; the general principles adopted must apply to all countries alike. In this connection he successfully attacked the proposals of the French delegates, made at the instigation of the French Admiralty, for the neutralization of the Kiel Canal. He declared that this was preposterous, and won the support of the British, Japanese, and Italian representatives for his stand. At the same time, he refused to yield to the British pleas for a general convention. Asserting that the United States was not prepared on short notice to enter into any such broad agreement, he pointed out the advantages of postponing it to a later date. Here, too, he had his way, and with happy results. The convention on freedom of transit was left to a conference which met at Barcelona in 1921, in a much more harmonious atmosphere and with a larger representation.[22]

Of the treaty as a whole White thought fairly well, but many of its parts he vigorously condemned. He had no patience with the assignment of the Tyrolese Germans to Italy, and felt indignant when he reflected that this had been done when neither he, Lansing, nor Bliss knew anything about it. It was Wilson's own indiscretion, and he blamed the President severely for it. Still more did he blame the Italians. The more he thought upon reparations, the more he regretted the decision to leave the totals indefinite. For years to come, he believed, the question would be a source of trouble. He was deeply disappointed in the clause finally adopted regarding Shantung, and heartily indorsed General Bliss's letter of protest to Wilson. He sympathized with China's desire to recover the province at once, and felt that Japan possessed no moral right to it; and though he realized that Japan held certain clear treaty rights, that Japanese pride was involved in the question, and that Japanese troops had physical possession of the area, he thought that the President should have maintained an unflinching stand.[23] The separate treaty for American military support of France he simply dismissed as impossible. White did not believe for a moment that the Senate either would or should consent to it, and he felt sure that Wilson had no real belief in it himself.

The great redeeming feature of the treaty, to White as to all other members of the American delegation except Lansing, was the League Covenant. Here, in his opinion, was a mechanism which should correct the worst faults of the peace. White was at the plenary session of the Conference on April 28th when the final amendments to the Covenant were inserted; and as he wrote to

[22] The Commission submitted its very able report early in April; it was returned for revision, and White sent the new report to Wilson on April 21st. In a covering letter he emphasized the American refusal to neutralize the Kiel Canal.

[23] Later, when more fully informed, White realized that Wilson had taken what was probably the only feasible course. Japan at once promised to restore Shantung to China, and honorably kept her promise.

Rogers, he now regarded the instrument as fairly satisfactory. He realized that for years to come the world would be full of friction and turmoil, and that some of the territorial decisions made at Paris would sorely plague Europe. But he felt that the League, in spite of its defects, would furnish a forum to the wronged peoples, would assist in correcting some of the errors, and would perhaps become the strongest guardian of world peace. He was still trying to conciliate Lodge on the subject. He wrote to the Senator in his letter of April 14th:

With regard to the League of Nations, you will doubtless have heard ere this that a paragraph covering the Monroe Doctrine, and in which it is mentioned by name, has been inserted in the final draft of the Covenant. I have contributed my mite toward the attainment of that end, by talking to many others of its importance from our point of view. There has been no objection on the part of any member of our delegation, certainly not of the President, who have all done their best to get it into the Covenant. There must be some reason as yet unknown to me why the idea was so universal at home that he objected to any amendments, for such was not my understanding, as I telegraphed you at the time; and it was perfectly clear at the plenary session of the Conference on the day of his departure that the French and several other delegations considered the draft provisional and intended—indeed Bourgeois so announced—bringing forward amendments when it should come up again for consideration in the committee. I have not yet seen the final draft, as it was only settled Friday night, and consequently there has not yet been time to print it, but sundry other amendments were introduced, and, so far as I hear (you know I am not on the committee) the chief objections which have been made at home by you and others to the draft taken to Washington by the President have been met. The newspapers have already announced to you how the Japanese amendment [for racial equality] was shelved.

You will be interested to know that Bourgeois and Larnaude spent more than an hour in combating the insertion of the Monroe Doctrine paragraph, not because of any objection in so far as the Doctrine itself is concerned, but because they said it would operate to prevent our coming to Europe and taking part in its affairs—particularly in those of France in case of her being attacked—which they, like the rest of their countrymen, consider to be of the highest importance to their future welfare. I forget whether I wrote you in a previous letter that Lloyd George held out against the Monroe Doctrine, with a view to making a bargain with us on another matter, which, if known, would, I think, create considerable interest, not friendly to him, in our country; but as he was persuaded to withdraw from his position, I will not put in writing what he had in mind, although I shall not fail to let you know the particulars when we next meet.

Lloyd George had shown a disposition to haggle over the Monroe Doctrine amendment in order to obtain some agreement for the limitation of the American navy. During Bourgeois's speech on April 28th, which was decidedly long, White noticed that Lloyd George kept asking Clemenceau how he happened to charge such a man with the League of Nations. Finally, his irritation mounting, Lloyd George demanded: "How on earth did Bourgeois ever become Premier of France?" Clemenceau whispered back: "It was when I was turning out Ministries one after the other; the supply of first-rate men ran out, and I had to stick him in!"

At last the long-sustained drama began to move toward its close. As April ended the German plenipotentiaries arrived at Versailles, where a large body of French troops hurriedly fenced in an area within which they might take their exercise. On May 1st the Allied committee, consisting of White, Cambon, Matsui, and Lord Hardinge, went to Versailles to meet the Germans and receive their credentials. The four men arrived at the Trianon Palace Hôtel just before three, and waited there for the enemy delegates. In a few moments they appeared: Count Brockdorff-Rantzau, who was the Foreign Minister, the Minister of Justice, and others. White was shocked by the agitation of Brockdorff-Rantzau, who seemed on the point of collapse. His face was chalky, his knees shook uncontrollably, and his hands trembled. A few curt and formal sentences were exchanged, documents passed from hand to hand, the two groups bowed stiffly to one another, and the Germans retired. White and his associates then drove to the Quay d'Orsay, where they related what had occurred; to White there was pathos in the humiliation of a once-great Empire, but Cambon said, coldly, that he was "glad to report the Germans seemed to be in just such a frame of mind as they should be." [24]

A week later, on May 7th—by chance the anniversary of the sinking of the *Lusitania*—there occurred in the Trianon Palace at

[24] White to J. C. White, Paris, May 7, 1919.

Versailles the dramatic scene of the presentation of the peace treaty
to the Germans for their study. The great event, as White wrote,
was admirably staged. A guard of honor saluted each Allied delegation and the four Americans as they arrived, and was then withdrawn while the Germans were sent for. White had an excellent
view of the scene as Clemenceau rose in his place and with a grim
stare at the German delegates before him announced: "You have
before you the accredited plenipotentiaries of all the small and
great Powers united to fight together in the war that has been so
cruelly imposed upon them. The time has come when we must
settle our accounts. You have asked for peace. We are ready to
give you peace." He listened carefully as Brockdorff-Rantzau, without rising from his place, began his reply: "We are under no illu-
sions as to the extent of our defeat and the degree of our helplessness. We know that the power of the German arms is broken."
Marshal Foch was prominent in the gathering; White was amused
when he heard Balfour ask why he was there, and some Frenchman
made the suave reply that it was because he was general-in-chief of
the Allied armies! He was struck by the salutation in Clemenceau's
speech, *"Messieurs les délégués de l'Empire allemand."* Brockdorff-
Rantzau's failure to rise displeased him, though he knew it might
be due to physical weakness. He was struck also by the tactlessness
of Brockdorff-Rantzau's reply, which nevertheless contained some
very good points. One of its chief statements, that Germany was not
solely guilty of the war, was of course far truer than most of the
spectators present then suspected.

The day after this event, White took time to write a summary
of his opinion of the whole Conference and treaty which merits
quotation in full. It was to a friend in the State Department whom
he completely trusted.

WHITE TO WILLIAM PHILLIPS, PARIS, MAY 8, 1919

You know the contents of the Treaty. . . . In many respects it is a
disappointment to three members of the Delegation—your chief, General
Bliss, and myself, who, I may add, were not consulted in respect to a
number of the decisions arrived at by that mysterious body, "the Council
of Five," "Four," or "Three," as the case may be from time to time.
Latterly it has been chiefly a Council of Three. The Treaty is naturally

much longer than it might have been, as our friends here insisted upon all manner of commercial and economic clauses which we should not have felt necessary, but of course, its worst feature is the abandonment of the Fourteen Points in a number of cases and the weakening of the League of Nations by the President's agreement to come to the rescue of France in case of her being attacked by Germany, thereby implying that the League of Nations does not afford sufficient protection in that respect. And Marshal Foch still says that the protection afforded France is entirely inadequate!

The three delegates previously mentioned consider the Chino-Japanese decision, or rather the handing over of Germany's rights in Shantung to Japan rather than to China, unfortunate—to put it mildly. Our opinion was asked in the matter, and while we were considering it, the decision was arrived at by the Three. That circumstance, combined with others of a similar nature, has convinced me of the danger which I have felt all along of the President's being alone and unprotected by anyone with him to take notes or whose testimony might be available in case statements attributed to him hereafter should be questioned, or to give advice relative to questions suddenly sprung upon him. He allowed himself to be persuaded to adopt the smaller Council as a better means of doing business, whereas, as I felt at the time and have been convinced ever since, it merely placed him in the power of the other Chiefs of State, chiefly those of France and England.

In any case, the friends of France cannot say that she has been "abandoned," to which the senior Senator from Massachusetts wrote me recently that France's friends in our country would never consent; but, between ourselves, there can be no doubt that French diplomacy, as shown by the Treaty, has had the advantage over American, and that in almost every case in which it clashed with the latter, the President in the end gave way, without always knowing it. Of course, concessions in respect to Japan make our firm stand, which so far as I understand is still maintained in respect to Fiume and the Treaty of London, much more difficult; although the President declares that he means to stand firm on both these points and even to retire from the Conference rather than give way on either of them.

You, of course, have realized that the Italian delegates returned yesterday without any invitation whatever from the Conference to do so; full of bitterness, I understand, against France and to a lesser extent against England, but not nearly so much so against us. The real fact is that the French and British were not anxious that they should return, fearing that if they were to do so, they would demand the carrying out of the Treaty of London, which I understand is exactly what they propose to do, and the President says he would rather leave the Conference than recognize the Treaty of London. I should have been disposed to support him to the hilt in this stand but for his concessions to Japan, which have so seriously weakened his whole position.

The fact is, my dear William, that the League of Nations, in which he has been more deeply interested than anything else from the beginning, believing it to be the best if not the only means of avoiding war in the future, has been played to the limit by France and Japan in extracting concessions from him; to a certain extent by the British too, and the Treaty as it stands is the result. The Italians overshot the mark and found themselves not only with the President but with France and England dead against them—the British, as regards Fiume, chiefly for commercial reasons.

White went on to say that although there was some doubt whether the Germans would sign the treaty, he felt fairly certain that they would. He continued:

The President has evidently pretty well made up his mind not to go home until he has either signed the Treaty or there is no immediate hope of getting it signed. He has called Congress for the 19th of this month, but has no intention of being there when it resumes its sessions, for the reason aforesaid. I cannot help feeling that he will be attacked in many directions the moment the session opens, and that in his absence there will be no one in a position either from full knowledge of what has taken place or from proper authority to do so, to defend him, and that the opposition will have taken a pretty good hold of the country before he returns.

There is much more that I might tell you as to the inner working of things than there is room for in this letter; but I should like to let you and also Frank Polk know that my opinion of Lansing's ability and strength of character has steadily increased since I have been associated with him. We have thought and felt alike on nearly every subject, and between ourselves, I think I have been useful in preventing friction between him and another member of the Commission, as a result of the latter's disregard of him in many questions respecting which he should have been consulted and brought forward. And I think the President has also been brought closer to him and depends more on him now than he did during the earlier period of the Conference, or than he had been in the habit of doing before they came abroad, as a result of certain quiet action on my part. General Bliss is also a much abler man than I imagined him to be before getting to know him. *Between our-selves*, he wrote a letter to the President, embodying Lansing's and my views, as well as his own, on the Japanese question, which thereby fortunately placed them on permanent record.

It may interest you to know, also in confidence, that I have established very friendly relations with Mrs. Wilson and Miss Benham, whom— particularly the former—I find a valuable channel for communication with the President. I have been surprised to find in her a much keener perception than I expected in respect to questions more or less compli- cated, and especially a right-mindedness on subjects whereof I shall tell you more particularly when next we meet.

In a letter to James Ford Rhodes a week later White expressed the same doubts. Though he hoped that his work had contributed something to world appeasement, "I am not sure that the Treaty as at present drawn will attain that end." But, he added philosophi- cally, "one can only hope for the best and trust that by means of the League of Nations the world may be got into a frame of mind tend- ing towards peace and to a realization that war does not pay, to say nothing of the horrors for which it is responsible." [25]

There followed the dragging weeks of delay as Germany sought to obtain modifications of the harsh terms of peace, while the Allies stubbornly responded to her arguments. We shall say some- thing on a later page of White's activities during this period, though the great hours of the Peace Conference were now past. He was of course present on the day of the signing of the treaty, and was somewhat surprised to find that the crowded Hall of Mirrors and the ceremonial gave him no thrill; advancing years, he reflected, and a life-long habit of taking events as they came, without excite- ment, had robbed him of the emotion he should have felt. That same evening, June 28th, the President sailed for the United States. Before he left White had been able to do him one more service. In his final week in France he was invited by President Poincaré to dine at the Elysée Palace, this being a natural act of hospitality;

[25] Lord Bryce wrote White on May 19th, offering to organize a demon- stration in the House of Lords in favor of the League of Nations. White replied, discouraging the proposal on the ground that it would strengthen the arm of American critics who assailed the League as a bulwark of British interests; and Wilson wrote that "you were absolutely right in the reply you made to him."—Wilson to White, Paris, May 23, 1919.

but Wilson hesitated to accept. He was full of resentment against
Poincaré for the part the latter had played during the Conference.
He believed that the French President and Marshal Foch had tried
at every step to balk his plans and to convert a peace of justice into
a peace of injustice. When Wilson confided this feeling to the American delegation and said that he was disposed to decline the invitation, White expostulated not only verbally but by a vigorous letter.[26]
In view of the fact that Wilson had been the nation's guest for so
many months, White pointed out that such a refusal would be
taken by the French as a national affront; so great was the sympathy of most Americans for France that such action would also be
resented in the United States. With some reluctance Wilson yielded,
and consented to sit at the board of the man whose whole course
during the Peace Conference he regarded as ignoble.

[26] White to Wilson, Paris, June 24, 1919. White wrote that he felt
strongly "that the relations between France and the United States should not
be jeopardized by any incident which can possibly be avoided, especially in
view of the effect which such a situation would produce upon the German
national mind at this very critical juncture."

CHAPTER TWENTY-THREE

The Peace Conference: Rejection of the Treaty

WITH the return of President Wilson to the United States at the beginning of July, the center of American interest shifted from Paris to Washington. Important work remained to be done by the Peace Conference, and White stayed on at the Crillon to do his share; but the battle that was beginning in the Senate attracted all eyes. Congress had been sitting in extra session since May. At the beginning of June resentment was manifested by many Senators because they had as yet no copy of the treaty, though it was now in the hands of many people in Europe. As a matter of fact, President Wilson was not responsible for the half-secrecy which surrounded the document; he would have given it out, but the Allied leaders insisted on keeping it from their respective publics till the last moment. The German Government had no such desire to suppress it, and it was soon being sold all over Germany for nominal sums. Copies were carried to the United States, and Senator Borah was able to reprint it in the *Congressional Record*, thus giving it a wide American circulation. On June 12th Senator Knox reported from the Foreign Relations Committee a resolution calling for the separation of the peace treaty and the Covenant, and thereafter the debate grew ominous for the League. On June 23rd Elihu Root made public a letter in which he suggested a program of reservations for the Senate to demand.[1] When on July 10th President Wilson formally laid the treaty before the Senate, it was clear that the Covenant would meet strong opposition.

By the letters he received from Lodge during May and June, White could measure the intensity of much of the Republican feeling. Lodge denounced various features of the Peace Treaty proper, and especially those relating to Fiume, Danzig, Shantung. It struck

[1] "Root's letter," Lodge wrote to White, "has consolidated feeling in the Senate," and "is producing immense effect upon public opinion throughout the country."—Lodge to White, Washington, June 23, 1919.

him as unfair that Italy was denied Fiume, which had been an enemy port, while Japan was given Shantung, which was the territory of an ally, containing forty millions of people. "To give Shantung to Japan is worse than anything the Holy Alliance did," he indignantly asserted.[2] To the special treaty for American military assistance to France in the event of German attack he had no marked objection, and in May he thought that if there had been no League and no Article Ten, it would have been well received.[3] Nor was he particularly opposed to an American mandate for Armenia, though he believed that the nation at large was utterly hostile to it.

But it was the Covenant upon which Lodge concentrated his attack. After the revision of this document in Paris, he wrote to White that "as to the new draft of the Covenant, the form is somewhat improved"; and he mentioned as changes for the better the amendment which gave member nations the right to withdraw, and the clause which made acceptance of a mandate voluntary.[4] But in other respects the safeguards struck him as inadequate. He thought the Monroe Doctrine amendment worthless, and predicted that the Senate would make a determined effort to rewrite it. He did not think that each nation's right to control its own immigration laws had been properly guaranteed, and he expressed the gravest apprehension regarding Article 10. "There is also the greatest possible resentment, I think," he added, "not only in the Senate but generally in the country—it is apparent wherever it is mentioned in public meetings—against the attempt which is to be made to force through the League by entwining it with the peace with Germany. That is a method of procedure which is extremely disliked by both the Senate and the people." In a letter on May 20 he was still more emphatic:

As to the amendment embodying the Monroe Doctrine, that and the amendments attached to it are perfect frauds. There is not one which is of any real value, and the one about the Monroe Doctrine to which you refer is very mischievous. It leaves it a great deal worse off than it was

[2] Lodge to White, Washington, May 6, 1919. Lodge wished the Poles to have Danzig.
[3] Lodge to White, Washington, May 20, 1919.
[4] Lodge to White, Washington, April 30, 1919.

in the first draft. It leaves it exactly as England says in her summary, for the League to decide upon its interpretations. Now the Monroe Doctrine is not an international engagement, which it has never been, and it is not a regional understanding, which is the most ridiculous phrase I have ever heard. It has been a policy of the United States and never anything else. We have declared and applied it and in my judgment we shall always continue to do so. As recently as the Hague Convention it was reserved by our delegates. Nobody has ever agreed to it. We have never asked anybody to agree to it. Article 10 was not amended at all. The privilege of a withdrawal at the end of two years was nullified by the condition that the nation offering to withdraw should fulfill all its obligations and the League was to decide by unanimous vote whether it fulfilled its obligations or not. Therefore if one nation dissented, no nation could get out. I use this merely as an illustration of the difficulties that leap to the eye. It does not, I think, meet the views of the Senate and there will be a very serious fight upon it.

Lodge expressed the hope that White was reading the American discussion on the League. "And what the final judgment of the people will be I do not know. They are, of course, very anxious to have the peace—we all are. There is no doubt the hostility to the League of Nations has grown, and if they adopt it, it will be a sorry day for the country in years to come which you and I are not likely to see."

White's position upon all this was fairly simple. He thought then, and later, that the Covenant would be improved by some clarifying reservations, including one to Article 10; but he never approved of all the reservations suggested by Lodge, for he thought some of them superfluous. He believed in the League, but he did not believe that it was his place to fight for it or to defend all its features. He wrote sharply, however, about some of the Senate extremists, such as Laurence Y. Sherman of Illinois, who was absurdly denouncing the League as founded upon the betrayal of Poland, the robbery of China, the abrogation of a sacred treaty with Italy, a base paltering with the principle of self-determination, and a duplicity unrivaled even at the Congress of Vienna.

What he wanted, above all, was more fairness in the discussion than he thought was likely to be shown: fairness to the League, to the American delegation and Wilson, to the Germans and the Jugo-Slavs and the Japanese. As regarded the critics of the League,

he was willing to go a great deal further with the liberals and ideal-
ists than with the hard conservatives. In one of his letters he mentioned with sympathy the protest signed near the end of May by the
Bishop of Oxford, Gilbert Murray, H. G. Wells, John Masefield,
and other British intellectuals, who declared that the Saar and
Polish settlements would poison international relations, and that
the indemnity would reduce Germany to economic servitude. A
great many Americans felt in the same way. White could understand this. He could not understand men who denounced the
treaty because the Italians did not get a port which plainly belonged to Jugo-Slavia, or because the Poles did not get a great city
of German population. Strongly as he condemned some of Wilson's steps and much as he regretted that before certain momentous
decisions Wilson should have taken no counsel with the Commissioners or the experts, he did not wish the President criticized
on unjust grounds. He still defended him as having done all he
could to expedite the treaty—a defense which drew from Lodge
the following retort: [5]

What you say about my criticism of the President for holding up discussion in the beginning is misquoted. What I said was this, and I
said it on the floor of the Senate: That the President asked me and
others not to discuss the first draft of the League of Nations until he
had had an opportunity of meeting us at the White House. That injunction I religiously observed, and did not open my mouth till after
the White House dinner. The President, however, landed in Boston,
my own town as it happened, and made a violent speech in behalf of
the League, having closed my mouth as a preliminary. I dare say this
is all right under the modern fashion, but to me it is contrary to the
principles of conduct on which I happen to have been brought up.

White entirely sympathized with the feeling of Lodge and others
that the treaty should have been made public to the whole world
soon after it was presented to the Germans. He knew that Wilson
shared this view, and had not been responsible for the delay. In
his letters to Lodge he vigorously defended the President, explaining that it was Lloyd George and Clemenceau who, fearing a storm
of criticism at home, had temporarily suppressed the document.
This was true. It was also true, as Elihu Root pointed out, that

[5] Lodge to White, Washington, June 12, 1919.

when Germany made the treaty public it was public, and Wilson
would have done better to recognize the fact. White's correspondence indicates that a good many copies reached the United States
in a clandestine way early in June. Root showed one to Lodge which
came from Henry P. Davison of J. P. Morgan & Company, who
had received it from Thomas Lamont. Lodge also procured one
from the Chicago *Tribune*, and handed it to Borah, who, as we
have seen, had it published. "It was perfectly silly management,"
wrote Lodge, and it was; but White was anxious that this should
not be attributed to sinister motives on the part of Wilson.

The other subjects on which White and Lodge exchanged confidences were the question of mandates and the Irish problem, and
on the former they were in agreement. At first White had an open
mind as to the American acceptance of a mandate in the Near East.
He did not like entanglements in Old World affairs; he equally
disliked to see the Armenians abandoned to what threatened to
be an awful fate. Lodge also had an open mind. As late as June
23rd he wrote to White: "I think it would make infinite trouble
if the present peace delegation undertook to commit the United
States to being a mandatary anywhere, and would irrevocably lead
at a later day to the revocation of the mandate by Congress. I can
see the great advantage it would be to have the United States take
a mandate in certain cases—I refer to Constantinople and Armenia—
and I have written you before that I have no such prejudice against
it as have many other people, but I think the general feeling
throughout the country as well as in Congress is against our being
mandataries anywhere. It does not appeal to the American people."
Both became more and more hostile to the idea of a mandate.
White came to object to the rôle of participant in what he regarded
as the inevitable squabbles of France, Italy, and Great Britain for
territory and trade in Asia Minor; he pointed out that the United
States had no trained personnel, such as the British and French
possessed, for administrative work in a foreign land. In midsum-
mer he wrote to Lodge that he was flatly against taking any mandate for Armenia alone, the most troublesome, difficult, and poorest
part of Asia Minor, and Lodge agreed with him.

On the Irish question they differed. The American Commission
for Irish Independence, which consisted of Frank P. Walsh, Ed-

ward F. Dunne, and Michael J. Ryan, had visited Paris in May
to demand a hearing for Irish representatives. White viewed them
with dislike. He thought they were meddlers. The Irish question
seemed to him no business of the American peace delegation at all.
Lodge, who knew that there were Irish as well as Italian voters in
Boston, took a different view. Early in June the Foreign Relations
Committee reported a resolution earnestly requesting the American
delegation to try to secure a hearing before the Peace Conference
for De Valera, Arthur Griffith, and Sir Horace Plunkett. White
thought this was improper, and wrote to Lodge that, so far as he
could see, the Irish question had "nothing to do with the making
of peace with Germany and Austria, which seemed to me to be the
particular job of the American delegation." [6] He thought that the
whole business was cheap politics, unworthy of a great nation.
Lodge's reply was spirited: [7]

As to the Irish matter, you say that it did not come within the
jurisdiction of the Peace Conference, which was what the President said
at the White House and which was quite true. Neither did the Monroe
Doctrine come within the jurisdiction of the Peace Conference. Still
less were we disposed to take in silence the British explanation of what
the Monroe Doctrine was, and their entirely just claim that under the
new draft it was for the League to decide what it was. This produced
a great deal of irritation in this country and led to the unanimous vote
—that is, only one man voted against—on the Irish resolution. The
English attitude has not been fortunate.

In his next letter, July 2nd, his comments were even more caustic. Wilson could do nothing for the Irish-Americans, any more
than for the Egyptians, and after honestly presenting the Senate
resolution to the Peace Conference, he let the matter drop. Lodge's
letter is worth quoting in full for the light it throws on his and
White's relations and on the Senator's attitude toward the treaty:

[6] White to Lodge, Paris, June 6, 1919. The House of Representatives just
before its adjournment in March passed the Gallagher resolution asking that
the President and Peace Conference "favorably consider the claims of Ireland
to self-determination." A few hours before he sailed back to Paris Wilson
cordially received a group of Irish-Americans—first making them purge their
delegation of Judge Daniel F. Cohalan, whom he regarded as disloyal.

[7] Lodge to White, Washington, June 23, 1919.

UNITED STATES SENATE,
July 2, 1919.

Personal

MY DEAR HARRY:

My best thanks for your letter of June 12th. Since you wrote it the Germans have finally signed, as I expected they would, and I suppose next week will see the President here with his treaty. There are things in the League as formed which I can never assent to; but I know the situation in the Senate pretty thoroughly. I do not believe that the League can possibly be ratified without some very strong reservations, such as those outlined by Mr. Root, whose masterly letter no doubt you have seen. If the President adheres to his position that we must ratify it without crossing a "t" or dotting an "i," my best judgment is that he will fail. The treaty will be sent to him with reservations, and then it will be up to him to hold it back. I am giving a good deal of thought and time to it. It is perfectly evident at this moment, although things change of course, that the Republican majority in the Senate is practically solid for the Root reservations. They will have two or three Democratic votes, at least, and there is more than one rift in the Democratic party already.

Wilson's attitude has forced the Irish question to the front. The resolution of sympathy for Ireland, demanding a hearing—which I think their representatives were entitled to—was brought about by Wilson's attitude and it may assume a very much more serious aspect. You know what the Irish vote is in this country. As far as I can make out, they are bitterly opposed to the League, and the fate of the Democratic party in the Northern States is in their hands. They are having great meetings and all pronouncing against the League. Cardinal O'Connell presided at one of these meetings in Boston. I know what the feeling of Cardinal Gibbons is, and I wish that Mr. Wilson by his manœuvres had not roused this question.

As for Shantung, as I said to you before, I cannot say how gratified I was that you took the same view. That question is growing in importance all the time. There is a great deal of feeling about it in the country and that feeling will grow enormously when the question is debated and exposed, as it will be in the Senate with great force. Mr. Wilson may get the votes, but he has got to get Republican votes and he has not got them now, and the opposition is stiffening and not weakening. In fact, I think the opinion throughout the country—despite the press, which does not, I believe, represent the real feeling of the people— is hardening everywhere against the League as it stands.

Your little word in regard to the third term is very interesting, but I shall not comment on it.[8]

I shall not enter into any argument about Fiume, but it does amuse me a little to think that France and England are so disturbed about Italian selfishness. We have a right, if we choose, to criticize other people for selfishness because—although I do not mean to say we are any better than our neighbors—we have no national interest to serve. We ask nothing and we get nothing. But I notice that England has managed in one way or another to secure an immense deal of territory, and I fancy that in Asia Minor she is going to get a good deal more. I also notice that France has looked after her own interests fairly well. I am in full sympathy with her demands, but she has certainly managed to get a good deal. And I very much fear that behind Shantung there is a plan between Japan, France, and England ultimately to partition China. But this is a mere suspicion so far.

I shall not attempt to go into all the very interesting things you tell me, for I am worked to death just now and I have not much time to write. . . .

Always affectionately yours,

H. C. LODGE.

Some time afterward White heard from Lord Reading, the British ambassador, that before his departure from the United States he was visited by two "prominent Republicans." Reading did not state whether they were Senators. They called to explain that it would be necessary to make every possible effort to defeat the Democrats in 1920, and that in using the Irish question for that purpose they would attack England mercilessly, but that they wished him to inform his government that there was no real animosity in the matter.

After Wilson's departure on June 28th, White's responsibilities were materially increased, and on July 12th, when Lansing left for home, they became still greater. From July 12th to 29th he represented the United States on the "Council of Five" and with General Bliss carried on the work of the American Commission. Of this there was a great deal. The partition of Austria-Hungary involved the most extensive territorial changes, and it was not until

[8] White had been told by Mrs. Wilson that President Wilson would under no circumstances accept a third term.

September 10th that the Austrian treaty was finished and signed. Nine days later the Supreme Council handed the Bulgarians their special peace treaty. Meanwhile the affairs of Rumania—which was running amuck and had to be sharply halted by an ultimatum from the Allies—of Turkey, and of all Asia Minor, presented urgent and painful problems. Italy still had to be dealt with, and when White's old friend Tittoni arrived in July at the head of a delegation, declaring that he deeply regretted the course pursued by his predecessors, Orlando and Sonnino, and would do his best to seek an agreement, White carried on prolonged negotiations with him. White repeated that the United States could never agree to Italian sovereignty over Fiume and Dalmatia, but that it was by no means committed to Jugo-Slav sovereignty in the former, and had always been ready to arrange for an international administration there. Tittoni, in the true spirit of the Conference, thereupon set about seeking "compensations" from the British and French in Africa.

There were also innumerable routine matters to be supervised. During July almost daily sessions were held by the two American Commissioners, White and Bliss, in the beautiful "Salon des Aigles" at the Hôtel Crillon, at which a weird and confusing variety of problems were dealt with. The work of the various field commissions was supervised; the sale of arms, munitions, and military equipment in Europe was discussed; special agents or representatives were heard upon conditions in German East Africa, in Hungary, in Armenia, and indeed all over the map; Herbert Hoover was consulted upon coal and food for Central Europe; the request of the Italian Government for an immediate credit of $162,500,000 in the United States was debated—and so on endlessly. Meanwhile, White attended daily, and sometimes twice a day, the meetings of the Council of Five, usually consisting of Clemenceau, Balfour, Tittoni, Makino, and himself, which was attacking the urgent problems of all southeastern Europe and Asia Minor. From time to time White made long reports by cable to Wilson, summarizing the negotiations upon Dalmatia, Western Thrace, and other disputed territories.

The work of the Council of Five, or Supreme Council, was particularly harassing and perplexing, and White found that for some of its delays the United States was responsible. For example, at the end of July the Allies were unwilling to fix the southern frontiers of Bulgaria until they knew whether the United States would accept a mandate for the proposed "international state" of Constantinople. The solutions of a good many territorial questions in Asia Minor were held in uncertainty for the same reason. It was of course clear that the American delegates would sign the Austrian treaty. But for some time nobody was certain that they would sign the treaties with Bulgaria and Turkey, and the experts attached to the Commission declared that much depended upon the decision. If Washington were to guarantee the treaties, then the terms would be different from those imposed if it did not. In the end, the United States signed only the Bulgarian treaty, abstaining from the Turkish treaties of Sèvres and Lausanne, and refusing utterly to accept any commitments in the Near East. White, it should be mentioned, always strongly condemned the temporary suppression of the King-Crane report on Syria, under pressure from France—the report having stated that a French mandate would be wholly unacceptable to the people. He thought it deplorable that the Syrian preference for American or British supervision should be roughly ignored.

While thus employed, White had duties of other kinds. He helped to review the parade of American battalions in Paris on July 4th, and had an opportunity for a few words with Marshal Foch, asking him whether, as a result of his recent visit to the eastern border, he felt any safer against German attack. The marshal replied emphatically, *"Monsieur l'Ambassadeur l'Allemagne n'existe plus"* [9]—of course meaning in a military sense alone. White also witnessed the great celebration of July 14th, and thrilled with pride at the fine appearance of the American troops. "Pershing's appearance was admirable—the perfect type of what an American commander ought to be. He rode a fine horse and headed our body of troops, which latter impressed everyone who saw them. As several persons have said to me since, they looked like a marching wall of invincible strength; and so they really did, and they all seemed, as they marched past me, to be of a superior type of manhood to that of any of the other troops." He included, in his letter to Lodge, some of the gossip of the occasion:

[9] White to Lodge, Paris, July 22, 1919.

WHITE TO LODGE, PARIS, JULY 22, 1919

I do not know whether you have heard of the row that took place behind the scenes about Marshal Joffre. I think I have already told you of the extraordinary—and to us almost disgraceful—way in which he has been treated. And it was decided by those in authority that he should not ride in the procession. He thereupon decided to leave Paris for a fortnight, and so informed our artist who is painting his portrait. This decision in course of time became known, and so many were the protests which reached the Government that President Poincaré decided to ask Joffre to sit beside him, and thus to view the procession, which, however, did not suit the public at all, and a debate was threatened—I think even actually begun—in the Chamber of Deputies. Finally the Government wisely decided to give way, and it was then arranged that Joffre should ride with the leading generals behind Marshal Foch; but the public, with whom Joffre is extremely popular, would not stand even that; and insisted that he and Foch should ride side by side, as they did; and of course received a most enthusiastic ovation. Pershing was also received with enthusiasm, and as far as I could see or have since heard, so were our troops.

In the same letter he added some remarks on the city:

I have never had time to write to you about the appearance of Paris during the greater part of our stay here, with American troops constantly in evidence, messengers innumerable in American uniform dashing about in all directions on motor-cycle side-cars, and perhaps most extraordinary of all, members of our admirable military police force standing side by side with the French policemen at the principal crossings, both in the Champs Elysées and in other parts of Paris. Of course, they always tower above the French policemen in stature, and, I am bound to say, in general appearance, both as to "smartness"—"*tenue*," as they say here—as well as superior intelligence in the management of traffic. Then the Avenue of the Champs Elysées has been and still is lined from top to bottom with captured German cannon, whereof the Place de la Concorde also is full, the larger ones surrounding the Obelisk and also the Arch of Triumph. One of the most imposing and striking features of the decoration of the Champs Elysées for the Peace Celebration on the 14th was the dumping, with the assistance of steam cranes, of a vast number of captured German artillery and piling it up high on each side of the Round Point, the whole being surmounted by a French cock in plaster, crowing. It is a wonder to me that the subway, which runs beneath this pile of useless artillery, should not have collapsed under the weight of the crowds which made use of it as a coign of vantage from which to see the procession.

At the end of July, Frank L. Polk, the Assistant Secretary of State, arrived as the new head of the American Peace Commission. From both Lansing and Lodge, on opposite sides of the political fence, White had heard of his ability, and he quickly found that everything they had said of him was true. At once Polk took White's place in the "Council of Five." He was much liked there. At one meeting White saw old Clemenceau nod his gray head slowly at Polk as he entered and say to the prefect of the Seine, who was standing near by, "*Il est tout-à-fait étonnant.*" For some much-needed rest, and above all for his first visit to his daughter, White left Paris on August 14th for a ten days sojourn in Scheveningen, where she and her family were staying. It was his first absence from Paris for more than a day or two at a time since his arrival in the preceding December.

When he took this trip Europe was still feverish and seething with turmoil. The Rumanians, by their ruthless invasion of Hungary and their wholesale looting of the country through which they passed, had excited the indignation of the world.[10] A bitter feeling had arisen between the French and Italian peoples, and Clemenceau and Tittoni passed anxious hours trying to keep it in check. In Fiume there exploded a small but bloody riot between the troops of the two nations. Meanwhile, from far-off Armenia there came news which wrung every humane heart. The British had been compelled by the stern popular demand for peace to withdraw their troops in that region, and an overwhelming Turkish army was reported to be advancing from one quarter upon the almost helpless Armenians, a Soviet force from another. There loomed up the danger of another great massacre. Fighting was constantly going on between the Poles and Ukrainians, and the threat of a great Russian assault upon Poland troubled everyone who looked eastward. White enjoyed to the full the week he spent with his daughter, her husband, and their three children at Scheveningen, the long

[10] The French had encouraged the Rumanians in their advance into Hungary, and were disconcerted when they got out of hand.—White to Lodge, Paris, August 13, 1919.

half-days on the sands being varied by trips to Haarlem, Amsterdam, and other cities. But he went in a sad mood, and when he came back he was still more depressed by a visit to the worst of the war-stricken regions. He sent Lodge an account of his observations:

WHITE TO LODGE, PARIS, SEPTEMBER 10, 1919

The most interesting day of my trip, however, was the last, from Ostend to Paris, *via* Dixmude, Ypres, Arras, Lens, Bapaume, Péronne, Ham, Noyon, Compiègne, and Senlis, a considerable part of it through an absolutely desolate and devastated country. At certain spots where fighting had been heavy, tanks, overturned and twisted into every conceivable shape, could be seen along or near the roads, as well as periodical camps of German prisoners working to clean up the country, which the British appear to be still doing in their section with German assistance. An officer to whom I spoke said they were still picking up dead bodies, and happened to discover one in a tank just as I passed by. As far as the eye could reach along certain parts of the road, there were no signs of farm work, and the only vegetation was a sort of rough grass growing on the hillocks, which seem to extend for a long distance on either side of the road and to render ploughing a matter of impossibility to one unversed in agriculture, such as myself, for all time to come. I was told that the idea is to plant a good deal of this territory with pine trees, which will grow in time and thereby increase the forest land of France. Not a city or village for more than two hundred miles, including the town of Senlis, which is almost in sight of Paris, that is not more or less badly damaged, and some of them, such as Lens and certain villages, without a single house standing.

In this same letter White included a reminder to Lodge that the unsettled and troubled world was in some measure waiting upon the action of Washington:

Everyone here is following the vicissitudes of the Treaty in the Senate with much interest. I do not mean only in Paris, but on this side of the ocean. Clemenceau told me this morning that he thought the Treaty would be ratified by this country next week. The Chamber of Deputies is supposed to do so tomorrow, or, at the latest, Saturday, and the Senate is not likely to take more than a day or two over it next week. All the necessary steps for ratification have been taken in England, and Tittoni assures us that Italy will ratify within a similar period; and those three will, as you know, set the Treaty with Germany in operation, as far as Europe is concerned. The newspapers state today that the Treaty will be reported out of the Foreign Relations Committee today or tomorrow, and that discussion will begin in the Senate on Monday next. As the importance of the situation is now entirely on our side of the water and not in Europe, there is nothing I can say from here which will further elucidate the situation, and we must just await the issue of events, which I hope for the world's sake may not be very long delayed, whatever the outcome.

Soon after his return White went to St.-Germain on September 10th to sign the treaty with Austria. It was a solemn occasion, and he fully appreciated the historic significance of an event which brought to an end all that remained of the Holy Roman Empire. He also made a trip about this time with various Frenchmen and Americans to the Pointe de Grave, from which Lafayette slipped away to take ship to the United States. There were speeches by President Poincaré and Ambassador Wallace, after which they all lunched in a marquee on the banks of the Gironde and returned to Bordeaux. "The President in his speech," wrote White to Lodge, "referred to our action in the war as 'decisive,' the nearest approach I have heard made by anyone high in authority here to an admission that our intervention won the war, except by Joffre and Chambrun." M. Loucheur took him later from Paris to a historic house in his possession, the château of Louveciennes in which Mme. Du Barry had lived. "In the beautifully painted dining-room," he told Lodge, "the cupboard in which Mme. Du Barry was discovered when they came to arrest her, still exists, and the terrace wall close by, from which the decapitated head of her lover, Cossé-Brissac, was thrown, is still there. Loucheur has a number of her letters and a number of documents, showing that after the death of Louis XV she must have been pretty hard up for money. I thought of you, as I always do on occasions of historical interest, and felt that, having established relations of a friendly nature with Loucheur, I may perhaps have the pleasure one of these days of going there with you."

It was in September that the so-called Bullitt affair made a commotion out of all proportion to its real importance. In White it aroused a feeling of indignant disgust. William C. Bullitt, an erratic young man who had held a minor post in the American peace delegation, testified on September 12, 1919, at a public hearing of the Senate Foreign Relations Committee. Part of what he said was sensational. He retailed a confidential conversation with Lansing, who according to him had stated that he considered many parts of the treaty thoroughly bad; that he thought the League "entirely useless," and that if the Senate and the American people only understood what the treaty really meant, "it would unquestionably be defeated." Clemenceau dryly remarked that "I got my bullet at the Conference, but Lansing got his afterward." White knew the man. He at once wrote to Lodge minimizing Bullitt's knowledge and pointing out that he had committed a gross breach of trust:

He was not one of the regular experts of the Delegation, but merely an attractive and rather brilliant personality, who had been taken on by the State Department for a while during the war, and got himself attached to the Commission. His chief duty while here, so far as I can make out, was to visit each Commissioner every morning and bring him a summary of the news of the previous twenty-four hours, as ascertained and boiled down—in an attractive form, certainly—by him.

His trip to Russia, to which he refers, was in no sense as an official representative of our Delegation, although I am afraid he gave that impression to Lenin and Trotsky. He was merely sent by Lansing and Colonel House to ascertain conditions, as he was particularly anxious to do so, and they felt that he might obtain information tending eventually to the solution of the Russian situation. Neither General Bliss nor I were even aware that he had gone until some time after his departure. It may interest you to know, furthermore, that after his resignation he went to England, and, I am told, endeavored to persuade Asquith to take up the mantle, as champion of the emancipation of the masses, which he felt the President had allowed to fall so ignominiously from his own shoulders. My information is that Asquith could not be persuaded to do this; but that London society, or at least a part of it, took Bullitt up for a time as quite a lion. . . .

And to this statement White added a careful expression of his own feeling as to the merits of the treaty. He emphatically wished it to be ratified:

I am not prepared to say that I never expressed to Bullitt during his morning visits, to which I have referred, any dissatisfaction with the terms of the Treaty; on the contrary, it is not impossible that I may have done so, as I certainly have in my letters to you; but I naturally assumed that I was talking to a man who could be trusted not to make public views expressed at random and not as the result of mature deliberation or in a formal way. No one whom I have yet come across connected with the Treaty is satisfied with it in all respects, which is perhaps the best thing that can be said in its favor. I have already told you why the French are not, and of course no group has got all that they wanted. But we came here to make a Treaty and a Treaty had therefore to be made, and of course it was a matter of judgment on the part of those connected with the making of that Treaty as to what concessions should be made to attain the end, dominating in importance all other objects: namely, the conclusion of a Treaty and the restoration of peace to a war-worn and chaotic world. I am not prepared to say that certain concessions might not have been avoided, or that I would not have refused assent to some of those which were adopted, had I been at the head of this Delegation; but an agreement having been reached with the greatest difficulty, amid conflicting interests, intrigues, and other obstacles such as never before were encountered in the making of a Treaty—because no treaties have ever been made of such world-wide range and affecting so many nations—I am of the opinion that it should be put into operation as soon as possible and the world thus restored to a peace basis.

This was a statement that, as addressed to Lodge, had the force of a plea. White always blamed Lodge for the Bullitt episode. "Really," he wrote to Representative Rogers, "it requires some patience at times not to become indignant with him."

Meanwhile, the Senator, busy as he was in Washington, was finding time to send White letter after letter explaining his views; many of these seemed to White prejudiced and narrow, but he recognized their complete sincerity. What they were may be seen in these extracts from Lodge's letters:

[August 7.]—My best thanks for yours of the 22d. I read with great interest your account of the 4th of July and the 14th, and I was particularly struck by what Marshall Foch said to you. Of course he spoke only in a military sense, but it is the undoubted truth that Germany's undertaking to invade anybody at present is a mere bogey. The fight has gone out of Germany for the time being and under the treaty nothing is left for her in a military way.

I am sorry that you are to be delayed so long, but I suppose somebody must be there. The treaty cannot get through the Senate without some very strong and effective reservations. Without the reservations there is considerably more than a third of the Senate who will vote against it. That is the situation today. We had Mr. Lansing before us for four or five hours yesterday, but the only result was that he did not seem to know much of anything about the treaty and did not seem to have been consulted. I did not suppose he had ever been, but I was sorry that the Secretary of State should have been put in such a position.

[August 19.]—Thank you for your letter of August 2d which I am glad to get. I am glad also that Polk has arrived. He is a first-rate man in every way. I have great personal regard for him and I am sure he cannot fail to be of the best service there.

I am sure there are many perplexing questions in the treaties that still remain, but I cannot but be a little amused by their putting the blame on us. The Committee had a long interview with the President this morning. I asked him about Armenia. He has not made up his mind what to do or what ought to be done in regard to it and he agrees with me that the feeling of the country would be very much against our taking any such mandate. I am also amused at the load that is put on the delays in the Senate. How about the ratification of the treaty in France? They have not even taken it up for discussion at the moment at which I write. The President took seven months to make the treaty. We have had it in the Senate Committee a trifle over one month and have been working on it every day. I have not been able to find anybody yet who thoroughly understands it either on the committee or off— and we are asked to jam through without consideration a treaty which is going to change the American Government in its entire future in a few days. If it were not for the League the Treaty with Germany would have been ratified long ago. Objectionable as many features of it are, I think the feeling in the Senate would have been to dispose of it with the least possible delay, but the League holds up everything. That commits the whole country to an indefinite future, to a situation which is growing more unpopular in this country every moment.

As for its delaying the peace, business is going on with Germany. The New York papers have quantities of advertisements of ships sailing and carrying goods to Germany not only through neutral countries, but they advertise sailings direct. They go under licenses issued by the Board which releases them from the obligations of the Trading-with-the-enemy Act. That form of pressure is very familiar to us here. It is being used by the President and everybody. The President says the cost of living will go down if we can only ratify the League—a proposition which I take leave to doubt, but it serves its turn. . . .

There is going to be no unnecessary delay about the treaty here, and as our power in the premises is equal to the President's I do not think that we should be reproached for taking five weeks in considering an instrument where he took seven months. How long the Senate will take in dealing with it after it is reported by the Committee I cannot say. As it stands today there will be some effective reservations put on. If they are not put on, as it stands today there are considerably more than a third at this moment who will vote to reject the treaty. Therefore I think the reservations will go on. All things may change but the opposition to the treaty has been stiffening steadily. I say this all to you frankly and perhaps you may think bluntly, but the trouble with all our people in Paris is that in making the treaty and making these agreements they seem to have considered feeling and opinion in every country but their own. Now this country has got an opportunity to study the treaty and look at it and we shall see how they feel about it.

Do not think I do not feel badly about Armenia. I do, but I think there is a limit to what they have the right to put off on us.

[October 2.]—I have received your letter of September 10. I am sending you by this mail a copy of Bullitt's testimony. You had better read it before you say that it amounts to nothing. He was fortified with papers at every stage. You speak of his not occupying a responsible position in the Commission. He occupied a most confidential place. He held a place in the State Department, where he had been for a year. He went out with the President on his own ship. You say he slipped away to Berne. He was ordered to Berne. He did not go of his own motion. He was ordered to go to Russia, and he put in the record Lansing's letter ordering him to go. He was sent, of course, with the approval of the President. As to Lloyd George and Lloyd George's denial, which he has been modifying since and he had better modify, he produced a letter from Lloyd George's secretary, Mr. Kerr. They not only knew but they approved his mission. He breakfasted with Lloyd George on his return and had a long talk with him. He was one of Mr. Wilson's confidential men of a type which ought to be well known to you by this time. He would have given all the conversations of which he made notes, but

Knox and I stopped him. He insisted on giving the report of his conversation with Lansing, which Mr. Lansing has not denied. I have no defence to make of Mr. Bullitt's breach of confidence. That is his affair. But that he was in a confidential position and that his statements backed by documents throughout as you will see, were true, I think there can be no doubt. He was not asked to resign. He thought that Mr. Wilson had betrayed the views which he and others represented. With all these views I have no sympathy whatever. He simply turned state's evidence. . . .

I appreciate what you say about the treaty. But the League of Nations as it stands is in my judgment in the highest degree dangerous to the United States. It is too long a subject to argue about. Strong and effective reservations will be put on. I feel very sure that there is now a decisive majority for them, not only Republicans but some Democrats; and this is certain: if they are not put on, the treaty will be killed on the floor of the Senate.

We are not so ignorant as you may think. We have given months of study to this matter. We have had many sources of information which probably were closed to you. Although the President has refused us all possible information, we have obtained it from other sources. They talk about delays and the necessity of peace. They ought to have thought of that before they attached the League to the treaty of peace with Germany. That is what has made delays here and everywhere else. If they had made the treaty of peace with Germany it would have been in force last April. But the President insisted that it should be tied up with the treaty of peace. The result has been a misfortune to the world. It is not our fault.

Clemenceau was far the strongest man at the Conference. I sometimes wish it had all been in his hands, and if it would give the old man any pleasure I hope they will elect him President.

I am in great haste and can only thank you for your letter, which I have read with great interest as I always do.

By the time this last letter had reached White, much had occurred in the United States. The President had begun his tour of the country in defense of the treaty early in September, and on the 26th of that month had suffered the collapse which for weeks kept him at the door of death and left him permanently shattered in health. Meanwhile, on September 10th the treaty had been formally reported to the Senate by the Foreign Relations Committee, and debate upon it had begun. All the amendments submitted were rejected by the Senate; but a list of fifteen reservations to the Covenant of the League were attached to the treaty by a majority vote. Then, on November 19th, the treaty with these reservations came up for ratification. It was defeated by the supporters of President Wilson and the so-called irreconcilables, the vote being 41 yeas and 51 nays. A resolution was then presented for ratification of the treaty without any reservations, and this was even more decisively defeated by Lodge and the opponents of the League, the vote being 38 to 53. On that same day the special session of the Sixty-sixth Congress came to an end, and the treaty went over to the new session.

Meanwhile much had been happening in Paris also. Writers on the Peace Conference have too often tended to assume that the curtain was rung down when Germany signed the Versailles Treaty and Wilson went home. Problems of the utmost difficulty in all eastern and southeastern Europe remained to be threshed out, and Bliss, White, and later Polk had to face them. First, as we have noted, was Austria.[11] The Conference was executor of the vast Hapsburg estate. Before Wilson left, the preliminary terms of peace had been presented to the Austrian representatives on June 2nd, and had been fiercely denounced in Vienna as a "death sentence." Great areas of the old Austro-Hungarian territory went to Czechoslovakia, Poland, Rumania, and Jugo-Slavia. To give proper historic, strategic, or economic frontiers to the neighbors of Austria and Hungary, it was necessary to assign numerous Magyars and Germans both to Czechoslovakia and the enlarged Rumania. The Austrian Government strove desperately to obtain some amelioration of the terms, and demanded also that the union of Austria and Germany be permitted. During July and part of August it was necessary to give a careful re-study to many of the proposed conditions of the Austrian treaty. White was intensely interested in the subject; he gave close attention to Austria's protest against the inclusion of several million Germans in the Czechoslovak republic, to the Klagenfurt question, to the guaranties for the rights of minorities, and to the reparations demands upon Austria. In the end the Allies made a number of concessions. White would gladly have given Austria permission to unite with Germany, but the French

[11] Scott, A. P., *An Introduction to the Peace Treaties*, p. 211 ff.

attitude made that impossible. He equally objected to the heavy reparations burden contemplated for Austria, its precise size being left to the Reparations Commission.[12]

Bulgaria and Turkey also had to be dealt with. During the first three weeks in September the treaty with the former nation was being given its finishing touches, and its territorial, financial, and military clauses were debated at length. Again the Americans stood for moderation. Polk, Bliss, and White opposed certain small cessions of Bulgarian territory on the west demanded by Jugo-Slavia; while they argued vigorously against the claim of Greece to the whole of Thrace. The problem of Thrace was especially troublesome. Frank Polk had one plan, by which part of western Thrace was to become an international state under the supervision of the League, and the rest to be divided between Bulgaria and Greece; Tardieu had another plan. American influence was waning, and in the end Jugo-Slavia and Greece were given practically what they wanted. As for Turkey, men still talked of an American mandate for Constantinople, but White assured everybody that the chances were a hundred to one that the Americans would never take a mandate anywhere. The British and French had arrived at that conclusion already. As a result, the Governments of those two nations inclined more and more toward the maintenance of a great part of the Turkish Empire in its existing condition, feeling that this would better serve the interests of everyone.

American prestige was weakened by the Senate's hesitancy over the Treaty, by the rapid departure of our army and principal leaders, and by the return of Mr. Hoover to America. White's letters were warm in praise of Hoover. The American people would probably never appreciate, in his opinion, the magnitude of Hoover's work, the number of lives he had saved, and the suffering he had alleviated. He had kept railroads running, telegraphs in operation, and more than a hundred ships plying on the seas, showing marvelous executive ability and an exceptional capacity for the selection of able subordinates. Some day, White confided to Lodge, "I shall tell you of some of the efforts to keep the knowledge from the

[12] Cf. Temperley, H. W. V., *A History of the Peace Conference*, vol. i, p. 272 ff; vol. v, p. 170 ff.

general public of what he was doing, by those jealous of his work, who, while using him and his organization, were anxious to cause the impression in Europe that it was the Supreme Economic Council or other organization, and not Hoover, that was really coming to its rescue." [13] As our influence waned, the other nations tended more and more to manage European questions in strictly European terms, and the mutual jealousy of France and England was painfully evident. Clemenceau gave as one reason why he was not anxious to deal with Asia Minor the fact that Lloyd George had lied to him "seven times," and Lloyd George, who flitted in and out of Paris as mercurial as ever—"he rarely remains of the same opinion during two consecutive days," wrote White—made equally scathing remarks about the French.

The French tried American patience once more when, at the beginning of November, they suddenly sprang upon our delegation a refurbished form of their old proposal for a permanent general staff, headed by Marshal Foch, to carry out the treaty. This had been rejected before the President and Lansing went home. "They cannot bear," wrote White to Rogers, "to give up having the command-in-chief, during the next fifteen years at least, of the military forces all over Europe, in peace as well as in war, to which we are absolutely opposed; and so, I may add very confidentially, is Marshal Joffre, with whom I discussed the matter a few evenings ago." The plan was again decisively rejected by Polk, Bliss, and White and never reëmerged, but it showed that the French insistence upon a strictly military type of security was by no means dead.

White enjoyed his labors, which were made the pleasanter by the presence of his brother Julian and his half-brother William Buckler, the latter having been assigned to the Peace Conference and occupying rooms in the same hotel. Mr. Buckler assisted him in many ways; for example, he drafted White's telegram of eight hundred words on July 18th, reporting to President Wilson the unanimous opinion of the American experts (A. C. Coolidge, D. W. Johnson, Buckler) that western Thrace should not be annexed to Greece. The British were annoyed by this telegram, declaring that a Power not at war with Bulgaria should have no part in the peace

[13] White to Lodge, Paris, September 10, 1919

with her; but Wilson replied ten days later agreeing to the withholding of the territory from Greece.[14] At one time White proposed to Lodge that Buckler should proceed to Washington to talk with Senators on the mandates question, on which he was an expert, but Lodge proved chilly to the plan. White was encouraged in his labors by a feeling that American signature to the Austrian and Bulgarian treaties was of the first importance to European peace.

As it became clear toward the end of October that the United States might reject the treaties and League altogether, a feeling of apprehension spread through the Conference and French Government circles. All Europe had counted on the United States participating in the peace and the League. Throughout the Old World there was a feeling that the American Government was impartial because disinterested; that its representation would be almost indispensable on the commissions created by the treaty; and that the removal of its steadying hand would be a serious misfortune. The German press was loud in its expressions of anxiety. Several German newspapers declared that Germany could hardly be bound to carry out a treaty when her only safeguard for its fair interpretation was withdrawn. The French also were frankly dismayed, and found too late that they had misconstrued the American attitude.

[14] Diary of W. H. Buckler, July 18, July 27, 1919. Mr. Buckler's diary gives us many glimpses of the work of the Conference during the summer. For example, he writes under date of July 16th: "At eleven, conference of Commissioners (H. W. and Gen. Bliss) with seventeen heads of departments, adjourned from 8th inst., in the Commissioners' room ('Salon des Aigles'). Present, Grew, J. B. Scott, Hoover, Johnson, Hornbeck, Dresel, Harrison, Coolidge, etc. At three-thirty attended Quai d'Orsay meeting of 'Five' (Clemenceau, Balfour, Makino, Tittoni, H. W.) to hear Venizelos expound his views as to the limits of the Greek occupation in Asia Minor; question referred to Tittoni and Venizelos for adjustment and report. H. W. kept at this meeting till very late." On July 23rd he writes again: "H. W. to dentist's and back in time to consult with Gen. Bliss. Had long interview with G. L. Beer; wrote to Col. House in London about 'A' mandates. At two, meetings of heads of departments with the two Commissioners; Hoover uttered pessimistic opinion as to coal situation in Europe. Dined at Crillon with H. W., J. B. Scott, Charles Russell, and Osma, just arrived from Spain. After driving Osma home heard J. B. Scott explaining at length to H. W. question of 'responsibilities' in Bulgarian Treaty." There is much mention of White's conferences with Hoover and Balfour.

Their disillusionment was graphically described by White in a letter to Lodge: [15]

In your letter of September 30th, you suggest that not the slightest attention appears to have been paid by any of the other countries to the fact that the President had just been defeated in the election and had lost control of Congress. You are mistaken on that point in respect to France, where they were well aware of the circumstance in question, but they worked out its operation in the wrong way. "Society" and the imperialistic and military elements, of whose aspirations I wrote you in my earlier letters, got it into their heads, in a general sort of way, without working out the details, that the President's idealism would be a bar in some way or other to their aspirations; but they considered the Republican majority in the Senate, being "the real friends of France," would *faire marcher le Président*—a term which was reported to me frequently, though it was never used in my hearing. Their idea, however, of making him march was not to prevent the United States from coöperating in European affairs, but on the contrary, to compel the President to agree to the Allied "pool" for the payment of the entire expenses of the war, to the huge International Army of Occupation in the Rhine Provinces, to say nothing—according to many minds—of the latter's annexation to France. Whenever this frame of mind was brought to my attention, I invariably endeavored to warn people that it was incorrect; but I might as well have talked to a stone wall. In their ignorance of the way things work with us, they were perfectly sure that such would be the result of the last November elections; and you may imagine, therefore, their disappointment at discovering the line adopted by the majority in the Senate.

As we have said, White believed in several of Lodge's proposed reservations to the Covenant; if he had been in the United States and had been summoned to declare himself, he would have taken a stand with the moderate reservationists. He wrote to Lodge a week before the decisive vote in the Senate that he did not criticize the additions to the treaty: "My experience with treaties during my public service has been that they have usually been improved by passing through the hands of the Senate. Such certainly was the case with respect to the Hay-Pauncefote Treaty and many others." What he wanted above everything else was a working compromise. As October ended and November began he felt that the withdrawal

[15] White to Lodge, Paris, November 13, 1919.

of the United States from world affairs would be a calamity. He wrote to Representative Rogers [16] that "it is really monstrous that they (the Senate and President) should be holding up here the peace of the world when four of the great Powers have already ratified and when the Treaty provides that it shall go into effect immediately after three have done so." He stated the same opinion to Lodge, though in more diplomatic terms, writing: [17]

Curiously enough, notwithstanding the fact that the Treaty has been for nearly a fortnight ratified by three of the great Powers—Italy, France, and Great Britain—and also by Germany, as a result of which, according to the terms of the Treaty, it should have at once gone into effect, the French are still holding up the exchange of ratifications, and the British seem to concur in that course. They say that it is because they are not yet ready with their appointees for the various Commissions which must begin operations the moment the exchange of ratifications takes places, which, of course, is nonsense, as they have had ample time to consider and decide upon all these appointments. I have no doubt in my own mind that the reason why the going into effect of the Treaty has been delayed, is simply that they are afraid to enter into all the arrangements and international commissions involved thereby, without us, for the reason that we alone, as I think I have written you previously, have the reputation in Europe for fair dealing, and there may possibly even be hesitation by Germany to participate in Commissions on which an American representative is provided for in the Treaty, without his presence. . . .

The fact is that during the last fortnight or so, the French Government has been in a state of profound alarm lest we fail to ratify the Treaty or ratify it in such a way as to preclude our taking part in many of its provisions; and their openly avowed interest in the League of Nations has been very much greater than ever before. I am not saying this with a view to urging you to hasten ratification; but merely to let you know the facts. Still less do I question the right of the Senate to do exactly what it thinks best about the Treaty, but no doubt the greater the delay in putting the Treaty into effect, the greater is the danger of one or more explosions somewhere.

This was an example of White's diplomatic mildness of statement. But a fortnight later, in another letter to Lodge, he assumed

[16] White to Rogers, Paris, November 1, 1919.
[17] White to Lodge, November 1, 1919.

a much more emphatic tone. He felt, he said, "that it is of the highest importance for the Treaty to go into effect and for peace to be restored to the world again, and I hope most sincerely that an agreement may shortly be reached between the President and the Senate majority, whereby it may be ratified by us. It will be a world disaster of great magnitude, in my opinion, if the Treaty be rejected, or be not ratified during this session." White keenly felt that Europe was in a state of suspense. He had argued that summer in a letter to Senator McCumber that it was fatuous to say that the United States should now keep out of European affairs.[18] The time to think of keeping out was in 1917. Had we kept out then there would have been a German peace in the spring or early summer of 1918; of that his observations in Europe had made him absolutely positive. But we did not choose that Europe should fall under the domination of Germany, and we alone prevented it. "Under these circumstances to say that we can divest ourselves of all responsibility for the condition which we have been chiefly instrumental in creating seems to me an untenable proposition, and I say this as one who throughout the whole of his life, and especially the many years of his public service, has always felt in the strongest way that we should keep out of European entanglements."

Before Lodge had received White's letter with the phrase "a world disaster," the disaster had occurred. The first rejection of the treaty on November 19th fell upon White as a painful blow. To the last he had been unwilling to believe that partisan bickering over a few dozen words in a document of eighty thousand could be allowed at one stroke to paralyze the much-needed labors of the United States. It was now left for Europe to put her house in order alone, and he feared that her unaided strength might be unequal to the task.

A mood of disillusionment had come over White as, during the summer, he had reviewed the course of the peace negotiations and talked of them with others. There were many facts to make him unhappy. Root had written to him that he did not at all agree with the general course of diplomatic policy which had been followed in Paris.[19] "I have felt that we occupied a very strong position before

[18] White to McCumber, Paris, June 23, 1919.
[19] Root to White, New York, June 5, 1919.

the Conference. We had nothing to ask for, and everybody wanted something from us which we were quite willing to give as long as they behaved decently. The situation plainly required on our part reserve and an avoidance of affirmatives in the first instance." For the so-called failures in the treaty White never blamed Wilson strongly. He had coped honestly and ably with a task far beyond the strength of any single man. But White did come to feel that one member of the delegation had pursued a devious course, had done much to cripple its work by willingness to make too many concessions, and had treated the President, his other associates, and the experts unfairly. White, we have often said, was a mild man. All the more emphatic is his letter to the Secretary of State in November, presenting an indictment with which more than one of the American experts agreed:

WHITE TO LANSING, PARIS, NOVEMBER 8, 1919

I have been thinking of writing to you for some time past about one or two situations which seem to me important with reference to the immediate or near future . . .

I was not aware until recently of the extent to which intrigue went on "upstairs" during the earlier months of the Conference, with a view to preventing any of the views of our experts, which happened to be contrary to those held there, from reaching the President. Still less had I any idea of the attempts made to get some of the experts to change their views and adopt those advocated in the small upper chamber previously mentioned.[20]

Since your departure I have realized more and more how grievously misled the Italians and others were by the tendency to compromise and by the assurances of friendship and sympathy, of a general nature at least if not actually with their particular views, expressed during their interviews upstairs; and there is no doubt in my mind that the Fiume and other questions would have been settled while the President was still here, if they had been left in your hands, or kept in the President's, and had not been hampered by a feeling upstairs that no decision should be attempted, much less reached, which would in any way be likely to cause jeopardy to the adoption of the Covenant of the League of Nations.

I am afraid the Shantung decision which, as you, the General, and

[20] By the "small upper chamber," White refers to the room in the Crillon used by Colonel House.

I felt, would arouse such serious opposition to the Treaty at home besides being wrong in itself, was another case in point.

Under these circumstances, and in view of the undue influence which I cannot but think our British friends exercise over our late colleague, I cannot help feeling anxious—and to a certain extent sharing the anxiety evidently felt in the Senate—about our participation in the League of Nations if we are to be represented there by a man (and a series of feeble advisers) given to compromise and not strong enough and willing to make a fight on every question in which our interests (which besides being commercial are those of world peace as against special national interests such as the land-grabbing and sphere-of-influence capturing now rife in Europe) are likely to be overridden unless carefully guarded and defended. And of course during the next few years such questions will constantly be arising in respect to commercial and financial matters in which our interests will be in jeopardy, and attempts will be made to make use of our influence at the League Council for the furtherance of European intrigue.

It seems to be generally assumed that Colonel House will be our first representative on the League of Nations Council, and if such be the President's decision of course there is, I suppose, nothing to be said. But I see no reason why it should follow that he have the selection of all American members of the staff, and I do not think —— and ——, to whom he has promised places on the mandates section, are suitable men for the purpose . . .

Reports of a breach between the President and Colonel House had long been current. On August 29, Wilson had cabled to House that he was "deeply disturbed by malicious story about break between us," and that "the best way to treat it is with silent contempt." Soon after a member of the American delegation asked White what he thought Wilson meant by this message. "What did he mean?" echoed White. "Of course his wording is tactful. But what he really meant is this: 'The story is true, and I do not wish you to deny it.'"

Some time before the Senate vote occurred, the American delegation had announced its impending departure. It stayed on until the first days of December. As the date of its sailing drew near, the apprehensions and anxiety of the European delegations and the French Government increased. White's final letter to Lodge, dated December 5th, contains a striking description of the confusion and the panicky last-minute efforts the French were making to keep the Americans a little longer in Paris. Clemenceau's Ministry was in a genuine fright, he wrote. He could not help feeling that it served them right for the way in which they had tried to impress Europe with the idea that France could manage everything, minimizing the wartime coöperation of the United States and refusing to admit that they were in the least dependent on American assistance; but now their alarm over what Germany might do when the Americans had gone struck him as "really tragic." Clemenceau had gone to Polk and begged that he remain until the Germans had signed the new "Protocol" (which covered certain provisions of the old armistice agreement that had not yet been properly executed by Germany), and until the Rumanians were made to behave themselves. The French Government had cabled to Ambassador Jusserand to use all his influence with President Wilson and Secretary Lansing to have the American delegation kept abroad a little longer.

Meanwhile the same French press which during the earlier months of 1919 had denounced Wilson in such unmeasured terms was now vigorously assailing the Senate, and especially Lodge. White frankly told his friend that the strongest indignation was being vented upon him, and that he had heard many prominent Frenchmen couple Lodge's name with maledictions. One leading journalist, Joseph Reinach, who had played a prominent part in the campaign against Wilson early in the Conference, told White that he never regretted any action of his life more bitterly than his participation in that campaign, for he now saw that Wilson had been the truest friend of France. White added:

Polk tells me this morning that he does not think that they yet believe that we can be really going, so impossible does such action on our part seem to be; and I have no doubt that when the fact is finally realized and we are actually off, there will be quite a journalistic outburst against us.

It is easy to understand how the French, after having imagined that they would capitalize our enthusiasm and affection for France into a huge sum of money in the Treaty of Peace, wherewith to pay the expenses of the war, and use our strength behind them to assume a dominating position in Europe, must be rather disappointed at finding not only the former but also the latter taken from under their feet.

All Europe, half resentful, half fearful, gloomily watched the
United States detach itself from her concerns. On December 9th,
Polk, Bliss, and White left France for their own shores. The last
great adventure of White's career was ending.[21]

[21] White's devotion to the cause of ratification comes out strongly in a
letter of November 27th to Lodge. "The line I am taking here," he writes,
"is to advise the French to accept any reservations upon which the Senate
may see fit to insist; adding that the effect upon our people of their so
doing will be advantageous to France, especially if they should get ahead
of the British in adopting that course." He was told that the British had a
special reason for regretting the failure of ratification. "They fear we shall
not be associated with them in doing our best to prevent the French from
crushing out all efforts of Germany to renew her commercial intercourse with
the outside world."

CHAPTER TWENTY-FOUR

Sequels of the Conference: Years of Retirement

IT was the army transport *America* on which White made his slow return across the Atlantic in December of 1919. The voyage gave him leisure to reflect upon what had occurred in Paris. It also gave him time to write at length to several friends, and in these letters to James Ford Rhodes, Representative Rogers, Lord Bryce, and others we may find his final verdict upon the Conference. As he surveyed President Wilson's acts, he was far less condemnatory than Secretary Lansing, far less favorable than the President's warmest admirers. He was in a measure disillusioned, and he feared that the quarrel between the Senate and Wilson was imperiling all hope of American participation in world affairs. But much of his inveterate optimism clung to him still.

To those who take an interest in the endless might-have-beens of history, White's more salient criticisms upon the American course in Paris must seem provocative. We may well wonder what would have happened if President Wilson had decided, as White always thought he should have done, not to return to Paris the second time. He went back to Washington in February with much triumphantly achieved—the groundwork laid for the treaty, the decision to include the League Covenant in it accepted. If he had remained, might not House, Lansing, Bliss, and White have carried on his work at the Peace Conference without faltering? Might it not have been possible, with Wilson standing aloof and firm against unwise concessions, to avoid some of the mistakes as to the Tyrol, reparations, Smyrna, and other issues? Would the President not have been in a position in the crucial spring months to rally American opinion behind the League? We can never know. Nor can we know what would have resulted if Wilson had refused to let Lloyd George, abetted by House, entice him into the Council of Four; or if he had insisted at the beginning of April, as White desired, on negotiating in a larger group, with more publicity, and

479

constant reference to his advisers. We cannot know what would have happened if, as White wished, he had been adamant on Shantung. White felt that there had been many blunders. Yet he also felt that Wilson's purposes had been of the highest character; and that the treaty, in view of the nervous prostration of Europe after its four years' hell, was on the whole "about the best that could have been obtained."

On landing, White went at once to Washington, where, his house being let, he took No. 1229 Nineteenth Street for the winter. He wished to be at hand if the Senate wanted him, and above all, he hoped that he might be of some use in effecting a compromise between the President and a majority of the Foreign Relations Committee. Wilson trusted him; Lodge was his close friend; why might he not be a peacemaker? The treaty was becoming, in his view, a football of politics and personal animosities. The action of the Senate on it he bluntly characterized as "intended more for domestic consumption than for the good of the world." It was plain to him that the American people were growing tired of the whole European mess, and that their indifference threatened the total rejection of the League. White himself had no objection to many of the reservations, and if necessary would have accepted all of them; he thought that in view of the unfair and unstable boundary arrangements in Europe, a reservation to Article 10 was distinctly needed. He did object very strongly to asking the other Powers to assent in writing to the American interpretation of certain clauses of the treaty. It would be much better, he thought, simply to embody the reservations in the instrument of ratification, and to assume that they would be accepted by the rest of the world.

But above all, and on any fair terms whatever, he wanted the League. He wrote to friend after friend that the soil in many parts of the world was fertile for conflict, and that the only hope of avoiding it was to get people "to think of settlements of disputes in terms of peace rather than of war—a condition of mind which I think a League of Nations will gradually bring about." He told Lord Bryce that the duty of the American delegates, Bliss, Polk, and himself, was plain. It was to go to the leaders on both sides in Washington, picture to them the appalling conditions prevailing over much of Europe, describe the disaster that American abstention from the healing process would constitute, and "try to make them realize the necessity for a compromise." In this spirit he gallantly journeyed to the capital.

Unfortunately, there proved to be little that White could do. President Wilson, when he arrived, was physically unable to see visitors, and could not resume active work until February of 1920; while even then he was unwilling to listen to pleas for an adjustment. White did not see the President. He did see Mrs. Wilson, renewing their very pleasant acquaintanceship of the Conference days. He told her, with the request that she convey the information to the President, that it would be necessary to accept a number of reservations in order to get a two-thirds majority. She seemed disappointed, and expressed the fear that White had been "keeping bad company." With Lodge he had somewhat better success. He saw the Senator repeatedly, and dined with him more than once; he talked to him at great length, and was told by mutual friends that he had succeeded in softening Lodge a good deal. In fact, Lodge told him that he would make distinct concessions as soon as a program was laid before him for which he could be certain that a two-thirds vote was obtainable.[1] There would be no use, he remarked, in permitting changes which would lose a considerable number of the votes behind him, without any compensating additions. White was temporarily heartened by this. He wrote to his brother with considerable hopefulness.

WHITE TO BUCKLER, WASHINGTON, JANUARY 20, 1920

You may have seen that at the Democratic dinner . . . Wilson came out with what would appear to be another decided stand against the reservations; but upon closer investigation it turns out that he affords a loophole of escape by saying that he is willing to accept any reservations which are interpretations and do not annul the Treaty. This may afford a loophole for some decided action soon.

And it is upon these lines that I have been working with the various Senators, my theory being that the Senate can take action without further intervention on the part of the President upon the Treaty, ratifying with such reservations as may be necessary, and then putting it up to the President to accept or reject them. I very much doubt whether he will assume the responsibility of not exchanging ratifications. I explained to

[1] White to Buckler, Washington, February 12, 1920.

Mrs. Wilson how much more important it is to get the Treaty into effect, so that we thus become engaged in trying to keep peace in Europe, than the acceptance or the reverse of a few reservations, more or less. It is along these lines that I have been working, and still am, with leading Senators on both sides—notably Lodge, Hitchcock, Underwood, Pomerene, Lenroot, etc., etc.

One feels keenly, however, how little they realize the terrible state of Europe, or realize how indispensable we are towards helping to restore normal conditions in that part of the world.

But during February his hopes waned, and long before the treaty received its death blow in the Senate vote of March 19, 1920, he knew what the result would be. He wrote his daughter on the eve of this vote: "What I have been trying to do," he explained, "is to get the Senate to ratify the treaty on any terms for which a two-thirds vote can be obtained (and which will mean substantially with the Lodge reservations), without any appeal to the President, who will not, I believe, when that is done, refuse to accept such ratification (which he has the power to do). But Senator Hitchcock, the Democratic leader, keeps consulting him and of course he says 'no' to every reservation of which he disapproves. It is one thing to do this before the Senate acts, but quite another to keep the country in a state of war and to have to take the blame thereof on himself, if the Senate has actually ratified." [2] White became highly irritated over Hitchcock's refusal to accept the reservations without regard to the President and then put ratification up to him as a *fait accompli*. Borah, Reed, and other irreconcilables, he wrote, were delighted by this. He thought the Nebraska Senator "a curious man." If Underwood had been the Democratic leader instead, White felt sure the treaty would have been carried. "Hitchcock has a light and airy way of treating the subject every time I talk to him about it," he wrote to his son on March 2nd, "the last occasion being two or three evenings ago, when he said he thought it would be rejected and then lie fallow for four or five weeks, and then the pressure on the Republicans would be so great to get it out of the way that they would have to make concessions to the President and that then it might be got through." It is interesting to

[2] White to Countess Seherr-Thoss, Washington, March 16, 1920.

speculate upon how much Hitchcock's casual and excessively optimistic way of regarding the treaty influenced the President.

At the end White placed more blame upon Wilson, or rather Wilson's short-sighted advisers—for he heard from medical specialists that the President's mind was far from normal—than upon Lodge. Most of all, of course, he blamed the total irreconcilables. But as he wrote his daughter, it was deplorable of the Administration not to accept the milder reservations. They "were only interpretations, were not to my mind of great consequence, and would probably not have been heard of after the Presidential election." [3] Unquestionably he was right, and a great blunder had been made. He heard that Wilson believed that the League idea would win a great victory in the presidential campaign. White himself was a better prophet. He predicted that the treaty would be smashed by an electorate which had unfortunately been deluded into believing that unless it were "Americanized" our troops would have to be sent abroad every year or two to fight.

With the rejection of the treaty, White's public career came to an end. He had supposed himself free in 1910, and now, a decade later, he was actually liberated. At seventy, after a sunny and happy career, there remained to him a half-dozen autumnal years which were fortunately to be as bright as any that had gone before. Except for a slight lameness, his physical faculties had in no wise failed. He still held a number of posts which cost him not a little time and labor, for he gave them devoted attention; he was a trustee of the George Washington University, of the Corcoran Gallery, of the National Geographic Society, of the Carnegie Institution, a regent of the Smithsonian Institution, and one of the most active workers for the Washington Cathedral. At infrequent intervals he still made public speeches. The most important was his address on April 12, 1923, at the first large meeting of the Baltimore branch of the League of Nations Non-Partisan Association. He had been grieved when Harding, under the influence of Senator Moses and Richard Washburn Child, turned his back squarely—and unnecessarily—on the League. Such Republicans as Theodore Burton, A. Lawrence Lowell, and George Wharton Pepper were still laboring for the

[3] White to Countess Seherr-Thoss, Washington, April 1, 1920.

League and White argued vigorously for American adherence.[4] To
the end his belief in it never faltered.

But the chief event of these years was his marriage at St. Bar-
tholomew's in New York on November 3, 1920, to Mrs. Emily
Vanderbilt Sloane, widow of William Douglas Sloane. It was one
of the happiest of unions. For years he had known Mr. and Mrs.
Sloane, and his first wife had always had a special affection for the
latter. The marriage gave him, for the first time in several years, a
real home, or rather several of them, for he and his wife had houses
in Washington, New York, and Lenox; at all three they now offered a gracious hospitality. It gave him three stepdaughters and
a dozen step-grandchildren, in all of whom he delighted. At an age
when most men's zest for life begins to contract, it gave him fresh
occupations and interests.

With his wife as companion, White found a new pleasure in
travel and entertaining. He had been abroad in the summer of
1920, before his marriage, and renewed many old friendships in
England, meeting St. John Brodrick (now Lord Midleton), the
Asquiths, the Curzons, the Cecils, Mrs. Alfred Lyttelton, and others
of the old group. In the spring of 1921 he went back again with
Mrs. White. The years that followed gave him long quiet summers at Lenox and busy winters in New York and Washington.
When Clemenceau came to the United States in the fall of 1922
to make a series of speeches that were not particularly well received,
he stayed with White at the Crescent Place house. White helped to
entertain Lord Robert Cecil in 1923 and 1925, and was rather proud
of his feat in inducing Senator Borah to breakfast with him and
Cecil. Numerous other foreigners who came to the United States
were at his house, and he took particular pleasure in introducing
them to leading members of the Administration or of Congress.
His relations with the Department of State remained close. He often
called there to visit the Secretary and such old friends as Mr. Joseph
Grew.

Of President Harding White saw much; of President Coolidge
very little, though it is evident that he had a much higher esteem
for the latter. Harding often came informally, in 1922 and 1923,
to the Crescent Place house, dining there with White and two or

4 *Baltimore Sun*, April 13, 1923.

MRS. HENRY WHITE
(née Vanderbilt)

three other congenial men. Late in the evening he would slip away from these dinners, of which few or none knew but the participants. But Harding did not apply to White for advice on his diplomatic appointments, while Mr. Coolidge welcomed it. The skill and firmness with which Mr. Coolidge and Mr. Mellon managed the European debt negotiations particularly pleased White, and at one time he hoped that Mr. Coolidge would break the third-term tradition by accepting renomination in 1928. Colonel House told him in 1927 that no matter whom the Democrats nominated the following year, Republican victory was certain.

Enjoying these contacts, reading widely, and keeping up a cosmopolitan correspondence, White was able to form shrewd judgments on current affairs. His letters during his retirement are full of interesting comments on the passing scene in Europe and America. Once more some illustrative excerpts may be quoted, each with but a brief word of explanation. In 1920 he was writing regularly to his brother in England:

[January 11th]—The situation is a most extraordinary one. There appears to be little or no communication between the President and Mr. Lansing, and, so far as I can gather, none of the latter's recommendations have met with any response, either favorable or the reverse. Only most urgent matters of routine are attended to, and all appointments seem to be held up. In fact, there would appear to be almost a suspension of government; certainly of any coördination or teamwork of a governmental character, each Secretary apparently running his own department, which, in the case of the Secretary of State, is particularly unfortunate. . . .

I saw Lord Grey the night before his departure, in New York; in fact, he dined at the Round Table Club, and he and I had a tête-à-tête conversation after dinner. A good deal of fuss is being made by those hostile to the President because he did not receive Grey before his departure. It is said that as he received the King of Belgium and the Prince of Wales, he should certainly have received Grey informally. I maintain, however, against all such critics, that the President was perfectly right, as there are three other ambassadors waiting to present their credentials, one of them having arrived before Grey, and about eight Ministers. You know how jealous diplomatists are, and certainly if Grey had been received and not the others, the latter would have been exceedingly jealous and dissatisfied. Moreover, of course, the reception of an ambassador when he presents his credentials is quite a different affair from a visit of a few moments, such as the King of Belgium and the Prince of Wales made to the President:—speeches have to be exchanged, and the Secretary of State and other officials should be present. Inasmuch as, according to all accounts, the President has so far seen only a few people, and even then was covered up to his throat with bedclothes, and only his right hand protruding therefrom, I do not see how he could with propriety have received Grey. The latter told me that he had had an interesting stay and had obtained a lot of valuable information which he could never have acquired without coming to this country.

[March 11th.]—I wish I could give you some encouragement as to the ratification of the treaty, but the President's last letter to Hitchcock seems to have put that out of the question, with or without reservations; and Lodge, with whom I have talked this morning, tells me he thinks it will disappear again in the next two or three days. I asked him what then, and he said, "Probably an attempt to pass the Knox resolution"; to which I replied, "But will not the President veto that?" He said, "Undoubtedly"; whereupon I asked, "And then what?"—to which he was unable to give me any reply, except that the President would receive the blame for defeating the treaty! So how we are going to get back to a peace basis I do not see very clearly at present.

[March 18th.]—The treaty is dragging its way slowly toward what everyone predicts will be its final death in the Senate, possibly tonight, certainly tomorrow. I shall not, however, give up hope until the vote is actually taken, owing to the fact that pressure upon both parties is so tremendous to keep the League of Nations out of the Presidential campaign, and it is not impossible that three or four Democratic votes may be obtained at the last minute to make up the two-thirds majority. On the other hand, those who ought to know say—notably two Senators whom I met last night and this morning—that any hope of that kind is out of the question. It is then proposed, I understand, to attempt to pass at once the Knox Resolution, but I see no reason why he should not veto that also, if it is sent to him, and then we shall still remain at war with Germany; a ghastly idea, in view of all that is happening now in that country.

From his letters to his daughter in 1922 may be quoted extracts dealing with the two great war chiefs of France and the United

States. When he speaks of the "failure" of President Wilson, he of course means only his failure to achieve full success:

[August 6th.]—I sent you a few days ago from Lenox the book you asked me for, by John Kenneth Turner, and I am adding this line in the same connection to say that it has evidently been written to discredit the better class, particularly those of means. . . . So far from being favorable to Wall Street *et id genus omne*, President Wilson was very hostile to all that it represented . . .

The President tried in every way possible to keep this country out of war and to bring about a peace in which no power would be overwhelmingly defeated or triumphant, and chaos might be avoided or certainly diminished; and it was only when he realized the determination of the German military party, by which that country was governed, to defeat him in that object, that he went into the war and devoted all his energies to winning it. Those are the facts known to me and to thousands of others, whatever anyone, Socialist, Bolshevik, or otherwise, may say or write to the contrary. Of course he failed most unfortunately at the Conference because (1) he does not know how to deal with men, (2) he has no idea of team-work, *i.e.*, of how to devolve work on others and get them to work with him and each other, and (3) because he is a one-idea man, and thought the League of Nations would be the sovereign panacea for the world's tragedy which he could not prevent, but a repetition of which he hoped might be thereby prevented; and he staked everything on its establishment.

[November 27th.]—I wrote you in a previous letter that Clemenceau is to stay here with us during his sojourn of three or four days. I was asked by House to take him in and could not well refuse. He is warmly welcomed everywhere personally; but his speeches have not at all met with popular approval and his coming (which I believe he hoped would persuade this country to join the League of Nations) is drawing out more of the latent antagonism which has been gradually permeating this country in respect to the course which the French are pursuing—a course so fatal in the long run to themselves.

In 1923 his indignation was aroused by Poincaré's invasion of the Ruhr, which he lost no opportunity to denounce. To an officer of the American Legion he sent a typical letter:

[January 30th.]—I deeply deplore the action taken by France, as fraught with great danger to herself and to the world at large, portions of which may at any moment as a result thereof reach a stage bordering upon chaos; and in my opinion France will lose rather than gain financially by her invasion of the Ruhr. If the French had been willing, as I so earnestly urged upon certain of their leading men in 1919, to fix a sum which our experts and other impartial financial experts believed the Germans could pay, I have not the least doubt in my own mind that a steady flow of money for reparations would have been coming into France during the last three years. . . .

The only course which our government can pursue is that which, so far as I understand, it has now adopted, namely, to wait until the French realize the futility of their invasion of Germany, when it may be possible for the committee of impartial experts suggested by the Secretary of State to be of some use, backed by his wise advice, in fixing an amount which the Germans can pay. Until such an amount is fixed not a dollar of American money should, in my opinion, be sent abroad.

The year 1925 brought the abortive French effort to fix their debt, and White sent Mr. Buckler some comments:

[October 27th.]—I forget whether I wrote you from Washington of my talks with Chambrun. They were very interesting and exceedingly frank. I gather that the reason why the debt parleys (as they are called in journalese) failed was (1) the age-long incapacity of the Anglo-Saxon and the Gallic races to understand each other; (2) the peculiar unsuitability of a skyrocket like Caillaux to deal in confidential conversation with a man of Mellon's extraordinary calmness and great financial ability; and (3) more than all, perhaps, owing to the fact that the French delegation had got completely out of hand, when they realized that instead of their mission resulting in a triumphant return to France with exceedingly easy terms, as they had been told would be the case by American aspirants in Paris to the Legion of Honor, and by certain bankers of the baser sort after their arrival in this country, they found nothing of the sort and began to be alarmed for the safety of their own political skins. Caillaux, therefore, thought it wisest to take them all back to France.

In 1926 there came a series of comments upon different events and personages. The following are all from letters to either his brother or his daughter:

[January 29th.]—Of course I am delighted at our having taken steps to join the World Court. The isolationists found themselves, even with the assistance of Alice Roosevelt, who, I believe, has been carrying on a lobby of her own, in a hopeless minority, and the worthy Dawes must be laughing in his sleeve at the practical proof of the necessity of an amendment to the Senate's rules, by the enforcement of the closure, in order to bring about a vote, which you will have seen by the newspapers. Those of today announce that the indomitable Borah and others are going to carry the "fight" to the country, as the "people" have been "cheated" by the "infamous gagging" of the Senate, or rather of free speech therein! If only President Wilson had been willing to accept the Senate reservations as the President has the similar reservations on our joining the World Court, what a difference there would have been in the history of the last few years!

[April 1st.]—You will find Colonel House's book interesting, which will be awaiting you at Rosnochau. He attributes more in the way of accomplishment to himself than was really the case, and also seems to think that he was taken much more seriously by the statesmen of Europe than he ever was. But his efforts were of the best, and it is tragic to read of the way in which the military party wrecked that magnificent country (Germany); not, however, fortunately, beyond repair. Incidentally, Gerard comes out a great deal better than I had supposed he did, at Berlin.

[September 24th.]—It is unfortunate that Stresemann should have committed the *faux pas* of alluding to the war guilt on top of Briand's wonderful speech, thereby getting Poincaré on his hind legs (who, as the world is beginning to discover, has reason to be very sensitive on that subject). If the Germans could only realize that the insertion of their war guilt in the Versailles Treaty, which they were obliged to sign at the pistol's point, is not history; on the contrary, that very circumstance, as the French were foolish enough not to see at the time, arouses the suspicion of historians and others. It is quite getting to be recognized in this country that Germany was not solely responsible for the war, although of course she could have stopped it, and Berchtold lied to the old Emperor of Austria to get him to approve of the declaration of war against Serbia.

[December 27th.]—I have never had much doubt in my mind that if Sir Edward Grey had announced to the Germans that, in the event

of their violating Belgian neutrality, England would at once enter the
war with France, it *might* have prevented the war. But equally I have
always felt and still feel that it would have been impossible for him to
make any such statement in advance, as the country had no desire to go
into the war and was not at all prepared to do so. As it was, he lost
three Cabinet ministers when he availed himself cleverly of the violation
of Belgian neutrality to get England into the war; and as you remember,
it was not for five or six months at least afterwards that the country
took the war seriously and realized what they were up against. Possibly
a man of great boldness might have risked it. But it seems to me that, had
Grey done so, there would have been a perfect outcry in Parliament and
throughout the country, that would have encouraged the Germans and
would in the long run have done more harm than good.

In the various pieces of legislation which in these years brought
about the reorganization of the foreign service and the purchase
of embassies and legations abroad, White took the most enthusiastic interest.[5] It had been one of his life-long hopes to see our
diplomatic service placed on a professional basis and to have it
properly housed. He was himself the first real "service man" of
prominence and the foremost representative of the merit principle
in our diplomacy. From the time when McKinley was President
he was repeatedly in correspondence with Representatives and
Senators, urging bills that would assist ministers and ambassadors
in their duties, asking for the confirmation of a good nomination,
or suggesting the purchase of a building in London or Paris or
Rome.

The Rogers bill which finally became law on July 1, 1924, embodied reforms for which White had in one fashion or another
been laboring for thirty years and more. He had been one of the
most vigorous supporters of Senator Morgan's bill of 1895 for the
reorganization of the diplomatic and consular service on a permanent professional basis. In 1899 he had written repeated letters to
Secretary Hay urging the purchase of an embassy in London. Mr.

[5] See White's address to the American Historical Association, December 30,
1915, on "Diplomacy and Politics"; and to the national convention of the
Navy League, April 11, 1916, on "The Baneful Influence of Politics upon
our Foreign Relations." Both were printed in pamphlet form and widely
circulated.

Choate's struggles to find a suitable residence had drawn public attention to the subject, and White learned that Hyde Park House, which he regarded as eminently suitable, could be had for £100,-000. Year after year, while he served in London, he took visiting Senators—Hoar, Lodge, Foraker, Bacon, Wolcott, an endless list—to see the fine embassies which other great nations owned, and to compare them with the improvised quarters which the United States was using. Year after year he told Americans of the harm that was done to the nation's prestige by the shabby quarters that our representatives had to use in many capitals. He liked to recall how once as a young man in Paris, struck by the fine appearance of the British Embassy there, he had asked his cabman to drive him to the American legation; how the cabman scratched his head, and finally took him to the building occupied by the representative of a small South American state. Year after year, also, he had descanted upon the irreparable harm done to our diplomatic service by the constant intrusion of the coarsest kind of politics.

White's friendship with Roosevelt had given him many opportunities to urge recognition of the merit principle upon the latter; and he did not need to urge the desirability of acquiring embassy buildings. "What an outrage it is," Roosevelt once wrote him, "that we do not properly provide quarters for our ambassadors abroad." During 1908-09 he and Roosevelt had hopes for a time that Senator Lodge's bill for the purchase of a $400,000 embassy in Paris would pass, but that hope faded. Under Wilson, White was encouraged by the President's retention of an important group of the best of the younger Republican appointees to the service, though he, of course, condemned Bryan's care for "deserving Democrats." Wilson had a genuine interest in the merit principle, and White more than once commended it. When Harding came to the Presidency, the outlook became even brighter. It happened that Harding offered President Butler of Columbia University the position of ambassador to Great Britain, and when Dr. Butler refused, said that he would at least like to have the fullest possible advice as to the condition of the diplomatic service. Dr. Butler very thoughtfully shared this request with White, and the latter wrote a long memorandum in January of 1921 which was laid before the President-elect. A copy of it went also to John Jacob Rogers, and this together

with a good many verbal suggestions which White made out of
his rich experience had their effect upon the Rogers Act.

In 1897, when White resumed his interrupted work in the American
embassy in London, the international position of the United
States was not such as to make a professional diplomatic service
indispensable. By 1921 any other kind of service was exceedingly
dangerous. As the greatest Power in the world, with important interests
in every part of the globe, the United States could no longer
intrust its diplomacy to hack politicians. White, in his letter to Dr.
Butler, pointed this fact out. He emphasized the lack of continuity
in our foreign policy. He showed how men of capacity were discouraged
from entering or continuing in the service as a career. In
the period during which Jusserand had been French ambassador in
Washington, he noted, the United States had sent seven ambassadors
to Paris. Not only did he suggest a wholesale reorganization of the
State Department, consular work, and diplomatic service on a
merit basis; pending this, he advised President-elect Harding that
there were a number of chiefs of missions who in his opinion
should be retained. The list he made out included Messrs. Henry
Fletcher, Edwin Morgan, Bailly Blanchard, William Russell, William
Phillips, Hugh Gibson, Peter Augustus Jay, and Percival
Dodge.

The passage of the Act sponsored by his friend, Representative
Rogers, which consolidated the foreign service and which he
thought would strengthen its position legally, financially, and in
the public estimation, gave White much satisfaction. Out of harness
though he was, he loved during the Harding and Coolidge Administrations
to keep in contact with the renovated system. Mr.
J. C. Grew has told how welcome he was in the State Department.
"His great-heartedness, his tolerance, his sympathetic understanding
of personal problems and difficulties and his Old World
courteousness not only endeared him to his friends but gave one
renewed zeal and inspiration after being in his presence. Frequently
on the busiest days in the Department of State, sometimes
when everything was going wrong, he would drop in for
a chat and with his cheery greeting of, 'Ah, my dear fellow,'
official troubles seemed to vanish. The foreign service was the
invariable theme of discussion; he followed every development

with keenest interest and watched the steady building-up of a profession, new in American life, of which he was one of the pioneers and most enthusiastic supporters. Often his wise advice was asked and followed in some difficult problem of administration. Promotion for merit he regarded as the basic principle of the service, and while he was far from advocating automatic advancement or anything that savored of bureaucracy, it was his earnest hope to see the greater number of our ambassadorships and ministerships eventually filled from the ranks. Whenever he himself could help some deserving officer by speaking to the Secretary of State or the President, he did so immediately, and frequently his recommendations were followed." No retired veteran ever kept more closely in touch with his calling.

Little by little, though his friends hardly noted it, White's age began to tell upon him. In the summer of 1926 he was seized with a serious inflammation of the leg and foot, in the nature of erysipelas, which confined him to bed or to the house, first at Lenox and later in New York, for almost three months. He suffered little pain, and was greatly cheered by a visit from his brother, W. H. Buckler, who came over from Oxford for a few weeks. They spent delightful days together; in letters afterward White spoke of the pleasure of their companionship in a way which showed his realization that they might never be together again. During December he was in New York with Mrs. White, but his recovery was imperfect. He had to be careful in diet, exercise, and hours. During the spring he grew feebler, and after his removal to Lenox an operation became necessary. On the evening of his last day he had a short conversation with his daughter, who had come from Germany, about an English book, *Where Freedom Fails*. It dealt incidentally with the war debts, and he surprised his listener by remarking emphatically, "I agree with him that we ought to remit the European debt." He elaborated upon the subject, saying that it was to the interest of America to cancel these obligations, since we should benefit from the increased economic well-being of Europe and her greater good will toward us. The next day, July 14, 1927, came the operation, and he never rallied from the shock, dying early on the morning of the 15th.

For years he had been among the most active workers for the erection of the new Washington Cathedral; though he saw the completion of only the crypt and part of the choir, he had taken peculiar pride in the progress of the structure. The time would come, he hoped, when it would be another Westminster Abbey, the burial-place of many of the country's most illustrious men. In the Bethlehem Chapel of its crypt, after a memorial service held on November 10, 1927, his ashes were laid to rest, not many feet from the grave of the great war President whom he had so loyally served.[6]

It was one of Henry White's earnest convictions, and a wise conviction, that the best work of a trained diplomatist is usually that of which the public is unaware. He believed that to be fully useful a diplomatist must keep in the background. If the Cabinet Ministers or ambassadors with whom he dealt felt assured that he did not wish to score any "diplomatic triumphs," or to make use of what he gained either for personal credit or for national prestige, but would instead give all possible credit to the other side— then he would be trusted and might attain much of what he desired. But if he sought personal glory and tried to keep a spotlight somewhere within reach, his negotiations would be likely to fail. White had an innate distaste for *réclame*. But he also cultivated unobtrusiveness for professional reasons. It was only slowly, as the cumulative weight of his services impressed close observers, that a few people like Roosevelt came to recognize in him one of the most efficient diplomatists of his time.

He must sometimes have rejoiced to think that he had himself demonstrated the prime utility of one trait which is seldom regarded as part of the diplomatic arsenal—honesty. He was the last man in the world to fit the Machiavellian conception of a foreign agent. Of guile, or sharpness, or duplicity, there was not a trace in his character. What he achieved was achieved largely by virtue of a candor and truthfulness which won the trust of everyone he met. He used to say that British diplomacy was the most expert in the world and the most honest in at least the Old World; and he liked to think of America as even franker and fairer in her

[6] Washington Cathedral, *In Memory of the Honorable Henry White,* 1927.

HENRY WHITE IN HIS LAST YEARS
(Above, with his grand-daughter; below, at Lenox, Mass.)

foreign relations. Diplomacy, as he viewed it, was not an art in which one nation was constantly getting the better of another nation; it was an art which enabled nations to help one another to mutual advantage. His whole career was an exemplification of open diplomacy—shrewd, tactful, reserved, but above all, straightforward. Next to honesty he placed sympathy. He believed that no diplomatist could succeed unless he understood the psychology of alien peoples, placed himself in their position, tried to look at issues through their eyes as well as his own, and paid their opinions proper deference. Without sympathy there could be no tact; without genuine tact, no spiritual agreement. The defectiveness of German diplomacy he traced chiefly to inability to sympathize with the minds of other nations.

The element of character thus played a larger part in his diplomatic work than the element of intellect. He never pretended to be a brilliant man in the sense in which John Hay was brilliant, nor a gifted man in the sense in which Lord Bryce was gifted. He had shrewdness, soundness of judgment, swiftness of apprehension, but he never laid claim to sparkling talents. It was his gifts of personality that were truly unique. He was a great gentleman, as Lord Pauncefote was a great gentleman, but he was something more. His courtesy went far deeper than surface politeness, for it expressed his warm and delicate personal sympathies and his utter unselfishness. He loved the people among whom he moved; he comprehended them, felt for them, wished to help them. For all his gentle dignity, this cordiality gleamed in his eye, rang in his voice, and charmed everyone he knew. If he ever made an enemy, there is no record of it among his multitudinous papers. But he made friends wherever he turned. From the poor clerk in the Vienna legation who wept when White left and said that his friendship had been an epoch, to the associates of his last days, this feeling was universal. The soldier who served him as orderly at Paris wrote to a friend on the day of White's departure a letter which, uncouthly phrased, is eloquent of the deepest emotion. There was something about him, too, that was restoring and heartening. As more than one of his friends had said with Lord Robert Cecil, when he entered a room it was as if a burst of sunshine irradiated it. Those who received his hearty handclasp and heard his voice felt, as Mr. Grew remarked, that the troubles of the day suddenly vanished. Ray Stannard Baker entered in his diary, during the early days in Paris, a description of White as he saw his tall figure pass in and out of the Crillon, ruddy, energetic, and cheery. Baker was still to some extent dubious as to White's training and grasp and he expressed these doubts, but he concluded in a burst of feeling, "I love him!"

If we add to these qualities his complete dependability and discretion, we can see why the most diverse men—Salisbury, Balfour, Lansdowne, Clemenceau, Roosevelt, Hay, Root—found him an ideal diplomatic intermediary. "As he was willing to trust others," writes Jusserand, "others were willing to trust him." As the years passed, he acquired a wealth of diplomatic experience which made his counsel on many subjects almost invaluable. Choate paid him a well-deserved tribute at the Pilgrims' dinner on his return from France. "Mr. White set up a school of diplomacy in London," he said. "He took fresh, green ambassadors and put them to school. What a group they were! Phelps, Lincoln, Bayard, Hay, and last of all myself. He is a wonderful diplomatist. Hardly a question that could arise did not arise under the five ambassadors under whom he served. You can imagine, with Harry White in the back room, how much of the responsibility they turned over to him." He mastered many subjects thorny in their intricacy, and no one knew more of form and precedent. But his special knowledge was always subordinated to his desire to be the interpreter of his country to the nation to which he was accredited.

If sweetness seemed one keynote of his character, strength was certainly another. He was strong in his loyalties, as when he followed Roosevelt in 1912 and stood stanchly by Wilson in 1919. He never failed a friend or turned his back on a conviction. He was strong in his patriotism. Few men have ever served the Republic so long in foreign lands, or lived so constantly abroad; from the Civil War till 1911 he was in America only at intervals, and those for the most part very brief. Yet he never lost his spiritual allegiance. Though he had a special fondness for England, it was never uncritical, while toward France and Italy his attitude was strictly objective; it was that of a friendly, unprejudiced American. He was strong in all the private relations of life. A career of unusual happiness and success never spoiled him. He suffered no premature bereavements, no illness, accidents, or quarrels, not even any losses of property; in a profession open to every vicissitude, he climbed the ladder steadily if slowly. He had health, money, the happiest of homes, a calling that he loved, friends in many lands, a gratifying degree of fame. Yet here, too, his character and self-discipline account for much. It was not merely that fortune emptied her cornucopia on him; he was worthy of his fortune.

He lived through one long and much-troubled era into the new and changed world of the post-war period. He adapted himself at Paris to this new world with surprising rapidity and vision. There, and later in Washington, he was far ahead of most Americans in his understanding of the nation's new responsibilities and duties. But some of the objects closest to his heart demanded effort in both periods alike, and this effort came naturally to fruition in his later years. A life-long believer in a close friendship between Great Britain and America, he lived to see the old hostility banished forever, and the two nations associates in war and partners in promoting disarmament and peace. A life-long believer in a professional diplomatic service, he lived to see the Republic do much to make his ideal her own. It was a life unostentatiously rich in useful activities, and no less rich in appropriate rewards.

APPENDIX I

Roosevelt on Disarmament, 1906

(This letter was written in reply to White's report of his conversation with Lord Haldane in London upon disarmament. Haldane, according to White, said that "the German Emperor is the kernel of the whole question," and that if Roosevelt could persuade him to stop any further increase in German military and naval expenditures, Great Britain would meet him more than halfway and would coöperate still more cordially in an international arrangement tending toward a general reduction of armaments. Roosevelt's rejoinder is here printed entire for the first time.)

OYSTER BAY, August 14, 1906.

DEAR WHITE:

You have such discretion that I feel able to say that you can make what use of this letter you desire, provided always that the man to whom you quote it realizes that in such a matter as the limitation or reduction of armaments it is not possible for me definitely to commit myself without knowing what the actual condition at the Hague Conference may be. Therefore what I am about to say may be taken as tentative and suggestive and not as definitely binding us, and still less the nation I represent. I agree entirely with Haldane that it is very advisable to put a check to the inordinate growth of armaments, and I further agree with Haldane that in one sense we are peculiarly in a position to propose their limitation or reduction; but in another sense we are not, because we have a small navy (and an army so much smaller as to seem infinitesimal) compared with the armed forces of the other great powers which in point of population, extent of territory, wealth, and resources can be put in the same category with us. Therefore we cannot ourselves reduce our forces. We could not possibly reduce our army; I have already reduced it since I have been President by about twenty-five per cent. Think what a similar percentage of reduction would mean to the continental armies of Europe! Yet with us it merely meant cutting down some twenty-five thousand men. We now have it at the very lowest possible limit. As for our navy, I think we have it as regards

498

number of units just at about the right point. All that I feel we should do is steadily, though gradually, to replace inefficient with efficient units. I should say that this would mean a program of building about a battle-ship each year. Now and then we could omit a battleship. Now and then we should have to add a cruiser or a few torpedo boats. Would it help to have a program for Europe and Japan with which the above program for us would be compatible?

So much for what I should like to go into—and I should very much like to put a stop to this rivalry in building up armies and navies. Now for the practicability of the program. You know all the inside of my dealings with the Kaiser at Algeciras, and know how very limited my influence on him is. My course with him during the last five years has been uniform. I admire him, respect him, and like him. I think him a big man, and on the whole a good man; but I think his international and indeed his personal attitude one of intense egoism. I have always been most polite with him, have done my best to avoid taking any atti-tude which could possibly give him legitimate offence, and have en-deavored to show him that I was sincerely friendly to him and to Germany. Moreover, where I have forced him to give way I have been sedulously anxious to build a bridge of gold for him, and to give him the satisfaction of feeling that his dignity and reputation in the face of the world were safe. In other words, where I have had to take part of the kernel from him, I have been very anxious that he should have all the shell possible, and have that shell painted any way he wished. At the same time I have had to speak with extreme emphasis to him on more than one occasion; and on one occasion (that of Venezuela) have had to make a display of force and to convince him definitely that I would use the force if necessary. At the time of the Venezuela business I saw the German ambassador privately myself; told him to tell the Kaiser that I had put Dewey in charge of our fleet to maneuver in West Indian waters; that the world at large should know this merely as a maneuver, and we should strive in every way to appear simply as coöperating with the Germans; but that I regretted to say that the popular feeling was such that I should be obliged to interfere, by force if necessary, if the Germans took any action which looked like the acquisition of territory in Venezuela or elsewhere along the Caribbean; that this was not in any way intended as a threat, but as the position on the part of the government which the American people would de-mand; and I wanted him to understand it before the two nations drifted into such a position that trouble might come. I do not know whether it was a case of *post hoc* or *propter hoc*; but immediately afterwards the

Kaiser made to me the proposition that I should arbitrate myself, which I finally got him to modify so that it was sent to The Hague. I need hardly say that in showing anybody any part of this letter, or telling him any part of this letter, you will of course have to keep all I have said to you about the Kaiser absolutely to yourself. I would not want any of your brother-ambassadors, save only George Meyer if you happen to meet him, to see it. The Kaiser, like Carlyle, is "gey ill" to live with, on occasions.

Therefore I have no knowledge whether I could accomplish anything whatever with the Kaiser. I will try, of course. That I can work with France and England I have no doubt; but I would like Haldane and Grey and would like the French people to understand that in my judgment it is essential that we should have some fair guarantee that a given policy will be carried out in good faith. I should feel it a great misfortune for the free peoples to disarm and leave the various military despotisms and military barbarism armed. If China became civilized like Japan; if the Turkish Empire were abolished, and all of uncivilized Asia and Africa held by England or France or Russia or Germany, then I believe we should be within sight of a time when a genuine international agreement could be made by which armies and navies could be reduced so as to meet merely the needs of internal and international police work. But at present we are far from any such ideal possibility, and we can only accomplish good at all by not trying to accomplish the impossible good.

Sincerely yours,

THEODORE ROOSEVELT.

HON. HENRY WHITE,
    The American Ambassador,
       Rome, Italy.

Appendix II

General von Falkenhayn on Mobilization

(For its complete detail, an extract is here given from Henry White's memorandum upon his conversation with von Falkenhayn in Berlin in early August, 1914.)

After dinner we went into the garden, and General von Falkenhayn took me off from the rest of the company for a talk, which I began by saying that I had been greatly surprised, after having been with him for nearly two hours, not to have noticed the receipt by him of any telegram or message or other indication that he was responsible for the movement of vast numbers of troops both to the eastern and western frontiers. He replied that he and his predecessors ever since the foundation of the German Empire in 1871 had been working as heads of the War Office to make the military machine as perfect as possible with a view to its working smoothly upon the outbreak of war. He added that his responsibilities, when war began, were largely transferred to the Great General Staff; that the troop trains were allowed a margin of four hours to reach their destination, but that he was to be notified whenever any of them happened to be ten minutes late, and that so far, he had received no such notification.

The General then remarked, "This is a very serious business," to which I replied that I was fully aware thereof. He went on to say that of course they never expected for one moment that England would enter the war, both in view of the civil war then threatening in Ireland, and of the well-known objection of certain members of the Cabinet, and indeed of the large majority of the British public (as their Intelligence Department had told them) to joining in any war; that the coming in of England had made all the difference in the world, both as to the probable duration of the war and possibly even as to its outcome. "Not," said he, "that the British army is large, or likely to weigh very heavily in the balance, but what there is of it is composed of extraordinarily good material. What is of far greater importance, however, in connection with England, is, from our point of view, the bulldog tenacity of that

501

nation, which will make them hold on to the bitter end in spite of obstacles which would be insurmountable to any other army."

I thereupon inquired whether the General had any possible doubt as to a German victory eventually; to which he answered that he would not like to say that he had any positive doubt in the matter, but he was certain of one thing, viz., that it was nonsense to talk of the war's being over in two or three months, as most people were saying in Germany at that time, and that he thought it was likely to last at least three or four years. He also said that "Those Peace People at the Palace," meaning the Emperor and his surroundings, "had held back the mobilization of the German Army for nearly forty-eight hours after he himself had thought it necessary because of a Russian mobilization, of which he was aware several days before it was generally known." The General also remarked that it had been Bismarck's policy always to divide the powers of Europe, and have some of them on the side of Germany when any great international question at issue and likely to lead to war arose between Germany and other powers of Europe; but that in this case they had succeeded in getting, as he expressed it, "the whole world united against Germany," and it remained to be seen whether Germany could hold her own in the long run against such a combination.

A few days afterwards I left Berlin for Holland, on the way home, sailing from Rotterdam in the steamship bearing the name of that city, early in September, the 3rd, I think, for New York.

But I have often thought since of my conversation with General von Falkenhayn, who afterwards held high commands in the war, and of the doubts which he evidently felt in his mind as to the manner in which it would end. It also confirmed the idea which I formed at the time, that it was fear of Russia, as to whose condition the German General Staff were evidently very badly informed, which was the immediate cause of Germany's entering the war, and not a desire to crush France. His remark also, as to those "Peace People at the Palace," confirmed my impression at the time, which has been fully borne out from various sources since then, that the Emperor himself was very loath at the last moment to declare war, and refused for a considerable time to sign the mobilization order. When General Von Moltke, who was at the head of the Great General Staff when the war broke out, died a year or two later, his widow stated publicly that he had come home on the day upon which the Emperor signed the mobilization order, saying that he had had the hardest job in his life to induce his Majesty to take that step, so reluctant was he to set the war actually going. Like many other weak and vain men, the Emperor had played too long with fire.

APPENDIX III

Memorandum on the Question of Fiume

The proposed creation of a free state including Fiume as a *corpus separatum*, the territory through which passes the Fiume-San Pietro railway, and eventually also Susak and the Island of Veglia, cannot be considered as a solution of the *economic problem* set forth by President Wilson—the problem of preserving Fiume as a *free outlet to the sea* for the hinterland.

As the proposed free state solution fixes a plebiscite for Fiume at the end of fifteen years, this will mean that during the intervening period the city will be the victim of the most bitter political and racial struggles; and if, as now seems almost certain, the city then decides in favor of annexation to Italy, Italy will come into absolute possession not only of the city but also of its port, and in consequence the hinterland's outlet to the sea will remain completely in Italy's hands—so that at the end of fifteen years, that which one seeks to avoid today, will come about.

Is it not preferable to face the situation at once? Is it not possible to resolve the question once for all in a way to guarantee immediately and permanently the exercise of port activities in a way to best serve the hinterland—and this in such a manner as to accord with the principles stated by President Wilson and to give at the same time at least a partial satisfaction to Italy?

Italy claims Fiume on the principle of nationality. President Wilson, though not denying the Italian character of the city, finds it difficult to accede to the annexation of Fiume to Italy, on the principle of safe-guarding the economic interests of the hinterland. Is it not possible to find a solution which will be in harmony with both principles?

In order to meet the economic interests of the hinterland, *possession of the whole city of Fiume is unnecessary*; it would be sufficient for hinterland interests, to detach that part of the port essential to the work of hinterland transportation, together with the accompanying plant and railway construction destined to this use in the past.

On the other hand, in order to satisfy Italian national interests, it is not absolutely necessary to have possession of the entire port of Fiume.

The following project seeks to offer a solution, which may satisfy both

President Wilson's claims for the economic interests of the hinterland and Italy's national interests.

The entire *operations of transportation* for the hinterland were carried out in the past in the so-called free port and in the port of Barross, with its wood deposits—both fitted out with the necessary plants and railways.

By the cession by Italy to the League of Nations for 99 years, of the above-mentioned two districts and their accompanying port and railway facilities necessary to the service of the hinterland, these would be separated from the city and rendered perfectly independent; this separation would not be difficult, as it has already been largely effected under the Hungarian administration. These districts and their transportation facilities would be administered by the League of Nations, an organization whose administration would offer every guarantee of impartiality and permanence for the hinterland.

In order to effect this solution, the creation of an independent organism would be necessary—an organism consisting of two parts, as follows:

The first would include the so-called free port (excluding the Zichy Quay) with the necessary land, port facilities, warehouses, repair shops, offices, houses for railway employees, etc.—in short, a district such as that indicated in red A, on the plan, and separated and walled off from the city, as at present.

The second would consist of the Barross port, with the delta (wood deposits), and all the railway facilities existing in the Susak district which at present form an integral part of the port and transportation system of Fiume; this second district should likewise be walled off as indicated in red B.

These two districts thus set apart are already fitted out to serve immediately the transportation interests of the hinterland, as suggested.

The remaining small portion of the port would remain to Italy as a national Italian free port, and would serve the immediate interests of the city, its local commerce and local passenger service; the Maria-Theresa breakwater with its bath-houses, rowing club-houses, etc., would also remain to Italy, and serve, as it does today, for the unloading of the coal necessary to the city, and its local industries.

The Vichy Quay, situated off from the first district, would serve the Italian steamship lines Venice-Ancona, in compensation for that portion of the free port which was employed exclusively for the said service.

This arrangement, whilst it guarantees the outlet of the hinterland, reserves to the city that portion of the port which is indispensable to it, and which is not used for the hinterland's traffic; the said arrangement would offer no obstacles to an eventual enlargement of the port of Fiume, in both the districts assigned to the League of Nations.

Besides the port facilities and local railway thus assigned to the League of Nations, it would be necessary in order to assure proper transportation for the hinterland, to give to the League also the administration of the two railway trunk lines, that leading to Zagabria and that leading to San Pietro.

This having been done, it would no longer be necessary to create an independent free state to comprise the territories through which these trunk lines pass.

The above solution would seem to be in full accord with the principles put forward by President Wilson in protection of the economic interests of the hinterland; it would also meet with his ideas as to the administrative functions of the League of Nations.

At the same time it would place under Italian sovereignty the greater part of the city and territory of Fiume, thereby largely satisfying Italian aspirations.

Appendix IV

Henry James to Mrs. Henry White

21, CARLYLE MANSIONS,
CHEYNE WALK, LONDON S. W.
February 23rd, 1913.

MY DEAR OLD FRIEND:

Let this mechanic form and vulgar legibility notify you a little at the start that I am in rather a hampered and hindered state, and that that must plead both for my delay in acknowledging your dear faithful letter of the New Year time, and for my at last having to make the best of this too impersonal art. I hate to tell you dismal things—and only do so now because they, after their nature, impose themselves. I have been having difficult times, quite stricken months, and even now, after a good deal of emergence, the end seems not altogether yet. After quite a large rift in the clouds, and at the moment I was about to seize the pen to greet and thank and bless you, I found myself from one day to the other laid straight up by my Doctor with a mild dragon of a Nurse placed in charge, and that is my present status. There is good appearance that it can't last much longer, but meanwhile I am unable to drive the pen with any grace at any point—and I blush for my delays and my general poor show in every direction. Thus I try to help myself to brazen the situation out, and I feel how absolutely I can count on your gentle understanding. I won't go into the history of my woes—all the more that I really hope I have shuffled the worst of them off. Even in this most recent form they have been part and parcel of the grave illness that overtook me as long ago as at the New Year, 1910, and with a very imperfect recovery from which I was struggling during those weary American months of winter-before-last when we planned so in vain that I should come to you in Washington.

I have deeply regretted, ever since, my failure of that pleasure—all the more that I don't see it now as conceivably again within my reach. I am restored to this soil, in which I am rooted, for whatever may remain to me of my mortal career. The grand swing across the globe, which you and Harry will again nobly accomplish—again and yet again—now simply mocks at my weakness and my reduced resources. Besides, I am but too thankful to have a refuge in which *continuously* to crouch.

Please fix well in your mind that continuity—as making it easy for you some day to find me here. The continuity is broken simply by my reverting to the country for the summer and autumn—a mere change from the blue bed to the brown, and then from the brown back again to this Thames-side perch, which I call the blue.

I hang here, for six months, straight over the River, and find it delightful and interesting, at once ever so quiet and ever so animated. The River has a quantity of picturesque and dramatic life and motion that one had never appreciated until one had thrown oneself on it *de confiance*. But it's another London, this old Chelsea of simplifications and sacrifices, from the world in which I feel that I for so long lived more or less *with* you. I feel somehow as much away now from that as you and Harry must feel amid your new Washington horizons—and it has of itself, for that matter, gone to pieces under the sweep of the big broom of Time, which has scattered it without ceremony. A few vague and altered relics of it occasionally dangle for a moment before me—I was going to say "cross my path"—but I haven't now such a thing as a path, or it goes such a very few steps. I try meanwhile to project myself in imagination into your Washington existence—and, besides your own allusions to it, a passing visit a few days since from Walter Berry helped me a little to fix the shining vision. W. B. had been, I gathered, but a day or two near you, and wasn't in possession of many particulars.

Beyond this, too, though you shine to me a bit fearfully—for I can't rid myself (in this world of Chelsea limits and fashions) of a sense of the *formidable*, the somehow—at least for the likes of me!—difficult and bristling and glaring, side of the American conditions. However, you of course lightly ride the whirlwind—or at any rate have only as much or as little of the storm as you will, and can pick out of it only such most musical thunder-rolls and most purely playful forked lightnings as suit you best. What I mean is that here, after a fashion, a certain part of the work of discrimination and selection and primary clearing of the ground is already done for one, in a manner that enables one to begin, for one's self, further on or higher up; whereas over there I seemed to see myself, speaking only from my own experience, often beginning so "low down," just in that way of shifting and selecting, that all one's time went to it and one was spent before arriving at any very charming altitude. This you will find obscure, but study it well—though strictly in private, so as not to give me away to a sniffy critic. Heaven knows I indulge in the most remorseless habits of criticism *here*—even if I make no great public use of them, through the increasing privacy and antiquity of my life.

I kind of wonder about the bearing of the queer Democratic régime that seems as yet so obscurely to loom upon any latent possibilities (that might have been) of Harry's and your "career"—just as I wonder what unutterable queerness may not, as a feature of the whole conundrum, "representatively" speaking, before long cause us all here to sit up and stare: one or two such startling rumours about the matter, I trust groundless, having already had something of that effect. But we must all wait, mustn't we? and I do indeed envy you both your so interesting opportunity for doing so, in a front box at the comedy, or tragedy, the fine old American Show, that is, whatever turn it takes; it will all give you, these next months, so much to look at and talk about and expertly appreciate. Lord, how I wish I were in a state or situation to be dining with you tonight! I am dying, really, to see your house—which means, alas, that I shall die without doing so. No glimmer of a view of the new Presidential family as a White House group has come my way— so that I sit in darkness there as all round, and feel that you can but say that it serves me right not to have managed my life better—especially with your grand example! Amen, amen! . . .

It's a jump, but I once in a while have a glimpse of Lady Ripon, of Evan Charteris, of George Curzon and one or two other slightly spectral reminders of the old time. That was at least the case a little last winter —and during a queer little monstrous visit that I paid in the summer at Cliveden (where the ancientries struck me even more than the novelties). Lady Ripon holds her own in marked gray, silver-gray, maturity, even as she did in the *beaux temps*; though she seems at present mainly remarkable for her intense artistic interest, which somehow has a funny public effect, in the unspeakably small Nijinsky, the acrobatic Russian dancer, about whom, as about his beautiful companion Karsavina, even dear little old Chelsea is now full of chatter. Sargent, round the corner, has painted and drawn him to superabundance, and dear Wilfrid von Glehn, also my near neighbour, can't sufficiently paint and repaint *her*, who sits to him with repeated affability: so that we feel immensely in the movement.

I rejoice to hear of your having had your grandchildren with you, though you speak, bewilderingly, as if they had leaped across the globe in happy exemption from parents—or a parent. However, nothing does surprise me now—almost any kind of globe-leaping affects me, in my *trou*, as natural, possible, nay probable! I pat Harry ever so affectionately on the back, I hold you both in the most affectionate remembrance, and am yours all faithfully

HENRY JAMES.

INDEX

Bryce on Bryan as Sec. of State — p. 322
White " " " " — p. 330 n.
Opposed to League to Enforce Peace — p. 333
Public opn. on League of Nations in 1915 — p. 350
Roosevelt on League at bedside conf., Nov. 26, 1918 — p. 352
Lodge memo. to White — — p. 352

DATE DUE